HISTORY OF
ENGLISH LITERATURE
1837 TO THE PRESENT

HISTORY OF ENGLISH LITERATURE
1837 TO THE PRESENT

Martin S. Day, Ph.D.

*Professor of English
at the University of Houston*

A COLLEGE COURSE GUIDE

DOUBLEDAY & COMPANY, INC., GARDEN CITY, NEW YORK
1964

Yeats's Epitaph from *The Collected Poems of W. B. Yeats.* Reprinted by permission of Mrs. W. B. Yeats, Macmillan & Company, Ltd., The Macmillan Company of Canada, Ltd.

Preface

This book examines the course of English literature from the accession of Queen Victoria in 1837 to the present. It thereby concludes a series of three volumes, the first of which traces English literature from the beginnings to 1660, and the second of which covers the period from 1660 to 1837. All three volumes attempt to provide for everyone interested in English literature a succinct, factual introduction to the works of every notable writer in our language in the British Isles.

Major figures are treated at some length, including attention even to their minor writings. Authors presenting few problems in interpretation receive relatively less space; therefore, length of scrutiny is not in itself a measure of an author's importance.

Minor writers are considered in sufficient fashion to show their contribution to, and revelation of, their age. Where desirable, lesser writers are considered in order to demonstrate the scope and variety of a period or a genre. Background material in history, cultural conditions, and development of the language is provided in order to orient the reader and to place each author in his milieu. Every effort has been made to offer the maximum amount of information about the literary works themselves.

The goal has been to achieve as much usefulness and thoroughness as possible. For each significant literary work the reader will find:

(1) THE CIRCUMSTANCES OF PUBLICATION, DATE, SOURCE, ETC. The dates in parentheses after a work should be read in the following manner: *the date in italic type is the work's date of composition, and the date in roman type is the date of publication.* Thus (*1898*, 1902) means that the work was written in 1898 but first printed in 1902. Unless otherwise stated, this dating scheme holds true for dramas as well as other literary forms, since plays of this era have regularly seen print at the time of first performance.

(2) BRIEF SUMMARIES. The reader is specifically informed about the exact contents of a work so that plot and characters are clearly understood. The summaries, except for wholly minor pieces, appear in separate paragraphs but in the same size of type as the biographical and other data which precede them.

(3) ANALYSES. Instead of rhapsodizing or censuring, this book seeks to explain what an author said and meant in each piece of writing. Interpretations hew as closely as possible to what seems to be each author's actual intent. Where other interpretations are likely, they are indicated.

While the divisions of the book are generally based upon chronological historical or cultural periods, those literary or art forms of special interest or importance to the period under discussion have been kept separate. It is therefore possible in using this series of books to follow the development of a major art form (such as the novel or the essay) from its beginnings to the present by tracing it through the table of contents.

A pronunciation key has been provided where any difficulty in pronunciation might occur. Sounds follow standard Middle American:

> cat, dāte, bär, âsk, bāre
> bet, bē, pér
> din, dīne
> dot, dōte, prŏve, bôre, cŏw
> but, fūse, bŭll
> þ as in then, th as in thin

Though the author's indebtednesses are too numerous to record in detail, he would particularly like to acknowledge the invaluable assistance of Lawrence W. Lamm and Harry L. Wagner of Copeland & Lamm, Inc. And special thanks go to Rosalie P. Day, the author's wife, for preparing the drawings for the illustrations which appear in the book.

Houston, Texas   MARTIN S. DAY
May 1964

Contents

PART TWO

The Celtic Renaissance

PART THREE
Twentieth-Century English Literature

Part One

THE VICTORIAN PERIOD

Chapter 1

Introduction to the Victorian Age

BACKGROUND INFORMATION

MAJOR HISTORICAL EVENTS. During the Victorian Age, England reached its pinnacle of power and prestige. Not since ancient Rome had any nation so dominated Western society and the entire world. The basis for this glory was England's economic productivity. As the inaugurator of the Industrial Revolution, England itself along with the rest of the world marveled at the grimy Midlands, "Workshop of the World." Between 1839 and 1849 the West Riding of Yorkshire alone expanded its fabric exports from 2,400,000 yards to over 42,000,000 yards. In 1848 Great Britain produced as much iron as all the rest of the world put together, but that figure was trebled by 1880. Between 1850 and 1872 the annual value of British exports soared from £90,000,000 to £315,000,000. By the latter year the country's foreign trade exceeded that of France, Germany, and Italy combined and was almost four times that of the United States.

Trade was the stimulus to the growth of the vast empire. The private merchant adventurers of the East India Company had brought under English control an India that was thirty-four times the size of England in area and fifteen times in population. The practically empty continent of Australia, almost forty times the size of England, was open to colonization and commerce, as was Canada, the second largest nation in the world. Indeed, English colonialism expanded in the 19th century with almost the rapidity of its 20th-century dissolution. No other country emerged as a rival to England in territorial acquisition until the century's close, and thus relatively small English armed forces were able to conquer over a tenth of the globe, although tombs and plaques in many a quiet English church commemorating a son who died fighting testify to the cost of empire building.

The economic power of England extended not merely within the empire but throughout the earth. The pound sterling was the standard money exchange of the globe, and world prices of all major commodities from grain to furs, and from cotton to steel, were determined in London. Almost every country was a debtor to England: much of 19th-century construction and development in the United States was financed from London; and the British owned buildings in Shanghai, mines in Mexico, and the entire railroad system of the Argentine. This wealth and imperial grandeur mounted to unprecedented heights during the reign (1837–1901) of Queen Victoria, and the English faculty for transforming institutions while maintaining their outward semblance is nowhere more clearly illustrated than in the noble lords of this era. For in the 19th century peerages were no longer conferred on the landed gentry as in the past but on the moguls of textile and railroad, steel and finance. Moreover, the reform spirit of the earlier 1830s continued under Victoria. The Poor Law Bill of 1838 extended benefits to the Irish, and the Tithe Law of the same year reduced the money sums paid by landowners to the Church of England. The Municipal Act (1840) further extended voting privileges. But reform had not kept pace with the discontent of workers. Britain's enormous productivity had been achieved by a frightful exploitation of the laboring classes, who were usually condemned to dire poverty, filthy conditions of work and living, debility, and painfully short lifespans. Popular resentment had caused a Workingmen's Association in London to submit a charter to parliament in 1836, calling for universal manhood suffrage, vote by secret ballot, abolition of property qualifications for members of parliament, payment of salaries to members of parliament, equal electoral districts, and annual parliaments. When the first national convention of the Chartists had its petition rejected by parliament in 1839, serious riots occurred in Birmingham, Newport (Wales), and elsewhere. The second national convention of the Chartists in 1842 again presented its petition in vain, and the long-threatened "turn-out" followed. In the first great strike of modern industrialism the vast machinery of the Midlands ground to a stop. The new railroads, however, quickly poured troops into the troubled Midlands, and the insurrection petered out before armed might. The goals of the Chartists were to be obtained but not by violence.

The English genius for pragmatism and compromise turned what might have become a bloody revolution into peaceful evolution. Moderate elements among the workers in 1845 formed the National Association of the United Traders for the Protection of Labour. This group was a revival of trade unionism, abandoning strikes and violence in favor of conciliation and arbitration. Prime Minister Peel, although a Conservative, in 1846 pushed through parliament the repeal of the Corn Laws. British agriculture thus lost its protectionist tariffs, and the workers were able to buy cheaper imported foodstuffs. Economic reality had compelled England to a position it has maintained ever since: unable to feed its own people, it must import food as well as raw materials to keep its industrial system functioning.

Crop failures in Ireland during the 1840s caused widespread suffering and forced multitudes of the Irish to emigrate to the Americas. The first great modern figure in the struggle for Irish nationalism was the moderate Daniel O'Connell, but after his death in 1847 radical groups stirred up an abortive rebellion the next year.

Chiefly at the urging of Prince Albert, the German husband of Victoria, the Great Exhibition of 1851 in London lavishly displayed the riches of the world. This was the prototype of all subsequent "world's fairs." Prosperity was the keynote, and Victorian England saw the exhibition as the summit of human ingenuity and productivity. The breathtaking focus of the exhibition was the gigantic Crystal Palace, fabricated from iron girders and vast expanses of glass.

The Crimean War (1854–56) was the only European conflict directly involving the British between the Napoleonic period and World War I. Although Russia was not a major military power, the Allies (England, France, Turkey, Sardinia) fought against her inconclusively. The British army showed itself tragically outmoded and inadequate; the famous Charge of the Light Brigade at Balaklava demonstrating incredible courage and incredible administrative bungling. The horrible suffering of the troops due to unsatisfactory supplies was only partly alleviated by the Herculean nursing efforts of Florence Nightingale.

The Sepoy Rebellion of native Indian troops in 1857 impelled the British government in the next year to remove India from the political jurisdiction of the East India Company and place it under the crown. England's war with China (1857–58) was part of the European maneuvers for power in a rich but weakly governed land. General Charles George Gordon led the Ever-Victorious Army of Chinese against the T'ai P'ing rebels, finally crushing them by 1863.

The Companies' Act of 1862 has been termed as momentous as any parliamentary measure in history. This act permitted the formation of corporate entities with limited liability of stockholders (hence the Ltd.— "limited"—after the title of most English business firms). Previously a shareholder in a firm was entitled to his proportion of a company's profits and was also obligated to his proportion of its liabilities. When the City of Glasgow Bank (not Ltd.) failed in 1879, shareholders were called upon to meet obligations hundreds of times greater than the value of their shares. Under limited liability a shareholder can lose no more than his initial investment. Limited liability therefore encouraged fantastic creation and expansion of concerns and produced the modern phenomenon of the multitudes of shareholders completely ignorant of the business in which they have invested and for all practical purposes excluded or self-excluded from the operation of the business. The modern corporation thus developed as an enterprise conducted by salaried executives and financed by vast sales of stock to many investors.

Benjamin Disraeli emerged as the dominant Conservative politician, but he surprisingly "dished the Whigs" by the Second Reform Bill (1867), which doubled the number of eligible voters and reapportioned more equitably the seats in parliament. With the triumph of the Liberal Party under William Gladstone, the reform movement continued: the Disestablishment Act of 1869, removing government support from the Church of Ireland (Protestant); the Irish Land Act of 1870, mollifying some of the evils of Irish land tenure; the Education Act of the same year, providing minimum essential education for all English children for the first time in history; the introduction in 1870 of competitive examinations for civil service posts; the University Tests Act of 1871, removing most of the religious restrictions upon students and faculty at Oxford and Cambridge; the Army Regulation Bill of the same year, reorganizing the military largely in the light of deficiencies revealed by the Crimean War; and the Ballot Act of 1872, first introducing the secret ballot. Under Gladstone the government followed chiefly a "Little England" policy, seeking to avoid foreign entanglements.

Disraeli returned to office in 1874 avowing a "Big England" policy to further British prestige and interest throughout the world. By purchase of Suez Canal shares in 1875 Disraeli established English dominance of the link between East and West and initiated English penetration of Egypt. In the next year Disraeli by the Royal Titles Bill had Victoria proclaimed Empress of India. Domestic measures during the second Disraeli ministry included: the Public Health Act (1875), still the backbone of English sanitary law; the Artisans' Dwelling Act (1875), the first real attempt of the government to improve the housing of the poor; and the Merchant Shipping Act (1876) to regulate seaworthiness and loading of vessels. Unpopular colonial wars against the Afghans in Central Asia and the Zulus in South Africa, coupled with the poorest harvest of the century in 1879, caused Disraeli's ministry to fall.

The second Gladstone ministry, starting in 1880, was highlighted by two spectacular personalities. Pious Victorians were shocked at the 1880 election to parliament of the militant atheist Charles Bradlaugh. The long quarrel about his taking of the oath (including "So help me, God") finally resulted in his seating in 1886 and the passage, under his sponsorship, of the Affirmation Bill of 1888, removing all religious qualifications for membership in parliament. Charles Parnell, though a Protestant, led the Home Rule for Ireland Party in repeated and eloquent demands for a separate legislature for Ireland. Parnell suffered political disaster in 1890 when named as co-respondent in a divorce suit, and he died the next year.

Under Gladstone the Employers' Liability Act (1880) for the first time assured compensation for workers injured at their employment, and the Corrupt and Illegal Practices Act (1883) limited the expenditures of political parties in campaigning. Gladstone's Franchise Bill of 1884 virtually provided manhood suffrage, excluding only domestic servants, bachelors living with their families, and men of no fixed abode.

As the century neared conclusion, England's dominance of the world was being challenged. Industrialization of continental nations was belatedly catching up with England's production, and Germany, united for the first time in 1870, was rising with the greatest rapidity. A worried Conservative administration, led by Lord Salisbury after Disraeli's death in 1881, saw the key to global power in the British fleet. The Naval Defense Act of 1889 stipulated that Britain should maintain a navy equal to the combined fleets of the next two strongest powers; this policy was followed until World War I.

Further to worry the Conservatives was the rising tide of English socialism. In 1883 the Fabian Society (named for the ancient Roman conqueror of Hannibal, Fabius, "the delayer") was founded, sparked by Sidney and Beatrice Webb along with George Bernard Shaw. The group believed that universal suffrage and fully representational government would eventually insure socialism. Labor showed its mounting strength and self-awareness with the London dock strike of 1889. The Independent Labour Party, frankly socialistic, was founded in 1893; by 1906 it had twenty-nine members in parliament.

In the Diamond Jubilee of 1897 the British empire and the entire world lavishly celebrated the sixtieth anniversary of Victoria's accession, and Kipling's words of warning in the "Recessional" sounded hollow to an England intoxicated with majestic power and world dominance. Sobering was the onset in 1899 of the Boer War in South Africa, where a small number of resolute white Afrikanders fought the empire almost to a standstill. The death of Queen Victoria in 1901 deeply affected the empire. Hardly any of her subjects could remember a previous English monarch, for her reign was the longest in European history, except for that of Louis XIV. During her reign England had achieved prosperity and power previously unparalleled in human history, but England's star, almost imperceptibly, was on the wane, and even the least sensitive of Englishmen knew that an era had passed.

Victoria, ascending the throne in 1837, counted about seventeen million subjects in the United Kingdom; at her death the population of the United Kingdom exceeded thirty-seven-and-a-half million. Most of this huge increase took place in the cities. Although many English villages in 1837 still looked much as they had in Chaucer's day, before the century's end almost every village had been transformed. Arnold Bennett recalled from his childhood the separate "Five Towns" that in 1910 were united into the giant Stoke-on-Trent. Into many a sequestered village the railroads breathed the soot of coal dust and lured village youth to the mushrooming industrial cities. Whole counties were blanketed with the smoke pouring from factory smokestacks, and a nation of agricultural yeomen had been transformed into a nation of factory workers.

The real beneficiaries of this labor were the members of the triumphant middle class. Even a sophisticated French author and critic like Hippolyte Taine, visiting England in the 1870s, was awed by the display of national wealth. "Paris," he declared, "is mediocre compared with these squares, these crescents, these circles and rows of monumental buildings of massive stone, with porticos, with sculptured fronts, these spacious streets. . . . Assuredly Napoleon III demolished and rebuilt Paris only because he had lived in London." But even this London splendor paled before the baronial magnificence of the Midlands manufacturers, where the magnates of the north ruled industrial empires from palaces that a Roman emperor would have envied.

The foreign world disliked the English merchant, but it greatly envied him and grudgingly admired him. The honesty and integrity of the English manufacturer and merchant were a global byword; to this day Argentinians assert *palabra inglés* (the word of an Englishman) when they mean the unqualified truth. Thus, we can see that Victorian repressive morality was largely due to deep-seated conviction, not to hypocrisy as it has often seemed to the 20th century. The Victorians possessed an English conscience and were not exclusively unfeeling exploiters of their fellows; the hosts of reform measures in the era testify to a humanity behind the wall of stockholders. Private charity and public service often showed the bourgeoisie to be worthy inheritors of the best traditions of a superseded aristocracy and bulwarks of a stable England.

CULTURAL CONDITIONS. "Victorian," as we use the word, is wholly accurate as a label simply for the chronological period 1837–1901, the reign of Queen Victoria. Much more dubious is the use of Victorian to characterize the British spirit during this era. In the inevitable reaction of the early 20th century the term meant smug, stuffy, narrow-minded, prudentially moral, hypocritically righteous, and naïvely optimistic. The later 20th century has tended to see Victorianism as moral earnestness, astounding material progress, confidence, and a serenity strange to our troubled times. In truth, the Victorian age was an era of extraordinary complexity and variety of viewpoint, as its writers demonstrate. But, oversimplified, the spirit of the period falls into three broad categories: Victorian Orthodoxy, Traditionalists, and Innovators.

VICTORIAN ORTHODOXY. The orthodoxy of the period (what we usually mean when employing the term Victorian) is the middle-class spirit of the

19th century. It is this spirit that dominated the age and put its impress upon the queen herself. The early Victoria was a vivacious girl who was a bit annoyed by the repressions of the time, such as the dull, pious Sundays, but the aged woman had fully conformed to the sedate image desired by her middle-class subjects.

The principal factor in the mind-set we usually term "Victorian" was Evangelical Protestantism, as noted by the Frenchman, Halévy, perhaps the greatest authority upon this era. A sizable proportion of the middle class consisted of Wesleyans (Methodists), intent upon transforming all society into a decorous, moral institution consonant with the preachings of John Wesley. The nonconformist groups (Baptists, Congregationalists, etc.) were almost all staunchly middle class and evangelical. Within the Church of England itself, the same evangelical forces were manifest; the sporting and drinking clerics of the 18th century (as Trollope notes in his novels) vanished in favor of sober and moralistic parish clergymen. Evangelicalism invested 19th-century English nobility (frequently middle-class in origin) with a dignity and rectitude seldom found even as late as the Regency. Evangelicalism also established amid the proletariat a number of workmen inspired by virtue and self-restraint. The reform movement of the age sprang not from the radicalism of a Shelley or an Owen but from the Evangelicals. Indifferent to tradition, the Evangelicals sought to form the Holy Society right here and now in each heart. This spirit exuded Protestant individualism.

Only slightly less instrumental than evangelicalism in forming Victorian orthodoxy was the economic and political philosophy of Jeremy Bentham. Benthamite reform was as potent during the "Conservative" regimes of Peel and Disraeli as during the "Liberal" administrations. Benthamism worked in two directions, occasionally at cross-purposes. In its insistence upon *laissez faire* it sought to insure freedom of action for all individuals capable of useful and intelligent conduct. Hence such measures as the repeal of the Corn Laws; but, even more important here, was its firm support for the unrestrained competition of a free enterprise system. Thus it worked hand-in-glove with the triumphant bourgeoisie, who benefited spectacularly under free capitalism. On the other hand, the insistence of Benthamism upon "the greatest happiness of the greatest number" called for the restraint of criminals and lunatics and the protection of women, children, and paupers in the interest of a wholesome society. It must be remembered, therefore, that the reform spirit of the era was fundamentally a defense, a shoring-up, of the bourgeois capitalistic system, intent not upon altering the system but upon strengthening and smoothing its operation.

Most Victorians were conditioned, by Benthamism and their own bourgeois origins, to view art and literature with two entirely different attitudes, which led to two entirely different expressions of popular art.

On one hand, average Victorians frequently looked upon art as a pleasant superfluity that provided occasional enjoyable relief from the persistent drive for wealth. The taste of the populace therefore often equated art with a treacly romanticism, a glamorous escapism devoid of the rebellious and disturbing characteristics of the great Romantics. This demand resulted in an abundant supply of sweet, coy, sentimental art of the type Meredith called "rose-pink." The medievalism of the age distilled the colorful and charming aspects of the past, avoiding the vulgar, violent, and sensual. Perhaps the ultimate of romanticism in the era, possible only with the complete victory of the bourgeoisie, was the romanticizing of the middle-class career itself.

On the other hand, many Victorians of the practical middle class considered realism as "the real art." Properly, 19th-century realism is best termed "bourgeois realism," and it demonstrated the following aspects:

(1) Bourgeois characters central to the portrait. Most Victorian novels depict the middle class and ascribe bourgeois viewpoints to the admirable aristocrat and proletarian. Even in historical fiction and poetic medievalism the characters in effect are transplanted Victorian bourgeoisie.

(2) Bourgeois experience of life. It is the everyday vicissitudes of bourgeois struggle, the urge to financial security and social acceptance, and the problems of domestic and commercial life that preoccupy these realistic characters.

(3) Bourgeois ethics. Realistic 19th-century literature demonstrates the success of those who conform to the middle-class concepts, and the failure of the unconventional and rebellious.

(4) Bourgeois surroundings. Middle-class places of residence, work, and resort dominate the backgrounds. Solid, comfortable, often cluttered and tasteless settings mirror the possessive goals of the characters and symbolize their purposes and natures.

Largely a middle-class product anyway, the novel in the Victorian period became the most popular form of literature and, for most writers, the only reasonably certain way to earn a living. Through the bourgeois realistic novel the Victorian age offers a fuller picture of its life than we find in the literature of any previous epoch.

The most admired writers of this age obviously were those who supported the Victorian orthodoxy. Tennyson was the poet laureate of the bourgeoisie, Macaulay its historian, Spencer its philosopher. When Tennyson in irate fashion deplores the passing of "old England," it is actually the weakening of the (Victorian) orthodoxy that he regrets. In his militant reform spirit, Dickens is really a true Benthamite, resolutely working to maintain the middle class. The so-called "laughing critics," like Gilbert and Sullivan, are generally attacking the deviations from the bourgeois orthodoxy, and Matthew Arnold sought not to overthrow the bourgeois ascendency but to render it more enlightened.

Broadly it can be hazarded that the majority of English writers reaching their maturity between 1837 and 1875 accepted the Victorian orthodoxy and in essence expressed it.

TRADITIONALISTS. We would label this group conservative, but the term is avoided because 19th-century conservatism differs significantly in meaning from 20th-century conservatism. Essentially what is meant here is that the intoxication with material progress in Victorian England did not entirely eradicate a persistence of traditionalism and a desire for institutions unaffected by change. To some, Evangelical Protestantism and its individualism seemed an abandonment of structure in favor of chaos. The powerful religious need for an unchanging rock amid the convulsions of the era produced, most notably, the Oxford Movement (detailed more fully under Cardinal Newman). Newman himself entered the Roman Catholic Church, and many other religious and intellectual figures of the period were also converted to Roman Catholicism. Within the Church of England the same spirit produced Anglo-Catholicism (often termed High Episcopal in the United States), which differed essentially from Roman Catholicism only in ritual and Mass in English instead of Latin, optional vows of celibacy for secular clergy, and refusal to admit primacy of the Bishop of Rome (the Pope). To many moderate Englishmen (as Trollope reveals of himself in his Barsetshire novels) Anglo-Catholicism proved more attractive than evangelicalism because of its dignity, color, and sense of long-continuing tradition. Within the last one hundred years Anglo-Catholicism has probably been the most dynamic element in the Church of England, has moved the entire Established Church in a more Catholic direction, and has tended to diminish the English antipathy to Roman Catholicism.

Traditionalist reaction to Benthamism produced, especially in Carlyle, a distrust of and a distaste for a free competitive society and extended franchise. Carlyle deeply regretted the passing of a paternalistic, agricultural system in favor of wage-slavery, and he contrasted the protected peasant of the past with the rootless proletarian of the industrial age, concluding that modern society had produced far less happiness and security for the average man. Carlyle saw the vast increase in the electorate as producing vulgarity and demagoguery, for he deeply believed that men must be led by great leaders rather than electing officials to be mere tools of the popular voice. In many respects he was a belated feudalist or possibly a protofascist. His age listened to him respectfully, but continued on the Benthamite path.

Both of the reactions discussed in this section are fundamental criticisms of the Victorian middle-class dominance not for the sake of its correction but rather with an eye to its demise and a desire to return to an earlier pattern of life, either real or supposed.

INNOVATORS. We might label this trend liberalism, but again the term is avoided because of the great difference between 19th-century liberalism and 20th-century liberalism. As early as 1859 Fitzgerald in *The Rubáiyát* expressed the intellectual's scorn for Victorian evangelicalism and, in fact, for orthodox faith generally. It can be said, broadly speaking, that most of the significant English writers reaching their maturity between 1875 and World War I had lost religious faith. Some, like Hardy, were deeply pained by the loss; others, like Wilde, professed faith at the approach of death or in severe psychological disturbances; most, however, had abandoned any sincerely felt conventional religion and were not much incommoded thereby. The major causes for this break with orthodoxy can be found in the emergence of the intelligentsia and in the contentions of science.

At the century's end many intellectuals were sufficiently disillusioned with the middle-class ascendency to sympathize with or vigorously advocate socialism. This, of course, was a native English brand; relatively few Englishmen became Marxian socialists, even though *Das Kapital* (1867–94) by Karl Marx was written in London. English socialists were intent not upon improvement of the capitalistic system but upon a complete change to a regulated economy, a nationalized industry, and a transfer of power from the middle class to the workers.

Both these "leftist" tendencies (seeking an overthrow of the Victorian orthodoxy and looking to a new and different system ahead) may be traced largely to the development of the 19th-century intelligentsia. We use this latter term in the sense of the rebellious intellectuals of recent generations who are at odds with their age and impatient with any orthodoxy whatsoever. The major Victorian authors (Tennyson, Arnold, etc.) had made the transition from being voices of an educated elite, as were 18th-century authors, to being voices for and to the triumphant Victorian middle class. By the last quarter of the century, however, most young writers and thinkers had lost sympathy with the bourgeoisie, even though the intelligentsia had itself developed from the middle class. Since the spectacle of the intelligentsia bitterly railing against current society is still with us deep into the 20th century, it is advisable to explore the reasons for this hostility:

(1) The 19th and 20th centuries have produced more educated and articulate persons than there are jobs commensurate with their abilities. Many of the intelligentsia (as yet greater in percentage in Europe and England than in the United States) are annoyed with every aspect of a system that will not support them adequately or provide them with the artistic and creative expression they desire.

(2) The middle-class mind still harbors a distrust of intellectualism and

pursues a materialistic bent that relegates culture to the category of the superficial and superfluous. In addition, many of the intelligentsia have so attacked all the characteristics of bourgeois society, that they have alienated themselves all the more.

(3) The 19th-century bourgeois society unleashed forces of change which initially seemed to its benefit but which by the century's end had proved profoundly disturbing. The drives to individualism, reform, and so on continued to snowball, eventually producing an intelligentsia that wished to push on somewhere, anywhere, while the startled middle class wanted to stop or even turn back. Thus, what the mid-19th century called "liberalism" became the nostalgic dream of later "conservatives."

(4) The revelations and theories of 19th-century science proved increasingly difficult for the Victorian orthodoxy to accept. The intelligentsia, becoming thoroughly impatient with what it deemed ignorance and backwardness, condemned the entire Victorian world and all its attitudes.

(5) Many theorists of history, such as Toynbee and Spengler, posit for every culture a late stage where the challenging, rational, individualistic mind turns upon society and itself, destroying confidence and mental stability. In such a period the centrality of a culture is lost as every thinker of the age pursues a path different from that of his fellows; the intellectual is no longer a voice for society, but a separate tortured spirit. The disillusioned intelligentsia of the late 19th century and of our own century may therefore be a participant in an enormous cultural groundswell underlying the surface phenomena discussed above in this section.

IMPACT OF SCIENCE. When Thomas Henry Huxley in 1894 was asked how the future would label the 19th century—Age of Darwin, Age of Gladstone, Age of Pasteur—he refused to commit himself to a name, but he was certain that the 19th century would be labeled an Age of Science:

> I conceive that the leading characteristic of the nineteenth century has been the rapid growth of the scientific spirit, the consequent application of scientific methods of investigation to all the problems with which the human mind is occupied, and the correlative rejection of traditional beliefs which have proved their incompetence to bear such investigation.
>
> The activity of the scientific spirit has been manifested in every region of speculation and of practice.

The Victorian orthodoxy found itself fearfully perplexed and disturbed by this Age of Science. It was deeply in debt to science for its increase in material comforts and the sober, factual nature of science appealed to the bourgeois mind; in fact, most 19th-century scientists themselves sprang from middle-class backgrounds. Also, the deep Victorian conviction in the idea of progress seemed to be supported by the theory of evolution.

Still, the supposed implications of the evolutionary hypothesis sent a spasm of horror across many 19th-century minds.

The evolutionary concept can be traced, along with almost all other ideas, back to ancient Greek philosophers, such as Heraclitus and Anaximander. In 18th-century France the theory had vociferous proponents in Laplace and Count Buffon, and in 18th-century England it was supported by Lord Monboddo and Erasmus Darwin, grandfather of Charles Darwin. In 1815 Jean de Lamarck in Paris propounded the environmental theory to account for evolutionary change, i.e., the giraffe lengthens its neck by stretching upward to eat high foliage, the gazelle develops fleetness of foot in fleeing from pursuers, horns sprout from the skulls of animals that practice butting. These accumulated characteristics are then passed on to offspring. The Lamarckian theory, though supported by some Soviet scientists, has been substantially abandoned by most Western scientists.

Lyell's *Principles of Geology* (1830) advanced considerable evidence of evolution as revealed in the earth's strata; Tennyson was vastly impressed with this work; and indeed it influenced the entire English-speaking world. *Vestiges of the Natural History of Creation* (1844) by Robert Chambers, whose name is still retained in the English *Chambers' Encyclopaedia*, popularized the concept of biological evolution in the general mind. Evolution, however, was parlor talk and pure intellectual speculation until Charles Darwin.

As the full discussion of Darwin and his works will be found later in Chapter 3, we will deal here only with the effect his concepts of evolution had on his contemporaries. This effect was stupendous, for, although the real or supposed conflict between science and faith did not bother Darwin, it rocked England to its intellectual and spiritual depths. With or without warrant, countless people deduced the following conclusions from Darwin's pronouncements:

(1) The Biblical account of creation in *Genesis* was completely inaccurate, a revelation merely of poetry and folklore. All scriptures similarly could be relegated to anthropology and fiction.

(2) The entire concept of separate creation was false. The denial of this idea seemed the final and inexcusable indignity. The Copernican revolution had removed our planet from a position at the center of the universe to the status of a minor satellite circling a middling-sized star. Darwinism then removed mankind from its special place on earth. Man was a superior animal but assuredly an animal.

(3) The idea of a human soul was false, and the belief in immortality a delusion. The death of a human being or, in fact, the extinction of mankind, would be no more in the process of cosmic evolution than the crushing of a gnat or the disappearance of the dinosaurs.

(4) The Creator of the universe, if such a being existed, was impersonal, as heedless of entire species as of individuals.

It must be emphasized that these assumptions were not Darwin's and were seldom proclaimed by any scientist. The vociferous supporters of these contentions were "progressive" laymen, and actually many of these ideas came from religious people, especially clerics, who thereby sought to dismiss Darwinism as blasphemy. If the 19th-century quarrel about Darwinism seems old-fashioned, we must remember that in its time it was a fearsome thing. Many conscientious Victorians lost their faith amidst anguished soul-searching, and most of the pious regarded modern science as the most despicable assailant that religion had ever known. Whenever we think of the serenity of the Victorians, we must realize that to many of them their period appeared the most agonizing era ever inflicted upon the human spirit.

A few of the notable authors of the time—Browning, Thackeray—were impervious to the evolutionary concept; and from his writings it would seem that Dickens had never even heard of Darwinism. The witty Disraeli, dismissing the evolutionists in 1864, imbedded a phrase in the language: "The question is this: Is man an ape or an angel? My lord, I am on the side of the angels." Most Victorian authors, however, can be understood only in the light of this controversy. Almost all of them were profoundly disturbed, some, like Tennyson, winning back religion, others, like Clough, permanently losing what they thought was religion and suffering mightily, and still others, like Meredith, embracing the new evolutionary convictions with joy.

As to the Victorian era in general, now that its wave of detractors has ebbed, it is possible for G. M. Young to assert as he did in 1945 that the world has witnessed two great ages of the human intellect, one the age of Pericles, the other the age of Victoria. Even as early as 1922 Dean Inge labeled the 19th century "the most wonderful century in human history." To understand the Victorian period we must be aware both of its inherent orthodoxy and of its extraordinary flood of new and overwhelming ideas.

LANGUAGE. The archaisms in "medieval" poems of Tennyson, Rossetti, and others, and the verbal pyrotechnics of Carlyle should not confuse the modern reader: the educated Englishman of the 19th century employed the same grammar and syntax as educated 20th-century Englishmen. Vastly improved transportation and communication by the second half of the 19th century practically eliminated dialectal speech among cultured Englishmen, and since the Education Act of 1870 dialect even among the masses has rapidly been vanishing in favor of Standard London English. Dialectal forms introduced into fiction and poetry, and the dialect verse of William

Barnes and others in this period, demonstrate not the potency of dialect but nostalgia for a passing way of speech.

In Victorian England the gap between Standard London English and all other varieties of the language tended to widen. For the triumphant bourgeoisie Standard London English became a status symbol. The enriched middle class created long waiting lists of merchants' sons intended for the "public schools" (i.e., private preparatory schools) with their attendant prestige, not the least of which was an "impeccable" English. Macaulay, one of the most admired writers of the era, was especially assiduous in maintaining the "purity" and "correctness" of English. The first known objection to the split infinitive (first termed "cleft infinitive") was that of Richard Taylor in 1840. "Some writers of the present day," he complained, "have a disagreeable affectation of putting an adverb between *to* and the infinitive."

The extreme self-consciousness of 19th-century speakers of English and their drive for language "purity" is demonstrated by the endless controversy in the correspondence section of *The Times* over "there let him lay," from Canto IV of Byron's *Childe Harold's Pilgrimage*. The imbroglio began in 1873 and continued in desultory fashion until 1922. Formalists from the numerous followers of Lindley Murray's grammar of 1795 vigorously affirmed the English language to be a species of logic and, where stymied logically, appealed to tradition of the few previous generations. The rigid examination system of English schools tried resolutely to inculcate "correct, logical" English. Alexander Bain's *An English Grammar* (1863) foreshadowed the later historical study of our language's growth that produced in Henry Sweet's *A New English Grammar Logical and Historical* (1892–98) the first truly modern and scholarly grammar of English. Dean Alford's *The Queen's English* (1864), often reprinted in the age, claimed to follow usage (apparently that of the circle of the learned cleric).

While essentially static in grammar and syntax, British English of the Victorian era expanded enormously in vocabulary. An unwillingness to alter linguistic patterns, coupled with eagerness to add numerous new words, is characteristic of a mature, self-conscious language. The increase of English words during the Victorian period actually exceeds the great expansion of the Renaissance vocabulary. It can be stated that from 1800 to 1900 English virtually doubled its vocabulary for these reasons:

(1) The impulses that brought about Romanticism encouraged the language to extend the constricted 18th-century vocabulary by huge additions of new and foreign expressions: *vaquero* (1837), *poi* (1840), *leitmotif* (1876), *mousse* (1892).

(2) England's role as empire builder and world merchant vastly increased contacts with most of the globe's tongues and demanded vocabulary for

previously unfamiliar geography, exotic products, and foreign ways of life: *cantaloupe* (1839), *hara-kiri* (1856), *jinricksha* (1874), *tabasco* (1898).

(3) The recognition by intelligent Englishmen that their language was no longer the provincial tongue of a medium-sized island, but a world language, compelled a drawing upon the vocabulary resources of every language that could contribute new and significant ideas: *sanatorium* (1840), *vulcanization* (1846), *agnostic* (coined by T. H. Huxley in 1870), *feminism* (1895).

(4) The science and technology of the era required many new words, and almost as important as new words were the new meanings applied to words long current: *turbine* (1842), *short circuit* (1873), *transformer* (applied to electrical equipment in 1883), *periscope* (for submarines, 1899).

By far the most voluminous contributor to English vocabulary in the 19th century was modern science. The term *scientist* was coined in 1840 by William Whewell, who at the same time suggested the modern use of *physicist* (earlier employed rarely as synonymous with *physician*). Most, in fact, of today's scientific specialties were given their present designations during the Victorian age, from *algology* (1849) and *bacteriology* (1884) to *zoögeography* (1868). Many now commonplace scientific terms were created during this period: *amoeba* (1841), *bacteria* (1847), *carbohydrate* (1869), *poliomyelitis* (1880), *bacillus* (1883), *psychopath* (1885), *appendicitis* (1886). The 19th century produced names for various, newly-discovered chemical elements: *actinium* (1881), *argon* (1895), *beryllium* (1863), *erbium* (1843), *gallium* (1875), *germanium* (1886), etc.

Perhaps most far-reaching of all vocabulary tendencies was scientific word coinage from Greek stems. This practice has been employed in English as early as the Renaissance—e.g., from the Greek *anthropo-* (man) and *logia* (study) the word *anthropology*, which never existed in ancient Greek, was introduced in 1593. In the 1830s and 1840s Lyell and other distinguished English scientists gave fresh impetus to this method of word creation, which in our own day continues to be the standard practice of science when it needs a new term. The 19th-century scientists exercised such a daring ingenuity in the invention of these pseudo-Greek words as English had never before witnessed. Typical is the creation by T. H. Huxley in 1870 of *abiogenesis*, combining the Greek *a-* (negative prefix), *bio-* (stem meaning "life"), and *genesis* (birth) to form a wholly new word. There seems no end to the possible combinations. From *lith-* (stone) both *neolithic* and *paleolithic* were coined by Lubbock in 1865. From *saur-* (lizard) Owen concocted *dinosaur* (1841), *stegosaur* (1877), and other combinations. Dictionary makers are overwhelmed by the multitudes of chemical terms invented on the same basis. One merely scratches the surface of a small nitrocarbon group with *trinitroglycerin* (1864), *trinitrocarbolic acid* (1866), *trinitrophenol* (1869), *trinitrocellulose* (1875).

In contrast to the awesome word fertility of the scientists, Victorian literary writers paled considerably. Except for the introduction of occasional archaic and dialectal terms, they generally proved as conservative as Macaulay, who apologized for using *constituency.* The most courageous word-coiner among men of letters was Carlyle. Many of his wordings were translations from the German, like *mischief-joy* (from *Schadenfreude*), but he also contributed Scottish words like *feckless, lilt,* and *outcome.* Apparently the indispensable *decadent, environment,* and *self-help* are his own inventions. Most writers of the era capitulated to the widespread euphemism of Victorian bourgeois speech by which *limbs* replaced *legs,* and even *serviette* was preferred to *napkin.*

Chapter 2

Victorian Poets

THE POETRY OF TENNYSON

Alfred Tennyson, first Baron Tennyson of Aldworth and Farringford, commonly **Alfred Lord Tennyson** (1809–1892). Following is a list of the more important events in the life of Alfred Lord Tennyson:

1809. Born August 6 at Somersby, Lincolnshire, fourth of eight brothers (he also had four sisters). Father was George Clayton Tennyson, rector of Somersby. Mother was Elizabeth Fytche. The Tennyson youngsters frequently played at being knights of King Arthur's court. Alfred started versifying at about the age of six. Early education at Louth Grammar School.

1827. First published volume, *Poems by Two Brothers,* in collaboration with brothers Charles and Frederick. (Frederick's modesty prompted this title.)

1828–31. Student at Trinity College, Cambridge, where his best friend was Arthur Henry Hallam, son of the historian. In 1829 won Chancellor's gold medal for poem "Timbuctoo." First published separately in 1830 and 1832.

1833–42. No publication, probably because of sorrow over Hallam's death (1833) and because of severity of professional critics toward his verse. Engaged to Emily Sellwood, sister-in-law of his brother Charles, in 1837.

1842. Established reputation with two volumes of verse. Extensive regular publication thereafter until his death.

1845. Assigned annual pension of £200 by Sir Robert Peel.

1850. Married Emily Sellwood. Succeeded Wordsworth as poet laureate.

1852. Birth of Hallam Tennyson, first child to survive birth.

1853. Resided until his death at Farringford, summering at Aldworth from 1869. Most leading figures of the age, Gladstone, for example, were visitors and friends. Most literary men from Palgrave to Swinburne and Hardy and American writers such as Bayard Taylor and Hawthorne were acquaintances. Traveled in British Isles and on the continent.

1884. Raised to the peerage as baron.

1892. Died at Aldworth on October 6. Buried near Chaucer in Poet's Corner of Westminster Abbey.

The idol of one age frequently becomes the target of the next. As the Victorian oracle, Tennyson in his lifetime commanded a larger audience and commanded more veneration from that audience than any other English poet has ever enjoyed. After his death and on into the early 20th century, the almost universal distaste for the bourgeois orthodoxy among intellectuals caused his reputation to decline drastically. Joyce dismissed him as "Alfred Lawn Tennison," and critics vied with each other in assigning the poet lower and lower ranking as a minor figure in English literature. Tennyson's reputation at mid-20th century, however, was rising, and he is now again rated highly, though significantly not for the qualities that brought him fame in his era. T. S. Eliot in 1936 acclaimed Tennyson as a great poet because of his "abundance, variety, and complete competence."

As an aid in distinguishing the dominant characteristics of Tennyson's poetry, we will follow each one of his poems with an identifying letter. The key for the letters is as follows:

(A) THE ARTICULATE VOICE OF THE BOURGEOIS ORTHODOXY. No other poet laureate in English, except Dryden, has been so productive during his term of office. Absolutely no other poet laureate has made himself so much the spokesman of the ascendancy of his period. Tennyson is the only English writer elevated to a hereditary peerage solely on the basis of his writings.

(B) THE CHAMPION OF THE BOURGEOIS ETHOS. In addition to being the voice of orthodoxy, Tennyson was its propagandist and its prophet, offering moral edification and stimulating ideas. He is largely credited with having given the English people their flattering image of the Prince Consort, the German husband of Queen Victoria. Many Victorians felt that *In Memoriam* reconciled their evangelicalism with the theory of evolution. In his later years, as the Victorian orthodoxy was toppling, Tennyson increasingly became the moralistic preacher, exhorting the age not to fall away from its beliefs. This and the previous category were chiefly responsible for his 19th-century fame.

(C) THE ROMANTIC LYRICIST. The young Tennyson inherited the mantle of Keats, and surprisingly many of his now celebrated poems date from the 1842 volume or earlier, i.e. before he consciously adopted the role of Victorian apologist. By nature Tennyson was a gifted poet, and it is this ability and the following characteristic upon which his present reputation is largely based.

(D) THE MORBID MYSTIC AND PERVERSE DREAMER. Concealed beneath an exterior of Victorian respectability was a dark strain in Tennyson that featured violence, flashes of bitter realism, and even irreverent humor. Emphasizing this unexpected Tennyson, modern critics often detect the submergence of the more desirable and truly poetic bard beneath the cloak of respectability and conformity.

These tendencies in Tennyson often overlap and are suggested merely as dominant characteristics in specific works. The poet constantly revised his poetry, and although they are here treated in the order of their first publication, the poems will be discussed in their final versions.

Poems, Chiefly Lyrical (1830) marks the emergence of the poet from the imitative style of the earlier poems into his own authentic voice.

"Mariana" (C) pictures a maiden despairing of her absent lover. An "experiment in atmosphere," it masterfully expresses the feeling of stagnation in the Lincolnshire fen country. Suggestion comes from Angelo's desertion of Mariana in *Measure for Measure*.

"The Poet" (C) in stanzas of rime and accentual pattern, *5a 3b 5a 2b*, states essentially the Romantic credo of the poet as the inspirer of mankind to freedom and true wisdom.

Poems (1832 but dated 1833) was generally derided by the official reviewers, though praised by John Stuart Mill. It includes some of the best-known verse of Tennyson.

"The Lady of Shalott" (B) is based upon an Italian romance *Donna di Scalotta*, the lady being ultimately Malory's "fair maid of Astolat." Weaving exquisite tapestry in her isolated isle, the Lady of Shalott, under a spell, has withdrawn from the world. She becomes hopelessly in love with Lancelot, and, turning from the "shadows of the world" in her mirror to gaze upon reality for the first time, she dies. Tennyson here first hit upon his immensely successful formula of lyric medievalism with a Victorian overcast. His medievalism is smooth and graceful, a dream vision of beauty and color. The implicit moral is soundly Victorian in its denunciation of a withdrawal from life.

"The Palace of Art" (B) employs a stanza with the rime and accentual pattern, *5a 4b 5a 3b*, to echo the moral of "The Lady of Shalott." The poem begins in Tennyson's best decorative manner to portray art for art's sake, a hedonistic refuge of the artist in beauty free of the taint of reality. After four years the soul feels sinful and gravely disturbed at the separation from humanity and everyday problems. In humility the artist descends to the world of men, sharing the riches of art with others. As in many of Tennyson's poems, the writer is struggling with contending forces within himself. The shrill harangue and inferior poetry of his evangelical conscience suggest that perhaps the poet's heart was unconsciously with the "devil's party."

"Oenone" (B) is the first significant example of Tennyson's formula of romantic classicism with a Victorian overcast. The blank verse monologue laments the desertion of the nymph Oenone by her lover Paris, and in a word-painting that challenges the many oil paintings on the subject it describes the Judgment of Paris in favor of Aphrodite. Although Pallas Athene is dishonestly offering a bribe to Paris, her advice for "Self-reverence, self-knowledge, self-control" is the summary of Tennyson's conscious philosophy.

"The Lotos-Eaters" (C) expands the portion of the *Odyssey* that deals with the succumbing of the sailors of Ulysses to the mysterious addiction of the Lotophagi. Even his inspirers, Keats and Spenser, could not have more effectively conveyed Tennyson's atmosphere of seductive luxury and blissful enervation.

Poems (1842) broke the ten years' silence with two volumes. The first consisted chiefly of revisions of previous verse. The second volume included most of his writing over the silent decade, except for *In Memoriam*. With this collection Tennyson definitely emerged as the poetic spokesman for the Victorian orthodoxy. The aged Samuel Rogers wrote to Tennyson: "Very few things, if any, have ever thrilled me so much." The youthful Dickens promptly dispatched copies of his works to the man "whose writings enlist my whole heart and nature in admiration of their truth and beauty."

"You ask me, why, though ill at ease" (1833) (A) in the *In Memoriam* stanza arose from Tennyson's annoyance at the hostile reception of his 1832 volume. He meditated a flight, like that of Shelley and Byron, to Italy; but in this lyric he justifies his remaining in England, chiefly because it is the land "Where Freedom slowly broadens down/From precedent to precedent."

"Ulysses" (*1833*) (B) was prompted by Hallam's death, Tennyson observing, "It was more written with the feeling of his loss upon me than many poems in *In Memoriam*." The suggestion comes not from the *Odyssey* but from Canto XXVI of Dante's *Inferno*. Instead of Dante's condemnation of the ancient voyager for daring beyond the limits ordained by God, Tennyson sees the forward-looking spirit of Ulysses as the 19th-century drive for fullest achievement and experience regardless of age and physical weakness. The dynamic force of this blank-verse poem, not at all typical of Tennyson, is in striking contrast to "The Lotos-Eaters." Probably this is the poet's most popular poem for the 20th century.

"Locksley Hall" (B) in couplets of rimed fourteeners is a dramatic monologue by a disturbed Victorian youth. He leaves a hunting party to meditate upon his old home, Locksley Hall. His personal distress is caused by the marriage of his beloved Amy to another. In familiar Tennysonian manner he debates withdrawal to the East (associated by the poet with license and passion), but he scorns such a choice in favor of participation in the momentous progress of the West. "Forward, forward let us range" is his cry, as he gazes idealistically toward a future of peace and universal prosperity. Although, by the poet's admission, the speaker displays considerable immaturity and egoism (indicative of strains within the writer), the period saw in this poem one of the finest expressions of its aspiration and confidence. The poem was a favorite of Browning.

"Sir Galahad" (A) in twelve-line stanzas is a dramatic monologue by the Arthurian knight, son of Lancelot and Elaine, as he searches for the Holy Grail. Increasingly, Tennyson was convinced that self-restraint and conformity to bourgeois morality were the keys to happiness and well-being; the theme of the *Idylls of the King* was in embryo.

"The Vision of Sin" (D) ostensibly preaches Tennyson's familiar doctrine of spiritual love as superior to physical love and sensuality. Nonetheless, the poet is morbidly fascinated in this nightmarish dream by the problem of man's perverse vulgarity and his attraction to vice.

"Break, break, break" (*1834*) (C) is a cry for Hallam in the poet's great sorrow. Metrically daring and effective is the use of three accents to the line, varying the number of syllables from as few as three to as many as ten.

The Princess (1847) contained Tennyson's first attempt at a lengthy poem.

"The Princess" (B), the title poem, in blank verse, is related by a party of young Cambridge men picnicking in the ruins of a medieval abbey in Kent. The subject is a woman's university barring all males whatsoever. Amid vague settings, medieval and Renaissance, the subjects of instruction even include modern science. The inevitable battle of the sexes that ensues is sometimes treated with high seriousness, sometimes farcically. Though advocating the stimulation of female intellectuality, the poet insists that woman's true career lies in marriage. Conjugal felicity is Tennyson's exalted Victorian ideal. From the poem's appearance to the present neither critics nor readers have shown enthusiasm for the narrative. Gilbert and Sullivan burlesqued the work in *Princess Ida* (1884).

Lyrics interspersed in *The Princess* are among Tennyson's best and among the best in English. The poet excels in the lullaby of "Sweet and Low," the bugle call of "The splendour falls on castle walls," the sentimental "Home they brought her warrior dead." "Come down, O maid, from yonder mountain height" and "Now sleeps the crimson petal" are often termed the greatest unrimed lyrics in English. The implicit sexuality in the latter poem is sublimated in exquisite harmony. All these lyrics display consummate art in melody and onomatopoeia.

In Memoriam A. H. H. (1850) (B), written as an elegy on the death of Arthur Henry Hallam, was composed over a seventeen-year period from 1833. Instead of a pastoral elegy like Milton's *Lycidas* or Shelley's *Adonais,* Tennyson recorded his grief in a series of one hundred and thirty-one short poems ("swallow-flights of song" he called them) in iambic tetrameter quatrains riming *a b b a*. This is termed the *In Memoriam* stanza, for although this quatrain was employed infrequently in earlier English poetry (by Lord Herbert of Cherbury and Ben Jonson) Tennyson apparently reinvented it and established its fame. Remarkable is the variety of poetic effects in the hundreds of stanzas, ranging from epigrammatic concision to long-sustained paragraphs and from meditative contemplation of death and scientific fact to the gaiety of New Year's and wedding parties.

Tennyson termed this work "The way of the soul." It is the progress from bitter grief and doubt to acceptance, from a fear that the cosmos is governed by indifference to the certainty that it is dominated by love. Stages in the gradual rise of spirit are marked by Christmas seasons, but the rise is interrupted even in the middle sections by torments of heart. Chiefly responsible for the gloom is the scientific depiction of man as a misbegotten animal in a heedless universe. Tennyson surmounts his despair partly by intuitive belief in benevolence as the guiding principle and partly by accepting evolution as divinely ordained. Mankind will evolve on earth toward the higher man, and the spirits of the dead will in an afterlife continue the evolutionary pattern toward full realization.

On the basis of this poem the Prince Consort secured the poet laureateship for Tennyson, and with this work Tennyson fully came into his own as the Victorian oracle. The first five thousand copies were sold almost immediately, and within less than a year the poem went through three editions, selling over sixty thousand copies. Except for the Romantic narrative poems of the previous generation, it set an all-time record for English poetry sales in its own day. Clergymen quoted *In Memoriam* from the pulpit, numerous "keys" appeared to explicate it, and multitudes revered it as the inspired voice of the prophet. Queen Victoria told Tennyson, "Next to the Bible, *In Memoriam* is my comfort." Many humanists of the age saw it as the definitive answer to the quarrel of science versus faith, and deemed it the 19th-century work most likely to speak to posterity. Our century has ignored it as philosophical preachment but still admires many of its sections for their eloquent lyricism and the poignant evocation of moods, especially in a tortured soul.

"The Eagle" (C) appeared in the fourth edition (1851) of *In Memoriam*. Its crisp, incisive six lines are among the most effective nature descriptions in verse.

"The Charge of the Light Brigade" (A) first appeared in the *Examiner*, December 9, 1854. Late in October of that year the Earl of Cardogan had led the Light Brigade (reconnaissance cavalry) at Balaklava in the Crimea in a gallant but ridiculous assault upon fixed Russian guns. *The Times* report stated that "someone had blundered" in issuing the preposterous order.

From Chatterton's "Song of Aella" Tennyson secured the rhythm for what he termed his "ballad."

"Maud; a Monodrama" (D), published in *Maud, and Other Poems* (1855), is a Romeo-Juliet narrative in verse. The speaker of this dramatic monologue is a bitter youth, living in rural isolation after his father's suicide. Basically he is appalled by the "lust of gain," the materialism, and the commercialism of the era. Speaking wildly, the youth explores the depths of morbidity and approaches insanity. Maud (only character named in the poem), daughter of a landowner hating the speaker's family, accepts the young man's proposal of marriage, starting him back to wholesome balance. After a seemingly fatal duel with her brother he flees, losing Maud. Tennyson termed it "a little *Hamlet*" and made it his favorite reading selection.

The theme, in proper Victorian manner, is the power of pure love to rescue a man from selfish despair. Virtually all contemporaries, however, except Browning, condemned the poem for its dark morbidity and inner terrors. Its portrait of a warped soul makes it one of the poet's more "modern" pieces. The metrics vary from idyllic love lyrics to purposely roughened lines of tortured introspection. Significantly, the narrative grew out of short lyrics such as "Come into the garden, Maud" and "O that 'twere possible."

Idylls of the King (1859) (B) printed four blank-verse poems on the Arthurian legends. Tennyson added and revised for more than a quarter of a century until in 1888 he had completed and organized the entire series of twelve poems into the present form. Pursuant to his final concept, the work is here considered as a unit.

"I intended Arthur to represent the ideal soul of man coming into contact with the warring elements of the flesh," stated the poet. Arthur is also obviously the Victorian spirit of rational self-control "working out his will to cleanse the world." Many of the age saw Arthur as modeled after the queen's husband, the Prince Consort. Dominant theme is the attempt by the moral Arthur to establish the Victorian virtues of marital faithfulness, fair play, gentlemanly conduct, and useful action for self and society. The Lady of the Lake presents to Arthur the Sword of the Spirit, Excalibur, with which he may fight against weakness and lust. The knights of the Round Table further represent the better faculties of human nature. Counter theme is the destruction of the spiritual by the physical, the uprising of materialism and sensualism. Lancelot symbolizes the valiant and essentially good man who succumbs to the blandishments of the flesh. Guinevere stands for the emotions of mankind, which must be properly directed by rational self-control if they are not to slip into error.

Obvious moralizing often supersedes veiled allegory and renders some of the work rather unpalatable to the 20th-century reader. The dream world

of medievalism, organs pealing in Gothic churches at midnight and knights
picturesquely caracoling at tournaments, is difficult to reconcile with the
characters—all Victorian in self-conscious sensibility, seeking "To lead sweet
lives in purest chastity." To our age the *Idylls* still speak, nonetheless,
with haunting romantic description and enthralling melody.

I. "The Coming of Arthur" (1869) announces the dawn of a new era,
radiant in sunshine and hope. Tennyson delicately evades the original illegitimate birth of Arthur and suggests both a normal, though unhappy,
union of Ygerne and Uther, and a miraculous presentation of the infant
Arthur to Merlin in a dragon-shaped vessel. The youthful Arthur reunites
and revivifies a disorganized kingdom, saves the realm of Leodegran, and
weds that monarch's daughter, Guinevere. At the marriage, insolent Roman
emissaries demand tribute; refusing, Arthur wars with Rome. Malory is
chief source.

II. "Gareth and Lynette" (1872), Fitzgerald's favorite, continues the mood
of youthful high spirits and optimism. Gareth, youngest son of King Lot
and Queen Bellicent, is fired by the glamour of the Round Table. Distressed
at the prospect of losing her darling, Gareth's mother persuades him to
serve one year incognito as a scullery boy at Arthur's court. Lynette pleads
for Lancelot to free her sister, Lyonors, captive of three wicked knights in
the Castle Perilous. Arthur, knowing Gareth's identity, picks him to go over
the snobbish objections of Lynette. The lad overpowers the villainous cap-
tors and releases Lyonors, forcing Lynette to apologize. Gareth is joyous,
idealistic youth; Lynette, charming but proud. The allegory is so overridden
by the vivacity of youth as to form perhaps the most charming tale of the
series. The *Mabinogion* is a source as well as Malory.

III. "The Marriage of Geraint" and the next idyll (IV), forming one continuous narrative in 1859 under the title of "Enid," were first separated
into the present division in 1884. Both parts stem essentially from the
Mabinogion. In this tale Geraint weds Enid, whom he saved from the
vicious knight Sparrow Hawk. Suspicious because of the mounting scandal
about Lancelot and Guinevere, Geraint removes his wife from the influence of the court. Waking one morning Enid sheds tears over her sleeping
husband. He awakes to hear her murmuring that she is a bad wife, unworthy
of him. Jumping to the false conclusion that she has confessed adultery, he
forces her to ride silently ahead of him.

IV. "Geraint and Enid," split from the second half of "Enid" simply to
create twelve books of equal length, continues the previous narrative.
Geraint refuses to listen to Enid even when she tries to save his life.
After vicissitudes with knights along the way, Geraint is wounded. Arthur
effects a reconciliation of husband and wife that lasts until Geraint's death
in battle against the Saxons. Geraint is an unattractive bully, a dominating
Victorian husband. Tennyson obviously intends Enid as a perfectly admi-

rable wife, but her obsequiousness is totally unacceptable to a modern reader.

V. "Balin and Balan" (1885) condenses and slightly alters Malory's account. The four types of malignity that are to shatter the court of Arthur are personified: Modred (envious ambition, rebelling against law and order), Mark (selfish treachery, injuring all righteousness for momentary gain), Garlon (slander, delighting in destruction of good reputation in order to comfort a mean egotism), and Vivien (sensuality and vice, joying in reducing others to its baseness). Balin, a good knight but easily aroused to blind anger, is duped by the evil forces into battle with his brother Balan. As they slay each other, the heartless Vivien rides off, leaving their corpses to the wolves. The heavy-handed moral preaches that undisciplined anger destroys oneself and others.

VI. "Merlin and Vivien" (1859) is Tennyson's elaboration of a mere suggestion in Malory. The aged wizard Merlin (pure intellect) is seduced by Vivien (voluptuous sensuality). He relinquishes his powers to her, and she uses her newly gained magic to imprison him forever in a hollow oak, Tennyson thereby symbolizing how the higher faculties of man may be rendered impotent by yielding to low passion. Through it all Merlin senses the growth of corruption, arising from Guinevere's infidelity, that is eventually to blight the entire court. Tennyson is unable to present passion tastefully, and so the characterizations of Vivien and Merlin are unpleasant rather than convincing.

VII. "Lancelot and Elaine" (1859) closely follows the story line of Malory but introduces almost unbearable sweetness. Hopelessly in love with Lancelot, Elaine nurses him back to health from severe wounds. She confesses her love, but Lancelot tenderly informs her that he can love no other than Guinevere, and Elaine is left to pine away to death. Victorians wept copiously at the tender sentimentalism of this poem, but modern readers are often cloyed with the ineffectual purity and femininity of Elaine.

VIII. "The Holy Grail" (1869), considerably modifying Malory's narrative, is told as dialogue between Percivale (former knight of the Round Table, now a hermit) and the aged parish priest Ambrosius. Percivale relates the vision of the San Graal, the chalice in which Joseph of Arimathea supposedly caught the blood of the crucified Christ and bore it to Glastonbury in Britain. Seeing the pulsating Grail is a sign that one has obtained complete "union" with Christ. While Arthur is absent putting down outlaws, his knights vow to search for the vision. Their quest is fruitless, as the annoyed Arthur predicted, except for Galahad, who is translated to heaven along with the Holy Grail. Tennyson believes that except for rare cases like Galahad, emotional and sensational religion generally partakes of superstition. The impractical quest by the knights neglects the proper and useful tasks they should be fulfilling. This marks the turning point of the entire work, for the fortunes of Arthur now begin to ebb. Boasting some of Tennyson's finest blank verse, this rates second only to "The Passing of Arthur" among the idylls.

IX. "Pelleas and Ettare" (1869) derives from Malory. Pelleas is one of the new knights created to fill the gaps caused by the disastrous quest for the Holy Grail. Innocent and trusting, he believes the pledge of friendship from Gawain and the pledge of love from Ettare. Finding Gawain and Ettare embracing amorously, he is shattered. Sensing the imminent downfall of Arthur, the scheming Modred mutters, "The time is hard at hand." The corruption induced by the liaison of Lancelot and Guinevere has pervaded the court. Pelleas is hopelessly naïve, and Ettare is a less interesting version of Vivien.

X. "The Last Tournament" (1871) partly utilizes Malory but leans especially on the later amplification of the Tristram account. Lancelot listlessly presides at a dispirited tournament, replete with constant infractions of the laws of chivalry. Arthur is away purging the realm of the last bandits. Tristram wins the tournament and hastens off to Isolt, his mistress and wife of King Mark. Discovering the lovers, Mark slays both. Arthur returns to find that Guinevere has fled. Lust and cynicism, symbolized by the sordid intrigue of Tristram, have swept away the old ideals. Like Matthew Arnold in his earlier version of the Tristram legend, Tennyson interprets Tristram as essentially a low adulterer.

XI. "Guinevere" (1859) is elaborated from a mere hint in Malory. Taking refuge in the convent of Almesbury, the unfaithful queen hopes to do penance for her sin by prayers and remorse. Arthur comes to lecture her on marital fidelity as she grovels at his feet. Though he forgives her for her crimes and her spoiling of "the purpose of his life," he shall never see her again. Unfortunately, Arthur seems to 20th-century readers insufferably self-righteous.

XII. "The Passing of Arthur" (1869) incorporates the "Morte d'Arthur" of 1842. A wholly exemplary character and a splendid ideal collapse before the baseness and sensuality of lesser men. The excellences of Arthur came too early to a world not ready for them. However, Arthur in fatal struggle carries the treacherous and ambitious Modred to the same destruction, and the way is prepared for a new era of heightened virtue. By general consent, this is the best of the idylls with its melodic blank verse and calm beauty.

"Tithonus" (*1833*, 1860) (C) was first published in *Cornhill Magazine*, under Thackeray's editorship. It is a monologue by Tithonus, the mortal lover of the goddess Aurora, who conferred upon him the gift of immortality. Unfortunately, immortality for Tithonus did not mean immortal youth, and the fantastically senile Tithonus pleads for the boon of death. The moral, the necessity for man to accept death as the lot of all men, is mercifully overshadowed by perhaps the purest, most classic-sounding blank verse of Tennyson.

"Enoch Arden" (A) was the poet's most popular work to his contemporaries. It was published in *Enoch Arden, and Other Poems* (1864) and translated into eight foreign languages before his death. Even though today's anthologies scrupulously omit this blank verse narrative, newspapers still herald the reappearance of a man given up for dead as an "Enoch Arden story." The title character, much changed by years of vicissitudes, is not recognized in his native village. Until death he maintains his disguise rather than destroy the happiness of his rewed wife.

Locksley Hall Sixty Years After, Etc. (1886) is remarkable testimony to the continued fertility and fluency of Tennyson as he neared eighty. Only Landor among English poets has displayed similar poetic vitality at far advanced years.

"Locksley Hall Sixty Years After" (D) portrays the central figure of the earlier "Locksley Hall" poem, now eighty, as he looks back to the blighted love affair with Amy and his own tragic loss of an only son. His youthful hopes for a better world have been crushed under heartless commercialism and crazed "liberalism." Nonetheless, he cleaves passionately to the conviction of the spirit's immortality and perfectibility. Amy's husband, whom he had scorned in the earlier poem, he now realizes has proved the better man in his life of simple service. Gladstone replied in a *Nineteenth Century* magazine article that the poem should not be the excuse for the indulgence "of a carping and also of a morbid temper" and listed the numerous reform measures passed by parliament under Victoria as a counter argument.

"Crossing the Bar" (C), from *Demeter and Other Poems* (1889), by the poet's request is placed at the end of all editions of his poetry. An old sailor's superstition asserts that a tide "moaning" as it ebbs across a harbor bar foretells a tragic voyage. Still another superstition claims that men die only as the tide flows out to sea. Likening his own passing to the ebb of the tide, Tennyson hopes for a quiet journey to an afterlife.

THE POETRY OF BROWNING

Robert Browning (1812–1889). Following is a list of the more important events in the life of Robert Browning:

1812. Born May 7 at Camberwell, London, only son of banker Robert Browning and Scotch-German Sarah Anne Wiedemann, a pious Congregationalist. The poet's father gave their home a rich atmosphere of art, books, and vivacious domesticity.

1821-26. Boarding school offered no intellectual challenge to the precocious boy who found his father's library infinitely more stimulating. Unable in 1826 to interest a publisher in *Incondita,* his first volume of verse, Browning destroyed all but two of the poems.

1826. Enraptured with Shelley, Browning briefly was "a vegetarian, a scoffer, an atheist."

1828. Quit University of London shortly after enrolling. Continued private study along with riding, singing, fencing, boxing, piano-playing, clay modeling, and theater-going.

1833. First published work, *Pauline,* was complete failure. The reception of this confessional piece apparently caused the poet thereafter to present objective, dramatic characters in his verse rather than stressing himself.

1834. Accompanied the Russian consul general to St. Petersburg.

1835. Paracelsus, first work to bear Browning's name, sold poorly but obtained high reputation in literary circles.

1837. Induced by actor-producer William Macready, Browning prepared his first drama, *Strafford,* which lasted for only five performances.

1838. First visit to Italy.

1840. Obscurity and supersubtlety of *Sordello* clouded his reputation for a quarter of a century.

1844. Second visit to Italy.

1845. Attracted to the invalid poetess, Elizabeth Barrett, by her compliments to his verse. Romantic courtship proceeded in spite of her tyrannical father's bitter opposition.

1846. Secret wedding of Elizabeth (forty) and Robert (thirty-four), followed by immediate departure for Italy.

1847. Settled at Casa Guidi, Florence, their Italian home for fourteen years. Browning later declared that Italy was his university. Landor was a close friend. Numerous literary figures from England and America visited the Brownings, chiefly lured by the poetic fame of Elizabeth.

1849. Birth of son, Robert Wiedemann Barrett Browning.

1855. Men and Women his first truly successful work, though not immediately winning an audience comparable with that of Tennyson.

1861. Death of Mrs. Browning at Florence. Abandoning his former life, Browning settled in London.

1867. Honorary master's degree and fellowship from Oxford signaled belated recognition.

1868. Popular acclaim first widespread with publication of *The Ring and the Book.*

1869. Marriage proposal to Lady Ashburton rejected.

1871–89. Most extensive publication, though varying in quality.

1878. Revisited Italy.

1881. Founding of Browning Society by Dr. F. J. Furnivall.

1889. Died December 12 at his son's residence in Venice. Buried in the Poet's Corner at Westminster Abbey.

Browning is probably the most attractive and certainly the most vigorous exponent of evangelical Protestantism. After a brief teenage infatuation with Shelleyan radicalism, he maintained thereafter an unshakable Christian faith, although he never attached himself to any religious sect. Admitting evolution, he felt none of the perturbations assailing Tennyson and Arnold. His age saw him as a pillar of faith, and the eminent Victorian bishop Westcott listed his principal teachers as St. John, Origen, and Browning. Later rebels against the Victorian orthodoxy, like Havelock Ellis, have tended to scorn Browning's serene convictions.

Throughout his mature work Browning consistently maintained:

(1) Individualism. Requiring no intermediary, the soul works out its own destiny with God as its only judge.

(2) Optimism. Simple goodness far outstrips the evil in this world. The enormous prospects of human happiness quite outweigh the magnitude of human suffering. Intuitively he feels absolute confidence in a personal deity who loves man and grants him immortality.

(3) Moral virtue. The spiritual quality of the universe can be properly grasped only by a man without significant blemish, and genius carries with it no warrant to abandon fundamental moralities.

(4) The zest and challenge of life. Human progress is inevitable, and aspiration instead of attainment is the test of the soul's excellence.

(5) Delight in observing people. Perhaps only Shakespeare surpasses Browning in the intense desire to understand his fellow men. Browning may well be the greatest descriptive psychologist among English poets.

(6) Benthamism. Browning resolutely proclaimed himself a political liberal, but he used the term in the sense of the Benthamites and would today be labeled a conservative, as the term is used in England. Although he strongly supported representative government and detested any arbitrary rule, he nonetheless opposed woman suffrage and Home Rule for Ireland. To Browning the English country gentleman was "the salt of the earth," and he deplored the excesses of continental republicanism.

Browning in his lifetime never received the public acclaim accorded Tennyson, and until his middle years he was overshadowed not only by the laureate's reputation but by that of Elizabeth Browning. Robert generously saw his wife as the greater poet. His fame came late and never subsequently fell to the abysses suffered early in the 20th century by Tennyson's reputation. Intellectuals have consistently praised Browning not as the religious teacher he seemed to his age but for his psychological portraits and his poetic style. Browning could write mellifluous verse like Tennyson's and Swinburne's, but he much preferred either a conversational quality catching the idiom and cadence of actual speech or a cerebral diction challenging the brain power of his readers. Too often Browning's verse becomes tortured, obscure, and enigmatically condensed; but in spite of their frequent patronizing of Browning's Victorian convictions, 20th-century poets in their often crabbed and highly intellectualized style probably owe more to Browning than to any other Victorian poet. Browning is the great exemplar of a revolutionary new poetic diction for his age, as Spenser, Dryden, and Wordsworth had been in earlier periods of English poetry.

Works are here considered in their order of publication but in their final titles and versions. Dramas are indicated by (D) and dramatic monologues, Browning's forte, by (M). In the dramatic monologues the speaker is an imagined character, not the poet himself.

Paracelsus (1835) (D) in blank-verse dialogue examines five highlights in the spiritual career of Theophrastus Bombastus von Hohenheim (c. 1493–1541), a German physician who in Renaissance fashion adopted the Latin name Paracelsus. From his father's library Browning obtained his sources: the works of Paracelsus edited by Bitiskius, *Vitae Germanorum Medicorum* by Melchior Adam, and the *Biographie universelle*. This is the first Browning work to explore the Renaissance that was to intrigue the poet throughout his career; he saw in the Renaissance the great upsurge of aspiring individualism. Astonishingly mature from a poet of twenty-five, it expounds Browning's lifelong philosophy in what some critics deem his greatest work.

Paracelsus, the searcher for knowledge, is countered by Aprile, the devotee of poetic life and beauty. On his deathbed the Faustian Paracelsus finally realizes that perfect love is not the quest for abstract knowledge or beauty but the divine condescension to human frailty. The best course is that of Festus, who sees God not as perfect knowledge or beauty but as perfect love. This love, the dying Paracelsus finally comprehends, offers to man the challenge of continuous rise to ever greater heights of creativity and expression. Though Paracelsus failed in his full purpose, he served humanity toward its betterment, found at last a deep realization of truth, and will continue in after life toward completion of the broken arc.

Pippa Passes: A Drama (1841) (D) is a by-product of Browning's search for materials for *Sordello*. Plot is apparently original except for indebtedness to Lytton's *Lady of Lyons* for the Jules-Phene episode. Prose and blank-verse dialogue are interspersed with the lyrics of Pippa, most famous of which is the innocent optimism of "All's right with the world!" The scene is contemporary Asolo, a silk-mill town in northern Italy. Pippa, a girl working in the factories, has but one holiday in the entire calendar— New Year's Day. She plans on this day to walk past the residences of the four most envied people of the community; she will imagine herself as each of them, and imaginatively share their favored lives of happiness.

I, Morning. At his mistress' instigation, Sebald has just slain Luca, husband of Ottima. As Pippa sings outside, the guilty pair realize their horrible crime and in repentance begin redemption.

II, Noon. Waggish students have pawned off the boorish Phene upon the sculptor Jules. He is about to cast her aside after the marriage ceremony when Pippa's song wakes him to his responsibilities and effects a reconciliation.

III, Evening. "Patriot" Luigi, seeking the liberation of Italy, is almost persuaded by his mother to remain overnight, not knowing that the police are planning to seize him. Pippa's song spurs him to immediate departure and consequent safety.

IV, Night. The Monsignor from Rome almost accepts the urgings of his wicked superintendent to let Bluphocks, an English scoundrel, entrap and ruin Pippa, for she is the legitimate child and heir of the superintendent's brother, whose property is wrongfully held by the superintendent. Hearing Pippa's song, the Monsignor is awakened in conscience and orders the villains seized.

The souls of men are mutually interdependent, and the simple goodness of the most naïve may have profound repercussions in transforming the lives of others to virtue.

Dramatic Lyrics (1842) was printed at the suggestion of the publisher Moxon to secure popularity with short pieces. Here appear the first Browning poems to be continuing favorites.

"My Last Duchess" (M), though one of his earliest dramatic monologues, is often considered among Browning's best. Probably it is another offshoot of his studies for *Sordello*. The model seems to be Alfonso II, of the ancient house of Este, fifth Duke of Ferrara, whose first wife, Lucrezia de Medici, died perhaps of poison in 1561 at the age of seventeen. Alfonso then negotiated for a large dowry to accompany his second wife, Barbara, niece of the Count of Tyrol, whose capital was Innsbruck. The heroic couplets superbly capture the rhythms of natural conversation, as the Duke talks of the portrait of his first wife, his "last Duchess." The duke, speaking familiarly as a high grandee to the count's agent, wishes to make two points: the second wife must flatter his ego and must bring a sizable dowry. His easy pretense as art connoisseur and polished gentleman does not conceal the consuming pride, greediness, and heartlessness of the duke. From the mouth of her destroyer the "last duchess" shines as a simple, sweet girl.

"Count Gismond" (M) was originally planned as a contrast with the previous poem, portraying the gallant French attitude toward woman as an adored ideal against the calloused Italian view of woman as a chattel. Gismond's wife relates how, just as she was to be crowned virgin queen of the tourney, the base Count Gauthier accused her of misconduct with him. Gismond leaped forward as her champion, slew the liar, and forced Gauthier in his dying gasp to acknowledge her innocence. They were married soon afterward. The imaginary episode illustrates Browning's contention that virtue is immediately recognizable and will properly overcome or be defended against evil. He supports the old chivalric belief: "God will have a stroke in every battle."

"Incident of the French Camp" was probably inspired by the sumptuous second burial of Napoleon in Paris in 1841. Although Browning asserted that the anecdote was true, the incident is unknown to history. A proud French youth dashes from the battle lines at Ratesbon (German Regensburg) in 1809 to announce victory to Napoleon, and dies as he delivers the message. The delight in romantic action and devoted heroism has made the poem a perennial favorite of the young.

"Soliloquy of the Spanish Cloister" (M) is an experiment in trochaic tetrameter. The speaker is a warped monk who desperately schemes to damn the soul of the innocent (yet probably boring) Brother Lawrence. Though the reference to the "scrofulous French novel" seems contemporary, the atmosphere is reminiscent of the intense Renaissance desire for revenge (as in *Hamlet*) that damns a man's soul as well as injures him physically. The speaker considers both perverting Brother Lawrence's morals and trapping him in heresy; apparently the speaker will even risk selling his own soul to the devil to destroy his enemy. In Protestant fashion Browning gravely challenges the monastic principles as a breeder of narrow, selfish spirits. The speaker resembles Robert Burns's Holy Willie.

"In a Gondola" was written to accompany the painting "Serenade" by Maclise. In a Venetian gondola a lover and his mistress sing of their stolen reality of love upon the gliding vessel. Ashore are the shams and illusions of life—and lurking assassins. The lover is poinarded as he helps the lady off the boat, but he has no hate for his slayers. Briefly but ecstatically he has lived to the full.

"Porphyria's Lover" (M), first printed in 1836 by the *Monthly Repository,* is Browning's first excursion into abnormal psychology. During a storm the speaker is visited by Porphyria whom he loves but whose love in return he has doubted. Convinced by her of her deep love for him, he strangles her with her own hair so that he shall never lose her. He rationalizes that his slaying is perfectly right, terminating her life at its highest moment. "All lost for love" was a sentimental slogan appealing to Victorian readers, who failed to sense the antisocial consequences of Browning's advocacy of complete surrender to the intensity of love. The imaginative poet carries his doctrine to its full conclusion in a disordered mind. The monologues of Tennyson are primarily mood pieces, but those by Browning are vivid objective characterizations, bringing to life a unique temperament and viewpoint. Browning vigorously objected to any interpretation of himself through these monologues, declaring his purpose to be the unbiased delineation of psychological states in intriguing personalities.

"The Pied Piper of Hamelin" was written for Willie Macready, son of the distinguished actor-manager, as the boy fretted in bed from a cold. The pied piper for a promised sum piped the rats out of the town to drown in the nearby river. Refused payment, he then piped away the children of the town, never to be seen again. The rat episode could refer to the migration of lemmings; the piping away of the children might refer to the Children's Crusade of 1212. Browning acknowledged as sole source Nathaniel Wanley's *Wonders of the Little World* (1678), but his account is actually closer to that of Richard Verstegen from 1605.

Dramatic Romances and Lyrics (1845) appeared at the urging of Moxon to gain popularity. Though reception was moderate, except from Elizabeth Barrett and the Rossettis, it has gradually become recognized as one of the most notable single volumes by an English poet.

"How They Brought the Good News from Ghent to Aix" (M) supposedly concerns an incident during 17th-century wars in the Low Countries, but there is no historical basis. The speaker and two fellow horsemen gallop one hundred and twenty miles in a circuitous route, the speaker's horse Roland proving the only steed capable of carrying its messenger to Aix. The stirring effect of galloping horses is largely achieved by use of the amphibrach (a metrical foot consisting of an unaccented, an accented, and an unaccented syllable). Browning stated that the meter came from Vergil, probably Book VIII of the *Aeneid*.

"The Lost Mistress" (M) is spoken by a man whose beloved has broken off the affair. Intensest emotion is thoroughly under the control of a strong, resigned, Browningesque spirit.

"Home-Thoughts, from Abroad" is an ecstatically lyric contemplation of an English spring supposedly by an Englishman in Italy.

"The Bishop Orders His Tomb at St. Praxed's Church" (M) was probably conceived during 1844 in Rome when Browning visited the church of St. Prassede, named for a charitable Christian virgin of the 2d century. An imaginary Renaissance bishop of the 16th century on his deathbed asks his illegitimate sons to provide him with a sumptuous tomb within the church. He glories in his triumphs over the rival Gandolf, especially with the mother of his children, but it is clear that he shall never have the tomb he yearns for. Ruskin asserted: "I know of no other piece of modern English, prose or poetry, in which there is so much told, as in these lines, of the Renaissance spirit,—its worldliness, inconsistency, pride, hypocrisy, ignorance of itself, love of art, of luxury, and of good Latin."

Browning develops ironic contrasts between the bishop's sense of powerful success and his actual failure in human relationships, between the narrow sensuous materialism of the bishop and his pathetic expectation of immortality, between the bishop's sense of command over people and things and the pitiful ineffectuality of his "orders" as his ownership is proved as brief as life itself. The deathbed monologue approaches "stream of consciousness" technique, following emotional rather than logical patterns.

"The Laboratory" (M) seeks to capture an aspect of the *ancien régime* of France in depicting a court lady like the 17th-century Marie Brinvilliers, whose lover died when his glass mask fell off during the preparation of poison at her request. The speaker gleefully contemplates the mortal agonies of her feminine rivals after she poisons them.

"Meeting at Night" and "Parting at Morning" actually form one love lyric. Browning explained about the male speaker: "it is *his* confession of how fleeting is the belief (implied in the first part) that such raptures are self-sufficient and enduring—as for the time they appear." The sharp visual images and intense emotion have made these among the most respected of Browning's poems.

Men and Women (1855) in two volumes constitutes Browning's greatest mature creation, except for *The Ring and the Book*. Critical enthusiasm was high, especially from William Morris, but general popularity grew slowly. The chief poems are:

"Love among the Ruins" (M) in a twelve-line stanza of Browning's invention is a meditation by a lover amid the ruins of an ancient city, probably the Nineveh excavated by Layard. The poet concludes that all the power and greed of man pales beneath the greater glory of love.

"Up at a Villa—Down in the City" (M) probably dates from the Brownings' residence in the hills near Siena during 1850. The speaker is an "Italian person of quality" who yearns for the color and excitement of the city but is marooned in the country by genteel poverty. Probably no other poem in literature so sparklingly captures the vivacious Italian spirit.

"Fra Lippo Lippi" (M) probably arose from Browning's viewing of "The Coronation of the Virgin" at the Accademia in Florence and from Landor's employment of the 15th-century painter in "Fra Filippo Lippi and Pope Eugenius the Fourth" in *Imaginary Conversations*. The account follows the vivid personal portrayal by Vasari, but it is a hint from Baldinucci that causes Browning to interpret Lippi as the first realistic painter. Lippi is molded into the Browning image of the individualist, rebellious against artistic convention, vigorously insistent upon robust, actual life, the very antithesis of "Pictor Ignotus." Lippi is caught by the nightwatch of Florence as he is carrying out an assignation. By naming his mighty patron, Cosimo of the Medici, he gains his release. He explains that he is not naturally inclined to the ascetic life but as a child was placed in the monastery because of extreme poverty. In spite of ecclesiastical preference for the traditional ethereal art, he will continue to paint the "simple beauty" of genuine observation, confident that therein lies God's truth. Vasari indicates that a generous pope permitted Lippi to drop his vow of celibacy and

marry Lucrezia Buti, his mistress and model for the Virgin in "The Coronation of the Virgin."

"A Toccata of Galuppi's" (M) is Browning's first poem exclusively upon
music. An unsophisticated Englishman, listening to a toccata ("touch piece,"
a rapidly-paced work) by the Venetian composer Baldassare Galuppi
(1706–85), observes two themes emerging. One treats of the frivolous, fun-
loving Venetians, kissing and dancing until stopped by death. The other,
with its solemn note of intellectuality, suggests the seekers after knowledge, who likewise miss the point of life if they live for nothing but cold
science.

"My Star," apparently a tribute to his wife, states that while others will
conceive of a world in a star, the poet has found therein a soul. When his
autograph was sought, Browning would generally write out this poem.

"Childe Roland to the Dark Tower Came" (M) takes its title from
Edgar's song in *King Lear*, but the account is admittedly a nightmarish
dream of the poet. Landscape details come from *Art of Painting* by Gérald
de Lairesse, read by Browning in childhood. The questing knight is assailed
by outer horrors and inner fears but resolutely pushes on to the goal of
his pilgrimage, a dark, squat tower. Browning agreed upon the meaning
of the poem as "He that endureth to the end shall be saved," and the
work has therefore become a favorite of those seeking the resolute, un-
wavering life of moral convictions. (Shackleton recited this poem at the
South Pole to keep his courage up.) In spite of Browning's disavowal of
allegory, the poem has been variously interpreted as the search for truth, a
modern *Pilgrim's Progress*, the sustaining power of love, an indictment
of materialism. The conclusion may be the knight's realization that the
end of his quest is simply to die bravely.

"Respectability" comes out in favor of nonconformity. If one does as
the world prescribes, one is accepted, but thereby runs the danger of forfeiting the riches of individualism and full living.

"The Last Ride Together" (M) is spoken by another of Browning's im-
possibly noble lovers. Even when love is unrequited, being in love is superior
to all other arts and talents. The hopeless lover has been stirred to the
ideal, which he can never lose.

"Memorabilia" ("Things worth remembering") was occasioned by Browning's overhearing in a bookshop, probably in 1851, a stranger's casual mention of talking with Shelley. The nonchalance of the stranger is incomprehensible to this worshiper of Shelley.

"Andrea del Sarto" (M) arose when a friend asked Browning for a photo-
graph of a del Sarto painting in the Pitti Palace at Florence; as a substitute, Browning wrote and sent the poem. The monologue depicts the
artist on the evening when he conceives the painting. He tries to bribe
his wife Lucrezia into some pretense of love, but she is eager to run to her

lover, the waiting "cousin." Their house is built with money entrusted to the painter by King Francis of France for royal art purchases. Consequently del Sarto is neither loved nor honorable. His craftsmanship is faultless, but he lacks the soul for great art. Account is derived from Vasari. Often deemed among his best monologues, it is remarkable for its portrayal of a wholly un-Browningesque character.

"Two in the Campagna" (M) is one of Browning's most successful lyrics. Amid the decay of the area surrounding Rome, the male speaker seeks the woman's love, since the heritage of the past and the struggle of the present do not satisfy him. But even love, when earthbound, is insufficient for a soul yearning for the infinite love of God.

"A Grammarian's Funeral" (M) is spoken by a disciple of an early Renaissance scholar as the followers of the learned man bear his coffin upward for burial upon a high mountain. Browning captures the grammarian's intense desire for knowledge, which ignored the world about and all physical ailments in his study of Greek. "The philosophy of the imperfect" perceives the meaning of life in the struggle for the unattainable goal. It may be argued that the grammarian is no more than a hairsplitting pedant, confusing any goals with high and worthwhile goals, but whatever his limitations, he has striven valiantly and has bequeathed inspiration to his followers.

Dramatis Personae (1864) and subsequent volumes of short poems contain many excellent pieces, but the later poet often deviated from poetry in his fascination with argumentative ideas and involved psychology. Because many of these later works repeat familiar Browning themes they will not be treated as intensively. With this work Browning first began to enjoy general popular regard.

"Rabbi Ben Ezra" (M) apparently arose as a reply to the pessimism of FitzGerald's *Rubáiyát,* especially in the potter's image of stanzas 26–32. Although fond of rabbinical lore, Browning proffers only the general temper and concept of Abraham Ibn Ezra (1092–1167), a learned Hebrew of Toledo, Spain, forced by persecution to extensive wanderings. The poem's structure is not truly logical, but a series of cheerful, robust affirmations, expounding Browning's own optimistic philosophy. All of life must be viewed as a whole; age and death are as vital to the plan as youth. Physical joys will not suffice, and disappointments and dissatisfactions are the promptings of human greatness, drawing us to the perfect deity. Aspiration, not achievement, will be God's criterion for judging us. Though only dimly comprehending, we must believe faithfully that we are made for His purpose.

"Caliban upon Setebos; or, Natural Theology in the Island" (M) is Browning's satire on anthropomorphic theology, ridiculing those who, lacking any revelation of God except through reason and the senses, create a God in their own image without acknowledging their own fearful limitations. Darwin's *Origin of the Species* started the poet thinking about primitive man, and Shakespeare's *Tempest* provided the "missing link" Caliban, his dam Sycorax, and his mother's deity Setebos. The Quiet, as supreme deity, is Browning's addition, probably suggested by Unitarian thought. Setebos is conceived by Caliban in Caliban's image, a superior savage creating or destroying by caprice, and anxious in petty fashion for servile worship and flattery. Haltingly Caliban senses beyond this nasty little deity the Quiet, a nonanthropomorphic spirit answering to Caliban's intuitive soul needs. Caliban refers to himself in the third person perhaps because of his rudimentary subhuman mentality, perhaps as a crafty device to deceive Setebos if the god should overhear him. One of the most remarkable scrutinies ever attempted of a half-bestial mind, it was chosen by Browning in 1885 as his most successful dramatic verse.

The Ring and the Book (two volumes in 1868, two volumes in 1869) is generally considered Browning's masterpiece, the ultimate exploring of his dramatic monologue technique. Its 21,116 lines of blank verse were written between 1864 and 1867.

SOURCE. In June 1860 for eight pence Browning purchased at a Florentine bookstall *The Old Yellow Book* consisting of printed and ms. documents relating a 17th-century Italian murder case. The volume is now exhibited at Balliol College library, Oxford. Browning also made use of a 17th-century pamphlet, termed "Secondary Source" by scholars, supplied to him in 1862 by an English friend in Rome. It is possible, but incapable of proof, that Browning secured some information from another pamphlet discovered in the Royal Casanatense Library in Rome in 1900.

HISTORICAL BASIS. At Rome in 1693 Guido Franceschini, a minor Arezzo noble, married Pompilia, supposed daughter of Pietro and Violante Comparini. In the next year Violante revealed that Pompilia was a child purchased from a harlot and brought up as the Comparini's daughter to enable the couple to secure a legacy conditional upon their having offspring. Bitter litigation followed between Guido and the Comparinis, with Pompilia subjected to a miserable domestic tyranny. In 1697 Pompilia fled from her husband under the escort of a young canon, Giuseppe Caponsacchi, but her husband had the pair arrested. Caponsacchi was banished, and Pompilia, after brief confinement in a convent, was permitted to join her foster parents, since she was expecting a child. Shortly after she bore a son, Pompilia along with the Comparinis was murdered by Guido and four of his minions. The slayers were sentenced to die in 1698, and Guido's appeal to Pope Innocent XII was denied. After the executions, a later court session cleared Pompilia's name. While Browning contradicts none of the essential facts, he makes his own additions (notably in the speeches by Guido, Caponsacchi, and the Pope) and develops his own characterizations.

SUMMARY. Book I. The Ring and the Book. The book is *The Old Yellow Book*. The ring belonged to Mrs. Browning. As a Roman jeweler adds some alloy to make the ring workable, so the poet will mix poetic fancy with the legal evidence in the book. The poet summarizes the story from his source and also blocks out the eleven following books. Conclusion is "Lyric Love," a dedication to the memory of Elizabeth.

Book II. Half Rome. The speaker is an unhappily married man who sympathizes with Guido. He speaks on the day after the murder of the Comparinis, while Pompilia is dying of her wounds. His facts are inaccurate, and he is hasty to applaud "the blow of honor" against a faithless wife. Though vigorous, the speaker is coarsely brutal and dirty-minded.

Book III. The Other Half Rome. The time is probably two days after the murders. This speaker is a Roman bachelor of greater sensitivity than the lewd gossiper of Book II, and is roused to pity by the plight of Pompilia and especially by her beauty. The Comparinis and Caponsacchi are sympathetically viewed. The facts are essentially correct as observed from a distance by a worldling sentimentally enthralled by a melodrama involving a lovely woman.

Book IV. Tertium Quid ("A third something"). A cold, cynical nobleman seeks impartially to sum up both sides, though the monologist is unduly deferential to Guido's rank and condescending to Pompilia because of her illegitimate birth. This detached observer, superbly evoking the aristocratic atmosphere of 17th-century Rome, is wholly Browning's creation. Style is formal and dignified, in contrast with the easy conversational tone of the previous two books.

Book V. Count Guido Franceschini. A few days after the crime and just after release from the torture rack, Guido pleads his case before the judges. Brilliantly clever, he confesses with apparent candor, making the Comparinis appear wholly treacherous and Pompilia faithless. The tone of this book changes to intensity and eloquence, for a man is struggling for his life. There is no record of Guido's testimony before the court, for the actual man presented his case solely through his lawyers. The unctuous casuistry is Browning's invention.

Book VI. Giuseppe Caponsacchi. From brilliance the drama now moves to lyric magnificence. Still in the throes of wild grief at the butchery of Pompilia ("Pompilia is dying while I speak"), the canon expounds the impact of mystic love—the radiant face of Pompilia is darkness before the infinite beauty of her soul. An average priest before knowing her, he is transformed by her spirit into a "soldier-saint," a St. George. His heart is suffused with idealistic love for Pompilia, bitter hatred for Guido, and scorn for the muddles of the law that permitted the tragedy and now seem unlikely to mete out justice. There is no record of the priest's appearance at the historical trial.

Book VII. Pompilia. From her deathbed Pompilia makes her deposition. The actual seventeen-year-old girl, pathetically and desperately suffering, is transformed by Browning into a profoundly wise saint. Gentle, tolerant, graciously simple, deeply understanding, instinctively pious, and truly forgiving, she embraces life. To all her agonies she proclaims: "This is the note of evil, for good lasts." Dominating all else is her mother love, an unusual motif for Browning. The limpid blank verse is as fervently touching as anything in English. Elizabeth is probably the model for Pompilia.

Book VIII. Dominus Hyacinthus de Archangelis. In a letdown from the heights of two previous books, Guido's genial, garrulous lawyer, Archangeli, prosaically writes a defense of his client on the basis of *honoris causa*. The legal quibbling and intertwining of law Latin are clever, but the effect of this satire on lawyers is rather dull.

Book IX. Juris Doctor Johannes-Baptista Bottinius. In further slackening of pace, the prosecuting attorney laboriously marshals the evidence against Guido. Technicalities occupy much of his attention, and in his desire to convict the murderer, Bottini places little emphasis upon Pompilia's purity.

Book X. The Pope. The second great climax, after Books VI and VII, is the refusal of the Pope (he was temporal ruler of the Papal States in which the crime was committed) to heed Guido's plea for clemency chiefly on the basis of the nobleman's holding of a minor church office. Pope Innocent XII actually transmitted his curt denial through subordinates, but Browning devises an incomparable monologue from the papal mouth. The eighty-four-year-old pontiff is essentially the poet's spokesman.

The first part of this book reviews the entire case, mercilessly dissecting the iniquity of Guido and praising the soul of Pompilia. No obliquities force the astute and virtuous old man from his clear-sighted analysis. The second part considers the religious and moral grounds for the judgment. The opinions are neither 17th-century nor papal, but Browning's own credo. Alone with himself and freed by his many years from the world's conventions, the Pope ponders the ultimate questions of faith. His position elaborates that of St. John in "A Death in the Desert." He decides that man has been created to wring from all his pains the ecstasy of eternity ("This life is training and a passage"), and even Guido in the afterlife may run the race and win the prize. Men will err by their God-given power of free will, but from their instinctive needs will emerge a stronger and purer instinctive belief. His generous heart is tempted with mercy as he reviews Guido's claims, but he decides to do justice, confident that God's mercy will envelop the soul of Guido.

Book XI. Guido. Awaiting execution, the murderer is visited in prison by two high ecclesiastics. In the longest and most powerful of all the books, Guido eloquently boasts of his towering height of villainy. He demands the right to live, mercy from the church, and clemency from the law. He

becomes increasingly loathsome as he lewdly attacks Pompilia and Caponsacchi. He threatens to return after death as a monster of vengeance. His
blasphemous pride changes suddenly to cringing terror as the executioners
approach, and the killer is dragged out to die. The source ascribes a conventionally repentant end to Guido, and this book is therefore wholly
Browning's invention.

Book XII. The Book and the Ring. In tying up loose ends Browning
gives four concluding reports. The first, essentially imaginary, is the letter
of a visitor to Rome, a gay Venetian gentleman, written just after the
execution. It was a completely diverting spectacle, and Guido exited from
life with a decent show of noble piety. The second, based fundamentally
upon the source, is sent by Archangeli to friends of Guido. The lawyer has
further quibbles which the Pope ignored; he will be glad to see this dotard
Pope dead. His son, by the way, enjoyed the execution. The third, wholly
imaginary, is a professionally calloused note from the prosecuting attorney.
Had the Fisc been defending Guido, he would have succeeded where that
bungler Archangeli failed. He is readying himself, as the historical lawyer
did, to oppose Pompilia in the subsequent civil suits over her property.
The fourth is a sermon preached by Fra Celestino at the church of San
Lorenzo following the execution. Browning leaned heavily for his entire
interpretation of Pompilia upon the historical affidavit of Fra Celestino,
Pompilia's confessor. The views ascribed to the Augustinian friar are Browning's own final pronouncement. He who trusts to human testimony is a
fool; we must trust in God to set the record straight. The ring has come
full circle.

COMMENT. *The Ring and the Book* is the most ambitious and most
successful attempt in English literature, except for *Paradise Lost,* to justify
the ways of God to man. The theme is demonstrated in a psychological
epic, where the same story is told a dozen times by a dozen different viewers
or participants. No single narrator presents the definitive truth, for each
supplies details and interpretation missing in other accounts.

The narrators fall into two broad camps: the way of the world, and the
opponents of social conventions in favor of a spiritual ideal. Society, as
represented in Books II, III, IV, and part of XII, is too much dominated
by its selfish interests ever to judge honestly the conduct of individuals.
Books VIII and IX demonstrate that the machinery of social justice is as
horribly biased as the popular voice and equally incapable of discriminating
right from wrong. The ultimate social institutions, church and state, are not
operating for justice but for the maintenance of selfish superficialities—
property, subjugation of women, and conventional appearances of morality. Guido, who adroitly appeals to these selfish social motives, is the
horribly logical product of such a society. The good people (Pompilia,
Caponsacchi, and the Pope) have all risen above society by following

intuitive good instead of selfish conventions. Pompilia defies society by fleeing with Caponsacchi from Guido's bondage. Caponsacchi dashes his
chances for a pleasant, profitable career in the church by becoming a St.
George (familiar in Renaissance art but an inconceivable anomaly in
Renaissance society). The Pope repudiates the world's judgment to seek the
spiritual reality.

The *Athenaeum* extravagantly termed this work "the *opus magnum* of
this generation, the supreme poetic achievement of the age, the most precious and profound spiritual treasure that England has produced since
Shakespeare." Certainly it can be said that Pompilia, true possessor of the
wisdom of the heart, is the only near match to Shakespeare's pure heroines.
Guido is probably the only clear rival to Shakespeare's Iago and Milton's
Satan. Caponsacchi and the Pope are two of the rare portraits of great
virtue allied with intellect, but their success lies in their minds' recognition
of the heart's superiority.

In 1912 Henry James considered the writing of a novel based upon this
poem, centered about Caponsacchi, and in 1926–27 Walter Hampden on the
New York stage achieved one of his greatest triumphs in *Caponsacchi,* a
dramatized version by Rose Palmer and Arthur Goodrich.

Jocoseria (1883) has its title explained by Browning as "a collection of
things grav*ish* and gay*ish*." Three of the ten poems are drawn from
rabbinical lore, the rest roaming countries and eras in the poet's well-known
manner. Perhaps best is "Adam, Lilith, and Eve" in which the fear of
lightning causes Lilith, the woman Adam might have married, and Eve,
whom he did marry, to tell the truth. Lilith would have given herself to
Adam if he had sought her passionately; Eve would have run off with her
true lover if he had appeared at her wedding to Adam. When the lightning
ceases, both women change their confessions to jests.

Parleyings with Certain People of Importance in Their Day (1887) consists of monologues in which the poet frankly addresses seven mute spirits
summoned before him. In lieu of providing an autobiography, the poet discusses the major intellectual interests of his life, hints at the growth of his
ideas, and contrasts his own current concepts with those of contemporaries:

Figure	Topic	Browning's view	Contemporary opponent
Bernard de Mandeville	Philosophy	Evil is illusory, trust God	Thomas Carlyle
Daniel Bartoli	History	Give all for love	The Pragmatists
Christopher Smart	Poetry	Divine inspiration makes the true poet	Swinburne and the Aesthetes
George Bubb Dodington	Politics	Serve the people, and make them free	Benjamin Disraeli

Figure	*Topic*	*Browning's view*	*Contemporary opponent*
Francis Furini	Painting	Depict accurately the gifts of God	The Darwinians
Gérald de Lairesse	Greek Classicism	Christianity surpasses Hellenism	Matthew Arnold
Charles Avison	Music	Music plumbs "mysterious motions of the soul"	Musical Aesthetes

Asolando: Fancies and Facts (1889) was published on the day of the poet's death. The title means "to disport in the open air, amuse oneself at random," a fanciful verb form derived from Asolo, the Italian community where Browning resided. The thirty poems fit roughly into three categories: (1) Philosophical and personal reiteration of standard Browning concepts, (2) Narrative poems derived from the poet's enormous reading, (3) Love lyrics of surprising lightness and charm for a man of seventy-seven, probably induced by his son's marriage in 1887.

"Epilogue," concluding this work and the poet's career, is as appropriate a finale as "Crossing the Bar" was for Tennyson. Browning vigorously proclaims the resolute, courageous breasting of life with unshakable faith in God and immortality.

THE POETRY OF ARNOLD

Matthew Arnold (1822–1888). Following is a list of the more important events in the life of Matthew Arnold:

1822. Eldest son of Dr. Thomas Arnold, born on Christmas Eve at Laleham on the Thames.

1828. Accompanied family to Rugby where his father started the most famous headmastership in the history of English "public schools." Matthew was educated at Winchester and Rugby. At the latter wrote his first published verse, the prize poem, "Alaric at Rome" (1840).

1841. Entered Balliol College, Oxford, where he paraded as a dandy. With "Cromwell" he won the Newdigate poetry prize at Oxford in 1843. His affected manner concealed a studious mind that won for him second honors at graduation in 1844. Best friend at college was Arthur Hugh Clough, who died in 1861 and in whose memory Arnold wrote "Thyrsis" in 1866.

1845. Elected to fellowship at Oriel College, Oxford. Briefly assistant master at Rugby in 1846.

1847. Private secretary to Lord Lansdowne, president of the council.

1849. First book of poetry published.

1851. Appointed inspector of schools by Lord Lansdowne. Arnold retained this post for thirty-five years. In same year married Frances Lucy Wightman. Three of their six children were to die in rapid succession.

1857. Elected professor of poetry at Oxford. His lectures turned his interest to prose, literary criticism at the outset.

1861. First published volume of prose, his lectures on Homer.

1865. Highly influential *Essays in Criticism.* Thereafter lectured extensively in England and America, and traveled on the continent.

1867. Last volume of poetry. Thereafter considerable publication in prose.

1870. Received Doctor of Civil Laws degree from Oxford at the same time as Darwin.

1883. Granted pension by Gladstone in spite of Arnold's constant attacks upon the Liberal Party.

1886. Retired from post as inspector.

1888. Died of heart attack at Liverpool. Buried at native Laleham.

The poetry and prose of Arnold represent in time, tone, and subject matter two separate and distinct creative efforts. We will discuss the poetry now, and the prose will be considered independently in the next chapter.

The poetry of Arnold occupied only his earlier years, up to 1867. It has been stated that Browning never lost faith, Tennyson struggled from doubt to faith, and Arnold always doubted. Arnold was not a rebel against Victorianism; rather he was a strongly intellectualized Victorian, unwillingly cut off from his milieu by his own sensitivity and cerebration. As a poet Arnold felt acutely the collapse of traditional faith from the assaults of science, "higher criticism" of the Bible, and utilitarianism. Pervading his verse is a profound sense of loneliness. The bonds between man and God and between man and Nature, have been shattered, leaving man in an indifferent cosmos of mechanical laws. The older social system has been equally shattered by industrialization and bourgeois democracy, bringing about an impersonal urban society. Arnold's poetry seeks rather desperately for individual meaning and purpose amid such isolation, but by his own admission his search was fragmentary, no true consistency ever emerging from his various searchings. Some influences were:

(1) The intellectual tradition of Oxford. Arnold is the pre-eminent "university" poet in English. It is not undergraduate camaraderie that appeals to him but the sense of withdrawal from a bustling chaotic world into a sphere of thought and intellectualized feeling. The fellow of Oriel and the professor of poetry deeply cherished the island of refined dignity and gentlemanly scholarship represented by Oxford.

(2) The peace and beauty of Nature. Although troubled by doubts unknown to Wordsworth, Arnold sought even more the comfort of natural

loveliness. Though fearful that it was illusory, he desired its consoling ministry.

(3) The stoicism of Epictetus and Marcus Aurelius. Arnold believed that depending upon external things for happiness resulted only in frustration and disappointment.

(4) The Christian ethic as distinguished from Christian faith and theology. Arnold asserted that Christianity's supreme virtue was that "it has lighted up morality; that it has supplied the emotion and inspiration needful for carrying the sage along the narrow way perfectly, for carrying the ordinary man along it at all."

(5) The decisive hero of constructive action and noble character. Diffident himself, Arnold honored such a hero in his father. He wrote his friend Clough that such an example was sought by the multitudes "to animate and ennoble them."

Of the three major Victorian poets Arnold received the least popular recognition during his own era and has in the 20th century enjoyed the best reception, certainly among fellow intellectuals. Our own troubled and unresolved mind discovers greater kinship with him than with the more complacent Browning and Tennyson. Because he was greatly influenced by his extensive reading, the sources for his poetry were often literary and can readily be traced.

Poems are here considered in order of publication but in their final versions.

The Strayed Reveller and Other Poems (1849) is dominated by the contrast of the life of strained action with the life of detached serenity.

"Quiet Work" is an Italian sonnet on a subject suggested by a poem of Goethe. Nature is silent and strong, while man is restless and noisy. Men should seek the serenity of Nature by resolute performance of what they deem significant work, in the world but not of it.

"Mycerinus" arises from an account of an Egyptian king (Menkaure of the fourth dynasty) by Herodotus. The young monarch is informed by an oracle that he has but six years left in life. The ruler is enraged at the injustice of the gods, for he has lived an exemplary life, while his dissolute father was spared until advanced age. Abandoning his throne, the young king turns to revelry in the cool glades of the Nile. Strangely, perhaps, Mycerinus obtains self-knowledge in his defiance of the gods and fate, as he had not in the feverish city where he had dutifully followed the gods.

"To a Friend," probably addressed to Clough, is an Italian sonnet in tribute to Sophocles, the ancient Greek tragic dramatist, "Who saw life steadily, and saw it whole."

"The Strayed Reveller" portrays a young shepherd poet, coming to the rites of Iacchus, who wanders into the courtyard of Circe and drains a winebowl there. Intoxicated by the wine of ecstatic vision, he observes the spectacle of human life as the gods observe it, but must also suffer pain for his vision, for poetic insight must be paid for by suffering. He is contrasted with Ulysses, the active man who learns from bitter experience. Oriental descriptions come from *Travels into Bokhara* (1834) by Sir Alexander Burnes. Concept of poetic mission seems indebted to Keats.

"Fragment of an 'Antigone'" is a chorus imitating rather than translating the ancient Sophoclean tragedy. It is Arnold's first attempt at a type of poetry that always delighted him—the austere classical scrutiny of ethics. This fragment supports the law of the family, followed by Antigone with fatal results, as opposed to selfish hedonism.

"The Sick King in Bokhara" examines an anecdote that Sir Alexander Burnes had attributed to sheer madness. During a drought a Moslem of Bokhara stores a secret supply of water for himself. When his family discovers his horde and drains it, he curses his brothers and his mother. In deep remorse for his disloyalty to his family and his violation of Moslem precepts, the man asks the king to slay him. At first the king dismisses the man as insane, but gradually the monarch with human sympathy realizes the man's compulsive sense of guilt and reluctantly permits him to die. The king with his own hands prepares the body for burial. Contrary to the conventional concept of punishment as social restraint and education, Arnold sees punishment as the deep-seated need of the violator.

"Shakespeare," an English sonnet, is perhaps the most famous poetic tribute to the dramatist after Ben Jonson's. Arnold suggests that Shakespeare is an enigma because he was the supreme poet, aloof from mankind, observing the human struggle with rare sensitivity but thoroughly mastering his own suffering to achieve detached serenity.

"Written in Butler's Sermons," an Italian sonnet, is Arnold's first attack upon rationalistic psychology. The blueprint concept of the human spirit, detailed by the 18th-century cleric, ignores the ceaseless and multitudinous movement and creativity of the mind, and epecially the reality of wholeness in human personality.

"Written in Emerson's Essays," an Italian sonnet, regrets the insufficient attention paid to the American prophet, whom Arnold venerated. Of greatest appeal to Arnold is Emerson's romantic assertion of self-reliance.

"To an Independent Preacher Who Preached That We Should Be 'In Harmony with Nature,'" an Italian sonnet, probably derives from Goethe's "Das Göttliche." The preacher is evidently imaginary, giving the poet an opportunity to object to the submissive following of Nature and to urge man to rise above natural limitations. Nature seems here conceived of as "the world of things" to which Arnold opposes the moral world that man can create.

"The Forsaken Merman" ultimately derives from a Danish ballad, "The Deceived Merman." Margaret is lured into the sea by a merman; she shares his life and bears him children. The sound of Easter bells from the church draws her back to her home town, and her merman spouse (the narrator) and her children call in vain for her return to the sea. This is a supernatural poem following the Coleridge formula of injecting just enough reality into the world of fantasy to beguile the reader. It may be an allegory of moral Protestantism (plain grays and whites) against the pagan sensuality of Nature (golds and reds).

"The World and the Quietist," probably addressed to Clough, suggests the poet's role of providing "adverse voices." He disturbs the complacencies of those locked in the conventional business of life and stirs men to a heightened awareness of life. The concluding image of the slave whispering the *memento mori* to the reveling monarch comes from Herodotus.

"In Utrumque Paratus" ("Prepared for either alternative") attacks human pride. If the world was initially a divine idea that later was worked out in the form of matter, man is only one cog in a vast concept, his human assertions paling before the universal. If, however, the world is solely material in origin, man's struggle for knowledge and belief may be illusion, with no relation to the "one all-pure" mind of God.

"Resignation" is addressed to Fausta (his elder sister Jane) in recollection of their mountain walks together in the English lake country. His sister is conceived of as a female Faust, insatiate in her romantic urge for adventure and achievement. Arnold contrasts for her the romantic yearning for action and power with the contemplative life of the poet. The poet's more admirable choice is impersonality, the recognition of the Higher Self ("the general Life") beyond the feverish charms of everyday existence. The chiseled verse employs the octosyllabics that Arnold used most effectively to convey the sense of a pensive landscape and the meditative serenity of the poet.

Empedocles on Etna and Other Poems (1852) arose from a slight shift in Arnold's theory of poetry. Increasingly he felt that poetry must be charged with thought, especially religious and philosophical.

"Empedocles on Etna," the title poem, is a short dramatic piece of two acts, which Arnold subsequently suppressed until Browning encouraged him to reprint it in 1867. Nature is examined from the viewpoints of the physician Pausanias, the philosopher Empedocles, and the poet Callicles. The briefest, least interesting, and most practical view is that of Pausanias, who seeks to learn the secrets of Nature for immediate and beneficial human purposes. Most extensive presentation is that of stoicism from Empedocles. Nature is impersonal, and the only cosmic morality requires all things to fulfill the laws of their own beings. Drives within man urge him to leap over these barriers of Nature, but the result is only frustration. The philosopher, incorporating within himself more of Arnold than the author would ever admit, realizes that extreme intellectuality ("devouring flame of thought") causes men to be false to their true selves. Empedocles finally leaps to death in the volcano, convinced that desire is fruitless pain and that death is committing oneself to the ultimate life and movement of the elements. Arnold's main source was the edition of the works of Empedocles by Simon Karsten in 1830. Callicles finds beauty and solace in Nature, believes in the gods he celebrates, and unites human life with the scheme of surrounding things.

The "Marguerite" poems consist of eleven pieces starting with "The River" and ending with "To Marguerite." Arnold's rearrangements in later editions have encouraged some scholars to consider other amatory verse part of the Marguerite canon, but such ascription is dubious except for "Separation" (1855) and "The Terrace at Berne" (1867), and of course the second "To Marguerite" (1857). Although Arnold termed her imaginary and T. S. Eliot has dismissed her as "a mere pretext for lamentation," Marguerite on the basis of Arnold's letters to Clough (published 1932) seems to be a French girl with whom the poet flirted briefly at Thun in 1848. Marguerite is romantic pagan passion, "clear, positive, happy." Arnold is intellectually torn by religious and philosophical doubts; more importantly here, his male drives are thwarted by a sense of social duty and his concept of the imperturbable, aloof poet. As a result he is self-frustrated, unable to respond to the earth-call of Marguerite, just as she finds him incomprehensible. Modern intellectuals in striving for love uncover only their own uncertainty, insufficiency, and meagerness of true emotion. The series forms a virtual sequence. The earlier poems such as "Excuse" and "Indifference" suggest the troubled conflict of opposing personalities. "Parting" recognizes the incompatibility of temperaments. In "Isolation" the poet abandons all hope of fulfilment through shared experience. "To Marguerite" laments that there is no longer any channel for communication on the level of the deeper sensibilities.

"Self-deception" is a mood of despairing bewilderment as the poet asks why man is gifted with potentialities and then is thwarted in any attempt to make constructive use of them. In an impersonal cosmos there is nothing to bind man to his fellows, to life, or to a deity.

"Tristram and Iseult," Arnold's first attempt at an extended verse narrative, is the earliest modern English rendering of the legend, preceding Tennyson's version (1872) by twenty years. Chief source is an 1841 article by Théodore de la Villemarqué in *Revue de Paris*. Though influential, the Malory account is incomplete. Instead of sympathizing with the tragic lovers and exalting their grand passion, Arnold interprets the story as almost a Tennysonian domestic tragedy. Tristram returns from Ireland with Iseult, they drink the love potion (Brangien or Brangwain, the servant responsible for the mistake, is altogether absent from this poem), and Iseult marries Mark of Cornwall although in love with Tristram. Their liaison discovered, Tristram flees to Brittany and there marries Iseult of the White Hands. Seeking forgetfulness, he engages in knightly adventures, receiving a fatal wound. Iseult of Ireland is summoned to his deathbed, dying with him in a final embrace. Iseult of the White Hands lives on, devoted to their two children (Malory explicitly states that this marriage was never consummated). Arnold interprets Tristram as the victim of physical passion. Iseult of Ireland seems a figure from the Marguerite poems, and the really central character is Iseult of the White Hands, who resembles Arnold's wife. In confronting the seductive woman with the pure Victorian spouse, Arnold is exorcising his earlier infatuation with Marguerite. As a coda Iseult of the White Hands tells her children of Merlin's ensnarement by Vivien, a moralistic parallel to Tristram's enslavement by Iseult of Ireland.

"Memorial Verses" (first printed in *Fraser's Magazine,* 1850) was written at the request of Edward Quillian, son-in-law of Wordsworth and neighbor of the Arnold family. Except for the sonnets, this is Arnold's first printed literary criticism. The recently deceased Wordsworth as the poet of deep satisfaction in the relations of man and Nature is set above Byron, the poet of passion, and Goethe, the poet of thought.

"Courage" praises the younger Cato and Byron for "strength of soul." Although they did not clearly discern "the tendency of the whole," they were magnificent in valor, force, and self-assertion.

"Self-Dependence" parallels the sonnet "Quiet Work." The poet cries to the stars in his unsuccessful efforts to define himself morally in a universe alien to human striving. The answering voice preaches essentialism (the opposite of existentialism), commanding a stoical renunciation of desire and struggle. Self-dependence turns out to be a dependence upon Natural law.

"A Summer Night" considers the two apparent paths of man, "madman or slave." The latter path is the familiar treadmill of urban conformity, where the individual is no more than an atom in a chaotic heap. In conclusion the poet suggests a possible way out: the tranquilizing effect of Nature (here the heavens) symbolizing intellectual freedom founded upon breadth and clarity of spirit.

"The Buried Life," perhaps the classic expression of isolation, foreshadows much 20th-century denunciation of the social life as a flight from self-consciousness. A social order founded upon pretense and subterfuge necessarily brings about the disintegration of the individual personality. Rarely, the communion of love can stir the modern heart to the awareness of eternal verities and a sense of complete living. Cf. "The Love Song of J. Alfred Prufrock" by T. S. Eliot where the search of a similar individual ends in complete futility.

"Obermann" is a memorial poem to Étienne Pivert de Sénancour (1770–1846) whose *Obermann* (1804) depicted a modern man with personality disintegrated by Arnold-like tortures of the spirit. Though not a noted figure in French literature, Sénancour greatly influenced Arnold. The poet sees Sénancour, along with Goethe and Wordsworth, as one who, self-schooled and self-scanned, truly saw his own way through life. Arnold was particularly impressed by Sénancour's blend of sentiment and stoic honesty with the call for the disinterested character. Without satisfactory explanation, the poet turns from Sénancour to enter the "world."

"Morality" offers a maturer version of the concepts in "To an Independent Preacher." Nature is the symbol of an amoral existence devoted to rich and varied experiences, freed from the struggle of disciplining the moral will. Nature and morality are both divine in origin, but morality is higher, closer to God, and more difficult and painful to achieve.

"The Future" is the most readable poem in English upon the familiar metaphor of the individual life likened to a ship on the river of time. The path of life is followed from origin through the city-girded channels of the stream to the wide expanses of the ocean. The conclusion suggests oriental mysticism (highly appealing to the poet) in the absorption of the self into the infinite whole. Apparently conscious mortality is drowned in eternity.

Poems; A New Edition (1853) for the first time bore the author's name upon the title page. Much of the collection reprinted verse from the previous volumes.

"Sohrab and Rustum," the most popular Arnold poem in its day, derives its tale of ancient Persian heroes from Sir John Malcolm's *History of Persia*. Arnold had no direct contact with the major rendering of the account by the 10th-century Persian epic poet Firdausi. Echoes of Homer and Vergil are extensive in Arnold's poem. Rustum, the famed Persian warrior, while at war was informed by his wife that a girl was born to him. The mother thus wished to spare her son the military career of his father. Years later, Rustum incognito meets on the battlefield his son Sohrab, who heads invading Tatars. Recognition comes too late, and the son perishes at his father's hands.

The original story is a version of the familiar Indo-European myth of the son's search for a father and subsequent death at the hands of the father because of inadequate recognition. Arnold senses the theme as symbolic of his own complex relationships with his distinguished father, Thomas Arnold. W. H. Auden has suggested that the earnest voice of the elder Arnold finally killed the poet in Matthew.

Rustum responds to the inadvertent death of his son in proper stoic fashion. While clearly intended as epic tragedy, the work creates rather the effect of pathos, for the participants are blameless pawns of unheeding fate. The attractiveness of the poem lies in the melodious oriental names and the extended similes, especially the concluding figure of the Oxus River flowing to the sea. The latter underlines the familiar Arnold exaltation of the philosophical subduing of the individual to Nature and fate instead of the heroic spirit that elevates epic struggle. Violence is transformed into beauty and death into peace.

"Requiescat" ("May she rest") is an elegy to a probably imaginary woman. In simple three-beat lines Arnold celebrates the blissful peace now ordained for an active woman, tired by the feverish pace of modern social life.

"The Scholar Gipsy" derives its narrative from the story of an Oxford student who abandoned college studies to wander with the gypsies, according to Glanvil in *Vanity of Dogmatizing* (1661). Arnold molds the tale to his concept of the independent scholar, gazing with interest and penetration upon all human activity, but not selling his soul to any program of men.

Stanzas 1–3 urge an Oxfordshire shepherd (possibly Thyrsis, i.e. Clough) to join in the search for the scholar-gypsy, who is conceived of as still wandering. The third stanza almost diagrammatically sets the time, place, and narrator.

Stanzas 4–14 recount the story of the scholar-gypsy, who is pictured as a quiet awaiter of knowledge and intuition amid the exquisite countryside surrounding the university. Arnold welds the long pastoral tradition of poetry to his own deeply felt love of the gentle English landscape.

Stanzas 15–23 contrast the simple faith and straight-line course of the scholar-gypsy with the tortured doubts and "divided aims" of the mid-19th century.

Stanzas 24–25 urge Arnold's interpretation of the true path for modern intellectuals. Just as the ancient Phoenicians let the rising Greeks seize commercial power in the Eastern Mediterranean and expanded their voyaging far to the west, so the modern thinking man should abandon the hurly-burly of social and business triviality and break new grounds of thought and creativity in his lonely quest.

The purpose of the poem is twofold: a passionate denunciation of contemporary intellectual confusion and frustration ("our mental strife") and an idealized vision of youthful integrity of the spirit, victorious over division and change. The poem is often considered the poetic masterpiece of Arnold, but, rather strangely, he considered it inferior to "Sohrab and Rustum." It is certainly the best of English "college" poems and one of the best poetic evocations of English pastoralism. The stanza (*a b c b c a d ee d,* iambic pentameter except for iambic trimeter in line 6) is apparently Arnold's invention.

"Balder Dead," the one significant new poem in *Poems, Second Series* (1855), is the first handling of Scandinavian mythology by a modern English poet after Gray. Source is the translation of the Norse prose Edda in Mallet's *Northern Antiquities*. The concluding report by Hermod of his conversation with Balder in the underworld is Arnold's chief addition. The awkward hominess and rough humor of the original are transmuted by Homeric and Vergilian influences.

In Valhalla, abode of the Norse deities, no other was "so bright, so lov'd a God" as Balder. His mother Frea had asked all objects everywhere to refrain from harming him. The wicked Lok, in disguise learning from Frea that the mistletoe had not taken the vow, quickly shaped a twig of mistletoe into a dart and persuaded the blind Hoder to hurl it at Balder. The poem begins with lamentations for Balder's death, led by his father Odin. Frea calls upon Hermod to go to the underworld and persuade Hela (Death) to restore Balder. Hela agrees if all things will weep for Balder. All things do weep except an old hag, probably Lok in disguise. Hermod therefore returns without Balder but with word from that resigned spirit, prophesying a new age of peace and glory ahead.

Balder is an Arnold hero in a Valhalla symbolic of 19th-century England. He dislikes the ceaseless activity and strife of the gods, who respect him but do not adequately understand him. Hoder in his blindness clearly resembles the well-meaning average Victorian who blunderingly slays the intellectual and artist of the period, and Balder, therefore, prefers the gloomy peace of the underworld to the futile battles of Valhalla. Though a severe critic of his age, Arnold reveals his essential link to the Victorian orthodoxy in Balder's vision of hope for a subsequent era of a new heaven and a new earth.

Fraser's Magazine first printed the following poems:

"Stanzas from the Grande Chartreuse" (1855) arises from Arnold's honeymoon trip to the continent in 1851, during which he visited the venerable Carthusian monastery near Grenoble. Musing, he thinks of himself as "Wandering between two worlds, one dead,/The other powerless to be born." Dead to him are past faiths—Norse, classic Greek, Roman Catholic, Anglican—supplanted by "the high white star of Truth," emblazoned by modern rationalists and intellectuals. He does not relish the "sciolists" (champions of the new industrial and democratic age) but hopes that a better age might supersede his own soul-racked era. Meanwhile he finds solace in the peace and silence of the monastery.

"Haworth Churchyard" (1855) appeared several weeks after the death of Charlotte Brontë. Arnold is mistaken in many of his statements of fact (e.g. Anne Brontë is buried at Scarborough) and he critically held strong reservations about the famous novels.

Poems, Third Edition (1857) adds only the second "To Marguerite" ("We were apart"), wherein the poet laments the era's horrifying loneliness.

Merope. A Tragedy (1858), Arnold's longest attempt at verse, was a cold failure. This blank-verse play arose from Arnold's lectures at Oxford upon ancient Greek literature. The extensive preface persuasively argues against self-pitying Romanticism and proffers instead the dignified classical ideal of "distinctness and depth of impression." Unfortunately Arnold tried to exemplify his cherished classicism in a wooden, ill-versed drama about Merope, ex-queen of ancient Messenia, who almost slew her unrecognized son Aepytus. Arnold sincerely admired this work, even striving vainly to have it produced on the stage, but it must be considered as an unhappy attempt of a professor of poetry to prove his case with an academic exercise.

Macmillan's Magazine in 1866 first printed Arnold's poem on Clough's death.

"Thyrsis" in the same stanza as "The Scholar Gipsy" echoes much of the earlier poem in a pastoral elegy to Clough. Arnold's work stems from the tradition of Milton's "Lycidas" and Shelley's "Adonais," and is often rated as high as these predecessors. The original Thyrsis was a herdsman in the *Idylls* of Theocritus; extensive references to the pastorals of Theocritus also occur in stanzas 9, 10, and 19.

Stanzas 1–15 constitute the traditional lamentation for the dead poet Thyrsis (Clough). Revisiting the beautiful scenery about Oxford, Corydon (Arnold) seeks in vain for the signal-elm, which to both had been a symbol of the quest of the scholar-gypsy. Arnold views Clough's death as a surrender; first forfeiting the spiritual tranquility necessary to the poet, he had then forfeited life itself. Arnold renders poignantly the ancient protest that Nature persists while man quickly departs. Nature's beauty is now an impersonal mocker of vain human desires. In stanzas 9–11 Arnold foreshadows the conclusion of the poem as he laments the passing of old pieties; he cannot utter the conventional assurances of personal immortality from past faiths. The fearful complexities of modern life and the inaccessibility of "the throne of Truth" suggest that resignation to extinction may be best.

Stanzas 16–24 offer Arnold's consolation, a far cry from the radiant assurances of Milton and Shelley. The turn comes in stanza sixteen where a party of Oxford huntsmen invade the field where Corydon muses. Arnold's instinctive revulsion from human bustling drives him to a farther field where he glimpses the signal-elm, "bare on its lonely ridge." As long as the tree survives, he can believe in the unworldly quest of the scholar-gypsy. Though Clough is gone forever, the imaginative, creative drive of life still persists. The only immortality he can offer Clough is the immortality of his idealistic search, the example to other spirits to seek an escape from the world's contagion to the realm of the scholar-gypsy.

Arnold criticized "Thyrsis" as containing too little about Clough, thus sensing that the poem is not only a lamentation for his dead friend but also a lamentation for the passing of poetic inspiration from Arnold.

New Poems (1867) prints quite a few later poems which are declarations rather than questions, dismissals of the knotty problems vexing youth.

"Dover Beach" probably was written much earlier (c. *1851*), for it parallels the poems Arnold wrote fifteen years before. The tide going out at night from the cliffs of Dover suggests to the poet the retreat of faith in the modern age. He is left with a world devoid of spiritual consolation. The communion of souls between two lonely lovers is the only consolation he can offer. The famous concluding simile of ignorant armies clashing by night is suggested by the description of the battle of Epipolae by Thucydides. Although beautiful, the world before his physical eyes is not real but a dream. The real world is shrouded in darkness and wild confusion. This has often been termed the one perfect poem by Arnold. Instead of mere "thinking aloud," as in much of his verse, melodic lyric and sharp visual symbols are molded into a gripping, sorrowful depiction of what he deems to be the modern predicament.

"Rugby Chapel" is dated 1857 though probably not completed for sometime thereafter. An agnostic son pays sincere tribute to his deeply pious father. The poem abounds in Christian symbolism and ends with the quite un-Arnoldian "On, to the City of God." A noble life such as that of Thomas Arnold confirms our belief in human greatness, which the pettiness of most lives would discredit. Matthew yearns for, though he cannot truly believe, an immortality for his father, who served mankind and sought valiantly to lift it upward.

"Obermann Once More" writes finis to Arnold's poetry of doubt. In quiet, fertile Glion, Obermann's spirit speaks to Arnold in review of human morals since the days of ancient Rome. Although Arnold is not naïve enough to succumb wholly to contemporary blandishments, he joys in the prosperity of the day that foretells the opulent 1870s. "Hope to a world new-made!" After long straining at the tether, the strayed reveler has returned to haven. While still heterodox in faith and viewpoint, he welcomes the hope of progress in contemporary society and breathes with confidence the air of Victorian optimism.

OTHER POETS OF THE EARLY VICTORIAN PERIOD

The following two poets, Elizabeth Barrett Browning and Arthur Hugh Clough, were both closely connected with the major figures we have just discussed. The other poets treated in this section are James Bailey, Sydney Dobell, and Sir Alfred Austin.

Elizabeth Barrett Browning (1806–1861). Born Elizabeth Barrett Moulton in Kelloe, Durhamshire, Elizabeth Barrett Browning was the eldest of the eleven children of Edward Moulton. Along with her father she added the surname of Barrett upon his inheritance of family property. Before the age of eight she was reading and imitating the ancient Greeks. As a teenager she became proficient in Hebrew, Latin, and the important languages of modern Europe. Her father paid for her first publication, *The Battle of*

Marathon (1819). At the age of fifteen she injured her spine while trying to saddle a pony, and consequently remained a semi-invalid throughout later life. After moving with her father to London, she first received extensive recognition for *The Seraphim and Other Poems* (1838). A compliment to Browning in her 1844 volume began a correspondence and then a courtship. Her father opposed her marriage partly from concern for her health and partly because of his overly possessive nature. Elizabeth and Robert eloped in 1846, leaving immediately for Italy. Their love affair is one of the world's supreme romantic idylls, and from all accounts their marriage was incredibly happy. She died and was buried in Florence, Italy.

Elizabeth Barrett Browning throughout her life sympathized with the dominant attitudes of contemporary English bourgeoisie:

(1) Deeply pious and idealistic, she supported strict evangelical morality and opposed ritual religion and any intermediary between God and man. Her love and her love poetry display emotional individualism restrained by middle-class ethics.

(2) A determined humanitarian, she called for improvement in the lot of all the world's underprivileged. All reforms, however, she confidently expected within the framework of the existing social order.

(3) More politically naïve than Robert, she enthusiastically supported all causes she considered fights for freedom, including the *coup d'état* of Louis Napoleon. *Casa Guidi Windows* (1851), its title derived from the Browning residence in Florence, is an impassioned plea for Italian independence.

(4) Her sentimentalism was dear to an age enraptured with her romantic elopement. "Cowper's Grave" (1838) and "The Cry of the Children" (1844) were considered at the time to be the last word in pathos; a later age has dismissed them. Elizabeth had a commendable facility in verse but often committed every poetic error except vulgarity. Feminists, especially, elevated her to the top rank, asserting that she had proved woman's competence in verse as George Eliot had in prose.

Sonnets from the Portuguese (1850) takes its cue from "Catarina to Camoëns" (1844), E.B.B.'s poem upon the beloved of the noted Portuguese epic poet, Camões. The guise of translation, adopted when her husband insisted upon publication, is intended to hide a highly personal lyricism. The forty-five sonnets in the Italian rime scheme form a sequence ringing the changes upon the theme of the writer's humility. Elizabeth is rapturously grateful to Robert for whisking her from the lonely seclusion of an invalid into a bright world of color and affection. The tone varies from the playful flights of No. 37 through the calm beauty of 43 ("How do I love thee?") to the majesty of 22. As the intimate outpouring of a woman ardently in love, they probably will constitute her only sure claim to poetic fame. Certainly no other love affair in history has produced such an ecstatically lyric outburst from both parties as did the love of Robert and Elizabeth.

Aurora Leigh (1857), a four-hundred-page novel in blank verse, though possessing little appeal today, was joyfully read by contemporaries. Marian Erle, an innocent daughter of the people, breaks her engagement with the exalted and priggish philanthropist Romney Leigh, rather than drag him down to her level. Romney's cousin Aurora, a bluestocking friend of Marian, finally accepts him. Victorian readers shed copious tears over the nobility of Marian. The poetess Aurora extensively worships the beauty of Nature, decries the evil in this world, and calls upon poets to interpret the complex modern society, and she herself versifies many social issues of the day, pleading for humanitarian reforms. Too enthusiastically, Dobell praised the work for displaying "poetry such as Shakespeare's sister might have written if he had had a twin."

The Love-Letters of Robert Browning and Elizabeth Browning (1899), though overshadowed by their love poetry, forms one of the world's most attractive bodies of correspondence between lovers. Passion is sublimated in idealistic love, as the perfect affection for a divine being is supplanted unconsciously by perfect love for a human being.

Mrs. Browning was the most cherished of poets to the Victorian evangelicals. She never presented the poetic problems of her husband or the spiritual tortures of Tennyson or Arnold, and she was esteemed above her husband by most middle-class readers. Indeed, the most characteristic verse of evangelical Victorians was lyrical hymnology, as can be seen in the famous—and still used—"Nearer My God to Thee," and "Abide with Me," which were written in this period.

Arthur Hugh Clough (kluf) (1819–1861). A native of Liverpool, Arthur Hugh Clough lived in South Carolina from the age of four until ten. Upon his return to England he fell under the spell of Thomas Arnold at Rugby. At Balliol College, Oxford, he established a lifelong friendship with Matthew Arnold. At Oxford his mental certitude, crystallized by Arnold of Rugby, disappeared before the crosscurrents of intellectual conflict. Briefly attracted to the Tractarians, Clough was shaken from faith by the contemporary skeptical and scientific theories. Regretfully, for Oxford provided the most congenial atmosphere Clough ever knew, he resigned his fellowship in 1848. His sympathies with the Parisian masses during the Revolution of 1848 caused Matthew Arnold to address him as a "republican friend." In 1849 he was named head of University Hall, a division of the University of London, but the experiment failed and Clough turned in 1852 to writing in the United States. An appointment to the Education Office brought him back to England and enabled him to marry in 1854. Tuberculosis, from which he had long suffered, caused him to visit Italy for his health, and he died in Florence.

His age universally testified to the brilliance of Clough, which unfortunately is never fully realized in his writings. His name is forever tied to that of Matthew Arnold, who likewise was a poetic seeker rather than a finder. Far more than Tennyson and Browning, Clough and Arnold in verse contended with the disturbed intellect of the period. Like Arnold, Clough desperately sought faith and comfort within the framework of the bourgeois dominance, but Clough died without the support of self-confidence that Arnold was to achieve. In an age of shaken ideologies, Clough unsuccessfully attempted to discover God through intellect and a sense of duty instead of through will, tradition, or love. His poetry demonstrates surprisingly different moods, indicative of a spirit never firmly anchored. He fluctuates between a biting satiric intellect and a painful moral sensitivity.

The Bothie of Tober-na-Vuolich (1848) proved to be not the theological manifesto expected upon his resignation from Oxford but a long vacation pastoral narrative full of good spirits generated by the sense of freedom. "Bothie" is a forester's hut in the Scottish Highlands visited by holidaying Oxonians. A radical young student proposes marriage to a Highland girl who rejects him because of their different stations in life; however, when he proposes their emigration to New Zealand, she accepts him. Beneath the surface jest and bubbling youthful nature is a sincere appreciation of the rugged Highland scenery and a serious debate on contemporary social problems. The meter is the classic dactylic hexameter of Homer and Vergil, inspired by Longfellow's use of the same meter in *Evangeline*.

Ambarvalia ("Going around the fields") (1849) contains short poems on the theme of abandonment of supernatural faith yet retention of the ideal of moral integrity. One of his best-known poems, "Qua Cursum Ventus" ("As the wind their course [directs]") exemplifies this rather stoical conviction.

Dipsychus ("Twin-souled") (1850), Clough's most ambitious work, depicts a soul divided against itself in its struggle with pleasure and pain, good and evil, faith and doubt. Obvious influences are Goethe's *Faust* and Bailey's *Festus* (discussed below). Unlike his predecessors, Clough can provide no resolution, as thesis and antithesis work upon each other. The net result provides neither salvation nor damnation for the individual soul but exposes ruthlessly the hypocrisies of a materialistic culture.

"Say Not the Struggle Naught Availeth" (*1849*, 1855), his most popular poem, is not typical Clough. The clusters of consonants and the abrupt phrasing admirably convey the sense of labored difficulty. The note of confident outcome made the poem a favorite with Winston Churchill, who publicly recited it during the darkest days of World War II as he looked hopefully for assistance from the New World where "the land is bright."

Poems (1862), a posthumous collection, assembles most of the verse of

Clough. The new selections reinforce the picture of a conscientious Victorian earnestly desiring to believe and to hope, though wracked by doubts. The good and the true, he fervently believes, will somehow survive though man can no longer take literally the confident creeds of his forefathers. Best known is the satire, "The Latest Decalogue," revising the Ten Commandments to indict sham religiosity that conceals selfish greed.

Philip James Bailey (1816–1902). William Aytoun (discussed later) applied the deprecatory label "Spasmodics" to a number of early and mid Victorian poets who incongruously sought to wed flamboyant Byronism to evangelicalism. From the Romantics they inherited the concept of the poet as the divinely inspired prophet with a license to fervent eccentricity. Philip James Bailey headed the school with *Festus* (1839), a vast epic-drama upon the Faust theme proclaiming the doctrine of universal salvation. Before this torrent of emotion, purple rhetoric, and religious sententiousness, Tennyson felt "like a wren beating about a hedgerow." With each succeeding edition Bailey worked in passages from his less successful pieces until the unreadable eleventh edition (1889) contained over forty thousand lines. Richard Hengist Horne praised the "unrepressed vigour of imagination," and countless Victorians thrilled to the wild glories of *Festus.*

Sydney Thompson Dobell (dō-bel') (1824–1874). Sydney Thompson Dobell evoked Aytoun's epithet with *Balder* (1853), the most extreme product of the "Spasmodics." In an isolated Gothic tower Balder meditates darkly upon life, his only action proving the "mercy killing" of his insane wife Amy. Dobell conceived of this work as first in a trilogy tracing "the progress of a Human Being from Doubt to Faith, from Chaos to Order." This first part seems incapable of getting beyond chaos.

Though discredited in their own era and now forgotten, the Spasmodics influenced greater poets (e.g. E.B.B. in *Aurora Leigh* and especially Tennyson in "Maud," probably the best piece of Spasmodic verse).

Sir Alfred Austin (1835–1913). Alfred Austin wrote abundantly but without distinction. Carping at his betters in *Poetry of the Period* (1870), he called Clough, Morris, Swinburne, and Browning (who maintained a running battle with Austin until death) inferior poets. Austin took himself seriously and solemnly draped himself in the robes of Tennyson whom he succeeded as poet laureate in 1896. Indicative of then-current intellectual trends, Austin's appointment arose simply because no major living poet was acceptable to the Victorian orthodoxy.

EARLY VICTORIAN LIGHT AND SATIRIC VERSE

Unlike the 18th century and Byron, the Victorian satirists eschewed Juvenalian thrusts in favor of gaiety and whimsy. Instead of invective satire their chief weapon therefore was parody.

Richard Harris Barham (bar'am) (1788–1845). Richard Harris Barham began *The Ingoldsby Legends* in 1837 in *Bentley's Monthly Miscellany,* collecting them in a first series (1840) and second and third series (1847). Prose and verse tales spoof Romantic taste in a prankish medievalism. Barham displays wild ingenuity in obscure lore, fantastic imagination, and odd rimes that even the 17th-century Samuel Butler or the 19th-century Browning could not surpass.

Edward Lear (1812–1888). Edward Lear based his reputation upon painting, producing over two hundred drawings to illustrate the poetry of his friend Tennyson. While painting animals and birds at the estate of the Earl of Derby, he amused the earl's grandson by penning nonsense verse, especially limericks. *The Book of Nonsense* (1846, followed by over forty editions), with later kindred volumes, far outshone his professional artistic reputation. "The Owl and the Pussy-Cat" (1871) is an established nursery favorite. Only Lewis Carroll can match Lear in the rare ability to break down the adult viewpoint and re-create the make-believe and illogical logic of childhood. Modern psychologists see beneath Lear's idle diversions a serious indictment of the painful 19th-century thought pattern and a joyous escape into a comforting world of free association of the mind.

William Edmondstoune Aytoun (ā'ton) (1813–1865). William Edmondstoune Aytoun contributed regularly to *Blackwood's* a group of parodies reprinted in 1855 as *The Book of Ballads, edited by Bon Gaultier.* All the poets of the day are mimicked, with probably the most effective barbs directed against the slipshod sentimentalism of E.B.B. in "The Rhyme of Sir Lancelot Bogle" and the frenetic unbalance of Tennyson's "Locksley Hall" in "The Lay of the Lovelorn."

POETS EMPHASIZING TRADITIONAL RELIGION

The following writers manifest religious reaction against romantic faith and evangelical Protestantism. They generally emphasize the sacred structure of the visible Church, the inherent sinfulness of man, the necessity of Christ's Atonement, the sacraments, the intercession of the Church between sinful man and God, and the inevitability of Judgment accompanied by damnation for the unrepentant. They deny the inherent goodness of man, emotion and sentiment as a substitute for orthodox faith, self-reliance, and free grace to all seekers. The poets discussed in this section were the ones writing early in the Victorian period; later Victorian traditionalists will be taken up further on in this chapter. Also, although the Oxford Movement is a most important part of the swing to traditional religion, we will reserve a discussion of it until the next chapter, where it can be taken up with its leading figure, Cardinal Newman.

Although often inextricably mixed, two main forces led these poets:

(1) Romantic medievalism and the desire to unite with the millennium-old tradition of Western Christendom, and (2) Catholic theology and the organic concept of the Church.

It is wrong to assume that adherence to Catholicism automatically meant thoroughgoing conservatism. Not infrequently, Englishmen of long-standing Roman Catholic families, notably Lord Acton, associated themselves with liberalism. Anglo-Catholics, however, were uniformly conservative. Most of the Catholic literature of the era was produced by converts, drawn by conservative appeals; and, of course, the chief expression of all Catholic poets was conservative religion.

John Keble (kē'bl) (1792–1866). A native of Fairford, Gloucestershire, John Keble graduated from Corpus Christi College, Oxford, and from 1831 to 1841 was professor of poetry there. Newman asserted that Keble's Oxford sermon, "National Apostasy" (1833), marked the beginning of the Oxford Movement. From 1836 until death Keble was Anglican vicar at Hursley, Hampshire.

The Christian Year (1827) proved one of the most popular 19th-century books. It consists of hymns and sacred verses chiefly upon all the holy days of the Christian calendar as well as general pious meditations. Nature references are extensive, but throughout runs the claim that "Christian hearts" are needed to let the visible universe symbolize the invisible doctrines of Christianity.

Lyra Apostolica (1832) was a co-operative effort by the early leaders of the Oxford Movement. Of this devotional poetry the most famous pieces are "Hail, gladdening light" (Keble's translation from the Greek) and "Lead, kindly light" by Newman. The outstanding idea is man's total inadequacy except as he yields to God and His Church.

John Mason Neale (1818–1866). Born in London, John Mason Neale became the best-known ultra-High Churchman of 19th-century Anglicanism. In 1855 he founded the Anglican nursing sisterhood of St. Margaret. In 1857 wrathful Protestants burned him in effigy for his Anglo-Catholicism. He was probably the most learned ecclesiastical historian of his era, but he is now remembered chiefly for his hymns. Numerous volumes, from 1843 until his death, rate him as the most important English hymn-writer since the Wesleys. The familiar Christmas carol "Good King Wenceslas" is his original composition, but he excelled in translation. From the Latin he translated *The Rhythm of Bernard of Morlaix* (1859), including the famous "Jerusalem the golden." *Hymns of the Eastern Church* (1862) first introduced to English a knowledge in translation of much liturgical and devotional poetry of the Greek Orthodox Church.

Aubrey Thomas de Vere (1814–1902). Born at Curragh Chase, County Limerick, Ireland, Aubrey Thomas de Vere was the son of Sir Aubrey de Vere (1788–1846), an orthodox Anglican poet who revived 17th-century

Anglo-Catholic themes and foreshadowed the Oxford Movement. The younger de Vere, educated at Trinity College, Dublin, was a prominent literary figure of his age, a friend of Wordsworth, Tennyson, Newman, and Carlyle. In 1851 the younger de Vere was converted to Roman Catholicism, and his Catholicism, strongly supported by medievalism and Irish patriotism, reached its best expression in the versified *Legends of St. Patrick* (1872). Sympathetic to the Romantics, de Vere particularly admired the later Anglican Wordsworth and saw Shelley as a potential Catholic idealist diverted by the drives of the Reformation.

Coventry Kersey Dighton Patmore (1823–1896). A native of Woodford, Essex, Coventry Patmore was the son of Peter Patmore, literary editor and critic, friend of Hazlitt. Irregularly educated, the young Patmore served as assistant librarian at the British Museum from 1846 to 1866. After the death of his first wife in 1862 he became a Roman Catholic convert largely through the urgings of de Vere. He proved one of the most impressive of secondary Victorian poets.

The Angel in the House sold many thousands of copies as the definitive poem upon respectable and happy Victorian married life. The poem consists of four successive installments: *The Betrothal* (1854), *The Espousals* (1856), *Faithful for Ever* (1860), and *The Victories of Love* (1860). Man's love of woman is the dominant theme, and his model is his wife, Emily Andrews, who appears in "A Face" from Browning's *Dramatis Personae*. Felix marries Honoria, daughter of an ecclesiastical dean. Patmore displays commendable subtlety in analyzing the problems of even a calm and uneventful marriage. Later critics have often scornfully dismissed Patmore altogether as the poet of "domestic bliss." Housman labeled this work "a nasty mixture of piety and concupiscence."

The Unknown Eros (1877) collects forty-two pseudo-Pindaric odes written over a ten-year period. Though never as successful as his earlier work, this religious verse, reminiscent of the 17th-century metaphysical poets, and written after his turn to Roman Catholicism, is Patmore's greatest achievement. Its theme is God's love of man. In daring imagery that resembles Donne's, Patmore sees God lovingly possessing mankind as a man lovingly possesses a woman.

Christina Georgina Rossetti (rō-set′ē) (1830–1894). Christina Rossetti was the London-born daughter of Gabriele Rossetti, and hers was one of the most talented families of the century. Her brother William was an agnostic intellectual, her brother Dante was the Pre-Raphaelite "aesthetic" painter-poet, and her sister Maria was an Anglican nun. Christina's whole life was dominated by pious Anglo-Catholicism. She rejected the two men who proposed marriage, the first (Collinson) because of his Roman Catholic leanings, the second (Cayley) because of his agnosticism. Much of her life was spent in religious rites and in Christian charities. Because of her beauty she was model for many Pre-Raphaelite paintings, but she was sick for much of her life and in later years was disfigured by goiter. She contributed verse to *The Germ* under the pseudonym of Ellen Alleyn.

Her verse proved the most popular Christian poetry of 19th-century England. Although influenced by her brother Dante, she is his antithesis: where he is all sensual, she is all ascetic. No other English poet since medieval times has been as preoccupied as Christina with the other world to the exclusion of this world.

Goblin Market and Other Poems (1862) has been termed the first literary success of Pre-Raphaelitism. Many of her short lyrics ("When I am dead, my dearest," "Dream Land," "After Death," "Remember," "Uphill") are among the best of the century. Resembling Emily Dickinson, she wrote with a refreshing simplicity and sincerity, generally lacking in the minor Victorian poets. Pervasive are a melancholia, a wistful dwelling upon death, and a fervent piety.

"The Goblin Market," in a sinister medieval setting, tells of two sisters regularly going to a stream for water. They hear goblins hawking their wares, "Plump unpecked cherries" and other luscious fruit. Lizzie (Maria), knowing that their sister Jeanie had bought goblin fruit and then pined away to death, urges Laura (Christina) to turn a deaf ear. Laura, however, buys goblin fruit with a snipped curl and thereafter begins to pine away. Lizzie goes to the goblins, has her face smeared with delicious fruit juices, but refuses to buy. The restorative power of the juices upon Lizzie's face cures Laura. Beneath the girlish tale is a religious theme of temptation, the snaring by evil, the offer of sacrifice, and the rescue from evil. In its striking word pictures, incantatory quality, and the magical evocation of the supernatural, it is the only poem in English that seriously can be compared with the eldritch poems of Coleridge.

The Prince's Progress and Other Poems (1866) in its title piece offers another Coleridgian lyrical ballad replete with long-sustained medieval glamour. On his way to his destined bride, the handsome prince dallies too long with wayside pleasures, only to find the bride dead upon his belated arrival. The broken betrothal theme is recurrent in Christina's verse; she was so affected by the experience with Collinson that upon a chance meeting in later life she fainted.

The keynote of the devotional poems appears in "Despised and Rejected." Christina obviously loved the world and bitterly condemned that love as sinful. She renounced the world, thereby felt miserable, and denounced her unhappiness as sinful. Instead of medieval resignation, her self-abasement and morbidity reveal a warring soul. Her avoidance of sentimentality and her straightforward honesty make memorable poetry of "If Only," "After This the Judgement," "The Lowest Place."

Sing-Song (1872) consists of poems for children and gay little occasional pieces for the family circle. These reveal a sprightliness quite in contrast to the world-renouncing humility of the devotional poems.

A Pageant and Other Poems (1881) includes the sonnet sequence "Monna Innominata" ("Nameless lady"). Christina explained that the speaker of the fourteen sonnets was one of the unnamed women celebrated by poets before Dante and Petrarch. Her brother William declared that Christina was the actual speaker, expressing her love for Cayley. The sequence challenges Mrs. Browning's *Sonnets from the Portuguese* but deals with a love affair ending unhappily. Its substance is renunciation of physical love for heavenly love.

New Poems (1896) and *Complete Poetical Works* (1904) include poems published in periodicals and within her prose devotions. "Amor Mundi" (1865) recounts her perennial "love of the world" and her insistence that such love leads to damnation. Throughout these religious poems is the theme not so much of Christian consolation as of the fearful tearing of the psyche between the world and the soul. She looks forward to death as a release from this struggle to an embrace by the Heavenly Bridegroom.

Richard Watson Dixon (1833–1900). A native Londoner and son of a Wesleyan cleric, Richard Watson Dixon associated with Morris and Swinburne at Oxford. Admiring Rossetti, he mingled Pre-Raphaelitism with High Church Anglicanism in his poetry. His friend Robert Bridges edited his *Selected Poems* (1896). Dixon's most important work was the still authoritative prose *History of the Church of England from the Abolition of the Roman Jurisdiction* (five volumes, 1877–1900). From his ordination in 1859 until his death he held various posts in the Established Church in the north of England.

POETS OF DISILLUSIONMENT AND DESPAIR

The complexity and impersonality of modern industrialization and urbanization, coupled with the embittered Victorian contest between science and faith, caused some poets to throw up their hands in pessimistic disgust. Thomas Hardy in his poetry displayed just this attitude; however, as he is such an important novelist, his works will all be discussed later in Chapter 5, which is devoted to the Victorian novel.

Edward FitzGerald (1809–1883). Born Edward Purcell, Edward FitzGerald along with his father adopted his maternal grandfather's surname in 1818 upon succeeding to the family estate. His birthplace was Bredfield House, near Woodbridge, Suffolk. After graduation from Trinity College, Oxford, FitzGerald married the daughter of Bernard Barton, the Quaker poet of Woodbridge, but the couple soon parted. A well-to-do landowner, he lived a quiet country gentleman's existence, and he possessed such friends as Carlyle, Thackeray, and Tennyson. The Orientalist E. B. Cowell taught him Persian in 1853, preparing him for his masterpiece:

Rubáiyát of Omar Khayyám (1859 in seventy-five stanzas, 1868 in 110 stanzas, 1872 and 1879 in 101 stanzas).

THE PERSIAN ORIGINAL. Omar, surnamed Khayyám ("tentmaker," possibly from his father's occupation), was born at Nishapur, Persia, about the middle of the 11th century and died c. 1123. By profession he was a mathematician and astronomer to the Seljuk sultan, Malik Shah. A period of political upheaval and uncertainty apparently induced him to free-thought and free-living. As an avocation he scribbled numerous quatrains (plural *rubāʿīyāt* from *rubāʿiy*, "composed of four") whose themes vary from gaiety to despair, but are always dominated by a revolt against ortho-dox Moslem faith (which particularly forbids alcoholic beverages). His verse is actually less significant in Persian literature than that of Hafiz or Firdausi, but FitzGerald has made him the one Persian poet generally known to the English-speaking world. About five hundred surviving quat-rains, lacking any structural continuity, are ascribed to Omar. The Bodleian Library ms. used by FitzGerald contains 158 quatrains arranged in alpha-betical order of rime. While some of these repeat the rime throughout, most employ the scheme *a a x a,* with the third line "wild," that FitzGerald adopted. The swooping effect at the quatrain's close makes it an appropriate vehicle for pagan defiance.

FITZGERALD'S MODIFICATIONS. Although this work has often been ranked with the Authorized Version of the Bible and North's Plutarch as one of the monumental translations into English, it is better to say, as FitzGerald did, that it is a "rendering." The arrangement of the quatrains (juggled about in each edition) is purely FitzGerald's. Of the 101 quatrains in the standard text (fourth edition, 1879) forty-nine are relatively faithful transla-tion from the original Persian, two are translations from a French version of Omar by J. R. Nicolas, forty-four are "composite" stanzas from scattered Omar quatrains, two reflect general Omar attitudes but do not appear in the original, two are from the Persian poet Perid ud din Attár, and two are an amalgam of Omar and Hafiz. "But at all Cost," FitzGerald wrote to Cowell, "a Thing must *live.*" He therefore felt at liberty to sharpen and alter Omar's original statements and imagery. Competent judges agree that this English "translation" is greater poetry than the Persian original and probably the greatest single poem of the Victorian era.

IDEOLOGICAL CONTENT. The guise of "translation" permitted the Suffolk gentleman to vent his repressed hostility toward Victorianism. A scornful dismissal of Victorian high seriousness in the quarrel between science and faith is pervasive, especially in stanzas 28 through 30. Agnostically he denies that either side can produce truth. Anti-intellectually (54–55) he brushes aside all constructed systems.

Many scholars, including Cowell, have ascribed allegory to Omar, who may have been a Sufi mystic, but FitzGerald insisted that when Omar called for wine he was not calling for "the wine of life," "intoxicating inspiration," or anything but wine (74). The sexual references (41) were purely decorative to FitzGerald, who, in and out of marriage, was never much stirred by love of woman. The sophistical argument of 61 justifies any conduct whatsoever.

Complete denial of any afterlife is stated in 66–67. The most audacious assault upon orthodoxy appears in 81, which at his own request was read to Hardy on his deathbed. Unwarranted by the original, this stanza sees God as a bunglingly unjust Creator.

The hedonism in the poem is not the "message," which often has been stated as "eat, drink, and be melancholy." The most consistent spirit of the work is despair. Life is achingly brief (3), and a quick end is the lot of both striver and sluggard (15). Individual existence is insignificant; for any one life is a mere bubble, ignored by the immensity of time and the heedlessness of earth (46–47). A fatalistic attitude and the futility of effort can be seen in 73, and a counsel to live for the day comes in 13. The longest connected series (82–90) likens man to a clay pot, briefly useful and then broken and discarded. Browning utilized the same metaphor optimistically in "Rabbi Ben Ezra"; understandably, FitzGerald derogated Browning for "cockney enthusiasm."

VERSE STYLE. The effectiveness of the work arises in large part from an almost 18th-century restraint in the expression of rebellion and license. "Laurence Hope" (Mrs. Adela Nicholson) in *India's Love Lyrics* (1901)— e.g. "Pale hands I loved beside the Shalimar"—generously employed the sentiment and eroticism of the East, but except for 33 FitzGerald avoided rich ornamentation. Stanza 94 perfectly embodies the combination of bemused smile and wistful melancholia that envelopes the entire poem.

RECEPTION. The first edition (1859), at FitzGerald's own expense, was completely ignored. In 1861 Whitley Stokes, a scholar of Celtic, introduced the poem to Rossetti, who in turn called it to Swinburne's attention. While standard Victorianism still gripped most Englishmen, these rebellious figures found FitzGerald to their liking. By the century's end widespread antipathy had developed toward orthodox Victorianism, and a copy of the *Rubáiyát* upon an Oxford table was a symbol of sophistication. Today, often in sumptuous gift editions, it remains the most popular single poem of the Victorian era.

Letters (1902–03 with subsequent additions) establishes FitzGerald as one of the English masters of correspondence. Withdrawing from the press of men and affairs, FitzGerald is a detached onlooker. Unwilling or unable to express any deep emotion, he has in the letters a most graceful quality of repose and self-sufficiency, lit with easy humor and occasionally shadowed with gentle sorrow.

James Thomson (1834–1882). James Thomson must not be confused with his fellow Scottish poet of the 18th century bearing the identical name. This Thomson, born at Port Glasgow, was the son of a merchant marine officer who was prematurely an invalid. Thomson's extremely pious mother struggled against poverty in their subsequent East London hovel, but died when the poet was eight. From the Royal Caledonian Asylum, a charity institution for boys, he proceeded to the Royal Military College in Chelsea for training as an army schoolmaster. In the army he met Charles Bradlaugh, who steered him to radicalism and atheism, and Matilda Weller, whom he deeply loved but soon lost because of her early death in 1853. Thomson identified himself with the German poet Novalis (1772–1801) and Matilda with Sophie von Kühn, the lost love of Novalis. Hence the pen name Bysshe Vanolis (the middle name of Shelley plus an anagram of Novalis), usually "B.V." In 1862 Thomson was discharged from army service for refusal to reveal the name of a soldier violating a minor camp regulation. Subsequently employed as a law clerk, he lived with Bradlaugh and wrote frequently for Bradlaugh's periodical, *National Reformer.* In 1872 he worked in the Rocky Mountains of the United States for an English mining firm and in the next year went to Spain as special correspondent for the New York *World.* Alcoholism dogged him for most of his remaining years, which were spent in London amid poverty.

"Give a man a horse he can ride" (*1865*), still a popular baritone solo and perhaps the best-known piece by Thomson, is completely unrepresentative. Its hearty masculinity is contrived, when Thomson as a member of the Secular Society sought to substitute the worship of physical vitality for the worship of God.

"William Blake" (1866) is probably the best poem written about the great Romantic, but its sense of fearful loneliness stems from the unhappy Thomson, not from the happy Blake. Thomson's hostility to religion arose chiefly from his revulsion against an ultrapietistic household in his childhood. In even his most bitterly atheistic writings, however, sounds a deep sorrow at the loss of faith.

The City of Dreadful Night, first printed in 1874 in *The National Reformer,* proclaims probably the bleakest despair in English literature. The poet told George Eliot, "It was the outcome of much sleepless hypochondria." She was enthusiastic about the "distinct vision and grand utterance" of the poem. Certainly, ultimate negation and pessimism are expressed in sincerity and grandeur. Thomson's City might be characterized as Dante's City of Dis, existing alone in a universe without solace. Each source of consolation (including the spirit of Matilda in IV and IX) is destroyed.

"There is no God . . . no secret to express . . . no light beyond the curtain." The mood seems less inspired by scientific revelations of the age than compelled by the "infinite void space" in Thomson's subjectivism.

THE PRE-RAPHAELITES AND OTHER OPPONENTS OF VICTORIANISM

The poets of this group comprise an intelligentsia who rebelled against the Victorian middle-class society. The Pre-Raphaelites and then the aesthetes (believers in art with no moral purpose; discussed later in the chapter), in denial of the age's religiosity and utilitarianism, took a common refuge in the cult of beauty, essentially "art for art's sake." Sharing strong aesthetic impulses, the poets who advocated complete change bitterly denounced what they felt were the inadequacies of the era and proposed substitute social systems for mankind.

In 1848 Dante Gabriel Rossetti noted in Milnes's *Life and Letters of Keats* that the Romantic poet preferred the early Italian painters to Raphael, who was generally revered as the first modern painter of finished technique and proficiency. In the same year Rossetti together with William Holman Hunt and John Everett Millais formed the Pre-Raphaelite Brotherhood of seven artists. Believing that painting of the Raphael type (especially honored in England since at least the time of Reynolds) had become conventional and sentimental, they proposed to emulate Raphael's predecessors in canvases of artistic individuality, imagination, and rich color. The label Pre-Raphaelite, originally applied to these artists in jest, was defiantly adopted, and they signed their paintings with a P.R.B. after their names in contrast to the Royal Academy, R.A. Also contributory to the Pre-Raphaelite concepts was the plea of Ruskin in *Modern Painters* (1843) for increased idea and story in paintings. The Brotherhood's insistence upon each picture telling a story insured an alliance between painting and poetry unparalleled in English art except with Blake. Where Pre-Raphaelite paintings were not illustrations to literature, the artists would frequently, especially in the case of Rossetti, compose verse or prose comment upon their paintings.

The group also created *The Germ*, a literary periodical beginning in January 1850; it changed its name to *Art and Poetry* with the third issue, and expired with the fourth issue in April. "Hand and Soul," a prose romance by Rossetti in the first issue, pictured the P.R.B. purpose as the fostering of individual, original ideas against slavish, traditional imitation. The nearest thing to a manifesto by the group was "The Purpose and Tendency of Early Italian Art" by F. G. Stephens (1828–1907), painter and charter member of the organization, in the second issue of *The Germ*. Stephens called for fidelity to Nature's truth and exact reproduction of details in painting. The monumental study of the group by an insider was *Pre-Raphaelitism and the Pre-Raphaelite Brotherhood* (two volumes, 1905–06) by William Holman Hunt (1827–1910). The only member of the group to maintain his position unaltered throughout life, Hunt characterized the movement as supporting health and integrity in art, and opposing foreign models, glittering sentimentalism, and theatrical attitudinizing. "Pre-Raphaelitism," Hunt insisted, "in its purity was the frank worship of Nature, kept in check by selection and directed by a spirit of imaginative purpose."

In the 1850s the example of Rossetti set the style of Pre-Raphaelite painting that it maintained thereafter: sensuousness, dreaminess, and decorative medievalism. Such art consciously turned its back on the modern industrial-urban world. Rossetti in his earlier writings also set the style for Pre-Raphaelite poetry: deliberate simplicity of manner, sharp particularization of visual and auditory detail, archaic technical vocabulary, a preference for ballad and other "medieval" verse forms, a lush decorative quality, rich sensuous description, and a moody predilection for twilight and autumn (hence decay, desolation, listlessness, death). Extensive religious references reveal evocative and pictorial qualities but no real religiosity.

By 1854 the P.R.B. had informally dissolved as its members' paths diverged, but its influence was strong upon the group (Morris, Swinburne, Burne-Jones) who gathered about Rossetti after 1857, and Pre-Raphaelite verse qualities appear in many poets wholly beyond the Rossetti circle: Tennyson (intrigued with the escape theme and pictorial color), Gerard Manley Hopkins (in his earlier work), and even an opponent like Browning (e.g. in "The Flight of the Duchess").

THE POETRY OF ROSSETTI

Dante Gabriel Rossetti (rō-set'ē) (1828–1882). Because of his high regard for the medieval Italian poet, Dante Gabriel Rossetti preferred this order of his name to the baptismal Gabriel Charles Dante Rossetti. All the Rossetti children were three-quarters Italian in blood and only one-quarter English. Italian was the household tongue. The father, a political refugee, was professor of Italian at King's College, London, where Dante Gabriel was born. Young Rossetti studied at King's College but left in 1842 to study painting. Before the age of twenty he had written some of his best verse. He founded the Pre-Raphaelite Brotherhood and was the major contributor to that group's organ, *The Germ*. In 1850 he met Elizabeth Eleanor Siddal, a beautiful but tubercular milliner, who became his favorite model and who, under his tutelage, displayed commendable talent in both poetry and painting. They were married in 1860, but she died in 1862 from an overdose of laudanum, possibly a suicide. Impulsively he thrust the manuscripts of his poetry into her coffin. Rossetti lived thereafter in Chelsea as a

Bohemian with many friends, somewhat consoled by a lovely model, Fanny Cornforth.

At the urging of friends he had his wife's coffin exhumed in 1869 and secured his manuscripts for publication. About the same time he became addicted to chloral and suffered considerable physical though not mental debility. Watts-Dunton was virtually his keeper during the later periods of despondency and feelings of persecution. Rossetti was especially drawn to Jane Morris, wife of William Morris. Late in 1881 he suffered a paralytic stroke and died the next year.

Rossetti is almost unique among English poets as completely the artist, a type more familiar on the continent. He had no genuine interest in political, social, or scientific movements of his era. Watts-Dunton listed Rossetti's loves as: poetry, painting, medieval mysticism, and women; all of which might be summed up as the search for ideal aesthetic beauty. Religion, Nature, or any subject Rossetti employed was material not for the determination of objective truth or the reforming of men but for the stimulation of the imagination and the evocation of beauty.

The Early Italian Poets (1861), Rossetti's first published book, was later revised and enlarged as *Dante and His Circle* (1874). Rossetti translated from about sixty Italian poets who preceded or surrounded Dante Aligheri. These poems offered to English readers a previously untapped literature so faithfully and effectively rendered in the original meters as not yet to be superseded. The most notable piece is Dante's "Vita Nuova."

Poems (1870), the first volume of Rossetti's original verse, includes many poems previously printed in periodicals.

"The Blessed Damozel" (*1847*) was first printed in *The Germ* and subsequently went through three further recensions. Rossetti himself stated, "Poe had done the utmost it was possible to do with the grief of the lover on earth [in "The Raven"], and so I determined to reverse the conditions, and give utterance to the yearning of the loved one in heaven." The spirit of a beautiful woman in heaven laments for her still-living lover on earth; the parenthetical statements are his earth-bound musings. The dominant mood of the double plaint is frustration, but harmoniously integrated are a Miltonic effect of the vast abyss of space, colors like an exquisite medieval illuminated ms., and Rossetti's fusion of sensuous and spiritual love. Stanza is accentual and rime pattern *4x 3a 4x 3a 4x 3a.* Rossetti never surpassed this early Pre-Raphaelite picture in decorative, detached verse.

"My Sister's Sleep" (*1847*), first printed in *The Germ,* relates the death of a sister, Margaret, on Christmas Eve and the sublimating of family grief in praise of the newborn Lord. There is no autobiographical basis for this essentially plain statement. By a few weeks this poem anticipated in its stanzaic form the *In Memoriam* stanza of Tennyson.

"The Portrait" (*1847*) is a lyric meditation, without autobiographical basis, for a dead woman whose portrait the speaker painted and now gazes upon. The effect is visually vague but poignant. Surprising for Rossetti is the absence of sensuous sexuality.

"Jenny" (*1847*) is the one truly "English" poem by Rossetti, displaying typical English moralizing, prudishness, genteel wholesomeness, and kindliness. Although about a prostitute, it proclaims no "raptures and roses of vice." The narrator tells of accompanying Jenny to her room after a dance. Exhausted, she falls asleep with her head upon his knee. He departs quietly, leaving the money she had sought. Much of the poem regrets man's inhumanity to women and the depths to which well-intentioned women may be thrust. Style is straightforward simplicity in four-beat couplets.

"The Sea-Limits" (*1849*) observes the sea as the symbol of the great life force, mournfully eternal. It is typically early Rossetti verse in its artful simplicity and perfect phrasing.

"The Burden of Nineveh" (*1850*), when published anonymously, evoked Ruskin's delighted "It is glorious" and a desire to know the author. Rossetti had witnessed the unpacking in the British Museum of giant sculptures unearthed by the 1845–51 English expedition to ancient Nineveh. Shall London's glory depart even as Nineveh's, perhaps because men of today are worshipers of mercantile idols, equally grandiose and vain? The poet seems constricted by an elaborate stanza (*a a a a b c c c c b*) in octosyllabics.

"A Last Confession" (*1850–52*) is strangely unlike Rossetti's other work, much as though Browning were writing a dramatic monologue version of Byron's *Lara*. During the 1848 Italian uprisings a patriot confesses to a priest. He adopted an orphan girl toward whom his emotions gradually changed from parental affection to a lover's attachment. When she spurns him and all the causes for which he stands, he kills her. The priest is present not for absolution but for shock effect. The patriot dies defiantly, whirling off to hell. Rossetti here demonstrates his ability to write some haunting verse and some sinewy blank verse.

"Sister Helen" (*1851–52*) was termed "that terse fierce masterpiece" by Christina Rossetti. In a medieval Scottish setting the jilted Helen melts the wax image of Keith of Ewern, thereby through "sympathetic magic" causing her former lover to waste away and die. Her small brother, uncomprehending, keeps asking her about her actions and relays the messages of those unsuccessfully pleading for her to stop her machinations. In league with the devil, Helen destroys her lover but also sends her own soul to hell. Bitter hate and implacable determination produce a double spiritual tragedy. Effective dramatic devices of the folk ballad are interwoven. Impressive is the recurrent and varied burden, the voice of an imaginary medieval throng gasping horrified echoes or anguished prayers after each ironic comment by Helen. In spite of its length and feverish attempt to cap one climax with another, it is one of the most successful art ballads in English.

"The Ballad of Dead Ladies" (*1869*) is a translation of "Ballade des Dames du Temps Jadis" by François Villon (fl. 1450). Rossetti was one of the important popularizers of French stanzaic patterns in 19th-century English verse. Strictly speaking, the French *ballade* requires precisely the same rime throughout (*a b a b b c b c* with envoy of *b c b c*), but Rossetti employs new *a* and *b* rimes in each stanza. "Where are the snows of yester-year?" is the sorrowing refrain for the passing of time that obliterates the beauty and wonder of woman.

"Troy Town" (*1869*) was suggested to Rossetti by Browning. The ancient Pliny recounts a legend that Helen dedicated a goblet molded in the shape of her breasts to Aphrodite, the goddess of love. The tale of fearful destruction induced by the world's most renowned beauty evokes a familiar Rossetti alternation between the ecstasy of passion and the remorse of death. The contrast is highlighted by the unvaried, agonized refrain.

The Athenaeum of December 16, 1871, carried Rossetti's defense of himself and all Pre-Raphaelitism against "The Fleshly School of Poetry," a diatribe by Robert Buchanan (1841–1901) in the October 1871 issue of *The Contemporary Review*. In lively journalistic fashion Buchanan snorted at Rossetti's sensuality, imitative quality, mingling of poetry and painting, off rimes, and drawn-out refrains; he concluded that Rossetti would be forgotten like Skelton and Donne, "once prosperous nonsense-writers each now consigned to his own little limbo." Rossetti's detailed reply, "The Stealthy School of Criticism," is restrained and dignified, demonstrating Buchanan's frequent misrepresentations. Before his death Buchanan rescinded his adverse judgments about Rossetti.

Ballads and Sonnets (1881) is most important for its completion of the following works:

"The House of Life" consists of 101 sonnets in the Italian form written between 1848 and 1881. Although many had been published in periodicals and in the 1870 volume, forty-seven previously unprinted sonnets appear in this collection and for the first time truly round out the series. The title is taken from astrology and means "the house of the ascendant," i.e. the first and most important of the twelve segments into which the heavens are arbitrarily divided by astrologers. Rossetti's series is not a true sonnet sequence but an assembly of sonnets (occasionally falling into consecutive groups) meditating the trinity of love, life, and death. Both the poet and his brother William, who edited the poems, sought to present the sonnets as purely imaginative; nonetheless, it is abundantly clear that the poems are intensely personal. Strongly presented is the love for woman, and the attempted Rossetti synthesis of the sensuous and the spiritual. A powerful sense of guilt suffuses the poet as he blames himself for his wife's death and feels a violation of her memory in his attraction to other women. Toward Jane Morris he feels deep frustration because she is securely married, and chagrin that he is likely to hurt her husband, one of his close artistic friends. The major sonnets are as follows.

The introductory sonnet (*1880*) is one of the best sonnets on the subject of the sonnet. Here Rossetti states that "A sonnet is a moment's monument," the expression of one concentrated mood or single incident.

I, "Love Enthroned" (*c. 1871*), exalts love above all other powers and human experience.

II, "Bridal Birth" (*c. 1860*), commemorates not merely the first birth of love but also the final spiritual rebirth of the lovers from the union of Love and Death.

IV, "Lovesight" (*c. 1860*), was first planned as the initial sonnet of the series. The poet wonders when he most clearly perceives his beloved: in daylight gazing upon her beauty, or at night contemplating her soul.

XIX, "Silent Noon" (*c. 1871*), celebrates a pastoral rendezvous of the lovers amid the quiet beauty of Nature's sex symbols.

XXIV, "Pride of Youth" (*1880*), sees the succession of youthful loves as natural growth and change rather than flighty heedlessness.

XXXIV, "The Dark Glass" (*1871*), sees love as the remotest bounds of the known, the ultimate revelation. This is perhaps Rossetti's most impressive *mystique d'amour*.

XLIX–LII, "Willowwood" (*1868*), is a connected series of four sonnets using weeping willow as a symbol of love grief. Ambiguously the series can refer to either Lizzie or Janey. The ecstasy and anguish of joined and sundered love affect the poet like tragic catharsis.

LIII, "Without Her" (*c. 1871*), is one of the most impassioned expressions in literature of painful grief for the absent beloved. Either Lizzie or Janey may be the unnamed woman.

LV, "Stillborn Love" (*c. 1869*), was regarded by Rossetti as his best sonnet. Apparently referring to Janey, it claims that love is an event not of time but of eternity, consummated only in "The house of Love" in an afterlife.

LVI–LVIII, "True Woman" (*c. 1881*), in a series of three sonnets, perceives the ideal woman in medieval fashion as bodily beauty and spiritual mystery. Rossetti ignores Victorian exaltations of wifehood and motherhood, and 20th-century respect for female intelligence.

LXXI–LXXIII, "The Choice" (*1848*), are three sonnets hesitatingly included, for they run counter to the all-for-love theme. The first attacks the earnest, scientific Victorian mind and proffers instead a sensual hedonism. The second denies the Victorian confidence in progress and suggests religious asceticism as preferable. The third scorns Victorian smugness and advises Browningesque self-development.

LXXIV–LXXVI, "Old and New Art" (*1849*), state the artist's Pre-Raphaelite credo. Art is the most sacred of all things to Rossetti, and it must recapture the simple directness of the Primitives.

LXXVII, "Soul's Beauty" (*c. 1866*), was written to accompany Rossetti's painting, *Sibylla Palmifera* ("Palm-bearing Sibyl"). The power of the soul's beauty is manifest both in Nature and in woman.

LXXVIII, "Body's Beauty" (*1868*), forming a diptych with LXXVII, was written to accompany Rossetti's painting, "Lady Lilith," with voluptuous Fanny Cornforth as model. Lilith, according to the Talmud the wife of Adam before Eve, is the eternal *femme fatale*.

LXXXVI, "Lost Days" (*1858*), one of the last of his earlier stark simple statements before the later mannered style, poignantly sees each lost opportunity as a form of self-murder.

XCVII, "A Superscription" (*1869*), is haunted by an old love, apparently Lizzie, but suggests a palimpsest with a new love, probably Janey, written over the old.

CI, "The One Hope" (*1869*), in pagan conclusion yearns in heaven to meet "the one Hope's one name," probably Janey Morris, possibly the ultimate mystical Love.

William Allingham (al'ing-em) (1824–1889). A native of Ballyshannon, Ireland, William Allingham held various professional posts in London from 1847 to 1870, when he became subeditor of *Fraser's Magazine* under Froude. In 1874 he succeeded Froude as editor-in-chief. Rossetti illustrated some of Allingham's books, and Tennyson and Carlyle were his friends. Many of Allingham's poems are lyrics to traditional Irish music or narratives about Irish fairies and the supernatural. Yeats was largely drawn to Pre-Raphaelitism by these works. The best-known Allingham piece is "Up the Airy Mountain." Allingham was the most gifted of the host of poet-painters who clustered about Rossetti in the P.R.B.

THE POETRY AND PROSE OF MORRIS

William Morris (1834–1896). William Morris bore the same name as his father, a wealthy London broker. Born at Walthamstow, Essex, he was educated at Marlborough College. Inclined toward medievalism and Anglo-Catholicism, he entered Exeter College, Oxford, intent upon becoming a clergyman. His interests shaded from religion to Pre-Raphaelitism, and he was instrumental in publishing the *Oxford and Cambridge Magazine* (1856), the successor of *The Germ*. After brief experience in an architect's office, Morris studied painting with Rossetti and married one of that artist's beautiful models, Jane Burden. Near London he erected the Red House, which he completely designed and decorated himself. This experience, arising from his profound distaste for the general ugliness of Victorian design, caused him in 1861 to establish a firm for the creation of household articles both useful and beautiful—textiles, furniture (he invented the Morris chair), ceramics, stained glass, wallpaper, carpets, etc. Opponents referred to him as the "poetic upholsterer." Turning to printing in his later years, he founded the Kelmscott Press in 1891 to produce probably the most beautiful books in England since illuminated medieval mss. Morris rode the crest of swelling radicalism to found the Socialist League in 1884 and became the most vocal literary supporter of socialism before the rise of the Fabians.

Very few men have ever demonstrated the proficiency of Morris in so bewildering a variety of arts and skills. Perhaps his many talents and breadth of interests militated against his pre-eminence in any one of them. Poetry was but one of his many abilities and came so easily to him that he took it lightly. All verse, he felt, was merely craftsmanship. "If a chap," he asserted, "can't compose an epic poem while he's weaving tapestry, he had better shut up, he'll never do any good at all." All the figures of his verse and prose tales are vigorous, healthy-minded people who struggle valiantly and take life and death as they come. Morris himself was a truly happy man, too much enjoying life to feel perturbations of the spirit even in his shifts of position. Our age, tortured by self-division, can discover and elevate a Hopkins while it almost forgets a Morris, whom it often brands as naïve.

PRE-RAPHAELITE PERIOD (1856–65). *The Defence of Guinevere, and Other Poems* (1858) has been termed the best single volume of Pre-Raphaelite verse. Its subjects are almost entirely British and French medievalism, falling into four types:

(1) Decorative aesthetic verse of the dreamy Rossetti style, foreshadowing the later aestheticism of Wilde, Dowson, etc.

"The Blue Closet" tells of Lady Louise's Christmas Eve lament for Arthur, the knight who rode off wearing her scarf and was never heard of again. His ghost appears to lead Lady Louise, Lady Alice (her sister), and their two handmaidens to the land of the dead. But the story is insignificant beside the tapestry-like evocation of eerie sorrow, a mood transporting the reader not only from the embattled 19th century but from life itself.

(2) Pictorial verses that seem to describe a Pre-Raphaelite painting. Although frequently dramatic character studies, they pointedly omit the moralistic strain of Browning.

"The Defence of Guinevere" in terza rima pictures Arthur's queen speaking in her own defense at her second trial for adultery. Persuading Arthur to inform Guinevere that he would not return at night from a hunting trip, Agravaine and Modred succeed in trapping Launcelot in her room.

Lines 242–81 present her claims of a perfectly innocent rendezvous. Incomprehensible to her medieval mind is the rehashing by Gawain, brother of Agravaine and here her chief accuser, of all the allegations at her first trial. Launcelot had then saved her in trial by battle with Mellyagraunce, and she interpreted his victory as God's vindication of her innocence. The poem concludes with Launcelot's arrival to defend her a second time. The beautiful and courageous Guinevere is the personification of Love and Beauty defying staid Victorian mores. Medieval intensity and passion are Morris' retort to the moralistic bourgeois domesticity in Tennyson's treatment of the same theme.

(3) Brutal realism derived from medieval chroniclers, notably Froissart. "The Haystack in the Floods" in octosyllabic couplets relates an incident of 1356 following the English victory over the French at Poitiers. An English knight, Sir Robert de Marny, and his mistress, Jehane, dashing for the English-held area of Gascony, are intercepted by Godmar, a villainous French knight. Robert is brutally decapitated, and Jehane is dispatched to Paris for trial as a witch. The concluding lines suggest that she may have found an escape in madness. The starkness of description and taut, sharply etched vigor make this the best Morris poem and one of the finest narrative poems in English.

(4) Ballad imitations with a strong Scott influence. Morris emphasizes not the dreamy or weird effects sought by Coleridge and Rossetti but medieval bravado and bold impetuosity.

"The Eve of Crécy" in four-beat triplets with refrain is spoken by Sir Lambert du Bois, an impoverished French knight who dreams of the wealth and glory he expects to win in the next day's battle, permitting him to wed the beautiful Marguerite. The poem's irony and pathos arise from the bitter defeat soon to be suffered by the French at Crécy (1346).

THE EPIC NARRATIVE (1865–76). The major effort of Morris was expended upon long narrative poems in which he saw Chaucer as his master, though the effect is often more that of Malory. Subjects were from ancient Greek or Scandinavian sources. Poetic reputation first came to Morris with *The Life and Death of Jason* (1867), a retelling of the Argosy quest for the Golden Fleece and Jason's life with Medea.

The Earthly Paradise (1868) was Morris' longest and most ambitious venture in verse. It consists of twenty-four verse tales, two for each month of the year. Viking wanderers in the 14th century, journeying westward, encounter an isolated Greek colony in some Atlantis or El Dorado, and exchange stories. Although Morris claims Chaucer as his model, the account is static rather than dynamic; and most of the tales (Greek in origin—e.g. "Atalanta's Race," "The Hill of Venus") show no individuality in the narrator but sound much alike. Only in the few Scandinavian accounts

("The Lovers of Gudrun") appears the muscular vigor of the sagas. Generally abandoning the stark realism in much of his earlier work, Morris lengthily spins out dreamy romance. The "Apology" states in "Of Heaven and Hell I have no power to sing" his refusal to moralize in the fashion of most Victorian poets. This work might well be termed decadent romanticism, for it is a poetry almost wholly of mood, and the recurrent theme is of the hero who aspires to sensuality, wealth, fame, or mere restlessness, only to find disillusionment in his success. Despite the underlying hatred of modern civilization, the work won numerous readers because of its escapism. It is the nearest thing possible to a Pre-Raphaelite epic.

Sigurd the Volsung (1876) arose from Morris' interest in Scandinavian literature and from trips to Iceland in 1871 and 1873. Though the poet's favorite, this grim, tragic version of the Siegfried story was not to current taste, though the young G. B. Shaw was thrilled by Morris' readings from the poem. The work breaks completely from *The Earthly Paradise* in its omission of archaisms, its substitution of raw action and stark description for dreamy glamour, and its clear-cut application to the contemporary situation. Unlike Matthew Arnold's quiet hopes for a cleansed world in "Baldur Dead," this poem rings with *ragnarok* ("Death of the Gods") and the revolutionary overthrow of the established order to create a new era. Greed, in 19th-century fashion, becomes the motivating force of the characters. Sigurd becomes a champion of the lowly. Therefore, the poem is less a translation of the *Volsungasaga* (half the length of the Morris poem) than a revolutionary 19th-century poet's reaction to the story.

MILITANT SOCIALISM (1876–96). The doctrinaire writings of Morris tended to prose. By the admission of socialists themselves, he was the one spokesman for their cause who could command the public ear.

Hopes and Fears for Art (1882) consists of a series of lectures published to raise funds for the Society for the Protection of Ancient Buildings (nicknamed "Anti-Scrape" by Morris). These lectures embody most of Morris' mature concepts about art and society.

"The Lesser Arts" (*1877*) stigmatizes an urbanized, mechanical culture in which the lesser or popular arts "become trivial, mechanical, unintelligent, and incapable of resisting the changes pressed upon them by fashion or dishonesty; while the greater arts, unhelped by the lesser, are sure to lose their dignity and become nothing but the dull adjuncts of unmeaning pomp." His hope for the future lies in increased leisure that will permit a return to native and traditional forms of art and life, eschewing the affectations introduced from the continent. In vigorous lesser arts he sees the foundation for all art and for a healthy culture.

"The Art of the People" (*1879*) sees history as concentrating upon the parasitic warrior caste and ignoring the infinitely greater significance of the creative populace. For a civilization to be truly wholesome, art must be popular. All "golden ages" have originated in folk art, and all decadence has come from repression and distortion of popular art. Desperately needed in our age is "an art made by the people and for the people, as a happiness to the maker and the user."

"The Beauty of Life" (*1880*) derides the ugliness of contemporary life and declares that a satisfaction of man's aesthetic impulses is essential to worthwhile society. Morris sees the downfall of folk art starting with the Renaissance and accelerating since. He sees the 20th century as "The Century of Education, not of the select few, but of the many" in true arts and skills.

"Art and the Beauty of Earth" (*1881*) elevates medieval popular art as the truly wholesome art of our civilization and again sees the Renaissance as a baleful sundering of art from the populace to be a gaudy plaything of wealthy patrons. All modern men should be educated to appreciate and themselves create a living popular art.

News from Nowhere (1890) stems ultimately from the *Utopia* by Sir Thomas More (in Greek *utopia* means "nowhere"). Immediately Morris revolts against the bureaucratic state socialism, the ultramodern, mechanistic paradise in Bellamy's *Looking Backward,* and sympathizes greatly with Butler's *Erewhon.* After a Socialist Club meeting discussing the future socialist society, Morris goes to sleep at his Hammersmith (London) home with "If I could but see it!" on his lips. In dream he visits the future socialistic England. "How the Change Came," perhaps the most interesting chapter, bears remarkable resemblance to the events in 20th-century Russia, though in Morris' England there is virtually no bloodshed in the revolution. The keynote of the ideal society is man as a social being rather than a selfish, acquisitive, unsocial creature. Men perform noble and worthy actions not for reward but for the sake of the deed. Money, political parties, crime, private property have all vanished. Wants are few, pleasures many. Life is simple, and the individual is free from restraints for the purpose of creativity. Wiser than most utopians, Morris actually underlines a grave defect of his paradise: with no obstacles to overcome, a stimulating, challenging intellectual life is absent. He awakes in his bed, nonetheless determined "to build up little by little the new day of fellowship, and rest, and happiness."

Poems by the Way (1891) consists of socialistic verses in which the theme runs completely away from poetry. It seems strange that such a competent craftsman would permit such shoddy work. The intent, of course, was a people's poetry understandable to anyone and satisfactory for chanting in meetings and parades of socialists. Bitter denunciation of a capitalistic society alternates with joy for the socialist future.

THE POETRY AND PROSE OF SWINBURNE

Algernon Charles Swinburne (swin′bérn) (1837–1909). A native Londoner, Algernon Charles Swinburne descended from nobility. His father was a British admiral and his mother was daughter of the Earl of Ashburnham. Both parents were devout High Church Anglicans. Smallest of the six Swinburne children, Algernon became the maverick, influenced by his paternal grandfather, an 18th-century freethinker. Proving a disciplinary problem at Eton, Algernon was removed for three years of private tutoring. At Balliol College, Oxford, he again proved troublesome and was forced to leave in his fourth year without a degree. Oxford friends included Jowett, Tennyson, Ruskin, and especially Morris, Rossetti, and Burne-Jones. In spite of his erotic verse Swinburne apparently had only one love affair, in which the adopted daughter of Sir John Simon laughed in his face in 1865. Thereafter liquor seems his chief diversion from poetry and impressionistic criticism. In 1879 Theodore Watts-Dunton rescued the poet from acute alcoholic dysentery and sheltered him at Putney until his death.

No other versifier in English has ever spun such intoxicating, hypnotic lines as did Swinburne. Even the most puritanical were enthralled by his dazzling virtuosity in every conceivable meter and stanza. But puritans were, as Swinburne wished, horribly shocked by the contents of his poetry. With the passing of the proper Victorians, Swinburne's insinuating melody no longer possessed the excitement of profanation and ecstatic rebellion. He is frequently dismissed today as a facile poet of meager and repetitious content. His best work, however, still stands in the forefront of English poetry.

THE DEFIANT PAGAN (1860–66). *Atalanta in Calydon* (1865), cast meticulously in the form of an ancient Greek tragedy, recounts a tale from Ovid. Althaca, queen of Calydon, was warned by the Fates at the birth of her son Meleager that he would live only as long as the firebrand before her was unconsumed. The wrath of Artemis, aroused by a snub from Oeneus, king of Calydon, causes a wild boar to ravage the domain. When the Arcadian beauty Atalanta arrives to join in the boar hunt, Meleager falls in love with her. When he offers Atalanta the spoils of the dead boar, his uncles (brothers of Althaea) snatch the booty from Atalanta and are slain by Meleager. In anger Althaea hurls the brand into the flames, and as it is consumed, so is the body of Meleager. Many readers find the story difficult to follow amid the corruscating raptures of Swinburne. Instead of the austere Hellenism of Landor or the moralistic Hellenism of Tennyson, Swinburne pictures a Hellenism of splendid nudity and unabashed sensualism. Though strange to the English tradition, this reading of ancient Greece was more familiar on the continent, especially in Théophile Gautier. The choruses from this drama are rated among the most melodic verse in English.

Poems and Ballads (1866) was motivated, as Swinburne later admitted, by the desire "to be thought an eminent and terrible enemy to the decorous life and respectable fashion of the world." The result is a decadent romanticism that goes beyond the rebellious titanism of Byron to the lush perversions of de Sade and Baudelaire. Sadism and masochism are lovingly caressed to demonstrate "art for art's sake," and to show horrified bourgeois respectability that "flowers of evil" could blossom on England's immaculate soil. Genteel reviewers, conscious mouthpieces of Victorian morality, raised a chorus of righteous indignation. *Punch* labeled the poet "Swineborn"; the *Saturday Review* denounced him as "the libidinous laureate of a pack of satyrs."

"A Match" belongs essentially to decorative Pre-Raphaelite poetry, generously represented in this volume, though overshadowed by the spectacular poetry of passion. It is a graceful, misty love lyric rising in the last stanza to a celebration of the paradoxical pleasure and pain of passion.

"Hymn to Proserpine" in a drawn-out six-beat line, fundamentally anapaestic, is supposedly a pagan lamentation of 313 A.D. when Constantine's Edict of Milan proclaimed Christianity to be the state religion. The speaker bitterly regrets the passing of pagan beauty and prophesies an eventual overthrow, likewise, of Christianity. Swinburne's assault is essentially directed against Victorian Christianity, drab and puritanic. The mood is one of intense weariness and a longing for the peace of death. Seldom in English literature have all the poetic devices of onomatopoeia, alliteration, chiming vowels, nature and sex symbols been fused into such mesmerizing lines.

"Ilicet" ("Let us go," the dismissal phrase ending an ancient meeting) laments the passing of time and the meaninglessness of human existence. It is a quieter expression of the pessimistic quatrains of FitzGerald.

"Laus Veneris" ("Praise of Venus") in sad, voluptuous stanzas defiantly chooses Venus over Christ, sensual ecstasy over salvation. The medieval Tannhäuser who speaks is really a late 19th-century decadent reveling in the sense of violation, and melancholy in his sinning. Lush sexuality vies with the self-pity of the self-damned.

"Faustine" celebrates Faustina, wife of the 2d-century Roman emperor Marcus Aurelius. Gossips of the age ascribed gross profligacy as well as bewitching beauty to her. Swinburne luxuriates in her sadistic pleasures, and as in most of his passionate verse, the source lies not in his meager sexual experience but in erotic art and literature.

"Dolores" sings of "the raptures and roses of vice," emphasizing masochism. "And good shall die first, said thy prophet,/Our Lady of Pain."

"The Garden of Proserpine" rejoices in the eerie and noxious underworld gardens presided over by Pluto's wife "With cold immortal hands."

Instead of the tempestuousness of Byron, this poem is suffused with the sense of a blasé, burnt-out era, welcoming its own dissolution, comforted "That even the weariest river/Winds somewhere safe to sea."

"Satia Te Sanguine" ("Satiate thyself with blood") contemplates sadistic love and finds death a blessed surcease from the savage flames of passion.

"In Memory of Walter Savage Landor" is a simple and eloquent tribute to the poetic classicist and his "faultless fame" in striking contrast to the surrounding verse of passion.

THE FREEDOM FIGHTER (1866–79). *Songs before Sunrise* (1871), declared Swinburne, "is myself." Renouncing his early sensual orgies, the poet now consecrates himself to the religion of freedom and man, and to hatred of all political and ideological despotism. Dominant is the struggle for Italian freedom, in which the patriot Mazzini is idolized by Swinburne. Although the freedom-loving world of the period rang with praise for these songs of the *Risorgimento* and thrilled to a new heroic age (as Conrad notes in *Nostromo*), most of these poems are shrill propaganda rather than notable poetry. The best pieces treat more generally of liberty and its great heroes.

"To Walt Whitman in America" sees the American poet as the symbol of American freedoms and calls upon him to "Send but a song overseas for us" to inspire Europeans to overthrow tyrants and inaugurate a new era free of kings and supernatural faith.

"Cor Cordium" (the inscription upon Shelley's tombstone, "Heart of hearts") calls upon the spirit of Shelley to reinvigorate men to the cause of liberty. Here, as throughout this volume, the sea to Swinburne is the symbol of purity and freedom.

"Hertha" (the ancient Teutonic earth goddess) achieves better organization and unity than most of Swinburne's rhapsodic verse, and probably is his fullest statement of a positive philosophy. The poet asserted, "I rate 'Hertha' highest as a single piece, finding in it the most of lyric force and music combined with the most of condensed and clarified thought." Hertha is conceived of as the eternal Life-Principle, the Goddess of Liberty. All gods are creations of man, and the one all-embracing truth is the human oversoul that demands only the fullest expression by each man of his human possibilities. Swinburne sees the evolutionary drive of mankind throwing off the old hates and the old faiths to produce "Even love, the beloved Republic, that feeds upon freedom and lives."

Poems and Ballads: Second Series (1878) contains echoes of *Songs before Sunrise*. Most notable are:

"A Forsaken Garden" mournfully observes the mutability of human love, the sad erosion of time, and the eventual total obliteration of the universe. Characteristic of his later verse, the sorrow and pain are present but muted, while the sensual is deleted.

"A Ballad of François Villon" carefully follows the form of the French *ballade* in praise of the 15th-century French lyricist, whom Swinburne rates as the first truly modern poet. The 19th-century English poet praises in Villon the strain of passion and grief celebrated in his own writings. The eleven translations from Villon in this volume help to establish Swinburne as one of the significant translators of French verse.

"Ave Atque Vale" ("Hail and farewell") takes its title from an elegy by Catullus in memory of his brother. Swinburne wrote this poem in April 1867 upon a false rumor of the death of Baudelaire, who actually expired in August. Certainly the greatest elegy by Swinburne, it is also one of the best elegies in English. Although in part echoing Catullus, Moschus, Milton, and Shelley, it displays considerable original power. Swinburne pictures himself beside the bier of the dead French poet. His farewell is no Christian rite but a despairing pagan libation. Quiet, sober lines assure the dead man of the relief from pain and struggle in the bounty of death.

THE LAST YEARS (1879–1909). Rescued by Watts-Dunton from a dying condition, Swinburne surprisingly survived for another thirty years, during which he published twenty-three volumes (five more followed posthumously). His poetic technique remained unimpaired, but his fiery rebellious spirit had almost vanished.

Heptalogia ("Seven jests") (1880) consists of seven excellent parodies upon contemporary poets, notably Patmore, Tennyson, and the Brownings. "The Higher Pantheism in a Nutshell" wickedly reduces Tennyson's "The Higher Pantheism" to idiocy. Most delightful is Swinburne's parody of himself in "Nephelidia" ("Cloudlets"), where he burlesques to absurdity all of his own stereotyped mannerisms, especially alliteration. His harshest critics have suggested that this bit of fun is perilously close to his serious pieces.

Tristram of Lyonesse (1882) was intended as Swinburne's masterpiece. The "Prelude" certainly stands with the very best of English lyricism, but the subsequent episodic narrative cannot sustain its torrential ecstasy. In opposition to the Arnold and Tennyson versions, Swinburne makes the medieval Tristram a disciple of the "Hertha" philosophy, and the Tristram-Iseult passion is the triumph of natural love over Victorian inhibitions. Although the love-death scene cannot match the ending of Wagner's *Tristan* (first London performance one month before the publication of Swinburne's poem), the intensity and imagery of this version, told in a purity of line not general in Swinburne, make it perhaps the best rendering of the story in English.

A Century of Roundels (1883) contains little memorable poetry but leaves the reader stunned at the sheer *virtuosi* ability of Swinburne. His *roundel* is not that of Chaucer but his own modification of the French *rondeau*. Though the poet uses a variety of forms, the fundamental pattern is a poem of three short stanzas utilizing two rimes and employing the beginning of the opening line as a refrain to the first and last stanzas. "The Roundel" upon the form itself is probably the outstanding piece.

Poems and Ballads: Third Series (1889) contains the incredible poem "Commonweal," in which the former republican and Victorian "bad boy" extolls the jubilee of "a blameless queen."

THE PROSE. The bulk of Swinburne's work consists of prose studies of literature. As a critic he accepts essentially the impressionistic criteria of Pater. As a gifted poet himself, he has a superb feel for poetry in others. (This propensity injures his examination of Shakespeare, whom he virtually ignores as a dramatist.) His judgments are intensely subjective, glorifying his heroes, especially Victor Hugo, and thoroughly damning his aversions, such as Carlyle. Often fearfully discursive and disorganized in verse, he can become monstrously repetitive and convoluted in the less obviously disciplined medium of prose. Probably his greatest contribution was *William Blake* (1868) in which he refurbished the reputation of a great Romantic in an age when few but Rossetti and Thomson had much of a taste for Blake's verse.

OTHER POETS OF THE LATER VICTORIAN PERIOD

THE AESTHETES

In propounding "art for art's sake" the aesthetes represented a reaction against the Ruskin mind-set and the entire evangelical-utilitarian spirit of Victorianism, as well as a flight from their contemporary commercial and mechanical world. They drew their inspiration from the native sources of Pre-Raphaelitism and from the French Parnassians. Théophile Gautier (1811–72) was the vehement continental advocate of art for its own sake, rejecting all moral, social, and political implications. Charles Baudelaire (1821–67) proclaimed that a poet with a moral purpose had vitiated his poetry. As an artist he wished to taste of all sensations, and evil was especially delicious. Extravagant, too, was his pleasure at shocking and disgusting the staid and complacent bourgeoisie.

Except in some aspects of Swinburne, the English aesthetes proved generally to be only slightly mauve copies of Gautier and Baudelaire. They are less significant for intrinsic content than for demonstration of a growing intellectual revolt against everything "Victorian." The works of Oscar Wilde were, of course, influenced by the aesthetes, and they will all be discussed together in Chapter 4, which is devoted to the Victorian drama.

Austin Dobson (1840–1921). Austin Dobson was born Henry Austin Dobson at Plymouth. He early studied engineering, his father's profession, both in England and France, but abandoned this career for a clerkship in the Board of Trade. He rose to high administrative posts before his retirement in 1901. Government employment was merely a livelihood to Dobson; literature was his profession. Dobson virtually fled from his own era to take refuge in the 18th century when "electric light/Not yet had dazed their calmer sight." He wrote numerous and commendable studies of his cherished past from *Hogarth* (1879) to *Fanny Burney* (1903). He could write heroic couplets with much of Pope's polished conversational ability, as in "A Dialogue to the Memory of Mr. Alexander Pope" (1888). Few Englishmen could reproduce the elaborate French stanzas with the finesse of Dobson: triolet ("A Kiss" and "Urceus Exit" of 1874), ballade ("On a Fan That Belonged to the Marquise de Pompadour" in 1878, taking none of the riming liberties of Rossetti's "Ballad of Dead Ladies"), and rondeau ("When Burbage Played" in 1885). Dobson did much to popularize such stanzaic patterns in English. A genteel bureaucrat, Dobson derived from the French the graceful insouciance of *vers de société* rather than the "flowers of evil."

Arthur William Edgar O'Shaughnessy (1844–1881). A London native, Arthur O'Shaughnessy was privately educated. As an assistant in the zoological department of the British Museum, he produced some important work in herpetology. His co-workers were astounded to find this quiet, reserved little man the author of *An Epic of Women and Other Poems* (1870). He won the regard of Rossetti for his excellent translations of French poetry and for his reproduction in English of melodious, sensuous lyrics *à la* Baudelaire. Like many an unassuming and innocent fellow, he liked to sport with savage violence and lush sexual imagery, though his characteristic style is the standard anthology lyric, "We are the music makers" (1874), proclaiming the prophetic Shelleyan ability of poets.

Arthur Symons (sim′onz) (1865–1945). Born at Milford Haven, Wales, Arthur Symons as a child wrote religious verse but soon rebelled against the pious atmosphere of his family to associate in London with Wilde and Dowson. Although he continued to publish as late as 1931, he is always associated with the 1890s, when he was an important contributor to the *Yellow Book* and editor of the *Savoy* (1896), both periodicals of the new aestheticism. In hostility to his Wesleyan upbringing, Symons reveled in the stylistic and moral decadence of many contemporary French poets; for, he states, they display "all the qualities that mark the end of great periods, the qualities that we find in the Greek, the Latin decadence: an intense self-consciousness, an over-subtilizing upon refinement, a spiritual and moral perversity." Such writing, he concludes, "is really a new and beautiful and interesting disease."

More suffused with French *fin de siècle* spirit than any other Englishman, Symons in his verse varied from delicate impressionistic pieces like "On the Beach" (*1890*) to titillating lust as in "Bianca" (*1894*). But Symons in life failed to live down to the principles he asserted; as William Rothenstein noted, "he began every day with bad intentions and broke them every night." Symons' translations from his revered French Decadents and his critical studies of Blake, Hardy, Swinburne, and Rossetti will probably be his best-remembered works. He was an important bridge between Pater impressionism and French symbolism.

Ernest Christopher Dowson (dŏ'son) (1867–1900). Though a native of Kent, Ernest Dowson spent much of his youth in France. At Queen's College, Oxford, he read erotic Latin poetry and took hashish. Without graduating, he drifted to London in 1887, when he attended sessions of the Rhymers' Club at the Cheshire Cheese and associated with Yeats, Symons, and Lionel Johnson. During sober moments in France he translated French poets and wrote original lyrics. Back in London he was rescued from alcoholism by a friend but he soon died of tuberculosis. His verse is always graceful and melodious. His two opposing strains are represented by:

"Nuns of the Perpetual Adoration" (1891) celebrates the withdrawal to an existence that is "Calm, sad, secure," because "Outside, the world is wild and passionate." Dowson seems to yearn for a heaven-haven from the spotted and blasphemous world.

"Non Sum Qualis Eram Bonae sub Regno Cynarae" ("I am not such as I was under the spell of sweet Cynara") (1896) takes the lady's name but nothing else from the *Odes* of Horace. For two years Dowson dined almost nightly at a Soho (London's foreign section) restaurant run by a Polish émigré. He fell in love with Adelaide Foltinowicz, the proprietor's daughter, but she married her father's waiter. She is the Cynara of this, the most famous poem of the English Decadents. The poem unites the Decadent themes of sensuality and sadness. To multitudes of the young, the refrain "I have been faithful to thee, Cynara! in my fashion" was a catchphrase of cynical nonchalance; but the work is really a lament on the incapacity to love truly.

LATER VICTORIAN SATIRISTS AND WRITERS OF LIGHT VERSE

Frederick Locker-Lampson (1821–1895). Born Frederick Locker, Frederick Locker-Lampson did not add the second surname until 1885. *London Lyrics* (1857 with additions and revisions up to 1893) shows him to be the truest disciple of Winthrop Mackworth Praed and of the *vers de société* of Landor. His subjects are the social trivia (a lady's glove, a soirée, a hansom cab) of everyday experience in upper-class London, treated with the witty pathos of a man who must hide the dire problems of life behind the façade of urbanity. These verses are hardly equaled in English for neat, polished dignity.

Charles Stuart Calverley (1831–1884). Born Charles Stuart Blayds, Charles Stuart Calverley produced much good tomfoolery and some sound criticism in *Fly Leaves* (1872). "The Cock and the Bull" is a clever sally at Browning's *The Ring and the Book,* "Butter and eggs and a pound of cheese" ludicrously parodies the Pre-Raphaelite ballads, and Tupper, Macaulay, and Tennyson are shrewdly satirized. The tones and meters rival those of Praed, his master.

Sir **William Schwenck Gilbert** (1836–1911). A native of London, W. S. Gilbert was educated at London University. His successive careers in the Gordon Highlanders, in government offices as a clerk, and in law as a practicing barrister provided him with rich material for his later humorous verse. In 1861 he started writing verse for *Fun,* and his *Bab Ballads,* chiefly collected from *Fun,* made Sir Arthur Sullivan (1842–1900) choose him as librettist for a series of light operas beginning with *Thespis* (1871). The spectacular success of Gilbert and Sullivan caused Richard D'Oyly Carte in 1881 to erect the Savoy Theatre specifically for the performance of their works. The two friends frequently quarreled bitterly, and they parted violently in 1896. Though they were reconciled, their subsequent effort, *The Grand Duke* (1896), proved a failure. The portrayal of Admiral Porter in *Pinafore* supposedly so irritated Queen Victoria that she refused to knight Gilbert, but he received belated knighthood from her son in 1907. Both Gilbert and Sullivan worked independently or in collaboration with others, but their truly memorable work was in partnership. However, *Bab Ballads,* by Gilbert alone, is also outstanding.

Bab Ballads (1869, second volume in 1873) derives its name from Gilbert's childhood nickname of "Bab." Although without any formal art training, Gilbert prepared the amusing line drawings that illustrate the verses. Some 20th-century critics such as Chesterton have considered these poems superior to the operetta lyrics, which often draw material from *Bab Ballads.* These remarkable nonsense pieces are dominated by a tone of farcical ferocity, gaily riming accounts of shocking violence in language of bizarre gusto, bewildering aplomb, or absurd, sentimental pathos. Psychologically these ballads provided a necessary escape valve to the confused intellect of the age, a jest giving assurance that the only proper response to the silliness of existence is laughter. Everybody was quoting the ballads at the time; even the sober Victorian peers laughed when some of Gilbert's verse was read in the House of Lords. Later intent upon "big things," Gilbert deprecated these poems; but "The Yarn of the 'Nancy Bell,' " "Etiquette," and others have apparently achieved a permanent place in English literature.

Trial by Jury (1875) was the first real success by the team of Gilbert, librettist, and Sullivan, composer, and it has been called the best one-act comic opera in English. It is the only "thorough-composed" work by the pair, as it contains no spoken dialogue. In a wild parody of English court proceedings, a breach of promise suit is tried. Angelina, the plaintiff, appears in a wedding gown accompanied by a bridesmaid chorus in order to gain the sympathy of the jury. The defendant, Edwin, stating that Nature has shifted his affections, offers to marry both his new love and Angelina. This admirable solution is received enthusiastically until the counsel discovers a prohibition against bigamy. The judge solves the problem by himself marrying the plaintiff. Social criticism is at a minimum in this opera, and, as always in Gilbert, proves wholly acceptable because of its geniality and wit.

The Sorcerer (1877) was the team's first full-length comic opera to be a resounding success. Gilbert adapted one of his own short stories, "The Elixir of Love." Alexis, a democratic guardsman, is about to marry Aline in Ploverleigh village. Believing that marriage should ignore rank and wishing everyone to share his felicity, Alexis persuades the very businesslike sorcerer, John Wellington Wells, to distribute a love philtre to all the villagers. In the resultant amatory confusion, all the wrong people fall in love with each other. To break the spell, someone must be sacrificed to the infernal powers; a popular vote sends John Wellington Wells to perdition, and lovers are then properly sorted out. The most interesting character is the sorcerer, whose impeccable top-hat-and-frock-coat manner mocks the pretensions of the respectable bourgeois businessman. His patter song, "My name is John Wellington Wells," is the first of many brilliant Gilbert sallies in this genre.

H.M.S. Pinafore (1878) has rivaled the *Mikado* as a long-lasting operetta delight. Its First Lord of the Admiralty obviously referred to W. H. Smith, the head of the admiralty at the time, who having started as a newsboy and risen to be the most successful bookseller of the age, had quite literally "never been to sea." "Pinafore," a child's apron, is a ludicrously inappropriate name for a fighting ship. By Gilbert's own admission he used at least seven of the *Bab Ballads* for material.

The Pirates of Penzance (1879), except for a makeshift performance to establish English copyright, was first performed in New York. The idea may have come from Gilbert's childhood experience when in Naples he was kidnaped for ransom by bandits. The success of Stevenson's *Treasure Island* and the continuing triumph of Gay's *Beggar's Opera* may also have influenced this whimsy. Its superb patter song, "I am the very model of a modern Major-General," pokes fun at the gross military incompetence demonstrated by the Crimean War and not yet fully rectified even by the 1870s. The general is a snobbish *nouveau riche* who purchases an ancient estate and therewith insists that the dead in the vaults are his ancestors. Thus did the risen bourgeoisie attempt to graft itself artificially upon the traditional and superseded aristocracy.

Patience (1881) topically rewrites "The Rival Curates" from *Bab Ballads* to make "aesthetic" poets Reginald Bunthorne and Archibald Grosvenor rivals for the hand of the dairy maid, Patience. Oscar Wilde has often been considered the prototype of Bunthorne, but actually the generic "aesthete" is intended, an amalgam of Swinburne, Wilde, Whistler, and the like. Gilbert gloriously mocks the artificiality of the aesthetes and suggests rather than proclaims their effeminacy.

Iolanthe (1882) contains the most extensive and pointed of Gilbert's political satire, mocking the House of Lords, with its conservative tendency to obstruct bills from the House of Commons, and all parliamentarians for their lack of personal convictions and the meaninglessness of party labels.

Princess Ida (1884) is based upon an earlier unsuccessful Gilbert play, *The Princess* (1870), which in turn is a comic version of Tennyson's poem. Gilbert, in proper Victorian fashion, thinks that woman's place is in the home.

The Mikado (1885), perhaps the most complete success of Gilbert and Sullivan, was supposedly inspired by a Japanese sword that fell from Gilbert's study wall. Topical satire against a wide variety of petty social pests appears in this operetta, but the chief butt is inflated bureaucracy, typified by the many-officed Pooh-Bah.

Ruddigore (1887), entitled *Ruddygore* until Victorian prudery intervened after opening night, is a burlesque of Victorian melodrama. Although the 20th-century reader or audience cannot recognize the parodies of forgotten thrillers, the work is still good fun in its spoofing of grisly atmosphere and ancestral curses. Sir Ruthven Murgatroyd is haunted by the necessity of committing a daily crime. He claims a false income-tax return, but the ghost of one of his ancestors sneers, "Everybody does that." The curse is removed and the good citizen Murgatroyd weds May Rosebud.

The Yeoman of the Guard (1888) very nearly approaches grand opera in its tale of Colonel Fairfax sentenced to death in the medieval tower of London as a sorcerer. Romantic and amatory complications eventually obtain for him both freedom and the lovely Elsie. Satire and humor are less than in the other operettas, but the music is perhaps Sullivan's best.

The Gondoliers (1889) captures the sunny atmosphere of Venice in a comic plot about who is the king of Barataria (it is another case of switched infants). The principal Gilbert contention is an attack upon equality or republicanism. "When every one is somebodee,/Then no one's anybody."

James Kenneth Stephen (1859–1892). A fellow of St. John's College, Cambridge, James Kenneth Stephen died young from head injuries. He revered Calverley, whom he could not match in grace but whom he surpassed in wit. *Lapsus Calami, and Other Verses* ("Slip of the pen") (1896) collects virtually all his verse. In clever parody he can pillory the slipshod manner of Byron ("Of Lord B.") and the occasional inanity of Wordsworth ("Two voices are there"). Especially sharp is his indictment of the Kipling cult of violence and masculine dash in "To R.K." Though often deriding Browningisms, he rated Browning second only to Shakespeare.

DIALECT AND CELTIC THEMES

After Robert Burns the Lallans verse fell back into a worse obscurity than it had ever previously experienced. Its distinctive qualities of robust vigor and wild grotesquerie were muted by the prevailing Victorian atmosphere, and thus the Scots poetry of this era sentimentalized native scenery and characters in the mood of "beside the bonnie brier bush." The only accomplishment of such pieces was to keep the tradition somewhat alive in anticipation of the 20th-century resurgence of Lallans.

William Barnes (1800–1886). A native and lifelong resident of Dorsetshire, William Barnes was a clergyman with a scholarly interest in philology. His good friend Hardy introduced occasional Dorset expressions in his verse but wrote in what Barnes called "national English." Barnes himself wrote in his native dialect, producing the only dialectal English verse since medieval times that can seriously be compared with modern Scots poetry. *Hwomely Rhymes* (1858) gained the approval of Tennyson, Patmore, and other poets as well as a popular following. All his Dorset verse was collected in 1879. Scrutinizing Hardy's country, Barnes found only gentle pathos and much pastoral beauty. Often his descriptive pieces display the Old Dutch Masters fidelity that Hardy praised or the sunny Arcadian quality of a gracious countryside. Perhaps his greatest poem is the lyric "Woak Hill," almost certainly about his dead wife, though presented as the monologue of a simple countryman leaving his old home with the memories of "My bride at Woak Hill."

Sir Samuel Ferguson (1810–1886). A native of Belfast and a graduate of Trinity College, Dublin, Samuel Ferguson practiced as a lawyer and privately dabbled in Irish antiquities. His collection of Ogham inscriptions (Ogham was a system of writing peculiar to the early Irish alphabet) from ancient Ireland is the most complete ever assembled. *Lays of the Western Gael* (1865) and *Congal* (1872) are poetized tales of the ancient Gaels properly romanticized and moralized in pseudomedieval language for Victorian taste. *Hibernian Nights' Entertainment* (1887) consists of prose accounts based on early Irish history and legend.

Fiona Macleod (William Sharp) (1855–1905). Fiona Macleod is a rare example of a man writing under a feminine pseudonym. The Scottish author William Sharp wrote extensively and without distinction under his own name. Not until his death came the revelation that the supposed Highland poetess "Fiona Macleod," writing from 1894 to 1904, was his alter ego. Both the verse and the prose of Fiona, from *Pharais: A Romance of the Isles*

(1894) to *Winged Destiny* (1904), are misty romanticizing that Sharp and many others thought to be the soul of Celtic imagination.

REACTIONS AGAINST THE AESTHETES

William Ernest Henley (1849–1903). William Ernest Henley was the son of a bookseller in Gloucester, where he was educated. Tuberculosis of the bone, crippling him at twelve, made it impossible for him to attend college. In 1877 he began a distinguished career as editor of various periodicals that made him a prominent literary critic and won him friendships among many current writers. Henley was the model for Long John Silver in Stevenson's *Treasure Island,* and his only child (d. 1894 aged five) is pictured as Wendy in James M. Barrie's *Peter Pan.*

A Book of Verses (1888) has a notable section "In Hospital" (1873–75) written during his stay at the Edinburgh Infirmary under the famous surgeon Dr. Joseph Lister. The twenty-eight poems offer a realistic-sentimental picture of hospital life (essentially a new vein for poetry); the exhilarating conclusion, "Discharged," is exultant free verse, a form in which Henley was a noted English pioneer. The best-known poem by Henley is "Invictus" (*1875*), a favorite of Theodore Roosevelt, which idealizes an undaunted spirit and an agnostic defiance of fate. "To W.A." became famous as the butler's favorite poem in Barrie's *The Admirable Crichton.* Perhaps his best piece is "Ballade of Dead Actors," to his actor brother, E. J. Henley, with its memorable refrain, "Into the night go one and all."

For England's Sake (1900) contains militantly patriotic verse evoked by the Boer War, with "England, My England" perhaps the most rabid conviction in verse that fate has ordained England to rule and to obliterate all adversaries.

A Song of Speed (1903), celebrating a headlong ride in a Mercedes, still remains the best poem about an automobile, its surging power an intoxicating joy to the sick man.

John Davidson (1857–1909). Born at Barrhead, Renfrewshire, Scotland, John Davidson studied and taught science in Scotland until coming to London in 1889. His earliest attempts at a literary career were handicapped by publishers' apathy and his own illness. Toward the end of his life (1906) a government pension briefly relieved his poverty. His drowning near Penzance, Cornwall, probably was suicide.

Davidson's early poetry, often in effective ballad form, shows him as both an English nature poet and a member of the *fin de siècle* group (he contributed to the *Yellow Book*). Much of his best verse of this period is found in his volumes *Fleet Street Eclogues* (1893) and *Ballads and Songs* (1894).

Under the influence of Carlyle and especially of Nietzsche, Davidson became a self-appointed prophet of materialism and the "overman."

The Theatrocrat (1905) and the two parts of an uncompleted Mammon trilogy, *The Triumph of Mammon* (1907) and *Mammon and His Message* (1908), might well be termed the first truly modern poetic dramas in English. Davidson uses the verse play as a vehicle for social criticism, denouncing Christianity and exalting sexualism as the pre-eminent universal principle. He was a forerunner of D. H. Lawrence. His diatribes against faith and chastity were coldly received.

Between 1901 and 1908 Davidson published a series of "testaments" culminating in *Testament of John Davidson* which contained disturbing proclamations on the religion of the blood and the right of might. His own final words epitomize his major doctrine: "Men are the universe become conscious; the simplest man should consider himself too great to be called after any name."

LATER VICTORIAN POETS OF RELIGIOUS EMPHASIS

Alice Christiana Meynell (men'el) née Thompson (1847–1922). A lifelong Londoner, Alice Meynell was the mother of seven children by her husband, Wilfrid Meynell, the editor. She was at the center of Roman Catholic literary life of the era. Patmore was long her friend, and she rescued Francis Thompson from his lowest depths. An infant prodigy in verse, she dropped poetry writing for twenty years after her marriage in 1877. She resumed with *Poems* (1893) and a volume of collected poems in 1913.

The outstanding quality of her verse is a fastidious reticence, due not so much to Victorian prudery as to her inherent nature. Her religious verse does not contain the ecstasy or awe of faith as much as it embodies the sense of everyday stability and refined consolation. Her "A Song of Derivations" (1875) is an example. Her genteel love poetry cherishes the security of a woman who knows that she is loved. Rossetti said that her most emotional poem, "Renouncement" (1877), was "one of the three finest sonnets ever written by women."

Francis Thompson (1859–1907). A native of Preston, Lancashire, Francis Thompson was educated for the Roman Catholic priesthood at Ushaw College, Durhamshire, but dropped these studies for equally unsuccessful medical training at Owens College, Manchester. Between 1882 and 1888 he made futile attempts to earn a living as bookseller, shoemaker, soldier, errand boy, and match peddler. In 1888 he hit the depths of starvation and opium addiction, and attempted suicide. The Meynells took him into their home, where he spent most of his remaining years.

Contemporary critics often disparaged Thompson as "the poet of a small Catholic clique," or as merely bizarre. However, his mixture of religious fervor and astounding conceits, much like his master Crashaw, has made him more attractive to the 20th century.

"The Hound of Heaven" (*1890*, 1893), his most famous work, is one of the finest odes in English. In brilliant, impassioned imagery Thompson recounts the struggle of the mystic in the "war within." Fearing that submission to God is loss of selfhood, the poet seeks refuge in human love, in sensuality, in Nature, in art. Always benignly pursuing, God finally reveals Himself as the supreme embodiment of all love.

"The Kingdom of God" (1908), taking its title from Luke 17:21, likewise proclaims: "The kingdom of god is within you." We may search the uttermost depths of the universe only to find God's omnipresence where we are. The simple quatrains of four-beat lines make excellent use of feminine endings.

Lionel Pigot Johnson (1867–1902). Born at Broadstairs, Kent, Lionel Pigot Johnson was educated at Oxford. Influenced by Newman, he joined the Roman Catholic Church in 1891 and briefly considered a career as a priest. In 1893 he emerged as a vociferous champion of Ireland, even calling himself an Irishman, though without ancestral connections.

The precise craftsmanship and calm cadences of Johnson have proved more congenial to many 20th-century readers than the frequent sentimentalism and romantic self-indulgence of much 19th-century verse. Editing Johnson's collected verse in 1915, Ezra Pound praised him for "constant feeling of neatness [and] sense of inherited order." Typical is "The Precept of Silence" (1895), quietly asserting the soul's refuge from tumult in a receptive God. "The Dark Angel" (1895) refers to both Satan and Johnson's sinful other self; the poet revels in his homosexuality like any French Decadent but glories in the struggle to overcome his debasement.

A MAJOR FORERUNNER OF MODERN POETRY

Gerard Manley Hopkins (1844–1889). A native Londoner of a staunch Anglican family, Gerard Manley Hopkins entered Balliol College, Oxford, in 1863. Walter Pater was briefly his tutor, and Robert Bridges his best friend. Hopkins was deeply affected by the Oxford Movement and turned to Roman Catholicism; he was received by Newman at Birmingham in 1866. In the next year he obtained his degree with first-class honors in classics. Determining on the priesthood, he applied to the Society of Jesus in 1868. Considering the writing of poetry inappropriate to his vocation, he burned all his completed verse. He resumed poetry writing in 1875 shortly before his ordination in 1877. Parish work proving not too successful, he spent the rest of his life teaching in Roman Catholic colleges, at Stonyhurst in England (1882–84) and thereafter at University College, Dublin, as Professor of Greek.

The poetry of Hopkins was unknown to the public during his lifetime. His friend Robert Bridges gradually insinuated Hopkins verse, first in the anthologies *Poets and Poetry of the Century* (1893) and *The Spirit of Man* (1916), then in the collected edition of 1918. Fuller editions of 1930 and 1948 have been enthusiastically greeted. The daringly experimental verse of Hopkins, which would have bewildered his contemporaries, has gained widespread attention in the 20th century, has profoundly influenced numerous poets of our age, and has caused some to consider his slender amount of verse equal to the work of Browning, Tennyson, or Arnold. He is certainly the most important devotional poet in English since the 17th century, but although Hopkins is a thoroughly "modern" poet and a vital discovery of our age, we must remember that he lived and wrote entirely within Victorian times.

The "modern" qualities in Hopkins' poetry which have greatly intrigued today's readers and today's poets are:

(1) Dramatic lyricism which, he claimed, combines "markedness of rhythm . . . and the naturalness of expression." In an attempt to violate as far as possible the contemporary expectation of what poetry should sound like (Hopkins called this "Parnassian"), he mingled the startlingly colloquial with the startlingly unusual to make a poem "explode." The fusion might be viewed as a speaking voice set upon a singing base, thus differing radically from the sheer melody of Tennyson and Swinburne and the sheer cerebration of Browning. Hopkins extensively employed assonance, alliteration, and internal rime not primarily for musical effect but dramatically.

(2) Extraordinary compression and density, discarding superfluities (e.g. articles, relative pronouns) to catch the fullest intensity of feeling. Urgency and excitement are generated by charged language and unexpected rhythms.

(3) Multiple meaning and ambiguity. The American "New Critics" have particularly admired Hopkins for his layers of meaning and his unified vision of several facets of observation simultaneously.

(4) Elliptical statement. Hopkins' poetry leaps from image to image and reproduces the actual movement of the mind in thought or the emotions in feeling.

(5) Preoccupation "with inner division, friction, and psychological complexities in general." Hopkins welcomed the rigid Jesuit discipline to chasten his individualism and love of the world, and the 20th century finds in Hopkins a reflection of its own intolerable tensions, as in him the man and the artist are in ceaseless conflict with the Christian priest.

Of all poets theorizing about their art Hopkins is perhaps the one who most fully practiced what he preached. In letters and especially in the preface written for Bridges in 1883, Hopkins explains his new techniques in his own terminology:

(1) "Running rhythm" (also "common" or "standard") is the conventional syllabic meter of English verse.

"Logaoedic rhythm" ("mixed") is the employment in running rhythm of variant metrical feet within the same line (e.g. an anapest in a line of iambic feet).

"Counterpointed rhythm" is a reversing of metrical feet within running rhythm (e.g. a trochee backed up against an iamb). This juxtaposition of stress was Hopkins' usual method of giving fresh surprise to traditional metrics.

(2) "Sprung rhythm" (by "sprung" Hopkins meant "abrupt") measures a line of verse solely by stress; the number of unaccented syllables ("slacks" to Hopkins) being immaterial. (Although Hopkins developed his concept primarily from music, this is actually the old Anglo-Saxon principle of versification.) Most of his memorable verse employs sprung rhythm.

"Rising rhythm" in sprung verse achieves the effect of the conventional iamb or anapest by lifting from unstressed or lightly stressed syllables toward heavy stress.

"Falling rhythm" in sprung verse achieves the effect of the conventional trochee or dactyl by dropping from heavy stress to lightly stressed or unstressed syllables.

"Rocking rhythm" in sprung verse achieves the effect of the conventional amphibrach by massing lightly stressed or unstressed syllables upon both sides of a stressed syllable.

"Rove-over" is Hopkins' term for more running-over of lines than intended in traditional enjambement. Sprung rhythm should be scanned from the beginning of the stanza to the end without a break. Hence in "The Windhover" the first syllable of *king*dom rimes with rid*ing* in the second line.

"Rests" as in music have the effect of sounded syllables.

"Outrides" or "hangers" Hopkins explains as "one, two, or three slack syllables added to a foot and not counted in the nominal scanning . . . so called because they seem to hang below the line or ride forward or backward from it in another dimension."

Observe the application of his principles to the first line of "Hurrahing in Harvest":

Summer ends now; now, barbarous in beauty, the stooks arise.

Hopkins intended this as a sonnet in "sprung and outriding rhythm" with rising rhythm pattern. It contains fifteen syllables instead of the conventional ten of an iambic pentameter sonnet line. The second and third syllables of *barbarous* are considered outrides.

(3) "Inscape," a Hopkins coinage apparently from *landscape,* is the unique, essential form and meaning of any object or of any experience. In-

scape can range from sharp sense perception to the Platonic idea. Every Hopkins poem is an attempt to apprehend an inscape.

"Instress" is the perceptive response to experience, the bridge by which the inscape of experience is intensified and communicated.

The early poetry of Hopkins (1860–75) survives only in fragmentary and incomplete fashion. It is conventional, reflecting Romantic tendencies (especially Keatsian) and Pre-Raphaelite influences. The one memorable piece from this period is "Heaven-Haven" (c. 1865), upon a nun preparing to take the veil.

"The Wreck of the Deutschland" (1876) is Hopkins' longest poem and the first in his mature manner, i.e. in sprung rhythm and with his characteristic style. On December 7, 1875, the Deutschland was wrecked in the Thames Estuary; among those drowning were five Franciscan nuns exiled from Germany because of the Falck laws and bound for America. The ostensible subject of the poem, lament for the nuns, is superseded by pain for the spiritual well-being of the unshriven crew and especially by the poet's internal sufferings and sorrows.

Stanzas 1–10 show the poet's soul-sickness at evil and violence in the world. We learn, however, not only from beauty and joy but also from agony and hurt. God must master his rebellious creature, man, who must learn either by gradual intuition or by sudden, shocking apocalypse. The Crucifixion, to which this disaster is likened, is divine sharing of human suffering, which sensitizes the soul and draws it closer to its Maker.

Stanzas 11–17 dramatically relate the horrors of the shipwreck.

Stanzas 18–31 depict one of the nuns, amid the uproar and confusion, calling upon Christ to "come quickly." In her the meaning of Christ is reborn. Suffering humanity seeks deliverance not from stimulating danger but from the daily round of trivia and frustration. The otherwise "unshapeable" existence of man is given full meaning and promise of heaven in the Passion of Christ.

Stanzas 32–35 adore the inscrutable wisdom and towering majesty of God. The dead nun is asked to intercede for the conversion of "rare-dear Britain."

Dixon termed the poem "enormously powerful." Its power lies not so much in its orthodox Roman Catholic contentions but in its corruscations of language, mind, and emotions. The problem of tragedy and the triumph of faith have not elsewhere in English been communicated with such disturbing ecstasy.

"God's Grandeur" (1877) states a familiar Victorian contention that a modern industrial culture has lost contact with elemental things, but the unceasing return of daylight symbolizes the immanent brooding of the Holy Ghost over the unheeding world of man. The effectiveness of this unconventional sonnet in "standard rhythm counterpointed" rests in its extraordinary intensity.

"The Starlight Night" (*1877*) opens with a Crashaw-like extravagance of images for starlight. Such expressions as "fire-folk" and "circle-citadels" resemble the *kennings* of Anglo-Saxon poetry. All the beauties of Nature can be bought by prayer and patience, which will enable us to see God in Nature. Possessing God and Nature, we have complete protection against the shocks of life. "Standard rhythm opened and counterpointed" ("opened" here refers to the sprung rhythm lines beginning both the octave and the sestet).

"Spring" (*1877*) sees springtime as symbolic of primal innocence, summed up in the Immaculate Virgin. Sonnet in same metrical pattern as "The Starlight Night."

"The Lantern out of Doors" (*1877*), a sonnet in "standard rhythm, with one sprung leading and one line counterpointed," reflects a familiar Hopkins manner of developing devotional attitudes from commonplace experiences. A moving lantern in the night suggests how casually we note and then forever lose interest in those who cross our path. But God's watchful care ignores none.

"The Sea and the Skylark" (*1877*), a sonnet in "standard rhythm, in parts sprung and in others counterpointed," shows distress with man's immersion in materialism and, presumably, the degrading theory of evolution. The ocean and the bird symbolize the purity man has lost.

"The Windhover: To Christ Our Lord" (*1877*) challenges Eliot's *The Waste Land* as the most discussed poem in the 20th century. In form it is the most daring sprung-rhythm sonnet by Hopkins; the poet termed it "the best thing I ever wrote." The kestrel (a hoverer in the wind) provides a dramatic inscape: it is the *anima Christi* speaking to the poet's "heart in hiding," showing it the beauty, strength, and glory of Christ, for the most commonplace things of Nature can suddenly flash out their own peculiar beauty and their symbolizing of Christ's wounds and suffering. Written in Wales, as were all the Hopkins poems from 1875 through 1877, this work particularly displays the influence of the Welsh *cynghanedd,* an elaborate pattern of alliteration and internal rime: "Fall, gall themselves, and gash gold-vermilion." Notable also is the prepositive attributive, a favorite Hopkins device:

"the rolling level underneath him steady air"=the steady air which was rolling in level fashion underneath him.

"Pied Beauty" (*1877*) is an eleven-line lyric ("curtal sonnet" in sprung rhythm) praising all "dappled things" whose twofold nature is emblematic of Christ's human-divine attributes. It is one of the most sensuous of poems in English, but it unfolds the world's magnificent diversity as a cause ultimately for venerating God.

"Hurrahing in Harvest" (*1877*) gleans from the rich harvest the presence of Christ, and the human will that lifts to praise and unite with Him. Sonnet in sprung rhythm.

"The Caged Skylark" (*1877*), a falling sprung-rhythm sonnet, conceives of man as an aspiring soul caged "in his bone-house." Man's spirit, however, will be "uncumbered" after the resurrection of the body.

"Binsley Poplars" (*1879*) effectively uses falling sprung rhythm for the sense of desecration of natural beauty in the cutting down of these trees near Oxford. Man's muddling with the landscape is his own self-blinding.

"Duns Scotus's Oxford" (*1879*), a sonnet in sprung rhythm, builds up a nostalgic picture of medieval Oxford and praises the 13th-century scholastic philosopher who spread the cult of the Virgin in France.

"Henry Purcell" (*1879*), a sprung-rhythm sonnet in alexandrines, seeks to reproduce the musical swell and roll of the 17th-century English composer. The musician's effect is likened to the crescent-shaped markings upon a sea-bird's quill feathers—a wonderful and unexpected beauty and regularity.

"Peace" (*1879*), using the image of a "wild wooddove," sees God as providing Patience that will eventually become Peace. However, Peace is not dead calm: "He comes with work to do." An eleven-line "curtal sonnet" in sprung-rhythm alexandrines.

"Andromeda" (*1879*), a sonnet in sprung rhythm, pictures the Roman Catholic Church in England tortured as was the mythical Andromeda, especially by the industrial mob violence then directed against the church in the nation's West. Her rescuer, Perseus (i.e. Christ), is called upon to save her.

"Felix Randall" (*1880*), a sonnet in sprung rhythm with numerous outrides, has been termed by George Orwell "the best short poem in the language." The subject is the death of a powerful blacksmith after he has received extreme unction. The poem balances the pain of dissolution with the ecstasy of salvation, the waning of physical prowess with the resignation of the blessed.

"Spring and Fall: To a Young Child" (*1880*) seems to manifest pagan grief over the brevity of life. All sadness arises from one source: like leaves, all humans must wither and die, and in the lament for the dying year we are symbolically weeping for our own demise. Four-beat rimed couplets in sprung rhythm.

"The Leaden Echo and the Golden Echo (Maidens' Song from St. Winefred's Well)" (*1881*) begins with the echoing lament for the loss of beauty and eventually of life. The "Golden Echo" is the consolation delivered by the spirits of the virgins who at the instance of St. Winefred, a 7th-century Welsh saint, dedicated themselves wholly to God (the saint's well at Holywell, Wales, was noted for miraculous cures). Bridges thought this poem showed undue influence of Walt Whitman, but Hopkins ascribed the effects to Greek choric rhythm. It may well be described as riming free verse. "The Leaden Echo" is falling rhythm of gloom, "The Golden Echo" a rising rhythm of hope.

"Spelt from Sibyl's Leaves" (*1884*) in sprung rhythm is, by Hopkins' own statement, "the longest sonnet ever written." Where a normal decasyllabic sonnet would employ 140 syllables, this sonnet calls for approximately 253. The Cumaean Sibyl, Apollo's votaress, conducted Aeneas to the underworld. Hopkins perceives evening as indeed evening (leveling), symbolic of the Last Judgment, when all the earth's rich variety shall be gone and the decision shall be starkly reduced to "black, white; right, wrong."

"Carrion Comfort" (*1885*) is the first of what Hopkins termed his "terrible sonnets," terrible, that is, in the sense of frustration and separation from God. Probably because their agonies mirror the psychic pain of the 20th century they have become in recent decades the most compelling Hopkins verse to modern intellectuals. The title of this sprung-rhythm sonnet was affixed by Bridges. Mystics thus describe the "war within" as the poet renounces selfhood and seeks purgation by which to unite with God. Although the end is submission, the sonnet labors throughout in fearful combat.

"No worst, there is none" (*1885*) is a sonnet generally in running rhythm but with occasional sprung rhythm; the seventh line is a rove-over in the middle of a word. This poem plumbs the utmost depths of what St. Ignatius termed "desolation," when the soul feels cleft from God and comfortless. Desperately grasping, the human spirit will cling to even a hand-to-mouth spirituality in its tortures.

"To seem the stranger" (*1885*) is a running rhythm sonnet with occasional counterpointing and outrides, as are the next three sonnets. Writing in Ireland, Hopkins feels dire loneliness; his family was unsympathetic to his conversion, and in Ireland, though a Roman Catholic, he is deemed an alien.

"I wake and feel" (*1885*) again expresses the sense of separation from God, an aching apartness more grievous than any hellfire.

"Patience, hard thing" (*1885*) reveals a slight easing of spiritual pain. No matter what the cost in anguish, we must bend our souls to the divine purpose.

"My own heart" (*1885*), last of the "terrible sonnets," calls for an abandonment of tortured introspection and a turn to the light of God waiting to shine all about him.

"To What Serves Mortal Beauty?" (*1885*), a relatively regular sonnet though with some outrides, is directed against both extreme puritanism and extreme aestheticism. It is equally foolish to reject natural blessings and to cleave only to them. Natural beauty is a part, but only a part, a heavenly grace.

"Thou art indeed just" (*1889*), one of his most conventional sonnets, is one of Hopkins' best. He is distressed at the prosperity of the wicked and the productivity of others than himself, but ends with a prayer for God's benison.

"To R.B." (*1889*), a relatively regular sonnet to Bridges, superbly describes in the octave the onslaught of poetic inspiration. The sestet ends prosaically, as the poet's inspiration has passed.

The intense interest in Hopkins has resulted in the publication of his prose, far larger in bulk than his verse. His journals and miscellaneous papers appeared in 1959, his letters to Dixon and to Bridges as separate volumes in 1935, and his letters to Patmore in 1938. In sum they constitute one of the most important bodies of 19th-century criticism. To Hopkins the fundamental quality of poetry is sincere and earnest conveyance to the reader of the inscape of experience. Next, Hopkins advances a completely individualistic style fully exploiting the language's resources to reveal the poet's own instress. Both Dixon and Bridges corrected their verses extensively on the basis of Hopkins' advice, but Patmore paid less heed to the Jesuit's comments. Hopkins took Tennyson and Swinburne to task not for their ideologies but for their substitution of melody for deep, honest feeling, and he considered both Browning and Carlyle to be emphasizing violent manner and bounce instead of true instress. Dickens he likewise assailed for consciously seeking the sentimental response of readers rather than probing the ultimate problems of humanity, but Wordsworth he judiciously supported against the attacks of Dixon. No other 19th-century critic approached so closely the general estimates of the age now held by the 20th century.

Chapter 3

Victorian Prose

In the Victorian era, due to the success of the novel, prose became the dominant literary form. As learning and letters drifted apart during this time, non-fiction changed its emphasis from style to content, although there were still men like Macaulay and Newman who could command both. Therefore, this chapter will treat a great deal of writing which may not qualify as literature in the belletristic sense, but which played a major role in shaping the period's intellectual and artistic world.

MAJOR EARLY VICTORIAN PROSE WRITERS

PROPHETS OF PROGRESS

Thomas Babington Macaulay first Baron Macaulay of Rothley, commonly **Lord Macaulay** (1800–1859). Born at Rothley Temple, Leicestershire, Thomas Babington Macaulay proved extraordinarily precocious, assembling a historical compendium and writing an epic poem before the age of eight. His father's home at Clapham, near London, was the gathering place for the "Clapham sect," a group of evangelicals active in missionary effort and in the abolition of slavery. At Trinity College, Cambridge, he twice won the prize for poetry, graduating in 1820. With his essay on Milton in the *Edinburgh Review* (August 1825) he established a literary reputation that was to increase throughout his life. In 1830 he was elected as a Whig to parliament, and in the reform debates of the next year he established himself among the noted political orators of English history. Macaulay was also a key figure in the passage of the 1833 bill eliminating slavery throughout the colonies. Under the Whigs he was appointed to the Supreme Council of the East India Company, and he resided in India from 1834 to 1838.

In India he prepared a humane penal code and stimulated native education. From 1839 to 1841 he was secretary of war in the Melbourne administration. Under the Russell government he was paymaster general (1846–47). With the return of the Tories to power, Macaulay concentrated upon writing. Following his 1852 election to parliament, he suffered a heart attack but continued writing until his death. He was buried in the Poets' Corner of Westminster Abbey.

Booksellers testified that the *Edinburgh Review* sold well only when it contained a Macaulay article. Crammed with information, his prose was thoroughly lucid and fluent, and though reaction against Victorianism has caused his eclipse, he must be recognized as the outstanding spokesman of Victorian orthodoxy.

Essays (1843) collected thirty-six articles, all but three from the *Edinburgh Review*. Macaulay was the chief popularizer of the technique of employing the subject of a review volume as a springboard for an extended critical study. In the review of Henry Neele's *The Romance of History* (1828), for example, Macaulay never even mentions Neele but criticizes past English historians and proposes the method he would later employ himself: fidelity to fact but evoking past life with the vividness of fiction. Among the more significant essays are those on the following subjects:

Milton (1825). The first prose of Macaulay to obtain wide recognition. As civilization advances, poetry declines perforce. Milton became a great poet by overcoming the incubus of a polished classical education.

Machiavelli (1827). Machiavelli in historical perspective appears as an honest observer of politics in the Italian Renaissance. Macaulay exceeded all previous English critics in a fair appraisal of Machiavelli.

Dryden (1828). Macaulay's opinion was largely responsible for Dryden's long relegation to "the second rank of our poets." Macaulay labeled Dryden a satirist in an age of science and criticism who wrote "poetry by courtesy."

Southey (1830). Occasioned by the poet laureate's *Colloquies*. Southey's Tory politics and his protest against the industrial revolution irritated Macaulay, who favored the idea of progress and the glorious present, "the most enlightened generation of the most enlightened people that ever existed." Such sweeping confidence is largely to blame for Macaulay's denigration by Arnold and later critics.

Byron (1831). Occasioned by Moore's biography. Macaulay upholds a fellow Whig, and points to the hypocrisy of Regency society displayed in its condemnation of the "Pilgrim of Eternity."

Bunyan (1831). Macaulay compares the allegory of *Pilgrim's Progress* to that of *The Faerie Queene* and finds Bunyan far superior to Spenser.

Boswell (1831). It was the 20th century that raised Boswell from the abyss to which Macaulay lowered him. Delighting in paradoxes, the essayist marvels that the best English biography by some chance accident should come from such a "servile and impertinent" character.

Horace Walpole (1833). Walpole was too "Frenchified," asserted Macaulay, and he dismissed to the rank of third-class artists the sociable Walpole, who would not work assiduously to improve his mind.

Pitt the Elder (1834). While praising the noted 18th-century statesman for injecting new life and courage into the nation's spirit, Macaulay reveals much of his own bias by annoyance at Pitt's complexity. Here, frowns the essayist, is an almost unique example of a man of true genius "who lacked simplicity of character."

Bacon (1837). Although scornful of Bacon the man, Macaulay exalts Bacon the philosopher far above Plato. This lengthy study is one of the most significant as well as typical expoundings of the 19th-century deification of material progress.

Clive (1840). Although enthusiastic about the renowned soldier, Macaulay censures him severely for accepting bribes from natives, because of the moral weakness involved and because such actions embarrass English dealings with the East Indians.

Von Ranke's *History of the Popes* (1841). A German work by perhaps the most eminent contemporary historian. Macaulay admits in this essay that in theology his idea of progress seems invalid. He praises the wisdom of Roman Catholicism and its ability in the Counter Reformation to regain much of the ground lost in the Reformation. Nevertheless, he insists that northern Europe owes its "great civilization and prosperity chiefly to the moral effect of the Protestant Reformation, and that the decay of the southern countries of Europe is to be mainly ascribed to the great Catholic revival."

Restoration Comic Dramatists (1841). Macaulay refuses to accept Lamb's ascription of such drama to the never-never world of "pure comedy." The Victorian critic is as condemnatory of the immorality in Wycherley, Congreve, and Vanbrugh as his 17th-century predecessor Jeremy Collier, and on the same bases.

"Warren Hastings" and "Frederick the Great" (both 1841) are character sketches of the colorful type with which Macaulay was later to encrust his *History*. Both dramatize historical events with all the vividness and raciness of fiction.

Later essays include "Addison" (*Edinburgh Review* 1843), perhaps his soundest piece of literary criticism, for the temperament and attitudes of the early 18th-century essayist were especially congenial to Macaulay. For the *Encyclopaedia Britannica* (eighth edition, 1853–60) he wrote five biographies. That on Dr. Johnson has been retained into the 20th century. This well-known article clearly displays the virtues and defects of Macaulay. A brilliant observer of the outside, Macaulay cannot penetrate beneath the surface. All his figures are checked off upon a list of positive or negative traits, as compiled by Macaulay's own rigid morality.

Lays of Ancient Rome (1842), Macaulay's bid for poetic fame, consists of four narrative poems based upon legends of early republican Rome. In his preface he regrets that the native literature of Rome was submerged under the superior prestige of Greek models. In his verse he attempts to re-create the ballad quality assumed to be characteristic of those lost narratives. All four poems imitate the gusto and gallop of Scott, and the most famous is "Horatius," which remained a standard declamation piece well into this century.

The History of England (I, 1848; II, 1855; III, 1861), a massive fragment, actually chronicles in detail only a sixteen-year period starting with 1685. Professional historians have deplored the distressing insularity of the work: the colonies and relations with the continent are virtually ignored. Macaulay was woefully unfair to personalities he disliked, such as William Penn and the Duke of Marlborough. Nonetheless, this is the most fascinating and readable history in English. No other historian has so strikingly welded the techniques of fiction to historical writing to bring to life the entire sweep and color of an era in sparkling vignettes, brilliant descriptions, and exciting character sketches. Macaulay frankly admitted that he wanted to write a history that would displace novels upon a lady's dressing-room table, and he succeeded spectacularly. The history is really a giant success story, demonstrating the triumph of Whig principles, such as the right of the people to determine who shall rule them, the supremacy of parliament over the monarch, and religious toleration along with the established church. Macaulay was the chief impresser upon the English of the Whig view of history, asserting that these principles led to national prosperity, reform, and the prospect of limitless future progress. Nowhere else could the Victorians find such a flattering confirmation of their optimism and self-confidence. The work's continuing popularity is largely a result of its perfect clarity of style and rich evocation of everyday 17th-century life.

John Stuart Mill (1806–1873). Born in London, John Stuart Mill was the eldest of the nine children of James Mill. Psychologists assign to the younger Mill one of the highest IQ ratings of modern times, setting him in the company of Newton, Leibniz, and Einstein. Young Mill studied Greek at the age of three, Latin at eight; by thirteen he had covered most of history and philosophy, and by sixteen most of science and political theory. His father carefully planned this program for him, scrupulously omitting literature and religion. His father's "system" sought to develop in the youth an association of his own happiness with positive service to society. Hence he was started as a clerk in the East India Company in 1823; he rose to the second highest office in the company before it was nationalized in 1858. In his spare time he was groomed as heir apparent of the leadership of Utilitarianism.

In 1826 Mill suffered a severe nervous breakdown; one of the results of his recovery was a turn from his father's emphasis upon better institutions to his own emphasis upon better men. In 1830 he and Mrs. Harriet Taylor fell deeply in love, but Victorian mores, represented by Mill's wrathful father, caused the lady to stay with her husband until the latter's death in 1849. Two years later she and Mill were married. Mill was occupied with writing and editing the *London and Westminster Review,* and from 1865 to 1868 he represented Westminster in parliament, in 1866 making the first motion in English parliamentary history for woman suffrage. He continued to support reform measures until his death, when he was buried beside his wife (d. 1858) at Avignon, France.

European critics rightfully regard John Stuart Mill as the most representative thinker of his age and the greatest proponent of English empiricism. Though essentially faithful to the principles of Utilitarianism—agnostic in faith, positivistic toward science, and associationistic in psychology—Mill displayed an extraordinary breadth of sympathy, especially remarkable in his break from the rigid cocoon spun by his father. Mill developed from a rather narrow individualism to a widely tolerant liberalism. Although always rather coldly detached and never guilty of "literary" airs, he was responsible more than any other writer for stimulating philosophic interest in the Victorian public.

"Bentham" (*London and Westminster Review* 1838) recognizes the founder of Utilitarianism as one of the greatest practical benefactors of mankind but, as a "boy to the last," deficient in spiritual values. In the momentous task of personal and national formation of character, Bentham by his ignoring of conscience, honor, and self-respect contributes very little.

"Coleridge" (*London and Westminster Review* 1840) diagnoses the sociopolitical struggle of 19th-century England as the opposing philosophies of Bentham (progress) and Coleridge (order). Although clearly identifying himself as a Benthamite, Mill sympathetically portrays the "higher conservatism" of Coleridge that would satisfy the human craving for continuity and tradition. This and the preceding essay demonstrate one of the most impressively tolerant and self-critical minds in English thought. Mill here also displays most significantly his lifelong insistence upon synthetic truth. That is, every honest viewpoint achieves an aspect of the truth, and the honest critic seeks to obtain all truth and reconcile it in a greater whole. As Coleridge failed to perceive truths excluded by tradition, Bentham failed to realize the truths contained in tradition.

A System of Logic (*1830–43,* 1843) established Mill as the chief empiricist of the century. Assuming that Nature is uniform (and thus leaving himself prey to Humean criticism and later theories of subjectivity), Mill attempted to set induction as the only valid method of determining truth. Intuitive thought is dismissed, and deduction is but a handmaiden of induction. The moral sciences, he asserted, transcend the physical sciences but like them are based upon causation. Human actions are predictable, and humanity can therefore control its own destiny. Until the century's end this text was the foundation for most English science and philosophy.

Principles of Political Economy (*1845–48*, 1848), the standard work in the field for most of the century, strongly defended private property against all forms of communal or state ownership (except public utilities). Mill opposed absentee landlords, however, and set as an ideal the principle of peasant ownership with each man enjoying the income he works for upon his own property. Industrial monopolies should be prevented and small business encouraged in order to strengthen competition and equalize individual wealth. With these principles established and a stable population achieved by self-restraint, Mill believed that utopian happiness would loom ahead.

On Liberty (1859), which Mill termed "a kind of philosophical textbook of a single truth," has often been bracketed with Milton's *Areopagitica* as one of the monumental treatises on human freedom. Mill's work was occasioned not by a specific repressive event, as Milton's was by the Licensing Act of 1644; rather, Mill felt a mounting conviction that Victorian England was "not a place of mental freedom" and that the nation had fallen into a "deep slumber of a decided opinion" that forestalled free expression. The first section of the work advocates the full airing of all viewpoints:

(1) The opinion being suppressed may be true. Socrates and Christ were both killed as heretics. What we summarily dismiss or persecute can turn out to be valid.

(2) Even if a stated opinion is false, its expression will cause the truth to reveal itself more fully. A creed without the strengthening of discussion and scrutiny becomes empty form.

(3) A detested or unnoticed opinion may contain part of the truth. Mill elaborates one of his favorite contentions: the truth is complex and multiform. Changes in thought patterns are not simple replacements of truth in place of error but the rise of a fragment of truth to be fixed into a new mosaic of truth-seeking.

In the second section Mill derides the modern movement toward uniformity: "The general tendency of things throughout the world is to render mediocrity the ascendant power among mankind." Intellectual progress and personal happiness can be secured only through the freedom of the individual to search throughout life and society for the fullest self-development. In all matters that affect him alone, the individual must be completely unhampered, and the state should intervene in individual conduct only when a person is demonstrably doing harm to another.

Although a mid-Victorian, Mill responds favorably to the 18th-century ideas of *philosophes* like Turgot and Condorcet. From them he inherits the concepts of perfectability and individualism. His work *On Liberty* is the fullest pronouncement of the principles that most Western democracies still claim to exemplify (except, notably, state paternalism). His two other popular works in this field, *Considerations on Representative Government* (1861) and *On the Subjection of Women* (1869), both maintain a libertarian outlook. Mill argues that free institutions are far better suited to promote healthy growth and freedom than the best of dictatorships, and he presents a very convincing case for the advancement of women's rights.

Utilitarianism (1863) seeks to elevate utilitarianism so that it may create as lofty a morality as any religious system. "Actions are right in proportion as they tend to promote happiness, wrong as they tend to promote the reverse of happiness." To answer the objection that life has a "nobler" end, Mill modifies Bentham's contentions. Where the father of utilitarianism had admitted only a quantitative difference between degrees of pleasure, Mill posits a qualitative difference: "better to be Socrates dissatisfied than a fool satisfied." In foreseeing a world where the distinction between individual and universal happiness will eventually have vanished, Mill actually preaches the ethics of Christianity with the religion left out.

Autobiography (1873) was scornfully labeled "autobiography of a steam-engine" by Carlyle, but it remains one of the most revealing documents of the 19th century and of a prodigious mind. The opening section somewhat justifies Carlyle's slur, as Mill details the rigorous inculcation of his father's concepts in the following areas:

(1) Politics—the supremacy of representative government and complete freedom of thought and expression. Education and reasonable persuasion could cause the people to effect an administration for the general welfare.

(2) Religion—agnosticism and anticlericalism. Mill states that he never had to throw off religious faith, because he never had any.

(3) Psychology—Hartley's associationism. Proper environment and education would permit "unlimited possibility of improving the moral and intellectual condition of mankind."

(4) Ethics—Bentham's utilitarianism, the backbone of his father's convictions.

Chapter 5, "A Crisis in My Mental History," is the most frequently anthologized portion, for it is the most "human" passage in all Mill. In 1826 at the age of twenty he suffered a severe nervous breakdown and in fearful depression meditated suicide. Leslie Stephen attributed this mood to overwork arising from the terrifying mental burden imposed by his father. Religious readers have analyzed it as the awakening of his soul. Although Mill offers no explanation, it may well have been a wish for his father's death.

Consolation came through Wordsworth, partly through the intrinsic values of the poet, partly through the sense of independence in a youth breaking from his father's regimen and for the first time delving into belles lettres. The healing power of Wordsworth's poetry impelled Mill to declare: "The cultivation of the feelings became one of the cardinal points in my ethical and philosophical creed." He therefore modified Benthamism by realizing that fundamentally social progress rests upon "the internal culture of the individual."

Mill's despondency proved a blessing in disguise, for he thenceforth extended his reading and contacts far beyond the utilitarian circle drawn by his father. Carlyle was a friend for some time; Mill explored Coleridge, German thinkers such as Kant and Goethe, and French philosophers such as Saint-Simon and Comte. More significantly his revolt against his father led him to the conviction that all earnest seekers for the truth possess some of the truth and that the truth from each should be assembled toward a fuller truth. In one of the world's noblest pleadings Mill asks us to "consider one's opponents as one's allies, as people climbing the hill on the other side."

INTERPRETERS OF CULTURE

Both Arnold and Ruskin as prose writers were enlightened members of the middle class speaking to a middle-class reading public. Earnestly they sought to lead their age to what they considered superior viewpoints. Though highly critical of Victorian deficiencies, they were not rebels.

Matthew Arnold (1822–1888). Matthew Arnold as a poet was discussed in the previous chapter. His verse, emphasizing his intellectual doubt, is largely a product of his youth, which was essentially concluded by 1867. His prose, in which he is an urbane and assured oracle of the era, extends from 1862 to his death. In prose Arnold was fundamentally a teacher, the apostle of culture, seeking to enlighten and direct the middle class ("Philistines"). Not always successfully, he adopted the role of the detached observer, gazing ironically upon human foibles and gracefully setting men aright. He proved a master of English prose style, writing a calm, elegant language of perfect grace and clarity.

Literary criticism was his forte. His three guiding principles were: (a) design, proportion, and wholeness in the total work, (b) the grand style, (c) literature as a "criticism of life."

On Translating Homer (1861) and *On Translating Homer: Last Words* (1862) consists of lectures Arnold delivered as professor of poetry at Oxford. He examines English translations of Homer from the 16th century to his own time, noting the failures to capture Homeric qualities. The outstanding Homeric virtue (summing up the others) is nobility, the product of an aristocratic society. With the departure of aristocracy, literature must reaffirm and sustain nobility in mankind. Truly great art arises from a culture stable and confident of its position.

Essays in Criticism, First Series (1865) established Arnold's prose reputation. T. S. Eliot has declared that Arnold formed the academic literary viewpoint dominant down to the present. The Arnold criticism combines the curiosity and dispassionate objectivity of the French Sainte-Beuve, Arnold's acknowledged master, with the moral earnestness and English gentility of Thomas Arnold. Arnold's fundamental premise is that literature is a criticism of life and that literary criticism is a discovery and analysis of the best ideas advanced by literature. The success of Arnold's contentions in his age arose from his recognition and attempted reconciliation of faith with rationalism, poetic imagination with objective fact. Most important essays in this volume are:

"Preface," probably his most famous prose piece, indulges in playfulness and eloquence that Arnold usually restrains. Assailing the provincialism of the English middle class and the drab narrowness of utilitarianism, he announces his purpose of disinterested search for the truth. Included here is the most famous of all prose paeans to Oxford University.

"The Function of Criticism at the Present Time" is often considered Arnold's most important pronouncement. Its keynote is disinterestedness. Arnold calls upon his age to abandon the narrow views of party and sect, and the provincialism that ignores anything non-English. True criticism seeks "to know the best that is known and thought in the world."

"The Literary Influence of Academies" considers the problem of a national body arbitrating the use of the language; such a prescriptive body had earlier interested Dryden and Swift. While praising the French Academy, Arnold asserts that such a legislative group for language is antipathetic to the English spirit. He declares that Burke is the supreme master of English prose.

"Maurice de Guérin" typifies Arnold's wish to widen English appreciation to include little-known but significant continental authors. Comparing this romantic French writer to Keats, Arnold praises him for "the most profound and delicate sense of the life of Nature." The scholar-gypsy in Arnold cherishes Guérin for "listening, observing, and saying nothing."

"Heinrich Heine" pictures a romantic youth who is the antithesis of Guérin who was deeply religious. Heine, in emotional rebellion, is stigmatized by Arnold for failure to believe in the primacy of intellect and spirit.

"Eugénie de Guérin" contrasts the Catholic piety of this Frenchwoman with the Protestantism of Emma Tatham of Margate. He finds in the spiritual life of the English girl a severe want of charm, grace, spaciousness, and sense of tradition, as compared to her Gallic opposite.

"Joubert: or a French Coleridge" praises this French author for his

Platonism and his abstention from controversy. Joubert is celebrated as "the most prepossessing and convincing of witnesses to the good of loving *light*."

"Pagan and Mediaeval Religious Sentiment" sympathetically urges an understanding of medievalism and Roman Catholicism, and even of paganism, for the religious impulse in man far outweighs any sectarianism.

"Marcus Aurelius," termed "perhaps the most beautiful figure in history," appeals to Arnold because of his stoic philosophy, and because of his refinement and delicacy, his blending of the intellectual and the spiritual. Especially do the self-restraint and detachment of the Roman emperor recommend themselves to Arnold.

"Spinoza and the Bible" distinguishes between the Christian's emotional love of God and Spinoza's essentially intellectual grasp of "the love and knowledge of God." Arnold here stands as a spokesman of Jewish excellence, as elsewhere in the volume he seeks to open the stops of that "narrow-toned organ, the modern Englishman" to noble values in paganism, medievalism, and modern European thought.

On the Study of Celtic Literature (1867) accepts (as did all major Victorians except Buckle and Mill) the now discredited theory that races of men biologically transmit psychological attitudes. Arnold here examines the contribution of Celtic "blood" to the modern British amalgam. In sum, he states, the Celt will "react against the despotism of fact" and hence will display remarkable imagination and spirituality corrective to the phlegmatic and practical Saxon. Arnold's contention reinforces the dubious idea that the poetry in any Britisher is to be explained by "Celtic blood." Arnold is more pontifical than knowledgeable in Celtic literature.

Essays in Criticism, Second Series (1888) selects his outstanding critical works over the preceding ten years. After excursions into social and religious criticism, he returns to literature because the qualities most needed by contemporary England—"flexibility, perceptiveness, and judgment"—are best exemplified in belles lettres. Important essays:

"The Study of Poetry" states that the supreme power of poetry is "consolation and stay," and that poetry eventually will replace religion. Growing more Platonic in his later years, Arnold calls for the removal of personal idiosyncrasies in favor of discovering absolute and unchanging beauty and truth in poetry. Chaucer, Rabelais, Molière, and Voltaire are excluded from the highest rank where Homer, Sophocles, Vergil, and Dante stand. Wordsworth is especially praised for the evocation of the transcendental. Dryden and Pope are denigrated as prosers in verse, probably because Arnold makes spiritual agony a touchstone of poetic greatness, and these men of the Enlightenment gave no indication of such a struggle.

"Milton" claims that the author of *Paradise Lost* was the ultimate master in recent centuries of the "grand style," and the closest modern equivalent to that manner in the classics of antiquity.

"Thomas Gray" dismisses that 18th-century poet as the "scantest and frailest," but Arnold blames Gray's era for providing him with no sense of the mystery of life and no dynamic energy.

"John Keats" praises the Romantic poet but, in the spirit of a classicist, regrets the superabundance of feeling as the excesses of freedom.

"Wordsworth" highly praises the poet laureate whom both Arnold and his father had known personally for many years. Wordsworth releases his readers from prosaic concerns, from the tyrannies of passion and set critical patterns, and lifts him to the plane of essential humanity.

"Byron" admits that the dashing lord was often coarse and sloppy as a poet. The later Arnold, after many shifts of judgment about Byron, finally perceives him as fundamentally an ally against the limited minds of the middle class. Byron recognized as few others did the decay of the old political and cultural order, and waged war for the liberation of the human spirit. Significantly, Arnold ignores Byron's sexuality.

"Shelley," which has strongly influenced the reputation of the poet down to the present, damns Shelley as "a beautiful and ineffectual angel, beating in the void his luminous wings in vain." After lengthy beratings of Shelley's private life, Arnold perfunctorily assures us that the "former beautiful and lovable Shelley nevertheless survives," but the poetry of Shelley is unexamined.

Social and cultural criticism represented merely an expansion of Arnold's position as a literary critic. Ruskin wanted good art and therefore proceeded to demand the good society from whence such art would spring. Arnold wanted disinterested literature and therefore proceeded to demand the disinterested society which would produce that literature. Arnold reached the apogee of his fame in Great Britain and America as the "apostle of culture."

Culture and Anarchy (1869) really means "Culture or Anarchy," for this lover of peace misinterprets minor disorders and noises of the period as symptomatic of approaching anarchy. Here, in clear-cut opposition to Mill, Arnold seeks to establish an authority principle instead of the idol of individual freedom. In a utilitarian age that often regarded past knowledge as a mere badge of social distinction, Arnold advanced as the most vociferous defender of the humanistic tradition. Significant essays:

"Preface" enunciates Arnold's principle of authority as applied especially to religion. He considers the Established Church of England as a cultural necessity to nourish ample minds. English Puritanism and Nonconformity (Protestant sects outside of the Anglican Church), he claims, have uniformly produced narrow minds since the writings of Milton and Bunyan.

"Sweetness and Light" takes its title from Swift's *Battle of the Books.*

England has a pitiful "faith in machinery," i.e. coal, railroads, wealth, population, freedom. The perfection for which men strive should not be mere machinery but "a harmonious expansion of *all* the powers which make the beauty and worth of human nature."

"Doing As One Likes" sees anarchy if, as utilitarianism approved, individuals continue freely to pursue their own selfish interests. Instead of personal or class concerns, Arnold urges, Englishmen should seek their best selves in the total national interest. Such a national spirit will act authoritatively to prevent disorder and violence.

"Barbarians, Philistines, Populace" applies these labels respectively to the aristocracy, the middle class, and the masses. The Barbarians he dismisses as adhering to an exterior culture of fox-hunting, racing, and etiquette. The Populace is too preoccupied with sheer physical survival to generate significant thought and leadership. The hope for England lies with the Philistines, who must be aroused from their provincialism and prejudice to spaciousness and amplitude of cultural vision. The term Philistines was derogatively applied by medieval university students to townsfolk, who, unlike university people, were obviously not children of light.

"Hebraism and Hellenism" sums up Western culture in these two aspects, both of which seek "man's perfection or salvation." "The uppermost idea with Hellenism is to see things as they really are" (as a quotation from Plato, "things as they really are" means the Platonic essences, or in Christian terms "the will of God"); "the uppermost idea with Hebraism is conduct and obedience" (rigid Puritanism). The Philistine middle class of England has overemphasized Hebraism. The balance of Hebraism with Hellenism will produce a harmonious and enlightened culture.

Friendship's Garland (1871) consists of a dozen imaginary letters supposedly written by Arminius von Thunder-ten-Tronckh, modern scion of the German royal house that expelled Voltaire's Candide. The German liberal excoriates the English middle class for betraying liberalism and the basic concepts of democracy: "the victory of reason and intelligence over blind custom and prejudice." The irrationality of English institutions and the smug narrow-mindedness of the middle class will bring England low.

Mixed Essays (1879) collects nine essays written over almost two decades. Although literary criticism is strong, even stronger is the insistence upon literature as the means of cultural elevation to the sane, ordered society. Major essays:

"Democracy" rebukes the middle class for its concept of democracy as individual freedom from government interference. Democracy has destroyed the earlier fortresses of aristocracy and priesthood without producing a new central power to bring stability to a nation. Arnold's solution is the state, i.e. the united nation collectively and corporately. A truly enlightened middle class will support a state that works for all citizens positively instead of a state that is merely hands-off.

"Equality" urges the egalitarian watchword of the French Revolution. Arnold realizes that the biggest problem of equality is financial, and strangely ignoring industrial inequality he advocates the increase in small landholders to offset the absorption of real property into the hands of a few.

"Irish Catholicism and British Liberalism" indicts the English and Scottish middle class for its refusal in 1878 to permit a Roman Catholic university for Ireland. Arnold points to the toleration accorded religious minorities elsewhere and demands the same freedoms for religious minorities in the United Kingdom.

Discourses in America (1885) consists of three essays that Arnold considered his chief claim to remembrance.

"Literature and Science," originally delivered at Cambridge in 1882 as a rejoinder to T. H. Huxley's "Science and Culture," was revised for delivery in the U.S.A. This is considered the classic defense of the humanistic tradition against the assaults of science. Arnold posits four essential human powers: "the power of conduct, the power of intellect and knowledge, the power of beauty, and the power of social life and manners." Science serves only the power of intellect and knowledge. All modern men must take full cognizance of science, but they must also cultivate to the full the other three powers. Belles lettres do not comprise the only path to the complete man, but no man is complete without them.

"Emerson" pays tribute to the American transcendentalist with whom Arnold greatly sympathized, but the most interesting parts praise Carlyle and Newman, with whom Arnold disagreed, but whom he genuinely respected.

"Numbers: The Majority and the Remnant" discusses what Toynbee terms the "creative minority." Arnold's hope for the future lies not in mere numbers but in the enlightened "remnant." Since America has a large and expanding population, it should produce a sizable "remnant" to elevate all its society. Singularly he ignores the problem of proportion whereby the numerically larger American "remnant" need be no more effective than in smaller nations.

Religious criticism by Arnold created quite a stir in its time but is now deemed his least significant contribution. Arnold felt that he was performing necessary criticism upon contemporary faith, for science had so questioned the supernatural that he believed religion's only chance lay in morality. His chief sources are Spinoza and Coleridge, especially as the approach of both was essentially literary and intuitive.

Literature and Dogma (1873) examines the history of the religious idea to interpret religion as a developmental process. Rejecting miracle and prophecy, dogma and metaphysical theology, Arnold defines religion as "not simply *morality*, but *morality touched by emotion.*" In trying to save Christianity he was ready to discard all but its ethics.

John Ruskin (1819–1900). John Ruskin was the son of a puritanical Scottish wine merchant, resident in London. As a child Ruskin knew a rigorously pious household, but also wrote verse, sketched paintings, and studied science. At Christ Church, Oxford, he won the Newdigate prize for poetry and graduated in 1842. His defense of the paintings of Turner burgeoned into the five volumes of *Modern Painters* (1843–60) and established his reputation. In 1848 he married Euphemia ("Effie") Gray. Their unhappy union, probably exacerbated by irreconcilable personal interests and Ruskin's dour parents, was annulled after six years, and Effie married the painter Millais. From 1854 Ruskin delivered lectures at the Working Men's College, established in London by F. D. Maurice. With impetus from Carlyle, Ruskin became increasingly a social critic. Although a professor of art at Oxford from 1870, he devoted extensive time to the St. George's Company, a co-operative enterprise, "to slay the dragon of Industrialism." Among his other activities was a London tea-shop dedicated to low prices and unadulterated products, a London street-cleaning project in which he himself wielded a broom, and practical road repairs along with his Oxford students. In 1877 he retired to Brantwood in the Lake Country. Except for intermittent periods of lucidity he spent the last fifteen years of his life mentally deranged.

Ruskin was the pre-eminent art critic of the century. In identifying morality with art he keynoted the temper of Victorianism and made a bourgeois society accept art as an essential part of meaningful culture. Subsequent critics have severely attacked his yardsticks of religion and morals applied to art, but his descriptions of art objects and natural scenery are classics of English prose. His art criticism is expressed in an ornate, poetic prose of long, sonorous sentences.

Ruskin's transition to social criticism logically developed from his assumption that art must be moral and must proceed from a moral society. His later writings sought to create the moral community from whence great art would emerge. He proved to be a highly influential reformer and bolsterer of English socialism. Most of the social measures he advocated have since been adopted in England. Seeking to appeal to all classes of readers, his later writings display a simple, colloquial, unadorned style.

Modern Painters in the first volume (1843) sought to exalt contemporary English landscape painters, especially J. M. W. Turner, over the established favorites—Salvator Rosa, Nicolas Poussin, and Claude Lorrain. Much of this work also praises the landscapes of Renaissance painters. Ruskin's thesis begins: "The picture which is looked to for an interpretation of nature is invaluable, but the picture which is taken as a substitute for nature had better be burned." He then proceeds to find in Turner an interpretation of nature as revealing divine majesty, eternal mystery, and breathless infinity. Ruskin is the focal point for the merging of Romanticism (especially in the Wordsworthian imagery), science (as an observation of facts), and fervent evangelicalism. Beauty and nobility are his criteria of great art. Beauty is achieved by apprehension of what is the hidden perfection in the world and in man. In his overall argument Ruskin inserts many impressive passages upon a variety of subjects, often irrelevantly. Some psychologists scent thus early the mental flaws that would result in the author's eventual derangement.

The second volume (1846) claims art to be the expression of "human dignity and heavenward duty." All art must be moral, and an impious or unrighteous man is incapable of producing significant art. Contemplative imagination is able to perceive "the Divine form among the mortal crowd." In this volume, particularly, is seen the influence of the 17th-century Richard Hooker upon Ruskin's prose style.

The third volume (1856) maintains that the Grand Style is faithful to particulars and not, as Reynolds had asserted, given to abstract and general treatment. Idealism, however, must dominate any true art vision, generating in the viewer or reader a heightened virtue and ethical standard. The most famous expression of Ruskin is "Pathetic Fallacy," the ascribing to natural objects of the emotions that actually reside in the beholder.

The fourth volume (1856) consists largely of a hymn of praise to the Alps. Nature is herself an artist working for man's joy, but Ruskin's deep concern for the wretchedness of many mountain folk indicates his trend toward social reform. His attempts to trace literary and artistic developments to the influence of mountains are more ingenious than successful.

The fifth volume (1860) in its "investigation of the beauty of the visible world" minutely examines how artists have depicted natural objects. After long excursions he returns to a defense of Turner and of the Pre-Raphaelites. The most important statements express Ruskin's belief in the necessity of the good society for all men. He appraises the entire series: "It declares the perfect and eternal beauty of the work of God; and tests all work of man by concurrence with, or subjection to that."

The Seven Lamps of Architecture (1849) is a paean to architectural beauty. This work brings to a head the Gothic Revival in architecture; the efforts of numerous Victorian architects (notably Augustus Pugin) and the enthusiasm of Ruskin still insure the building of many new ecclesiastical structures in imitation Gothic. From continental and British Gothic Ruskin deduced:

(1) Lamp of Sacrifice (self-denial to praise God or give happiness to fellow men)

(2) Lamp of Truth (materials and spatial arrangements honestly designed for proper use)

(3) Lamp of Power (sense of glorious aspiration, soaring, and vigor)

(4) Lamp of Beauty ("all most lovely forms and thoughts are directly taken from natural objects")

(5) Lamp of Life (bold ingenuity and vitality; the product of vibrant men, not machines)

(6) Lamp of Memory (expressing and preserving the history and personality of a people)

(7) Lamp of Obedience (restraint and self-discipline)

Ruskin prefers the Gothic of northern Europe to that of the Latin south because of its reputed superiority in purity and majesty. With this work Ruskin brought the word *Gothic* to its present elevated connotation after the long climb from its early 18th-century meaning of "crude," "barbaric." He also seizes the opportunity for a social message. Instead of constructing railroads, England should have built beautiful churches and houses. Instead of selling their souls to individual gain, Englishmen should have combined their efforts for the erection of and worship in superb cathedrals.

The Stones of Venice (I, 1851; II, 1853) attempts to establish the concept that art is a direct function of national morality. "The rise and fall of Venetian Gothic art depends on the moral or immoral temper of the state." Ruskin's thesis is oversimplified, for it cannot explain excellent art in the not overly moral Italy of Leonardo da Vinci. Ruskin also overplays his hand by denunciation of the "poison-tree" of the Renaissance. Gothic symbolizes virtue and faith; the Renaissance means corruption and hypocrisy. Nonetheless, this work definitely led the way to a realization of medieval achievements, and it contained in its description of Venetian architecture some of Ruskin's best word pictures. In social criticism Ruskin attacked modern industrialization and division of labor; truly it is not the work but the man who is divided. Three of Ruskin's principles are:

"1. Never encourage the manufacture of any article not absolutely necessary. . . .

2. Never demand an exact finish for its own sake; but only for some practical or noble end.

3. Never encourage imitation or copying of any kind, except for the sake of preserving records of great works."

Carlyle acclaimed the work as a "true and excellent *Sermon in Stones.*"

Pre-Raphaelitism (1851) vehemently defended the Pre-Raphaelites against their detractors. He declared their work to be the "most earnest and complete" since Albrecht Dürer. Ruskin thus established himself as the encourager of new and youthful artists. The pamphlet then discusses Ruskin's favorite, Turner, and his difficulties in securing approval.

Unto This Last (1860 in periodical form, 1862 as book) marks the climactic turn of Ruskin from art critic to preacher of social reform. The title (Ruskin affected poetic, cryptic labels) is taken from the biblical parable of the laborers in the vineyard. "There is no wealth but life." National wealth is not a selfish personal treasure but a public responsibility that must be employed in action for social justice.

"The Roots of Honour" pleads for the professionalization of industry, with the merchant and manufacturer as consecrated to public service as a physician or cleric.

"The Veins of Wealth" asserts that the true goal of wealth is to create happy, virtuous men.

"Qui Judicatis Terram" declares that justice should rule social and economic conduct. Competition that injures any worthy man is unjust.

"Ad Valorem" attacks the traditional economists, including J. S. Mill. "The real science of political economy . . . teaches nations to desire and labour for the things that lead to life."

Thackeray, editor of *Cornhill Magazine* in which the series first appeared, was compelled by popular clamor to suspend publication. The assault upon the orthodox economic philosophy of the age was distasteful to the average Victorian businessman, especially when it came from, of all people, an art critic. Ruskin believed that this work embodied most of his significant social criticism.

Sesame and Lilies (1865) in title means "nurture of the mind" (sesame) and "beauty of womanhood" (lilies).

"Sesame: Of Kings' Treasuries" pleads for the right evaluation and employment of books. Before the extensive public libraries of today, he called for far more fully accessible libraries.

"Of Queens' Gardens" is Ruskin's advice to women, which can well be taken as the classic Victorian dictum on the subject. It is addressed, of course, to ladies of the privileged classes who are expected to be superlative examples of morality and generous dispensers of alms to the needy. Ruskin advocates education for women in the same subjects studied by men, but he scrupulously excludes theology because of feminine fanaticism in religion and does not insist upon as thorough knowledge of a field as required of a man.

Editions after 1871 generally include the following Dublin lecture of 1868.

"The Mystery of Life and Its Arts" starts with Ruskin's mystification over the public indifference to the notable canvases of Turner. Then he proceeds to the baffling indifference of mankind to all the eternal verities. From unanswerable questions he falls back upon his elevation of the artist who loves nature and studies the beauty of her truth above the artist who loves his own skill and seeks first the pleasure of beauty.

The Crown of Wild Olive (1866) refers in title to the prize awarded a victor in the ancient Olympic games. Ruskin contends that man should work for the spiritual satisfaction of a job well done, not for material reward. Ruskin would wholly supplant the competitive system with fair wages, stimulating working conditions, and craftsmanship to delight in good work. All convenience or cheapness gained by degrading labor should be eliminated. The land should be made beautiful, and cities should be small but attractive with open countryside nearby.

Time and Tide (1867) consists of twenty-five letters written to a Sunderland cork-cutter, Thomas Dixon, an intelligent laborer who had sent letters on his economic concepts to Ruskin. Ruskin's replies promulgate the Laws of Work in a frankly utopian picture of the ideal society. By this time Ruskin has come to the point of pleading for a deferment of all civilization's arts and graces until the poor have been adequately provided for. He calls for a revival of the trade guild concept with men laboring for the joy of work and the satisfaction of service, instead of selfish competition for material gain. Like his master Carlyle, Ruskin tends to advocate an authoritarian society where the right leadership will consist of pastors and overseers instead of greedy tyrants.

Fors Clavigera: Letters to the Workmen and Labourers of Great Britain (1871–84) consists of ninety-six papers best described as the precursor of the modern newspaper column. Current events, personal experiences, and pure digressions crop up continually amid the recurrent theme of redress of human deprivation. The mystifying title derives from an Etruscan mirror case in Geneva engraved with the figure of Atropos (one of the Fates) ready to drive home a nail with a hammer. *Fors* variously symbolized to Ruskin Force, Fortitude, and Fortune. *Clavigera* symbolized Club-bearer, Key-bearer, and Nail-bearer; hence, respectively: the deed of Hercules, the patience of Ulysses, and the law of Lycurgus. In this series Ruskin has little to add to his previous statements, but many of these papers sport a racy idiom, a facility of phrase-making, and an impassioned vigor unmatched in his previous utterances.

Munera Pulveris (1872), meaning "gifts of the dust," borrows a phrase from Horace. The articles comprising this work had originally started as a sequel to *Unto This Last* in *Fraser's Magazine* during 1862–63, but Froude, the editor, was forced to discontinue the series just as Thackeray did. This is one of Ruskin's more difficult writings because of its involved phraseology and especially because of its multitude of erudite allusions to classical literature. Its technical discussion of Ruskin's revision of contemporary economics, when shorn of decoration, is not too abstruse. His important definitions:

Value—the power of anything to sustain and enhance true life;

Cost—the amount of labor required to produce value;

Price—the amount of labor which the possessor will accept in exchange for value.

Praeterita (1885–89), meaning "things passed by," is Ruskin's autobiography, penned during periods of lucidity. Sir Kenneth Clark has asserted that this is Ruskin's only book written purely to give pleasure, and it captures, as do none of his other writings except his correspondence, the easy conversational style of a brilliant talker. As a biography it has many defects. The influence of Carlyle is strangely minimized; there are many omitted periods of his life; and mania prevented the completion of the work. Nonetheless, it possesses a quiet charm, humor, and a naïve egoism that make it perhaps his most attractive volume.

TWO CONSERVATIVE APPROACHES

The Victorian Age had witnessed a religious ferment unequaled in English history since the Commonwealth period, from which it markedly differed in many important respects.

(1) Vociferous agnosticism and atheism were added to the religious debate. Even the strongest rationalists of the 18th century were shadowy deists and mild skeptics rather than militant critics of faith. The Victorian period saw the first genuine emergence in English thought of straightforward attacks on all religion.

(2) Religious agitations did not disturb the masses of Englishmen but were essentially confined to the clergy and the evangelical middle-class. The majority of Englishmen, ranging from devout to indifferent, remained at least nominally in the Established Church. Countrymen were unmoved by the religious upheavals (cf. Kilvert's parishes). The proletariat of the metropolises and industrial communities continued loyally or apathetically, but as the century neared its end, the proletariat increasingly turned its former religious energies into the socialist movement.

The spectacular conversions and sharp alterations of religious viewpoints occurred generally to Victorians subjected in their youth to pronounced evangelical influences. From the evangelical ranks arose diametrically opposite responses. George Eliot became an agnostic, Samuel Butler an atheist. George Eliot's brother Isaac and Mrs. Browning's sisters Arabella and Henrietta became very High Church. From the Clapham Sect of evangelicals most of the Wilberforces turned to Roman Catholicism. The astoundingly varied escapes from evangelicalism carried the three Newman brothers: Charles to total disbelief, Francis to non-Christian theism, and John to Roman Catholicism and eventually a cardinal's hat.

Most dramatic and far-reaching of the Victorian religious impulses was the Oxford Movement (also known as the Tractarian Movement and Puseyism), largely responsible for the potent Anglo-Catholicism which has gained enormously in the Established Church of the 19th and 20th centuries. Just as Oxford in the 1730s had been the nurturer of Wesley and evangelicalism, so in the 1830s the university produced another religious revival. The Wesleyan Movement had reacted fundamentally to religious apathy and the 18th century's failure to provide an emotional faith. The Oxford Movement reacted in a distinctly rightist and ritualistic fashion due to the following events:

(1) The Irish Church Bill of 1833. This bill called for the suppression of ten of the twenty-one episcopal sees of the Established Church of Ireland, which Anglicans considered an integral part of the Established Church of England. To loyal churchmen this bill seemed to be a monstrous threat against the very existence of the Established Church. Under Gladstone in 1869 the Irish Established Church was disestablished, but the Church of England was untouched.

(2) The general rise to political power and hence the pressure upon the Established Church of its opponents. With the English union of church and state, parliament broadly controls the Established Church. In 1829 Roman Catholics were freed from all former legal restrictions, and the Reform Bill of 1832 added to the electorate a sizable middle-class composed largely of evangelicals (Methodists, Baptists, Congregationalists, etc.). The Anglican clergy feared that parliament would henceforth be swayed to hostile actions against the Established Church. The Anglican clergy were thus aroused to seek a more dominant role in the operation of their own church.

(3) The "Higher Criticism," largely of German origin and perhaps reaching its peak in David Strauss's *Das Leben Jesu* (1835), in its cold dissection of Christian scriptures challenged the very basis of orthodox faith. Such criticism claimed gross inconsistencies in the Bible and announced that Christianity was a compound of ancient Near Eastern mythology and mystery cults. The attack upon the evangelical's prop of faith, the supposed infallibility of the Bible, elicited the clerical response of emphasizing the organic (i.e. Catholic) nature of the Christian Church.

(4) Contemporary liberalism and utilitarianism were distinctly thisworldly, minimizing spirituality and opposing religious institutions. In reaction churchmen bristled against liberalism and re-emphasized tradition.

(5) Science of the 19th century proved strongly materialistic and mechanistic. What was not demonstrably concrete, physical reality was assumed to be nonexistent or illusionary. The religiously-inclined therefore tended to respond with the most assertive religious conservatism, vigorously denying the scientific viewpoint.

(6) The era's general recognition of fragmentation (especially keynoted by Arnold's poetry) motivated many thoughtful people to seek refuge in the oldest still-continuing institution of Western society and in its oldest surviving rituals.

The beginning of the Oxford Movement was ascribed by Newman to Keble's sermon "National Apostasy" in 1833. Keble denounced the Irish Church Bill as "direct disavowal of the sovereignty of God." Later in the same year Keble, Newman, and a few others began the publication of *Tracts for the Times*, which insisted that the Established Church was not an institution created by the state but the "local presence and organ" of "the Church Catholic and Apostolic, set up from the beginning." Every English-man reciting the Apostles' Creed was declared to be affirming this faith in the phrase, "I believe in . . . the holy Catholic Church." Although directed primarily toward clergymen, the tracts gained an ever-widening audience because of the supple, graceful prose of Newman. The climax came with *Tract XC* (1841) in which Newman asserted that the Thirty-Nine Articles (a statement of doctrine for the Established Church of England) although "the offspring of an uncatholic age, are, through God's good providence, to say the least, not uncatholic, and may be subscribed by those who aim at being Catholic in heart and doctrine." Protestant ire rose alarmingly, and the tracts were thereupon discontinued at the request of the Bishop of Oxford.

With Newman's conversion to Roman Catholicism in 1845, the leaders of the Oxford Movement were Keble, R. Hurrell Froude (brother of the historian-biographer J. A. Froude), and Edward B. Pusey. Gradually the spirit and the outward form of Anglo-Catholicism began to exert them-selves through an ever-increasing number of Anglo-Catholic bishops and they began to permeate cathedral closes and vicarages (as portrayed by Trollope in *Barchester Towers*). But the driving force of Anglo-Catholi-cism lay rather in the clergy than in the laity, which was still essentially Protestant. Disraeli in 1875 pushed through parliament a bill to "put down ritualism," but, undeterred, the churchmen continued to gravitate in a clearly Catholic direction. Anglican clerics hailed the movement as greatly strengthening the religiosity of the Established Church, but unquestionably Anglo-Catholicism caused increasing numbers of Protestant laymen to drop their support of the church or to become lukewarm.

Thomas Carlyle shared with Newman and the Oxford Movement dis-illusionment in the materialism of the 19th century. He too believed that the universe was spiritual in nature and that the individual human being was of paramount importance. However, he turned to German transcendentalist philosophy rather than Roman Catholicism, and, particularly in his later years, he came to advocate a society built on strictly autocratic principles.

John Henry (Cardinal) **Newman** (1801–1890). John Henry Newman was the eldest of six children (three boys and three girls) born to a London banker. His early evangelicalism was tempered by a love of medievalism which had been induced by the novels of Scott. His undergraduate years (1816–20) at Oxford were largely influenced by the liberal theology then dominant. As a young Anglican cleric he was swayed to conservative religion by Keble and R. H. Froude; and as vicar of St. Mary's, the university church of Oxford, from 1828 he exerted increasing influence for clerical traditionalism. His Mediterranean cruise with R. H. Froude in 1832–33 drew him closer to Catholicism, though he continued to denounce Roman Catholicism. While on ship between Palermo and Marseille he wrote the famous hymn, "Lead, Kindly Light," consecrating himself to a religious task as yet imperfectly perceived. Some of the best devotional lyrics in *Lyra Apostolica* (1836) are Newman's. In the pulpit and through his writing of about a third of the *Tracts for the Times* (1833–41) he developed as the major spokesman for Anglo-Catholicism.

Extensive study of patristic writings convinced him that the Roman Catholic Church was the only true ecclesiastical line from Christ, and after the furor aroused by *Tract XC* he retired in 1842 to Littlemore. In the next year he resigned his vicarage at St. Mary's, and in 1845, just two days after the Frenchman Ernest Renan renounced the Roman Catholic priesthood in favor of atheism, Newman was admitted to the Roman Catholic Church. At the *Collegio di Propaganda* in Rome during 1846–47 he was ordained a Roman Catholic priest and granted the degree of Doctor of Divinity. Back in England he joined the monastic order of Oratorians and founded the Birmingham Oratory in 1848. His subsequent role as the most influential Roman Catholic voice in Victorian England will be discussed in conjunction with his writings. With old sores healed, his Oxford college, Trinity, made him an Honorary Fellow in 1877. His disapproval of the timing of the proclamation of papal infallibility in 1870 discredited him in the eyes of Pius IX, but the new Pope, Leo XIII, elevated him to the cardinalate in 1879. At his request his tombstone at Rednal bears a Latin inscription meaning "From shadows and semblances into the truth."

Like the later Carlyle, Newman was a vociferous opponent of "liberalism"; for instance, he opposed any increase in the suffrage, though he hoped that power would awake voters to responsibilities. In theology he saw the problems of faith with a clarity that delighted the agnostic Huxley —"apart from an interior and unreasoned conviction, there is no cogent proof of the existence of God." But he utterly rejected materialism, convinced that the visible world is only a shadow. Secularism he countered with dogmatic Christianity, its insistent otherworldliness, its incompatibility with nature and history, and its uncompromising principles of spirituality and morality. His conclusion followed that "the difficulties of creed and Scripture Canon are unsurmountable unless overridden by the authority of an infallible Church." His extended works sometimes offer arid patches, but in selection and especially in short pieces he proves one of the consummate masters of English prose due to his pure diction, cadenced rise and fall, elegant simplicity, smooth fluency, and fastidious restraint.

ANGLO-CATHOLICISM (1833–1845). *Lectures on the Prophetical Office of the Church* (1837), republished in 1877 and subsequently as part of *Via*

Media ("middle way"), consisted of St. Mary's lectures in 1835–36. They constitute the classical statement of Anglo-Catholicism down to the present: Anglo-Catholicism stands in the middle as the true Church, unblemished by "corruptions" of Romanism and "errors" of Protestantism.

Oxford University Sermons (1843) was the last in a series of a dozen volumes of Newman's Anglican sermons, which rank among the most eloquent in English homiletics. Perhaps most important in this volume is "The Theory of Developments in Religious Doctrine" (1843) in which Newman designates growth as the truest test of life. Revelation in the Bible provides the chief outlines for Christian dogma which then gradually builds toward an ever greater whole.

ROMAN CATHOLICISM (1845–1890). *Essay on the Development of a Christian Doctrine* (1845) was begun before his submission to Rome and helped him to determine his course. Newman now proclaimed what he had previously denied with vigor, that Roman Catholicism of today is the true lineal continuation of primitive Christianity. The operation of the divine spirit within the Church conserves the original sacred truth and develops new truth through a continuous organic growth. Certainly the most significant work for Newman's own development, it has been termed by many Roman Catholics his greatest writing.

The Present Position of Catholics in England (1851) was considered by Newman "the best written" of all his works. It consisted of lectures delivered at Birmingham in 1851 to counterbalance the strident "No-Popery" agitation following the papal bull of 1850 which re-established the Roman Catholic hierarchy in England for the first time since the Reformation. Newman spelled out all Protestant objections to Roman Catholicism and replied with every brilliant retort of withering satire, imaginative illustration, and dramatic sally at his command. No other Newman work displays such a full spectrum of literary light and power. It is perhaps the only piece of the past two hundred years that can seriously be matched with Swift.

The Idea of a University (1852), his most popular work, consists of nine discourses delivered in Dublin, to which Newman came in 1851 to found a Catholic university. Although Pope Pius IX had approved the project, it failed because of the disagreements of Irish bishops and because state recognition was refused by Protestant England. The book ironically was released almost simultaneously with the Royal Commission report recommending liberalization and secularization of Oxford and Cambridge. The time-honored "education by the parsons" was to be superseded in the noted English institutions by instruction in modern sciences and humanities by lay specialists.

Newman's superbly persuasive plan seeks to recapture essentially the Oxford concept of his youth—a nonutilitarian cultivation of "intellectual excellence" under ecclesiastical supervision. He specifically excludes any research or experimental functions from his university, which is wholly a teaching institution. Although he contemplates no seminarian indoctrination, theology would be the queen of studies, and the task of his university would be the creation of true gentlemen, amply developed in mind and manners. Newman's is the incomparable and incomparably felicitous statement of the conservative ideal of a "liberal education." Many educational theorists of the 20th century are thinly echoing his objection to the substitution of compartmentalized training and skills for a broad and deep disciplining of the mind.

Sermons Preached on Various Occasions (1857) contains the best Roman Catholic sermons in English. Most famous is the prose lyric "The Second Spring" preached in 1852 at the Synod of Oscott, the first assembly of the Roman Catholic hierarchy in England since the early 16th century. A major theme of the work is the law of permanence beneath the transience of earthly things. Seemingly swept out of England irretrievably, the Roman Catholic Church had returned in full force to the land of St. Guthlac and St. Boniface. The humility and wholly conciliatory tone of this poetic sermon of triumph allayed many Protestant fears that Roman Catholicism would aggressively combat Anglicanism or the English state.

Apologia pro vita sua ("Explanation of his life") (1864) arose from the slurring remarks in *Macmillan's Magazine* (1863) by Charles Kingsley: "Truth for its own sake had never been a virtue with the Roman clergy. Father Newman informs us that it need not be, and on the whole ought not to be." The revised edition of 1865, now the standard text, details the author's journey of religious search from childhood evangelicalism to Roman Catholic conversion in 1845. The autobiography transcends mere refutation of Kingsley (whose name is unmentioned) to relate with simple sincerity Newman's spiritual quest. There is little "human interest" in the sense of Boswell's journals, and meager portrayal of the era's scenes and personalities as in the Crevy papers. The work concentrates on Newman's wrestling with theology and his own soul. Critics have suggested that Newman's hindsight gave to his life a more logical development than it actually displayed, and that he minimizes the psychological factors in his background which may largely have determined his course. Readers, however, generally agree with the Anglican bishop E. A. Knox who in 1933 ranked this work "for all time among the greatest of the world's autobiographies" because of its flawless prose, its impressive dignity, and its utter absence of pose (somewhat rare in autobiography, especially by clerics). In the final chapter, for which all that precedes is a prelude, he details the appalling futility of the "human situation." Only from outside nature can deliverance come; the "direct, immediate, active, and prompt means" for this is Roman Catholicism, which offers "renovating grace," infallibility in doctrine and morals, ministry to rebellious man who must learn the peace of submission, and ultimate and sole rescue of "human nature from its misery." As Mill's *Autobiography* is the greatest English self-searching of a mind, so the *Apologia* is the greatest autobiography of a soul.

The Dream of Gerontius (1865) was first published in the Jesuit periodical, the *Month*. In the first part of Newman's only long poem, Gerontius ("old man") dies contrite after receiving the last rites of the church. In the second part his guardian angel conducts the soul of Gerontius above the blasphemy of hell to a vision of divine radiance, ending in committal to purgatory until the cleansed soul may forever sojourn in heaven. Though deficient in visual imagery the poem is impressive in its psychological depiction of a dying man and in its appeal through blank verse and stanzaic lyrics to the ear and to the imagination. The 20th century is most familiar with the piece through the oratorio (1900) by Sir Edward Elgar.

An Essay in Aid of a Grammar of Assent (1870) analyzes the psychology of religious belief in an era of mounting skepticism and apathy toward faith. The first part treats of apprehension and belief, emphasizing "real assent," i.e. "the absolute acceptance of a proposition without any condition"; such belief embraces the whole man and not merely the faculty of abstraction which produces the "notional assent" of science. The second part shapes toward "the illative sense," which like Coleridge's *Vernunft* means total comprehension. Transcending and including logic, the illative sense is the divine implantation in man by which the mind reveals certitude in the riot of converging possibilities. Newman avoids the technical language of the philosophers to examine the way that the true believer actually does believe. The fluent, conversational prose and the wealth of concrete illustrations make an abstruse subject clear and cogent.

Thomas Carlyle (1795–1881). Second of the ten children of a puritanical stonemason, Thomas Carlyle was born at Ecclefechan, Scotland. Determined to be a Kirk of Scotland clergyman, Carlyle at the age of fourteen walked a hundred miles to Edinburgh University. There the powerful influence of Hume and French skeptics shook his religious convictions, and he left in 1814, without a degree, to teach school at Annan Academy. While teaching at Kircaldy (1816–18), he fell in love with Margaret Gordon, but his peasant origin was unacceptable to the girl's guardians. In 1818 he first complained of "dyspepsia," which dogged him throughout all later life; 20th-century diagnosticians have analyzed history's most famous stomach disorder as neurosis of the stomach, a psychosomatic condition arising from emotional stress and disappointment. After a brief study of law, he turned to writing and to translation from the German. He was encouraged by the brilliant Jane Welsh whom he married in 1826 and whose farm at Craigenputtock he moved to when unsuccessful in obtaining university posts.

On the basis of *Sartor Resartus,* John Stuart Mill persuaded the Carlyles in 1834 to move to 5 Great Cheyne Row, Chelsea, where they lived for the rest of their lives. The friendship with Mill ended by mid-century when Carlyle had become a vociferous opponent of Mill's liberal democracy. The former friends became bitter enemies because of the Jamaican riots of 1865 in which Governor Eyre imposed martial law and executed a civilian. Mill headed the Jamaica Committee to prosecute Eyre, and lined up with Mill were the liberals Darwin, Huxley, Lyell, Spencer, and Stephen. Carlyle chaired the Eyre Defense Committee, and backing him were the conservatives Dickens, Tennyson, Kingsley, and Froude. Carlyle saved Eyre but lost on principle, as the Lord Chief Justice affirmed the final authority of civil justice throughout the Empire. In 1866 Carlyle was triumphantly inaugurated as Rector of the University of Edinburgh. His advanced age saw him showered with many honors, but he refused a noble title and burial in Westminster Abbey.

Carlyle was a crabbed, moody individualist, and his style peremptorily brushes aside rational argument, trim exposition, or logical analyses in favor of intuitive force. He uses imperatives, direct address, bizarre metaphors and illustrations, arresting word-coinages (especially compound nouns in literal translation from the German), exclamations, and "shock" tactics of startling shifts of thought or phrasing. Throughout his writings (for he withheld utterance until overcoming his youthful skepticism) he stresses the spiritual nature of the universe and the necessity of not tinkering with the physical machinery of society but rather of achieving a genuine spiritual rebirth of every human being. With dramatic suddenness, however, he transforms himself in 1845 from the earlier Romantic to the later reactionary.

German transcendentalism dominated the youthful Carlyle as he identified Universal Spirit with the ultimate reality. The "Sage of Craigenputtock" professed horror at war and useless aristocrats, and advocated social improvement for the people's welfare. He was strongly touched by medievalism, and he appeared to be an embryonic socialist.

"The State of German Literature" (*Edinburgh Review*, 1827) first revealed Carlyle as the exhorting prophet. Here, after discussing Fichte and Kant, he launches into an attack upon Lockean reason. Eloquently he admonishes his readers to abandon logic and to commune with the immanent deity, yielding to impulses of the heart.

"The Signs of the Times" (*Edinburgh Review*, 1829) was Carlyle's first declaration of his social gospel. Attacking the statistics-worship of Macaulay, he asserts that Britain's increased prosperity had benefited only a fraction of the population and that the masses had suffered much more under industrialization and urbanization than under the previous rural economy. Belaboring orthodox laissez-faire, he champions government regulation to insure truer equality and genuine social justice.

Characteristics (1831) actually states or adumbrates most of Carlyle, but since it is written without appreciable Carlylisms, it is often ignored. Rejecting reason, Carlyle appeals to spiritualized emotions and the moral will. Through "communion of souls" mankind may become a "new collective individual" guided by the ideal of "united, victorious labour." More than any other figure of the 19th century, Carlyle compelled his age to realize that it lived amid crises, that it suffered from deep-rooted ailments, and that it had to make decisions of fearful magnitude.

Sartor Resartus ("The tailor retailored") (*Fraser's Magazine,* 1833–34) purports to be the biography of Herr Diogenes Teufelsdröckh ("god-born devil's dung"), Professor of Things in General at the University of Weissnichtwo ("know-not-where"), and author of a book on the philosophy of clothes. It all sounds like Swift (whose *Tale of a Tub* supplied the tailor metaphor) and Sterne (who would have envied the discovery of the professor's biography in six paper bags crammed with everything from laundry bills to a metaphysical speculation on the steam engine) at work expounding the transcendentalism of the German philosophers and the utopian dream of the French Saint-Simonians. The 19th-century followers of the Comte de Saint-Simon sought an ideal society where the resources of the world would be pooled for the greatest good of all, a reorganization of industry modeled upon the military would rescue mankind from the chaos of laissez-faire, and human energy would fight against natural forces instead of fellow men. Carlyle's work, an extraordinary piece of writing for which the language in despair has coined the word *Carlylean,* is simultaneously an intellectual and spiritual autobiography, and a diatribe against current conditions in England.

Book I assails scientific contentions and their basis in empirical philosophy. Matter, Carlyle asserts (paraphrasing Fichte), is not man's master but his servant. It is a creation of man's spirit to provide the challenge for the development of morality. Man is pure spirit, subject solely to the laws built into his conscience by God.

Book II details Carlyle's own spiritual journey from "The Everlasting No" through "The Centre of Indifference" to "The Everlasting Yea." The episode actually happened to him in Leith Walk, Edinburgh. Initially he is a slave to an impersonal, meaningless materialism. He wakes to realize that the physical body is simply the clothing of the divine within man and the entire material universe simply the clothing of cosmic divinity.

Book III further observes that institutions of society are but the clothing of the "Social Idea." Such institutions (church, state, economic system) have been revered in their outward garments, while men forget the ideal truth behind them. Carlyle prophesies the cremation of these outworn, superficial institutions, with a new Golden Age rising like a phoenix from the ashes.

Brotherhood and the duty to work usefully will grip mankind's true leaders and assure a theocracy, a reborn humanity ruled by the divine spirit within.

The French Revolution (1837) was begun in 1834, largely at the instigation of Mill. Carlyle lent Mill the manuscript of the first book, which happened by mistake to be burned, so that Carlyle was forced to rewrite it.

Interpreting the Revolution as God's vengeance upon a tyrannical, parasitic aristocracy, Carlyle appealed to the liberals and for the first time swayed general English sentiment to some sympathy with the French Revolution. Lord Acton praised Carlyle as the first to release the English mind from "the thraldom of Burke," but Conservatives were soothed by the condemnation of the Revolution for failing to achieve lasting constructive purposes. Carlyle covered dramatic French events from the death of Louis XV in 1774 until Napoleon's triumph in 1795, dealing only sparsely with legal, financial, social, cultural, and international affairs. Scholarly historians are justifiably critical, but the interpretations of personalities seem essentially valid and the tension-charged scenes still make this one of the most-read histories in English.

Chartism (1839) arose from Carlyle's fear that parliamentary rejection of the proposed Charter would trigger a proletarian revolution in England. He advised the propertied classes to accept their responsibility to the entire populace or face the same downfall as the French aristocrats. His concrete proposals are for public education and subsidized emigration in one of his most spirited and effective pieces. The title of the first chapter, "The Condition-of-England Question," provided a catchphrase for the rest of the century.

On Heroes and Hero-Worship (lectures in *1840*, 1841) infuses a deep-seated conviction, which Shakespeare shared in his history plays, that great men make history (rather than historical events produce great men), with Fichte's ascription of the "divine idea" embodied in the leading spirits of an age. Calvinism and Puritanism cause Carlyle to see the hand of God inevitably willing the leadership by the righteous, divinely inspired hero. Carlyle discusses the hero as: divinity (Odin), prophet (Mahomet), poet (Dante and Shakespeare), priest (Luther and Knox), man of letters (Johnson, Rousseau, Burns), king (Cromwell and Napoleon). Throughout the work is heard the urgent cry for powerful leadership in a disorganized age (Carlyle thought he had such a leader in Sir Robert Peel until the statesman's death in 1850).

Past and Present (1843) attacks the social, economic, and political injustices of the Victorian age and proclaims the need for a hero to guide England from its present predicament. Carlyle finds an example of his true leader in Abbot Samson of St. Edmundsbury in the late 12th and early 13th centuries. Derived from the contemporary medieval account by Jocelin of Brakelond (published by the Camden Society), Carlyle's portrait shows a paternalistic clerical administrator reforming a run-down monastery, imparting to it justice and efficiency. The conclusion points the moral: a New Aristocracy must supersede the present politicians and the indolent rich, and it must be obeyed as it attempts to rescue a now-foundering society. The vivid re-creation of medieval monasticism profoundly influenced Ruskin, Morris, and Rossetti, and caused some Roman Catholics to predict Carlyle's conversion.

From 1845 on Carlyle bitterly derides liberal democracy of the Mill variety and comes to embrace his previous enemies—economic and hereditary aristocrats. He contends that the social ideal can be achieved only through the God-fearing dictator, and that war is the ultimate means of revealing the hero. Now the scientists more than the Benthamites are the target of his fury.

Oliver Cromwell's Letters and Speeches (1845) was suggested by Mill, who was horrified at the outcome. Carlyle had found his hero. Justifying the means by the ends, Carlyle completely excused Cromwell for the dictatorial dissolution of the Long Parliament and the savage massacre of the Irish. The almost universal contemporary opinion of Cromwell was expressed by John Forster: "he lived a hypocrite and died a traitor." Carlyle's brilliant piece of historical research is chiefly responsible for refurbishing the memory of the Lord Protector.

"The Nigger Question" (*Fraser's Magazine*, 1849) forced an open break with Mill. Contemplating the idle Jamaican Negro, Carlyle advocated a resumption of slavery. The "wiser" Englishman, holding Jamaica as a fief from God, should ignore economic liberalism and compel the Negro to be productive under the divine mandate of labor. In the very next issue of *Fraser's* in 1850 Mill indignantly replied with a defense of democracy and racial equality.

Latter-Day Pamphlets (1850) collects eight articles by Carlyle against liberalism, which he denounces in phrases like "philanthropic twaddle" and "malodorous phosphorescence of *post-mortem* sentimentalism." Attacking reforms and humanitarianism, he calls for a national dictator who will override parliament and conscript the unemployed and assign worthwhile work to all. Carlyle here and later ignores facts (he insists that convicts enjoy better conditions in prison than a duke does in his mansion) in his determination to argue his case for the hero's rule. It must be admitted, however, that he saw better than any of his contemporaries the problems of the power state, government regulation, and the rising proletariat. Throwing himself against the stream of Western democracy, Carlyle nonetheless possessed a prophet's vision of the inner weaknesses of his period.

The Life of John Sterling (1851) is Carlyle's most attractive work. Unintentionally it reveals a mellow Carlyle who loved good friends and good talk. Most memorable of the volume's vignettes is a portrait of the aged

Coleridge. Sterling was a minor disciple of Coleridge, but his life to Carlyle was a parable of the course of a 19th-century Englishman from youthful incendiary radicalism to the conservative haven delineated by the later Coleridge.

History of Frederick II of Prussia (1851–65, 1858–65) occupied thirteen years of Carlyle's life, and seemed to him his masterwork. Though Froude ranked this work with that of Thucydides, posterity has been distressed at Carlyle's blind hero worship. The duplicity and cruelty of Frederick the Great are wholly excused in the exaltation of the divinely inspired hero. The writer who expertly handled great masses in the French Revolution is virtually oblivious to all but his absolute military despot. Portraits, however, are brilliant (though, as with that of Voltaire, often grossly unfair) and the battle scenes are among the most stirring in English literature.

Shooting Niagara: and After? (1867) is a furious diatribe against democracy evoked by Disraeli's 1867 Reform Bill extending the franchise. Disraeli is called "a superlative Hebrew Conjuror," but his political opponent, Gladstone, no better, is representative of "the multitudinous cants of the age." "The whole of our hope depends" upon the hereditary aristocracy not upon mere democratic "Count of Heads."

Reminiscences (1867, 1881) is slightly embarrassing in its fulsome tribute to Jane Welsh Carlyle. With fantastic memory Carlyle records scenes and phrases forty years in the past, all impressively portraying a devoted wife. He catches much of her wit and sprightliness, but ignores the tartness of a frustrated woman tied to the intractable Carlyle. Some critics now exalt Jane as the greater of the two Carlyles, largely on the basis of her shrewd and charming letters, collected for the most part in 1883, 1891, and 1903.

LEADERS IN SCIENTIFIC THOUGHT

The year 1887 dramatically marks the culmination of one epoch of science and the inauguration of another.

The German physicist Hertz in 1887 produced radio short waves confirming the belief of the Britisher, Sir James Clerk Maxwell (1831–79), that light was an electromagnetic phenomenon. The structure of classical science, developing since the early 17th century, appeared absolutely complete. Victorian science seemed fully buttressed in its mechanistic, materialistic interpretation of the universe. The one and only reality of the world consisted of minute hard particles (the unbreakable atoms) operating under exact mathematical forces. With calm certitude John Tyndall (1820–93) could in his presidential address of 1874 assure the British Association for the Advancement of Science that science had within its grasp the power to explain absolutely everything in the "ultimately purely natural and inevitable march of evolution from the atoms of the primaeval nebula to the proceedings of the British Association for the Advancement of Science."

Such a sense of unalterable fact gave to 19th-century scientists a majestic certainty and placid acceptance that made conventionally pious or idealistic contemporaries look like foolish dreamers. The realism of the scientists, strengthened by their spectacular discoveries and demonstrable contributions to material progress, caused many Victorians to feel toward scientists as awed and acquiescent as earlier eras had toward clerics.

Though Victorian science produced no towering genius like Sir Isaac Newton, it contributed some of the most important scientists of history. Michael Faraday (1791–1869) in *Experimental Researches in Electricity* (1839–55) established today's vast technology of transforming electrical into mechanical energy and vice versa. Sir William Thomson, Lord Kelvin (1824–1907), in an 1851 paper to the Royal Society of Edinburgh firmly established the principle of dissipation of energy and the absolute scale of temperature. Probably no other single man has done so much to alleviate human suffering as Joseph Lister, Lord Lister (1827–1912), whose article "On the Antiseptic Principle in the Practice of Surgery" in *The Lancet* (1867) inaugurated modern medicine.

But the most disturbing of scientific explorations lay in the biological sciences where many a Victorian ship of faith foundered upon the rock of evolution.

Charles Robert Darwin (1809–1882). Born in the same year as Tennyson, Charles Darwin came from an intellectual family, highlighted by his grandfather Erasmus Darwin, the physician. After education in his native Shrewsbury, he went to Edinburgh and Cambridge. Upon graduation he accepted a post as naturalist aboard H.M.S. *Beagle,* embarking in 1831 upon a five-year round-the-world scientific expedition. After his return in 1836 he published the results of his biological observations in *Journal of Researches into the Geology and Natural History of the Various Countries Visited by H.M.S. Beagle* (1839). These findings, plus the Malthusian theory that population increases in a geometric ratio while food supply increases arithmetically, caused Darwin to arrive at the doctrine of natural selection. Another English naturalist, Alfred Russel Wallace (1823–1913), independently reached the same conclusion; Darwin fully acknowledged the contributions of Wallace. Honoring science above his personal reputation, Wallace refused to contest the fame of Darwin.

On the Origin of Species by Means of Natural Selection, or the Preservation of Favoured Races in the Struggle for Life (1859) sold out the first edition on the day of publication and has ever since remained the most important and most influential work on natural philosophy in English. The sober dignity and systematic massing of facts and evidence give it more authority than any colorful and spectacular harangue. Darwin begins with the breeding of horses and other domestic animals, by which man consciously seeks to develop in lower creatures characteristics he desires. Darwin then sees processes of nature following the same pattern. "Natural selection," he asserts, "is daily and hourly scrutinizing, throughout the world, the slightest variations; rejecting those that are bad, preserving and adding up all that are good."

With the limited resources of our planet, superabundant life proliferates into an unceasing struggle for existence, an unrelenting contest between the hunter and the hunted, the eater and the eaten. The slightest peculiarity that will aid an organism in this battle will assure survival of the individual, who thus can reproduce and pass the superior faculties on to descendants and his species. The terrifying pressure of fertility and selection compels species to specialize and alter, the strong remaining alive and the weak perishing. Completely new species of plants and animals thus emerge from the fray. The concept of progress in this ceaseless warfare impresses Darwin even more than the struggle itself, as he assures us "that no fear is felt, that death is generally prompt, and that the vigorous, the healthy, and the happy survive and multiply." Sex is a means partly of dividing labors, largely a means of improving and stablizing desirable traits by cross-fertilization. Genetically, however, Darwin left unanswered the momentous question of what causes the minute variations within a litter of animals or a podful of seeds.

With this work Darwin did not create the concept of evolution, which was already old, but his identification with the concept arises from:

(1) His original theory of natural selection, which accounts for the enormous variety of living things and the means by which new species emerge.

(2) His huge accumulation of scientific facts and his astute marshaling of evidence to substantiate the theory of evolution.

In the eyes of many this volume rendered the concept of evolution no longer a speculative theory but an established scientific truth.

The Descent of Man, and Selection in Relation to Sex (1871) took the logical step that Darwin had cautiously avoided in *Origin of Species* and proclaimed that man was also the product of natural selection, probably a scion of the anthropoid apes. The consciousness and intelligence of man have developed as adaptations to environment and as superior weapons in the struggle for survival. Two-thirds of the book analyzes sexual selection to account for race and other human characteristics.

Recollections of the Development of My Mind and Character (1887) is usually titled *Autobiography*. Written between 1876 and 1881, it is intended solely for his children, displaying the frankness and intimacy of family correspondence. Conceived in the scientific spirit, it attempts to trace the evolution of the man himself. Darwin is quite amazed to contemplate Darwin. Once he had loved music. Once he had enjoyed Wordsworth and Milton. In essentially Lamarckian fashion he traces the external influences that molded him into the scientist. The bitterest anti-Darwinite is charmed by the honesty, modesty, and thorough wholesomeness of the narrative and the man. Significantly, Darwin traces his religious attitudes from early evangelicalism to undogmatic agnosticism. The man long considered chance versus design, free will versus determinism, spirit versus matter; the scientist became too preoccupied to worry about these problems, and, all faith deserting him, he "felt no distress."

Thomas Henry Huxley (1825–1895). Thomas Henry Huxley was the youngest of the seven children of George Huxley, who as schoolmaster at Ealing numbered Newman among his pupils. From childhood Thomas was an omnivorous reader; an early reading of *Sartor Resartus,* he later declared, "led me to know that a deep sense of religion was compatible with the entire absence of theology." A brilliant medical student, at the age of nineteen he discovered a membrane at the root of human hair which is still termed "Huxley's layer." From 1846 to 1850 he served as assistant surgeon aboard H.M.S. *Rattlesnake,* his researches upon Pacific jellyfish establishing him as one of the top zoologists of the century. His appointment in physiology and comparative anatomy at London University in 1857 started a lifetime career as a distinguished scientific educator, researcher, and mainstay of many scientific organizations. *The Origin of the Species* (1859) struck him "like a flash of light to a man who had lost himself on a dark road."

Darwin was not combative, but Huxley, as "Darwin's bulldog," preached the gospel of evolution throughout the English-speaking world. Huxley coined the word *agnostic* to explain his position toward faith and was grateful for his name, since indeed he was "doubting Thomas." He maintained his views even in the face of the death of his eldest child Noel in 1860; the famous letter in reply to Kingsley's conventional consolations constitutes a noble agnostic credo. Huxley proved a withering controversialist against upholders of orthodox faith, notably Gladstone. Respecting, however, the right of others to their opinions, he vigorously opposed any pressure upon the Established Church to violate its principles by burying the agnostic George Eliot in Westminster Abbey.

Huxley shared with that equally brilliant Victorian, Newman, a fundamentally skeptical mind, a passionate love of truth regardless of consequences, and a superlatively honest fluency. The goals of these bitterly opposite spirits were identical: human happiness, dignity, and spiritual integrity. Militant for science and agnosticism, Huxley at heart was a Victorian puritan, as rigorously ethical and solidly English as any of his indignant opponents. For the English-speaking peoples Huxley created the image of the scientist as the successor to the priest in moral rectitude, unflinching honesty, and consecration to the cause of humanity. Although locked in dispute with Arnold, Huxley was not the antithesis of humanism, but the blending of modern science with the long humanistic tradition. If Newman is the artist of English prose, Huxley is its craftsman. Devoid of literary pretenses, Huxley nevertheless proved a model of exposition in prose of precision, clarity, and simplicity united with striking illustrations and imaginative power.

"The Method of Scientific Investigation" (*1863*) demonstrates Huxley's notable facility in explaining scientific concepts in layman's language. With appropriately commonplace examples he explains the inductive and deductive methods and the bases for scientific hypotheses.

"On the Advisableness of Improving Natural Knowledge" (*1866*) briefly surveys the development of science since the Renaissance and states the case for science: (1) the vast store of factual and useful knowledge gained, (2) the creation of the scientific spirit, fearlessly and honestly seeking the truth.

"On a Piece of Chalk" (*1868*) from a homey reference to the ubiquitous English chalk, gradually moves to enormous vistas of geological strata and their fossil evidence. It is the acknowledged masterpiece in English of inductive movement from the familiar and recent to the strange and remote.

"A Liberal Education and Where to Find It" (*1868*) demands a well-rounded education which must include a strong tincture of science. Instead of the fashionable training in the classics, instruction should emphasize the useful. Included is a classic definition of "liberal education," which makes man live "in harmony with nature." Huxley's definition and objectives remarkably parallel those of Arnold, but where Arnold emphasizes self-knowledge and the inner life, Huxley stresses knowledge of the world outside the individual and action in that world.

"On the Physical Basis of Life" (*1869*) gives nearly all Huxley's ideas. The 19th-century scientist belabors religion in demonstrating the basis of all living things in remarkably similar protoplasm, differing from inorganic matter only in molecular structure. Mind itself is but "the result of molecular forces." Then the 18th-century Humean skeptic in Huxley leaves the door open to ethical responsibility by questioning matter as an unknown and apparent natural law as simply a probability.

"Scientific Education" (*1869*) suggests that since most of Huxley's contemporaries are devoted to "getting on," science should be their means. A scientific education surpasses all others because it inculcates the concept of causality and provides abundant useful facts. Training should proceed from the most concrete science (physical geography) toward the most abstract (physics), always employing the inductive method.

"Administrative Nihilism" (*1871*) was aimed at the laissez-faire advocates and especially at J. S. Mill. Government regulation is necessary, for a neighbor who neglects his sanitation is as dangerous as a neighbor brandishing a revolver. Huxley, examining the role of government, even favors an established church, provided it eliminates theology and concentrates upon "an ideal of true, just, and pure living."

"On the Hypothesis that Animals Are Automata, and Its History" (*1874*) was read to the B.A.A.S. immediately following President Tyndall's address and reaffirmed its mechanism and materialism. Psychic events arise from purely natural causes, and consciousness itself is a mere echo of molecular movement.

"Address on University Education" (*1876*) was delivered at the opening of The Johns Hopkins University, Baltimore, Maryland. Huxley's idea of a university favors the tendencies now dominant in American higher education. Huxley conceives of the university as balancing instruction and research, producing graduates who can ably direct the world's business and constantly expand the realm of verifiable knowledge.

"Lectures on Evolution" (*1876*), delivered in New York City, consists of three speeches constituting a unified masterpiece of expository argument typical of Huxley's warfare on behalf of Darwin's theory. Huxley considers three hypotheses of the earth's history: present conditions existing eternally, the creation according to Genesis, and the evolutionary concept. With illustrations from American geological formations (Niagara Falls and the Connecticut sandstone) he delivers a devastating attack upon the Pentateuch and erects the opposing edifice of evolution. Loyalty to truth, he pleads, must supersede loyalty to creed.

"Science and Culture" (*1880*) ruptured a friendship as Huxley apparently tilted head-on with Arnold's humanism. Speaking at the opening of the Science College in Birmingham, Huxley boldly asserted that scientific study of society was the best preparation for citizenship and scientific study of nature the best preparation for life. Education in science was as "liberalizing" as training in the dead classics, and far more useful.

"The Principal Subjects of Education" (*1882*) advocates the educational program now general in the English-speaking world. The place of science is secure, as it meshes with nonscientific subjects in aesthetic appeal: the comprehension of "unity in variety." Huxley accords an honored place to the "liberal arts," insisting that English literature and translations into English can confer full cultural values, obviating the traditional indoctrination in the classics.

The Evolution of Theology: An Anthropological Study (1886) is probably Huxley's most solid contribution to a verbal battle over theology with Prime Minister Gladstone that raged for more than half a decade. Dead controversies, especially those involving religion, are usually tedious reading; but Huxley, like H. L. Mencken, still delights with witty sallies, sarcastic denunciations, and sparkling illustrations. In this sober volume Huxley explains the Old Testament as the gradual evolution of Judaism, always in response to purely natural stimuli, from primitive animism to an advanced ethic. Religion, Huxley asserts, is debased by dogma and ritual but is elevated as the scientific spirit purges it of theology in favor of pure ethics.

"The Struggle for Existence in Human Society" (*Nineteenth Century,* 1888) foreshadows the Romanes Lecture. Grieved by the misery of the underprivileged, Huxley refuses to accept laissez-faire and its unregulated battle for human survival in the machine age. In the evolutionary pattern mankind has developed a social consciousness, and this higher nature must succor his brethren.

"Autobiography" (*1890*) was contributed to a collection of biographical sketches edited by C. Engel. It is as pleasantly disarming as any thumbnail sketch ever written, modestly recounting a distinguished career. Huxley sees his life purpose as a dedication to the furtherance of science, "the New Reformation."

Ethics and Evolution (1893), the Romanes Lecture, contrasts the cosmic process with the ethical process. The cosmic process is ceaseless change and, for conscious beings, an arena of suffering and death. The ethical process ("the organized and personified sympathy we call conscience") counters with mutual cooperation and brotherly love to minimize the pain of existence. Huxley expresses high regard for Buddhist mysticism but rests his hopes upon science. With the forward thrust of experimental science man can improve his physical environment, his social community, and his own nature; within a hostile, irrational universe he can create a benign and rational world.

OTHER PROSE WRITERS OF THE EARLY VICTORIAN PERIOD

PHILOSOPHERS AND HISTORIANS

Herbert Spencer (1820–1903). Herbert Spencer was largely educated in his native Derby by his schoolmaster father. He was articled to a civil engineer in 1837 but abandoned engineering in favor of writing in 1845. Spencer was interested in George Eliot but after coldly drawing up opposing lists of the advantages and disadvantages of marriage, he decided to remain a bachelor. As part of his eccentricity he carried ear plugs constantly, and in company placed them in his ears whenever the conversation became trivial and he preferred to meditate with himself.

Spencer was the Victorian philosopher of evolutionary progress. Though scorned by the universities, his vast and tedious tomes achieved the best popular sale ever among English philosophers. An evolutionist before Darwin, he is credited with coining the phrase "survival of the fittest." He optimistically averred, as the biological scientists would not, that evolution is synonymous with progress; and he is chiefly responsible for indoctrinating many popular minds down to the present with this conviction. "Progress," he wrote, "is not an accident but a necessity. What we call evil and immorality must disappear. It is certain that man must become perfect."

Ambitiously attempting a task as vast as that of St. Thomas Aquinas in the *Summa Theologica,* Spencer in what he called Synthetic Philosophy sought to summarize all knowledge into one great focal theme; but, unlike the Doctor Angelicus, Spencer established not God but evolution as the all-embracing principle. Spencer placated the contemporary religious mind by positing God as the Unknowable and then proceeding to explain absolutely everything by evolution. Quite literally he took everything, for, by his own statement, his concern ranged "from principles of ethics to a velocimeter, from a metaphysical doctrine to a binding-pin." Although the enunciation of his purpose was categorically stated in *First Principles* (1862), his Synthetic Philosophy embraces a huge shelf of volumes written from 1855 to 1893. The progress of evolution was traced in life, mind, morality, society, and the cosmos.

His contemporary devotees glorified Spencer as the supreme philosopher, but subsequent skepticism toward optimism and progress has greatly dimmed his radiance. The 20th century, at any rate, refuses to digest his ponderous polysyllabic style. Note Spencer's definition: "Evolution is an integration of matter and concomitant dissipation of motion; during which the matter passes from an indefinite, incoherent homogeneity to a definite, coherent heterogeneity; and during which the retained motion undergoes a parallel transformation."

The remaining writers treated in this section are the major Victorian historians.

Henry Thomas Buckle (1821–1862). Inheriting a sizable fortune from his ship-owning father, Henry Thomas Buckle devoted all his time to study and writing. His poor health, which caused him to be educated privately, eventually forced him to travel and in Damascus, Syria, he died.

History of Civilization in England (I, 1857; II, 1861) from 1866 on has more accurately added *France, Spain, and Scotland* to the title. This massive fragment on modern European history was planned as the introduction to a fifteen-volume study. It was the first history in English to exemplify a monumental theory of history. Buckle minutely examined climate, soil, food, and other natural influences governing the forward march of intellect.

James Anthony Froude (fröd) (1818–1894). James Anthony Froude came under the influence of Newman at Oxford, where his brother Richard became one of the leaders in the Tractarian movement. Breaking with Newman, James Froude was attracted to Carlyle. He and the novelist Kingsley married sisters. From 1860 to 1874 he was editor of *Fraser's Magazine,* and from 1892 until death he was a professor of history at Oxford.

History of England from the Fall of Wolsey to the Defeat of the Spanish

Armada (twelve volumes, 1856–70) is the Protestant epic upon the 16th century. With heavy indebtedness to Carlyle for spectacular scenes, hero worship, and impassioned character sketches, Froude lavishly portrays the Reformation as the polestar of English history. The murders of Rizzio and Darnley and the last scene of Mary Queen of Scots at Fotheringay are worthy of an excellent novelist. Froude is the first English historian to prepare a detailed study from unpublished mss. Though strongly biased, the work is factually accurate and still remains the fullest survey of that tumultuous epoch.

Thomas Carlyle (I, 1882; II, 1884) was the authorized biography, since Froude was Carlyle's literary executor. Unlike the standard pious tribute, this unique authorized biography honestly depicts Carlyle in all his atrabilious and explosive moods. Loyal followers of Carlyle protested, but this still remains one of the masterful biographies in English. Carlyle emerges as a tough-minded individualist, a stout moralist with a vitriolic nature.

William Edward Hartpole Lecky (1838–1903). An Anglo-Irish native of Dublin, William Edward Hartpole Lecky was educated at Trinity College, Dublin, and served as a Liberal member of parliament. He declined an Oxford professorship in history.

History of the Rise and Influence of the Spirit of Rationalism in Europe (1865) shows Lecky as a disciple of Buckle. This is the first significant English approach to the history of ideas. Lecky analyzes the advancement in European culture as resulting from emancipation from superstition, magic, and persecution through the growth of intellect and tolerance. The governing concept closely parallels that of Mill in *On Liberty*.

John Richard Green (1837 1883). An Oxford native, John Richard Green was an Anglican cleric until his doubts about Christian theology, generated by Renan and other 19th-century rationalists, caused him to leave the church in 1869 and become a librarian at Lambeth. Fear of early death from tuberculosis forced him to condense a contemplated great-scale work into the following:

Short History of the English People (1874) has proved ever since publication to be the most popular one-volume history of England. The careful title indicates that it is people who concern Green more than the dramatic climaxes of history. Constitutional, intellectual, and social advances are seen partly as a result of England's security from invasion after 1066 but chiefly as a logical progressive development from the inherent tolerance and practicality in the English temperament. Green's success may stem largely from his neat balance between the two major schools of Victorian historians: the Carlyle-Froude-Macaulay school of colorful personalities and spectacular events, and the Buckle-Lecky school of ideas and cultural forces.

John Emerich Edward Dalberg-Acton, first Baron Acton of Aldenham, commonly **Lord Acton** (1834–1902). Lord Acton was born in Naples, Italy, the son of an English baronet and a German countess. He studied in Paris, Edinburgh, and Munich, traveling extensively in Europe and America. He was a Liberal member of parliament and a close friend of Gladstone, who had him elevated to the rank of baron in 1869. From 1895 until his death he was regius professor of modern history at Cambridge. His magnificent historical library of sixty thousand volumes was purchased by the American philanthropist Andrew Carnegie and is now at Cambridge University.

British Protestants were puzzled by the position of Lord Acton. He was a pillar of Liberalism, intent upon writing a vast but never completed History of Liberty, resulting in *History of Freedom and Other Essays* (1907), collected from his periodical articles. In the liberal Roman Catholic journals *Rambler* and *Home and Foreign Review,* Acton sought Roman Catholic acceptance of modern science and social concepts. He was an outspoken opponent of the doctrine of papal infallibility proclaimed in 1870. Nonetheless, he always remained a devout Roman Catholic, explaining that while he opposed reactionary policies of his church, he steadfastly accepted her doctrines.

Never producing a great work, he still ranks as one of England's top historians. He founded the *English Historical Review* (1886–   ) and was the inspirer and first editor of *The Cambridge Modern History.* He conceived of history as demonstrating the spiritual evolution of man toward higher ethical and social standards. His profound distrust of entrenched authority appears in his famous dictum: "Power tends to corrupt, and absolute power corrupts absolutely."

TRAVELERS AND EXPLORERS

With gusto matching their Elizabethan forebears, Victorians pushed into the unknown to remove what Burton termed "that huge white blot which disgraces our maps." By the century's end the far corners of the globe had been penetrated, except for the remotest north and south, but most of the accounts of far journeys fall outside the realm of belles lettres. *Missionary Travels in South Africa* (1857) endures largely as a revelation of the dauntless courage and abiding faith of David Livingstone (1813–73). The accounts of Sir Henry Morton Stanley (1841–1904), especially *How I Found Livingstone* (1872), are exciting journalism. John Hanning Speke (1827–64) probably is the ideal explorer—methodical, tireless, infinitely patient and watchful—but his *Journal of the Discovery of the Source of the Nile* (1863) reduces almost to a dull business venture the discovery of the magnificent Lake Victoria as the headwaters of the fabled Nile.

Alexander William Kinglake (1809–1891). Born near Taunton, Somersetshire, Alexander William Kinglake was educated at Eton and Cambridge, and was called to the bar in 1837. After widespread travels in the Near

East, including the battles of the Crimean War, he returned to sit in parliament (1857–68).

Eothen, or Traces of Travel Brought Home from the East (1844) records a journey of 1835 to Turkey, Syria, Egypt, and Palestine. Though dealing with some of the most familiar monuments and shrines of history, this is one of the most unconventional of travel accounts. A whimsical and independent mind faithfully reports how these experiences impressed him, and his responses are seldom predictable. The volume amounts to an engaging autobiography.

The Invasion of the Crimea (eight volumes, 1863–87) is one of the most readable of war histories, in spite of its bulk. Kinglake's prejudices, particularly in favor of Raglan, render it somewhat dubious, but Gladstone quipped that the book was too bad to live and too good to die. Todleben, an enemy Russian general generously portrayed, labeled the work a romance rather than a history.

Sir Austen Henry Layard (lā'ard) (1817–1894). Born in Paris, Sir Austen Henry Layard was the son of an Englishman in the Ceylon civil service. After youthful travel and study in England and on the continent he set out for Ceylon in 1839 but became fascinated en route with the Near East. In 1845 he led an English expedition to explore the ruins of Assyria, and in 1849 headed another party excavating at Babylon and in southern Mesopotamia. From 1852 he rose in governmental posts to become ambassador to Constantinople (1877–80). Thereafter he lived in Venice, writing on Italian art.

Nineveh and Its Remains (I, 1848; II, 1849) has been the most popular volume on archaeology in English. Although always sober and calm, Layard communicated to his countrymen the thrill of discovery of ancient civilization, backed up by the colossal statuary he shipped to astound even today's visitor to the British Museum. The spectacle of an awesome and vanished might stirred imagination, as in Rossetti ("The Burden of Nineveh") and Kipling ("Recessional").

Sir Richard Francis Burton (1821–1890). A native of Torquay, Devonshire, Sir Richard Burton enjoyed upon the continent an undisciplined childhood that scarcely prepared him for Oxford. Challenging a fellow undergraduate to a duel and other unruly behavior forced him to leave the university. As a subaltern in the Bombay Native Infantry in 1842 he abhorred discipline and spent his time gaining remarkable proficiency in Hindustani, Persian, and Arabic. His ability to pass himself off in the Sind as a Moslem induced him to make the *hajj* to Mecca and Medina in 1853 in the guise of an Indian Pathan. African adventure engaged him for most of the remaining decade. From 1861 until death, serving the British Foreign Office, he roamed over much of the world.

Burton admitted regretfully that he had never killed anyone, but abandoning civilization to revel in the last of the earth's wildness, he encountered every other savage experience. His energy was superhuman and his temper ferocious. His rebelliousness, however, rose from a cantankerous personality, not from any real ideological hostility to Victorianism.

Pilgrimage to Al-Medinah and Meccah (1855) recounts the first visit of an Englishman to the holy cities of Islam. The grim humor, headlong vigor, brilliant descriptions, and insatiable love of adventure make it one of the most exciting and personal volumes in English. The intensive knowledge of Arab life and history give the work the weight of a historical document.

First Footsteps in East Africa (1856), though less famed, is possibly the greater book. Certainly it was an even more hazardous exploit. Burton and Speke vanished into the interior of Somaliland in 1854 to be the first white visitors to the capital. On their return, running the gauntlet of Somali spears, Speke was wounded in eleven places and Burton had a javelin lanced through his jaws.

The Thousand Nights and a Night (sixteen volumes, 1885–88) was privately printed, for its extensive treatment of Middle Eastern pornography was too much for the era. This unexpurgated translation of the famous Arabian Nights stories shows Burton's deep understanding of Arabic life and language and it is an extraordinarily felicitous reproduction of the original, though archaisms and a rugged style detract from its literary quality, and also Burton can be dull where the original was equally dull.

Charles Montagu Doughty (dŏ′ti) (1843–1926). Charles Montagu Doughty was born at the rectory of Theberton Hall, Suffolk. An impediment of speech prevented him from entering the navy, but he spent many years of travel and study in England and on the continent. In 1876 he left Damascus for two years of wandering through Arabia that carried him to Madâin Sâlih and many other points previously unexplored by Westerners. His later years, spent largely in Italian isolation from the contemporary social and literary world, were devoted to the writing of long narrative poems. At Doughty's funeral one of the mourners was his chief admirer, T. E. Lawrence.

Travels in Arabia Deserta (1888) offers rare knowledge of the geography of interior Arabia and the life of its inhabitants, but the volume's style is its most extraordinary achievement. Renouncing post-Elizabethan developments in vocabulary and syntax, Doughty writes a sonorous, majestic prose that sounds precisely like that of a fluent and poetic Elizabethan. Not an affectation, the style is thoroughly a part of Doughty; "God has sent a son, and the father cannot contrary him in anything, whilst he is a child." The idiom proves exactly right to depict a Semitic people still living the life of Old Testament patriarchs in a still-continuing heroic age. Many consider this the best travel account in English.

The Dawn in Britain (1906–7), a twenty-four-book epic of about thirty thousand blank-verse lines, is one of the longest poems in the language. Its composition involved about eleven years, and Doughty considered it his masterwork. Covering a span of 450 years, the work treats of three tidal movements of history from West to East and back again: the Gallic invasion of Rome and Delphi, the conquest of Britain by Rome, and the arrival of Christianity in Britain. Civilization comes to "the utmost isle" (original title of poem) as a fusion of British, Roman, and Christian elements. The grasp of sweeping forces in history, occasional narrative grandeur, and an impressive Elizabethan cadence and diction induce a few to rate it the greatest completed epic since *Paradise Lost,* but the unepical 20th century has paid it scant heed.

NATURE WRITERS

The greatest celebration of Nature during the Victorian era sounded not from versifiers but from two poets in prose.

Richard Jefferies (jef'riz) (1848–1887). Richard Jefferies was born John Richard Jefferies at Coate, Wiltshire. After a brief education he began at seventeen to write descriptive sketches for local newspapers. His periodical articles gained him mounting attention, but his brooding solitary spirit preferred rural obscurity. Poverty and ill health brought him to an early death at thirty-eight.

In his brief career Jefferies rapidly progressed from a rural sportsman, *The Game Keeper at Home* (1878), to an unpretentious but profound poetizer of Nature. His contemplation of Nature became that of a mystic, sensing as deeply as Wordsworth the soul behind the exquisite beauty of the English countryside. "The Pageant of Summer" (*Longman's Magazine* 1883) is characteristic of his high-level maturity. A smoothly flowing description of summer loveliness with all the details of a painter and a thoroughly knowledgeable countryman ends: "To be beautiful and to be calm, without mental fear, is the ideal of nature."

The Story of My Heart (1883) is subtitled "My Autobiography," but it is so only in the sense of an "Autobiography of a Soul." Jefferies concerns himself solely with his maturing Nature viewpoint over a sixteen-year period. He seeks an age of soul-cultivation as ancient Greece cultivated the body and his own age cultivates the mind. The mystic soul finds orthodox concepts of deity inadequate in its expansion and heightened acuity: "the full stream of ocean beats upon the shore, and the rich wind feeds the heart, the sun burns brightly; the sense of soul-life burns in me like a torch."

Robert Francis Kilvert (1840–1879). Born at Hardenhuish, Wiltshire, of a clerical family, Robert Francis Kilvert took holy orders after graduation from Oxford. His brief career was spent largely in Welsh parishes. He died suddenly of peritonitis a month after his marriage. He was unknown until the eve of World War II.

Diary (three volumes, 1938–40) consists of twenty-two notebooks of almost daily entries from January 1870 to March 1879. Resident far from the arena of great affairs and actually no intellectual, Kilvert offers no picture of the contemporary mental struggles, and his responses to big issues (e.g. the Franco-Prussian War) are conventional. As a depicter of everyday village life, however, Kilvert rivals Dorothy Wordsworth. There are enough brilliant vignettes of small-town life and drama to equip a prolific novelist. But most of all, Kilvert is a prose Hopkins, studding his diary with poignant Nature perceptions like: "Last night there was a sharp frost, the crescent moon hung cold and keen, and the stars glittered and flashed gloriously. Orion all in a move of brilliance."

BIOGRAPHERS

The Victorian era produced no one comparable to Boswell, but it labored upon mountains of biography. These biographies generally were titled *The Life and Times of* . . . and monotonously detailed almost everything about their subject. One thing they did omit—the indecorous or embarrassing in their subject's life that would lessen his stature in proper Victorian eyes.

John Forster (1812–1876). Born at Newcastle, John Forster was educated at University College, London, and at the Inner Temple. Lamb and Leigh Hunt encouraged the brilliant student to criticism and periodical writing. Financially secure with government sinecures, Forster spent his life as one of the best-known literary men of London. He foreshadowed the professional biographers of the 20th century as he ranged in studies from the 17th century to contemporaries.

The Life and Adventures of Oliver Goldsmith (1848) was rewritten twelve times before publication. This full and accurate study is chiefly responsible for the sustained interest in the pleasant, if feckless, personality of Goldsmith. Success unfortunately impelled Forster to expand the work into *The Life and Times of Oliver Goldsmith* (1854), where the canvas became overcrowded with late 18th-century personages.

Life of Dickens (I, 1872; II, 1873; III, 1874), probably the best Victorian biography, was a labor of love by a devoted friend. No one else was so qualified to be the biographer of Dickens (the Forster Collection, bequeathed to the nation, contains most of the ms. copies of Dickens' novels). The novelist emerges as a character greater than any of his vivacious creatures, an intense and vital being of charm and drama. Today's readers perhaps unwisely ignore the work because the discreet Forster will not tell the truth about Dickens and Ellen Ternan.

David Masson (1822–1907). David Masson was born at Aberdeen, Scotland, and there educated through the university. Periodical and educational writing took him to London where he became a friend of Carlyle and Thackeray. In 1853 he succeeded Clough as professor of English literature at University College, London. After the death of Aytoun, Masson succeeded to his chair at the University of Edinburgh and resided there until death.

Life of Milton (six volumes, 1859–80) is the first of the truly monumental, painstakingly scholarly biographies of noted English writers. Masson is meticulously accurate and encyclopedic in his knowledge of Milton's period. While the interpretation of Milton and his works will always proceed, it is unlikely that this detailed factual study will ever be wholly superseded.

MAJOR LATER VICTORIAN ESSAYISTS AND PROSE STYLISTS

Denying the utility of art and ignoring morality, aestheticism and impressionistic criticism clashed directly with the orthodox concepts of Victorianism and encouraged the *fin de siècle* spirit of the poets discussed in the previous chapter. Sources of this critical movement were:

(1) Continental aesthetes, especially the French Parnassians and Johann Winckelmann. The German strain was essentially aesthetic, the French more rebellious and amoral.

(2) The native current of Pre-Raphaelitism and the intellectual revolt against Victorian evangelicalism and utilitarianism.

Walter Horatio Pater (pā'tér) (1839–1894). A native Londoner, Walter Pater was early made an orphan by his father's death, and passed his youth at Enfield in a household of female relatives. At Queen's College, Oxford, he attracted the attention of Jowett but graduated with only second-class honors in 1862. From 1864 until death he was a Brasenose College professor, leaving Oxford only for brief residence in London and for continental visits. Shy and reticent, he lived simply and quietly.

As acutely as Arnold, Pater sensed the "sick hurry," the "divided aims" of his era; but instead of the inherent stoicism of Arnold, Pater was by nature an epicurean in the true meaning (i.e. seeking withdrawal from the feverish world to minimize pain and maximize pleasure).

Studies in the History of the Renaissance (1873) established Pater's reputation as a leader of the aesthetic cult. Botticelli, della Robbia, Michelangelo, and other Renaissance figures are exalted as artists working for no other end than the joy of created beauty. The appreciation of "Mona Lisa" in the essay on Leonardo da Vinci is the best example of impressionistic criticism; whatever the famous painting means to the artist and to others, it means to Pater all the unfathomable mystery of womankind. The only essay upon a modern, "Winckelmann," elevates as supreme truth the German's adoration of sensuous beauty.

"The School of Giorgione" epitomizes the aesthetic doctrine in its insistence that all art must seek "to be independent of the mere intelligence, to become a matter of pure perception, to get rid of its responsibilities to subject or material."

"Conclusion," the *locus classicus* of aestheticism and impressionistic criticism, was later to be regretted by Pater. Its statements and implications along with those of the "Preface" expound the following aesthetic articles of belief:

(1) Hedonism the end of life. Intellectual and emotional intensity permits one "to burn always with a hard, gem-like flame."

(2) Art the only true basis for a poise and unity in life.

(3) Pure subjectivity. Art is primarily an expression of the artist's personality. The perceiver of art benefits solely from the uniquely personal stimulation that he derives from the art object.

(4) Destruction of the genre. Each work of art is a self-creative experience to both creator and consumer, and rules of form (e.g. epic poem, landscape painting) are brushed aside.

(5) Amorality. Art is not the handmaiden of social problems, faith, or morals.

(6) The evanescent. Art captures the fleeting, the transitory.

The effect of *Studies* upon aesthetes particularly and upon the public generally has not yet been broken, although all subsequent Pater writing labors at an amplified concept of art.

The Child in the House (1878) imaginatively re-creates Pater's own childhood in the person of Florian Deleal ("flowering of loyalty"), obviously in the feminine household at Enfield. Pater's first piece of avowedly creative rather than critical writing idealizes his early years, portraying them not as they were but as he would wish them to have been. From many sensuous details the boy's spirit develops toward the ideal of untarnished beauty, unalterable by the trivial and the mean of the world. Few pieces in English match this poetic and sensitive unfolding of a boy's soul.

Marius the Epicurean (1885) in the form of fiction traces the religious and aesthetic quest of an imaginary Roman in the days of Marcus Aurelius. In turn Marius passes from the ancestral "religion of Numa" through intellectual epicureanism, stoicism, and theism to Christianity. Like his creator, Marius is an idealist, seeking to transcend the sordidness of the real world. In Christianity his vision of the Eternal Companion and Universal Creator provides "the *Great Ideal*" beside which the physical world fades. Such *seeing* and *being* "he had always set above the *having*, or even the *doing*, of anything." Wilde stated the purpose clearly: "Pater seeks to reconcile the artistic life with the life of religion." Yeats considered this work "the only great prose in modern English."

Appreciations, with an Essay on Style (1889) is aptly titled, for instead of evaluation, each essay concentrates entirely upon a single idea in a piece of literature that intrigues Pater.

"Style" essentially explains and defends his own writing techniques. Pater agrees with Buffon's dictum: "The style is the man himself." The craftsmanship lies in the perfect combining of form and content to give unified expression to the writer's concept. Polish, precision, and nuance are sought as zealously in prose as in verse.

"Wordsworth" (*1874,* one year after *Studies*) finds in the poet a deep perception of the fundamental human passions, expression of the calm dignity and sober contemplation of man close to Nature. In remarkable contrast to earlier writings this piece exalts an artist for his reinforcement of moral and spiritual values.

"Coleridge" sees the tragedy of the noted Romantic in his search for an absolute, whereas, Pater claims, "to the modern spirit nothing is, or can be rightly known, except relatively and under conditions." Such relativism was always characteristic of Pater.

"Lamb" admires one of Pater's favorite critics, particularly for delicacy and reserve, and pre-eminently for his goal of sympathetic understanding. Lamb is praised for maintaining a personality and viewpoint undisturbed by contemporary events or even his own unhappy family life.

"Shakespeare's English Kings" is the volume's only essay previously unprinted in periodicals. Pater considers solely the irony of kingship, the human beings that Shakespeare contrasts with their royal trappings.

"Dante Gabriel Rosetti" (*1883*) analyzes the Pre-Raphaelite's objective as art for art's sake but, significantly, does not commit Pater. Rosetti's attempted union of the sensuous and the spiritual is praised as true medievalism and true life.

"Postscript" (published as "Romanticism" in *Macmillan's Magazine* 1876) provides famous and still influential definitions of classicism ("order in beauty") and romanticism ("the addition of strangeness to beauty" arising from intense curiosity and emotion).

John Addington Symonds (sim'ondz) (1840–1893). A native of Bristol, John Addington Symonds was educated at Harrow and Oxford. Lung ailments sent him to Italy where he lived much of his life, dying in Rome.

History of the Renaissance in Italy (1875–86) is largely responsible for the enthusiasm of the English-speaking world for the Italian Renaissance. Symonds minimizes all other aspects of that age to portray it as the supreme flowering of art. Amazingly, the *Encyclopaedia Britannica* had carried no article on the Renaissance until that of Symonds in the ninth edition (1885), where he explained that the aesthetic movement (from him and from

Pater) had lifted the reputation of the Renaissance from Ruskin's scornful derogation of its sensuality and paganism.

Symonds was also a poet, albeit a minor one. Two of his volumes, *Many Moods* (1878) and *New and Old* (1880), amply show his characteristic defect as a poet—he was overly literate.

OTHER PROSE WRITERS OF THE LATER VICTORIAN PERIOD

PHILOSOPHERS, LIBERAL THEOLOGIANS, AND FREETHINKERS

Beyond thinkers already discussed the dominant schools of 19th-century British philosophy were fundamentally derivative—idealism from Germany, pragmatism from America.

The leading idealist was Francis Herbert Bradley (1846–1924), whose excellent prose in *Appearance and Reality* (1893) is still often seen in anthologies. Bradley refused to accept the traditional linking of idealism with religion. John McTaggart Ellis McTaggart (1866–1925) completely severed idealism from theology. Although an atheist, McTaggart (*Nature of Existence,* 1921) believed in the immortality of the soul on the basis of all events occurring not within the mere tyranny of time but within the "simultaneous now."

Strangely enough, the leading British pragmatist was a naturalized German, Ferdinand Canning Scott Schiller (1864–1937), who spent most of his life at Oxford, teaching in the United States late in life. In *Plato or Protagoras* (1908) he labeled himself a "neo-Protagorean," intent upon a denial of Platonism in favor of a "rehumanizing" of philosophy. Schiller is one of the most vivacious and readable of academic philosophers.

Disturbing liberal thought of the 19th century caused many evangelicals to become even more fundamentalistic in their interpretation of the Scriptures and, as we have noted, caused a reaction among many Anglican clergymen by turning them more toward Catholicism. Broad Churchmen (i.e. latitudinarians) found it difficult to reconcile new thought to the old institution of Christianity.

Essays and Reviews (1860), now tame reading, aroused a Victorian whirlwind. Science and Germanic "higher criticism" of the Bible thread through most of the seven papers of this Broad Church volume. Miracle, prophecy, divine inspiration for the Scriptures are all challenged. Analysis of Jewish history places the Hebrews in Semitic culture and minimizes any unique or self-generated aspects of Hebraic thought. Intended as free discussion and reconciliation of faith with science, the book was condemned as heresy by a conference of Anglican bishops. When the lay Privy Council overrode the ecclesiastics, much of England chuckled at the quip that "hell was dismissed with costs."

John William Colenso (ko-len'sō) (1814–1883). Of an old Cornish family of St. Austell, John William Colenso became Anglican bishop of Natal, South Africa, after making a name as a Cambridge mathematician. In attempting to convert an intelligent Zulu chieftain to Christianity, the bishop was induced by the native's penetrating queries to ask some deep questions of his own on the Old Testament, resulting in:

Critical Examination of the Pentateuch (1862–79) scrutinized the first five books of the Old Testament with modern insistence upon accurate statement. Colenso's revelation of many inconsistencies and inaccuracies in the account (Arnold in "Function of Criticism" smiles at the "eighty and odd pigeons" which Colenso from Leviticus 10:16–20 calculated as the daily diet of Jewish priests) caused angry ecclesiastics to seek Colenso's excommunication. The bishop held his diocese only to arouse further ire by his support of the Zulus. Today enlightened clerics recognize the truth of Colenso's major criticisms, but in his own day he openly said what the clergy felt was wise to conceal from their congregations. Though no monumental work, this is the most influential excursion by a Britisher into the German preserve of biblical "higher criticism."

Sir Leslie Stephen (1832–1904). A Londoner by birth, Sir Leslie Stephen was the son of Sir James Stephen, the major power for decades in the Colonial Office. His mother belonged to the evangelical Clapham Sect. His Cambridge education culminated in his priesthood in 1859. During the American Civil War he visited the North and became one of its leading supporters in England. The gradual shift of his opinions toward agnosticism compelled him to relinquish holy orders in 1875. His first wife was the younger daughter of Thackeray, and by his second wife he was the father of Virginia Woolf. As editor and critic he was one of the most influential men of letters in the last quarter of the century.

Like Huxley, Stephen was a Victorian agnostic who claimed contemporary admiration by his staunch morality and intense sincerity. His was one of the powerful intellects of the era, expressed in a workmanlike prose, polished and quietly ironic, that has well stood the test of time. His literary studies, *Hours in a Library* (1874–90), lack the imaginative touch of Arnold or Swinburne but impress with their sound, weighty judiciousness.

History of English Thought in the Eighteenth Century (1876), his most massive work, is still the definitive survey of the subject because of its fairness and exhaustiveness. Probably no other work has matched this in making the current English-speaking world appreciate its profound debt to 18th-century ideas.

Dictionary of National Biography began under the editorship of Stephen in 1882; and although he relinquished his post in 1891, he continued to contribute until 1901. Publication began in 1886. Stephen's share of writing consists of 378 articles, totaling over one thousand pages. The standards established by Stephen insured one of the monumental pieces of English scholarship, unsurpassed by any comparable work in any language and a worthy mate for the scholarship of the *Oxford English Dictionary*. Every notable deceased Englishman in history is carefully chronicled. Meticulously accurate, the work ignores all legendary and unsubstantiated material. Judgments are deliberate and unprejudiced. Stephen is the unchallenged master in English of the short biography.

An Agnostic's Apology (1893), the most personal and self-revelatory of his works, depicted Stephen's imperceptible ebbing of faith, which was as painless as Darwin's. Stephen scrutinized the Old and New Testaments as purely human documents and denied the divinity of Christ. The difference between 18th-century skepticism and Victorian agnosticism appears in the comparison of Hume with this work. To the destructiveness of Hume, Stephen added an enthusiasm for science, a religion of humanity, and secular idealism. He believed that all intelligent men of his era, whatever their outward acquiescence, were actually agnostics. He contended that a purely social ethic superseded Christianity in instructing a man to live like a gentleman, and, as he was soon to demonstrate after a protracted illness, "to die like a gentleman."

Charles Bradlaugh (brad'lô) (1833–1891). Son of a solicitor's clerk in London, Charles Bradlaugh suffered physically and legally for much of his life because of his militant atheism. From 1860 he was editor of the *National Reformer,* which he founded as the first journal of professed atheism in the English language. Elected to parliament by Northampton in 1880, he was refused a seat because of his atheism until 1886 when he became the first avowed atheist in parliament.

Bradlaugh stood in the same position in England that his contemporary Robert Ingersoll cut in America. His atheism, however, essentially sprang not from the influence of science but from the radical undercurrent of 18th-century thought, especially that of Tom Paine. Like contemporary agnostics, he was astonishingly Victorian—rigorously moral and even a teetotaler. With an Englishman's sense of fair play, even the pious Gladstone supported Bradlaugh's attempt to sit in parliament, and as Bradlaugh was dying parliament voted to expunge from the record its half decade of resistance to him.

Edward Carpenter (1844–1929). Son of a Brighton barrister, Edward Carpenter took holy orders after graduation from Cambridge in 1868, but, revolting against conformity (and especially stimulated by the writings of Walt Whitman), he left the university and the church in 1874. Though considered quite bizarre in the 19th century, he was much sought after by "advanced" thinkers in his later years, particularly because of his strong influence upon D. H. Lawrence.

Civilisation, Its Cause and Cure (1889, enlarged 1921) foreshadows the later glorification of Irrational Man and the 20th-century intellectuals' despair over our culture. Carpenter sees the emergence of ancient civilization as a curse and not a blessing to mankind. The elevation of reason cut man off from his proper unconscious bond with nature and fostered the cruel selfishness of individualism. Carpenter postulated in primitive man a spirit of "unanimism," unifying all elements into harmony within himself, with his fellows, and with the world. Human emphasis upon cerebration was liable to doom our species as overspecialization did for the dinosaurs.

SCIENTIFIC ANALYSTS AND SOCIAL SCIENTISTS

Sir **Francis Galton** (1822–1911). First cousin of Darwin, Francis Galton was born at Birmingham and educated at King's College, London, and Trinity College, Cambridge. Extensive travels in Africa between 1845 and 1850 interested him in anthropology, but his wide-ranging studies stretched from meteorology, in which he first established the theory of anticyclones, to criminology, in which he laid the foundations for modern fingerprint identification. His greatest contribution was the creation of the science of eugenics. In a series of volumes starting with *Hereditary Genius* (1869) he advocated the improvement of the race by conscious selection of human mates and planned procreation. Human society, he contended, should deliberately and systematically control the choice of the fit and the elimination of the unfit that occurs automatically in nature.

Karl Pearson (1857–1936). A native Londoner, Karl Pearson was educated at Cambridge. He became eminent in mathematics and biology. The leading disciple of Galton, he held the Galton professorship in eugenics at London University.

Grammar of Science (1899) is probably the best exposition in any language of classic science. The only reality is the motion of discrete particles in space. Metaphysics and theology are completely abandoned; mind is nothing but the sum total of physical perceptions. The quest for the "why" of the universe is pointless, as science will encompass the entire range of knowledge in determining the "how." The only credo for the future is that of science: "I believe because I understand." The ethic for the future is the scientific spirit by which men shall subordinate individual selfishness to the welfare of mankind.

Ironically, scientific investigation had already undermined classic science before Pearson's definitive statement. In 1887, the very year of the Hertz experiment, the American physicists, Michelson and Morley, shook the foundations of 19th-century science by their experiment with the speed of light. Their astounding results disclosed that: the speed of light + the rotation speed of the earth = the speed of light − the rotation speed of the earth. This bewildering discovery was confirmed by subsequent researchers, and the explanation by Albert Einstein (then a young scientist in Germany) in 1905 ushered in the Age of Relativity and a new era for science.

Sir **Edward Burnett Tylor** (1832–1917). Edward Burnett Tylor was the son of a Quaker brass foundryman in suburban London. As a Quaker he was denied university training. An 1856 residence in Mexico determined his lifetime career in anthropology, as Darwin's voyage in the *Beagle* had determined the lifework of the biologist. Tylor's reputation was established with *Researches into the Early History of Mankind* (1865). In 1896 he was appointed the first professor of anthropology at Oxford.

Tylor is the acknowledged founder of cultural anthropology, and Max Müller always termed ethnology "Mr. Tylor's Science." A thoroughgoing Darwinian, Tylor convinced many of the evolutionary pattern of man's customs and beliefs. Tylor liked to bait clergymen by demonstrating the origin of their most solemn theological tenets in primitive superstition and their most exalted ceremonies in savage rites.

Primitive Culture (1871) inaugurates the scientific study of culture. Tylor marshals colossal evidence of similar patterns of human thought and behavior in widely dispersed societies; "the mind of uncultured man works in much the same way at all times and everywhere." His "doctrine of survivals" finds the nonfunctional beliefs and practices of civilization to be a sort of vermiform appendix from our primitive past. Denying any need for divine revelation, Tylor traced man's religious impulses by logical growth from animism (Tylor gave to this word its modern meaning) through successive phases to monotheism.

Sir **James George Frazer** (1854–1941). James George Frazer was born in Glasgow, Scotland, to eminently pious Presbyterian parents. After graduation from Glasgow University, he became a fellow of Trinity College, Cambridge, where he remained for the rest of his life. Tylor's *Primitive Culture,* he stated, "marked an epoch in my life," and it turned him into a cultural evolutionist. Never meeting a savage in the flesh, Frazer distilled several hundred anthropological studies from the first-hand observations of others. Most of his lifelong researches denied the literal truth of the Scriptures, so sacredly true to his parents.

The 20th-century emphasis by many anthropologists upon a psychological and psychoanalytical approach to the primitive mind has dimmed the professional reputation of the rationalistic Frazer, even though Malinowski has termed him "the greatest anthropologist of our age." To the lay reader, however, Frazer remains the most-read English anthropologist because of his literary powers, which produce brilliant thumbnail sketches, imaginative color, and peaks of dramatic emotion.

The Golden Bough (1890, two volumes; 1900, three volumes; 1911–15, twelve volumes) gathers vast anthropological examples about the primitive motif of the slaying of the sacred king for the benefit of the tribe. The title refers to the bough plucked in Vergil's *Aeneid* to gain entry for Aeneas into the underworld; ancient legend associated this sprig with the mistletoe bough used to strangle the priest-king of Diana's grove in the Alban hills of Italy. Frazer conceives of cultural evolution proceeding from magic to religion and thence to science. Magic is pseudo-science by which the primitive attempts to control nature. By "sympathetic magic" (Frazer's coinage) a savage believes that his performance of an act will cause a connected event in nature (e.g. killing the sacred king before his decline of strength will prevent the decline of soil fertility). Subsequent religion casts off all relations to science; religion is "a propitiation or conciliation of powers superior to man which are believed to direct and control the course of nature and human life." Science shares with magic the belief in a uniformity of nature but ascertains the sequence of cause and effect through physical laws. A. E. Housman extolled the work as "learning mated with literature."

Walter Bagehot (baj'ot) (1826–1877). Born at Langport, Somerset, Walter Bagehot was the son of a banker. He worked in his father's business and in addition was able to spread his talents into many other fields. He edited a newspaper, the *Economist*, and wrote several books on widely diverse subjects. His *The English Constitution* (1867) and a work on banking, *Lombard Street* (1873), were well received. *Literary Studies* (1879), published after his death, shows him as an astute and quite readable critic of literature. *Physics and Politics* (1869) had wide influence even outside of England. It examines the evolution of communities of men, using Darwinism as a starting point.

THE FABIAN SOCIETY

The study of sociology and the very word itself were instituted in 1837 by Auguste Comte in France. Sociological research in English begins with Beatrice and Sidney Webb; Mrs. Webb significantly stated that her studies had to begin with the novels of George Eliot, the only previous English writer with a genuine sociological approach. Verses in the *Spectator* of 1953 saw the Webbs as marrying not for vulgar procreation:

> But for the nobler, purer aim
> Of hatching out statistics
> The life blood of enchanting tomes
> On humble-life logistics.

The numerous sociological treatises of the Webbs probably reached their peak in *English Local Government,* a series of seven volumes issued between 1906 and 1927. Individually and in collaboration the Webbs produced one of the largest bodies of sociological studies in English, the foundation for countless works since.

Along with George Bernard Shaw, the Webbs were the leading spirits in the Fabian Society, founded in 1884. The organization name is taken from Fabius, the Roman general whose delaying tactics eventually brought the downfall of Hannibal. Patience was the Society's watchword in its campaign for the ultimate victory of socialism. As Sidney Webb defined it: "Socialism is the conscious and deliberate substitution, in industrial as well as political matters, of the collective self-government of the community as a whole, organized on a democratic basis, for the individual control over other men's lives, which the unrestrained private ownership of land and industrial capital inevitably involves." Although the Fabian Society has never exceeded four thousand members in any year, it has consistently included many of the best minds in England: H. G. Wells, John Galsworthy, Robert Graves, Clement (later Lord) Attlee, William (later Archbishop) Temple, Ronald (later Monsignor) Knox, G. K. Chesterton, Bertrand Russell, Leonard Woolf, C. E. M. Joad, G. D. H. Cole, H. J. Laski.

The Fabian Society is the oldest and most successful of the world's socialistic organizations; it has never experienced a split, and its principles and methods have remained virtually unaltered since its founding. It has proved one of the most potent forces in modern Britain. It sponsored countless lectures and pamphlets on socialism; the London School of Economics was established by the Webbs in 1895; and the *New Statesman* was founded in 1912 by the Webbs. The Fabian Society has been the ideological branch of the Labour Party, and with the Labour victory of 1945 its 229 members in parliament and the government dominated the administration and put into effect almost the entire Fabian platform enunciated more than half a century before. The return of the Conservatives to power in 1951 has forced the Fabians back to their original policy of patient waiting.

Fabian Essays in Socialism (1889), the most influential work by the group, has thus far sold well over two million copies. Its original editor, G. B. Shaw, was able at ninety-two to write a triumphant new preface for the jubilee edition in 1948. The volume consists of seven lectures delivered by seven Fabians at Cambridge and Leicester. It may be considered the manifesto of British socialism. Wholly a native outgrowth, Fabian socialism dismisses both Marxist revolutionaries and Morris-like utopians. Sidney Webb's favorite phrase, "the inevitability of gradualness," expressed the Society's confidence that the democratic process will eventuate in the welfare state. Denying a class struggle, the Fabians simply place all who contribute to society by their efforts against those who enjoy income unearned by their labor. The contemplated welfare state would provide the minimum necessities for all (eliminating unemployment and parasites) and permit everyone to secure the just rewards for his specific contribution to society.

Sidney James Webb, first **Baron Passfield** (1859–1947). A native Londoner, Sidney Webb entered the civil service in 1878 after studying at the City of London College. He was the leading spirit in the founding of the Fabian Society. In 1892 he married Beatrice Potter, his collaborator thereafter in numerous works on economics, sociology, and socialism. He resigned from the civil service in 1891 to serve on commissions of the government and the Labour Party. His highest position was as secretary for the colonies and dominions under the MacDonald administration of 1929, which elevated him to the peerage. Webb is chiefly responsible for the 20th-century pattern of British socialism and the Labour Party. Shaw termed him "the ablest man in England."

Beatrice Webb (née Potter), **Lady Passfield** (1858–1943). Daughter of a wealthy London businessman, Beatrice Webb had J. S. Mill and Herbert Spencer as early friends and mentors. At first scornful of the Fabians as faddists, she was converted to socialism by 1890 on the basis of living incognito among the poor of England's north. She married Sidney Webb in 1892. The team of Webb and Webb was "augustness radiating" to E. M. Forster. Even close friends considered the childless marriage as essentially the partnership of two great brains, but her autobiographical works, *My Apprenticeship* (1926) and *Our Partnership* (1948), reveal a thoroughly feminine and human personality in a woman of monumental intellect.

History of Trade-Unionism (1894) is the classic work in its area and probably has influenced the development of the Labour Party more than any other single book. The Webbs interpret the development of unionism not as shaping toward compromise with capitalism in the exaction of higher wages or the acceptance of a dole but as moving inevitably toward the realization of a socialistic society.

TRANSLATORS AND SCHOLARS

The Victorian era and the 20th century are second only to the Renaissance as a notable age of translation. By the end of the 19th century the English-speaking people were almost universally literate, but only a small percentage could read any foreign language easily. A large reading public created by increased population and prosperity made it feasible to translate innumerable works into English. The reader of English has therefore been placed in an enviable position: he has available in his language virtually every significant piece of world writing.

The Victorian age caught up with the backlog by complete translation for the first time of such past masterworks as:

Aquinas, *Summa Theologica,* by E. O'Donnell (1859).

Beowulf, by J. M. Kemble (1837).

[East] *Indian Poetry,* by Sir Edwin Arnold (1881).

Classical Poetry of the Japanese, by B. H. Chamberlain (1880).

Mabinogion [Celtic lore], by Lady Charlotte Guest (1838–49).

Nibelungenlied, by J. Birch (1848).

Talmud, by D. M. Schwab (1885).

In addition, all contemporary European writers of prominence were translated during this period.

Benjamin Jowett (jŏ'et) (1817–1893). A native of London, Benjamin Jowett enjoyed a brilliant undergraduate career at Balliol College, Oxford, and later rose through academic ranks to be regius professor of Greek (1855) and master of Balliol (1870). He was a liberal theologian, a Broad Churchman, highly popular with students but suspect to the deeply orthodox. The list of his pupils and friends embraces the entire panorama of current English intellectual life and also includes the Americans Holmes and Lowell, the French Renan, and the Russian Turgenev. He translated from Thucydides (1881) and Aristotle (1885), but his most famous work is:

The Dialogues of Plato (1871) and *The Republic* (1888), which in their idealistic philosophy and broad tolerance were a refuge to Jowett from the inhospitable reception of his liberal theology. The translator meticulously worked and reworked every phrase to convey the nuances and conversational grace of the original. Although today's readers may feel the version to be a bit stiff and old-fashioned, it still remains the standard translation.

Andrew Lang (1844–1912). Andrew Lang was born at Selkirk, Scotland. His grandfather had been a close friend of Sir Walter Scott, and Lang was devoted to Scott throughout life. At the Edinburgh Academy he "loathed Greek" until converted by studying Homer. His university training was at St. Andrews, Glasgow, and Oxford (he was a student under Jowett at Balliol). Irked by academic life, he turned to journalism in 1875 and for forty years produced an amazing variety of writings ranging over poetry, biography, Scottish history, fairy tales, novels, and essays. For the ninth edition of the *Encyclopaedia Britannica* (1875–89) he wrote such entries as "Ballads," "Family," "Molière," "Name," "Scotland," and "Totemism." Lang prided himself chiefly upon his anthropological works, which, especially *Myth, Ritual, and Religion* (1887), may be said to establish the modern view that similar folk themes demonstrate a common human experience and thought pattern, underlying mythology, religion, and art. His interest in abnormal psychology made him one of the founders and later president of the Psychical Research Society.

Odyssey (1879), in collaboration with S. H. Butcher, proved one of the most famous books of the century. This prose version attempts to archaize through a style based upon the Authorized Version of the Bible. Though sonorous and dignified, it now seems rather affected. Contemporaries honored it as the definitive translation of Homer, and Gilbert Murray, famed Greek scholar, later termed it a "beautiful book."

Iliad (1883), in collaboration with Walter Leaf and Ernest Myers, is less accurate than its predecessor, but along with it has achieved the largest sales of any translation of Homer into English.

Aucassin and Nicolette (1887) was the first English translation of this charming medieval French tale. Lang's first printed volume was *Ballads and Lyrics of Old France* (1872), and throughout his career he was a significant popularizer of French themes and verse forms.

Revised Version of the Bible. The Revised Version, the first since the Authorized Version of 1611, was instituted by the Anglican bishops in 1870. The revisers consisted of sixty-five English biblical scholars, forty-one from the Church of England and the rest from Protestant denominations in the British Isles. After 1872 the group co-operated with American Protestant revisers, but both national groups published independently. As few changes as possible were made in the text of the Authorized Version, but revision was deemed necessary because:

(1) The Authorized Version contains some mistakes, ambiguities, and inconsistencies (A.V. for Cor. 4:4 reads, "I know nothing by myself"; R.V. reads, "I know nothing against myself.").

(2) Semantic alterations in the language since 1611 require modernization (A.V. for Matt. 17:25 reads, "Jesus prevented him, saying . . ."; R.V. reads, "Jesus spake to him first").

(3) Discovery since 1611 of valuable early texts of the New Testament: Sinaitic and Vatican of the 4th century, Alexandrine and Ephraem of the 5th century, Beza and Claromontane of the 6th century.

The New Testament revision was published in 1881, arousing such interest that the entire text was telegraphed to Chicago to appear as a newspaper supplement. The Old Testament revision appeared in 1885. Some of the revisers later co-operated upon a revision of the Apocrypha (1896). Although textually superior to the Authorized Version, the Revised Version has never gained as wide a popular esteem.

Frederick James Furnivall (férn'i-val) (1825–1910). One of the leading scholars of the period, Frederick James Furnivall was born in Egham, Surrey. He was the son of the physician who attended Mary Shelley in 1817. Furnivall was educated at London University and Cambridge. Early attracted to Christian Socialism, he taught at the Working Men's College in London. He was an active figure in the Philological Society (secretary from 1862 until death) and the Roxburghe Club (research in early English literature). In 1864 Furnivall founded the Early English Text Society (Ruskin and Tennyson were charter subscribers) which has performed invaluable service in printing the texts of medieval mss. In 1868 he founded the Chaucer Society, which published extensive 14th-century material. Furnivall also founded the New Shakspere Society (with Browning as first president), the Ballad Society, the Wyclif Society, the Shelley Society, and the Browning Society. Probably no other scholar has individually contributed so much to the stimulation of precise examination and scholarly study of English literature.

Sir **James Augustus Henry Murray** (1837–1915). James A. H. Murray was born at Denholm, Scotland, and because of his studious ability he rose to be headmaster in nearby Hawick grammar school at the age of twenty. His wife's ill-health forced him to move to London, where he taught at Mill Hill School and received his B.A. from London University (1873). His philological articles caused him in 1879 to be placed in charge of the new dictionary compilation. His death came before he could see the final installments of his giant task.

A New English Dictionary on Historical Principles sprang from the Philological Society proposal in 1857, apparently on the suggestion of Furnivall, who served as editor and chief compiler from 1861 until Murray took over in 1879. Actually, thousands of readers throughout the British Isles and the United States contributed over eight million slips from which the work was assembled. The first installment (A to Ant) appeared in 1884, the concluding installments (Wo–Wy) in 1928. This dictionary attempts to list every word and every sense of every word ever used in English. The earliest ascertainable appearance of a word meaning is noted, and then quotations of subsequent appearances are cited up to the present (quotations amount to about 1,800,000). The exhaustiveness of this dictionary may be indicated by the word *set,* which occupies over eighteen pages of small print in three columns and is analyzed into 154 main divisions; the last division, *set up,* is broken down into forty-four subdivisions. Since 1895 installments have borne the title *Oxford English Dictionary,* the label frequently used today. Many, however, still call it "Murray's dictionary."

The supplement in 1933 dramatically indicates the alteration of English within a few decades. The first installment in 1884 does not possess such a commonplace word as *allergy* (first noted in 1913) and has no knowledge of *addict* in the sense of someone habitually using narcotics (first noted in 1909). Future supplements will undoubtedly maintain this work as the world's crowning piece of linguistic scholarship.

LITERARY PERIODICALS

The Victorian period represents the high-water mark of English periodical writings. As noted throughout the chapters discussing this age, many significant English writings first appeared in contemporary magazines. In the year 1859 an incredible total of 115 periodicals started in London alone. The first issue of the *Cornhill* in the next year sold 110,000 copies. Periodicals provided the chief vehicle of communication in the age preceding 20th-century mass media. Newspapers engrossed only moderate attention until the 1890s instituted the sensational press ("Yellow Journalism"), which provided reading matter for the universal reading public created by the National Education Act of 1870.

The important periodicals appeared mostly as monthlies, weeklies, and reviews brought out quarterly. *Punch,* the oldest surviving humor magazine in English, was begun in 1841, and some famous magazines that began in the Romantic era continued in full strength (*The Edinburgh Review* and *Blackwood's Magazine*). *Athenaeum* (1828–1921) established a century-long reputation for critical excellence and progressive independence. To show the enormous role played by these periodicals in disseminating 19th-century literature and thought, an issue of *The Fortnightly Review* (1865–1954) chosen at random, the November 1874 issue, contains a scientific essay by Huxley, Shakespearean criticism by Pater, a poem by Swinburne, and an installment of Meredith's *Beauchamp's Career.*

Chapter 4

Victorian Drama

THE NINETEENTH-CENTURY THEATER

The Theatre Act of 1843 is perhaps the most important event in English theatrical history since the Restoration. The monopoly of London drama granted to Covent Garden and Drury Lane by the Act of 1737 was at last broken, and the modern theater was free to develop. Although the way was now open for the Second Renaissance of the English theater, it had fifty more years to wait, chiefly because of the mind-set of the Victorian audience.

Most of the expansion permitted by the Theatre Act of 1843 was devoted to a popular clientele, roughly equivalent to today's mass moviegoers— lower middle class and some of the working classes. For these viewers the Victorian stage provided countless melodramas, all stamped from the same mold.

(1) Suspenseful plot. Characterization was wholly subordinated to exciting conflict.

(2) Pseudo-realism. Settings were contemporary, suggesting that romantic excitement lurked beneath the everyday world.

(3) Stereotyped figures. Valiant seamen, virtuous shopgirls, and cruel mortgage holders all inhabit the world of melodrama, which is black and white without shadings.

(4) Sentimentalism. By definition, melodrama is based on excitement and sympathy purely for their own sake.

(5) Naïve moral concepts. The virtuous are always munificently rewarded and the villainous always taste the bitterness of their just punishment.

The origins of the melodrama can be found in the 18th century, partly in the native English tradition demonstrated by "Monk" Lewis, and partly in the French *boulevard* theaters with plays by dramatists like Pixerécourt ("the Corneille of Melodrama"). Even though many 19th-century melodramas were translations from the French, the genre was completely domesticated.

The fashionable Victorian theater-goer belonged to the upper middle class and made theater attendance a badge of social prestige. Until the wartime relaxation after 1914, this class attended evening performances in formal garb, to see and to be seen. Appreciating elegant magnificence, it was treated by Victorian stage directors to probably the most sumptuous Shakespearean stagings in theatrical history. It expected acting in the grand manner, elevated even in comedy above the prosiness of everyday. Great actors abounded throughout the era from Edmund Kean to Sir Henry Irving, the first English actor to be knighted.

Nonetheless, the modern theater was being born in Victoria's age. At her accession London had only two legitimate theaters and a total of less than a score of houses offering some sort of acting. By 1899 there were sixty-one theaters in London. At Victoria's accession theaters maintained a steady glare of light throughout a performance; by 1850 today's practice of darkened theater during performance had become standard. W. C. Macready and Charles Kean introduced in the 1840s the limelight that since has passed from the stage to become a cliché. The arc light came in the 1870s and the incandescent bulb in the 1890s. Today's picture stage, replacing the former wing-and-backdrop, was apparently introduced in 1841 for *London Assurance,* Dion Boucicault's most successful play. Henceforth audiences would regularly expect upon the stage the three unbroken walls surrounding normal house furnishings, and at about the same time Macready enforced the modern fidelity to historical stage settings. Macready was also one of the leaders along with Robertson in originating today's stage director. By the 1870s the director had fully emerged as the dominator of the actors in giving shape and interpretation to the drama. The rise of the director to supremacy during this era is probably the most significant single contribution to stage history by the Victorian theater. However, it must be kept in mind that only in the 20th century has directing become a separate profession. In earlier times the author or more generally the leading actor (actor-manager in the 19th century) fulfilled the task of directing the play.

The Victorian theater established the "well-made play" that has essentially endured as staple theatrical fare until the present. The *pièce-bien-faite* was created by Augustin Eugène Scribe (1791–1861), a French playwright who from 1815 on produced several hundred plays by formula. Staunchly middle class, Scribe reacted against the formlessness of romantic drama and inaugurated a clever, financially sound manipulation of a few characters. The "well-made play" carefully follows these patterns:

(1) Characters generally from the upper middle class. Outside of a few minor servant roles, four to eight parts are specified, each character essential to plot and equipped with an approximately equal number of lines.

(2) Simple plot concentrated upon one problem, usually love and marriage. "Logic of events" controls the structure. The playwright's skill is demonstrated by his tying of the characters into an apparently hopeless knot from which he smoothly extricates them. Neat foreshadowing convinces the viewer of the utter rightness of the solution. Scribe insisted upon a threefold statement of every important fact: first, for the intelligent and attentive; second for the intelligent and inattentive; third, for the unintelligent and inattentive.

(3) Authentic contemporary settings and costumes, luring the fashionable audience to believe that its own life and problems are being delineated.

(4) Dialogue simulating upper-middle-class speech but free of the slurrings, garblings, or fragments of everyday conversation.

The playwrights of this era are very much precursors of the modern theater. The four who will be discussed here are Thomas William Robertson, Henry Arthur Jones, Sir Arthur Wing Pinero, and Oscar Wilde. (The article on Wilde covers not only his plays but also his writings in other forms.)

Thomas William Robertson (1829–1871). Thomas William Robertson was to born a theatrical family at Newark-on-Trent. As a child actor in his father's company he picked up only a smattering of formal education. From 1848 he was an actor in smaller London houses, doing minor writing on the side. With *Society* (1865) he began a series of highly successful dramas that continued until his death.

Robertson, the first really significant English dramatist after Sheridan, is the first truly modern playwright in English. As a man of the theater turned dramatist, he made a twofold contribution. For stage history he was the first stickler for complete contemporary stage realism, so that the Green Room smiled at his preoccupation with "doorknobs." Gilbert ascribed to Robertson the beginning of modern stage direction. Robertson introduced the "well-made play" and endowed it with a serious central theme. His Victorian sentimentality did not detract from the successful London revivals of *Caste* in 1946 and 1947, which demonstrated that Robertson's innovations have become the accepted patterns of today's English drama.

Caste (1867) is one of the most representative of Robertson's works. The Marquise de St. Maur attempts to break up the marriage of her son, the Honorable George D'Alroy, to the dancing girl, Esther Eccles. George's burdens are increased by a vulgar, drunken father-in-law, the elder Eccles, and by a vulgar, jolly sister-in-law, Polly Eccles, with her cockney beau, Sam Gerridge. The dowager noblewoman is finally brought around by her baby grandson; and Captain Hawtree, George's sophisticated friend, sends old Eccles to Jersey where he may drink himself to death.

Hawtree dashingly enunciates the drama's problem: the incompatibility of marriage partners from different levels of society. Robertson's frequently proclaimed retort is that "true hearts are more than coronets." Each of the eight acting roles is sharply individualized and equally developed though Wilde branded the Marquise as a "monster without being a myth." Old Eccles, the stock drunk, is the one genuine holdover from earlier forms of drama. The dialogue marks an impressive advance in simulating contemporary speech patterns.

Henry Arthur Jones (1851–1929). Henry Arthur Jones was the son of a tenant farmer at Grandborough, Buckinghamshire. After village schooling to the age of twelve, he worked in a draper's shop (dry-goods), and from 1869 to 1879 was a commercial traveler. Successful playwrighting, at first as an avocation, permitted him after 1881 to devote his time entirely to the theater. His dramatic achievements won him an honorary degree from Harvard University in 1907. He became almost equally prominent as a lecturer and analyst of the contemporary theater. Attracted to socialism in his earlier years, he ended as a rabid Tory, spending the last decade of his life denouncing all "radical" ideas in government.

Literary historians of the 20th century have held it against Jones that he started as a melodramatist and that he interspersed his serious plays with flashy box-office attractions. He has been overshadowed by the greater wit of Wilde and the greater genius of Shaw. Nonetheless, he was the first modern English dramatist to seek a high literary place for his plays (Robertson was strictly a man of the theater). Jones led the fight for international copyright, a national theater subsidized by the state, and the removal of censorship. The Berne (Switzerland) Convention of 1886 realized his first project. Disagreement about details among English theatrical and literary men thwarted his hopes for a state theater. Although unsuccessful in his struggle to eliminate censorship, Jones did effect a notable relaxation. For all writers Jones demanded the same "freedom of treatment . . . allowed to the Bible and to Shakespeare." By his commissioning of William Morris to create the sets for *The Crusaders* (1891), Jones inaugurated the modern art of stage design.

Saints and Sinners (1884) has often been termed the "first modern serious drama" by the intelligentsia, for this is the first play to strike out at Victorianism. The drama might have been run off the stage if Arnold had not risen to its support.

Jacob Fletcher, minister of Bethel Chapel, Steepleford, refuses to preach against the co-operative store which endangers the grocery business of his sanctimonious parishioner, Samuel Hoggard. Irked by the narrowness of small-town evangelicalism, the minister's daughter Letty permits herself to be seduced by the sprightly Captain Eustace Fanshawe. Hoggard uses the scandal as a lever to pry Fletcher out of his position, and Letty dies miserably (original ending). A happy outcome was later supplied by having the sturdy farmer, George Kingsmill, make Letty an honest woman.

Though sentimental and melodramatic, the play is the theater's opening attack against the deadening morality and hypocritical respectability frequently characteristic of Victorian evangelicalism. Hoggard exemplifies Jones's theme of the shocking difference between the bourgeois profession of religion and the actual practice. Arnold praised the play because "by strokes of this kind faith in the middle-class fetish is weakened."

Michael and His Lost Angel (1896) was regarded by Jones as his masterpiece. Because of the vehement protests over a wholly secular scene staged in a church and a clergyman portrayed as an adulterer, the play when first performed lasted only ten days in London and eleven nights in New York.

The Reverend Michael Faversham, taking vows of celibacy as an Anglo-Catholic priest, compels Rose Andrew, a parishioner, to confess her illegitimate child to the assembled congregation. Michael's dearest project is the restoration of the ruined church. The wealthy Audrie Lesden, whom he considers frivolous and flighty, makes a large donation and forces her attentions upon him. Michael in agony retires for contemplation to St. Decuman's island where Audrie appears and spends the night with him in the shrine. He confesses his sin before the congregation and flees to Italy. There Audrie pursues him to die in his arms.

Even for moribund Victorianism the theme that earthly love can overpower the most fervent of spiritual love and moral conviction was too strong. Shaw suggested that instead of his excruciating penance, Michael should have proclaimed the new-found glory of love. Although it comes close to success, the play misses because Jones lacked the poetic intensity for tragedy.

Sir **Arthur Wing Pinero** (pi-nēr'ō) (1855–1934). Of Portuguese Jewish extraction, Arthur Wing Pinero was the son of a London attorney. Initially studying law, he turned to acting at nineteen. By 1882 he was able to devote his entire time to writing farces and sentimental comedies, but his literary reputation rests upon a set of serious dramas beginning with *The Profligate* (1889). In 1909 he became the first playwright to be knighted solely for dramatic writing.

Pinero was the best craftsman in 19th-century English drama. He brought the "well-made play" to its epitome, but he followed Ibsen, at a distance, by injecting social issues and genuine contemporary problems. Unlike Jones, he accepted current mores without protest and let the audience depart, certain that its cherished beliefs were sound. Today's successful revivals of Pinero demonstrate that, like Robertson, he was primarily of the theater rather than of literature. Among his works are such plays as *Trelawny of the Wells* (1878), *Iris* (1901), and *Mid-Channel* (1909).

The Second Mrs. Tanqueray (1893) still remains the most deft treatment of a much-belabored theatrical theme: can a woman with a past obtain a respected position in polite society?

Aubrey Tanqueray, a handsome widower of forty-two and London's most eligible man, marries Paula, an ex-courtesan of twenty-seven. Paula is snubbed by local society and by Ellean, Aubrey's nineteen-year-old convent-bred daughter by his first marriage. Entrusted to Mrs. Cortelyou, Ellean proceeds to Paris where she becomes engaged to Captain Ardale, a former lover of Paula. Feeling duty-bound to reveal Ardale's character, Paula is scathingly denounced by Ellean. After Paula commits suicide, Ellean sobs down the curtain: "I helped to kill her. If I'd only been merciful!"

Pinero assures his viewers that their conviction is true—the marriage of a demimondaine and an honorable gentleman is doomed to failure in spite of his perfect solicitude and her complete reformation. The play's perennial stage success rests upon the dramatist's superb skill in giving the sense of easy, natural realism to every plot development, even to the coincidence of a stepdaughter falling in love with her stepmother's old flame. Verisimilitude, preparation, and economy are blended to produce the model of the well-made play.

Oscar Fingal O'Flahertie Wills Wilde (1856–1900). Oscar Wilde was the son of a distinguished Dublin physician, Sir William Wilde, and Jane Francisca Elgee, a poetess who under the pseudonym of "Speranza" wrote fervent pleas for Irish self-government. Oscar proceeded from a brilliant student career at Trinity College, Dublin, to even greater brilliance at Magdalen College, Oxford. In 1878 he won the Newdigate prize for poetry and first-class honors in classics. Ruskin influenced the undergraduate, but Pater was his idol. Proceeding to London, Wilde emulated the painter Whistler in posing as an eccentric genius. His bizarre get-up (velvet jackets and knee breeches accompanied by gilded lilies), taste (for sunflowers and peacock feathers), and conversation (intoning "Nothing succeeds like excess") made him notorious before he ever published a book and invited sallies from *Punch* and Gilbert and Sullivan (*Patience*, 1881).

He displayed the same Wildisms before Americans in 1882. His marriage in 1884 was the society spectacle of the year. For the first half of the 1890s he sparkled as England's wittiest conversationalist and its most talked-about writer. The blow fell in 1895 with his conviction on the charge of homosexuality, chiefly with Lord Alfred Douglas. After two agonizing years in Reading Gaol (American *jail*) he fled to France under the alias of Sebastian Melmoth (St. Sebastian was martyred by arrows, which appear on English prison garb; Melmoth was the wanderer of

Charles Robert Maturin's novel). Wilde was converted to Roman Catholicism just before his death.

Among English men of letters only Byron and Shaw have surpassed Wilde in the craft of conscious posing and self-publicizing; with all three the legends have substantially improved upon the reality. Friend and foe alike took Wilde for the consummate exemplar of aestheticism, but after his disgrace he was cast into darkness, many discussions of literature ignoring him altogether. The 20th century's antipathy to Victorianism and its open-handed treatment of perversion have often worked together to bring Wilde to a kind of martyrdom. From our present perspective it is at last possible to evaluate Wilde as the capable literary artist he actually was.

DRAMAS. In the guise of "the well-made play," Wilde's dramas restore to the theater the sparkling comedy of manners which had been unknown since the time of Sheridan; Wilde is actually closer to the Restoration dramatists than is any other subsequent playwright.

Lady Windermere's Fan (1892), praised today almost solely for its epigrammatic wit, supports the anti-Victorian contention that right and wrong are purely relative terms and that moral compromise is essential.

The puritanical Lady Windermere quarrels with her husband because of his attentions to the much more mature Mrs. Erlynne. Lady Windermere does not know that she is actually Mrs. Erlynne's daughter, abandoned as an infant. Lord Windermere's secret assistance to Mrs. Erlynne causes the piqued Lady Windermere to flee to a lover, Lord Darlington. Mrs. Erlynne destroys Lady Windermere's farewell note to Lord Windermere and dashes to Darlington's quarters, where she persuades Lady Windermere to return to her husband. Lord Windermere, accompanying Darlington to the latter's room, finds his wife's fan on the floor. Mrs. Erlynne claims that she took the fan by mistake and lets it appear that she was keeping a rendezvous with Darlington. Mrs. Erlynne marries Lord Lawton, stipulating that they shall live outside of England.

"There is a bitter irony in things, a bitter irony in the way we talk of good and bad women. . . . Oh, what a lesson!" muses Lady Windermere, the "good" woman saved by the sacrifice of the "bad" woman. Wilde rather crudely underlines his theme because his genuine interest lies both in the witty delineation of an elegant *fin de siècle* society and in displaying his scintillating epigrams. Darlington is given most of the brilliant remarks in his Wildean role as commentator upon high society. The coldly calculated arrangement for the marriage of her daughter to an eligible bachelor by the Duchess of Berwick shows a realistic touch in contrast to the two romantic triangles.

The Importance of Being Earnest (1895) has proved the most durable English drama of the 19th century. Wilde termed it "A Trivial Comedy for Serious People" and asserted: "The first act is ingenious, the second beautiful, the third abominably clever."

As a cover-up for holidaying, John Worthing invents a dissolute younger brother Ernest who compels John to leave his ward Cecily in Hertfordshire and go up to London. Jack's friend, Algernon Moncrieff, has invented an imaginary invalid, Bunbury, which he uses as an excuse to get away from London. Jack proposes to Algy's cousin, Gwendolyn, who is enamored of the name Ernest, supposedly Jack's name. Algy is accepted by Cecily, who thinks he is Ernest, Jack's younger brother. Both young men decide to be rechristened, but Jack turns out to be Algy's long-lost brother, abandoned as a baby in a handbag in Victoria station—and his actual name is Ernest.

(1) The play's lasting appeal arises from some of the most brilliant dialogue of the English stage. Even where irrelevant to the plot, Wilde's wit dazzles.

(2) Only Pope's "Rape of the Lock" can match this work in dexterously maintaining a rococo atmosphere with no obvious intrusion of the serious. Underlying both works, however, is an implied denunciation of a frivolous, vacuous high society.

(3) Wildely burlesquing the clichés of the farce, the drama reduces to inanity all the stock features of coincidence, mistaken identity, and incredible dénouement. The master of comedy of manners for the last century and a half neatly scores the theater for its long trough of weak comic farce. H. G. Wells recognized this satire as the play's real forte.

Wilde wrote two other comedies, *A Woman of No Importance* (1893) and *An Ideal Husband* (1894).

Salomé (Paris 1893) was written in French by Wilde in 1891; the English translation of 1894 is by Lord Alfred Douglas. The world première with Sarah Bernhardt in the title role occurred in Paris in 1896. First London performance in 1905 was "private"; the public ban was not lifted until 1932. The New York Metropolitan Opera forbade the operatic version, with music by Richard Strauss, until 1934. The original account of Salomé appears in Matthew 14 and Mark 6, but Wilde is chiefly indebted to the operatic version by Massenet (1881) and the novelistic version by Flaubert (1887). The atmosphere owes much to Baudelaire and Huysmans.

Herodiade, Salomé's mother, divorces Herod Philip to marry his brother, Herod Antipater, governor of Judea. John the Baptist (Iakanaan) scathingly denounces the remarriage and is imprisoned by Herod Antipater. Salomé, attracted by the prophet, continues her unsuccessful attempts to seduce John even when her thwarted lover, Narraboth, commits suicide in her presence. Salomé performs the "dance of the seven veils" before her entranced stepfather, who as reward offers her whatever she wishes. Herodiade's bidding and her own rage at the moral prophet induce Salomé to demand John's head on a silver platter. As Salomé rapturously kisses the lips of the severed head, Herod nods and his soldiers crush her to death under their shields.

Wilde's addition to the account is the towering lust of the virgin Salomé. No other work in English so epitomizes perverted lusts, its characters representing not human beings but passions incarnate. The high-pitched emotions of this play, its atmosphere of Byzantine violence, and its somber brooding over evil create something utterly alien and unique in English drama. The language kindles also a unique hypnotic effect of lush, ripened sin in the most intoxicating passages Wilde ever wrote. This is the supreme example of *fin de siècle* decadence in English.

SHORT STORIES AND NOVEL. Some critics believe that Wilde's best work appears in the short narratives of *The Happy Prince and Other Tales* (1888) and *A House of Pomegranates* (1891); certainly Wilde proves himself the ablest teller of fairy tales in English, with Andrew Lang a distant second. His one novel, *The Picture of Dorian Gray,* is a masterpiece of its kind.

While supposedly intended for children, Wilde's short tales have proved even more attractive to adults. The earlier volume has a deceptively simple style, wholly appropriate to the genre. The later volume is sensuously decorated with jewels, flowers, fruits, etc. Until his imprisonment Wilde considered "The Young King" from the 1891 volume his best work. Another famous story from this book is "The Birthday of the Infanta."

The Picture of Dorian Gray (1891) had its idea of an aging portrait and an unaging man suggested to Wilde by the painter, Basil Ward, who appears in the novel as Basil Hallward. Though unnamed, "the yellow book" which Dorian reads in the novel is *À Rebours* by Huysmans. This "poisonous book" strongly affected Wilde.

Dorian Gray half in jest expresses the wish that he might remain young and handsome and that his portrait by Hallward age instead. The miracle occurs, while Dorian is tempted to wild debauchery by the sophisticated Lord Henry Wotton. Dorian abandons a lovely young actress, Sibyl Vane, who in despair commits suicide, and the deeper he plunges into vice, the fouler the portrait becomes, but Dorian himself appears outwardly unchanged. Attempting to reform him, Hallward persuades Dorian to reveal the hidden portrait, is horrified at the hideous figure on canvas, and is slain by Dorian. James Vane, Sibyl's brother, and Alan Campbell, a chemist who helped dispose of Hallward's body, meet violent deaths. Dorian in rage stabs the painting with the knife that killed Hallward. Servants find the picture as their master always looked, but on the floor with a dagger in its breast is the dead body of a foul debauchee.

Wilde admitted that all three major characters were self-portraits. Hallward represents conventional morality; Lord Henry, aesthetic contemplation untroubled by desire or conscience; Dorian, cynical hedonism. Tempting is the psychoanalytic interpretation of Dorian as Wilde's Id, driven to self-destruction by too literal an application of aestheticism from Wilde's Ego, Lord Henry; the Super-Ego, Hallward, is killed when he remonstrates against Dorian's craving for sensuality. Pater saw the novel's moral as the platonic concept of an ugly soul forming an ugly body. Moralists, led by Henley, excoriated the volume, and the prosecution quoted extensively from the novel at Wilde's trial.

VERSE. Wilde's poetry from his first published volume in 1881 until his incarceration belongs to the aesthetic school, in which Dowson and Symons were probably his superiors.

The Ballad of Reading Gaol (1898), written in France in 1897, is his greatest poem. "C.3.3" was Wilde's identification number in Reading prison. The poem's central subject is Charles Thomas Wooldridge, formerly a trooper in the Blue Royal House Guards, who was executed during Wilde's imprisonment because he murdered his wife in a fit of jealousy. The theme of the work is society's cruelty in inflicting of punishment without understanding. The greatest pain is the one the wrongdoer suffers within himself. There is a clear indebtedness to Coleridge's "Rime of the Ancient Mariner," Thomas Hood's "Eugene Aram," and A. E. Housman's "Shropshire Lad." Except for the implacable Henley, the English critics generously praised the poem.

PROSE. *De Profundis* ("From the depths") was Wilde's sole literary writing in prison (*1897*). The title was given by Wilde's literary executor; Wilde originally termed this extensive letter to Lord Alfred Douglas *Epistola: In Carcere et Vinculis* ("Letter in prison and fetters"). It is his only truly serious and sincere prose. The earlier portion is bitter self-justification and recrimination against Lord Alfred Douglas, but the latter part achieves resignation. Wilde asserts that suffering is a greater teacher than prosperity, sorrow more noble than joy, humility more godlike than pride.

Chapter 5

The Victorian Novel

The Victorian reading public firmly established the novel as the dominant literary form of the era. Virtually the entire literate population consisted of novel-readers. Spencer, that rigorous apostle of science, excepted George Eliot's works from his general condemnation of "mere" novels; Newman and Arnold were avid readers of fiction; and Darwin stated in his *Autobiography* that to him novels were "a wonderful relief and pleasure." Carlyle, however, dourly excluded the novelist from the category of the hero as writer. Amazingly, Tennyson compared the novel to verse drama and gave it higher rating: "I am of the opinion that if a man were endowed with such faculties as Shakespeare's, they would be more freely and effectively exercised in prose fiction with its wider capabilities than when 'cribbed, cabined, and confined' in the trammels of verse." Certainly the novel may well be termed the most distinctive and lasting literary achievement of Victorian literature.

At the outset of the Victorian period no one, except possibly Thackeray, considered the novel a significant art form. By 1853, however, Clough, writing in the *North American Review,* recognized that cultured readers had turned their attention from poetry to the novel. By the century's end the novel had completely triumphed over poetry as aesthetic and spiritual nourishment for English readers. The novel by this time claimed writing talents that in earlier eras would have developed elsewhere—Meredith and Hardy who were essentially poets, Gissing and Wells who were essentially essayists.

Scott had created a large novel-reading public and had made novel-reading respectable. He was also responsible for strengthening the tradition of the three-volume novel and for kiting the price up to one-and-a-half guineas. Publication of novels in monthly installments, especially those of Dickens, enabled even the poor (often pooling their pennies) to purchase novels. Both the three-volume and installment formats encouraged novelists to be diffuse and picaresque. Henry James toward the century's close was chiefly responsible for the "well-made" novel, substituting for the lengthy, rambling Victorian form a more compact novel with a handful of characters working out one clearly defined problem.

THE NOVEL OF VICTORIAN ORTHODOXY

Below are listed some of the major reasons for the spectacular success of the Victorian bourgeois novel.

(1) The English novel originated as a middle-class genre, and it was the logical reading matter for the triumphant 19th-century bourgeoisie.

(2) Unburdened by tradition or status, the novel was flexible, and hence adaptable to the portrayal of the multitude of changing situations in Victorian life.

(3) Escapism had become a psychological necessity to an era bedeviled by chaotic industrialism.

(4) Realism was the ostensible justification for the conscious reader as escapism was the actual satisfier of his unconscious needs. Just as Defoe had earlier beguiled his middle-class readers with the pretense of genuine reportage, so the Victorian novelists appealed to their audience with the semblance of the real world.

(5) The earnest Victorians sought and found in contemporary novels instruction for living amid bewildering complexity and change. Novelists made sense out of the enormous variety of choices and experiences.

(6) The novel assumed for the 19th century the mission fulfilled in earlier eras by the epic: formulation of the "myth" of the age. There was no Spenser or Milton to perform such a task in verse for the Victorian age. The most ambitious attempt to do this in verse was Tennyson's somewhat pallid *Idylls of the King,* and any casual novel reader can name a score of Victorian novels of far greater myth-making power.

The outstanding characteristics of the bourgeois novel were:

(1) Acceptance of middle-class ethics and mores. The "good" characters conform to principles of bourgeois orthodoxy and are properly rewarded.

(2) Social orientation. The major human problem treated by the bourgeois novelists is the adjustment of the individual to his society.

(3) Emphasis upon characters. The bourgeois novelists strove to produce fascinating, rounded characters who resembled people their readers knew or would like to know. Most characters were middle class, in middle-class settings, and with the typical middle-class preoccupations, even in "historical" novels. Their complexity was almost wholly emotional. Lower-class

figures were subordinate, usually treated patronizingly. Upper-class personages were viewed with a mixture of envy and scorn.

(4) The hero. The central figure, though demonstrating human weaknesses, is molded to the bourgeois ideal of the rational man of virtue.
Human nature is believed to be fundamentally good, and lapses from the
bourgeois code are errors of immature judgment which are corrected by
maturation.

THE NOVELS OF DICKENS

Charles John Huffam Dickens (1812–1870). Charles Dickens was the
grandson of a footman and a maid. His father, a minor government clerk,
consistently lived beyond his income. From the birth of the novelist at
Landport, family fortunes grew increasingly worse, and the deprivations
and insecurity of his childhood colored the entire lifetime and writings of
Dickens. In 1824 the elder Dickens was thrown in Marshalsea Prison for
failure to pay his debts, and Charles had to drudge in a factory making
shoe blacking. His formal schooling ending at fifteen in 1827, the novelist
became a legal reporter and in 1831 a political reporter. Meanwhile his
first love affair fizzled out, as Maria Beadnell and her parents saw no prospects for the poor youth. His first literary pieces, published sporadically in
periodicals between 1833 and 1835, were collected in 1836 as *Sketches by
Boz* (*Boz*, a family nickname for his youngest brother, was a childish corruption of *Moses*). The success of *Pickwick Papers* induced him to marry
Catherine Hogarth in 1836. His sister-in-law, Mary Hogarth, came to live
with the married couple and induced in Dickens the first of his attachments
to other women; he was desolate at her sudden death soon after. Another
sister-in-law, Georgina, lived in Dickens' home from 1842 until his death.
Meanwhile he wrote prodigiously, often keeping more than one novel
going in separate monthly installments or in his own periodicals, *Master
Humphrey's Clock* (1840–41), *Household Words* (1850–59), and *All the
Year Round* (1859–95).

His American tour in 1842 was highly successful, but his severe criticisms
of the United States in *American Notes* (1842) elicited shrill protests from
Americans. Dickens' readings and actor-manager roles in private theatricals suggest that he might have enjoyed a spectacular career upon the
stage. Now well-to-do, the Dickens family traveled extensively between
Catherine's regular childbirths (ten altogether). Dickens was the first editor
(1846) of the *Daily News*, followed by Forster, his lifelong friend and
biographer. In 1856 Dickens purchased Gadshill Place, a Kentish mansion
that he had longed for when a child. In the next year he met an actress,
Ellen Lawless Ternan, who was largely responsible for the separation of
Dickens from his wife in 1858. The novelist's fiery energy and drive for

wealth resulted in a triumphant reading tour of the United States in 1867–68, clearing £20,000. His heart weakened by his nervousness and great exertions, Dickens died at Gadshill in 1870 and was buried at Westminster Abbey.

No other writer in English history, not even Shakespeare, so engrossed the attention of his age. At least one out of every ten persons in the English-speaking world had read him or had heard his novels read. No other novelist in English has had such complete success with readers from the highest to the lowest members of society. To his contemporaries he was the master of sentiment, even the dour Carlyle was moved and even the ferocious critic Jeffrey shamelessly wept for Little Nell. Victorians also admired him as a militant reformer, but his popularity arose from his denunciation of specific ills that everybody hated and his advocacy of improvements that everybody supported. Even the most devastating attacks by Dickens upon contemporary society are primarily aimed not against bourgeois ideals but against the failure of men to live up to those ideals. His success sprang too from the romantic treatment of characters within realistic settings (since used in many best sellers).

With the 20th century, Dickensian reform is a dead issue, and his sentimentality often cloys. Critics have also flayed his sloppy style, his frequent lapses of taste and judgment, his lamentable weakness in structure. His continuing stature rests upon:

(1) Fantastic fertility in character creation. Dickens gave English literature an enormous gallery of living characters. Although often labeled "caricatures," his people possess a vivacity as great as life itself.

(2) The depiction of childhood and youth. Perhaps from Victorian taboos, emotional underdevelopment, and the ineradicable impressions of his childhood, Dickens could not really work himself into the adult mind as Browning could; but his entry into the very fiber of David Copperfield and Pip is unmatched elsewhere in world literature.

(3) Robust comic creation. Reading Dickens in Polish translation, the youthful Joseph Conrad far away on the continent was transported with laughter and given the first impulse to a literary career.

(4) Unconscious artistry. When Dickens worked consciously, he was an excellent inventor; but when he drew on unconscious sources, he proved a literary genius. Today's evaluation of Dickens sees him at his best in archetypal symbols that gripped his readers without their or his actual comprehension of his wizardry. His novels falter when, as in *Dombey and Son,* Dickens had to think his way through; but when, as generally, he wrote in a frenzy as though possessed, his characters enact symbolic roles as old as the race and as deeply ingrained in the psyche.

THE EARLY NOVELS. The best-liked works of Dickens are still the huge canvases of his earlier period. Glorious humor generally irradiates this period, as the novelist confidently believes that common sense and good will are the only requirements for successful living. Social criticism is chiefly of individual evils and specific character traits.

The Pickwick Papers (1836–37) arose from the desire of the publishers Chapman and Hall to compete with the very successful hunting accounts of Surtees. Emphasis was placed upon the illustrations of coaching, inn-life, and sport by Robert Seymour with the text by the young reporter Dickens. The suicide of Seymour before the publication of the second number left Dickens free to develop the account as he pleased.

The pleasure tours of the Pickwick Club (Samuel Pickwick, perpetual president) permit a picaresque string of sparkling encounters. A jaunt to Rochester involves saving Miss Wardle from the rascally Mr. Jingle. The novel definitely improves when Pickwick meets Sam Weller, the cockney bootblack of the White Hart Inn. Weller's homey wit and unshakable presence of mind thereafter extricate the Pickwickians from many a scrape. But the toils of the law thwart even the redoubtable Sam Weller. Pickwick is found guilty of breach of promise in a trumped up case by his landlady Mrs. Bardell. Refusing to pay, Pickwick is thrown into Fleet Prison whence Mrs. Bardell also goes when she cannot pay her scoundrelly lawyers, Dodgson and Fogg. To reconcile Mr. Allen to the marriage of his daughter to Mr. Winkle, Pickwick pays his fines and is free. Miss Wardle is properly married to Mr. Snodgrass. Pickwick dissolves the club and retires to the country, interrupting a quiet life only to be godfather to little Winkles and Snodgrasses.

Pickwick Papers is the despair of critics and the eternal delight of readers. What started as a waggish parody of 18th-century picaresque adventure blossoms out as a panoramic novel. With awesome creativity Dickens tosses out about three hundred characters, many of whom (like the immortal Fat Boy) appear and disappear as bewilderingly as foam flecks of the sea. The Pickwickians begin as silly butts and end up as valorous supporters of their imprisoned leader, where the joyous radiance of the earlier chapters is blackened in the squalor and filth of the prison. The characters are old comic stand-bys, but Dickens charges these clichés with a wild fantasy and an infectious gusto. André Maurois correctly diagnoses the novel's fundamental appeal: "A whole picture of rural England rose up, a very eighteenth century and rural England, alive with that sort of child-like delight which the English take in simple pleasures, the enjoyment of roaring fires on the hearth, sliding in snowy weather, a good dinner, and simple, rather absurd love-affairs."

Oliver Twist (1837–39) abandons the sunny landscapes of *Pickwick Papers* for the seamy, squalid city and the essentially picaresque narrative for wild melodrama.

Bumble, the bullying official of a workhouse, gives the name Oliver Twist to a child born by a dying, destitute woman. Horrified when the half-starved Oliver asks for more of the watery gruel, officials apprentice him to a harsh casket-maker from whom the lad escapes to London. Picked up by Jack Dawkins (nicknamed The Artful Dodger), Oliver is snared by old Fagin, who trains urchins as thieves. On the first mission, trying to pick the pocket of Mr. Brownlow, Oliver is caught but rescued by his intended victim. The gang recaptures Oliver and, led by the vicious Bill Sikes, breaks into the house of Mrs. Maylie. Wounded Oliver is befriended by the Maylies. Nancy, girl friend of Sikes, tries to help Oliver (whose real enemy is Monks, Oliver's elder brother, who wants the boy eliminated), but Nancy is murdered by Bill. In trying to escape pursuing police, Sikes accidentally hangs himself. Fagin is apprehended and executed. Monks flees to America. Oliver is revealed as the son of a gentleman, Edward Leeford, the best friend of Mr. Brownlow. Rose Maylie, the adopted daughter of Mrs. Maylie, is actually his aunt. Adopted by Mr. Brownlow, Oliver now turns to a life of happiness and well-being.

Oliver Twist frequently elicits the stock criticisms about Dickens: bizarre plot, cloying sentimentalism, caricatures instead of characters. The plot is indeed a farrago of the unacknowledged heir, incredible coincidences (Oliver's two robberies by sheer chance involve his unknown relatives and friends), and chilling melodrama. Though caricatures, Fagin and The Artful Dodger are among the more memorable figures in English literature.

The novel's lasting achievement is the symbolic power of the dark underworld of the poor. The pitiful figure of Oliver holding out his little bowl and asking for more is an ineradicable symbol of all the needy children in the world pleading for sustenance. In such universalizing lies the magic of Dickens.

Psychologically, Oliver rings false. From infancy he knows nothing but suffering and iniquity, yet throughout he remains uncorrupted, by even that master perverter of youth, Fagin. As though he had been born possessing indestructible middle-class virtues, Oliver is untouched by the sordid world through which he moves. And Dickens, instead of solving the original problems put forward by the book, simply rescues Oliver from his hideous background.

Nicholas Nickleby (1838–39), written concurrently with *Oliver Twist*, blends the dark aspects of *Oliver Twist* with the sunny radiance of *Pickwick Papers*.

Trying to support his sister Kate, the penniless Nicholas seeks help from his miserly uncle Ralph but is rebuffed. As tutor in Dotheboys Hall, Nicholas is shocked by the treatment of the boys, especially the half-witted Smike, at the hands of Squeers, the cruel master. Nicholas thrashes Squeers and takes Smike with him and makes a living first in a theatrical company with Mr. Crummles, then in the counting house of the noble

Cheeryble brothers. Nicholas barely saves his sister from the lascivious Sir Mulbery Hawk, who was egged on by Ralph. Nicholas falls in love with Madeline Bray whom Ralph wants to marry his partner, Gride. Trying to hurt Nicholas through Smike, Ralph learns that the dying half-wit is his own son and commits suicide. Nicholas marries Madeline, and Kate marries Frank Cheeryble.

Nicholas and the plot are rather hopeless, but the astounding fertility of Dickens creates some of the most extraordinary scenes in English literature; for instance, the almost illiterate Squeers teaching English, the theatrical Mr. Crummles bidding farewell, the mad suitor conducting courtship with vegetables. The Cheerybles are intended as models of benevolent businessmen, but Aldous Huxley dismisses them as "gruesome old Peter Pans." However, this is Dickens' first attempt to fathom Victorian economy, and he sees the philanthropic manufacturer (a Cheeryble) as the constructive, good man, while the money manipulator (Ralph Nickleby) is the destructive, evil figure of contemporary capitalism.

The Old Curiosity Shop (1840–41) achieved the firmest bond between writer and reader in English literature—before its end the novel was selling 100,000 copies of each issue of *Master Humphrey's Clock,* in which it appeared.

Little Nell and her grandfather Trent live in Old Curiosity Shop, but the improvident old man gambles away the last of the money borrowed from Quilp, a nasty dwarf. Forced to wander, the tiny girl and the old man work in puppet shows and Mrs. Jarley's Wax Works, finally settling down in a small house at Tong where Nell tends the graves in a nearby churchyard. A granduncle returns from abroad to help Little Nell, but she has already died, and her grandfather soon follows her. Quilp drowns in fleeing the police. Fascinating characters include Dick Swiveller, a vivacious "card," and the diminutive maid-of-all-work, "the Marchioness."

Landor asserted that the story of Little Nell might have beguiled Desdemona of her tears. Fitzgerald was deeply affected, and Bret Harte tells of coarse, blasphemous miners in Colorado weeping over her. In the 20th century Aldous Huxley stigmatizes the "sticky overflowings" of the novel as proof of abysmal vulgarity in Dickens.

The actual theme, which so gripped thousands of readers, is that of the persecuted innocent fleeing from the wicked city of wrath and finding refuge only in death. In realistic guise it is the old allegory of virtue and beauty hounded from a dirty world that cannot appreciate them.

Barnaby Rudge (1841) stands with the *Tale of Two Cities* as Dickens' only venture into historical fiction. Its depiction of the Gordon riots of 1780 is clearly indebted to Scott's *Heart of Midlothian.*

Geoffrey Haredale, a country gentleman, feuds constantly with Sir John Chester, but the two join forces to forbid the marriage of Emma, Haredale's niece, and Edward, Chester's son. Consent is wrung from the gentle-men when Edward saves the lives of Emma and her uncle during the Gor-don riots. Barnaby Rudge, whose father murdered Haredale's brother, is innocently involved in the riots but is pardoned just before his scheduled execution.

Side characters are the most interesting, especially Dolly Varden, Dick-ens' first attempt to portray a flirtatious minx. Even more impressive than any single character is the bestial swirl and wild destruction of the riots. This is probably the first English novel to make a mass movement the central figure rather than a background. Dickens interprets the riots not primarily as "Anti-Popery" protests but as social outcries of the destitute against their economic oppressors. Chester's casting off to the gallows of his illegitimate son Hugh is symbolic of a ruling class that refuses its own offspring in its selfish exploitation. Barnaby, the Innocent Fool, emblematic of the deep inherent good in the mass spirit, is twisted and manipulated by evil plotters. The implicit warning of proletarian uprising in *Old Curiosity Shop* is here made explicit during the "hungry Forties."

Martin Chuzzlewit (1843–44) by Dickens' own statement is to "show how selfishness propagates itself and to what a great giant it may grow from small beginnings."

Wealthy old Martin Chuzzlewit, attended by his adopted daughter, Mary Graham, seems dying. His pious fraud of a cousin, Mr. Pecksniff, and his villainous nephew, Jonas, are the chief ghouls seeking his fortune. Old Mar-tin recovers, however, and the obsequious Pecksniff obeys the aged man's order to dismiss Young Martin, his grandson, who is an apprentice ar-chitect to Pecksniff. Loving Mary, Young Martin tries his fortune unsuc-cessfully in America. Back in England he finds Old Martin apparently a senile tool of Pecksniff, but Old Martin turns upon the hypocrite and makes the noble youth his heir and husband of Mary.

Dickens' family chronicle clusters about Old Martin an unattractive gal-lery of Chuzzlewit cormorants. Old Martin feels the taint upon his hoard and purposely compels Young Martin to make his own way. Young Martin's purification through exile and suffering purifies the old man's money, making it thus a vehicle for good instead of evil. In both England and America Dickens portrays the gross contradictions between democratic shibboleths and the actual tyranny of Mammon.

By almost universal admission, Pecksniff and Sairey Gamp the midwife are among the most unforgettable characters of literature. Pecksniff is mid-dle class and Sairey lower class, but both are crass cupidity masquerading as moral ideals.

A Christmas Carol (1843) was the best of the Victorian Christmas books and the most popular Christmas story of the English-speaking world.

Ebenezer Scrooge, symbol of all whose better nature has been withered by avarice, is visited by three ghosts: Christmas past (his own joyous child-hood), Christmas present (the household of Bob Cratchit, his underpaid clerk, and especially the courageous cripple, Tiny Tim), and Christmas future (the unmourned corpse and neglected tomb of Scrooge). His better nature reasserting itself, Scrooge becomes the good master, the good friend, the good man.

This modern morality makes the Christmas spirit a criticism of man's perennial selfishness and relentless competition. The sense of brotherhood should suffuse mankind. To Dickens Christmas is purely human and secular rather than supernatural, an altruistic sharing of physical goods and mortal love with all one's fellows.

Dombey and Son (1846–48) is the first Dickens novel to emerge from the nostalgic stagecoach days of his youth into the railway age of the Forties.

Indifferent to his daughter Florence, Dombey rejoices in the birth of son Paul, even though his wife dies in childbirth, for now shall be preserved "the firm of Dombey, wholesale, retail and for exportation." Shocked by his son's death, Dombey coldly marries the aristocratic Edith Skewton simply to beget another son. Irritated with her calculating husband, Edith elopes with Dombey's manager, Carker. Carker, who had effectively wrecked the Dombey firm, is run over by a railroad train. Impoverished, Dombey is cared for by Florence.

Although Dickens stated the theme as pride, the dominating concept is the inhumanity of a system that reduces everything to the power of money. Dombey is the upper-middle-class businessman whose acquisitive-ness and unbridled competition are responsible for the misery of the masses. His denial of every human affection ironically results in the destruction of everything he values. Again it is the pure love of a noble woman that re-generates him.

David Copperfield (1849–50), essentially autobiographical, is one of the best-loved novels in English. It was also Dickens' favorite of his works.

A posthumous child, David is happy with his mother and servant Peg-gotty until his mother's marriage to Mr. Murdstone. Playing with Peggotty's relative, Little Em'ly, was fun, but the tyranny of Mr. Murdstone causes David to revolt and his mother to pine away to death. Schooling at Salem House proves unpleasant, but David makes friends with Tommy Traddles and James Steerforth. Toil at his stepfather's business is relieved only by the amiable but improvident Micawber family; so David flees to his great-aunt Betsy Trotwood. Lodging with the Wickfields, David is attracted by Agnes Wickfield and repelled by Uriah Heep, Wickfield's obsequious clerk. Study-ing law under Mr. Spenlow, he falls in love with and marries Dora Spen-low. Mr. Micawber reveals the thievery of Uriah Heep and emigrates to Australia. Little Em'ly is seduced by Steerforth, who is drowned at sea.

Dora dies as David is rising in the world of journalism. Finally David, the young novelist, marries Agnes.

The most moving quality of the novel is the re-creation of childhood and youth. The security of mother love and the ecstasy of puppy love, the bitter hatred of the male parent (transformed into the stepfather Murdstone = murder + stone), the helpless fears, the animal spirits, and the strange emotional waves of the growing child have seldom elsewhere been so hauntingly evoked and poetically symbolized.

The author's reshaping of his youthful experiences tells much about Dickens' psychology. The inept, volative Micawbers are his own parents. The orphaning of David is the Lost Child theme that threads through many of his novels, indicating Dickens' bitter feeling that his parents never surrounded him with the warm security essential to childhood. Dora, the "child-wife," suggests Maria Beadnell in courtship and Kate Dickens in marriage. Agnes is wish fulfillment, perhaps with Mary or Georgina Hogarth, or more likely with an imaginary woman who would properly appreciate him and share his interests.

THE LATER NOVELS. Although the general reader has seldom been as moved by the later Dickens as by his early magic, critics of the 20th century have steadily magnified the stature of his later works. These products of Dickens' novelistic maturity consistently demonstrate a structural unity missing in the early novels; possibly the influence of Wilkie Collins can be seen in this. Dickens' social criticism moves from specific cases to the indictment of an entire society and of general defects in human character. As Thackeray aged, he became increasingly reconciled to his social background, while Dickens with the passing years progressively intensified his hostility to current society. The robust energy and fertility of Dickensian creation are now somewhat modified by a somber realization of the complex interweavings of individual greed with the terrifying forces of modern civilization. Dickens' comic view of life moves toward a tragic vision.

Bleak House (1852–53) is the first Dickens novel to achieve a carefully-knit plot with every character involved in the central problem.

In the Court of Chancery the case of Jarndyce vs. Jarndyce has become hopelessly entangled through twenty years of legal arguments. The baleful effects of the snarl have permeated all strata of society, from the sumptuous mansion of Lady Dedlock to the foul tenements of Tom-all-Alone's. In her youth Lady Dedlock had a daughter by Captain Hawdon. She believes the child dead, but, actually, Esther Summerson, ward of Mr. Jarndyce, is that daughter. The secret is discovered by lawyer Tulkinghorn from Lady Dedlock's maid. Inadequately paid for her spying, the maid kills Tulkinghorn. Lady Dedlock is found dead at her lover's grave. Detective Bucket apprehends the criminal after exhaustive search.

Bleak House is one of the most incredible *tours de force* in literature. The staid machinations of the Court of Chancery are seen infecting a huge cross section of society, and for the first time Dickens achieves the novel of the social group. The dark fog that opens the novel shrouds the entire work. Dickens had in *Pickwick Papers* excoriated the law's delays and absurdities, but here the abysmal injustice of the law is a symbol of a vaster darkness— the dead hand of the past and of vested interests that thwarts all generous and progressive elements in man. Dickens sees the human spectacle as a contest of instinctive love, liberty, growth, and health against perverted selfishness, acquisitiveness, and cruelty. In the earlier works the forces of good generally triumph, but beginning with this novel, the forces of evil often defeat the aspiring, as typified here by the destruction of Richard Carstone, nominally the young hero.

It is a moral blindness from the past which blights the present in this novel. Dickens portrays the futility of society in Sir Leicester Dedlock, a representative of decaying aristocracy, in Turveydrop, a venal dandy, in Harold Skimpole, a futile pretender to art and culture, in Chadband (another Pecksniff), a pious hypocrite, and in the Smallweeds, viperous usurers.

Dickens offers only a few possibilities out of the morass. Boythorn (based upon Landor) represents untamable natural energy undaunted by the dreariest of muddled lawsuits. Mr. Jarndyce (a revision of Mr. Pickwick) retires from a crazy world and performs his acts of kindness within his immediate circle. Mr. Rouncewell, the sturdy ironmaster of the north, is the vigorous entrepreneur of industrialism; but Dickens fails to realize that this rugged individualistic industrialist was already vanishing beneath the mountainous structure of finance capital and giant corporations.

Hard Times (1854) is the first Dickens novel to eschew a vast canvas in favor of a relatively small number of characters concentrated in one locale.

Coketown, in a perpetual shroud of industrial smoke, resounds constantly with the unceasing rhythm of the great hammers and pistons. The rulers of Coketown are Bounderby, the banker, and Gradgrind, the hardware dealer. Admirable product of the Gradgrind principles is young Gradgrind, who robs Bounderby's bank. Suspected is Stephen Blackpool, a power-loom operator. Blackpool finds the expenses of current divorce proceedings entirely too high to let him divorce his drunken wife and marry Rachel. At Rachel's request he refuses to join the union and is therefore thought by Bounderby to be sympathetic to management. When Blackpool supports the principle of unionism, Bounderby fires him. Seeking work elsewhere, Blackpool falls into an abandoned mine shaft and dies.

The bourgeois reading public has never relished *Hard Times,* for it is the first Dickens novel that really hurts. Earlier sallies (even *Bleak House*) could be dismissed as Dickens' dislike of lawyers, parasites, aristocracy, and hypocrites; but this novel is frankly a tract attacking the entire system of industrialization and industrialists. The caricatures of *Hard Times* are not, as in earlier Dickens novels, quaint and amusing depictions of imaginary eccentrics but caricatures of the well-to-do reader himself or, to poorer readers, of the manipulators of the system under which they lived.

The opening schoolroom scene brilliantly expounds the Gradgrind worship of Facts. Fact is to obliterate imagination, emotion, humanity represented here by Cissy Jupe. The so-called Facts of Gradgrind wholly ignore the reality of breathing life. This worship of Fact dominates Coketown, and in Bounderby it possesses the lethal utilitarian weapon of greed for material possessions and power over other men. Human beings are percentage marks, statistical tables, and machine tenders to Bounderby. Carlyle never launched so devastating an assault upon the "cash-nexus" and the blight of laissez-faire capitalism.

In the personal life of the Gradgrind family the worship of Fact makes a thief out of Tom and a loveless wife to Bounderby out of Louisa. Sleary's tawdry horse-and-dog show is symbolically the inconsequential amusement to which Victorian utilitarianism had reduced art, but these poor circus performers radiate the natural creative force that in the person of Cissy will give some solace to the desolate Gradgrinds.

Little Dorrit (1855–57) marks the height of Dickens' sociological interests.

"Poverty," the first part, brings Arthur Clennam back to his decaying homestead, where he becomes interested in Amy Dorrit, a daily sewing girl. Her father, William, has been in debtor's prison for twenty-three years. Trying to help the elder Dorrit, Clennam gets bogged down in the hideous bureaucracy of the Circumlocution Office, run by the Barnacle dynasty, but from outside sources discovers a considerable legacy that rescues Dorrit.

"Riches," the second part, takes the Dorrits to Europe where their new wealth permits Fanny Dorrit to marry into the rich Merdle family. The failure of the Merdle Bank causes Mr. Merdle to commit suicide, beggars the Dorrits again, and sends Clennam to debtor's prison. His former partner frees Clennam, who marries Amy.

As the Court of Chancery was the oppressive symbol of *Bleak House,* the Marshalsea prison is the even more sober symbol of *Little Dorrit.* The release of Clennam from prison is a contrived happy ending, even a sardonic thrust. For all the world is a prison, all society a vast house of bondage. Even the power figures (the Barnacles and the Merdles) are hopelessly trapped in their own webs, as much as the little people within their toils. Like the medieval wheel of Fortuna, the incessant quest for material wealth inevitably swings downward even if in fickleness it occasionally shoots upward. Shaw, who labeled *Little Dorrit* "a more seditious book than *Das Kapital,*" declared that his youthful reading of this novel made him a revolutionary.

A Tale of Two Cities (1859), probably the least typical Dickens novel (humor and eccentric personalities are virtually absent), may be looked upon as a dramatization of Carlyle's *French Revolution.* London and Paris are the two cities.

Sidney Carton, a wastrel English lawyer, loves the young French girl Lucie Manette, but she marries Charles Darnay, a Frenchman whose appearance remarkably resembles that of Carton. During the Reign of Terror in the French Revolution, Darnay hurries to Paris to save the life of an old family servant. A wine-seller Defarge and his monstrous wife railroad Darnay to the guillotine. Carton, for love of Lucie, substitutes himself for Darnay and goes to death in triumphant serenity: "It is a far, far better thing that I do than I have ever done."

Carton is Dickens' one success in portraying a gentleman and a tragic figure. The description of Lucie fits Ellen Ternan, and it seems clear that the noble sacrifice for an unattainable love represents an idealization of the novelist's love for the young actress. With a deep sense of guilt, Carton in his great renunciation is not pathetic (as are most of Dickens' suffering characters); his act of conscious redemption and purification elevates him to heroic stature.

Central to the novel is the Carlylean concept of the Revolution as the inevitable bloody harvest from the long-planted seeds of suffering and injustice. The themes of the private lives and the public revolution clash against and blunt each other.

Great Expectations (1860–61), a more artistic *David Copperfield,* shows the old Dickens resurgent in intervals of hearty humor and in numerous fascinating characterizations, although throughout the novel is the sinister undercurrent of crime and criminals.

The escaped convict Magwitch is aided by young Pip, who lives at Cooling, Kent, with his older sister and her blacksmith husband, Joe Gargery. Some time after the convict's recapture and deportation, Pip is brought to the home of Miss Havisham, to play with her adopted child, Estella. Miss Havisham pays Pip's apprentice fees to Joe, and Pip assumes that she is the unnamed benefactor who through the lawyer Jaggers provides money to send him to London to be a gentleman. Pip loves Estella, but she marries the boorish Bentley Drummle. Magwitch illegally returns from Australia to reveal himself as Pip's benefactor. In the attempt to smuggle Magwitch out of England, the boat is swamped. Magwitch later dies and Pip tries his fortune in the East. A decade later he returns to marry the widowed Estella.

Bulwer-Lytton and the public compelled the happy ending; Dickens originally concluded, "Pip remained a solitary man." The original ending is far better, the logical outcome of all Pip's wrongheaded "great expectations." Pip's pretenses of gentility make him an intolerable snob, but his whole world of gentility is a sham built upon the generosity of the coarse criminal Magwitch.

The novel is penance by the mature, now clear-seeing Dickens for his earlier subservience to false values, his hatred for the job at the shoe-blacking factory, his desperate lower-middle-class passion to rise to gentleman's status. More broadly, the work condemns the entire leisure-class ideal of contemporary society. Pip's gentility is pure parasitism, and his return to useful occupation is expiation for trying to live by the labor of others.

Perhaps the enduring art of Dickens must rest upon unconscious symbology. The immersion of Pip when the boat is swamped constitutes, whether Dickens consciously realized it or not, a symbolic baptism, washing away the false values of Pip, anointing him with the true waters of life (from the wellspring of Joe Gargery), and thus transforming the youth spiritually. Beyond the art of *David Copperfield,* Dickens here achieved his one memorable success in depicting psychic growth and spiritual ripening in his central character.

Our Mutual Friend (1864–65) has bequeathed "Podsnappery" to the language but otherwise seems a diffuse, overly complicated story from a tired author.

Switching clothes with a steward who is subsequently killed, John Harmon ("our mutual friend"), back from South Africa, conceals his identity under the name of John Rokesmith. He resides with the Wilfers, whose daughter Bella had been designated by his father's will as bride for John. Boffin, manager of the Harmon estates, holds the Harmon money as residuary legatee. The generous Boffin, knowing John's secret, helps him win Bella, who believes that she is marrying a poor man. Boffin turns over the property to the true heir, and the John Harmons are taken care of.

Brilliantly, Dickens portrays the Harmon wealth as a dust-heap (that is, trash-pile), which actually amounted to considerable value as salvage in Victorian times. This mountain of trash is symbolically all Victorian materialism. Modern society is itself a dust-heap, empty of culture, devoid of integrity, honesty, and humanity.

Heading this cultureless culture are middle-class parasites such as the Veneerings, who flaunt their wealth and bribe their way into any place, including parliament. But the prize delineation is Mr. Podsnap, an embodiment of Philistinism beyond even Arnold's power of description. Mr. Podsnap is blind toryism, English insularity, bourgeois indifference to culture, money-worshipping Board-of-Directors respectability. With a grand imperious gesture of his right arm Mr. Podsnap utterly dismisses all of the world's unpleasantness and injustice.

Bella, perhaps also drawn from Ellen, is Dickens' attempt at female growth. Repudiating her monetary greed, she marries for love. A pitiful failure is Bradley Headstone, the self-educated schoolmaster, who has actually destroyed himself by accepting the Victorian standards of false knowledge and money values.

The Mystery of Edwin Drood (1870) remains a mystery because Dickens died halfway through writing it, and no completely satisfactory ending has yet been devised.

During his childhood in the East, Edwin Drood was betrothed by his parents to Rosa Bud. As a young student engineer he visits Cloisterham (Rochester), where Rosa lives, as well as his uncle, choirmaster John Jasper, an opium addict. Jasper is interested in Rosa as also is the violent-tempered Nevill Landless from Ceylon. Edwin comes to Rosa for a mutual breaking of their engagement, and then disappears. Jasper throws suspicion upon Nevill, but a dragging of the river discloses no body.

Wilkie Collins' influence and the incessant oriental associations suggest that Jasper, probably the murderer, is actually re-enacting a ritual thug slaying of Edwin, but Dickens carried the secret to his grave. Most discussions of the novel seek to puzzle out the conclusion.

The moldering Cloisterham is Dickens' final indictment of society. The intertwining of the colonial themes suggests that the blighting effects of Edwin's materialism, racism, and selfish pragmatism have now spread their infection throughout the world. The natural force of honesty and impulsive goodness remains within many minor characters but is all but overwhelmed by the pervasive evil and hypocritical conformity.

THE NOVELS AND OTHER PROSE OF THACKERAY

William Makepeace Thackeray (thak'é-ri) (1811–1863). William Makepeace Thackeray was born in Calcutta, India, the son of a high government official, Richmond Thackeray. His mother had been the reigning belle of Anglo-Indian society. His father died in 1815, and Thackeray was sent to England where he lived with relatives and experienced some unhappy school years. When his mother came to England in 1820 along with her second husband, Major Carmichael Smythe, Thackeray went on to pleasant years at Charterhouse and thence to Cambridge in 1829. During his two college years Thackeray wrote comic pieces for the *Snob* and a burlesque poem upon "Timbuctoo," subject of the Chancellor's prize in 1829 (Tennyson won the prize). Toying only briefly with law, Thackeray at the age of twenty-one went to Paris to study painting. A rash attempt at newspaper publishing, the failure of an Indian bank, and his heavy gambling destroyed his patrimony. Married in 1836 to Isabella Shawe, he had two small daughters on his hands in 1840 when his wife became deranged and had to be cared for until her death fifty years later. For a decade Thackeray under many pseudonyms contributed numerous short pieces, predominantly humorous, to periodicals. *Vanity Fair* established him as a novelist. He became successful as a lecturer and by his genuine liking for the United States, during several speaking tours, smoothed American feathers ruffled by Dickens. His own friendship with Dickens was cooled by personal misunderstandings, though the era's two most prominent novelists maintained a mutual respect. As first editor of the *Cornhill Magazine* from 1860 to 1862 Thackeray launched the periodical upon a distinguished career. One of his daughters became Lady Ritchie, while the other married Sir Leslie Stephen.

Upper middle class himself, Thackeray excelled at portraying his own social stratum, and with the confidence of secure entrenchment, he could view his peers with bland irony and a mild cynicism. The chief subject of Thackeray is the contrast between human pretensions and human weaknesses. Of the bourgeois novelists he was the greatest conscious artist; perhaps most noteworthy is his graceful 18th-century style of prose, admirably lucid and fluent.

Vanity Fair (1847) was a conscious innovation which discarded the conventional intrigue plot of contemporary novels. From *Pilgrim's Progress* Thackeray lifted his title for the shams and hypocrisies of "ready-money society."

Amelia Sedley and Becky Sharp are good friends at Miss Pinkerton's school for girls. The penniless Becky tries to snare Joseph Sedley, Amelia's brother, but he flees back to military service in India and she despairingly becomes a governess in the household of old, cantankerous Sir Pitt Crawley. Becky receives a proposal from Sir Pitt when he is widowed, but she has already married his son, the dashing Rawdon Crawley. George Osborne is forbidden by his father to marry Amelia when her father goes bankrupt, but George is persuaded by William Dobbin (secretly in love with Amelia) to go through with his vows. The two married couples meet at Brussels where George trysts with Becky on the eve of Waterloo in which he is killed. Amelia in poverty devotes her time to her son and to the memory of her unworthy husband. Becky and her husband cannot live upon his meager wins at gambling. Becky accepts the attentions of wicked old Lord Steyne until Rawdon discovers them and casts her off. Amelia, at last married to Dobbin, runs across Becky in Germany. Becky marries Joseph Sedley this time and collects his insurance when he dies under mysterious circumstances.

No previous English novel, not even from Thackeray's master, Fielding, so minutely depicts and anatomizes a whole class of society—the new leisured gentry, a parasitic class made possible by England's tremendous wealth. Constructive labor is unthinkable to such a group, and once admitted to its ranks, Becky would rather be a kept woman than descend to being a governess again. With monetary wealth as his sole criterion of value, old Osborne joyfully accepts the heiress Amelia as a daughter-in-law but in rage casts her off when she is destitute. Today's taste prefers *Vanity Fair* to all subsequent Thackeray novels, possibly because this is his most ferocious attack upon a hypocritical society, while later novels demonstrate his progressive accommodation to his milieu.

Untouched by the spiritual storms of the century, Thackeray seems to worship the Victorian deities of marriage, home, family, children. Rawdon Crawley's elevation to manhood from a dissolute braggart is accomplished solely by home and child, while Thackeray's severest charge against Becky is her incapacity to be moved by either. He recommends these Victorian sentiments as the only bulwarks against the destructiveness of a money-mad society.

The novel is built upon Becky and Amelia's contrasting curves of fortune. Thackeray's theme asserts that in a stable society the violator of accepted mores, such as Becky, may momentarily seem triumphant but will eventually be cast down, while the dutiful follower of accepted mores, such as Amelia, though momentarily in eclipse will eventually be rewarded. The resourceful and vivacious Becky enlists much sympathy today, for she actively struggles to achieve her goals. She is a brilliant study in duplicity, audacity, and femininity, all of which she uses in her struggle to survive. Although to us Amelia seems far too dependent, she is the Victorian ideal of womanhood and properly ends with assured fortune and respectable position in society. Beneath his unprepossessing exterior Dobbin is the bourgeois hero in his noble fidelity, altruistic principles, and stout virtues. In typically middle-class fashion Thackeray perceives the straightforward, simple people as good—the clever, complex people as bad. Becky springs from a dubious bohemian background and, particularly suspect, she is part French.

Pendennis (1848–50), one of the great autobiographical novels, is a Victorian expurgation of Fielding's *Tom Jones*.

Arthur Pendennis is a spoiled young man because of a doting mother, Helen, and an adoring adopted sister, Laura Bell. He falls in love with Miss Fotheringay, an actress ten years his senior, but is neatly extricated by his uncle, Major Pendennis, a sophisticated man-about-town. At the university Pen foolishly sports as a dandy, and Laura must pay off his gambling debts. Fanny Bolton, a pretty lass of the lower classes, loves him devotedly, but he leaves her as innocent as he met her. The flirtatious heiress Blanche Amory toys with him but merrily jilts him. At last Pen realizes the qualities of the patient Laura, whom he marries with the resolute intention of proving himself a solid citizen and a competent writer.

Thackeray's own drawing for the title page indicates his medieval morality—the pull of good versus evil in the life of a good-natured but naïve young man. From the corruptions of the world (and Blanche) Arthur is saved by the pure love of a good woman. Thackeray so modestly underplays his central character (portraying himself) that Pen becomes less interesting than the many other personalities of the book. Structural unity is sacrificed to a series of dramatic episodes, and because it was published serially, the development of the novel was powerfully affected by public opinion. Pen, the readers insisted, could not soil little Fanny. Irish objections to Costigan caused laudable Irishmen, Shandon and Finucane, to appear in later installments. Journalists took umbrage at the earlier treatment of their profession; so Thackeray elevated their position toward the end. The process of maturing, the novel's major concern, is conceived of as total conformity to prevailing bourgeois concepts. This work was a favorite of Tennyson and of the American novelist William Dean Howells.

Rebecca and Rowena (1849) is probably second only to Dickens' *Christmas Carol* among the multitudinous Christmas books that were produced by mid-Victorianism. Supposedly it is a sequel to Scott's *Ivanhoe*.

Henpecked by his bovine blond wife Rowena, who ignores him for their son Cedric and their neighbor Athelstane, Ivanhoe joins King Richard in battle. After long convalescence from his wounds Ivanhoe returns in disguise to find Rowena married to Athelstane. He reveals his identity to her only upon her deathbed. The widowed Ivanhoe finds a more satisfactory spouse in Rebecca.

This mock-heroic demonstrates the passage from Scott romance to Victorian realism. A romantic heroine will not wear as well in matrimonial traces as an intelligent woman with resources of humor, courage, and loyalty. The volume also contains some of Thackeray's best humorous verse.

The History of Henry Esmond (1852), Thackeray's only non-serialized novel, is often considered the greatest historical novel in English. Setting is late 17th and early 18th centuries.

Although the true heir to the Castlewood estate, Henry Esmond, deemed illegitimate, is a dependent of his second cousin, the titular viscount, Lord Castlewood, whose family consists of his young and lovely wife Rachel, his son Francis, and his daughter Beatrix. Castlewood's neglect of his wife exposes her to the unwelcome attentions of the wicked Lord Mohun who kills Castlewood in a duel. Wrongfully blamed by Lady Castlewood in her husband's death, Esmond proceeds to the continent as an officer in the campaigns of the Duke of Marlborough. Home on furlough, he falls in love with Beatrix, but that spirited young lady prefers the Duke of Hamilton, who also is quickly slain in a duel with Lord Mohun. Esmond secretly escorts the Stuart Pretender to England, but the plot to depose the monarch is thwarted by the Pretender's pursuit of Beatrix. When the Pretender flees to Paris, Beatrix joins him. Esmond marries Lady Castlewood and emigrates with her to family plantations in Virginia.

As narrator, Henry Esmond writes in the genuine diction and cadence of the early 18th century. He brilliantly depicts the following three facets of English history:

(1) The Jacobite plots to restore a Stuart to the English throne.

(2) The Marlborough campaigns. With the shrewdness displayed in *Vanity Fair* Thackeray ignores the vast battle effects in favor of up-close realism. Drudgery is relieved by comradeship. Heroism is a quiet, dogged affair.

(3) The social and literary life of the Queen Anne period. Thackeray buried himself in the 18th-century section of the British Museum to emerge with probably the most authentic picture of a past era ever sketched in English fiction. Steele, whom Thackeray strongly resembled, receives a very lifelike portrayal, but the savage genius of Swift is only half perceived, it not being congenial to a Victorian gentleman.

The major concern of the work, however, is a peculiar love story which only the constructive power of Thackeray could save from the ridiculous— a man falling in love with a young, flirtatious girl and ending up with a marriage to her mother. As always, characters and fundamental situations in his novels were constantly adapted by Thackeray from his own life. However, the essence of the novel, as Pater realized, is a domestic drama of the strange psychological shift from a mother-son relationship to a husband-wife relationship.

While Lady Castlewood is the most complex characterization in all Thackeray, the fascinating figure is Beatrix, another version of Becky Sharp, but one who chooses a butterfly career in reaction to her thwarted, love-starved mother. The Victorianism in Thackeray makes him thrust aside this exciting sex symbol and primly consign Beatrix to sensual France.

The Newcomes (1853–55), Thackeray's dynasty novel of three generations, is supposedly narrated by Pendennis.

Anglo-Indian Colonel Thomas Newcome lets his son Clive study art. Clive wishes to marry a cousin Ethel, but her family, seeking a more fashionable marriage, engage her to Lord Farintosh. Clive is persuaded to marry sweet Rosey Mackenzie. His father loses his fortune, and Clive's mother-in-law (the Old Campaigner) makes life miserable for everyone. The Colonel hands over everything to Clive and retires to die as a pensioner at Grey Friars, his and Clive's old school. Ethel refuses to go through with a marriage of convenience, and after Rosey's death she and Clive are free to marry.

These newcomers are the triumphant bourgeoisie replacing the former aristocracy. Intelligently critical, Thackeray depicts middle-class shortcomings in Newcomes such as Brian, Lady Ann (Brian's wife), Hobson, and Barnes. His concentration, however, is upon the admirable Newcomes. Clive is a somewhat feckless rewrite of Pendennis, but he is a good-natured, well-intentioned fellow whose conformity to bourgeois standards brings him eventual rewards. Ethel is Thackeray's most attractive heroine with a strength of character and intelligence unknown to Amelia Sedley.

Thackeray's greatest effort is expended upon Colonel Newcome, essentially a picture of his stepfather. Newman (who admired this novel) and many other Victorians expatiated upon the concept of the gentleman. Here, insists Thackeray, is proof that the new bourgeoisie can produce the complete gentleman as well as the discarded aristocracy. Totally English in concept, the Colonel is innately good and artless, his gentility arising instinctively, not by artifice.

The unifying theme is condemnation of marriage for the wrong reasons. Thackeray dissects six wrong marriages, contrasting, not too effectively, the happy marriage of Arthur and Laura Pendennis. The central love triangle consists of Clive-Ethel-Rosey with the right combination finally effected.

The Virginians (1857–59), a sequel to *Henry Esmond*, was Thackeray's last significant novel, though the fragment *Denis Duval* (1864) suggests his old power.

In Virginia, Colonel Esmond names his country seat Castlewood after the family's ancestral estate in England. His daughter, Rachel Warrington, is an affectionate but imperious colonial dame to her orphaned sons, George and Harry. In the French and Indian War under Washington's command, George is missing. Harry goes to England where he is a trifle repelled by the coolness and acquisitiveness of the English Esmonds. Under the direction of the aged Baroness Bernstein (formerly Beatrix Esmond) he plunges into social dissipation from which he is rescued by the surprising appearance of George, an escapee from a French prisoner-of-war camp. During the American Revolution, Harry follows George Washington into battle, while George renounces his American property and lives thereafter in England.

Although some critics consider this the best fictional portrait of Americans by an Englishman, it belongs fundamentally to romance instead of Thackeray's forte of social criticism. The basic plot is the hackneyed 18th-century contrast of the sober, plodding brother with the rakish, dissipating brother. Thackeray only partially employs this plot to set American innocence against Old World corruption. Many contemporary Americans were distressed by the unheroic picture of Washington as a stolid man of humorless sincerity. The impressive, though really distressing, figure is the fat old courtesan-emeritus, Baroness Bernstein, the all-too-predictable end of the saucy Beatrix. The novel virtually breaks into two separate tales—Harry's adventures to chapter forty-seven and then George's vicissitudes to conclusion. Thackeray hits his best stride when he depicts his beloved 18th-century England, but he now seems the aging observer rather than the intense participant of *Henry Esmond*.

NON-FICTION. *The English Humourists of the Eighteenth Century* (1853) consisted of lectures first delivered in 1851, the most popular lectures since those of Sidney Smith. Thackeray redefined *humorist* (an "eccentric" to the 18th century and a "comic" to subsequent centuries) as essentially a genial, almost sentimental spectator of life. His selection arbitrarily omitted Johnson and Sheridan. Fielding, Steele, and Goldsmith were his favorites. Thackeray delineated his subjects as unheroically charming, and the interpretations owe much to Macaulay's Whiggery. The graceful ease and urbane, witty phrasemaking lifted high the reputation of 18th-century authors, though for definitive portrayal the lectures reveal Thackeray much more accurately than his subjects.

Roundabout Papers (1863) collected familiar essays written chiefly for the *Cornhill Magazine*. Originally intended to imitate Steele, they actually prove closer to Lamb. The titles—"On Ribbons," "On Screens in Dining Rooms," "Thorns in the Cushion"—indicate Thackeray's ability to write with consummate conversational grace on the most trivial of experiences, and to render them wholly delightful. Thackeray assumes the wistful and roguish air of an old fuddy-duddy smilingly caressing the little joys of everyday life. If the familiar essay should again rise in repute, this work will be considered Thackeray's greatest achievement as well as his most characteristic.

The Letters and Private Papers (1946) is apparently the definitive edition, though portions of Thackeray correspondence have been printed ever since his death. The novelist superficially appears as probably the gayest, most effervescent of all English letter writers, and certainly as the finest of true gentlemen. But beneath the "kidding" (often more American than English in texture) sounds a troubled man, obsessed by personal difficulties but even more deeply influenced by the pessimistic conviction that virtue and taste may be futile in a world conquered by the strong and the unprincipled.

THE NOVELS OF TROLLOPE

Anthony Trollope (trol'op) (1815–1882). A native Londoner, Anthony Trollope was the son of an unsuccessful barrister and Frances Trollope, a remarkably successful author of about 115 volumes. Shabby gentility made Anthony's schoolboy days at Harrow and Winchester quite miserable and precluded university training. His ingenious mother secured Anthony a clerkship in the Post Office at the age of nineteen. Transfer to Ireland in 1841 was a new beginning. He married in 1844 and in the next year published his first novel, the unsuccessful *Mac Dermots of Ballycloran,* dealing with an Irish family. With *The Warden* (1855) he established himself as a consistently recognized novelist for the rest of his life. As an important official in the Post Office he traveled extensively throughout the British Isles and throughout the world. The pillar box, a receptacle for mail upon thousands of English street corners, was Trollope's idea. Trollope was a founder member of the *Fortnightly Review* and the *Pall Mall Gazette*. In 1867 he resigned from the Post Office to be editor of the short-lived *St. Paul's*. Although the later novels showed no diminution of competence, the reading public gradually turned away from him.

Middle middle-class, Trollope depicts the most solidly entrenched of 19th-century Englishmen. Industrial capitalists and laborers are virtually absent, but he ranges the entire bourgeois spectrum from little tradesmen to the new commercial peers and has a warm place in his heart for the surviving Tory squires. The 20th-century resurgence of Trollope is largely based upon nostalgia for the essentially secure Victorian world he portrayed in his earlier novels, a world of English gentlemen intent upon maintaining personal dignity, social respectability, and domestic sanctity. The central conflict in every one of his major novels concerns the struggle to retain his cherished way of life against the assaults of outward forces and/or inner traitors who would subvert it. No other English writer (not even Jane Austen) has so exhaustively delineated this fundamentally placid, genteel lost world.

Much of the inevitable post-mortem reaction against his novels was furthered by Trollope's *Autobiography* (1883), which distressed the arty by his unqualifiedly workmanlike approach to novel-writing. Trollope blocked out his novels and wrote them with all the methodical drudgery of a competent grocer. Wherever he was—even on train and ship—he placed his watch in front of him and wrote 250 words an hour for four hours a day. No other English novels seem so much the solid product of calm, dogged English craftsmanship. So consistent is Trollope that his novels rarely display the troughs and peaks of other writers; practically every one of his novels has been labeled his best by some devoted admirer.

The Barchester novels, still his most popular, have been termed "as English as roast beef." They portray the monumental stability of rural life in the English south, assailed by the disturbing forces from London but able to absorb and control that shock. The gentlefolk of this area are primarily intent upon maintaining rank and property. They are completely self-assured and sober, eminently respectable and conservative. Trollope also recognizes their deficiencies. Their unimaginative conservatism renders them incapable of perceiving the patterns of change. They display no intellectual questioning, no spiritual depths, and no artistic sensibilities.

The Warden (1855) apparently arose in reaction to a reforming article against Charterhouse appearing in Dickens' *Household Words* in 1852. Dickens is satirized in the novel as Mr. Popular Sentiment. Trollope presents the case for holders of clerical sinecures against militant crusaders like Dickens.

The Reverend Mr. Septimus Harding is appointed to a sinecure as warden of Hiram's Hospital, an institution for twelve old men. John Bold, a young physician with reforming zeal, encourages the inmates to seek a larger share of income from the endowment, and he enlists the editorial voice of the *Jupiter* (London *Times*). Harding wishes to resign in spite of the practical arguments of his worldly son-in-law, Archdeacon Grantly. Eleanor, Harding's younger daughter, addresses an appeal to Bold, who later proposes to her. She marries Bold, and her father resigns with dignity, content with his reduced income.

Contemporary clerics testified to the accuracy of Trollope's ecclesiastical portraits, an impressive feat of imagination from a layman. All Trollope's clergymen are English gentlemen first, and clerics second; good manners are infinitely more important than theology. Grantly's insistence upon the temporalities of the church is countered by Harding's unselfish gentility. He is one of the most convincing portraits in English literature of unostentatious goodness. The love story is quite subordinate to the novel's innovation: a moral dilemma with strong contemporary ethical overtones.

Barchester Towers (1857), the most popular Trollope novel, is a sequel to *The Warden*. In *Barchester Towers* we find a wide variety of people added to the cast. John Bold has died.

London politics thwart Archdeacon Grantly in his expectation of a bishopric. The new bishop of Barchester is Dr. Proudie who is henpecked by his redoubtable spouse. Mrs. Proudie and the bishop's chaplain, Obadiah Slope, attempt to impose Low Church practices upon the cathedral. Grantly counters by securing the living of St. Ewold's for an Oxford High Churchman, Francis Arabin. The bishop's order that absentee clergymen return to their pastoral duties drags from Italy the bizarre Stanhope family, featuring the exotic Madeline and the ne'er-do-well Ethelbert. Slope's interest in Madeline and the widowed Eleanor causes Mrs. Proudie to ship him off. Arabin succeeds to the deanship of the cathedral and marries Eleanor.

The stresses upon 19th-century Anglicanism are symbolized in the ecclesiastical politics of a provincial cathedral. Grantly is the survival of the 18th-century cleric to whom the church is a dignified but not particularly religious institution; to Grantly the chief role of the clergy is to set the community standards of social dignity and gentlemanly behavior. Slope is evangelical Protestantism, unsympathetically portrayed as vulgar and sanctimonious self-seeking. Arabin represents the Oxford Movement, proving much more attractive to the clergy than evangelicalism, which in fact drives Anglicans to the High Church. Indeed, every clerical type is represented, except the intensely pious. Trollope artfully introduces the outlandish Stanhope clan to set in greater contrast the staid, decorous citizenry of Barchester.

Doctor Thorne (1858) is one of Trollope's most heavily plotted novels.

Frank Gresham, heir of financially encumbered Greshambury Park, falls in love with Mary Thorne, who lives with her kindly old uncle, Dr. Thorne. Frank's mother tries to turn him from Mary and to Miss Dunstable, a rich heiress, but Frank marries Mary. The death of another uncle, Roger Scatcherd, makes Mary an heiress and frees Greshambury Park.

The love story is familiar sentimental Trollope—love and honor should triumph over rank and wealth. The intruder from outside is Scatcherd, a vulgar *nouveau riche* railway contractor, whose crass materialism and melodramatic rise are alien to Barchester. The traitor within is Frank's mother, Lady Arabella, whose schemes to marry her children to money are betrayals of the enduring genteel standards of Barchester. Dr. Thorne is the rock of English provincial stability, the epitome of quiet, natural virtue.

Framley Parsonage (1861), written at the prodding of Thackeray, is perhaps the most characteristic of all Trollope's novels and reputedly one of the most "English" of all novels. It was Trollope's greatest success during his lifetime.

The vicar of Framley, Mark Robarts, chafes at his indebtedness to Lady Lufton, his patroness. Seeking contacts to further his career, he is persuaded to sign a note for the influence-peddler, Sowerby, and gradually the debt closes in upon Robarts. Lord Lufton, against the wishes of his mother, Lady Lufton, woos Lucy, Mark's sister. Lady Lufton finally recognizes Lucy's qualities, and the marriage brings in Lord Lufton to save the shaky financial condition of Mark.

Mark and Lucy form a contrasting pair. His ambitions force him to compromises with his conscience, and his attempt to gain independence from Lady Lufton lands him into a mess from which he can be extricated only by Lord Lufton. Such is the fate of those questing for more than their place in society would warrant. Lucy could have Lord Lufton but she will not accept him without his family's approval; her own self-respect and her future social position require it. Lucy is probably the most Austen-like heroine outside of Jane Austen's novels.

The novel's lasting reputation rests upon the rich canvas of a 19th-century English town—surpassed only by Eliot's *Middlemarch*—from the splendor of Gatherum Castle to tight-fisted Hogglestock, the complete geological strata of provincial life in the upper and middle classes.

The Last Chronicle of Barset (1867) reaches Trollope's greatest heights after the weakest of the series, *The Small House at Allington* (1864). Trollope considered *The Last Chronicle of Barset* his best work.

Archdeacon Grantly is horrified when his son Henry wishes to marry Grace Crawley, whose father, the curate of Hogglestock, is accused of stealing a check for £20. Mrs. Proudie, the "she-bishop" of Barchester, tries to oust Josiah Crawley, but the ecclesiastical commission summoned by her husband, Bishop Proudie, reaches no decision about Mr. Crawley. Mrs. Proudie dies of a heart attack—but dies standing up! The Arabins, returning from abroad, clear up the mystery of the check. After Mr. Harding's death leaves St. Ewold's vacant, the exonerated Mr. Crawley is given the post, and Henry and Grace are married.

Crawley is Trollope's one deeply religious cleric. Perhaps the business of the check is too trivial, but with no other character does Trollope approach such tragic despair in an honest heart. Crawley is Trollope's most complex character and, as he displays in his superb denunciation of Mrs. Proudie, Trollope's one character of deep passionate intensity. Criticism of the Established Church is implicit in the portrayal of the lowliest clergyman in the hierarchy of Barsetshire as the most spiritually dedicated. The magnificent story of Crawley is encumbered with three other stories, and altogether there are ninety-four speaking characters.

Although the reading public continues to prefer the Barchester novels, 20th-century criticism has increasingly exalted the Political or Parliamentary novels by Trollope (these were also the favorites of the American president, Grover Cleveland). In this difficult and unusual genre Trollope is surpassed only by Disraeli. Though some of the Barsetshire characters appear peripherally, the main figures are Phineas Finn (notably in *Phineas Redux,* 1874), an Irish bourgeois parliamentarian modeled after the author, and Plantagenet Palliser, Duke of Omnium, an aristocrat who reaches the highest governmental office in *The Prime Minister* (1876). The rural comedy of Barchester is replaced by the deepening gloom of London politics. While the agricultural south might represent an idyllically ideal old England, the wide range of national interests is compelling a new world for all Englishmen. Trollope's political philosophy epitomizes the main-line English position: reform and change must proceed but without violence or abandoning of tradition. Above all, government is a product of men, with human faculties and foibles outweighing any abstract political theories. Although Trollope's political experience was limited to unsuccessful candidacy for parliament, insiders consistently testify to his astute grasp of political realities.

The Way We Live Now (1875), highly unpopular in its day, has been extravagantly praised in recent years. It is Trollope's one angry social satire, excoriating the corruption of England's gilded age. In the feverish craze for wealth and social prestige, all the stabilizing restraint of older virtues has been cast aside. Melmotte the swindler is the symbol of this age; all fawn upon him, knowing his criminality but entranced by the audacious scale of his swindles and the golden aura of big money it exudes. Aristocracy in the person of Lord Alfred Grendall and the squirarchy represented by the Longestaffe family make themselves pawns in the giant fraud. The only success now is money, however obtained, and money is God. This pessimistic diatribe is an outraged English gentleman's protest against the triumph of Mammon over a lost world of dignity and honor.

THE NOVELS OF THE BRONTËS

Charlotte Brontë (bron'tā) (1816–1855). Charlotte Brontë was the third child of Patrick Brunty, an Irish clergyman who at Cambridge borrowed the spelling of Nelson's title, Duke of Bronte (in Sicily). From 1820 the permanent residence of all the Brontës was Haworth, Yorkshire. Maria (b. 1813) and Elizabeth (b. 1815) both died in 1825 from tuberculosis contracted at Cowan Bridge School (Lowood School of *Jane Eyre*). Two younger sisters were Emily and Anne. Charlotte and her only brother Patrick Branwell (1817–48) developed from 1830 to 1835 an enormous cycle of stories about Angria, an imaginary African empire. Much of her later fiction drew its themes and personalities from the Angrian series. In 1835 to provide funds for Branwell's education, Charlotte became a governess, though there was no Rochester in her actual experience. From 1842 to 1844 she studied French in Brussels under Constantin Héger, from whom derives her first novel, *The Professor* (*1845*, 1857). In 1846 the three sisters unsuccessfully published *Poems by Currer, Ellis, and Acton Bell*, using their initials in these pseudonyms. The success of *Jane Eyre* brought Charlotte popular acclaim, but she was distressed by Branwell's alcoholic death from delirium tremens and Emily's death shortly afterward. In 1854 Charlotte married her father's curate and died the next year as a result of childbirth illness.

Jane Eyre (1847) received more initial praise than any other first published novel in English, unless *Pickwick Papers* is classified as the first by Dickens. Certainly the unbroken popularity of the novel since its appearance is unmatched by any other first novel.

Orphaned as a child, Jane Eyre experiences unhappiness in the household of relatives, the Reeds, and at Lowood School. As governess to the ward of Rochester, she is drawn to her employer; as she is about to marry him, it is revealed that his insane wife is imprisoned in an upper room of Rochester's mansion, Thornfield. Fleeing from him, she is befriended by St. John Rivers, a stiffly proper cleric whose marriage proposal she rejects. When Rochester's mad wife burns down the mansion killing herself, Rochester is maimed. Jane hurries to him, and they are married.

Jane Austen epitomizes the decorous femininity to which manners are all important; the Brontë sisters epitomize passionate femininity to which love is all important. Never before had the English novel trumpeted that a woman's passion can equal or exceed a man's. The love-starved governess wins the most unlikely male, Rochester, the Byronic libertine.

St. John Rivers is the right man in all respects but the transcendent one—love. Rochester is the wrong man in all respects save that of love. Nonetheless, Jane refuses to be Rochester's mistress when the insane Bertha Mason is revealed as his lawful wife. She pleads conscience (sufficient excuse to Victorians), but the real cause seems to be her unwillingness to accept the father-child relationship under his masculine dominance. When Rochester is blind and impoverished, she returns triumphantly to establish the mother-child dominance over him. The madwoman is less a symbol of Rochester's guilt and compulsory penance than of the irrationality in Jane that refuses marriage until it meets the terms of her inner nature.

The sense gained by readers of elemental life forces (powers of protecting warmth and sustaining continuity more basic even than sex) has completely excused the inept portrayal of high society, the grotesque coincidences, and occasional surfeit of sentimentality.

Emily Brontë (1818–1848). Emily Brontë and her younger sister Anne (1820–49) co-operated in a Gondal cycle of tales, set in the North Pacific, after Charlotte left home in 1835. Though little remains of this series, it probably provided the themes and personalities of Emily's later fiction. Emily accompanied Charlotte to Brussels in 1842 but was content to return to her native moorland late in the same year upon her aunt's death. Silent and reserved, she received far less publicity than Charlotte. Emily died of a cold contracted at Branwell's funeral.

Wuthering Heights (1848) gained relatively little attention at publication but has steadily mounted in stature to be acclaimed the greatest Brontë novel. *Wuthering* is a Yorkshire variant upon *weathering,* i.e. "stormy."

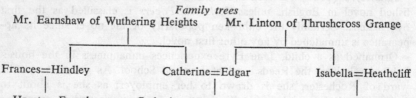

Family trees

Mr. Earnshaw of Wuthering Heights   Mr. Linton of Thrushcross Grange

Frances=Hindley   Catherine=Edgar   Isabella=Heathcliff

Hareton Earnshaw   Catherine (Cathy) Linton=Linton Heathcliff

In 1801 Mr. Lockwood, tenant at Thrushcross Grange, is marooned by snow in Wuthering Heights, home of his landlord, Heathcliff. Startled at night by the apparition of the elder Catherine, he exacts the local history from Ellen Dean, housekeeper of Thrushcross Grange. Years before, Mr. Earnshaw found in Liverpool a dark urchin whom he brought up under the name of Heathcliff. His daughter, Catherine, and Heathcliff are companions, but after Mr. Earnshaw's death his son Hindley mistreats Heathcliff. When Catherine decides to marry Edgar Linton, Heathcliff vanishes. Returning later, Heathcliff wins Wuthering Heights from Hindley by gambling and after Hindley's death treats Hareton as a servant. Heathcliff compels Edgar's daughter to marry his son by Isabella, and with Linton Heathcliff's death the older Heathcliff is master of Thrushcross Grange. In 1802 Lockwood learns of the death by heartbreak of Heathcliff and finds young Cathy and Hareton in possession of Wuthering Heights.

Thrushcross Grange represents the cultured amenities of life, the world of genteel society. Wuthering Heights represents primitive vitality. Catherine is torn between the two. With all its polish and beauty, Thrushcross Grange has an air of triviality and decay, and in spite of its natural force, Wuthering Heights displays crudity and awkwardness. Catherine wants the virtues of both and sees no incongruity in stating that she loves Edgar, the world of manners and respectability. Nonetheless, she also loves Heathcliff, but this is a love deeper than love, springing from elemental powers. Heathcliff is the symbol of all dark potencies in a being of unknown origin, impressively bearing but one name, that of looming natural landscape.

The appeal of the novel and its consummate poetry arise then not from a conventional love triangle but from a struggle of archetypes representing universal forces. The ties that bind Catherine to Heathcliff are beyond sex, and from the stormy tumult of their elders (resolved in the union of death), young Cathy and Hareton may effect a workable balance in life of the active and passive.

Anne Brontë (1820–1849). Less famous than Charlotte or Emily, Anne Brontë contributed poetry to their joint effort, *Poems by Currer, Ellis, and Acton Bell*. She also wrote what is still an underrated novel, *Agnes Grey* (1847), which was published with *Jane Eyre* and *Wuthering Heights*. She wrote another novel, *The Tenant of Wildfell Hall* (1847).

OTHER EARLY VICTORIAN NOVELISTS

Edward George Earle Lytton Bulwer-Lytton, first **Baron Lytton of Knebworth** (1803–1873). Bulwer-Lytton was born in London as Edward Bulwer, a general's son. As a youth he had a love affair with Lady Caroline Lamb, the pursuer of Byron. After graduation from Cambridge in 1826 he married Rosina Wheeler in 1827 and served in parliament from 1831–41 and from 1852–66. He separated from his wife in 1836, and for years thereafter she subjected him to every possible public embarrassment. His historical dramas, *The Lady of Lyons* and *Richelieu* (both 1838), survived on the English stage into the 20th century because of their bravura color. Inheriting his mother's property in 1843, he added her maiden name to his to form the hyphenated surname. During 1858–59 he was colonial secretary, and in 1866 was raised to the peerage. His only son, Edward, proved to be a brilliant diplomat and under the pseudonym of Owen Meredith a secondary but popular poet.

Bulwer-Lytton seemed another Byron to his age (incredibly, he was even offered the throne of Greece but declined). As a handsome young man he was a noted socialite, and his virtuosi writings made him a European personality; Wagner, for example, based his opera *Rienzi* upon Lytton's novel (1835). As the fashionable taste in novels veered, so veered Lytton with astounding dexterity.

Pelham; or The Adventures of a Gentleman (1828) is the best picture extant of high society in the transition from Regency to Victorianism. Pelham's insistence upon wearing only black as formal garb established the still-continuing practice of men's black evening clothes.

The Last Days of Pompeii (1834) purposely strives to outdo Scott by grandiose theatricality in treating an historical theme. It remains Lytton's most popular novel.

A wealthy young Greek, Glaucus, loves Ione, but her guardian, Arbaces, a sinister Egyptian priest of Isis, has designs upon her. Glaucus sends messages to Ione by the blind slave girl Nydia, who is hopelessly in love with him. Arbaces has Glaucus falsely convicted of murder, and the youth is thrown into the arena to face a wild lion. The eruption of Vesuvius frees Glaucus and kills Arbaces. In the darkness Ione and Glaucus are led to safety by Nydia. When the lovers awake in the boat the next morning, they find that the broken-hearted Nydia has drowned herself.

Lytton is concerned not with a version of history but with an overly elaborate, baroque depiction of Pompeii, the city of pleasure on the eve of destruction. The sinfulness of the pagan Pompeians is contrasted with the simple piety of the Christians, and the city's obliteration is righteous retribution upon the wicked. Seeking tragic sublimity, Lytton achieves horrific sensationalism.

The Last of the Barons (1843) is actually Lytton's best novel. In breaking the Scott formula, Lytton anticipates the 20th-century historical novel. The central figure is the 15th-century Warwick the King-maker during the Wars of the Roses, and Lytton uses fiction not to distort or alter historical facts but to provide motivation and dialogue illuminating actual events.

My Novel (1853) displays Lytton's remarkable versatility in a realistic domestic novel, probably the best examination of life in the Victorian country mansions.

Charles Reade (1814–1884). Charles Reade was the son of an Ipsden, Oxfordshire, squire. A brilliant Oxford University career insured him a life-long fellowship at Magdalen College, but he generally spent his time in London bachelor quarters. Reade considered himself primarily a dramatist, but his plays—like *Masks and Faces* (1852), later turned into a novel, *Peg Woffington* (1853)—though current successes, have since lost all favor. Most of his novels—principally *It's Never Too Late to Mend* (1856) and *Hard Cash* (1863)—follow the reforming ardor of Dickens, objecting to prison conditions, cruel insane asylums, and riotous conditions of labor. He wrote one masterpiece, quite different from his other works, a superb historical novel.

The Cloister and the Hearth (1861) applied to 15th-century Europe the Reade insistence upon making readers see, hear, and feel the tangible objects and atmosphere of an era.

Gerald Eliason, son of a Dutch merchant, has been destined to the priesthood since birth. Angered by his son's love for Margaret Brandt, the father, with medieval sanction, imprisons his disobedient boy, but Gerald is aided in escape by his sweetheart. Fleeing toward a contemplated art career in Italy, the youth is befriended through many adventures by Denys, a Burgundian bowman. A false report of Margaret's death causes Gerald to enter the Dominican order as Brother Clement. Years later the two meet, but he pursues his religious work and she cares for their son Gerald, who grows up to be Erasmus, great Renaissance scholar and humanist.

Probably no other historical novel has rendered so exciting its mass of erudition about the past. Yet for all his learning Reade still followed Scott's 19th-century pattern of the historical novel in implanting a contemporary in previous epochs. Gerald is essentially a 19th-century Protestant youth thrust into the Pre-Reformation period, and the novel's ferment of curiosity, experiment, and invention belongs more truly to the Victorian era than to 15th-century Europe. Reade's anti-Romanist viewpoints are strongly colored by the survival of compulsory celibacy for university dons that frustrated the novelist himself. Gerald's thrilling adventures on the road are among the best picaresque passages in English, and stout-hearted Denys is one of the most engaging of minor characters in literature. Successful in evoking an era of zest and tumult, Reade barely misses in elevating an unhappy love affair to profound tragedy through the irreconcilable claims of the religious life (cloister) and domesticity (hearth).

Elizabeth Cleghorn Gaskell (gas'kel) (1810–1865). Elizabeth Cleghorn Gaskell, née Stevenson, was born in Chelsea, London. Because her mother died a month after her birth, she was adopted by her aunt and brought up in Knutsford, Cheshire, the environment of *Cranford*. In 1832 she married William Gaskell, a Unitarian clergyman, and lived thereafter in Manchester. Her fiction won her the friendship of Carlyle, Dickens, and Landor. Her *Life of Charlotte Brontë* (1857) was the first biographical study of the Brontës and is still an invaluable contemporary account.

Cranford was first serialized in Dickens' *Household Words*, 1851–53. This classic of English small-town life is the author's best-known but least typical novel.

Cranford is a hamlet inhabited almost exclusively by spinsters and widows living in "elegant economy." Domineering Miss Deborah Jenkyns is the leader of this humble social set until her death. Her younger sister Matilda (Matty) is impoverished by a bank failure, but the new arbiter, Mrs. Jamieson, is willing to tolerate her because her father was a rector. A long-lost brother Peter returns from India to help Matty. Lady Glenmire, Mrs. Jamieson's sister-in-law, surprisingly marries the town physician and becomes plain Mrs. Hoggins.

Although it is more a collection of character sketches than a novel, *Cranford* offers some minor dramas, but hardly enough to disturb its genteel old-maidish placidity. To its own age, and to ours, the novel displayed a nostalgia for an island of quiet, gentle, prim English ladies in a tumultuous industrial age.

North and South (1855), more typically Gaskell, troubled Dickens as he serialized it in *Household Words*. The contrast lies between the industrial north and the agricultural south of England. Attempting to reconcile conflicting interests, Mrs. Gaskell tries to portray both employer and employee favorably, but the stark depictions of starving strikers are powerfully affecting and to many contemporaries seemed horribly subversive. The novelist preaches the compromise spirit of the Corn Law repeal against rampant laissez-faire. Although her grasp of economics can be challenged, Mrs. Gaskell shocked her readers profoundly by her graphic accounts of human suffering and industrial strife.

Charles Kingsley (1819–1875). Son of the vicar of Holne, Devonshire, Charles Kingsley spent his early years upon the south coast, scene of many episodes in his historical novels. After Magdalen College, Cambridge, he was presented in 1842 with the living of Eversley, Hampshire, which he occupied for the rest of his life. In 1859 he became chaplain to Queen Victoria; from 1860 to 1869 he was professor of modern history at Cambridge; in 1873 he was named a canon of Westminster.

Kingsley's unwarranted slurs against Newman have darkened his continuing reputation. In his own era, as a militant Christian Socialist, he was often termed a dangerous radical. Yet this "radical" joined Carlyle and other reactionaries in defense of Governor Eyre (see the life of J. S. Mill in Chapter 3). Marx's famous condemnation of religion as an "opiate of the people" is a misconstruction of Kingsley's objections in *Politics for the People* (1848) to the apathy of Christians toward their suffering fellowmen. Kingsley was actually a supporter of the "social gospel" and economic co-operatives rather than an advocate of any deep-seated changes. Social reform in England before Kingsley was generally associated with irreligion (like the atheistic unionist Higgins in Mrs. Gaskell's *North and South*); Kingsley saw reform as essential Christian brotherhood.

Alton Locke, Tailor and Poet (1850) is the first significant novel in

English to present a proletarian (not a mere picaresque) hero. Locke is a mystic whose universal love for mankind is diverted into the revolutionary Chartist movement. The failure of Chartism results in his spiritual re-enlightenment, in which he substitutes moral force and Christian love for any violence. The burning sincerity of Kingsley in his depiction of slums worse than pigsties and brutally-treated labor probably did more than any other 19th-century work to awaken the conscience of smug Victorians.

Westward Ho! (1855), Kingsley's most famous novel, is set in Elizabethan times. Kingsley's purpose, born of Crimean war times, was to preach "muscular Christianity."

Amyas Leigh, a blond giant from Bideford who has sailed with Drake around the world, promises to seek the child of Oxenham (who was slain by the Inquisition). Meanwhile, he fights under Ralegh in Spain and brings home a Spanish captive, Don Guzman. Amyas' love, Rose Salterne, elopes with Guzman. Pursuing Guzman in the new world, Amyas finds Rose content with her husband. A land hunt for a mythical treasure city turns up Ayacanora, Oxenham's lost daughter. Learning of Rose's death and that of his brother Frank at the hands of the Inquisition, Amyas vows to kill all Spaniards he can. He fights gallantly against the Armada, sinking Guzman's ship. Blinded by a thunderbolt, he has a vision of the true love of Guzman and Rose. Ayacanora marries and cares for the maimed giant.

Today's readers relish the spirited romance of dramatic duels, spectacular sea battles, and grisly tortures of the Inquisition. Quite unhistoric, Kingsley's exemplary Elizabethans possess the fierceness of Vikings and the moral delicacy of evangelical clerics.

Among Kingsley's other works: *Hypatia* (1853), a novel set in Alexandria about A.D. 400; and *The Water Babies* (1863), an imaginative story for children.

Benjamin Disraeli, first Earl of Beaconsfield (1804–1881). Benjamin Disraeli was the son of Isaac D'Israeli, a writer of literary anecdotes. Although descended from an ancient and aristocratic Jewish family, the young Disraeli joined the Anglican Church in 1817, symptomatic of the "erosion" induced by English tolerance toward Jews. Educated at home, he first entered parliament in 1841 and then sat without interruption in Commons from 1847 to 1876. His brilliance made him the head of the Conservatives from 1847 until his death. After three separate terms as chancellor of the exchequer, he became prime minister briefly during 1868 and then from 1874 to 1880. On his own initiative Disraeli engineered the 1875 coup by which England gained controlling interest in the Suez Canal. In 1876 he had Victoria proclaimed Empress of India and was himself elevated to the peerage. The "Peace with Honor" which he secured from Russia in 1878 at the Congress of Berlin brought his popularity to its peak and won him a Knighthood of the Garter. His funeral occasioned the greatest national mourning between the deaths of Wellington and Victoria. The English still observe the day of his death, April 19, as Primrose Day, for this was Disraeli's favorite flower.

Disraeli's external political philosophy was expounded in hundreds of speeches keynoting Imperialism, a "Big England" concept. Sensing the pride of Englishmen and the loyalty of the colonies, Disraeli inspired his age with the concept of empire that was to grip the national spirit until after World War II. His internal political philosophy, expounded chiefly in his novels, testifies to the remarkable emergence of the novel as a vehicle for wide popular communication. Opposing the middle class, Disraeli called for a working partnership of peers and proletariat with the monarchy serving as a vital principle, not a mere instrument. The impact of his novels had much to do with lifting him to the leadership of the Conservatives.

Coningsby (1844), propagandizing for the conservative "Young England" movement, has often been called the best political novel ever written. Instead of an essay or treatise, fiction, Disraeli asserted, "offered the best chance of influencing opinion."

Coningsby, grandson of the Marquis of Monmouth, is invited to explore the Manchester factories of his Eton classmate, Oswald Millbank. At the manufacturer's mansion Coningsby meets Edith Millbank and learns that her Whig father favors a natural aristocracy of able men instead of hereditary peers. At his grandfather's social functions he learns the Young England concepts from Sidonia, a wealthy Jew. Class conflicts weaken the nation, and upper and lower classes should unite in affirming English solidarity of property and labor against the disruptive mercantile spirit of the middle class. Coningsby wins Edith in spite of her father's opposition and in 1840 wins a parliamentary seat from which he may proclaim his ideas.

Trollope's political novels surpass Disraeli's as novels, but Disraeli grasps political philosophies as Trollope cannot. Lord Monmouth, perhaps Disraeli's most impressive fictional creation, represents Old Torydom, smug, cynical, urbane, and selfish. Millbank is the Whig spirit of laissez-faire, industrialism, bourgeois dominance. Sidonia is Disraeli himself, gifted with Rothschild millions, the outside observer who can chart the new and rightful course via Young England. Coningsby (drawn after George Smythe, active in the movement) is English youth proceeding through the novel to political maturity. Disraeli's wit is scintillating, matched in English fiction only by Peacock and Meredith.

A "Condition-of-England" trilogy is completed by *Sybil, or The Two Nations* (1845) and *Tancred* (1847). "The two nations" are the rich and the poor; in *Sybil,* Disraeli matches the social novelists in their disclosures of proletarian miseries. Whig and Tory simply represent conflicting interests among the wealthy; both ignore the genuine suffering of the populace. Conservatism (the New Tories) must weld a revitalized, just, and unified

England. *Tancred* preaches against materialism and seeks a religious awakening, though Tancred's search for spiritual rebirth in the Holy Land is developed inconclusively. Today's readers, conceiving of Victorianism as stable and satisfied, discover a surprisingly 20th-century attitude in the perceptive Disraeli: Europe is disillusioned, weary, psychically spent.

Richard Doddridge Blackmore (1825–1900). Son of the curate of Long-worth, Berkshire, Richard Doddridge Blackmore was educated at Oxford and at the Middle Temple of law. His early attempts at poetry proved unimpressive, but from his first novel in 1864 he established himself as a popular writer of fiction. In their shapelessness, most of his novels reveal the dangers of Victorian serializing.

Lorna Doone (1869) has been termed the first novel of the Romantic revival in fiction. It remains Blackmore's one famous work and the model for many subsequent best-sellers.

During the late 17th century Exmoor is terrorized by the savage Doone clan, which has, among other atrocities, murdered the father of the narrator, John Ridd. Lorna Doone, however, is a jewel among these brigands. Ridd wishes to bear her off from her savage relatives but is opposed by Carver Doone, a villainous giant. For services to the king during the Monmouth Rebellion, Ridd is knighted, and returns to marry Lorna. Carver wounds the bride but is overpowered by Ridd and thrown into the quicksand bogs.

Lorna Doone is a provincial rather than a historical novel. The autobiographical technique captures the flavor of West Country speech and spirit—rhythmic dialogue, rustic humor, robust honesty. Blackmore makes no attempt to think himself or his readers into the historic events or the mind-set of the era. Although distressingly superficial in comparison to the works of the Brontës, his novel provides the sure-fire formula often repeated thereafter.

George Henry Borrow (1803–1881). Of Cornish ancestry, George Henry Borrow was born at East Denham, Norfolk. After grammar-school education he was articled to a firm of lawyers, but neglected law for the extensive study of languages. His phenomenal grasp of other tongues included most European languages and went as far as Turkish and Chinese. Dissatisfied with current society, he began a tramp's life that carried him throughout the British Isles, with special interest in Gypsies. By an ironic quirk, he became an agent of the Bible Society to finance his foreign wanderings, ostensibly as a distributor of religious publications.

A handsome muscular giant towering over six feet, this remarkable linguist was probably the most extraordinary vagabond of history. Much of his writing seems clearly fictional, and even the ascertainable facts have been treated with the verve and freedom of a novelist.

The Bible in Spain (1842) is too inaccurate in facts and too unconcerned with conventional landmarks ever to be a guidebook to Spain, but no other work lays so bare and brings so vividly alive the feel of the land and the pulse of its people. Borrow's mission as colporteur of pious writings startlingly contrasts with his breezy worldliness, his zest for bravura adventure and sensation, his fascination with dark, primeval passions. It may be the masterpiece of romantic travel accounts.

Lavengro (1851) and *The Romany Rye* (1857) form one continuous narrative, a highly fictionalized autobiography covering Borrow's life until 1825. Enemy of all conventions and passionately fond of freedom and action, he associates with outcasts, particularly the Gypsies. He varies between a pedant's display of linguistic skill and the wild rakishness of the bohemian. Scenery has little interest; he is absorbed by the eccentric and the robust in human activity. Borrow's herculean battle with the Tinman and his idyllic love affair with Isopel Berners rank among the most emotive passages in Romantic prose. Lavengro ("philologist") and Romany Rye ("Gypsy gentleman") were both terms applied to Borrow by the Gypsies.

Frederick Marryat (mar'i-at) (1792–1848). A native Londoner, Frederick Marryat entered the Royal Navy in 1806 and through valiant service in the Napoleonic Wars by 1815 rose to commander (he is frequently called Captain Marryat). He was on duty at St. Helena in 1821 when Napoleon died there. During the Burmese War (1824–25) he performed with especial courage and success. In 1830 he resigned to devote his remaining years to novels about the "old navy," portrayed realistically but with much less savagery than Smollett sketched. Without psychologizing powers, Marryat displayed such narrative fluency that Ford Maddox Ford over-enthusiastically termed him "the greatest of English novelists."

Mr. Midshipman Easy (1836) explores ship life during the Napoleonic Wars.

Spoiled Jack Easy is initiated into a midshipman's life and serves with distinction aboard the *Harpy*, in the process falling in love with Agnes, a Sicilian girl in a captured Spanish vessel (while Spain was an ally of Napoleon). Even more thrilling adventures await him aboard the *Aurora*. Marrying Agnes, Easy retires to a country gentleman's life upon an inherited estate in Hampshire.

Few novelists can match Marryat in depicting stirring action, and his headlong dash generously sprinkled with camaraderie and cleaned-up Sterne-like humor, lured several generations of British youth to the sea.

Robert Smith Surtees (1803–1864). Born at Durham, Robert Surtees was educated at the local grammar school. He studied law in a lawyer's office and practiced in London. His avocation was sport, especially hunting, which increasingly monopolized his time. He considered his racy journalistic pieces improper for his own children to read.

Jorrocks' Jaunts and Jollities was serialized from 1831 to 1834 in *The*

New Sporting Magazine, edited by Surtees. *Pickwick Papers* by Dickens was commissioned as a competitive work to this phenomenal success.

Fox-hunting, rabbit-shooting, and stag-chasing are the weekend and holiday recreations of the cockney grocer, John Jorrocks. His episodic adventures are punctuated by ludicrous mishaps and gargantuan meals.

This is the classic English sporting volume. Jorrocks was intended as a lampoon upon the wealthy cockney copying his betters, but Surtees and his readers are wholly delighted with the vulgar, earthy, John-Bullish huntsman.

Joseph Sheridan Le Fanu (lef'a-nū) (1814–1873). A grandnephew of the dramatist Richard Brinsley Sheridan, Joseph Sheridan Le Fanu was born, lived, and died in Dublin. After Trinity College he was an active journalist for Conservative publications. After his wife's death in 1858 he lived in retirement, haunted by his own imaginary horrors. He was the British master of Poe-like stories in the 19th century; James Joyce, an avid reader of Le Fanu, incorporates many references to his works in *Finnegans Wake.*

Uncle Silas, a Tale of Bartram-Haugh (1864), according to Elizabeth Bowen, "is not the last, belated Gothic romance but the first (or among the first) of the psychological thrillers." It may be the masterpiece of the novel of terror.

Maud Ruthyn, by her father's will, is ward of her uncle Silas, a recluse in the decayed Derbyshire country house, Bartram-Haugh. Silas is under a cloud because of the mysterious murder of a bookie to whom he owed money. Maud's death would make Silas rich. She tries to escape but is kept a virtual prisoner. Silas and his coarse son Dudley come to murder Maud but kill the governess by mistake. Silas dies from an overdose of opium, and Maud is happily married to Lord Ilbury.

Few novels maintain so long the dreadful suspense of *Uncle Silas.* Maud, the narrator, is helpless apprehension personified, beset with ever mounting terrors. Not the trappings of the gothic novel but Maud's internal fears grip the reader. The pervasive autumnal atmosphere is a perfect background.

William Wilkie Collins (1824–1889). Son of William Collins, the noted landscape painter, Wilkie Collins was a native Londoner. In his teens the family lived for several years in Italy. Back in London, he studied law desultorily and embarked upon literature after his father's death in 1847. After 1873 his work was significantly weakened by the intrusion of propaganda.

Although Collins' plots are melodramatic, they anticipate Henry James and later novelists in their tight economy and careful dovetailing. Collins strongly influenced the later Dickens, though many consider Collins' influence more of ingenuity than sound construction. Collins actually has exerted more influence upon the English novel than any other minor novelist. *The Woman in White* (1860) was one of his most successful novels, and posterity has awarded high praise for *The Moonstone* (1868).

The Moonstone has been termed "probably the best detective story in the world" by Chesterton and "the first, the longest, and the best of modern English detective novels" by T. S. Eliot.

At the storming of Seringapatan, India, in 1799, John Herncastle steals an enormous diamond (the moonstone), which he bequeaths to his niece, Rachel Verinder. Young Franklin Blake, a distant cousin, brings the stone to Rachel for her birthday, but it immediately disappears. Sergeant Cuff of Scotland Yard finds innocent the trio of Hindus sworn to recover the stone and suspects Rachel herself, because she thwarts the investigation. Rachel becomes engaged to Godfrey Ablewhite, a personable charity worker, but she breaks the engagement when he is revealed as a fortune hunter. The gem is traced by Cuff to a pawnbroker who passes it to a bearded sailor. The bearded man, who is robbed and murdered, turns out to be Ablewhite in disguise. Franklin, as Rachel looked on, had taken the diamond while under sedation and had passed it to Ablewhite for safekeeping. When the awakened Franklin forgot his handling of the stone, Ablewhite simply kept it. Several years after Franklin and Rachel are married, a traveler tells them of seeing the moonstone upon the forehead of an Indian idol.

Dickens introduced the detective to the English novel in Inspector Bucket of *Hard Times,* but Collins here creates the pattern of the detective novel since followed by thousands of works. The plot is replete with clues and misdirections, and mysteries fit within mysteries like Chinese boxes; there is enough material for half a dozen detective stories. Rachel is a high-spirited girl, unexpected in Victorian life and most welcome in any life. The resourceful Cuff, lover of rosebushes, is the first of an immense progeny of astute, imperturbable sleuths. The narrative follows the older epistolary form, each writer blessed with Collins' fluency and eerie eye for atmosphere. The novelist adroitly exemplifies his own formula: "Make 'em laugh, make 'em weep, make 'em wait."

THE NOVEL OF INTELLECTUAL
AND PSYCHOLOGICAL EMPHASIS

In rebellion against the bourgeois ascendancy, the novel of the intelligentsia during the Victorian period and the early 20th century displays the following characteristics:

(1) Questioning of middle-class ethics and morals. The "good" characters refuse to conform to principles of bourgeois orthodoxy. If, as usually happens, they are punished for their nonconformity, they are not to blame; it is current society that is at fault.

(2) Individual orientation. The major human problem envisaged by nov-

elists of this group is the self-realization of the individual. Worthy characters defy conventions and social pressures to realize the fullness of their own natures.

(3) Emphasis on inner nature of characters. During this phase of the intelligentsia novel the character still maintains a fully rounded form, but the emphasis shifts from his social behavior to his inner life.

(4) The hero. In this phase the intellectual critic is rationalistic and confident of man's essential goodness, seeing society as responsible for the distorting of man. The hero in these works generally sees through society's limitations and molds his own life, but his necessarily awkward relations to his society and his own inward struggles militate against giant heroic stature. Frequently the central figure is not a hero at all but the compromiser, the defeated, or the benighted conformer.

(5) Seriousness. During this phase of the revolt, the rebels are still Victorianly sober, convinced that although the current mores are wrong there is a fixed standard of conduct and viewpoint that should be adopted.

THE NOVELS OF GEORGE ELIOT

George Eliot (real name Mary Ann [or Marian] Evans) (1819–1880). Mary Ann Evans was the daughter of a Warwickshire farm manager. Christiana, Isaac, and Mary Ann, all born at Arbury Farm, near Nuneaton, were children of a second marriage. For Mary Ann's first twenty-one years her home was Griff House, her father's residence. At the age of eight when her reading of Scott's *Waverley* was interrupted, she wrote her own second half for the novel. After strongly evangelical private education, she became her father's housekeeper first at Griff and later in Coventry. In the big city she became acquainted with freethinking Charles Bray and Charles Hennell, who effectively converted her to agnosticism. Hennell's wife abandoned her translation of Strauss's *Life of Jesus* (one of the most famous pieces of "higher criticism" of the Bible) and Mary Ann completed it for her first publication in 1846. Her remarkable intellectuality made her a book reviewer in Coventry and thence in London as assistant editor for the *Westminster Review*. She developed an emotional as well as intellectual interest in Herbert Spencer, but that philosopher was too wary to be snared in marriage. In 1854 she went to live with George Henry Lewes, a talented writer on various subjects, who was unable under Victorian law to secure a divorce from his estranged wife. Branded as an adulteress, Mary Ann was compelled to publish all subsequent writings anonymously or pseudonymously. The sons of Lewes, because of the scandal, had to be educated abroad; they testified that Mary Ann, who labored to support them, was the truest of mothers. Her penname (George from Lewes, Eliot because it "was a good mouth-filling easily pronounced name") was first affixed to *Scenes of Clerical Life* (1858), which consisted of three stories clearly revealing the notable characteristics of the novels which were to follow. A journey to Italy in 1860 provided the background for the later novel *Romola*. During another Italian visit in 1869 she met John Cross, an avid admirer. Lewes died in 1878, and in 1880 she married Cross, twenty years her junior. She died seven months after her marriage.

Lord David Cecil has called George Eliot "the first modern novelist." Hers was the first massive intellect to turn to the English novel. Henceforth the English novel would be not only the product of a sensitive observer and natural artist but also the vehicle for ideas based upon a conscious rational philosophy. George Eliot was a proponent of the Positivism of the Frenchman, Auguste Comte (1798–1857), which saw three stages in the development of civilization: theological, metaphysical, positivist. He believed that Europe was in the Positive or scientific era and therefore should discard the older concepts of god, faith, and immortality in favor of a "religion of humanity" which would channel religious impulses into love and sympathy for all mankind. George Eliot insisted that men receive their rewards or punishments here and not in the hereafter; such rewards are not material, as the bourgeois novelists believed, but in inner well-being. From Comte (who invented the word *sociology*) George Eliot also adopted the scientific attitude toward social behavior; cause-and-effect relationships in politics, economics, religion, and all other areas explain human conduct. Therefore, there are no villains in the novels of George Eliot, since all characters act as the influences upon them dictate.

THE EARLIER (RUSTIC) NOVELS. Still the most popular George Eliot novels are the ones set in the author's native Warwickshire. Charming pastoral idylls are given the memorable backbone of penetrating character analysis and some of the most convincingly realistic scenes in the whole range of English fiction. These earlier works really constitute the novelist's *Prelude,* a shrewd and poetic scrutiny of the forces that molded George Eliot and made her a novelist.

Adam Bede (1859) is a rural painting of the Dutch school depicting a pre-industrial agricultural area at the geographical and psychical heart of England.

It is late 18th century. Mrs. Poyser of Hayslope has two nieces—pretty Hetty Sorrel, and sober Dinah Morris, a Methodist lay preacher. The town carpenter, Adam Bede, loves Hetty but she prefers Captain Arthur Donnithorne, the young squire. Adam's brother Seth proposes to Dinah but she refuses on the basis of her ministry. Adam, finding Hetty and Donnithorne embracing, overpowers his rival and compels him to write a farewell note to Hetty. On the eve of her marriage to Adam, Hetty flees to Donnithorne, but his regiment has left for Ireland. Giving birth to Donnithorne's child and then abandoning it, she is tried for infanticide. Donnithorne secures her reprieve, but she dies. Adam is drawn toward Dinah.

This work did for the novel what Wordsworth did for poetry in the *Lyrical Ballads*. George Eliot produces a friendly Hayslope, fresh, robust, authentic. Donnithorne is not a petty seducer, but a thoughtless, young strayer, as Hetty is. Adam and Dinah display the firmly moral righteousness of the peasant, exemplifiers in spite of their priggishness of the melioristic virtues cherished by the novelist. As in all George Eliot's successful novels, *Adam Bede* proclaims that love without marriage or marriage without love is equally debasing. For all the characters their natures and environment determine their fate, and their degree of happiness is solely of their own making. Mrs. Poyser, garrulous but wise, the household pillar and oracle, is a masterpiece of comic realism. Suffusing all is the lyricism of rural Warwickshire.

The Mill on the Floss (1860) exorcises George Eliot's own emotional and spiritual struggles in childhood and girlhood.

Dorlcote Mill on the Floss near St. Ogg's, the very life of Mr. Tolliver, its owner, becomes increasingly in the debt of lawyer Wakem, Tolliver's enemy. The education of proud Tom Tolliver and his brilliant sister Maggie is ended by foreclosure upon the mill. Tolliver remains as manager but vows his son to eternal hatred of the Wakems. Against her family's wishes, Maggie becomes interested in crippled Philip Wakem, son of the new owner. However, Stephen Guest, beau of Maggie's friend Lucy Deane, takes Maggie for a boatride and urges elopement. Although Maggie refuses, they are forced to spend the night together in the drifting boat. Tom and his father cast off Maggie as a fallen woman. Tom is now running the mill that he has been able to buy back. When an autumnal flood inundates the Floss, Maggie hurries to her brother and is drowned with him.

The first section of the novel is dominated by the brother-sister relationship of Maggie and Tom (Marian Evans and her brother Isaac). Tom seems unworthy of Maggie's devotion, but even the highly intellectualized George Eliot felt the feminine need to lean upon a tower of masculine assurance and will. The unsentimental portrait of childhood was a refreshing innovation in Victorian literature, and its sensitivity and sharpness have yet to be surpassed.

Remarkable in the growing-up of Maggie is the depiction of her falling in love with Stephen. Until this work the English novel was distressingly content with confronting two attractive young people of opposite sexes and then informing readers that they were in love (the Brontës' work is the notable exception, but theirs is an ecstatic poetic heightening). The foppish Stephen appears an unlikely match for the intellectual Maggie, but George Eliot pictures convincingly and freshly the urgent sensual compulsion; in the process Stephen is at least partially transformed by his love for Maggie. Regrettably, George Eliot never attempted this depiction elsewhere.

Silas Marner (1861), with the "wise passiveness" of Wordsworth, is probably the nearest thing to a perfect George Eliot novel, though its field is admittedly small and its tone rather gray.

Unjustly accused of theft, the linen-weaver Silas Marner came to Raveloe fifteen years before the story commences. His whole life revolves around his horde of gold, which he nightly counts with his nearsighted eyes. Raveloe's leading citizen is Squire Cass, father of the decent Godfrey and the n'er-do-well Dunstan. Dunstan steals Marner's gold and drunkenly falls to his death in an abandoned quarry. Godfrey had married a common woman in a distant hamlet but conceals his marriage in order to woo Nancy Lammeter. The first Mrs. Godfrey Cass dies on the way to her husband, and the nearsighted Marner at first mistakes her golden-haired child for his lost gold. Caring for the foundling (whom he names Eppie) gives new meaning to Marner's life. The discovery of Dunstan's skeleton and Marner's lost gold causes Godfrey to confess. Childless Nancy wants Eppie but Eppie, now sixteen, clings to Marner.

The novel's theme is the regenerative power of humanity and love. Marner's miserly existence was a stultification of life, but Eppie is his means of regaining and renewing life. For once George Eliot eschews overt moralizing and lets the story carry its own weight. The novel is again a case study in a community, an early 19th-century village before the advent of factory industrialism.

THE LATER NOVELS. Later George Eliot novels generally move away from purely rural Warwickshire as she feels the need to explore the possibilities of the novel of intellectual content. A fervid intellectual idea permeates each of these works, sometimes to the detriment of realistic character portrayal.

Romola (1863), her one attempt at the historical novel, is set in late 15th-century Florence, Italy.

Money belonging to his foster father, Baldasare Calvo, and necessary to ransom the old man from slavery, is squandered by Tito Melema. He marries the beautiful, scholarly Romola but also consorts with Tessa, a lower-class girl who thought their mock-marriage at a carnival was genuine. Tito rises by being a spy for the opposing camps of the French and the Medici. Calvo reappears, is brushed aside by Tito, but denounces him. When his perfidy is revealed, Tito flees the populace but is killed by Calvo. Romola learns of Tessa and brings up her children by Tito.

The overriding theme is that moral excellence results from the incessant choice of good, while moral degradation results from selfish expediency. Tito begins by being merely weak, but ends as base and monstrous. The commendable characters, Savonarola and Romola, accept their moral responsibilities, aid their fellowmen, and grow in ethical stature. Although scenes and dialogue are often colorful and lively, George Eliot cannot successfully reconstruct Florentine life of this period.

Felix Holt, the Radical (1866) centers about a political election during the Reform Bill controversies of the 1830s.

Harold Transome, heir to Transome Court of Treby Magna, runs for election as a Radical, with the family lawyer Jermyn conducting the campaign. The rabble-rousing techniques are objectionable to Felix Holt, an educated youth who has nonetheless associated himself with the proletariat, working as a watchmaker. On election day Felix tries to quell a workers' riot but is arrested as ringleader in the slaying of a constable. His sweetheart, Esther Lyon, successfully obtains his release and is revealed as the true heiress of Transome Court. Harold wants to sue Jermyn as a thief, but the exasperated lawyer discloses that he is Harold's actual father. Esther relinquishes Transome Court to Harold and marries Felix.

Felix is supposed to carry the weight of a dedicated spirit, a grass-roots worker for the moral strengthening of the people. His ideals are supposed to awaken Esther, another Marian. Actually he remains George Eliot's spokesman for the Carlylean doctrine that a renovating of the spirit rather than political machinery is essential to progress. The plot is the novelist's most contrived. Nonetheless, the scrutiny of the provincial middle class is another engrossing sociological analysis. The Transome-Jermyn conflict is as deft as any George Eliot handling and should have been the central feature of the novel.

Middlemarch, a Study of Provincial Life (1871–72), also set in a Warwickshire town of the Reform period, is critically considered George Eliot's masterpiece. The title means "middle of the marches," i.e. typically provincial.

The intellectual Dorothea Brooke interests Sir James Chettam, but she marries the pompous scholar, Edward Casaubon. Sir James marries her vivacious sister Celia. Casaubon's second cousin, Will Ladislaw, loving Dorothea, causes Casaubon in his will to deny his property to Dorothea if she marries Will. Attending the dying Casaubon is Dr. Tertius Lydgate, a would-be medical researcher, who is drawn into the orbit of Middlemarch's influential banker, Nicholas Bulstrode. Rosamund Vincy sets her cap for Lydgate and captures him. The drunken Raffles, blackmailing Bulstrode because of the banker's shady past, dies under Lydgate's treatment and causes accusations of malpractice. Dorothea supports Lydgate, who moves to London and at his wife's insistence becomes a fashionable society physician. Will and Dorothea marry. Rosamund's weak brother Fred is assured of a better future by marriage to the excellent Mary Garth.

Virginia Woolf has termed *Middlemarch* "one of the few English novels written for grown-up people." In this century it has often been acclaimed as the greatest English novel, largely because it is the first novel in our language definitely concerned with the intellectual life. To any bourgeois novelist Lydgate's financial success and social position as a prominent physician would be perfect rewards; George Eliot makes the reader perceive that Lydgate's abandonment of research at his selfish wife's behest renders his inner life a sterile tragedy. To any bourgeois novelist the futile, meaningless scholarship of Casaubon would be a merry joke, but George Eliot conveys the bitter ache of a mind conscious of its uselessness. Indeed, George Eliot's characters achieve a mental complexity virtually unknown to the bourgeois novelists.

The novel indicts a society that denies ample scope to the intellect and to culture. The environment permits proper self-realization and creativity to the solid, nonintellectual Mary Garth, but Dorothea is endowed with a searching, constructive spirit fated to frustration. Lydgate would be right for her, but his defective regard for the role of women and the pressures of an acquisitive, superficial society make him choose Rosamund. Ladislaw is seen as an ampler, richer, truly international spirit unencumbered by current British limitations, but the very Englishness of George Eliot makes her incapable of lifting him above the well-intentioned dilettante.

George Eliot fills the canvas with a host of memorable minor characters. Her technical ability is proved by her flawless dovetailing of the Dorothea and Lydgate plots, originally planned as separate stories.

Daniel Deronda (1876) displays some of George Eliot's greatest strengths and greatest weaknesses.

Gwendolen Harleth is an intelligent society belle yet essentially cold and egotistical. She knows that aristocratic Henleigh Grandcourt has children by his mistress, Lydia Glasher, but she marries him to save her family from financial ruin. Her unhappy marriage is ended by Grandcourt's drowning, for which Gwendolen feels guilty. Although high society is alien to the experience of George Eliot, she performs a remarkable imaginative feat in depicting it convincingly. Marriage for the wrong reasons, usually monetary, is a familiar theme in the Victorian novel, but no contemporary matches George Eliot in the analysis of moral wretchedness and self-scorn as experienced by Gwendolen.

The second part deals more especially with Daniel Deronda, who plays a smaller role in the first part. Daniel has been brought up in ignorance of his ancestry by Grandcourt's uncle. Befriending a Jewish girl, Mirah Lapidoth, he comes in contact with Hebrew life and thought, especially through the inspired Zionist, Mordecai. Deronda departs with Mirah for Palestine to help establish a homeland for world Jewry. Deronda thus finds a mission worthy of him, as Dorothea Brooke never could. George Eliot sought to glorify a consecrated purpose far greater than selfish individualism, but her thesis runs away from her novelistic art.

George Eliot also wrote some verse, although it does not comprise an important part of her work. Her poetry included *The Spanish Gipsy* (1868), a verse drama, and *The Legend of Jubal* (1874); most noted is her lyric poem, "The Choir Invisible."

THE NOVELS, POETRY, AND OTHER WORKS OF MEREDITH

George Meredith (1828–1909). George Meredith was the son of a Portsmouth tailor and naval outfitter. Sensitive of his tradesman origin, Meredith encouraged mystification about his background. After schooling at Portsmouth and at Neuwied on the Rhine, he was apprenticed to a London lawyer but preferred London's literary Bohemia. Here he met Mary Ellen Nicholls, the brilliant widowed daughter of Thomas Love Peacock, and he married her in 1849. Their embattled marriage resulted in her elopement with an artist to Capri in 1858, leaving Meredith with their son. After her death in 1861 he married Marie Vulliamy in 1864; this second marriage proved happy. Although constantly writing both poems and novels, Meredith did not gain popular acclaim for three decades. He supported himself chiefly as reader for the publishers, Chapman and Hall, encouraging Hardy and Gissing but rejecting Butler's *Erewhon* and the novels of Shaw. Meredith eloquently advocated "advanced ideas," such as woman suffrage, that caused his era to label him "radical." A spinal ailment in the 1880s gradually forced him into a wheelchair. By the 1890s many of his contemporaries had caught up to Meredith's concepts, and among the intellectuals he became a virtual dictator of English letters. Even though at his death the monarch, Edward VII, requested his burial in Westminster Abbey, there was objection because of Meredith's vociferous free thought (he called himself a "practical Christian" but belonged to no sect). He was interred at Dorking beside his second wife.

Meredith and Hardy, close contemporaries, display diametrically opposite responses to the Victorian intellectual quarrel over the theory of evolution. While it induced (or substantiated) in Hardy the tragic view of life, evolution evoked from Meredith a sense of life as high comedy. He saw humanity as the loftiest evolution from Earth, and mind as the noblest evolution of humanity. His trinity consisted of mind, body, and spirit—all in continuous evolution to ever more splendid goals beyond our present conjecture. Like Browning, but shorn of evangelical Christianity, he urged activity, courage, faith in life. The 20th century has been intrigued by the intellectuality of his prose and verse but has often been dubious of his radiant optimism.

CRITICISM. *The Idea of Comedy and the Uses of the Comic Spirit* (1877), originally a lecture before the London Institution, is the best exposition of the Meredith philosophy that informs all his belletristic writings. Critical intelligence (Meredith's uncommon meaning for "common sense") must gov-

ern men and preserve genuine civilization. Its ally is the comic spirit, not
burlesque, not satire, but a clear-eyed, dispassionate perception of conceit,
sentimentality, and folly. In the novels such Olympian mockery of his
characters instead of sympathetic identification made Meredith unpleasant
to nonintellectual readers. Though only meagerly noted at the time, this
essay has since been rated among the top 19th-century critical essays and
among the best examples of a creative writer's analysis of his own purposes.

THE NOVELS. *The Ordeal of Richard Feverel* (1859) may be considered
Meredith's first novel, being preceded only by the oriental allegory, *The
Shaving of Shagpat* (1855).

His wife having run off with an indigent poet, Sir Austin Feverel trains
his son Richard by the System, which does not include women. As a boy,
Richard, in vengeance for a horsewhipping from farmer Blaize, bribes a
laborer to fire Blaize's hayrick. At the age of eighteen he meets Lucy
Desborough, Blaize's niece, and the System evaporates. When the elopers
marry, Sir Austin is irreconcilable. Richard leaves Lucy under the protection of Lord Mountfalcon and goes to London to plead with his father.
Seeking Lucy for himself, Mountfalcon pays Mrs. Mount to seduce Richard.
Ashamed of his fall, Richard flees to Germany from whence he is summoned by news of Lucy's bearing of his son. Richard's duel with Mountfalcon wounds him only slightly but causes Lucy's death from shock.

Meredith's novel is the Romeo and Juliet theme almost point by point,
especially to the blighting of youth by wrongheaded age. Sir Austin is
stuffily averse to his son marrying into a mere farmer's family, but his
grossest error lies in the "unnatural" System that disregards normal human
drives. Richard's abandonment of Lucy is hard to justify, and the conclusion
follows from Victorian melodrama, but Meredith is the last novelist to read
for plotting.

The most notable feature of the book is an unprecedented experimentation in style. Most of the novel is told with Meredith's ironic sophistication,
but Richard's tutor, Adrian Harley, offers sarcastic witticisms, and Sir
Austin keeps a book of philosophical aphorisms. Dialogue, especially from
Blaize and Mrs. Berry, is flavorfully realistic. At emotional climaxes, the
meeting of the lovers and the scene of Richard in the Rhineland storm,
Meredith soars with poetic extravagance; both episodes, of course, represent rebirth through Natural processes. Distracting to contemporary readers,
this versatility of style foreshadows the multiple viewpoint of 20th-century
experimenters.

Beauchamp's Career (1875), Meredith's own favorite, is his fullest scrutiny of contemporary problems.

Nevil Beauchamp revolts against his aristocratic origins, typified in his
uncle Romfrey, and becomes an avowed democrat and radical. In Venice
he is dismayed to see the *mariage de convenance* of the lovely French girl,

Renée. She refuses to flee with him and dutifully weds her father's choice, an aging marquis. Nevil plunges into English politics as a radical candidate for parliament, influenced by the republican Dr. Shrapnel and Jenny Denham, Shrapnel's ward. A summons from Renée forces his absence at election time and contributes to his defeat. Renée abandons her roué husband and throws herself upon Nevil, but he politely rejects her. Marrying Jenny because of suitability rather than love, he enjoys an increasingly affectionate union. In saving the life of a drowning urchin at Southampton, Nevil drowns. The bitter enemies, Romfrey and Shrapnel, leave the beach reconciled.

Often termed Meredith's "political" novel, *Beauchamp's Career* is much more. Perhaps no other liberal has perceived the genuine problems of reform with the clear vision of Meredith. The Comic Spirit recognizes equally the deficiencies of the conservative Romfrey and the radical Shrapnel. Although Nevil espouses Meredith's own convictions, he discovers how fallacious is the black-and-white view most men, especially idealists, take of life. He learns, essentially, that he must compromise with mankind.

The Egoist (1879), generally accepted as Meredith's masterpiece, applies *The Idea of Comedy* from overall concept to individual scene. The author labeled *The Egoist* "a comedy in narrative."

Sir Willoughby Patterne (the egoist) is loved by Laetitia Dale, but becomes engaged to Constantia Durham, who jilts him. Clara Middleton, daughter of the scholarly Dr. Middleton, is his next fiancée, but she too is repelled by his egoism. She struggles to get out of the engagement, with Vernon Whitford, Patterne's cousin, as her only ally. To avenge himself on the struggling Clara and to forestall her jilting of him, Patterne proposes to Laetitia, thus permitting Clara to escape. Clara marries Vernon, and Patterne is left with Laetitia.

The Comic Spirit chastises Patterne but, as Meredith states in his essay, still loves and understands him. His nasty egoism is a logical product of his class and era, the pattern of the highly praised Victorian gentleman (Willoughby Patterne refers to the "willow pattern" of Chinese porcelain picturing a girl escaping with her lover from a tyrannical father and a tyrannical fiancé). Patterne is the Romantic Victorian hero, but Meredith damns him and his numerous contemporary counterparts for caveman-like possessiveness and anti-intellectualism. The egoist is brought to heel when finally, embarrassingly, he must accept Laetitia on her terms, not his.

Clara is among the more successful female portraits by male novelists. She initially accepts Patterne, the "ideal husband" by Victorian standards, but gradually she apprehends Meredith's concept of marriage as a true expansion of a woman's life and as woman's intensified sharing of life's adventure as a partner. Meredith convincingly imparts an empathy for Clara as she desperately seeks to evade the enormity of Patterne's ego; as never before in the English novel, sexual revulsion is dramatically depicted.

Vernon Whitford, the quiet, unconventional freethinker, is Meredith's true anti-Victorian hero and the embodiment of the Comic Spirit. Vernon is modeled after Leslie Stephen, who is to reappear as an older and different man in Virginia Woolf's *To the Lighthouse*. Vernon, like Stephen, is a devotee of Comte's Positivism.

The entire situation is Meredith's own first marriage, now transferred to betrothal. With the magnanimity of few men but with the detachment of the Comic Spirit, Meredith sees his own failings in Patterne and the genuine distress of his first wife. Dr. Middleton obviously is drawn after Peacock, Meredith's first father-in-law.

Critical reception was belated recognition of a major novelistic talent in the writing of fiction. *The Egoist* remains as one of the few 19th-century novels still presenting a significant challenge to the intellectual 20th-century reader.

Diana of the Crossways (1885) poses the most difficult of novelistic problems to Meredith. His heroine is witty and intelligent, but commits horrible blunders. She traps herself in compromising situations, but must retain reader sympathy. Perhaps only Meredith could concoct so many devastatingly brilliant remarks to demonstrate conclusively the wit of Diana.

The attractive Irish beauty, Diana Merion, is besieged by suitors. Although the solid Thomas Redworth loves her, he is too late. To avoid unwelcome attentions she has already married the calculating politician, Augustus Warwick. While her husband is away, Diana associates with the elderly peer, Lord Dannisburgh. Warwick angrily sues the peer for seducing Diana. Although the suit fails, the innocent Diana believes herself stained and lives apart. When the ailing Warwick threatens to exercise his legal husbandly rights, Diana agrees to elope with Sir Percy Dacier, nephew of Dannisburgh, but Redworth dissuades her from this folly. Desperate for money, Diana sells to a newspaper Dacier's secret tip on the repeal of the Corn Laws. Chagrined at her violation of his confidence, Dacier marries an heiress. After Warwick's death Diana marries Redworth, who had patiently waited for her.

Meredith telescopes into about five years much of the long career of Caroline Norton, granddaughter of Richard Brinsley Sheridan and a noted writer (Diana writes a novel, *The Princess Egeria*). Meeting Mrs. Norton in her fifties, the awkward young Meredith had been delighted with her bearing and brilliance. Adhering too faithfully to what he deemed actual fact, Meredith leaves the reader incredulous that Diana would betray the secret.

Diana's mistakes are part of Meredith's concept. Purposely Meredith carries his heroine through what his Victorian readers considered unpardonable indiscretions only to assert that thereby a spiritually pure woman remains unsullied. Crossways, the family home of Diana, is also a word symbolizing womanhood at the threshold of modernity.

Among Meredith's other noted novels are *Evan Harrington* (1860), *Rhoda Fleming* (1865), and *The Adventures of Harry Richmond* (1871) in the early part of his career; and *One of Our Conquerors* (1891), *Lord Ormont and His Aminta* (1894), and *The Amazing Marriage* (1895) in the latter part.

THE POETRY. *Poems* (1851) consists of what the poet himself later termed "abstractly optimistic" verses, yearning for an end of war, for "the League of Nations" (actual title), for universal brotherhood and progress. Though mediocre as poetry, they are the grand visions of youthful idealism.

Modern Love (1862) cannot properly be compared to a sonnet sequence (in which each poem may be separately relished). It is a narrative poem diagnosing the breakdown of Meredith's first marriage, only slightly fictionalized. Each of the fifty units consists of sixteen lines formed of four quatrains riming *a b b a*. The poem basically studies the nuances of inner emotional conflicts between two highly sensitive and well-intentioned people, both of whom are equally culpable and blameless. Egotistically absorbed in his own concerns and still expecting his wife to be an unquestioning worshiper, the husband cannot appreciate her conception of the purely impulsive and sensual in marriage. The wife ("Madam") turns to a lover and the husband, not too vigorously, seeks another woman ("My Lady"). Both feel guilt in their extramarital relations, recognizing the superiority of each other to the interlopers; but all self probings and pathetic attempts at reconciliation fail.

In the last ten sections the husband through suffering achieves pity and forgiveness, but, uncomprehending, the wife commits suicide to free him. The memorable four "sonnets" that conclude the poem widen the application: demanding that marriage continue precisely on the terms of their premarital expectations, both partners failed to mature and to accept inevitable change. Only greater intelligence and deeper sensitivity and sympathy toward each other can save other couples from this unnecessary tragedy. Today's reader is astounded at the righteous indignation of the critics of the time, the *Spectator* claiming that it should have been entitled *Modern Lust*.

"The Old Chartist," perhaps best of the numerous Browningesque character poems in the volume, suggests a new pattern for English radicalism. After years of exile abroad because of his Chartist agitation, an aging shoemaker on the way home "to rouse the people up to strike" sees a rat washing itself in a brook. At first identifying the rat with the parasitical rich, he next changes his mind to perceive the rat as a fellow democrat, working his best in a hard world. The old man now sees his program as teaching his fellow workers to be better and more intelligent workers, preparing for the day of labor's true share in the world.

"Ode to the Spirit of Earth in Autumn" is Meredith's first significant Nature poem. Eschewing Wordsworthian divine Nature and any claim of individual immortality, the poet revels in participation with the life force and with sustaining Earth.

Poems and Lyrics of the Joy of Earth (1883) reprinted verse appearing in periodicals over two decades and added new pieces. The best of Meredith, it ranks as one of the most notable single volumes by any English poet, and both the virtues and difficulties of his verse strike the reader. A rebel like Hopkins against Victorian poetic diction, Meredith produces some poems of annoyingly crabbed verse; but at its best his syntactical legerdemain generates an unprecedented richness of movement.

"Love in the Valley" (first version 1851, present version 1878) was more intoxicating, Stevenson asserted, than any liquor. Tennyson and Rossetti also agreed that it is one of the best hymeneal (wedding) poems in the language. Following the bride-to-be through roughly the twenty-four hours preceding the marriage night, the poem merges the life of Nature and the girl, a child of Nature.

"Phoebus with Admetus" (1880) in complex stanzas considers the servitude of Apollo as herdsman of king Admetus because the god slew the Cyclopes. Meredith interprets Apollo as the creative impulse of man, expressed in labor. Devoted efforts in fulfilling Natural duties will harmonize man with universal forces and lift civilization upward.

"The Lark Ascending" (1881) in octosyllabic couplets contrasts vividly with Shelley's skylark. The bird is a real bird, symbol only in the sense of the poet who ascends to a higher vision while remaining the caroler of earth. Nature is a single living symphony with a completely non-egoistic bird important not for its lone note but as part of the symphony, linking "all hearers in the song they drink."

"The Spirit of Shakespeare" interprets the Bard in the light of the Meredithian Comic Spirit, penetratingly critical of man but loving him and seeking to open vistas of Natural amplitude in mind and soul.

"Lucifer in Starlight" is one of the most notable Italian-type sonnets in English. The devil is the principle of anarchy in the universe. Instead of overt manifestation of the divine, the harmony of the stars ("the brain of heaven") is all-sufficient proof of the universal principle of immutable Natural order.

"Melampus," in iambic pentameter stanzas (*a b a b c d c d*), resembles the sensuous flow of Swinburne. Melampus of Greek mythology could understand the language of birds and animals because serpents had licked his ears as he slept. Meredith conceives of Melampus as a militant humanist, loving all life, banishing fears, and welcoming Nature's process as completing his human wholeness.

"The Day of the Daughter of Hades" artfully employs a three-stress line to reproduce the fleeting of time. Skiageneia, daughter of Persephone, accompanies her mother on a one-day visit to the earthly realm of Demeter, mother of Persephone. In old age Meredith considered this his most important poem because it epitomized his optimistic doctrine of accepting life's brevity and sorrow, but in 1883 he preferred the following poem.

"Earth and Man" places Earth in the position most religious persons would ascribe to God. Our religious sense, he claims, originates in Earth and must be directed to Earth, for hers are the unalterable laws of universal order.

"The Woods of Westermain" specifically refers to the forest of Westermain near Wooton in Surrey, but the poem's broad implications summarize Meredith's philosophy of Nature. The courageous and imaginative will find Nature not "red in tooth and claw" (Tennyson) but a harmony to "touch a string" of exuberant joy in man, balancing the trinity of blood, brain, and spirit. Clearly, the ego that worries Meredith approximates the Freudian *id*, and Meredith demonstrates his Victorianism and essential difference from later viewpoints in his desire for "brain" to repress the inner darkness of man and thereby insure a wholeness and peace.

Ballads and Poems of Tragic Life (1887) consists largely of collected verses first published in periodicals.

"The Nuptials of Attila" (1879) is an excellent specimen of the narrative poem, a genre today in low repute. Momentous is the tension of the Hun encampment as the warriors wait impatiently to resume bloodletting. Ildico in the marriage bed drives a knife through the giant ribs of Attila, and his savage horde dissolves. Terrifying suspense and raw violence have seldom been so effectively evoked in English verse.

A Reading of Earth (1888) contains some of Meredith's best Nature poetry, though echoing his previous themes.

"The Thrush in February" (1885) sings of "the forward view," the idea of progress. "Full lasting is the song [of the thrush], though he/The singer, passes."

"A Faith on Trial" (1885) was wrung from the poet by the approaching death of his second wife from cancer. "Reality's flower" is mankind, and although men must perish, man and his triumphant destiny shall endure.

"Hard Weather" fuses the turmoil of earth with man's challenging task of shaping himself and his environment to new, progressive uses.

"A Stave of Roving Tim" in rollicking measure is Meredith's tribute to the life force seen in the creative work and vitality of humble people.

THE NOVELS AND POETRY OF HARDY

Thomas Hardy (1840–1928). Thomas Hardy was the son of a stonemason-builder at Higher Brockhampton, Dorsetshire. Almost all his long life was spent near Dorchester. Apprenticed to an architect at sixteen, he went to London for architectural work and study until illness in 1867 sent him back to his Dorchester employer. His early verse found no publisher, but the success of his novels (the first was *Desperate Remedies* in 1871, but recognition came with *Under the Greenwood Tree* in 1872) permitted him to abandon architecture after 1872. He was married to Emma Gifford from 1874 until her death in 1912, and then to Florence Dugdale from 1914 until his death. Pained outcries against *Jude the Obscure* in 1895 turned his attention again to poetry, which he continued to write almost until death. His later years were filled with growing recognition and acclaim; but, shy and reticent, he shunned publicity.

Evolutionary thought that provided Meredith with the comic view of life evoked the tragic view of life from the ultrasensitive Hardy, though his attitude was strongly reinforced by the immemorial folkways of his native Dorset. Hardy felt poignantly that man is an alien in an impersonal universe, and at the mercy of sheer chance. The biological urges implanted in him by the blind struggle for survival thwart his pitiful dreams for self-improvement. Though most readers assume that Hardy was a pessimist, he insisted that he was a meliorist, yearningly hopeful for a better world. By setting his chief novels in "Wessex" (the ancient Anglo-Saxon kingdom of Alfred) Hardy achieved the effect of man's long-protracted struggles on the timeless earth.

THE NOVELS AND SHORT STORIES. *Far from the Madding Crowd* (1874), the first of Hardy's most memorable novels, combines poetic description of Nature with a George-Eliot-like fidelity in picturing rustic life. With this piece Hardy added notable dimensions to the English novel. Meredith's erratic genius occasionally flashed poetry in the novel, but *Far from the Madding Crowd* from start to finish is a poetized novel. The title comes from Gray's "Elegy."

Gabriel Oak, a ruggedly honest farmer, is rejected in his bid for Bathsheba Everdene. Soon after, the loss of all his sheep forces him to work on Weatherbury Farm, Bathsheba's property. Well-to-do farmer Boldwood is turned down by Bathsheba, who prefers the dashing Sergeant Troy. After his marriage to Bathsheba, Troy is distraught by the death of Bathsheba's maid, Fanny Robin, and the child she bore to Troy. Troy flees and is reported dead, causing Boldwood to renew his suit. When Troy reappears, he is killed by Boldwood. Gabriel Oak marries Bathsheba and becomes the master of Weatherbury Farm.

The overpowering effect of the novel is that of a pastoral epic. Unlike the later Hardy novels, this work does not load the dice against man; mere casualty brings sorrow and pain but also happiness, even a happy ending. Appropriately named, Gabriel Oak is an elemental being with the patience of Nature itself. Attuned to the rhythms of Nature, he persists stolidly until his rocklike strength provides the prop Bathsheba needs. Many of Hardy's great characters are simple creatures, devoid of the inhibitions or the superficial gloss of polite society, sprung from the Dorset soil, re-enacting the immemorial attractions and repulsions of basic human life. No previous English novelist has displayed such myth-creating force, the sense of individuals performing the unchangeable rituals of the race. Bathsheba is fundamental femininity, swayed by momentary passion and superficial flirtation, but awaiting eventual union with the elemental male symbolized by Oak. Boldwood is Hardy's most extensive treatment of an emotional male, literally unhinged in mind by passion. The third type of male is Troy, the lady-killer, a romantic sentimentalist whose pursuit of shallow sensations ruins his own life and the lives of others. The overall theme suggests that the storms of Nature and life can never be eliminated but they can be borne by patient endurance. This work implicitly opposes the bourgeois novel by completely ignoring its standards of society and by confronting it with elemental verities.

The Return of the Native (1878) is the first English novel to achieve the tragic intensity of Shakespeare and the ancient Greek tragic dramatists. The tragic concept for both Shakespeare and the ancients lay in man's violation of the moral code of the universe, but Hardy insists that it is the violation of man's code that induces the tragedy. Both Shakespeare and the Greek dramatists posit man's free will and consequent obligation for his own downfall, while Hardy sees the tragic flaws in man as built in by natural forces and therefore compelling man irrevocably to pain and defeat.

Eustacia Vye, "the raw material of a divinity," yearns to escape from desolate Egdon Heath. Her lover, Damon Wildeve, is pledged to Thomasin Yeobright, whom he marries in pique when Eustacia becomes interested in Clym Yeobright (the "native"), a Parisian jeweler recently returned to his native heath. Against his mother's objections, Clym marries Eustacia, who is disillusioned when Clym determines to remain on the heath. Mrs. Yeobright comes for a reconciliation but is not admitted by Eustacia, who is trysting with Wildeve. Mrs. Yeobright's death from snakebite alienates Clym from Eustacia. In an attempted rendezvous, Eustacia, and Wildeve both drown. In a later edition Hardy married Thomasin to the faithful reddleman, Diggory Venn, and made Clym an itinerant preacher.

The central character is brooding Egdon Heath, the countryside near Dorchester, totally indifferent to the pathetic struggles of men. Impersonal Circumstance here cannot be contended with or, as in *Far from the Madding Crowd*, be appeased by Oak-like resignation. Eustacia's gifts, perhaps elsewhere a blessing, are here an insurmountable curse. Natural Law draws her to Wildeve and Clym, and them to her; but compatibility is impossible, and pain is inevitable. Eustacia yearns for realization of all the joys and poetry of life, but this "ill-conceived" world is contrived only to smash her dreams. Blind Chance assumes a cosmic significance, wrecking human lives not from hostility but from sheer indifference. Like his creator, Clym is a meliorist, but his inability to alter social circumstances in his attempt as an intellectual to uplift the stolid peasantry convinces him that the cosmic Circumstance is hopelessly bungled. Man is doomed to defeat in a heedless universe. No personal difficulties in Hardy's life account for his deeply tragic viewpoint; a sensitive man's reaction to evolutionary theory and Schopenhauer's philosophy of the Will appears the major explanation.

Critics have consistently praised the dramatic structure of the novel and the minor characters, who seem a Greek chorus; but especially momentous are the somber mood of the omnipresent Heath and the pitiful struggles of mortals trapped by relentless Fate.

The Mayor of Casterbridge (1884–85) foreshadows Hardy's later formulation of the working of the Immanent Will.

Early in the 19th century Michael Henchard in a drunken fit sells his wife and baby daughter to Newson, a sailor (although an incredible event, Hardy cited actual cases). Sober, Henchard searches for them in vain, finally settling at Casterbridge (Dorchester) where he becomes a prosperous grain merchant and mayor of the city. Farfrae, a young grain expert, becomes his manager. Henchard's wife returns with Elizabeth-Jane, Newson's daughter, for Henchard's daughter had died. After courting Elizabeth-Jane, Farfrae weds Lucetta Le Sueur, formerly Henchard's inamorata. Farfrae prospers in a separate business as Henchard's fortunes decline. Henchard is revealed as the wife-seller, and his relations with Lucetta cause a public scandal that results in her death through miscarriage. All that is left to Henchard is Elizabeth-Jane, and when her true father, Newson, appears to supplant Henchard, the bitter man pines away to death.

Henchard is doomed by his own wild impulsiveness, and his struggles for survival only intensify the ironic pressures of cosmic fate and chance that beat him down, but his "defiant endurance" lifts him to tragic stature. He is capable of true magnanimity and in suffering is purified to the point of deep, unselfish fatherly love for Elizabeth-Jane. Though his faults are severe, the scheme of things looks outrageously cruel in crushing him by natural selection.

All the characters of the book sense that the "iron hand of necessity" drives them. Lacking the sociological analysis of George Eliot, Hardy nonetheless displays a poet's sensitivity to places. Few other novels are so competent in evoking the atmospheric feel of a community, here the ancient city of Dorchester.

Wessex Tales (1888) and *Life's Little Ironies* (1894) are Hardy's most notable collections of short stories. With the same attitudes and locales as the novels, these miniature dramas, often ironic, include also fantasy and humor. Hardy's predilection for grotesquerie and melodrama is less successful in the short works where he cannot extend the atmosphere and surround the incredible with homespun characters and incidents. Even more than the novels, the short stories reveal Hardy's fascination with old folkways, superstitions, rituals, and dialect. Other stories are gathered in *A Changed Man and Other Tales* (1913).

Tess of the d'Urbervilles (1891) demonstrates Hardy's mounting defiance of Victorian standards as he resolutely makes a seduced girl his heroine, subtitling the novel, "a pure woman faithfully presented."

The shiftless loafer Jack Durbeyfield drops all pretense of supporting his poor family upon learning of his descent from the aristocratic Norman-French d'Urbervilles. Tess's mother sends the girl to seek connections with the rich Stoke-d'Urbervilles, *nouveau riche* who have assumed the ancient surname. Tess is seduced by Alec d'Urberville, but her peasant mother is only concerned about now marrying her to Alec. Tess's child by Alec soon dies, and she goes to work at the distant dairy farm of Talbothays. Angel Clare, the rebellious son of a cleric and an avowed liberal, marries Tess. On the wedding night he confesses his past sexual experience but is horrified by Tess's account of her relation with Alec. Clare flees to Brazil, and Tess labors at sterile Flintcomb-Ash. Her letters to Angel unanswered, Tess succumbs anew to Alec's blandishments. When Angel returns to forgive her, in despair she kills Alec and goes off with Clare. She is apprehended at Stonehenge and later executed.

This is a threefold tragedy.

(1) Personally to Tess, condemned by the wild blood of the d'Urbervilles and the permissive environment of the Durbeyfields. The Norman-French descent utilizes the oldest surviving tradition in England of glory and pride. Tess refuses to cajole her seducer, whom she detests, into marriage purely for social appearances, and her courage throughout and her noble resignation at the end elevate her to tragic heights.

(2) Socially to the peasantry and those long upon the land. Alec seems certainly to symbolize the new bourgeois intrusion into the English countryside, usurping the name and power of the old landed gentry and unscrupulously exploiting the people.

(3) Ultimately to life itself. The gods are cruel ironists. Tess is ready for love but meets Alec. Clare eventually wakes up, but too late. Happenstance is elevated to cosmic indifference in such episodes as Tess's letter of confession that accidentally slips under the carpet.

Such emphasis upon universal destiny cannot be handled by humdrum realism. Hardy moves to a higher key by poetizing Nature in the idyllic loveliness of Talbothays and the somber barrenness of Flintcomb-Ash. Symbolism occurs frequently from the minor touch of bloodstained butcher's paper flapping in the wind to the superlative penultimate chapter where the searchers find Tess upon the sacrificial altar of Stonehenge. The entire work reveals an aching poetic sensitivity to beauty and suffering.

Even the intelligent Clare does not perceive the falseness of the "double standard" when he expects Tess's forgiveness for his sins and is immediately thunderstruck at her parallel confession. Until he purges his limitations in distant Brazil, Clare is an indictment of the avowed middle-class liberal still deeply enmeshed in Victorian prudery. The incredible extent of current puritanism appears in the scene fording the stream where for serial publication Hardy had to change Clare's carrying of the milkmaids in his arms to carrying each in a wheelbarrow.

Jude the Obscure (1895) aroused such a storm of protest (*Pall Mall Gazette* termed it "Jude the Obscene" and the Bishop of Wakefield burnt a copy) that Hardy thereafter turned from the novel to poetry. Hardy explained that the book is "concerned first with the labours of a poor student to get a University degree, and secondly with the tragic issues of two bad marriages, owing in the main to a doom or curse of hereditary temperament."

Jude Fawley is encouraged by his schoolmaster, Richard Phillotson, to consider collegiate training, but poverty forces him to work as a stonemason. A vulgar country girl, Arabella Donn, traps the hardworking youth into marriage and leaves Jude when he becomes disillusioned. Jude tries unsuccessfully to enter Christminster (Oxford). Meanwhile he is charmed by his cousin, Sue Bridehead. Her marriage to Phillotson and his rebuff from college dons induce him to heavy drinking. Sue and Jude run off together but suffer severe deprivations since they are stigmatized for an illicit union. Arabella leaves them her child by Jude, a melancholy small boy nicknamed Little Father Time. In the depths of despair at Christminster, Sue tells Little Father Time that it is better not to be born, and when Sue and Jude are away he proceeds to hang the younger children and himself. Feeling horror and guilt, Sue returns to Phillotson, and Jude, deathly ill, lets Arabella snare him again. As Christminster resounds with festivity and Arabella is flirting with the spectators, Jude dies of tuberculosis.

"Predestinate Jude" is the toy of Schopenhauerian Will. The First Cause has implanted in him aspirations impossible of realization. He first seeks to be a scholar, but his social class is beneath Christminster's 19th-century condescension. Sex urgencies yoke him with Arabella. His diminishing hopes now suggest an "ecclesiastic and altruistic" career, but the attraction of Sue destroys this plan. Desperately he lowers his hopes simply to making Sue happy, but society, laws of nature, and blind chance produce the appalling murder and suicide of the children, sundering Sue forever from Jude. Her return to Phillotson seems total desecration to Jude, and his death ends the cruel play of the Will.

The novel's motto, "The letter killeth," keynotes Hardy's revolt against the indissoluble Victorian marriage. Sue's marriage and Jude's were both follies, but, asks Hardy, must such follies be punished by a life sentence? Many shocked contemporaries agreed with *Blackwood's* that Hardy headed "the anti-marriage league," though the novelist clearly states that the passionate and impulsive heredity of Sue and Jude make them special cases.

Until the bitter conclusion, when illness has destroyed all hope, Jude valiantly struggles against implacable fate. His efforts accord him heroic stature, and he is the vehicle for the most savage indictment in literature of a society and a universe that crush the underprivileged intellectual. Although Hardy offers the possibility of some future hope (Jude sees himself as "fifty years too soon"), the overall effect produces one of the most pessimistic, and powerful, works in all literature. Little Father Time embodies the "coming universal wish not to live," and all characters see life only as cruelty.

Among Hardy's other novels are *The Hand of Ethelberta* (1876), *The Trumpet-Major* (1880), *Two on a Tower* (1882), *The Woodlanders* (1887), and *The Well-Beloved* (1897).

POETRY AND DRAMA. Increasingly, 20th-century critics have been rating Hardy's verse as equal in importance with his novels. While anthologists vary widely in their selections, the following are representative of Hardy's themes and treatment:

Wessex Poems (1898), consisting of Hardy verse written from 1865 on, manifests the same characteristics as the novels. Hardy's people are elemental beings, thwarted by the irony of Circumstance. As poignantly perceptive of Nature as Meredith, Hardy concentrates upon the tragic waste in the Darwinian struggle for survival and ignores any justification in the emergence of higher types of life.

"Hap" (*1866*) typifies Hardy's tragic despair at the impersonal universe governed by "crass casualty" that strews man's path with pains.

"Her Dilemma" (*1866*) foreshadows the later *Satires of Circumstance*. To comfort a dying man a woman lyingly assures him of her love, though she is furious at the cruelty of fate that compels such falsehood.

"Heiress and Architect" (*1867*) has the designer of a wealthy woman's house (designer of her life) puncture her romantic dreams.

"Her Initials" (*1869*) contrasts the enduring power of art with the transience of human life and affections. The verse from a former poet still is magnificent, but the speaker no longer has love for the woman he had once associated with the poem.

"Nature's Questioning" is Hardy's questioning of Nature in the light of Darwinism. He cannot conceive any longer of Wordsworth's sustaining Nature. It all seems a confused accident, a bewildering conundrum.

Poems of the Past and the Present (1901)

"Rome, at the Pyramid of Cestius near the Graves of Shelley and Keats" (*1887*) celebrates two Romantics cherished by Hardy, especially Shelley, whose influence was extensive upon Hardy. It is the irony of things that an obscure ancient Roman is granted modern fame by the chance proximity of famous graves of modern men.

"A Christmas Ghost-Story" (*1899*) was induced by the surprisingly high casualties of the Boer War in South Africa. The ghost of a dead British soldier asks how men can reconcile their slaughterings of their fellows with their claims of following the Prince of Peace.

"An August Midnight" (*1899*) sounds Hardy's suspicion that man's consciousness and sensitivity have made him an alien in the universe. The humble insects attracted to his midnight lamp may be better attuned to things than man is.

"The Darkling Thrush" (*1900*) affirms the theme of the previous poem in witnessing the joyous song of the bird amid the death of the year and of the 19th century. With no outward "cause for carolings," the bird must sense some hidden reason for happiness, not discernible to man.

"God-Forgotten" is Hardy's agonized hope that the blind injustice of the universe can be ascribed solely to God's ignorance of what has happened to his creation.

"By the Earth's Corpse" is the meditation by the deity after the earth is cold and life is extinct. God repents of his ill-conceived and ill-executed scheme for earth.

"Tess's Lament" lyrically expresses the emptiness of the novel's heroine after Angel Clare has left her.

"Long Have I Framed Weak Phantasies of Thee" anticipates the concepts of *The Dynasts*. Melioristically, Hardy conceives of the Schopenhauer Will (that has blindly, impersonally shaped universal evolution) as gradually attaining consciousness and benevolence. The development in man of sensitivity and reasoning will be paralleled by such growth in the Cosmic Will. With percipience the Will can mend the present inadequacies of the universe.

The Dynasts (Pt. I, 1903; Pt. II, 1906; Pt. III, 1908) ranks with Milton's *Samson Agonistes* and Shelley's *Prometheus Unbound* as one of the monumental closet dramas in English. In nineteen acts and 130 scenes this vast epic-drama traces the Napoleonic Wars from 1805 to 1815. The historical passages are faithful to fact, though scenes range from rustics in Wessex through all the swirling courts and battlefields of Europe to "Phantom Intelligences" observing the titanic struggle from outer space.

Sources. Hardy drew upon an enormous body of printed matter and even from eyewitness accounts heard in his youth. Most influential work in suggesting the dramatic form and scope was the *Drama of Kings* (1871) by Robert Buchanan, whom we mentioned earlier in connection with his satirical attack on Dante Gabriel Rossetti.

(1) Summary. Part I begins with Napoleon as newly proclaimed emperor locked in battle with Pitt. All-conquering on the European continent, Napoleon is nonetheless fated for eventual downfall because of British determination.

Part II starts Napoleon at his height of power, but gradually the star of Wellington rises in the Peninsular campaigns. This portion sweeps with more variety and color than the other two parts.

Part III is Napoleon's catastrophe: Moscow, Spain, Leipzig, Waterloo. Wellington and England have risen to luster matching Napoleon's, and at the final showdown Napoleon in defeat rides into the wood of Bossu and out of history.

(2) Techniques. Prose passages (often of poetic intensity as in the stage directions about the battle of Albuera) intersperse the standard blank verse. Some stanzaic verse is employed, notably in the choruses of "Phantom Intelligences." Hardy deemed best the terza rima prelude to Waterloo.

Hardy's most impressive devices are distance and contrast. From their astral heights the spirits perceive the huge continental armies as slowly crawling caterpillars, a festering upon Europe's skeleton. Scenes of aristocratic splendor clash with bestial carnage and the brutal suffering of little people. Especially savage is the contrast of the arrogant, empty-headed Regent (later George IV) with the cold misery of his contemporaries. In English only the work of Gibbon matches Hardy's dramatic grasp of a stupendous historical spectacle.

(3) Theme. The Dynasts incorporates the philosophic position arrived at in the shorter poems. All mankind is part of the anatomy of the blind, heedless, unthinking Immanent Will. By evolutionary drive the Will has shaped man to consciousness, which renders all the more agonizing his compulsion to catastrophic conflict. More than any other character, Napoleon senses that he is an instrument of the Will. The dynasts carry the laws of the jungle into international politics, all their diplomatic protocol masking the animal lust for power and possessions.

The concluding "After Scene" set in the Overworld lyrically and melioristically pleads that the consciousness and sensitivity that have developed in man shall also develop in the impersonal drive of the universe, "Consciousness the Will informing, till It fashion all things fair!"

Time's Laughing-Stocks (1909) is strong in short narratives somberly contemplating the sad, ironic fate of man. "The Homecoming" (1901) is typical Hardy in its dialectal telling of a reluctant child-bride unhappy in the lonesome farmhouse of her new husband. "At Casterbridge Fair" (1902) is a series casting over the merriment the pall of time and death. "The Man He Killed" (1902) is a private's musing over the imbecility of war and its destruction of average people who don't know what it's all about. "George Meredith" (*1909*) in terza rima is probably the best poem written about the fellow novelist, whom Hardy sees as "trenchant, turning kind."

Satires of Circumstance (1911) takes its title from fifteen short, acid poems portraying bitterly ironic situations such as "In the Room of the Bride-Elect" where a girl in vexation realizes that she is marrying the wrong man, or "At the Draper's" where a tubercular husband overhears his wife ordering mourning garments. Actually, the volume includes many optimistic poems such as "When I set out for Lyonnesse," on the magic of youth, and "The Abbey Mason," praising the devotion and creativity of the imaginary inventor of Perpendicular Gothic. The 1914 edition included *Lyrics and Reveries.*

Moments of Vision (1917) collects poems going as far back as the 1870s and extending through the war years. "In Time of 'The Breaking of Nations' " (*1915*) has been termed one of the greatest poems ever evoked by war; human love and human labor will always continue, long after the memories of war have vanished.

Late Lyrics and Earlier (1922) and *Human Shows* (1925), including some verses dated as early as 1866, show no diminution of poetic power in pieces written during Hardy's ninth decade. There is much less bitterness in the aged poet, and much mellowed nostalgia for bygone days coupled with hope for a spiritual regeneration in this new age.

VARIOUS NOVELISTS OPPOSING VICTORIANISM

Lewis Carroll (real name **Charles Lutwidge Dodgson**) (1832–1898). Charles Lutwidge Dodgson was the son of the vicar of Daresbury, Cheshire. The name Charles Dodgson was latinized to Carolus Ludovicus and then reversed and anglicized to Lewis Carroll. After Rugby, Dodgson proceeded to a mathematical career at Christ Church, Oxford. From 1855 until 1881 he lectured on mathematics at Christ Church. Scrupulously, Dodgson kept his two selves wholly separate. The mathematician remained a staid, uninteresting, stiffly conservative bachelor don, who shunted to the Dead Letter Office mail addressed to Carroll. Lewis Carroll was the sublimation of Dodgson's anti-Victorianism in the writing of what are purported to be children's books but which actually are even more entertaining to adults.

Alice's Adventures in Wonderland (1865) sold over 150,000 copies in the author's lifetime and still remains the best-loved children's book in the English-speaking world.

Following a fully clothed rabbit down a rabbit hole, Alice blunders into the fantastic world of Wonderland, replete with bizarre talking animals. Her mistakes almost cause her drowning in her own tears, but she is befriended by a crusty old Duchess, a mad Hatter, a somnolent Dormouse, and a March Hare who take her to play croquet with the Queen of Hearts. During a jury trial at the Queen's court, Alice calls everyone nothing but a pack of cards. As they rise and swoop down upon her, Alice awakens on a bank beside her sister.

The Alice of the title was Alice Liddell, eight-year-old daughter of Dean Liddell. Many of the characters are playful references to Dodgson's Oxford acquaintances, Dodo being the author himself. To his age the work was the glorious nonsense of childhood. The 20th century has emphasized the following characteristics of the book:

(1) Logical nonsense. More than any other author in English, Carroll approaches the incredible inventiveness of Aristophanes, the ability to begin with an utterly preposterous situation and then work out its development with rigorous logic.

(2) Symbology of dreams. The work is frankly a dream vision with the guidance of free association. Carroll admitted, "I had sent my heroine straight down a rabbit hole, to begin with, without the least idea what was to happen afterwards." The major theme centers about the enchanted garden (adult life as viewed by childhood). Alice encounters annoying frustrations and misdirections until she finally enters this fertility symbol only to find it populated by disagreeable adults. Psychoanalysts are not in total agreement but suggest underlying motifs of oral fixation (eating or drinking causes extraordinary giantism or shrinking in Alice), re-entry into the womb, and in the water passages rebirth and even prenatal memories. Since the whole subject of the work is growing up, it is quite reasonable to expect Freudian parallels.

Through the Looking-Glass (1871) is usually rated only a trifle below its predecessor. The Alice is another girl, Alice Raikes, daughter of the Postmaster General, a distant connection of the Dodgsons.

In her next dream Alice steps through the looking-glass into a chessboard world; the country is divided into chessboard squares by little streams and hedges, and all the people are chessmen. Alice moves through the game to be crowned queen at the end, but her annoyance at all this nonsense forces her awake. Besides the chess pieces are characters such as Humpty Dumpty and Tweedledee and Tweedledum; "The Walrus and the Carpenter" and "Jabberwocky" are famous inserted verses.

The way of the adult world is more obviously castigated than in *Wonderland*. Alice is more clearly natural impulse forced into the rigid, unnatural squares of the world. The Red pieces are cruel and oppressive, the White pieces amiable but weak. The White Knight is the only creature with the kindness to help a lost little girl.

Most notable about this work is the surprising anticipation of 20th-century concerns. Space and time are so relativistically handled that Eddington frequently refers to this book when explaining scientific relativity

in *Nature of the Physical World*. The interest in semantics makes
obligatory in today's anthologies on semantics a selection from Humpty
Dumpty's musings about the meaning of words. Carroll's portmanteau
terms, especially in "Jabberwocky," foreshadow Joyce's experiments in
Finnegans Wake (e.g. *slithy* fuses "slimy" and "lithe," *mimsy* fuses "miserable" and "flimsy").

VERSE. Carroll also gave the world an immortal nonsense poem in "The
Hunting of the Snark."

Samuel Butler (1835–1902). Samuel Butler was born at Langar, Nottinghamshire, son of the Reverend Thomas Butler and grandson of a bishop.
Although educated at St. John's College, Cambridge, for the clergy, he
refused holy orders because of religious doubts. After considerable argument with his father, he emigrated in 1859 to New Zealand. Selling his
sheep ranch profitably in 1864, he returned to England, living the rest
of his life in London bachelor quarters. Although talented in painting and
musical composition, he is remembered for his widely varied writings,
among the most original and belligerent of the century.

A friend of Darwin, Butler disagreed with the theory of natural selection,
and in a series of volumes beginning with *Life and Habit* (1877) he asserted
that evolution was not the result of chance variations but "unconscious
memory" transmitted from generation to generation as habit and growing
constantly with the life of a species. Ignored by his contemporaries, Butler's
concept has since gained some favor with scientists.

In the last decade of the century Butler busied himself with the Homeric
question, finally deciding that the *Iliad* was written by a native of the Troad
sympathetic to the Trojans and the *Odyssey* by a Sicilian woman from
Trapani. Butler published translations of the *Iliad* (1898) and the *Odyssey*
(1900) in colloquial prose to counter the pseudobiblical flavor of the Lang
versions.

Erewhon, or, Over the Range (1872) is "nowhere" spelled backward,
plus a switch of the "w" and "h". A novel only by courtesy, it is the most
trenchant satire upon Victorianism. The imaginary land (interior New
Zealand) is an inverted Utopia, a scathing reversal of current England.

Crime in Erewhon is considered a sickness, and embezzlers receive
decorous condolences and are sent to the Straighteners for moral therapy.
Physical illness is considered a heinous offense punished by inflexible courts.
Thus the Victorian severity to the victims of ill fortune and "economic
law" is pilloried as cold inhumanity.

The evasion of parental responsibility in Erewhon contrasts with parental
tyranny in Victorian households. The Established Church is bitterly carica-
tured as Musical Banks patronized chiefly by women; everyone in Erewhon
piously lauds the currency of the Musical Banks, but the scrip is absolutely
worthless. Ydgrunism (Grundyism) imposes a vitiating conformity. The

Colleges of Unreason (Oxford and Cambridge) set great store upon a hypothetical language (classic Greek and Latin) whose consummate virtue is its utter uselessness.

The chapter on Machines seems prophetic of 20th-century worries. Erewhonians have obliterated all machines (except in museums), frightened that machines could dominate men. Higgs, the narrator, constructs a balloon and escapes.

Erewhon Revisited (1901) has unity and character portrayal missing from the brilliant variety of *Erewhon*. It is one of the world's most merciless assaults upon human credulity.

After twenty years Higgs returns to Erewhon, finding to his horror that his balloon ascent has been proclaimed a miracle and he is worshiped as Child of the Sun. The Musical Banks have exploited the "miracle" for a powerful religious revival and a vast proliferation of dogmas, proscribed heresies, and supposed relics. The reverend professors Hanky and Panky of the Colleges of Unreason have erected monumental systems of hairsplitting theology and supersubtle exegesis upon Sunchildism. Attempting to tell Erewhonians the truth, Higgs barely escapes the country alive.

Butler was shocked when readers assumed that he was deriding Christ in a parody of the Ascension. His butt, he asserted, was the ecclesiastical obscuring of noble teachings. Higgs experiences the frequent tragedy of truth seekers who witness the perversion of their ideas and actions.

The Fair Haven (1873) is an antitheological tract masquerading as a spiritual autobiography by one "John Pickard Owen." The alleged author had been swayed by Strauss's *Life of Jesus* and "higher criticism" to be an unbeliever. The work purports to be his winning back to faith. Its subtitle claims "a defence of the miraculous element in our Lord's ministry here on earth," but the entire volume is towering irony, for the more "Owen" defends Christian miracles, the more dubious they are made to appear. Butler's contention is that vital Christianity is best shorn of the miraculous elements.

The Way of All Flesh (1873–85, 1903) was withheld from publication to avoid family embarrassment. Though Butler made it a vehicle for his evolutionary concepts, readers have regarded the work primarily as a devastating indictment of Victorianism. It is Butler's one true novel and one of the masterpieces of English fiction.

George Pontifex, printer and bookseller, is a blustering household tyrant. His son Theobald is compelled by George to become a clergyman. The Reverend Allaby secures Theobald as curate (actually to take a daughter off Allaby's hands) and Christina Allaby in a card game beats her sisters to obtain marriage rights to Theobald. As a father the weak Theobald tyrannizes over his children, infuriating Ernest, the oldest son. Ernest's schooling at Roughborough under Dr. Skinner is an escape from parental tyranny to schoolmaster's tyranny. Aunt Althea Pontifex is his only true friend. Ordained soon after graduation from Cambridge, Ernest proceeds to London. His totally unrealistic upbringing renders him helpless in the real world, and he is jailed on the charge of improper advances to a woman. Unfrocked, Ernest marries Ellen, his mother's former maid, and runs a second-hand clothing store. Ellen's alcoholism proves intolerable, and she is revealed as previously married. Ernest sends his children to a happy, healthy family because he fears that his upbringing might make him as bad a parent as Theobald was. Inheriting Aunt Althea's money starts him upon a new and better life.

Except for the imprisonment of Ernest and the marriage to Ellen, the account is faithfully autobiographical, even to including an actual letter by Butler's mother over Christina's signature. Butler appears twice, his younger self in Ernest and his mature self in Overton, the supposed narrator. The iconoclastic Butler topples over the household gods so revered by Thackeray and standard Victorians. Behind the mask of Victorian family love Butler discovers cruel ignorance, sadistic tyranny, and disgustingly unctuous respectability. Like his 17th-century namesake, Butler sees the evils of mankind summed up in hypocrisy.

The only impossible character in the novel is Towneley, Ernest's (and Butler's) ideal man, gifted by instinct ("unconscious memory") and untrammeled environment with the serenity to live naturally and creatively. Butler conceives of Victorianism as a sour turning from proper evolutionary development, but Towneley is a portent of a more wholesome humanity ahead.

Mark Rutherford (real name **William Hale White**) (1831–1913). William Hale White was born into a fanatically pious evangelical family in Bedford. Educated for the Congregational ministry, White could not in conscience continue, and became a civil servant in the admiralty, rising to high posts. His wide-ranging interests extended from association with Chapman and George Eliot in the publishing business to extraordinary competence as an amateur astronomer.

Never generally popular and often dismissed as a minor specimen of Victorian agnosticism, White is a novelist's novelist, praised by Matthew Arnold, Joseph Conrad, D. H. Lawrence, and André Gide. Bennett termed *The Revolution in Tanner's Lane* (1887) "the finest example of modern English prose."

The Autobiography of Mark Rutherford (1881) and *Mark Rutherford's Deliverance* (1885) form a continuous introspective autobiography, supposedly edited by Reuben Shapcott. Rutherford pictures his evangelical upbringing in a narrow-minded "God of the Church." His spiritual awakening came from Wordsworth's *Lyrical Ballads,* providing him with a "God of the hills." Hounded from a Congregational pulpit by his fundamentalist congregation, Rutherford is briefly a Unitarian cleric but abandons this post for London as the *Autobiography* breaks off. In the sequel London is a "city of Dreadful Night" as horrifying as Thomson's, but Rutherford lives through to quietistic resignation, tranquil at last in realizing that it is pointless to question the three-fourths of life that is "unintelligible darkness."

White called Rutherford "a victim of the century." Certainly Rutherford is the classic portrayal of a deeply religious spirit tortured by the most bigoted aspects of Victorian evangelicalism. The agonized sincerity in soulsearching makes these two works the true pioneers in the use of fiction for probing spiritual autobiography.

George Robert Gissing (1857–1903). A native of Wakefield, George Gissing was educated at Owens College, Manchester. Poverty during his young adult life made him a bitter rebel, angrily throwing into the age's face the sordid, shabby life in London slums. *Demos* (1886) was his first novel to gain attention, but his relentless depictions of lonely people in hopeless struggle with fate always kept his reading public small. The slightly improved finances of his later life permitted him to study the classics and Italian antiquities. He died at St. Jean de Luz in the Pyrénées.

New Grub Street (1891), his best-known work, derives its name from the 18th-century nickname for Milton Street, the residence of indigent writers.

Jasper Milvain, a clever reviewer and essayist, accepts the current materialistic standards, writes what the public wants to read, and becomes a success. Edwin Reardon (Gissing) will not compromise with his artistic conscience. He writes two excellent but unappreciated novels, falls into mental depression that causes separation from his wife, and finally dies of deprivation and despair. Reardon's friend, Harold Biffen, who remains loyal to Reardon, is also a highly competent but ignored writer. Hopelessly in love with Amy, Reardon's widow, Biffen commits suicide. When Amy inherits a sizable fortune, Milvain marries her.

Milvain states: "Literature nowadays is a trade." He is assured worldly success by his shrewd cultivation of the people an author should know and by his astute marriage for money. The drab, understated realism makes Reardon, the dedicated artist, not so much tragic as pathetic. His destruction, Gissing avers, arises from the cruelty of an age that ignores intellectual integrity and authentic depiction of reality.

The Private Papers of Henry Ryecroft (1903) is a dreamlike account of what Gissing really wanted from life. Ryecroft, a defeated literary man, is enabled by a legacy to retire from Grub Street to rural meditation. In what amounts to a series of essays, he expounds a quiet epicureanism.

Opposing science and democracy, he dwells largely upon books and art and the necessity for artistic detachment. Although there are resemblances to Hardy and Mark Rutherford, Gissing refuses extensive self-analysis.

THE ROMANTIC REVIVAL

By the 1880s the novel of the intelligentsia completely dominated serious fiction. To provide for continuing bourgeois tastes and for the increasing mass of not overly cultured literates created by the Education Act of 1870 the "best-seller" emerged. As employed in this text "best-seller" is defined as fiction arising less from the creative impulse of the author than from the calculated purpose of satisfying the wishes of mass readers. The best-selling writers of the late 19th century consciously patterned their works after the characteristics of the bourgeois novel discussed earlier, while the original bourgeois novelists had acted upon unconscious assumptions. The so-called "Romantic Revival" of the late 19th-century novel was the best-seller formula of dashing characters in spectacular adventures against a picturesque background.

Readers were captivated by daring intrigues in the mythical central European realms of *The Prisoner of Zenda* (1894) and *Rupert of Hentzau* (1898) by Anthony Hope (Sir Anthony Hope Hawkins, 1863–1933). Wonder attended the African exploits in *King Solomon's Mines* (1885) and sequels by Sir Henry Rider Haggard (1856–1925). The world's most famous fictional sleuth ranged dramatically from *A Study in Scarlet* (1887) to *The Case-Book of Sherlock Holmes* (1927) by Sir Arthur Conan Doyle (1859–1930). Shivers played upon many spines because of the monstrous hypnotist Svengali in *Trilby* (1894) by George Du Maurier (1834–96). Characteristic of best-sellers, many of these works have been relegated by later generations to light or juvenile reading. All these competent bestsellers were surpassed by one master spinner of tales, whom we take up now.

Robert Louis (originally **Lewis) Balfour Stevenson** (1850–1894). Robert Louis Stevenson on his father's side came from a line of Scottish engineers, and on both sides devout Calvinists. Early affliction with tuberculosis prevented much formal schooling and caused extensive traveling for health. Parental opposition greeted his abandonment of engineering for writing, and parental wrath rose upon his proclamation of agnosticism. France aided his health and provided delightful bohemian companions. At Grez in 1876 he met Mrs. Fanny Osbourne, an unhappily married American woman, ten years his senior, from California. After further continental ramblings, Stevenson in 1879 cast off his past and journeyed to California with considerable difficulty, marrying Fanny in 1880 after her divorce. Still seeking a healthy climate, the Stevensons roamed the British Isles, the continent, and

America. In 1888 they toured the Pacific, finally settling down at Apia in the Samoan Islands. "Tusitala" ("the teller of tales," Samoan) was virtually a Scottish laird at his home, Vailima, until his death from cerebal hemorrhage.

Treasure Island (1882) is an accepted classic of younger readers not because of the results of treasure trove but because of the exhilarating joy of the quest by Jim Hawkins. *Treasure Island* superbly symbolizes what robust childhood expects of life: adventure into the adult world, camaraderie, clear-cut objective goals, the touching upon perils without injury, the clearing up of the hidden and mysterious, and, above all, the acceptance by adults because of displayed competence.

Other noted Stevenson adventure stories of this period are *Kidnapped* (1886) and its sequel, *David Balfour*, also called *Catriona* (1893).

The Master of Ballantrae (1889) almost rises to novelistic stature in the relentless 18th-century feud between two brothers, James Durrie, the Master and embodiment of evil, and Henry, the good man hounded to evil by evil. A taut psychological conflict is buried, however, in a picaresque romance roaming from India to the savage wildernesses of America.

Stevenson's genius for romantic narrative is best realized in notable and exciting short stories such as "The Sire de Malétroit's Door," "A Lodging for the Night" (about François Villon), and the masterly *The Strange Case of Dr. Jekyll and Mr. Hyde* (1886), which gained his first wide repute. A collection of short stories, *The Merry Men* (1887), included some very powerful tales like "Markheim."

Weir of Hermiston (1896), though a fragment, is Stevenson's masterpiece and one true novel. The work breaks off amid the bitter rivalry of Archie Weir (son of Weir, the hanging judge) and Frank Innes for the lovely Kirstie Elliot. Stevenson planned that Archie would kill Innes, be sentenced to death by his own father, and then be rescued by Kristie's brothers to flee to America with his sweetheart. The Scottish background and dialogue ring true and poetic.

ESSAYS. Stevenson's truest calling was that of romantic essayist. In an era when literature tended to drab naturalism or aesthetic detachment, Stevenson, like that other ailing countryman, Scott, proclaimed the vigorous joy of living, satisfying a deep popular need.

"Aes Triplex" ("triple bronze" meaning "courage") (*Cornhill Magazine*, 1878) urges creative, energetic life no matter how brief is existence.

"A Gossip on Romance" (*Longman's Magazine*, 1882) pleads for romance, "the poetry of circumstances." The pleasure of literature and art is seen as the stimulation to emotional excitement through vivid adventures and colorful backgrounds.

"Pulvis et Umbra" ("dust and ashes") (*Scribner's Magazine*, 1888) employs every device of language to assail the scientific, especially evolutionary, viewpoint.

Travels with a Donkey (1879) and *The Silverado Squatters* (1883)—travel accounts of trips in France and California respectively—are among the most engaging of romantic tours, for their joy is not in places so much as in the high-spirited, adventuresome narrator who savors to the full the exotic and the flavorful.

POETRY. *A Child's Garden of Verses* (1885) may be the best children's poetry in English. It avoids the usual pitfalls of this genre: didacticism and condescension. Without any of Lewis Carroll's power of penetrating unconscious depths, it caters beautifully to the conscious joys, imaginative flights, and moodiness of childhood.

Stevenson's verse for adults approximates the naïveté of his children's poetry, achieving a minor niche amidst the "muscular" verse of Henley and Kipling. His one remembered piece, marked by simple resignation, is "A Requiem" which is inscribed upon his tomb.

Part Two

THE CELTIC RENAISSANCE

Chapter 6

The Celtic Renaissance and Irish
Literature to the Present

BACKGROUND INFORMATION

During the initial quarter of the 20th century there arose in Ireland for the first time since the ancient Gaelic bards a group of writers who felt themselves to be distinctively and devotedly Irish. It was they who brought about what we call the Irish Literary Renaissance, and it is their turning to Irish myth and Irish folkways for their inspiration and subject matter that most particularly distinguished them from earlier Irish-born writers, like Swift, Goldsmith, Sheridan, Wilde, and George Moore, who had worked in the mainstream of English letters. Thus the authors discussed in this chapter, although they represent many styles and varied talents, all wrote in the spirit of Yeats's plea to maintain still their "indomitable Irishry."

The concentration of talent in this one important group did not, however, exhaust the amazing fertility of Irish writers in this period. Such eminent Irish-born writers as George Bernard Shaw, James Joyce, and Samuel Beckett appear elsewhere in this book, as being better understood in the broader contexts of English literature and even world literature than in the specific field of Irish national expression. All in all, Ireland in this period achieved an astonishing wealth of literary activity, and, in the writers discussed here, it presented a brilliant example of a modern nation seeking its identity through its poets from its past.

MAJOR HISTORICAL EVENTS. Although English suzerainty over Ireland began with the 1169 invasion of the Marchers (actually Norman-Welsh), the English rule was tenuous until the ruthless "Pacification" completed by Mountjoy in 1607. "No more," the Gaelic harpers wept, "no more the shield is seen slung on the broad back, nor hilt girt to the side at the coming of the moon." English policy sought an assimilation of the Irish by imposing the English language and Protestantism (Church of Ireland). Succeed the English did in language, for the economic and cultural prestige of English by the 19th century had generally swept Gaelic away except in obscure crannies of Ireland. Otherwise the English failed. Roman Catholicism represented a militant Irish defiance of England, and whenever England was imperiled (notably during the Civil Wars and the Napoleonic Era), the Irish rose in open rebellion; even in times of peace they maintained a ceaseless agitation for freedom, and the threat of revolt always persisted.

Daniel O'Connell (1775–1847), "the Liberator," successfully fought for Catholic Emancipation, achieved in 1829; significantly, O'Connell made English the vehicle for his eloquence. Disagreeing with O'Connell's wholly Catholic position, the Young Ireland group (eagerly espousing a label conferred in jest by English journalism) sought a united nation of all creeds. Its voice was *The Nation* (1842–48), which in prose and verse (some by Oscar Wilde's mother) demanded the restoration of Irish greatness in politics and culture. The Young Ireland group led the unsuccessful rebellion of 1848, provoked by the potato famine that starved to death thousands of Irish. *The Nation* was suppressed, and its founder, Sir Charles Duffy (1816–1903), emigrated to become a later prime minister of Australia. Returning, Sir Charles became first president of the Irish Literary Society in 1891.

Thomas Davis (1814–45), editor of *The Nation* until his death, was the first noted proponent of restoration of Gaelic as the living language of Ireland instead of "a medley of Teutonic dialects" as he scornfully called English. Davis was one of the founders in 1845 of the Celtic Society, dedicated to the publication of Celtic documents and the glorification of Gaelic.

Ireland's fondest hopes for Home Rule appeared near realization through the dedicated efforts of Charles Stewart Parnell (1846–91). His downfall because of alleged misconduct with Kitty O'Shea split Ireland apart with devastating effects such as Joyce records in *Portrait of the Artist as a Young Man*. Many observers interpret the subsequent upsurge of Irish politics and letters as a national reaction of guilt and reconsecration because of the Parnell debacle.

CULTURAL CONDITIONS. The first significant manifestation of modern Irish literature sprang largely from a romantic and patriotic interest both in the Irish past and in the contemporary, unspoiled peasantry. Almost forgotten heroes of legend were again exalted along with the surviving superstitions and customs of rural Ireland. Determinedly, the writers of this period attempted to supplant the conventional image of the stage Irishman (blustering, uncouth, volatile) with the depiction of an imaginative, mystic, bardic people. Many of the literary figures were middle-class or upper-class Protestants. Verse and poetic drama dominate what is variously termed the Celtic, Gaelic, or Irish Literary Revival or Renaissance.

Standish James O'Grady (1846–1928) is generally considered to have inaugurated the Celtic Renaissance with his *History of Ireland: Heroic Period* (1878) and *History of Ireland: Cuculain and his Contemporaries*

(1880). These and subsequent O'Grady volumes offered the first relatively complete history of the Gaelic bards and the first extensive formulation of the cycles of Irish heroic legends. Yeats (who termed O'Grady "all passion and all judgment") and most other writers of the Celtic Renaissance received their impetus from him. As a Protestant, O'Grady minimized the Catholic elements, and the movement continued thereafter to emphasize the pagan.

THE EARLIER POETS AND DRAMATISTS

Douglas Hyde (1860–1949). Born at Castle Hyde, County Roscommon, Douglas Hyde was the son of a Protestant clergyman. From neighboring peasants he learned Gaelic and was inspired to dedicate his entire life to promoting Gaelic as a living tongue and literary medium. After graduation from Trinity College, Dublin, he briefly taught literature at the University of New Brunswick, Canada, but returned to Ireland to help found the Gaelic Union in 1878. His first published work was a collection of Gaelic tales, *Leabhar Sgeuluigheachta* (1889). His many subsequent works, both in Gaelic and English, are devoted primarily to the cultural and literary history of Ireland. Hyde's best writing consists of translations into English of Connaught songs and several effective short plays dealing poetically with Irish regional life. The Gaelic League, which he organized in 1892, has been the most energetic and successful of organizations supporting a living Gaelic, and Hyde was the most influential single figure in the campaign. Although a Protestant and a sedulous avoider of political agitation, he was elected the first President of Ireland in 1938. No other person in the English-speaking world has received such high public office solely because of his literary and linguistic accomplishments.

William Butler Yeats (yāts) (1865–1939). Born at Sandymount near Dublin, William Butler Yeats was the son of J. B. Yeats, a Pre-Raphaelite painter and Protestant skeptic. He accompanied his father during several residences in London, but always felt that his true home was Sligo, Ireland. His education was divided between Hammersmith and Dublin. During his early twenties he was a member of the *Yellow Book* coterie in London and a founder of the Rhymer's Club. He threw himself wholeheartedly into the Celtic Renaissance, and proved to be its most impressive figure. He was instrumental in establishing the Irish Literary Theatre in 1899, and from 1904 until death he was a director of the Abbey Theatre. His fame brought him to various parts of the British Isles and to America, and in 1923 he was awarded the Nobel Prize for literature. He was named one of the first senators of the Irish Free State in 1922; in public office he waged a gallant but unsuccessful fight to loosen Irish censorship of literature. Yeats was correcting his poems until forty-eight hours before his death on the French

Riviera. The bearing of his body back to Ireland was the first act of the Irish navy outside of territorial waters. Many English and American critics consider Yeats the greatest poet in English since the time of Wordsworth. Masefield has termed him "the choicest poet and the greatest poetical influence of our time," and T. S. Eliot agrees.

As the following divisions indicate, the poetry of Yeats falls into three rather sharply distinguished periods. Yeats continually revised his poems, and the altered attitudes of a later period frequently cause revisions to be virtually new and wholly different works. Original versions are therefore used as the basis of our discussion, in order to avoid clouding his development. Dramas are treated along with lyrics, since his plays are now seldom performed but remain notable poetic achievements.

THE AESTHETIC PERIOD (to 1910). The early verse of Yeats has a dreamy quality, appropriately labeled *Celtic Twilight* (his collection of Irish stories in 1893). From the influence of the Pre-Raphaelites, the French symbolists, Pater, and the "decadents," he imbibed the Art for Art's Sake concept. "I believe," he wrote during this period, "that all men will more and more reject the opinion that poetry is a 'criticism of life' and be more and more convinced that it is a revelation of a hidden life."

The Wanderings of Oisin (*Usheen* in the first edition, 1899) first attracted critical attention and approval, Morris congratulating him in the Strand, "You write my kind of poetry." The title poem is chiefly indebted to the 18th-century Gaelic poem "The Lay of Oisin on the Land of Youth" by Michael Comyn and to the Middle Irish "Voyage of Maildun." Blind, bent, but undaunted, the pagan bard Oisin (Ossian) returns to Christianized Ireland and recounts to St. Patrick his three centuries in fairyland with the goddess Niamh ("beauty" or "brightness"). The first century is spent on the island of youth (and love), the second on the island of maturity (and accomplishment), the third on the island of old age (and contemplation). Paganism is preferable to Christianity as Yeats sees the bard tapping deeper roots of elemental mystic nature than does the formalized structure of the Church. Characteristic of the early Yeats, the poem abounds in haunting symbols and fairy magic generally alien to the English tradition. The same conflict between Celtic imagination and Christianity appears in the poetic drama *The Land of Heart's Desire* (1894).

The Countess Cathleen (*1889,* 1891) was the first drama by Yeats to be staged. Intended as a "counter truth" to the previous narrative poem, it depicts an Irish countess selling her soul to the Demon-Merchants to provide for her starving people. Her soul is saved because she humanely chose responsibilities against selfish dreams. Many Catholics attacked the play as heresy; students of University College (with only Joyce abstaining) petitioned and demonstrated against it. In spite of five revisions over thirty years, the exciting verse of the original is probably the best version.

Poems (1895) collects Yeats poetry from periodicals and adds new verse. "Crossways," the first section (dated 1889), consists of eight poems on Arcadian and East Indian themes, chiefly preaching subjective truth, as in "The Indian upon God"; and eight poems upon Irish themes, notably "Down by the Salley Gardens," which contrast age and youth and which evoke the pain of mortality.

"The Rose," the second section (dated 1893), in its prefacing poem "To the Rose upon the Rood of Time" specifies its three concerns: occult, Irish, personal. Suffusing all is a neoplatonism derived mostly from Spenser, Shelley, and London intellectual circles. The occult references spring from Yeats's 1890 initiation into the Order of the Golden Dawn, a cabalistic group examining Rosicrucian and other hermetic lore. Instead of the oriental lotus blossom, Yeats substitutes the European rose as the symbol of imperishable order and beauty, especially in "The Rose of Peace." Ireland is the soul's quiet repose in "The Lake Isle of Innisfree," a poem that thrilled Stevenson in the far Pacific; and Ireland is the abode of heroes in the pieces of Fergus and Cuchulain. In "Cuchulain's Fight with the Sea" Yeats perceives the ancient warrior as creative joy fearlessly plunging into the sea of life. Along with *Oisin* these works were attempts to unify Irish spirit through the heritage of legend. The most memorable poem in the collection is "The Rose of the World," arising from Yeats's love for Maud Gonne, a reigning Irish belle and a vehement advocate of a free Ireland; the ecstatic tribute to the loveliness of woman sees her beauty as a primary aspect of the deity.

The Wind among the Reeds (1899) transmutes Yeats's autobiography into art. Since their first meeting in 1889, Yeats had an idealized love for Maud Gonne. For Mrs. Olivia Shakespear, cousin of Lionel Johnson and wife of an elderly solicitor, he developed a more sensual love after their introduction in 1895. The warring elements within the poet are personified here and in the prose tales of *The Secret Rose* (1897) as three different males. Aedh ("fire burning by itself") is the vigorous, emotional man freely pouring out his affection. Michael Robartes ("fire reflected in water") is the intellectual man seeking wisdom while restrained by thought. Hanrahan ("fire blown by the wind") is changeable and erratic man. The volume centers about the complexities of love and the failure to resolve love's pains. Though the book shows strong leanings upon the French symbolists, all is sung with a Celtic magic strange to the Anglo-Saxon. Especially good is "The Song of Wandering Aengus" who at dawn catches "a little silver trout" which is transformed into "a glimmering girl/With apple blossom in her hair"; when she vanishes, he spends his life in unsuccessful but ecstatic search for her. The girl is evidently of the Sidhe ("the people of the Faery Hills"), frequently appearing to men in the sex symbol of fish. Though ideal beauty cannot be trapped and permanently held, it provides the incentive to life and striving.

The Shadowy Waters (*1885–1900*, 1900), acting version first staged in 1906 at the Abbey Theatre, shows Yeats's greatest indebtedness to the French symbolists, especially Mallarmé. Because it symbolizes his own story, it always remained a favorite of Yeats. The pirate Forgael captures and bewitches Queen Dectora; sending all others homeward on her ship, the two drift on his ship into the polar mists. Essentially it is a soaring lyric on a love of impossible beauty beyond human understanding. The roles are unsatisfactory for the stage, for they represent faery symbols of the voyage within the inner life.

Where There Is Nothing (1902), first performed in London in 1904, is a prose drama whose hero, Paul Ruttledge, throws away his existence as a country gentleman to preach a revivifying faith. History is the decline from God-given intuitive joy to a society that cherishes things more than life. "We must destroy the World; we must destroy everything that has Law and Number, for where there is nothing, there is God."

In the Seven Woods (1903) takes its title from forests upon the estate of Lady Gregory where Yeats wrote many of the lyrics for this volume. Most of the poems arise from the poet's disappointment over Maud Gonne's marriage in 1903. The note is not essentially pessimistic, for Yeats consciously feels that from their perishable pains men can fabricate the romantic imperishable delight of art. Key poem is "Adam's Curse," which in form marks a tendency away from Yeats's earlier ornamented style to dramatized conversation, one of his later fortes. The piece considers the three labors of poet, beautiful woman, and lover. Each must present the deceptive appearance of casual spontaneity but is actually the product of ceaseless organization and refinement of life into art.

Included in this volume is *On Baile's Strand*, the first of five plays (written over a span of thirty years) upon the Cuchulain cycle. All five center about the conflict between the institutionalized world of Conchubar—tame, fixed, calculating—and the personal world of Cuchulain—passionate, aspiring, untamable.

Deirdre (1907) like Synge's play is a poetic drama on the legendary "Irish Helen," but unlike Synge, Yeats plunges the conflict into the last hour of the heroine. Intended for King Conchubar, Deirdre marries Naoise. Conchubar traps them and slays Naoise. Pretending to acquiesce to Conchubar, Deirdre gains her chance and commits suicide. The work typifies Yeats's revolt against Ibsen, Shaw, and the entire naturalistic stage. "Remote, spiritual, and ideal" is his concept of drama; and his heroine defies the current trend by heroic energy and the assertion of her will against circumstance. Yeats was trying to create a new drama and a new audience, seeking to "bring the old folk life to Dublin . . . and with the folk life all the life of the heart." The attempt was doomed to failure in the Dublin of Joyce's *Ulysses*, but this work shows unprecedented dramatic construction for Yeats and rates among his poetic best.

THE MASK PERIOD (1910–25). As a famed public personage, Yeats in this period threw himself into Dublin and Irish life. His attention was drawn from "the land of heart's desire" to the impelling actualities of Ireland. The incantatory music of his earlier works is here superseded by terser, simpler poems, but instead of realism, his attitude is best described as the Mask, an idea introduced in his diary in 1910. He suggests that the poet best contends with society not, as he did earlier, by seeking escape from it but by shifting adoptions of its most vital and striking appearances. "I think all happiness in life depends on having the energy to assume the mask of some other self." This idea of the Mask will be further developed under our discussion of Yeats's work, *A Vision*.

The Green Helmet and Other Poems (1910) continues the laments for the loss of Maud Gonne, but instead of contemplating elusive, idealized beauty, Yeats in almost conversational fashion reveals the concrete problems of loving a beautiful political agitator. Maud had told the poet, "The world should thank me for not marrying you," and in the poem "Words" Yeats agrees: "I might have thrown poor words away/And been content to live." "The Mask" is the first poem to explore a theme later amplified; to remove the mask of the lover's pretense is to destroy the excitement of love and life. The specifically Irish poems, especially "Upon a House Shaken by the Land Agitation" (i.e. Lady Gregory's Coole Park), state Yeats's lifelong contention that a leisured class is necessary to foster the arts and provide disinterested administrators. *The Green Helmet* (originally *The Golden Helmet*) is another poetic drama in the Cuchulain cycle, demonstrating in the contest of the warriors for title of "the strongest" that not physical strength but grandeur of spirit will triumph.

Responsibilities (1914) has been praised by Ezra Pound and most critics for a "new robustness" in its dedicated commitments. Yeats's aestheticism is here superseded by the assumption of the following specific responsibilities:

(1) To the Irish past (dead poetic friends in "The Grey Rock," dead ancestors in "Pardon, Old Fathers").

(2) To the Irish present (defending Irish culture against the detractors of Synge's *Playboy* and the opponents of the Dublin Municipal Art Gallery).

(3) To himself and to art. A series of "Beggarman" poems glorifies the social outcast for his reckless gaiety of life and rejection of purely material values. "A Coat" is a renunciation of previous aestheticism and a vow of "walking naked" in forthright adherence to specific truth.

The Wild Swans at Coole (1917) moves from simple personal statement toward the elaborate "System" of cosmology devised by the later Yeats.

The title poem enunciates the major themes of the volume: death, life, and the patterns of life and death. The swans at Lady Gregory's estate suggest the pattern of immortality and eternity as for nineteen years their beauty has been unaltered. The death theme runs through a series of poems upon Major Robert Gregory, Lady Gregory's son, who had volunteered and was killed in action as a British aviator. Most memorable is "An Irish Airman Foresees His Death," where the perception of a "lonely impulse of delight" justifies the self-sacrifice. The theme of life in the aging poet finds the dreams and memories of later years as integral to life as the "burning youth" of the dead flyer. "The Double Vision of Michael Robartes" establishes the patterns. The first part of the poem is the dominance of pure body, the second of pure soul; in the third section is the compounding of body and soul, a grand design truly discernible only in precious moments of insight.

   The Dreaming of the Bones (1917, 1919) is probably the closest approach in English to the Japanese no dramas. Yeats was introduced to this genre by the American poet Ezra Pound, who in 1913 was Yeats's secretary. In the no drama ghosts gradually reveal themselves and their sufferings to mortals; one unifying episode and image is established symbolically with masks, dancers, and a chorus independent of the action. The Yeats play pictures a young revolutionary soldier fleeing from the English after the Easter Rebellion to the borders of Clare and Galway. The shades of Dermot and Dervorgilla, who "brought the Norman in," are tortured by remorse assuageable only by the soldier's forgiveness. He refuses to forgive, and they sadly dance in unappeased yearning. Suffering Ireland is the direct consequence of a crime seven centuries before, and the souls of the wrongdoers can never gain peace while their sin still endures. Yeats wrote four other imitations of the no drama, and no influence shows throughout his later plays.

   Michael Robartes and the Dancer (1920) treats the following three interrelated problems:

   (1) The Easter Rebellion and resultant disorders. Although Yeats had disapproved of violence, in "Easter 1916" he contrasts the "polite meaningless words" of Irish nationalism with the noble sacrifice of the revolutionaries, from which "A terrible beauty is born."

   (2) His developing "System" which predicts an age of destruction looming ahead. "The Second Coming" sees the ending of the Christian era, and has forebodings of the era to come.

   (3) Family concerns. "A Prayer for My Daughter" asks how his daughter Anne (b. 1919) can escape the horrors ahead. It postulates that her personal hopes lie in the symbols of the Horn of Plenty (aristocracy and courtesy) and the Laurel Tree (innocence and good customs).

   THE PROPHETIC BARD (1925 to death). Already world-renowned, the aging

Yeats awed the world with a late burst of creative energy almost unique in the history of poetry. Critics today frequently consider his later work his best and are astounded at its "modernity." Yeats's concluding period possesses the following distinct characteristics:

(1) A humorous and realistic view of life expressed in the taut, complex irony familiar to mid-20th-century poetry. His shadowy heroes of Celtic lore and the dead of the Easter Rebellion are supplanted by long-time personal friends and by 18th-century Protestant Irishmen like Swift, Berkeley, and Burke. The diction here approximates the fluency and vigor of first-rate conversation.

(2) His personal "System" of cosmography, long developing and stimulated by his marriage in 1917 to an Englishwoman, Georgie Hyde-Lees, a spiritualistic medium. Puzzled scrutinizers of Yeats's later works are not yet certain whether these poems are great because of or in spite of the "System." Even where difficult to follow, his blending of image and tightly packed phrasing produces richly textured and excitingly cerebral verse.

A Vision, an Explanation of Life Founded upon the Writings of Giraldus and upon Certain Doctrines Attributed to Kusta ben Luka (1925; extensively revised, 1937) is a prose exposition of Yeats's "System." Yeats eschewed all the 20th-century orthodoxies (Christianity, Marxism, psychoanalysis) in favor of a scheme supposedly dictated by supernatural commentators speaking through Mrs. Yeats. The following discussion is an extremely simplified version of this rather complicated "System."

Yeats envisioned life as patterned after The Great Wheel (a wheel with twenty-eight spokes representing the twenty-eight phases of the lunar month) instead of the more common astrological wheel of twelve houses.

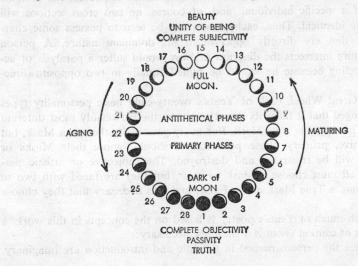

BEAUTY
UNITY OF BEING
COMPLETE SUBJECTIVITY

FULL MOON.

ANTITHETICAL PHASES

AGING   PRIMARY PHASES   MATURING

DARK of MOON

COMPLETE OBJECTIVITY
PASSIVITY
TRUTH

Every soul (and every civilization) passes through all twenty-eight phases of the wheel. Each phase is labeled and illustrated. Phase 19, the "Assertive Man," is illustrated by Byron. Phase 17, "Daimonic Man," includes Dante, Shelley, Landor, and Yeats himself. However, for Phase 1 and its exact opposite, Phase 15, which represent absolutely pure types, Yeats saw no human counterparts. One historical revolution of the wheel takes two thousand years, and each successive revolution mounts spirally toward the Great Year (26,000 years) which will break out of the wheel altogether.

Yeats also saw that each individual was composed of warring elements, and that this mingling of opposites held true for each country, and each era. He represented this conjunction of opposites as two interpenetrating cones ("gyres"):

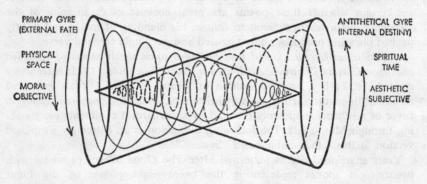

A cross section of these ceaselessly turning cones will reveal the mingled aspects of a specific individual, and, of course, no two cross sections will ever prove identical. Thus, each person can be seen to possess some characteristics that are directly opposite to his dominant nature. A person whose nature intersects the diagram midway would suffer a paralysis of action or feeling because he would be pulled equally in two opposite directions.

In the Great Wheel, each of Yeats's twenty-eight basic personality types is so arranged that it faces its direct opposite, the personality most different from it. This opposite is its Mask. For every personality there is a Mask, but the objective, primary phase personalities should ignore their Masks or else they will be frustrated and destroyed. The subjective or artistic personalities all must choose a Mask to wear, but they are faced with two to choose from, a True Mask and a False, and it is necessary that they choose correctly.

Although much of Yeats's poetry is based on the concepts in this work, a few words of caution about *A Vision* are necessary:

(1) Since the persons named in the title and introduction are imaginary,

the incredulous often argue that *A Vision* is tongue-in-cheek playfulness. Yeats was serious about it, but he recognized that his "System" was metaphoric, like Dante's.

(2) Much of the material and all the attitude stem from centuries-old hermetic writings and are foreshadowed in earlier Yeats pieces.

(3) All writings by Yeats after 1922 are fully explicable only in terms of *A Vision*, though they can still be appreciated as remarkable poetry. Constant revising by the poet imposed the "System" upon earlier originals.

The Tower (1928) takes its title from Ballylee Castle, which Yeats bought and restored in 1918. The tower's winding stair (giving the title to the next volume) is Yeats's gyre. Although written during some of his happiest years, these poems center about the poet's fearfulness for the approaching end of the two-thousand-year cycle that started with Christ. Masculine and political concerns dominate; the images are chiefly of sterility.

"Sailing to Byzantium" seizes upon Byzantine culture as the climax of a two-thousand-year cycle, coming at almost the midpoint (c. 1000), the full moon, phase 15. In the exquisite artifice of Byzantine art Yeats perceives the Unity of Culture he zealously sought to bring to Ireland. The first stanza shows the conflict of the sensual and the ideal, the world of becoming versus the real being. In the second stanza he triumphs over physical decay by the imposition of imaginative art. The fire of the third stanza represents neoplatonically the heavenly fifth element purging the four material elements of earth; spooling in conical fashion ("perne in a gyre"), the spiritual essences will grant him the vision of eternity. Out of this fire is born the phoenix of the last stanza, immortal art beyond decay.

"The Tower" sees in the structure itself a symbol of the turning of the cone, effecting in the aging man a heightened spiritualization largely through the study of Plato and Plotinus.

"Nineteen Hundred and Nineteen" (*1919*) savagely denounces the cruel civil conflict lacerating Ireland. Yet even if the priceless objects of art are obliterated, man retains the power and consolation of art.

"Meditations in Time of Civil War" (*1922*) consists of seven poems moving from the symbols of order such as ancestral houses through the cracked masonry of civil conflict to "the coming emptiness" as the two-thousand-year cycle swings to destruction.

"Leda and the Swan" (*1923*) goes back four thousand years to the beginning of the classical cycle, preceding the present Christian cycle. The rape of Leda by Zeus is an annunciation parallel to Mary's. Though the god's visitation initially excites terror, it also brings an insight into the momentous start of a new cycle. Even the reader unacquainted with Yeats's concepts is gripped by the vivid intensity of this Italian-type sonnet.

"Two Songs from a Play." The first poem (opening *The Resurrection*, 1927) considers the eruption of Christianity, starting the present two-thousand-year cycle. Yeats perceives Christianity as irrational force over-whelming the previous two-thousand-year cycle of classical culture. The second poem (concluding the drama) parallels the great historic cycles with the smaller ones in each man's life. Whatever happens to man arises from his own spiritual destiny, his own subjective truth.

"Fragments" is reminiscent of Blake (whose works were edited by Yeats in 1893). The present Christian cycle is running out as the machine age (drawn from the pragmatic Locke as Eve was taken from Adam) dooms a natural and instinctive life.

"Among School Children" (1926) arose from the Irish senator's tour of a convent school in Waterford. Observation of the youngsters (Maud Gonne was once a child, and her lover was once young) and of the sacred images (how separate them from the divinity they symbolize?) makes him con-template the nature of being and reality. He rapturously concludes that not parts but the complete whole is the essence of truth.

The Winding Stair (1929) is an astounding paean to life by the sick and aging poet.

"A Dialogue of Self and Soul" ascribes the victory to Self. Soul favors the "gyre" of the winding stair, leading to nirvana, but Self rejoices in the cyclic pattern of reincarnation and finds all living totally blessed.

"Byzantium" is a complete rewrite of "Sailing to Byzantium." The pre-vious poem carries the uninitiated from the material to the spiritual ideal. The new poem comes from an initiate contemplating the arrival of novitiates. The first stanza contrasts the artistic perfection of Byzantium at the full-moon phase of Christian culture with the gyre-confused human being. The second stanza features a specter, the animating dead spirit, urg-ing spirits to escape from the material world and from Yeats's round of reincarnations. The third stanza elevates the immutable beauty of art and spirit above changing physical things. The fourth stanza, at the midnight pealing from the cathedral, summons yearning spirits to the purgatorial dance. The concluding stanza, still in the dance, reverses mortal experience through a final purification to "Break bitter furies of complexity," which transcends reincarnation and achieves pure spiritual essence.

The section, "Words for Music Perhaps," in this book features two contrasting series. "Crazy Jane," appearing in seven poems, represents robust sensuality. The seven succeeding poems treat of two idealistic lovers, haunted by the fear of aging and loss of love's intensity; Yeats assures them that the image of true love is an eternal essence unravaged by change and time.

Concluding section, "A Woman Young and Old," traces a woman's en-counters with love from childhood to death. "O bitter sweetness" are life and love in the gyres of earthy sensuality and visionary spirit.

Last Poems and Plays (1940) collects later verse, especially from Yeats's three final years. "The Gyres" epitomizes this collection in its prophecy of a historical cycle crashing to its destruction but leaving the spectator artist free to create true visions. Yeats in his final poems joyously welcomes life and shows no fear of death, but always he possesses that uncanny un-English quality, as in the epitaph for his tomb in his last poem, "Under Ben Bulben":

> Cast a cold eye
> On life, on death.
> Horseman, pass by.

A.E. or **Æ** (pen name for **George William Russell**) (1867–1935). George William Russell had written "Æon" (Latin form of the Greek word meaning "lifetime") as his pen name, but the printer could decipher only the first two letters; Russell explained his use of *aeon* as the circular passage of the soul from revolt against God through reincarnations, eventually returning it to the deity. Russell was born at Lurgan, County Armagh, into a pious Protestant family against which he later revolted. Art classes at the Dublin Metropolitan School made him a schoolmate and lifelong friend of Yeats. He painted extensively throughout life but never professionally. When Yeats met him, Russell was immersed in oriental mystic writings whose fascination never left him. Between 1890 and 1897 his vocation was minor clerkship, his preoccupation theosophy, his avocation poetry. From 1897 to 1905 he organized agricultural co-operatives throughout Ireland. Under his editorship (1905–23) the *Irish Homestead* was one of the leading proponents for Irish nationalism. He then edited *Irish Statesman* until its termination in 1930. Disheartened by the course of Irish politics, he spent his last years abroad, dying in Bournemouth, England.

For a quarter of a century George Russell was the public debater, adviser, and conscience of Irish nationalism. The long memory of the Irish still cherishes him, but his reputation has grievously slipped elsewhere.

As he declared, Russell was his practical self, A.E. his spiritual self. From *Homeward: Songs by the Way* (1894) to *The House of Titans* (1934), A.E. contradicted Russell, for his poetry insists that this world is an insubstantial shadow of the Light of Lights, the heavenly home perceived solely through dreams and visions. The typical A.E. poem begins with a description of Nature (or earthbound experience) and ends in mystic ecstasy, sensing a pantheistic unity of all things in a harmonious universe. In spite of the recent interest in mysticism A.E. has continued to decline, in the judgment of critics, chiefly because of (1) fundamental, perhaps monotonous, repetition of the same themes from earliest to latest verse; (2) a Romantic diction and style, reminiscent of the Pre-Raphaelites and lacking the sinewy complexity of the later Yeats; and (3) an optimism and sweetness unacceptable to our age.

James Stephens (1882–1950). James Stephens knew considerable hardships during his early life in his native Dublin. A.E. (Russell), who seemed the head of the Celtic Renaissance to many young writers, rescued Stephens from clerical drudgery, found him congenial work in the National Gallery, and helped him get into print. Famous by World War I, Stephens then frequently traveled and resided abroad, dying in London.

More than any other writer, Stephens provided for the world the Irish image it wanted and found utterly charming. Through the World War I era his verse is primarily joyous imagination, ranging from amusing fantasy and whimsy through the sentimentally picturesque to the wildly grotesque. His verse forms are also imaginative and refreshing. His postwar verse up to his last volume, *King and the Moon* (1938), grows more serious. The later poetry, such as "The Crest Jewel," proclaims the Romantic doctrine of purely subjective truth, the soul's own creation of good and evil, the world and fate.

The Crock of Gold (1912) is one of the most delightful prose fantasies in English, poetic, wise, and humorous at the same time.

Knowing all there is to know, an aged sage and his wife spin themselves to death and are buried under the hearthstone of the Philosopher and his wife, the Thin Woman of Inis Magrath. When Meehawl MacMurrachu asks the Philosopher who took his wife's scrubbing board, the Philosopher sends Meehawl to recoup his loss by taking the Leprechauns' Crock of Gold. In revenge the Leprechauns send the Great God Pan to lure away Meehawl's daughter, Caitilin. The Philosopher has Angus Og, one of the old gods, persuade Caitilin to leave Pan and wed Angus Og. The thwarted Leprechauns next inform the police about the bodies under the hearthstone, and the Philosopher is jailed. The Thin Woman asks Angus Og to save her husband (the gods are anxious to help but have to be asked). Angus Og and the other Gaelic gods bring such merriment to the town that the charges against the Philosopher are forgotten and he is released. The gods await the birth of Caitilin's child and the return of their ancient rule of Ireland with laughter and song.

The contest between Pan and Angus Og for Caitilin represents the struggle within man between his sensual lusts and divine inspiration. Stephens believes that the ancient glories of Irish joy and melody await only the will of the Irish to generate them out of themselves.

Other notable and characteristic Stephens works are *The Charwoman's Daughter* (1912) and *Here Are Ladies* (1913).

Oliver St. John Gogarty (1878–1957). A Dublin native, Oliver St. John Gogarty was an irreverent medical student at Trinity College, and hence the model for Buck Mulligan in James Joyce's *Ulysses*. A distinguished throat specialist, he was also the literary friend of Yeats, Moore, and A.E. From 1922 to 1926 he was a member of the Irish Senate, but his hostility to Sinn Fein became a source of danger to him. From the 1940s he resided in the United States.

A.E. called Gogarty "the wildest wit in Ireland." The Celtic Renaissance is strangely missing from his works, which are essentially classical and pagan, but from *Poems and Plays* (1920) onward Gogarty is the embodiment of rabelaisian Irish wit.

Padraic Colum (pä'drik kol'um) (1881–   ). Born in County Longford, Padraic Colum came to Dublin during the flowering of the Celtic Renaissance. Yeats, A.E., Synge, and Lady Gregory were his friends and encouragers. He was an active participant in the early development of the Irish National Theatre. He was also active in the Irish Revolutionary Brotherhood. In 1911 along with Stephens he founded the *Irish Review*. In 1914 he came to the United States, where he has lived ever since.

More than any other poet of the Celtic Renaissance, Colum seems an inheritor of the old bardic tradition. Although he employs conventional English forms rather than Gaelic, his verses are steeped in Irish soil. *Wild Earth* (1909) is perhaps his best verse collection, but his imaginative and melodic quality remains high as seen in *Collected Poems* (1932).

Francis Ledwidge (1891–1917). Francis Ledwidge was son of a farm laborer at Slane, County Meath. Forced to leave school at twelve, he worked as farm hand, servant, grocer's clerk, miner, and road mender. Receiving some of Ledwidge's verse, Lord Dunsany became the youth's patron and introducer to Dublin literary circles. Ledwidge joined Dunsany's Battalion of Royal Inniskilling Fusiliers and was killed in action in Flanders.

Often termed a "peasant Keats," Ledwidge was a tragic war loss like Brooke, Owen, and other English poets. Dunsany, who edited *The Complete Poems* (1919), believed that Ledwidge would have equaled Burns, had he lived. The range, however, is limited, including some Irish nationalism and tales of the ancient Gaelic cycles, but chiefly and most tellingly relating the exquisite beauty of Irish landscape.

Lady Isabella Augusta Gregory (née **Persse**) (1852–1932). Lady Gregory was born into a staunch Protestant family of Roxborough, County Galway. In 1881 she married Sir William Gregory, a noted Irish member of parliament. She made the Gregory estate at Coole the unofficial headquarters of literary nationalism, especially after her husband's death in 1892. As director with Yeats of the Abbey Theatre she was instrumental in its success in the face of stormy protests. Lady Gregory was an indefatigable searcher for folklore and peasant customs, which she incorporated in numerous dramas written for the Abbey Theatre. Not a dramatist by nature, she made herself one to provide needed scripts for a burgeoning stage.

In 1898 Edward Martyn brought Yeats to meet Lady Gregory at Coole and there proposed a distinctly Irish theater. The resultant Irish Literary Theatre in the next year offered *The Countess Cathleen* by Yeats as its first play. Already functioning in Dublin was the Irish National Theatre which in 1902 became the Irish National Dramatic Company, with Yeats one of its leaders. The first playbill by this group offered a drama by A.E. and a drama by Yeats. In 1903 the combined efforts in the Irish dramatic movement inaugurated the Abbey Theatre, one of the most famous theaters of this century. Thriving on controversy, the Abbey Theatre launched the careers of a number of notable playwrights (including Yeats, A.E., and Colum noted above) and many distinguished actors.

Unlike the ethereal symbolism of dramas by Yeats and A.E., the plays of Lady Gregory are generally prose comedies of Irish country life. Her central themes appear in her first drama, *Spreading the News* (1903); in the typical Irish village quiet routine generates an appetite for the shock of disorder, and ignorance permits ludicrous confusion. Her attitude is noninflammatory, but she could elicit protests from both Nationalists and Unionists with the melodramatic *The Rising of the Moon* (1907), in which a political refugee, a ballad singer, by singing the folksongs of his native county enlists a policeman's assistance in escaping. Increasingly, Lady Gregory's contribution appears primarily of historical importance.

John Millington Synge (sing) (1871–1909). John Millington Synge was born at Newton Little, near Dublin, a descendant upon both sides of Protestant clerics. After graduation from Trinity College, Dublin, he wandered through Europe. In Paris in 1896 he was urged by Yeats to explore the authentic old Ireland of the Aran Islands in Galway Bay, where he thereupon spent most of his next six years. His first drama was *The Tinker's Wedding* (1902). In the succeeding half-decade before illness carried him off, he produced one of the 20th century's great tragedies and one of its great comedies.

Riders to the Sea (1903) finds elemental tragedy in a fisher family of Ireland's west.

The husband and four sons of Maurya have all drowned while fishing. Her daughters, Cathleen and Nora, examining the garments of a man drowned off Donegal, recognize them as belonging to their brother Michael. The distraught mother pleads with her only surviving son, Bartley, not to put to sea amid a threatening storm. He insists upon riding off, and is thrown from his pony to death in the sea. The keening from the mourning women ends with Maurya's resigned, "No man at all can be living forever, and we must be satisfied."

Eschewing modern bourgeois society as a setting for tragedy, Synge chooses a primitive, brutal world, stark in its simplicity. The stripping away of every superfluity and the cadenced, archaic speech of the peasants produce a drama of tragic intensity. Few plays since the ancient Greeks have displayed such power in the portrayal of human mortality and pain.

The stature of the people in this play is heroic, and they rise far above the mere pathos which characterizes most 20th-century bourgeois tragedy.

The Playboy of the Western World (1907) aroused wild protests, as Irishmen considered themselves maligned in the naïve admiration accorded a patricide. Cordons of police were necessary to maintain a semblance of order during Abbey Theatre performances. Padraic Colum's father was among those arrested. Yeats vigorously supported Synge's comedy.

Old Mahon is a bully and a tyrant. Rather than accept an aged fiancée chosen by his father, Christie, his timid son, hits Old Mahon over the head with a spade and flees, believing he has killed his father. At a distant public house, Pegeen, the publican's romantic daughter, falls in love with Christie because of his prowess and dismisses her cowardly suitor, Shawn Keogh, choice of her father and her priest. The Widow Quinn, an Irish Wife of Bath, tries to snare Christie, and all the local girls flock about him. Old Mahon appears to thrash Christie and his glamour disappears. Trying to kill his father, Christie finds the townsfolk turn from admiration to horror. At last, the two Mahons depart but with Christie now master.

Though carping over the wrong points, the enraged Irish were right. Christie's revolt against his father, Pegeen's casting off Shawn, and the townsfolk's admiration for the supposed father-slayer symbolize the unconscious urge of the Irish to break away from the tyranny that shackles them, but when the townsmen see the naked assault of Christie upon Old Mahon, they retreat, demonstrating that their courage lies solely in their dreams.

In broader application, the drama considers illusion and reality. Distance lends enchantment, glamorizing deeds; but the immediate reality, as Pegeen observes, is an apple off another tree, often harsh and disillusioning. Christie's career is everyman's (*Mahon* is pronounced *man*), as he must assert his independence, enter the adult world of competition and love, and supplant the previous generation.

The most compelling feature of this drama is the poetic prose of the dialogue, ranging from robust flytings to Christie's imaginative wooing of Pegeen. Although authorities deny that any Irishmen talk exactly this way, Synge compounded from his sensitive ear a diction utilizing much Irish speech and producing an incomparable lilt and harmony.

Deirdre of the Sorrows (1910), unfinished at Synge's death, is a remarkable attempt to tell the legendary epic account in the modern Irish speech employed in Synge's previous dramas. A.E., Yeats, and most writers of the movement tried the theme, but even in unpolished form Synge's is the best. Conchubor is a sad, lonely monarch driven to bloody deeds he regrets by the overpowering attraction of Deirdre's beauty. Naisi is a poetic lover but also a husband annoyed that his wife has softened him and deprived him of the comradeship of fighting men. No other work of the Celtic

Renaissance succeeds thus in welding the themes of Irish peasantry of to-day with the spacious grandeur of an epic past.

Edward John Moreton Drax Plunkett, 18th Baron Dunsany, commonly **Lord Dunsany** (dun-sā′ni) (1878–1957). Though born in London, Lord Dunsany came from an ancient family of Marchers who had been nobles of Ireland since the 12th century. Educated at Eton and Sandhurst, he inherited the title in 1899. He saw action with the Coldstream Guards in the Boer War and with the Royal Inniskilling Fusiliers in World War I. He first attracted attention with *The Glittering Gate,* performed by the Abbey Theatre in 1909. By 1916 five of his plays were running simultaneously in New York. In World War II he left Ireland to serve in England with the Home Guard. He was Byron Professor of English literature at Athens University until the German invasion of Greece in 1941.

Though the English-speaking world was overwhelmed by Dunsany during the first quarter of the century, it reacted from this and came to look on Dunsany as almost a museum piece in his last three decades. Maeterlinck was his stylistic master as he poured into fantasy conventional bourgeois ethics, ironic twists, and a protest against modern materialism. *The Gods of the Mountain* (1911) shows his ability at the romantic, imaginative one-act play. His forte lies with the brief evocation of a poetically stark, primitive world inhabited by his own mythological creations of monstrous deities and eccentric mortals. His talent for dramatic miniatures was impressive, and his short stories, equally imaginative, have caused O'Faoláin to rate him among the modern masters of this genre.

St. John Greer Ervine (er′vin) (1883–   ). A native of Belfast, St. John Greer Ervine spent his early teens in England, but returned to Ireland and had his first play, *Mixed Marriage* (1911), produced by the Abbey Theatre. For three decades he was a noted drama critic in England, becoming president of the Critics' Circle in 1929.

Ervine's earlier dramas are realistic problem plays of the Protestant North Ireland, especially *John Ferguson* (1915), exemplifying the Ulsterman's fear of Irish nationalism and Roman Catholic penetration. Far less satisfactory are the conventional later dramas, social comedies, written for the London stage.

MORE RECENT NOVELISTS AND DRAMATISTS

It was during World War I, while the German assault on Verdun occupied the world's attention, and while the English frantically grouped for the impending Somme drive, that Irish nationalists, chiefly the Sinn Fein ("ourselves alone"), hoisted the republican banner of The Plough and the Stars over the Dublin Post Office on Easter Sunday 1916. Hundreds were killed before peace was briefly restored, only to break out in the "Anglo-

Irish War" (1919–21). The outlawed Dáil (national assembly), spearheaded by De Valera, had declared independence in 1918.

A savage guerrilla campaign, called war by the Irish Republican Army and assassination by the English, brought to Ireland suffering unknown since Elizabethan times. Lukewarm support from the mass of Irishmen ballooned into fervid enthusiasm because of the daring ingenuity of the IRA and the repressive countermeasures of the "Black-and-Tans," a police force of tough English veterans nicknamed from their uniforms.

A wearied England in 1921 by treaty with the Dáil created the Irish Free State, which enjoyed the dominion status of Canada. Protestant Ulster, in the North, elected to remain part of Great Britain. Enraged at the prospect of a split Ireland, the IRA rose against the Irish Free State to add to Ireland's "troubles." With the new constitution of 1937, Eire became the official name of a republic embracing the primarily Catholic south, east, and west of Ireland, breaking off all political ties with England, and maintaining neutrality during World War II. The Republic of Ireland does not recognize the allegiance of Ulster to England and, while officially no action is being taken, the borders of Ulster are still an area where Irish nationalists struggle to create a unified Ireland from Bantry Bay to the Giant's Causeway.

The Easter Rebellion transformed Irish literature. Writers coming to maturity then and subsequently have been purged of the dreamy Celtic twilight and plunged into a real world of bloodletting and nation-building. Irish literature since the Easter Rebellion has generally displayed strong realism, even naturalism; however, the rigorous censorship of the Republic of Ireland, shying at any frank portrayal of sex or bodily functions, has cast a pall over many authors and has caused others to leave their native land. Fiction (especially the short story) and realistic prose drama predominate in recent Irish writers, and their subject matter tends to be contemporary urbanized Ireland.

Liam O'Flaherty (lē′am ō-fla′hér-tē) (1897–   ). Liam O'Flaherty was born into an intensely nationalistic, Gaelic-speaking family in the Aran Islands. He was educated at several Roman Catholic institutions, among them University College, Dublin, destined for the priesthood. His family was horrified when he enlisted in World War I to fight for the English. Shell-shocked, he returned to Ireland to participate in the Easter Rebellion. From 1918 he wandered as an itinerant worker around much of the world, and he became an agnostic along the way. His brother in Roxbury, Massachusetts, encouraged him to write in 1923. While bitterly anticlerical, O'Flaherty is staunchly nationalistic.

The Informer (1925) won the James Tait Black prize for fiction and was dramatized as an Academy-award-winning motion picture in Hollywood (1935).

During the "Anglo-Irish War" Gypo Nolan, driven by hunger, for a price reveals to the English constabulary the whereabouts of the fugitive Frankie MacPhillip. After Frankie's slaying, the Irish revolutionaries track Gypo down, give him a kangaroo trial, and shoot him. Gypo drags himself to Frankie's mourning mother and receives her forgiveness as he dies.

O'Flaherty seems to be a Romantic working through naturalistic materials. We are spared none of the squalor and degradation of the slums, but a thrilling manhunt culminates in the powerful drama of the forgiveness scene. Throughout this tale of brutality shines O'Flaherty's profound compassion for his physical and spiritual derelicts.

The Stories of Liam O'Flaherty (1956) show the changing interests of O'Flaherty. His earliest fiction seems prose Synge, depicting the starkly primitive folk of the Aran Islands. During the 1920s he was preoccupied with the contemporary Irish "troubles," but since the 1930s he has increasingly searched the Irish past, especially the Great Famine of the 1840s.

Seán O'Faoláin (shon ō-fal′an) (1900–   ). A native of Cork, Seán O'Faoláin holds an A.B. from the National University of Ireland and an M.A. from Harvard University. He was a staunch nationalist during the "Anglo-Irish War," and for a while was director of publicity for the entire IRA. Irish censors banned his first collection of short stories, *Midsummer Night Madness* (1932). From 1940 to 1946 he edited *The Bell*, the outstanding Irish literary periodical since the retirement of A.E. in 1930. Although a frequent traveler and lecturer in Europe and America, he resides in Ireland, where, since the 1940s, he has been its most distinguished man of letters. From 1957 he has been director of the Arts Council of Ireland.

O'Faoláin has proved a valiant defender of Ireland abroad and a severe critic of Ireland at home. He is the only first-rate Irish writer who has consistently remained within the fold of Roman Catholicism; his momentary lapse and return are explained in *A Summer in Italy* (1950), one of the best evocations of place in modern travel literature. Though pious, O'Faoláin is highly critical of repressive church influence in Ireland. More broadly, his short stories (probably the best in English from the 1940s into the 1960s) generally reveal the sense of frustration and limitation among bourgeois Irish in and around the author's native Cork. His short stories have become mainstays of recent anthologies because of their sensuous grasp of locale and their lyric moods of pain and anxiety. The author's own selection of twenty-seven items from three decades appears in *The Finest Stories of Seán O'Faoláin* (1957). In *I Remember! I Remember!* (1962) O'Faoláin is increasingly concerned with the disillusionment that occurs when Irish dreams and memories are confronted with bleak reality. O'Faoláin perceives his Ireland as irrevocably divided by "the impact of a complex and sophisticated civilisation on the quiet certainties of a simpler way of life." With *The Vanishing Hero* (1956) O'Faoláin demonstrates that he is one of the outstanding critics of modern fiction.

Frank O'Connor (real name **Michael O'Donovan**) (1903–   ). Frank O'Connor was born to a lower-class family in the Cork slums (O'Connor was his mother's maiden name). After an unpleasant schooling under the Christian Brothers, he worked unsuccessfully at minor jobs. Joining the IRA, he fought against the compromising Irish Free State until captured and imprisoned. He worked as a librarian from 1925 to 1938 and served as director of the Abbey Theatre, 1936–39. In 1952 he became a permanent resident of the United States, since lecturing at the universities of Northwestern, Harvard, and Chicago.

Though renouncing his faith and his native land, O'Connor is Irish of the Irish. He ranks with O'Faoláin as a master of the contemporary short story, into which he infuses an incomparable robustness. His first collection of stories was *Guests of the Nation* (1931). Deceptively simple, his short stories depict Irishmen unable to accept the rigid patterns of a theocentric and hidebound society, and thrown back upon their inner resources of instinct. The squalor and hurt inflicted upon his characters are more than compensated for by their abounding vitality. O'Connor significantly defines the short story as "the art form that deals with the individual when there is no longer a society to absorb him, and when he is compelled to exist, as it were, by his own inner light." Yeats termed him the Chekhov of Ireland. *The Mirror in the Roadway* (1957) has been praised by C. P. Snow as "the best book on the major novelists" from Jane Austen to Joyce. The title (a quotation from Stendhal) indicates O'Connor's analysis of each novelist as a creator of subjective truth, like a character in an O'Connor short story. Perhaps O'Connor's crowning work in criticism is his study of the genre upon which he concentrated, *The Lonely Voice: A Study of the Short Story* (1963).

An Only Child (1961), though an autobiography, is an imaginative masterpiece, one of the best of 20th-century self-analyses. The childhood of Joyce was almost luxurious in comparison with the juvenile hardships of O'Connor. His shiftless Irish father was as coarse as D. H. Lawrence's English miner father, but more improvident and temperamental. Maggie O'Donovan, his mother, unsentimentally portrayed, is one of the true saints, even though "the gutter where life had thrown her was deep and dirty." His blighted early years were a search for identity amid chaos. He found it in jail where the imprisoned IRA men went upon a dramatic hunger strike. He refused to join, eschewing the death wish and desire for martyrdom in favor of life.

Sean O'Casey (1880–   ). Sean O'Casey was born John Casey into a rare species, lower-class Protestants of Dublin. After sketchy education he moved from one laboring job to another. As a militant proletarian, he was

active in the Dublin strike of 1913. His earliest writings were nationalistic
and socialistic under the Gaelicized name Sean O'Cathasaigh. He was into
his forties when the Abbey Theatre produced *The Shadow of a Gunman*
(*1923*, 1925), the first work under the name Sean O'Casey. The success of
Juno and the Paycock (*1924,* 1925) permitted him to quit his job of mixing
concrete for road building. The tumultuous reception accorded *The Plough
and the Stars* (1926) caused O'Casey to move to England, where he has
lived ever since.

Exuberant vitality and passionate love for suffering mankind inform
everything O'Casey writes; but even into his eighties he is a wanderer, in
his own words "a voluntary exile from every creed, from every party, and
from every literary clique." O'Casey has never worn any badge but his
own, and consistently his literary expression has run counter to current
tendencies. His bitterest detractors, from Irish zealots to elegant London
reviewers, nonetheless recognize him as a genius. His supporters rate him
second only to Shaw among 20th-century British dramatists.

NATURALISTIC TRAGICOMEDIES OF IRELAND'S "TROUBLES" (1923–26). Juno
and the Paycock (*1924*) is set in 1922 during the civil war between the
Irish Free State and the IRA.

Against the background of the funeral of murdered Robbie Tancred,
fanatical IRA member, the shiftless "Captain" Jack Boyle (a peacock of a
man) evades the prodding of his wife Juno to go to work. Expectance of a
legacy moves Boyle to wild expenditures. His son Johnny has lost an arm
fighting for the IRA, and his daughter Mary becomes pregnant by a
jilting lover. Collapse of the legacy causes creditors to strip the Boyle
quarters of almost everything. Johnny, accused of informing on Tancred, is
dragged out by Irish Irregulars and killed. Juno and Mary abandon the
drunken Boyle, who is loudly protesting his patriotism and the miserable
state of the world.

O'Casey stakes his case upon "impure" drama, tragicomedy, blending the
broadest of robust humor with the bitterest of pains. Instead of the well-
made play with one central problem, he offers the Chekhov thematic type
of drama. The disintegration of a family results from separate downfalls,
all resulting from self-love. Boyle flees from all responsibilities and realities.
Mary gratifies solely her own pleasure. Johnny nurses a pathetic image of
himself as a maimed hero. The separate themes are drawn together in Juno,
whose departure dramatically symbolizes the broken family. Instead of conventional dramatic technique, O'Casey tries to infuse the complexity and
disorder of life. The men quixotically talk about patriotism and Ireland;
only Juno perceives that the real enemies are human hate and selfishness,
and the only true goal is the full assumption of mutual responsibilities.

The Plough and the Stars (1926) is set during the Easter Rebellion of

1916, the title referring to the revolutionary flag that symbolized constructive reality and noble aspiration.

While little Mollser Gogan is dying of tuberculosis in a Dublin tenement, Jack Clitheroe is awaiting the uprising and his wife Nora is expecting a child. When the rebellion begins, most of the tenement dwellers enjoy a wild spree of looting stores. Jack is killed in the street battles, Mollser dies, and Nora has a stillborn baby. Delirious, Nora peers out the window looking for Jack, but attracts English gunfire. Breaking into the Clitheroe apartment in search of snipers, the English soldiers take the occasion to rest and Nora is taken downstairs to Mollser's bed.

In this tragicomedy there are actually eight separate defeats for eight characters. The drama moves from broad laughter initially to final ironic tragedy. Irishmen were annoyed at O'Casey's contention that poverty and narrow minds were more fundamental problems than Ireland's struggle for independence, but even more they were enraged at the riotous scenes of looting that venomously countered the earlier speeches on idealism and stigmatized Dubliners as more concerned with plunder than with nationalism. The *Playboy* disorders were repeated, and Yeats shouted defense of O'Casey from an embattled proscenium.

EXPRESSIONISTIC PROPAGANDA (1928–40). Ireland's rejection of O'Casey was complete in 1928 when Yeats as director of the Abbey Theatre turned down *The Silver Tassie* (1933). Yeats's predilection for the Japanese *no* drama made him unsympathetic to the expressionism into which O'Casey was veering. Modern expressionism stems from the experimental German theater, with Ernst Toller and Georg Kaiser exercising the most influence upon O'Casey. Expressionism employs wholly unrealistic stage techniques in an attempt to transcend the limitations of the conventional stage; actually, expressionism is the old Morality in 20th-century guise. It avoids photographic reality to portray abstractions from the realm of ideas and values.

Within the Gates (1933), the first fully expressionistic O'Casey drama, is set within a park-world resembling London's Hyde Park, and many characters speak cockney English. O'Casey frankly labels the play a Morality.

The Young Whore (Jannice) is actually the daughter of the Bishop (Gilbert). The conflict arises from the struggle for her soul between the repression of life (Bishop, Salvation Army officer, Policewoman) and the celebration of life's poetry represented by the Dreamer. She dies with a song, dance, and prayer. The Bishop is moved to a more compassionate view of mortals and an ampler view of life.

This is the first powerful assertion of the later O'Casey conviction that energetic youth and life can and must prevail against traditional restraint. The obvious symbolism and occasional preachiness are relieved by verve and imaginative dialogue.

LATER PLAYS (1940–   ). The more recent O'Casey dramas return to Irish locales and in a mixture of realism and fantasy continue his protests against restraint, superstition, and the English. Among these plays are *The Star Turns Red* and *Purple Dust* (both in 1940), *Red Roses for Me* (1942), *Oak Leaves and Lavender* (1946), *Cockadoodle Dandy* (1949), *The Bishop's Bonfire* (1955), and the following last play to date:

The Drums of Father Ned was commissioned by the Dublin Tostal (Spring Festival) Drama Council in 1958 but was dropped when the Roman Catholic Archbishop of Dublin forbade the celebration of Mass during the tostal if an O'Casey play were produced.

Father Fillifogue, parish priest of Doonavale, is sabotaging the joyous tostal where Angus, Celtic god of youth and beauty, is trying to assert his old reign over the Irish. Mayor Binnington and Deputy Mayor McGilligan hate each other cordially but for money reasons cooperate on a shady deal to buy Russian lumber through Skerigan, an Ulster Protestant. Michael Binnington and Nora McGilligan fall in love against their parents' wishes and decide to run for office against their elders. Father Fillifogue wants the Russian timber destroyed, but the younger generation will use it to build needed homes. The discredited oldsters are abandoned as the community follows the life-sounding drums of Father Ned, who organized the tostal but never appears in person.

Ulster Protestantism is under attack as much as Eire Catholicism. It is not religion but puritanism, O'Casey contends, that tries to stifle the joy of living. From the eighty-year-old playwright pours a fervid conviction that youth and freedom must override the elders.

THE AUTOBIOGRAPHY. O'Casey's enduring reputation may eventually rest upon the sprawling autobiography collected in 1956 as *Mirror in My House*. In third-person narrative, O'Casey relates the life of Johnny Casside (Sean through the later volumes) in Irish splendor of language. *I Knock at the Door* (1939), covering 1880–90, and *Pictures in the Hallway* (1942), covering 1891–1904, are perhaps the most lyrically appealing as the small boy and youth, tortured by ailing eyes and bewildered at the prejudice and inconsistency of adults, tries to understand his world. *Drums under the Window* (1946), covering 1905–16, centers about the Dublin strike of 1913 and O'Casey's repudiation of religious and political goals in favor of bread and poetry. *Inishfallen Fare Thee Well* (1949), covering 1916–26, is perhaps the most impressive; in ironic, tragic mood a tenement dweller observes the wild fury of Ireland's "troubles" and his personal defeats as an uncompromising playwright. *Rose and Crown* (1952), covering 1926–34, and *Sunset and Evening Star* (1954), covering 1934–53, detail his self-imposed exile in England; he is still the outrageous Irishman but is moved to superb tributes to Yeats and Shaw, and he remains enamored of life whether at staid Cambridge or in dynamic America.

Brendan Francis Behan (bē'an) (1923–1964). A native of Dublin's slums, Brendan Behan joined the IRA at the age of thirteen. At sixteen he was sent to England to blow up the English battleship *King George V*, but was arrested in Liverpool and sentenced to prison for possession of explosives. After three years of English jails, he was deported but found Ireland uncomfortable, since the Roman Catholic Church continued to excommunicate him for his republican activity. A Dublin military court in 1942 again committed him to prison for illegal IRA agitation. After his release in 1947 he was often referred to as the "bad boy" of British letters.

The Quare Fellow (1956) Behan calls a "comedy-drama."

Convicts in an Irish prison await the execution or reprieve of a "quare fellow" (man sentenced to death). They dig his grave and therein sneak drags from the ends of "snouts" (cigarettes) he tossed away in final prodigality. When the quare fellow is refused a reprieve and is executed, the prisoners set up a horrendous din and then subside into silence in their "flowery dells" (prison cells). The play closes as the prisoners divide the quare fellow's last letters for sale to the Sunday papers.

Playgoers have been intrigued by the coarse vitality and cynical resilience of men in cages. Life goes on with energy and even humor amid the weird stratagems and stratifications of prison society, but implicit is a strong condemnation of capital punishment and the treatment of convicts.

Borstal Boy (1958) recounts Behan's three years in an English borstal (reformatory). Ignoring the forces that molded his previous sixteen years, Behan concentrates upon the problems of a youth maturing while in prison. This is thorough-going naturalism, censoring none of the obscenity and vulgarity of coarse wastrels. Nonetheless, Behan found rare stimulation in the challenge of getting along with his fellows and emerged more tolerant and understanding toward the English and his fellow man than before.

With the brilliantly individualistic vignettes of *Hold Your Hour and Have Another* (1963), he appeared to be the major Irish literary figure of the 1960s, but death silenced a robust voice that men could not.

Part Three

TWENTIETH-CENTURY ENGLISH LITERATURE

Chapter 7

Introduction to the Modern Period

BACKGROUND INFORMATION

MAJOR HISTORICAL EVENTS. After the downfall of Napoleon, England throughout the 19th century stood unchallenged as the world's greatest power; but as Queen Victoria expired and the 20th century began, a change set in. To be sure, it was less a decline of England than a rise of other nations. Across the Atlantic the generally friendly United States turned into an economic giant, still hesitant, however, to accept a global position; and on the continent a Germany unified in 1870 presented a formidable menace which compelled England to regroup its fleet in the British Isles and prepare for war. In internal matters, mounting trade unionism erupted in a rash of strikes and prodded Liberal administrations toward the development of the modern social security system: Old-Age Pension Law (1909), National Insurance Act (1911), and Minimum Wage Law (1912). The political giants of the Victorian era were gone, but a fiery Welshman, David Lloyd George, was ascending toward the role of national leadership in the war ahead. In 1910 George V began a reign that was to last until 1936.

A hundred-year period of peaceful European expansion and prosperity was shattered in 1914 by World War I. In the opening gambit on the western front, the British professional army was sacrificed to hold the French Channel ports. By the end of 1914, with the German army in northern France, the western front became so stabilized in trench warfare that the next three years of hideous carnage would not vary the line more than ten miles. Though the main British effort was concentrated in Flanders (Ypres, Passchendaele), the English had to conduct a world-wide struggle involving African colonies of the Germans and the Turkish empire in the Near East, and, proportionally, England's war losses equaled those of any other combatant. At home, prices more than doubled, taxation reached about five times the prewar levels, and the burden of domestic and foreign debt increased ten times between 1914 and 1918. A war-weary England had to demobilize and assimilate about eight million servicemen, placate labor, and fight for world markets now increasingly threatened by America and Japan.

Strikes at home and the unrest of a war-devastated world abroad in 1922 brought to an end the Liberal administration of Lloyd George and the effective life of the Liberal Party. In the general election of that year the Labour Party with 142 seats for the first time became His Majesty's Loyal Opposition. The brief Conservative government of Stanley Baldwin fell in the elections of 1923, and Ramsay MacDonald brought in the first Labour administration in English history, an avowedly socialistic government. In less than a year Baldwin was back as prime minister, and angered labor almost paralyzed the nation with the General Strike of 1926. In 1928 the cause of feminism was finally won with the extension of the franchise to women on the same terms as men. Mounting unemployment, the gradual drifting away of the overseas possessions and dominions from the mother country, and the deterioration of the uneasy continental peace caused another Conservative defeat and the second Mac-Donald Labour government in 1929.

The Great Depression from 1929 on, plus an increasingly belligerent Germany, brought about a coalition government first headed by MacDonald in 1931 and from 1935 by Baldwin. After the death of George V, Edward VIII reigned less than a year during 1936 and then staged the first voluntary abdication in English history. His younger brother became king, reigning as George VI until his death in 1953. Fearful of another war, England went along with the appeasement policy of Neville Chamberlain, the prime minister succeeding Baldwin in 1937. Sacrificing Czechoslovakia to Hitler at Munich in 1938, Chamberlain stepped from the plane at London, waving the peace pact and proclaiming, "Peace in our time." World War II broke out the next year.

England's leader in this time of peril was Winston Churchill, who followed Chamberlain as prime minister in 1940. The German *panzerdivisionen* swept over western Europe initiating the *blitzkrieg,* which allowed the Germans to overrun a whole country within a few days. Early 1940 found England the only nation still fighting Hitler, and the *Luftwaffe* stormed the island kingdom in the Battle of Britain, culminating in saturation aerial bombing of London. Thousands of civilians perished, and much of central London was destroyed. But England stood firm in a magnificent display of national courage. By engaging Russia in 1940 and the United States in 1941, the Axis Powers were forced to ease the pressure on Britain. A massive counterattack, first in 1943–45 by Russia in the east, and then in 1944 by the combined Western allies striking into Normandy, prostrated Germany, and in 1945 the Allies from East and West met in Germany to end the European conflict. A few months later in 1945 an atomic bomb destroyed Hiroshima, Japan, and ended World War II, but left the monstrous question mark of thermonuclear destruction to plague a battered world.

The defeat of Churchill in the British elections of 1945 astounded the outside world, but the British were jettisoning not the man Churchill as much as war and their anguished past. Exhausted in victory, they yearned for security. Under Clement Attlee's Labour government (1945–51) the British Welfare State emerged, nationalizing (i.e. socializing) many of the country's industries and, most importantly, providing cradle-to-grave protection for every English worker. The subsequent Conservative regimes of Churchill (1951–55), Eden (1955–57), Macmillan (1957–63), and Home (1963–) have attempted to turn away from nationalization of industry but have left untouched the structure of social security. The British Welfare State is the first of the two pre-eminent facts of contemporary English life, and its very fulfilment seems at the moment to have robbed English reformers and humanitarians of one of their major causes.

It is understandably difficult for Englishmen of the postwar era to realize that the great affairs of the world are no longer being decided in Downing Street (the prime minister's residence). In World War II the British Isles suffered over 400,000 killed or missing, and about the same number of wounded. The money cost exceeded £16,000,000,000 and the national debt more than trebled. In these cold figures lies the economic downgrading of Great Britain to a debtor nation, secondary in the world's financial structure. Weakened, England had to acquiesce to the dissolution of its vast colonial empire. In the most tremendous liberation of all time, Great Britain from 1947 to 1963 has given independence to over 600,000,-000 people in countries all over the globe. Almost all these newly-freed countries maintain a special tie with Britain as members of the British Commonwealth of Nations, an organization composed of British colonies, possessions, and independent states which were formerly colonies. Thus, England does maintain close trade and cultural relations with its former colonial empire. The second overpowering fact of contemporary English life is the loss of the empire and the consequent decline of English prestige.

Perhaps only England could display the political phenomena of the 1950s and 1960s. Conservative administrations, basically imperial, have presided with dignity over the dismemberment of the empire. In 1961 Macmillan opted to petition for British entrance into the European Common Market, abandoning the neutralist, nationalist traditions of the Conservatives, while the liberal Labour Party protested. The neo-Elizabethan era (Queen Elizabeth II ascended the throne in 1953) may inaugurate for England a rediscovery of Europe as the first Elizabethan age inaugurated England's discovery of the New World.

CULTURAL CONDITIONS. The upper and lower classes of 20th-century England have made terms with their environment. The well-to-do have gracefully accepted a drastic reduction of their incomes, and the workers are enjoying a substantial increase in their standard of living. The most noticeable discontent exists among the ambitious middle class, the one large emigrating group in England, whose frequent departure to Australia, Canada, or elsewhere for greater opportunity is draining off a significant portion of England's able, constructive population. Virtually all Englishmen have become acclimated to a secular society, residually Protestant. Evangelicalism has withered, and the Established Church has tended increasingly in a Catholic direction. Most Englishmen, like most men, sense a disturbing world they never made but which they fit into as best they can.

Intellectual currents in the first decade and a half of this century were largely an extension of the later 19th-century revolt against Victorianism. Intellectuals remained confident that human beings were rationally inclined and needed only a bit of clear-sighted direction to construct the better world. Non-Europeans cannot realize the cataclysmic effects of World War I upon the psyche of intellectuals. The outraged cries of protest (significantly muted in World War II) announced the destruction of an era's mind-set. The forward course of mankind seemed irremediably destroyed, along with the hopes for a rational society and for reason itself. The dominant note among intellectuals since World War I has therefore been pessimistic, a typical work being entitled *Studies in a Dying Culture* (1938) by Christopher Caudwell.

Perhaps Western culture is expiring, as the German historian Oswald Spengler hysterically maintained or as the American historian Carroll Quigley calmly states in fixing 2500 as the approximate date for the ultimate end of our civilization. Conversely, we may be on the brink of a new age of creativity, in which case our own era would correspond to the perturbed period of Mannerism that followed the High Renaissance and preluded the majestic achievements of the 17th, 18th, and 19th centuries. We have the rare good fortune of finding contemporary expression a case study of travail from the ruins of an impressive past toward the fabrication of a new and perhaps equally constructive future. The problem for the intellectual now is to find a new order because the older rationalism and progressivism of secular society have been largely destroyed.

The interbellum period (1918–39) witnessed a desperate search for order. Some sought a traditionalist course which reached back to the wellsprings of Western culture. The influential *Criterion* magazine was determinedly Catholic, royalist, and classical. Converts to Anglo-Catholicism included T. S. Eliot, C. S. Lewis, C. E. M. Joad. Converts to Roman Catholicism included Evelyn Waugh, Graham Greene, and, recently, Edith Sitwell. Others turned to communism, and among intellectuals maturing around 1930 few failed to flirt with Marxism; however, disillusionment with Stalinism has virtually swept English intellectuals out of communism. It is important to observe that both these searches for faith were essentially among the intellectual classes and did not profoundly influence the average Englishman.

Since science and the scientific approach have been the chief instruments in forging the modern mind and the modern world, it is no accident that many of the best English minds of this century (e.g. Whitehead, Russell, Keynes, Laski) have been concentrated upon the exciting factual exploration of the universe, man, and society. But the developments of 20th-century science have resulted in more intellectual heat than light. Science of the 19th century (cf. Pearson) plumped for a mechanistic, deterministic structure of the universe, which did away with any free will or individual choice. Physical and natural science of the 20th century has abandoned this position in favor of relativity, permutations and combinations, and theories of probability that encourage or at least permit an idealistic, voluntaristic appraisal of the universe. Remarkably, however, the major schools of 20th-century psychology retain the determinism of the previous century. Behaviorism treats of human beings as mindless organisms responding to stimuli according to rigid organic laws. The psychoanalytic schools of Freud, Jung, and Adler have proved immensely more stimulating to most intellectuals, but they too are deterministic, asserting that unconscious elements in the human psyche, beyond the control of the conscious or "rational" self, actually motivate human conduct to a great extent. The contradictions within scientific concepts mirror similar contradictions throughout modern thought and experience, heightening the bewilderment in the intellectual's search.

The English intellectual since World War II finds himself pretty much a rebel without a cause. The "Angry Young Men" of *Declaration* (1957), notably Osborne, Wilson, and Wain, casting about for victims, have attacked the Royal Family, the Established Church, and the London theater —institutions of only minor significance in molding contemporary English life. The British Welfare State has eliminated most abuses of defunct laissez-faire and utilitarianism, and Christianity, Marxism, and psychoanalysis have all lost their proselyting charms for most of the younger English intellectuals. Indeed, the concept of irrational man has rather universally gripped the intellectuals and cast mankind back upon the sole resource of individual experience.

LANGUAGE. Most observers think that 20th-century English continues to alter enormously in vocabulary but otherwise remains static, but perhaps we are too close to the subject to appreciate what is happening. Certainly the new grammarians are opening up exciting prospects in contemplating our language free of the Latin-grammar straitjacket imposed upon generations of schoolchildren. With the perspective of dispassionate foreigners, continental scholars have led in the objective study of English linguistics: the Dutchman Hendrik Poutsma (first study of English, 1904), the Dane Otto Jesperson (1909), and the Dutchman Etsko Kruisinga (1911). Much of contemporary linguistic study casts new light upon long-standing but previously ignored English practice, and some recent concentration (e.g. upon tonal patterns) unfortunately possesses no earlier materials to let us know what if any changes have occurred over the years.

Development is occurring in English verbs. Verb phrases are rapidly superseding simple verb constructions; e.g. the progressive present (*she is sobbing* or *she's sobbing*) has almost displaced the traditional present (*she sobs*) of many verbs, except for the historical present. In helter-skelter fashion, not realizing what they are constructing, English speakers have been building up an elaborate system of *aspect,* i.e. verb phrases (in English) indicating the nature of an action or the way in which it is regarded. For example, below is a collection of different aspects entirely in the past tense:

Preparation	She was about to sob
Quick incipience	She burst out sobbing
Slow incipience	She gradually began to sob
Quick completion	She broke off sobbing
Slow completion	She trailed off sobbing
Extensive duration	She kept on sobbing
Brief duration	She just barely sobbed
Repetition	She sobbed and sobbed

Apparently ancient Indo-European (like modern Slavic tongues) used aspect extensively, and English now appears to be increasing its subtlety constantly by new experiments in aspect.

Many of the examples of aspect above show another tendency of English verbs, unquestionably on the increase. In old-fashioned terminology it is called verb-adverb phrases. Apparently the English-speaking people have a deep-seated urge toward an analytic instead of synthetic language. Such a process eliminated many inflections during the three fallow centuries after the Norman Conquest. Today the same tendency often substitutes verb-adverb phrases for more formal, usually borrowed verbs: *bring about* (accomplish), *put up with* (tolerate), *turn over* (surrender).

The process of linguistic conversion, active since the Renaissance, seems to be accelerating in contemporary English, especially in the employment of nouns as adjectives: *government* problems and *machine* technology haunt this *space* age. More colloquial is the transformation of nouns into verbs, e.g. *beetle, pleasure, jet* (flying of airplane), all in the 20th century.

Schoolteachers may still be fighting against *It's me* and *Who do you want?* but theirs is a losing battle. The expectancy of nominative form before the verb and accusative form following the verb is overpowering the last major stronghold of English inflections, the pronouns.

American expressions are inundating England chiefly through Hollywood films and popular songs, but also through advertising, radio and television programs, and the newspapers and popular magazines. *The Concise Oxford Dictionary* (1951) chronicles such American contributions to British speech as *ballyhoo, blizzard, blurb, bobby-soxer, bogus, bulldozer.* Many older Englishmen sadly or bitterly assert that English communities look like neon-spangled American towns and their younger generation talks like the new-fangled Americans.

The British Bench of the Court of Appeal has solemnly pronounced that the American import *finalize* is "not English." Nonetheless, a favorite 20th-century method of verb creation uses the suffixes *-ize* (*hospitalize*, 1901) and *-ate* (*excalate*, 1900). New nouns ending in *-ism* (*fascism*, 1922) and *-ation* (*nebularization*, 1928) are rampant, as well as adjectives in *-istic* (*mutualistic*, 1902) and *-ational* (*vegetational*, 1926). Presumably almost any English word can be altered by the prefixes *anti-, de-, extra-, pre-, super-,* and *non* (e.g. *anti aircraft*, 1914; *antibody*, 1901; *anticathode*, 1907; *non-rigid*, 1909; *non-skid*, 1908, *non-smoker*, 1902).

The stupendous increase in English vocabulary during the 19th century continues undiminished into this century; expansion comes from new creations (e.g. *triphibian*, attributed to Churchill, 1943), borrowings from other languages (e.g. *Gestalt*, 1924), and adaptation of existing words to new conditions (e.g. *land* a seaplane in water, 1930). The greatest single corps of contributors consists of scientists and technologists. Almost every issue of scientific journals suggests a new term, usually a combining of Greek stems, and so vast is this proliferation that specialized publications such as *The Bulletin of Zoological Nomenclature* treat solely of scientific terminology. Belletristic writers of this century have been meager contributors except for their willingness to borrow or translate foreign terms (cf. Shaw's translation of Nietzsche's *Übermensch* as *superman*, 1903). The uninhibited word-creation of the English masses is demonstrated by Eric Partridge's *Dictionary of Slang and Unconventional English* (1937, fifth edition extensively enlarged in 1961), which also devotes far more attention to phrases than do most dictionaries.

Vocabulary and accent as badges of social status aroused a lively, albeit trivial, tempest in the English teapots of the 1950s. Professor A. S. C. Ross of Birmingham University delivered a lecture on sociological linguistics to a learned society in Finland in which he distinguished between "U" (Upper-class) and "Non-U" speakers of English. The vivacious Nancy Mitford seized upon this erudite analysis for a gay piece in *Encounter* and then for a collection of pieces, *Noblesse Oblige* (1956), by several authors. The leveling tendencies of current English society cause a search for class distinction, dubiously displayed thus:

"U"	"Non-U"
looking glass	mirror
chimneypiece	mantlepiece
false teeth	dentures
wireless	radio
What did you say?	Pardon?
I wonder if you would pass the mustard?	Would you pass the cruet?

Certainly the Englishmen of today, except for a few hardy recusants, tend to judge their countrymen by the "U" linguistic standard of the BBC (British Broadcasting Corporation) but are remarkably tolerant of the deviations by those bred to Irish-, Scottish-, Australian-, or even American-English.

Chapter 8

English Drama from Shaw to the Present

In 1879 Matthew Arnold complained, "In England we have no drama at all." At that time the same complaint could have echoed all over Europe. However, the last two decades of the 19th century and the beginning of the 20th century witnessed a remarkable resurgence of the drama throughout the continent and in England, too. Henrik Ibsen in Norway, Anton Chekhov in Russia, August Strindberg in Sweden, Luigi Pirandello in Italy, and Eugene O'Neill in the United States brought a new spirit and a new life to the almost moribund theater of the 19th century. In England, in the decade after Arnold's death, Jones, Pinero, and Wilde roused the English theater from nearly a century of somnolence, and in the first quarter of the 20th century, English drama came into its own once more.

The great age of English theater-building was during the years 1880–1900, with new theaters up to World War I being designed generally in Victorian rococo. Among the few genuinely modern structures are the Festival at Cambridge (1926) and the Stratford-on-Avon Theatre (1932). Every significant English community is provided with a theater, but most of the new construction since World War I has consisted of motion-picture palaces.

The Victorian stage setting beguiled its viewers by elegant splendor or persuasive realism. Edward Gordon Craig (son of the famed actress Ellen Terry) and Harley Granville-Barker in the decade and a half before World War I pioneered in simple, symbolic stagings, but their examples were followed extensively only after the rise of the cinema following World War I. In general, the scenic grandeur possible to motion pictures has encouraged stage designers to eschew strict imitation and offer imaginative settings except for farces, melodramas, and light comedies.

The most far-reaching development in stagecraft has been electric lighting, first introduced inside the Savoy Theatre in 1881. The harsh glare of the early electric lights aroused protests from actors, such as Ellen Terry, because it dispelled the subtle caress of misty gas lighting, but by the early 20th century the stage electrician had become a master technologist capable of creating varied and extraordinary effects unprecedented in the theater. The modern dramatist therefore relegates to technical stage directions much of the mood painting formerly requiring dialogue.

The West End of London, throughout this century, has consistently proved one of the world's most flourishing centers of living drama. Its frequent performances of Shakespeare and other dramatists of the past constantly remind viewers of a great playwriting tradition, and even in the lightest production of Coward or Novello there can be found the suggestion of a great acting tradition. The Royal Academy of Dramatic Art (founded 1904), one of the world's most prestigious schools of the drama, provides competently trained actors, and the numerous theaters throughout the British Isles provide extensive employment and have made virtually every educated Englishman theater-conscious. Except in costume drama the old-fashioned theatricality has vanished from acting in favor of commonplace realism.

Unlike the epochs of previous drama, 20th-century playwriting has been strongly individualistic, making it difficult to identify trends or schools. On the whole, 20th-century English drama has emphasized sociological problems and has been rather weak in areas stressed by continental dramatists: philosophy as in Jean Paul Sartre, psychology as in August Strindberg, imaginative fantasy as in Jean Giraudoux. Contemporary British drama has been particularly strong in realism or at least the guise of realism. Yet the greatest modern British dramatist, George Bernard Shaw, is first of all a master of the Drama of Ideas.

THE PLAYS OF SHAW

George Bernard Shaw (1856–1950). George Bernard Shaw was born into a Dublin Protestant family. His father was a poorly-paid government clerk, and Shaw quit school at fourteen to work as a rent collector until moving to London in 1876 to join his mother, a music teacher. His mother supported him while he wrote five novels, rejected by Meredith and published in minor socialist periodicals. An 1882 speech by Henry George insured his lifelong interest in economics and led him to the study of Marx and Engels. In 1884 he was one of the founders of the Fabian Society (discussed in Chapter 3), and proved one of its most vociferous propagandists. For the London *Star* (1888–89) and then the *World* (1890–94) he was a distinguished music critic, influential in popularizing the operas of Wagner, especially in his essay, *The Perfect Wagnerite* (1898). In 1895 he began distinguished drama criticism for the *Saturday Review*. Mounting success as a dramatist permitted him to give up drama criticism in 1898, and his world-wide reputation was established by World War I. In 1925 he was awarded the Nobel Prize for literature. His astounding vitality and barbed wit continued unabated until his death, well into his nineties.

Probably no one else has so fascinated and delighted the English-speaking peoples and yet failed to win many adherents to his views. He was a staunch vegetarian, pacifist, antivivisectionist, and champion of the Irish over the English. He has been the only major figure in English literature to cry down Shakespeare, albeit facetiously. Above all, his was an unswerving radical and independent voice even through the rabidly patriotic period of World War I.

Perhaps the most characteristic Shavian quality is the ability to make people think by compelling them to laugh. One of his key techniques is turning everything topsy-turvy and forcing an astounded audience to see "the other half of the truth." But always, from his first play in 1892 to *Buoyant Billions* in 1949, there flashes an unflagging wit, more coruscating than anything else in the history of English drama. No other playwright has ever matched Shaw in lengthy speeches and prolonged stage conversations that somehow never drag or lose out as theater. Whereas the opinions of Shakespeare remain an enigma, Shaw was never chary of exposing his complete collection of opinions.

The often bewildering (and, in its time, shocking) verbal perversity of Shaw actually rests upon Puritan Protestantism. An ascetic, he is scornful of romantic love and of pleasure instead of work. An antimaterialist, he is a vitalist believing in Creative Evolution, which man should further toward a perfect society, and in the Life Force, really the divine will. Nurtured in the same intellectual atmosphere that produced Hardy, Shaw affirms a strong individualism and a passion for reforming mankind because optimistically he conceives of the sentience behind the universe as gradually evolving toward beneficence and love.

The Quintessence of Ibsenism (1891), along with the impetus from William Archer (1856–1924), helped to establish the reputation of the great Norwegian dramatist, Henrik Ibsen (1828–1906), in England. Archer's translation of *Pillars of Society* provided the first public performance of Ibsen in England (1880), and Archer edited Ibsen's dramas in five volumes (1890–91). Shaw perceived three innovations by Ibsen: surprising viewers into thinking about themselves, fusing ideas into the "well-made" play, and portraying both characters and events realistically. Shaw emphasized the social-problem dramas of Ibsen and minimized the poetic and symbolic plays.

Discussed below are the most important of Shaw's fifty-three full-length plays.

FIRST PERIOD (1892–1901). These early dramas by Shaw have in some ways proved more durable theater pieces than his later works. He follows Ibsen in casting social criticism into the "well-made" play, but instead of the Norwegian's northern solemnity Shaw parades an Irishman's wondrous wit and humor. Since here the plot carries and exemplifies the ideas, these are perhaps the most stageable Shavian dramas. Shaw's chief role in this period is the debunker of falsehood and hypocrisy.

Widowers' Houses (1892) arose from Shaw's own youthful experience as a Dublin rent collector. It was first produced in the experimental Independent Theatre of J. T. Grein.

A young medical student, Harry Trench, is outraged to discover that the father of his beloved, Blanche Sartorius, derives his income from high rents on tenements. Harry wishes Blanche to disavow her father's money and live upon his modest income. To his horror Trench learns from the venal rent collector, Lickcheese, and from Sartorius that his own income arises from mortgages on the Sartorius property. Disillusioned and bewildered, he capitulates to the status quo.

This brilliant first play establishes a major theme of Shaw, the tragedy of well-intentioned men being used for base purposes by selfish men. The villain is bourgeois capitalism that feeds upon exploitation of the poor and corrupts men of good will. However, unlike most socialist authors, Shaw recognizes the monstrous complexity and interweavings of the system, and Trench is powerless by individual action to escape from or demolish the net entangling him.

Mrs. Warren's Profession, though written in 1894, was not produced until 1902, and then privately. Grein and the cast were ready in 1894, but the censor put a ban upon the play that was not lifted until 1924.

Vivie Warren is a modern independent girl distressed but understanding when she finds that her mother escaped from dire poverty by prostitution. Vivie insists, however, that her mother retire from her present position as the wealthy head of an international chain of brothels, in part financed by Sir George Crofts. Mrs. Warren refuses, and Vivie renounces her mother to live by honest work in London.

The play is a satiric, dramatic representation of Marx's contention that virtue is impossible in a capitalistic society. Mrs. Warren is a courageous entrepreneur in a system where anything and everything bear a price tag. The point to remember is that every sharer in capitalistic society is as guilty as Mrs. Warren, and Crofts is respectable because society conceals and ignores the despicable source of his wealth. The work has been uniformly hailed by critics for powerful realism. The first American performance in 1905 was shut down by the police, but the court acquitted the cast of a charge of indecency.

Arms and the Man (1894) is the first Shaw drama to hold the stage consistently to the present, both in its original form and in the musical comedy version, *The Chocolate Soldier* (1909). It is the "pleasantest" of all Shavian dramas.

Captain Bluntschli, a soldier of fortune, escapes pursuing Bulgarian soldiers by hiding in the quarters of Princess Raina, who finds this down-to-earth realist more satisfactory than her romantic officer beau, Sergius. Bluntschli turns out to be heir of a magnificent Swiss hotel chain, and he carries off the princess, leaving Sergius with the servant girl, Louka.

The audience delights in this inversion of Anthony Hope's Ruritania (*The Prisoner of Zenda* appeared during the same year). All the melodramatic trappings are present: the boudoir of a princess, armed pursuit by moonlight, and a hunted fugitive in uniform. Shaw turns these, however, into a comic comment on the romantic attractiveness of war. Military heroism is burlesqued in the pretentious Byronism of Sergius. Romantic love is satirized in the high-flown and bored courtship of Sergius and Raina. The genuine, permanent love offered by Bluntschli is based upon realistic mutual understanding.

Candida (1894), the "safest" Shaw play, was a favorite of the author, and is often considered his best, especially by those disliking his propaganda dramas.

The Reverend James Morell is a handsome, immensely successful Christian Socialist cleric, aged forty, of "advanced" views; his lovely and intelligent wife of thirty-three is Candida. The eighteen-year-old poetic genius, Eugene Marchbanks, falls in love with Candida and wants her to elope with him. In one of the stage's great scenes she chooses: "I give myself to the weaker of the two." Morell is thunderstruck, but Marchbanks understands and departs.

The male conflict is between Morell, the practical "advanced" man of present worldly success, and Marchbanks, the impractical genius whose true vision far surpasses that of Morell. Candida chooses realistically between the romantic idealist (Eugene) and the romantic Victorian (James) with his essentially conventional ideas of marriage. The genius will win out regardless, but the lesser man truly needs her. Candida is a figure of maternal love to whom sex and the home are the verities, and the world that men concern themselves with is but a play world of unreality. Eugene is actually a catalyst who forces husband and wife to a truer marriage by a genuine realization of their relationship.

The first performance of this play was in 1897. This is the last of seven early dramas published as *Plays, Pleasant and Unpleasant* (1898). The "unpleasant" plays satirize capitalistic society; the "pleasant" plays are witty intellectual pleas for realistic instead of romantic interpretations of love and marriage, war and heroism.

The Devil's Disciple (1897) and the next two dramas were published in 1900 as *Three Plays for Puritans*. All three are avowed attempts to offer exciting "sexless" dramas in opposition to the current rage for romantic sexuality on the stage.

Recoiling from a desiccated religion that proclaims gloom and self-denial as the acme of goodness, Dick Dudgeon of Websterbridge, New Hampshire, in 1777 announces himself as the disciple of the devil. When the British seek Minister Anderson, an advocate of independence, Dick lets himself be taken by mistake. The parson's wife assumes that Dick is motivated by love for her, but to her bewilderment he simply refuses to save himself by destroying another man. Anderson saves Dick in the nick of time. The source is an anecdote included in the novel *A Day's Ride* (1863) by Charles Lever.

By conventional standards Anderson's rescue of Dick is as noble as Dick's self-sacrifice, but Anderson's action arises from gratitude and a desire to regain the affections of his silly, sentimental spouse, while Dick's action arises solely from humane instincts. Dick is not at all the devil's disciple (except to the narrow-minded); rather he is revolting against an oppressive church and asserting the fundamental goodness of human nature. Dick is the anti-romantic hero within the framework of melodrama.

Caesar and Cleopatra (*1898*), Shaw averred, was to improve upon Shakespeare, who "never knew human strength of the Caesarian type."

To Caesar all else is subsidiary to the pacification of Egypt. He finds the scared Cleopatra between the giant paws of the Sphinx and makes a queen out of her. Cleopatra in the famous rug incident is smuggled to Caesar upon Pharos Island in the harbor of Alexandria. Attacked by the Egyptians, they leap into the sea and escape. Secure in power, Caesar spares the plotter Pothinus, but Cleopatra has the man slain by her nurse Ftatateeta. Caesar leaves Rufio as governor of Egypt and promises to send Antony as a present for Cleopatra.

Shaw's Caesar, largely suggested by the German historian Mommsen, is a compound of Plato's philosopher-king and Bluntschli. He is Shaw's first great portrait of the Shavian statesman, the superman exemplifying the Life Force. The ruler of men must be wise, mild, efficient, and above all, it is superior civilization, not superior might, that will win the world. In contrast to Shakespeare's Cleopatra, Shaw's heroine is young, inexperienced, and given to cruelty. She develops, though incompletely, under the influence of Caesar's sanity and culture. Remarkably, the first public performance of this play was in German translation at Berlin, 1906. First production in English was in the United States later in the same year.

Captain Brassbound's Conversion (*1899*) was written for Ellen Terry, whose famous correspondence with Shaw (published 1931) was then at its height.

In exotic Morocco (as derived from Cunningham-Graham) the hanging judge, Sir Howard Hallam, and his sister-in-law, Lady Cicily Waynflete, are lured into the barbarous interior by Captain Brassbound, a modern pirate and smuggler. Brassbound then reveals himself as Hallam's nephew and because of the judge's alleged mistreatment of Brassbound's mother, the freebooter proposes to submit Hallam to the wild justice of the Moors. Lady Cicily persuades Brassbound to release Hallam and later saves Brassbound from British justice.

Always the antiromantic, Shaw takes the familiar Robin Hood type of outlaw and makes a fool out of him. Brassbound's romantic rough justice of the wilds parallels the dignified justice of Hallam's refined court: both arise from the uncivilized passion for violent revenge. Lady Cicily exerts not sex but superior moral and intellectual power to establish truly civilized order. The plot itself is farce comedy, even to a gallant landing party from the U.S.S. *Santiago*. American, Oxonian, and cockney English clash with uproarious effect. First performance was in 1900.

Other Shaw plays from this period are *The Philanderer* (1893) and two plays published in 1898 with *Plays, Pleasant and Unpleasant, The Man of Destiny*, and *You Never Can Tell*.

SECOND PERIOD (1901–29). In this period Shaw reaches his greatest creativity. Now independent of Ibsen, he is most original and exciting. However, his incessant preaching so loads the plays with challenging ideas that while a few of these works may hold the stage (usually in revised form), their lasting appeal will probably be to the reader. Prefaces, notes, appendices, and elaborate stage directions create for each of these dramas something far more (or less) than a straight dramatic script such as Shakespeare's.

Man and Superman (1901–03) was first performed in 1905, omitting the "Don Juan in Hell" scene, which was first presented separately in 1907. The first entire production was in 1915. The play re-creates the Don Juan legend in modern, altered guise.

John Tanner (Don Juan Tenorio), a well-to-do radical, author of the *Revolutionist's Handbook* (which Shaw appends to the published version of the play), is co-guardian along with the conventional liberal, Roebuck Ramsden, of Ann Whitefield (Dona Ana). Octavius Robinson, deeply in love with Ann, is rejected because Tanner is actually her objective. Tanner, fleeing on a continental motor trip, dreams of Don Juan in Hell while in the Sierras. Awake, Tanner is cornered and secured by Ann at Granada. In the subplot, Violet, sister of Octavius, is pregnant supposedly out of wedlock, but she reveals a secret marriage to the Irish-American millionaire, Hector Malone.

This play may well be censured (as T. S. Eliot has censured *Hamlet*) for attempting to consider entirely too much. The witty dialogue and brilliant accompanying paraphernalia leap dazzlingly from one topic to another, but most important are:

(1) Don Juan interpreted not as a Lothario but as an intellectual rebel against conventions. Tanner is passionate about moral and social issues but

is oblivious of sex. However, he has been "selected by Nature to carry on the work of building up an intellectual consciousness of her own instinctive purpose."

(2) The Life Force manifesting itself through Ann, who is Everywoman. The mother-woman pursues and captures the artist-man. To Shaw romantic sex is superficial; the deep Life Force exemplified by Ann selectively seeks the advancement of the species. The procreative drive draws together the eugenically desirable partners even though they may be wholly unsuitable as marriage partners.

(3) The Superman through Evolution. Shaw sees evolution as advancing toward a superior mankind, not toward any "master race" or mere superior individual set over his lesser fellows.

(4) Progress lying with the transformation of human nature. Contemptuously Shaw (and his Devil in "Don Juan in Hell") dismiss "man's increased command over Nature," for what is essential to man's advance is "increased command over himself."

(5) Skepticism about democracy and socialism. A democratic majority will be no more than a preponderance of passion and ignorance unless mankind is fundamentally improved.

John Bull's Other Island (1904) was intended for the Irish Literary Theatre of Dublin, but inadequate facilities forced a première in London.

Irish Larry Doyle and English Tom Broadbent are successful civil engineers in London. Larry's native community, Roscullen, Ireland, becomes their property. Larry is proposed as member of parliament from Roscullen, but that cool realist refuses. Tom wins the candidacy and Nora Reilly (who had waited eighteen years for Larry) into the bargain.

Chesterton terms this the most real of Shaw's dramas. Long absence from Ireland has given Larry a mature perspective and an incapacity to play up to Irish limitations. Broadbent is sentimental about the Irish and with concrete plans for land development wins their support and can do them good. Nonetheless, Broadbent is a demagogue who, in the words of "The Revolutionist's Handbook" (*Man and Superman*), "stereotypes mediocrity, organizes intolerance, disparages exhibitions of uncommon qualities, and glorifies conspicuous exhibitions of common ones." Ostensibly a gay comedy, the drama belabors the inadequacies of both Irish and English.

Major Barbara (1905) is a brilliant reconsideration of the theme of *Mrs. Warren's Profession,* for Shaw suggested that he might have titled the work "Andrew Undershaft's Profession."

Lady Undershaft summons her son and two daughters to meet their father, Andrew Undershaft, whom they hardly know. She wants more money for the daughters, who are about to marry, and wishes her son to inherit the Undershaft munitions industry, traditionally bequeathed to a foundling. Daughter Barbara, engaged to Adolphus Cusins, a professor of Greek, is a devout major in the Salvation Army. Barbara counters her doctrine of God and salvation to her father's brazen doctrine of work and money. Shocked when the Salvation Army accepts a £5000 donation from Undershaft, Barbara quits the Army to live in her father's model village. God's work, she declares, should be done for its own sake, not for bribes, whether the Salvationist's promise of heaven or the employer's promise of bread. Technically a foundling by British law, Cusins inherits the munitions business.

Though observers have varied in their interpretation, the prefatory "First Aid to Critics" makes clear that the play deals with "our mercanto-Christian morality." Undershaft (i.e. the underpinning) is the logical result of a capitalism that feeds upon competition and power. In such a society the one cardinal sin is poverty (as Shaw quotes from Butler). Modern religion, like all else, is bought by capitalism to serve its purpose, here to make the poor accept their lot. Barbara is distressed to realize that her religious preoccupations and altruism were possible only because of Undershaft's financial support. Her "conversion" at the end is presumably the only recourse for a being of conscience in this society, but the triumphant Undershaft bears within his own industrial empire the means for social revolution, as he admits, "Whatever can blow men up can blow society up." Undershaft is an immensely interesting and virile figure, but essentially his is the cause of death. Barbara and Adolphus (who is based upon Gilbert Murray) are faith and hope, not in orthodox religion, but in life itself and in a better tomorrow for mankind.

The Doctor's Dilemma (1906) expresses Shaw's skepticism about scientists and especially about the medical profession. The actual dilemma seems weakened by alteration to a David-Bathsheba plot.

Jennifer Dubedat pleads with the renowned surgeon, Sir Colenso Ridgeon, to apply his treatment for tuberculosis to her dying husband, an artist but a scoundrel. Unable to treat both Dubedat and his own aged friend, Blenkinsop, a mediocre general practitioner, Ridgeon turns Dubedat over to Sir Bloomfield Bonington, knowing that Bonington's care will be fatal. It is. Ridgeon admits that he fell in love with Jennifer, but she marries another, and he wryly observes, "Then I have committed a purely disinterested murder."

The Preface, printed with the play in 1911, more vigorously than the drama itself enunciates Shaw's attack upon physicians for having a vested interest in ill health. His solution is socialized medicine, not realized in England until after his death.

Getting Married (1908) is a magnificent *tour de force*. Piqued by critics' protest that his plays were mostly talk, Shaw made this all talk upon the subject of marriage. Every view—religious, social, conventional, unconventional—is saucily presented, with Shavian emphasis upon the freedom of women and the disparity between eugenic partners and marriage partners. The concluding marriage of Edith Bridgenorth and Cecil Sykes suggests Shaw's contention that the best preservation of an institution consists of constant, merciless scrutiny of it and unceasing determination to improve it. In the bargain, the play completely follows the unities of time, place, and action without any breaks.

Androcles and the Lion (*1911–12*) was first performed in Berlin in 1912, with first London performance in 1913. Subtitled "A Fable Play," it was originally intended for children but was revised into adult fare.

Henpecked little Androcles removes the thorn from the lion's paw and wins the beast's undying gratitude. Androcles is captured with other Christians for a Roman holiday. Beautiful Lavinia, though losing her belief in Christian myth, finds spiritual strength to refuse to bow to Roman orders even under the persuasive logic of the pagan captain who loves her. Ferrovius tries to be a tame Christian but in the arena he yields to temptation and fights brilliantly. When the lion waltzes with Androcles instead of devouring him, the Roman emperor, impressed by the "Christian sorcerer," frees everybody.

Androcles is delightful, but the real point of the drama lies with Ferrovius and Lavinia. Ferrovius is natural man with good Christian intentions, but one who easily backslides into self-preservation and competition. Shaw's Preface, printed with the play in 1915 as World War I raged, considers Ferrovius the typical "man of God" who preaches the doctrines of the King of Peace and then fanatically advocates war in the name of Christ (Ferrovius was honest enough to admit his full shift of allegiance to Mars). Lavinia, instead of even a partial capitulation to the decadent society, offers her all to "strive for the coming of the God who is not yet." In the Preface, Shaw sees society as following Barabbas, a thief and therefore a capitalist; he urges the following of Jesus, who was a Christian and therefore a socialist. Discerning the essence of Jesus as the doctrine that "the kingdom of God is within you," Shaw sees true Christianity as assertion of his own cherished Life Force.

Pygmalion (*1912*) was initially performed in German at Vienna. First production in English was in London, 1914. The musical comedy version, *My Fair Lady* by Lerner and Loewe (première in New York, 1956), has proved the most successful musical comedy in history.

Linguistic expert Professor Henry Higgins because of a casual bet teaches impeccable English to the cockney flower girl, Eliza Doolittle. Made to speak and look like a duchess, Eliza, realizing that she is now a thoroughly useless lady, flees to Higgins' mother. The new Pygmalion is moved by his new Galatea, but in Shavian upset she marries Freddy Eynsford-Hill and with him runs a fashionable green grocery.

Shaw neatly revises the original legend to make the 20th-century Pygmalion transform a living flower girl into a marble statue; then it is the statue itself that insists upon coming to life. However, because Eliza will always be a flower girl to Higgins, she prudently chooses Freddy, who is more willing than her creator to accept her as she now is. In all fairness, it must be said that the ending as Shaw conceived it is given in a prose epilogue. On stage the relationship between Eliza and Higgins is, to say the least, left ambiguous. If it was Shaw's idea that Higgins was too confirmed an old bachelor for Eliza to want him for her husband, the audience has never yet fully accepted it.

Heartbreak House was written between 1913 and 1916 but was not printed until 1919 and not acted until 1920 (first in New York) because, as Shaw remarked, "Truth telling is not compatible with the defense of the realm." Although set in a Sussex country house, the play is an indictment of all European civilization, which has drifted without purpose in callous selfishness and indifference. Captain Shotover, eighty-eight years old, realizes the needs: "Youth—beauty—novelty—they are badly wanted in this house." War is unmentioned until bombs drop at the end upon the de-energized house of Western society. In spite of the references to Chekhov, the play is Shavian rather than Russian.

Back to Methuselah was written between 1918 and 1921, printed in 1921, and first performed in New York. The longest of Shaw's plays, it required three nights to complete the first performance. It might best be thought of as five plays constituting an optimistic rebuttal of *Heartbreak House*. The dominating theme insists that Creative Evolution will replace man if he stops where he is; man must will to live longer and better.

Part I in the Garden of Eden. Adam and Eve are troubled to learn of death by seeing a dead fawn, but death is a relief from the burden of immortality. The serpent offers the solution of birth by which individuals will die but the species will be immortal.

Part II in England after World War I. The Barnabas brothers, biologists, suggest that men must achieve fuller maturity by willing the extension of the individual lifespan to three hundred years, but the narrow-minded politicians Burge (Lloyd George) and Lubin (Henry Asquith) vulgarize and vitiate the concept.

Part III in the year 2170. A clergyman friend of the Barnabas brothers and their parlor maid from Part II have lived for 250 years. Although short-lived bigots are tempted to slaughter the long-livers, each man wonders, "Am I perhaps to be one of the elect?"

Part IV in the year 3000. Many humans now have become long-livers and constitute virtually a different species from the old-fashioned short-livers.

Part V ("As far as thought can reach") in the year 31920. Humans are now born from eggs at approximately the present age of eighteen. Death occurs solely by accident. True maturity is the exercise of creative power over oneself.

Shaw hoped that this drama would form part of the mythology of a new religion of Creative Evolution. Whatever its success, it is the fullest statement of Shaw's idea of individual betterment leading to the realization of the Superman through man's own willed control of evolutionary processes.

Saint Joan (1923), the last great drama by Shaw, has proved consistently successful. Its impetus was the canonization of the Maid of Orleans in 1920. The major features of the story are historically authentic.

Inspired by visions, the peasant girl Joan persuades the Dauphin of France to let her lead the French forces in expelling the English. After the coronation of the Dauphin, Joan is captured by the English, brought to trial as a heretic, and condemned to burning at the stake. In the epilogue Charles the Victorious (formerly the Dauphin) dreams about Joan and all her accusers up to her canonization. All express sorrow and repentance at her death and fervent reverence for her, but hastily demur at her suggestion of reappearance.

The central problem of the play concerns the world's treatment of a Superman ahead of his time—or in this case, ahead of her time. Creative genius inevitably conflicts with the frozen structures of organized society. In a magnificent trial scene Shaw presents her opponents not as one-dimensional villains but, as Joan states in the Epilogue, "As honest a lot of poor fools as ever burned their betters." Cauchon brilliantly argues the Catholic case against unrestrained personal religious judgment (Joan is offered as the first Protestant) and against nationalism as the destroyer of unitary Christendom. Warwick is dismayed at her role as God's direct messenger to the French king, for this threatens the entire feudal structure of the barons. The Epilogue is sometimes criticized, but it establishes the entire theme of the progressive genius against the inertia of the majority. Its comedy renders more poignant the one true tragedy by Shaw. The entire second period of the dramatist reaches its climax with a ringing insistence that mankind can and must alter and mature toward its grand destiny.

Other plays from this period are: *Misalliance* (1910), and *Fanny's First Play* (1911). Also from this period is Shaw's remarkable essay *The Intelligent Woman's Guide to Capitalism and Socialism* (1928).

THIRD PERIOD (1929 TO DEATH). The plays of Shaw's declining years are still clever and delightful (they would do honor to any other 20th-century English dramatist), but display essentially a reworking of familiar Shavian themes. Clouding their gaiety is the disappointment of many liberal hopes, a disenchantment that clearly marks Shaw as a holdover from a more expansive and optimistic era. The prescience of the old man never deserted him, as *The Apple Cart* (1929) shrewdly foresees the political and social problems of the coming Welfare State. *On the Rocks* (1933), while subtitled "A Political Comedy," is a depressing scrutiny of the decline of England and English democracy. *Geneva* (1939) is a not very successful topical work on the political state of Europe at that time. Confounding all, however, *In Good King Charles's Golden Days* (1939), the last completed drama by Shaw, offers a rousing battle of words that any young playwright would envy. Newton (science), Kneller (art), Fox (religion), and Charles II (government) scintillatingly dispute the significance of their specialities in 1680 and today. Always Shaw displayed a buoyancy and wit generally missing from any other contemporary writers of comedy.

CONTEMPORARIES OF SHAW

DRAMATISTS OF SOCIAL EMPHASIS

John Galsworthy. John Galsworthy (whose biography will be found in Chapter 11 along with a discussion of his novels) wrote well-knit realistic problem plays espousing the cause of the underdog. A scion of the upper middle class, he was emphatically critical of the Victorian orthodoxy.

The Silver Box (1906) contrasts the severe legal penalty inflicted upon Jones, husband of the Borthwicks' charwoman, for stealing a cigarette box, while young Gorthwick, son of a member of parliament, receives only a gentle rebuke from the judge for stealing his companion's handbag in a drunken pique. Galsworthy's first drama is a notable feat in playwriting efficiency and construction.

Strife (1909) depicts the tragic suffering and waste during a strike at the Trenartha Tin Plate Works on the Welsh border. Adamant old John Anthony champions "No compromise!" for the board of directors, while David Roberts retorts "No surrender!" for the strikers. When Roberts' wife dies, both sides cast off their leadership and yield to exactly the terms rejected four months previously. The personal tragedy of the strike leader injects a problem irrelevant to the strike and throws sympathy to his cause.

Justice (1910) castigates the brutal prison treatment of Falder, a clerk who altered a check for benevolent, though misguided, purposes. Immediate government action and reform followed, making this drama perhaps unique in English history for its direct sociological influence.

The Skin Game (1920) pits the old landed gentry, the Hillcrists, against the blatant *nouveau riche* manufacturers, the Hornblowers. Enraged by Hillcrist exclusiveness, Hornblower threatens to blight the countryside with factories. Mrs. Hillcrist uses the shady past of Chloe, daughter-in-law of Hornblower, as blackmail. Chloe attempts suicide. Mr. Hillcrist and his charming daughter Jill plaintively ask, "What's gentility worth if it can't stand fire?" Unscrupulous tactics defile the genteel as well as the bumptious.

Loyalties (1922) is one of the first English plays openly to denounce anti-Semitism. Retired Captain Ronald Dancy steals £1000 from De Levis, a rich young Jew, and spouts anti-Semitism to cover his tracks. Dancy's Mayfair friends support him until his unmasking and subsequent suicide reveal how misplaced were their loyalties.

Harley Granville Granville-Barker (1877–1946). A London native, Harley Granville-Barker was educated privately and at the Theatre Royal, Margate. His London debut in 1891 was followed by increasing acting success, climaxed by his actor-directorship of the Court Theatre from 1904 to 1907. The intellectual drama and imaginative stage designing and direction of the Court Theatre represent one of the most potent forces in creating the contemporary English stage. Barker was chiefly responsible for Shaw's fame (producing eleven Shaw plays in this period), the popularity of continental drama (Ibsen, Sudermann, Maeterlinck), and an outlet for new British talent (Galsworthy, Masefield, Hankin). During the first decade of this century Barker seemed the most promising of all English dramatists, but he apparently lacked sustained creative power. His Savoy Theatre productions of Shakespeare in 1912 may be the best of recent centuries. By himself or with his wife he later proved an important translator of the dramas of Martínez Sierra, the brothers Quintero, Arthur Schnitzler, Sacha Guitry, and Jules Romains. Toward the end of his life he concentrated upon dramatic criticism, lecturing at Yale (1940–41) and Harvard (1941–43) and writing in France, where he died.

The Marrying of Ann Leete (1901) is probably the most Chekhovian drama in English. The New Woman, Ann Leete, abhorring the stifling conventions of polite society as exemplified by a "right marriage," throws herself into the arms of the gardener, John Abud. Though in plot Robertson's *Caste* with the sexes reversed, the drama is charged with the Shavian Life Force that overleaps social barriers. Ann's parents, Sir George and Lady Leete, are the stiff fossils of a dying caste.

The Voysey Inheritance (1905) strongly underlines the persistent theme of Barker: private moral responsibility to oneself versus public moral responsibility. Extensive banalities of everyday speech produce convincing realism. From his father, Edward Voysey has inherited a business shot through with fraud. Idealistically he wishes to expose the dishonesty and clear his conscience, but he is persuaded by Alice Maitland to conceal the rottenness while working for genuine solvency and soundness. Clearly, man must serve society and keep it functioning in spite of troubles with his conscience.

Waste (1907), Barker's most powerful work, may be the nearest thing to genuine tragedy set in the 20th century. Henry Trebell, an idealistic politician and forceful progressive, is rising toward a cabinet post until the revelation of scandal. His sweetheart, Amy O'Connell, destroys herself and their unborn child in an illegal operation. Cantelupe, a High Churchman, blocks Trebell's appointment, and private and public frustration cause Trebell's suicide. Overwhelming social forces waste a talent that might have been greatly beneficial to mankind.

Prefaces to Shakespeare (1923 *et seq.;* collected as series 1, 1927; 2, 1929; 3, 1936) may stand as Barker's most significant writing. A master actor-manager-producer-playwright scrutinizes the stage meaning of a fellow man-of-the-theater. None of the scholarly studies is as revealing, and perhaps as fundamental, as this pragmatic examination of how Shakespeare's plays actually project in the living theater. No other single work has proved so influential upon contemporary Shakespearean performances.

St. John Emile Clavering Hankin (1869–1909). A native of Southampton, St. John Hankin was educated at Malvern College and Oxford University. Besides his dramatic works, he was a noted contributor to *Punch*. Like Shaw he rebelled against the sentimentalism of the late 19th-century stage, but he lacked the wit and idea power of Shaw. Although Hankin is one of the finest craftsmen and dialogue writers of the 20th-century theater, his drably commonplace characters and cynical view of man and society prevent wide popularity.

The Cassilis Engagement (1907), his most famous work, depicts the attempt of Mrs. Cassilis to make her son realize the folly of marrying the scheming Ethel Borridge. Her studied attentions and hospitality have a surprising effect—Ethel breaks off the engagement, aghast at the petty monotony of life in this country mansion. As usual, Hankin's people are "county," symptoms of a decaying, pointless social class.

The Manchester School. The Manchester School of playwrights sprang from the pioneer work of Miss A. E. F. Horniman, who proved the "angel" for the Abbey Theatre in Dublin. In 1907 Miss Horniman established the first modern English repertory theater at the Midland Theatre, Manchester, and in the next year "Miss Horniman's Company" took over the Gaiety Theatre, Manchester. Until her retirement in 1921, her group set the standards for the English repertory stage:

(1) Under repertory the "star" was replaced by ensemble activity.

(2) Repertory created an organic whole of designers, actors, playwrights, costumers, and producers instead of a makeshift assembly for each production.

(3) Repertory called for a varied fare instead of the "long-run" system.

Plays by the Manchester School employed strongly realistic characters and settings and emphasized rebellion against current bourgeois viewpoints. Most noted of the school was William Stanley Houghton (1881–1913), whose *Hindle Wakes* (1912) tells of the consequences of an amorous weekend involving Fanny Hawthorn, a working girl, and Alan Jeffcote, son of a cotton-mill owner. Alan's father insists that the youth break his engagement to the heiress Beatrice Farrar and marry Fanny; Fanny's mother sees the marriage as social advancement for her daughter. Fanny refuses, insisting against her shocked elders that she will not be chained for life to a vacillating weakling just because of a momentary indiscretion. This proved the most successful original drama at the Manchester Repertory Theatre. Allan Noble Monkhouse (1858–1936) railed against the narrowness of suburban existence, notably in *The Grand Cham's Diamond* (1924). Harold Brighouse (1882–1958), himself a director of a Lancashire cotton mill, objected to the evils of industrialism in *The Price of Coal* (1911).

DRAMATISTS OF MOOD

Sir **James Matthew Barrie** (bar'i) (1860–1937). James M. Barrie was born at Karriemuir (the Thrums of his fiction), Forfarshire, Scotland. After graduating with honors in English literature from Edinburgh University, he wrote for a Nottinghamshire newspaper and from 1885 for *The British Weekly* in London. With the novel *The Little Minister* and the play *Richard Savage,* both in 1891, he started his reign as one of the best-loved writers of 20th-century English letters. From his baronetcy in 1913, honors were heaped upon him, culminating in the chancellorship of his alma mater, 1930 to death.

A whimsical charm suffuses the writings of Barrie, a mixture of fancy and sentiment vastly appealing to the public during the lull before the holocaust of World War I. *Quality Street* (1903) and *What Every Woman Knows* (1908), the latter renamed *Maggie,* have been appropriately staged in recent years as musical comedies. His sentimental novels, charmingly reproducing Scottish dialect, have been condescendingly labeled "the Kailyard School of the Novel."

Peter Pan or The Boy Who Would Not Grow up (1904) has become a classic of childhood.

Wendy Darling and her brothers are carried off to Never Land by Peter Pan and his fairy attendant, Tinker Bell. Here Wendy becomes a mother substitute to the lost boys, youngsters fallen from their prams and never found again. Jealous pirates who desire Wendy for their mother kidnap the boys. The pirate leader is villainous Captain Hook, pursued by a crocodile who had eaten one of Hook's arms; since it had also swallowed a clock, the crocodile warns of its approach by ticking. Peter Pan tricks the pirates to their deaths, Hook finally leaping into the crocodile's jaws. The Darling youngsters return home. Wendy visits Peter Pan once each year to clean his house, but he becomes increasingly indistinct.

Adults as well as children have been engrossed by this wish-fulfilment, this escape from a grown-up world to perpetual childhood. In pleading for the imaginative view of life, Barrie recognizes that the Gothic and the vigorously competitive are as real to childhood as the cute and smiling.

Barrie's own admission that the play was automatic writing indicates the exploiting of unconscious fears and desires deep in the psyche.

The Admirable Crichton (crī'-ton) (1914) performs a Gilbert-and-Sullivan topsy-turvy.

When Lord Loam's steam yacht is shipwrecked in the Pacific, the butler Crichton gradually assumes leadership over the inept aristocrats. After rescue, the old order is reestablished with Loam as lord and Crichton as butler.

Barrie is a master at eating his cake and having it too. Class distinctions are artificial, and many subordinate Britishers are wholly capable of posts of responsibility. Nonetheless, every Britisher knows his place and willingly sacrifices ambition to social stability. What could be a tragic theme of waste to others becomes a comic relief of British resiliency and acceptance to Barrie.

Dear Brutus (1917) takes its title from *Julius Caesar:* "The fault, dear Brutus, is not in our stars,/But in ourselves, that we are underlings."

Lob (another name for the ancient Puck) assembles on Midsummer Eve several guests unhappy about their fate in life. Though the house is miles from any forest, a magic Wood of Might Have Been appears annually on this eve in place of the garden. Guests enter the wood to find how they would have lived if given a second chance. They learn that their other possible fates would have paralleled their actual careers.

W. Somerset Maugham. W. Somerset Maugham (whose biography will be found in Chapter 11 on the modern novel) revived the comedy of manners for the era after World War I. His sardonic satire and astringency appealed to a disillusioned audience. His craftsmanship in construction and his superb ear for dialogue are unsurpassed in 20th-century English drama.

Our Betters, written in 1915, was premiered in New York in 1917. Its pack of titled American expatriates in London, especially Pearl Grayson, are vicious sensualists, mocking the ironic title. The witty conversation and hothouse atmosphere are reminiscent of Restoration comedy.

The Circle (1921), probably Maugham's best drama, is one of the few plays in English comparable to the best of Congreve.

Priggish Arnold Champion-Cheney, M.P., and his wife Elizabeth invite his mother, Lady Kitty, who thirty years ago left Arnold's father to elope with Lord Porteous. Elizabeth, tiring of her furniture-collecting spouse, elopes with guest Teddie to the Malay States. The generations have come full circle.

The sparkling wit and apparent cynicism prepare for the hard-won wisdom of Porteous. His earlier elopement had been a horrendous violation of Victorian mores, resulting in the frivolous degeneration of Kitty and himself. Perhaps the younger generation in a less stuffy age may succeed where his generation failed: "You can do anything in this world if you're prepared to take the consequences, as consequences depend on character."

For Services Rendered (1932), set in the home of a minor Kentish solicitor, scathingly denounces the drift and futility of English life after World War I. Prophetically, a blinded serviceman sourly comments, "One day they'll muddle us all into another war."

Clemence Dane (real name **Winifred Ashton**) (c. 1895–   ). A native of Blackheath, Clemence Dane was educated in rural schools until she was sixteen. In 1913 she abandoned schoolteaching for the stage, where she acted under the name of Diana Portis. Her novel, *Broome Stages* (1931), is a family chronicle tracing several generations of a theatrical clan. Her proficiency and diversity in playwriting match those of most of her male competitors.

A Bill of Divorcement (1921), her most famous piece, urged that lunacy be recognized as grounds for divorce (as it now is in England). The play derives from her own novel, *Legend* (1919).

Will Shakespeare (1921) contains some of the best dramatic blank verse of this century and remains the best attempt among the impossible efforts to depict the bard himself upon the stage. *Wild Decembers* (1932) still seems the best of many dramas portraying the Brontë sisters.

MORE RECENT DRAMATISTS

WRITERS OF THE WELL-MADE PLAY

James Bridie (real name **Osborne Henry Mavor**) (1888–1951). A native of Glasgow, Scotland, James Bridie was educated at Glasgow University. He practiced medicine in his native city and served as an army surgeon in both World Wars. Local success in his avocation as a playwright caused his first London play, *The Anatomist* (1931). He offered a new drama almost every year thereafter until *The Queen's Comedy* (1950).

Often termed the Scottish Shaw, Bridie has proved one of the wittiest and most ingenious of 20th-century dramatists, but he lacks the shock quality in the play of ideas. His position is good-natured, middle-of-the-road liberalism. In an era when art has tended to fly militantly to the extreme right or left, Bridie has perhaps missed his due.

Tobias and the Angel (1932) is based upon the apocryphal Book of Tobit.

Tobias, son of the blind Tobit, sets out to win his fortune and is befriended by Azarius (really the archangel Raphael in disguise). Tobias overpowers a giant fish and upon his companion's advice cuts out and retains the fish liver. Tobias bluffs his way past a bandit, but it takes Raphael to overcome the devil Asmoday and release Sarah from demonic possession to be the bride of Tobias. On his return Tobias applies the fish liver to his father's eye sockets, restoring the old man's sight.

The dialogue is colloquially modern amid biblical story and surroundings. In addition to the Bible account, Bridie is evidently influenced by the folklore theme, the Grateful Dead motif, with the angel instead of ghost as companion. Viewers, however, are most charmed by the development of Tobias from insecure youth to poised maturity.

A Sleeping Clergyman (1933), Bridie's own favorite, is an attack upon eugenics through a depiction of three generations of the Cameron family.

Though talented, the first Cameron was drunken and tubercular. His immoral, illegitimate daughter commits suicide after slaying her lover. Nonetheless, her two illegitimate children give the lie to heredity, the son saving the world from dire epidemic through a new serum, and the daughter becoming executive secretary of the League of Nations.

Robert Cedric Sherriff (1896–   ). A native of Aylesbury, Buckinghamshire, Robert Cedric Sherriff was educated at New College, Oxford. His work for an insurance firm was first interrupted by army service in World War I and then terminated by his success in playwriting in 1929.

Journey's End (1929) at one time had nine companies performing the drama in England and America. The title is a quotation from *Othello*.

Captain Dennis Stanhope's infantry company in the trenches near St. Quentin awaits the German drive of 1918. Lt. Raleigh, brother of Stanhope's fiancée, is distressed to find his former idol now a battle-hardened cynic quieting his nerves with whiskey. Lt. Osborne, a middle-aged ex-schoolteacher, and Raleigh are sent on a dangerous daylight raid to obtain a prisoner for questioning. Osborne is killed, and Raleigh is outraged by the champagne dinner celebrating the successful raid. Stanhope tries to explain the fighting man's defensive mask of forgetfulness to Raleigh just before the youth dies of wounds. As the fury of the German drive mounts, Stanhope leaves the corpse to direct the defense.

Recent taste prefers the psychoanalyzing of combat troops, but this stark, simple piece still remains perhaps the greatest English drama about war. These Britishers are not heroes (the subaltern Hibbert is a coward), but they doggedly perform their duty, each trying to maintain his world of meaning and dignity amid the chaos of battle.

John Boynton Priestley (1894–   ). Son of a Bradford, Yorkshire, schoolmaster, J. B. Priestley served in World War I and subsequently studied at Trinity Hall, Cambridge. He first scored literary success with the novel, *The Good Companions* (1929), a James Tait Black prizewinner in the picaresque tradition about an itinerant theatrical company. His first drama was *Dangerous Corner* (1932), and his later career and probably his future reputation will rest upon his playwriting. His third wife is the noted scientific writer Jacquetta Hawkes, with whom he collaborated in *Journey* *down a Rainbow* (1955), a revealing account of travels in Texas and New Mexico.

Priestley's dramas (more than forty) may sport with "circular time," mental telepathy, and Labour doctrine, but always underneath lies the practical Englishman, anxious for a sane world. *Johnson over Jordan* (1939) is a modern morality whose Robert Johnson is Everyman or, at least hopefully, every Englishman. Masks, ballet, and music are employed. Among his other plays are *They Came to a City* (1943) and *Summer Day's Dream* (1944). The following work is perhaps his most popular play.

An Inspector Calls (1945) is a parable play set in 1912.

The prosperous Birling family is celebrating the engagement of their daughter to Gerald Croft when an inspector calls to query the group about the suicide of a girl. Probing, Inspector Goole reveals that Birling fired the girl from his factory, the daughter had the girl sacked from a store, the son had seduced her, and Mrs. Birling barred the girl from charity. Also, Gerald had discarded her as a mistress. After intensive grilling that shakes everyone, the inspector departs and the report comes that the girl has just now killed herself. The inspector appears to be the embodiment of conscience, striking home against a family of eminent respectability but also of cruel selfishness and social irresponsibility.

Terence Mervyn Rattigan (1911–   ). Terence Rattigan, educated at Harrow and Oxford, established himself as a popular dramatist through *French without Tears* (1936). Ever since, he has scored continual box-office successes in live drama and films. Among his numerous successes are *The Winslow Boy* (1947), which won the Ellen Terry Award as the best play of the year; *Playbill* (1948), composed of two plays, *Harlequinade* and *The Browning Version*, which also won the Ellen Terry Award: *The Deep Blue Sea* (1952); *The Sleeping Prince* (1953); *Separate Tables* (1954); and *Ross* (1960), which was based on the life of T. E. Lawrence.

Noel Pierce Coward (1899–   ). Born at Teddington, London, Noel Coward was educated at Chapel Royal School, Clapham, and at the Italia Conti Academy. His acting career began at the age of eleven, to be interrupted by army service in World Wars I and II. A thoroughly competent man of the theater, he has enjoyed success as playwright, actor, and song composer for stage and films.

Although Coward has tried his hand at every sort of drama except verse and first achieved fame with the serious play *The Vortex* (1924), he remains characterized as the comic playwright of the "smart set" from *I'll Leave It to You* (1920) to *Nude with Violin* (1956). He is glossily professional, very conscious of how lines will go on the stage, and extremely adept at knowing what will please theater-goers. His dialogue snaps with the fast return and sure placement of a good tennis player, and his characters are generally the amoral bright things of a standardless era. He is also a gifted song writer, and the composer-librettist for several musical comedies. Among his most successful works are *Hay Fever* (1925), *Bitter Sweet* (1929), the patriotic *Cavalcade* (1931), *Design for Living* (1932), *Red Peppers* (1935), and *Present Laughter* (1942). The following two plays are his most distinctive works.

Private Lives (1930) may be the best brittle farce in English.

Elyot Chase and his second wife, Sibyl, are honeymooning in a French hotel, where to Elyot's dismay they find Amanda, his first wife, honeymooning with her new mate, Victor Prynne. Sibyl and Victor refuse to relieve the embarrassment by departure, and Amanda and Elyot, thrown together, eventually elope. The emotional storms that broke up their first marriage bring Amanda and Elyot to a screaming, furniture-hurling donnybrook. Sibyl and Victor appear, preaching nobility and morality, but gradually fall to fighting between themselves. Amanda and Elyot tiptoe out with their suitcases.

The wild pace equals that of Evelyn Waugh's *Vile Bodies,* and the brilliant dialogue exceeds. Insouciant gaiety and glittering pyrotechnics mask a bleak world of rootless, undisciplined people who live only for momentary, epidermal pleasure.

Blithe Spirit (1941), billed by the author as "an improbable farce," was precisely the right formula—scintillating wit and fantastic escapism—for war-battered Britain. The title is saucily adapted from Shelley's "Ode to a Skylark."

Dabbling in spiritualism, novelist Charles Condomine is embarrassed when the "blithe spirit" of his first wife, Elvira, reappears. His second wife, Ruth, cannot see the ghost; but the two wives, living and dead, feud most felinely. Ruth is accidentally killed, and storms in as a specter. Charles tells off both ghosts and hastily departs as glassware and furniture smash and crash on an apparently empty stage.

Present Indicative (1937) and *Future Indefinite* (1954) constitute one of the liveliest autobiographical records in English. They supply perhaps the fullest portrait of the brisk London stage and the English "smart set" during the second quarter of the century. The critical suggest that Coward never deepens during this stretch of years but remains perennially the debonair sophisticate of the 1920s.

George Emlyn Williams (1905–   ). Emlyn Williams was born into a very poor Flintshire, Wales, family. Remarkable ability and the encouragement of sympathetic teachers helped him to win a scholarship to Oxford University. At the age of twenty-one he began a distinguished acting career, in which he is perhaps best known for his impersonation of Dickens reading from his novels. *Night Must Fall* (1935) has proved one of the most popular thrillers of the 20th-century stage. His *The Corn Is Green* (1938) is an autobiographical drama of a boy's maturing in a small Welsh town. *George*

(1961), his autobiography, traces Williams' course from Welsh childhood to London theatrical debut.

Peter Alexander Ustinov (yöz'te-nof) (1921–   ). London-born son of White Russian emigrés, Peter Ustinov proceeded from Westminster School to a bewilderingly varied and meteoric career on stage, screen, and television as actor, director, producer, and playwright. *Add a Dash of Pity* (1959), a collection of short stories, and *The Loser* (1961), a novel, are further proofs of a remarkably agile talent. Among his plays are two time-fantasies: *The Banbury Nose* (1944), which moves backward in time, starting in 1943 and ending in 1884, and *Photo Finish* (1962).

The following is perhaps Ustinov's best play.

The Love of Four Colonels (1951) consists of four brilliant sketches or parodies about a four-power commission of colonels at a German castle where the Sleeping Beauty awakes.

Each colonel woos his ideal beauty as he imagines himself to be: Rinder-Sparrow as an English gentleman out of Shakespeare, Aimé Frappot as the debonair Frenchman from a Marivaux drama, Ikonenko as a Russian character out of Chekhov, and Wesley Breitenspiegel as an American out of Saroyan.

Seldom has the theater so delightfully propounded the contention that beauty is in the beholder's eye and each eye is directed by a personal illusion about love and life. Seldom, too, since Shaw has the stage witnessed such ingenuity, bounce, and wit.

EXPERIMENTALISTS

John James Osborne (1929–   ). After education at Belmont College, Devonshire, John Osborne made his stage debut at Sheffield in 1948. His first drama was staged the next year. He was one of the leading contributors to *Declaration* (1957).

Look Back in Anger (1956) is the first significant pronunciamento from England's "Angry Young Men," the British equivalent of the American "Beat Generation."

Although college-trained, Jimmy Porter conducts a sweet-stall. He and his wife Alison quarrel bitterly, causing her to return to her parents. Jimmy thereupon takes Alison's actress friend, Helena Charles, as his mistress. Losing her child, Alison returns and Helena relinquishes Jimmy to her, although a bitter future lies ahead.

Defiant of his bourgeois audience, Osborne hurls out a savagely naturalistic picture of maladjusted contemporaries. To Jimmy all bourgeois values are blasphemously "phoney" or "wet." Alison's parents, remembering the placidity of an early 20th-century England, are bewildered by an age in which, Jimmy cynically snorts, "There aren't any good, brave causes left." The only alternatives ahead are boredom and annihilation. Although monstrously unpleasant, Jimmy is acidly real and powerful, a contemporary Promethean figure. In its shockingly honest language and brutally photographic quality, this is one of the most original and effective English dramas of the century.

Recently Osborne scored a success in another type of drama, the historical play, with his work *Luther* (1961).

Harold Pinter (1930–   ). Son of a Jewish tailor in East London, Harold Pinter studied acting at the Royal Academy of Dramatic Art and performed extensively under the stage name David Baron. Since his first drama, *The Room* (1957), he has written numerous works for stage, radio, and television. While Osborne displays an essentially English response to the contemporary world—it is a squalid tragedy in which we nonetheless keep fighting—Pinter more nearly resembles continental responses such as those from the Franco-Rumanian Ionesco—life is a comic absurdity. His most notable plays are *The Caretaker* and a television play, *Night School* (1960).

The Caretaker (1960), Pinter's first popular success, employs only three characters.

Slow-talking Aston brings home to his decaying property an old tramp, Davies, whom he rescued from a fight at a café. Ungrateful, Davies plays off Aston against his younger brother Mick. Although the brothers had dreamed of converting the structure into modern flats and letting Davies be the caretaker, his intransigence causes them to eject him.

The dismissal of Davies from the room that could have meant security and purpose echoes Adam's expulsion from the Garden of Eden. Strange indeed is the human nature that desperately needs to forge from the meaningless world a haven of self-sufficiency but that perversely destroys or vitiates its one hope of salvation. Pinter's mastery of everyday idiom and his verbal inventiveness quicken to poetry. The focusing of attention upon what everyone else considers nonessentials and the many threads left unexplained or mysterious keep an audience amused; withal, Pinter insists that this is a truly realistic portrayal of life's absurdity instead of the pseudorealism that "makes sense" of everything.

Samuel Beckett (1906–   ). Samuel Beckett was born in Dublin of Jewish parentage. After graduation from Trinity College, Dublin, he joined his fellow Dubliner, Joyce, in exile and for a period acted as Joyce's secretary. Since 1932 he has resided in France, and since 1947 he has employed French as his literary language.

As mentioned above, Beckett is a leading proponent of the "theater of the absurd." Thus his *Waiting for Godot* (1952), which he originally wrote in French and then himself translated, is a four-character play which fully dispenses with "plot" in any earlier sense of the word, and concentrates mainly on portraying the hopeless situation of mankind by means of bizarre happenings and elliptical dialogue. The scene appears to be the very edge of the world, a wasteland with only the remnant of a tree. The play, for all its seriousness, contains much humor and much theatrical skill. In *Endgame* (1957), also translated from his own French, the themes are loneliness and the essential absurdity of life. Beckett has created a style of theater which can poignantly dramatize the solitude and grim humor of modern life.

His novels, *Murphy* (1938) and *Watt* (*1942–44*, 1953), his last significant works in English, show the influence of Joyce and Kafka, as well as fore-shadowing Beckett's subsequent development in French. These two pieces exemplify the "novel of the absurd" as *En attendant Godot* (1952) was to demonstrate the "theater of the absurd." The outward meaning of the world has vanished, and a Beckett character existentially seeks wholly to spin the world from his own being. The Kafka-like quality is strong in *Watt*, whose name implies an eternal question to which his insane employer Knott (not), whom he can never meet, responds with the eternal negative. The postwar novels in French, notably the Molloy trilogy, lean definitely toward Sartre and Camus.

NARRATIVE DRAMA

Melodrama in the 20th century has been elevated above the crude banalities of Victorian theatricals. Edgar Wallace (1875–1932) in a series of thrillers culminating in his masterpiece, *The Case of the Frightened Lady* (1931), brought a convincing narrative technique and a craftsmanlike precision to the drama of crime. *Gas Light* (1939) by Patrick Hamilton (1904–62) was suffused with an unsurpassed atmosphere of dread. Aldous Huxley (discussed in the chapter on the Modern Novel) remarkably employed all the stock features of the melodrama in *The Gioconda Smile* (1948) to develop a tense psychological conflict.

The chronicle or history play in this century has vastly improved upon the mere spectacular pageants lavishly strewn across the Victorian stage. The pattern has followed a humanizing and domesticating of heroic figures. John Drinkwater (1882–1937) in *Abraham Lincoln* (1918) exploited high-lights of the Great Emancipator's career to assert that from the evil of war good might emerge if men could learn from their mistakes and from the wisdom of great spirits. *Mary Stuart* (1922), also by Drinkwater, offered a wonderfully fresh and well-intentioned Queen of Scots tragically ensnared by Renaissance intrigue and power politics. Laurence Housman (1865–1959), brother of A. E. Housman, wrote one of the century's smash hits in *Victoria Regina* (1934). Probably the best English drama upon literary figures is *The Barretts of Wimpole Street* (1930) by Rudolf Besier (1878–1942), Ibsen-like and with Freudian implications in its depiction of Elizabeth Barrett's tyrannical father.

VERSE DRAMA

At the outset of the century extravagant critical enthusiasm greeted the verse plays of Stephen Phillips (1864–1915), especially *Paolo and Francesca* (1902), based upon the ill-starred lovers immortalized by Dante; but the chorus of adulation fell silent and Phillips died in obscure poverty. The oriental phantasy *Hassan* (*1913*), by James Elroy Flecker (1884–1915), when first staged in 1923 proved the last sumptuous West End performance of new poetic drama; the sadistic revenge of Haroun al Raschid upon Rafi, his would-be assassin, echoes much of the cruel perverted beauty of Wilde's *Salomé*. Otherwise, English verse drama, though it has been extensively written and though the courageous Granville-Barker attempted Hardy's *Dynasts* on the boards in 1914, belongs essentially to poetry instead of the theater. (T. S. Eliot's contributions to verse drama will be discussed in the next chapter.)

Christopher Fry (1907–   ). A native of Bristol, Christopher Fry had extensive experience as an actor and producer in repertory, as well as in teaching English literature, before his verse dramas enthralled a poetry-starved theater audience. In 1950 four of his plays were appearing simultaneously on the London stage. In 1962 he received the Queen's Gold Medal for poetry.

Fry dramas are rather slender in plotting and simple in theme; their dominant note is an affirmation of youth and life over age and death. They are moods, the stuff of dreams, rather than structured drama. Their glory is a dazzling, dancing, imaginative poetry.

A Phoenix Too Frequent (1946), Fry states, "was got from Jeremy Taylor who had it from Petronius." The title is taken "from Robert Burton, quoting Martial."

Dynamene, widow of Virgilius, goes to his tomb at Ephesus, determined to die of grief. The lamp in the tomb during her vigils attracts Tegeus-Chromis, a soldier guarding the corpse of a gibbeted felon. When the felon's body is stealthily removed and the soldier's life is therefore forfeit, Dynamene practically suggests the substitution of her husband's corpse.

Neo-17th-century conceit writing produces the first significant verse comedy in nearly three centuries. As the title jestingly implies, Dynamene quickly soars from the ashes of her dead life in a smiling assertion that life must be lived and must triumph over death. Wryly, the dramatist probes romantic love. The soldier loved the matron because of her faithfulness to her husband's memory, but no sooner does he love her than he wants her to be the opposite of what he loved her for.

The Lady's Not for Burning (1948) is set in spring about 1400 in the little market town of Cool Clary. It probably is Fry's best work.

Jennet Jourdemayne is sentenced to burn as a witch for transforming old

Skipps, the rag and bone man, into a dog. Ex-soldier Thomas Mendip, wanting to die, confesses to murdering Skipps to insure his own hanging. Old Skipps turns up alive, and Thomas foregoes the pleasure of dying for another fifty years or so in order to marry Jennet.

Since fancy and imagination caused her troubles, Jennet wants no dreams or love, but she vigorously fights to live. Thomas finds life dull and base. Each proves a catalyst to the other in a paean of life and love. The play's forte is a bubbling, often humorous, poetry that asserts the exhilaration of living even amid the darkness of men's minds.

Thor, with Angels, designed for presentation at the Chapter House during the Canterbury festival of 1948, is an impressive 20th-century religious drama. In Kent, "A.D. 596," the Jutish landowner Cymen is torn between his pagan instincts and the new Christian ethic, but the monotheistic Christian god of love triumphs over the battle deities of Thor and Woden in a vividly poetic psychological conflict.

Venus Observed (1950), set in autumn, has an autumnal shower of poetry, perhaps prophesying that further Fry works would prove less appealing.

The aging, aristocratic amorist, Duke of Altair, while observing the planet Venus in his observatory, wishes his son Edgar to select one of three charming mistresses of the Duke as Edgar's stepmother. Perpetua (the eternal Venus of vivacious girlhood) appears and the Duke discards all three mistresses in seeking her hand. Finally, Edgar and Perpetua are united, and the Duke is content with Rosabel, who in disgruntled love had set fire to the place.

The dramatist states that loneliness is the theme, and perhaps one should see no more in the piece than the necessity of warming love and companionship equally for youth and age. Some see an allegory of contemporary England with the need for the young to assert themselves and the aged to train, and then yield to, their proper successors.

Among Fry's other plays are *The Dark Is Light Enough* (1954), subtitled as a winter comedy, which is written in a more restrained verse style. Fry also did translations from the French of plays by Jean Giraudoux and Jean Anouilh.

Chapter 9

Twentieth-Century English Poetry

Two of the most important poets of the new century have already been noted, Thomas Hardy under Victorian fiction and William Butler Yeats under the Celtic Renaissance. Though the career of Gerard Manley Hopkins was entirely in the 19th century, his works were first published in 1918 and have exerted immense influence upon contemporary verse; we have discussed him at the end of the chapter on Victorian Poets.

THE EARLY YEARS OF THE CENTURY

EMPHASIS ON EMPIRE

Kipling and Newbolt are prominent among writers who reacted with vigor against the decadent languor of *fin de siècle* verse (see Victorian Poetry); they were charged with enthusiasm for progress and the Empire.

Joseph Rudyard Kipling (1865–1936). Rudyard Kipling was born at Bombay, India. In 1871 his parents brought him to England where in 1876 he entered the United Services College at Westward Ho, Devonshire. At seventeen he returned to India where his father obtained for him a position with the *Civil and Military Gazette* of Lahore. In 1889 his increasing literary fame again drew him to England. In 1892 he married Caroline Balestier of Vermont and resided in Brattleboro, Vermont, until 1897. Thereafter he rapidly became the most famous English writer of his time, the first Englishman to receive the Nobel Prize for literature, in 1907. His later years were darkened by the World War I death of his only son and by his rabidly conservative distaste for burgeoning English liberalism. Probably no other English literary figure of this century has soared so high in reputation, only to fall so low. Even before his death, his fame was rapidly ebbing.

VERSE. Kipling is, thus far, the last English poet to appeal powerfully to all levels of English society.

(1) His verse opened up to the English-speaking peoples a previously unexploited vein of exotic material, chiefly East Indian in *Departmental Ditties* (1886) and *Barrack-Room Ballads* (1892). Their thrilling *élan* largely arises from a colonial's romantic memory of far places, but Kipling's romanticizing could equally invade the everyday, as "The King" glamorizes the railroad.

(2) People uninterested in poetry *qua* poetry were thrilled by the splendor and spread of empire as glorified in *The Seven Seas* (1896). Kipling's Toryism made the mediocre Alfred Austin the poet laureate in 1896, but Kipling was the unofficial laureate of the British empire, as in "Recessional" (1897). His brassy imperialism is largely responsible for his present condemnation as a period piece.

(3) Kipling proved to be the people's poet with a ballad lilt and infectious cadence that was resoundingly masculine. Undeniably, Kipling restored to poetry a vitality, long missing, through the vigorous slangy speech of pieces such as "Fuzzy-Wuzzy" and "Mandalay" (both 1890). The failure of any subsequent English poet to retain such a broad audience is one reason for the falling away of the general reading public from poetry.

Perhaps it is fame enough to bequeath, as Kipling has, a number of folk classics; it is unlikely that critical opinion (in spite of some kind words from T. S. Eliot) will ever again elevate his verse to its former reputation. Nonetheless, the best poetry of Kipling may be less strident pieces such as "Sussex" (*1902*) and "The Land" (*1910*), conveying a sense of the immemorial countryside and an old England as intuited most poignantly by a colonial upon his ancestral soil.

PROSE. Two books written in Vermont, *The Jungle Book* (1894) and *The Second Jungle Book* (1895), with their central character of Mowgli, the ultraromantic "nature boy," have gained a place in the mythology of childhood. Kipling's black-and-white view of life, his easy acceptance of opposites (East versus West, white skin versus colored skin, past versus present), render him particularly amenable to the youthful reader, as in *Captains Courageous* (1897), also written in America.

Like Maugham, Kipling was a born storyteller. He brought to an apogee the swift-moving, well-plotted short story, and from *Plain Tales from the Hills* (1887) onward, he spun a vast canvas that collectively created the myth of the Anglo-Indian. He is unsurpassed as master of the tale of picturesque adventure.

Kim (1901) is Kipling's one novel likely to survive, though the author dismissed it as "nakedly picturesque and plotless."

Kimball O'Hara, an Irish orphan fending for himself in the slums of Lahore, is befriended by an aged lama from Thibet. The two wander through India in search of the River of the Arrows, or stream of immortality. Recognized by the British, Kim is adopted by his father's former regiment and is educated at a Lucknow college. Colonel Creighton enlists Kim in the Secret Service, where he distinguishes himself by capturing in the Himalayas the documents of a dangerous Russian spy.

The work may be read as the cream of English picaresque fiction, swirling Kim through the exotic grandeur and sordidness of India and its people; but its central and enduring theme is the chasm between the world of the spirit (the lama) and the world of action (Kim) which love alone can bridge.

Sir **Henry John Newbolt** (1862–1938). A native of Bilston, Staffordshire, Henry John Newbolt practiced law from 1887 to 1899. In 1900 he founded the *Monthly Review* and edited it until 1904. From 1911 to 1921 he was professor of poetry at Oxford. In 1923 he became official naval historian, supervising the five-volume official history of the Royal Navy in World War I.

Newbolt made himself the stirring voice of English patriotism and naval glory, themes almost entirely preoccupying *Poems New and Old* (1912).

GEORGIAN POETRY

The term "Georgian poetry," referring primarily to the period of George V, was given prominence in the five volumes, *Georgian Poetry*, edited by Edward Marsh, the first of which came out in 1912 and the last in 1922. Many of the poets in this group tended to portray the quiet countryside. We include with them their contemporaries whose emphasis was on realism. The growing importance of the "modernist" movement overpowered the Georgians; and only recently is there revived interest in their work.

William Henry Davies (1871–1940). Born at Newport, Monmouthshire, William Henry Davies hoboed around much of the world until losing his leg in Canada while stealing a train ride. *Autobiography of a Supertramp* (1908) vividly details this adventuresome life. Shaw "discovered" him in 1905 and encouraged a poetic activity that produced over five hundred Davies poems by the time of his *Collected Poems* in 1935.

In poetry Davies is a "primitive," like Grandma Moses in painting. Always homey and spontaneous, his best work has a fresh simplicity and relaxed quiet in limning the gracious English countryside. Modestly conscious of his limitations, Davies attempts no social or philosophical profundity.

Ralph Hodgson (1871–   ). Ralph Hodgson has been reticent about his life, believing that "the poet should live in his poetry." It can be ascertained, however, that since his Yorkshire birth he has worked as printer, draftsman, reporter, and editor. From 1924 through 1938 he was visiting lecturer in English literature at Sendai University, Japan. In 1940 he established residence on a farm near Minerva, Ohio. In 1954 he received the Queen's Gold Medal for poetry.

The collected *Poems* (1917) show a narrow range of themes—chiefly a love of landscapes, an antipathy to all forms of cruelty, and a rather ecstatic joy in all living creatures. Verses written from then through the 1940s are generally similar. Within Hodgson's scope he is an excellent master of traditional rhythms. Perhaps unwisely he has recently been ignored, as an old-fashioned devotee of Nature and beauty.

Gordon Bottomley (1874–1948). A native of Keighley, Yorkshire, Gordon Bottomley always lived a sedentary life because of ill health. In *Georgian Poetry* (1915), edited by Edward Marsh, he seemed one of the most considerable poetic talents of the period. In 1925 he received the Benson Medal of the Royal Society of Literature for poetry. Later years were spent in Lancashire seclusion.

Bottomley began in *fin de siècle* vein but proceeded to bold, starkly primitive poetic dramas perhaps unduly neglected, because instead of the modern idiom of T. S. Eliot they are romanticized Shakespeare. *The Riding to Lithend* (1909), set in 10th-century Iceland, captures the cold northern savagery of the sagas in the account of the slaying of Hallgerd's husband, Gunnar. *King Lear's Wife* (1915) and *Gruach* (1921), the latter on the early life of Lady Macbeth, are probably the only convincing preludes ever written to Shakespearean tragedies. The atmosphere is grim and primordial, but the works are essentially lyric poems in dramatic form rather than true stage plays.

Walter John de la Mare (dé-là-mãr' or del'a-mãr) (1873–1956). Walter de la Mare was born at Charlton, Kent. Through his mother he was related to Browning. After education at St. Paul's Cathedral Choir School in London, he worked from 1890 to 1908 as a bookkeeper for Anglo-American Oil (subsidiary of Standard Oil). In 1908 Newbolt obtained for him a pension that permitted his subsequent concentration upon poetry. His very distinctive novel, *Memoirs of a Midget* (1921), won the James Tait Black prize; the pathetic life of tiny Miss M., told adeptly through her own words, is a veiled criticism of social heartlessness toward the abnormal and the handicapped.

If De la Mare's dates could be set back precisely one century, he would be labeled one of the great Romantics. The everyday realities of the world, including sex, are absent from his verse. Stillness, motionlessness, dark night (as in "The Listeners"), and dreamy suggestiveness suffuse his works with glamour and romance. Some of his most popular verse is addressed to children; *Peacock Pie* (1913) and *Down-a-Down Derry* (1922), for example, find the whimsical or the astoundingly lovely in the commonplaces of childhood. *Collected Poems* (1942) offers the adult reader similar charm.

Not since Coleridge has an English poet sung so melodiously and delicately about the strange and the mysterious.

Philip Edward Thomas (1878–1917). Born in Wiltshire and educated at Lincoln College, Oxford, Philip Edward Thomas devoted two decades to critical writing and hackwork. The English residence of Robert Frost, 1912–14, encouraged him to turn to poetry. Enlisting soon after the start of World War I, Edward Thomas was killed in action at Arras, France.

Poems (1917), dedicated to Frost and patently following the themes and rhythms of Frost, revealed one of the notable Nature poets in English, a countryman with an extraordinarily faithful eye for the little but poignant features of landscape and wildlife. *Collected Poems* (1922) contains less Frost idiom and a more deepening concern for the beauty and brevity of life. Aldous Huxley characterizes the atmosphere of Thomas poetry as "a nameless emotion of quiet happiness shot through with melancholy."

Harold Edward Monro (mun-rō′) (1879–1932). Son of a Scottish civil engineer living in Brussels, Belgium, Harold Edward Monro was educated at Caius College, Cambridge. With his establishment in 1912 of the Poetry Bookshop and of the quarterly *Poetry and Drama,* Monro became the leading arbiter of contemporary verse and encourager of youthful poets. As a critic and anthologist he vigorously supported "modernism" in poetry.

Monro's theory of verse as enunciated in *Some Contemporary Poets* (1920) called for: intellect instead of singing quality, total effect instead of single outstanding lines, avoidance of poetic diction (e.g. "e'er"), no obtrusive rhythm, no overworked regular meter, subjects from immediate personal experience rather than from books or tradition, and no propaganda line whether religious or social. Monro's own poetry is usually at its best when ignoring his theories, especially the point against lyricism. He is frequently condemned as a poet by intention rather than intuition, but he is remarkably effective in the animistic quality of sensing relationships with the inanimate objects around him. T. S. Eliot offers judicious praise of the *Collected Poems* (1933).

Lascelles Abercrombie (1881–1938). A native of Ashton-upon-Mersey, Cheshire, Lascelles Abercrombie was educated at Malcolm College and the University of Manchester. He taught English literature at Leeds University (1922–29) and at London University (1929–35) until the illness from which he died forced retirement.

His taut intellectuality and densely packed style should make Abercrombie an interesting modern poet, but his traditional diction and his addiction to the dramatic monologue and the long reflective poem have cursed him with the sobriquet "the latter-day Browning" and largely relegated his meager vogue to academic circles, especially since the lyric and short realistic poems dominate today's verse.

The Sale of St. Thomas (1911 in part, 1930 in toto), his most praised work, narrates the supposed trip to India by the doubting apostle. *Emblems of Love* (1912), with stupendous erudition explores all manifestations of love—historical, mythological, real, and symbolic. *The Theory of Poetry* (1924) and *The Idea of Great Poetry* (1925) for some observers establish Abercrombie as the most significant academic critic of poetry since Matthew Arnold, though his minimizing of psychoanalytic technique has caused his dismissal by many as old-fashioned. He sees the touchstone of great poetry as complexity in unity, "a confluence of all kinds of life into a single flame of consciousness," linking poet and reader.

Alfred Noyes (1880–1958). Alfred Noyes was born at Wolverhampton, Staffordshire. After Oxford studies he briefly followed the sea until settling down to the writing of poetry. His high reputation made him professor of modern English literature at Princeton University, 1914–23. In 1924 *Some Aspects of Modern Poetry* voiced his acid distaste for "modernist" verse. In 1925 he became a convert to Roman Catholicism, recounting his religious course in *The Unknown God* (1934). During World War II he toured America in support of the British war effort. Though almost forgotten by the general reading public, he continued to write extensively until his death.

The heartiness and fluency of "The Highwayman" and "The Barrel Organ" earned Noyes a popularity beyond that of any of his contemporaries except Kipling, but his marked beat and easy rime have caused him to be relegated today to adolescents. Composers such as Samuel Coleridge-Taylor and Edward Elgar have found his pieces ideal as lyrics for music. Perhaps his best work is the epic *Drake* (1908) in twelve books of rollicking verse upon the maritime England of the first Elizabeth.

Wilfrid Wilson Gibson (1878–1962). Born at Hexham, Northumberland, Wilfrid Wilson Gibson was educated at private schools, and served in the ranks during World War I. He has produced more than thirty volumes of poetry, most impressively upon the subjects of war and his native Lake Country (often in Northumberland dialect).

Gibson began as a belated Pre-Raphaelite and Tennysonian, but with *Stonefolds* (1907) he found his métier as a slightly sentimentalized George Crabbe. Gibson's typical verse deals with the hard lives of peasants and workers. Few of his poems stand out, but cumulatively they develop a rugged, authentic picture of narrow lives of unceasing toil.

John Masefield (mās'fēld) (1878–   ). John Masefield was the son of a Ledbury, Herefordshire, lawyer. At fourteen he went to sea, wandering about the world, and for a time was barkeeper and carpet factory worker in New York. While reading Chaucer in America, he determined upon a poetic career. Remarkably, he was the first English poet to be a genuine deep-water seaman. In 1897 he returned to England, and during World War I he served with the Red Cross in France and on the Gallipoli

Peninsula. Succeeding Bridges in 1930, he was the first proletarian poet laureate in English history, designated appropriately under a Labour government.

Salt-Water Ballads (1902), *Ballads* (1903), and *Ballads and Poems* (1910) contain much of the still memorable short poetry by Masefield. The best pieces celebrate a sailor's life with an infectious sea-chanty lilt, an exciting revelation of what Masefield calls "the rough, bawdy beautiful world." Masefield is especially skillful in long lines of trisyllabic feet, so singing that many have been put to music. The sonnet "Sea Fever" is a good example of Masefield's rhythm.

The Everlasting Mercy (1911) created Masefield's first big sensation. In this narrative poem of Jimmy Jaggard and his mother, the poet introduced extensive profanity, shocking to staid Georgian ears and eyes. Although Jimmy is converted to righteousness, the sordid account aroused protests, especially from Stephen Phillips, that the standards of literature were being destroyed.

Reynard the Fox (1919), the climax of Masefield's works, is supposed to have earned him the laureateship more than any other work. In a vigorous four-beat line Masefield offers perhaps the best depiction in verse of the English countryside and countrymen (about seventy characters) centered about the *mystique* of the fox-hunt. Chaucer is Masefield's mentor in energy, humor, picturesqueness, lyric moments, sympathy for man and beast, and, especially, the high spirits engendered by sun and wind amid a lovely landscape. The fox is "crossed" by another fox and finally escapes, but the hunting, not the killing, is the point.

Although Masefield's bibliography is enormous and varied, ranging through poetic drama, novels, children's tales, accounts of both World Wars, and even propaganda for woman suffrage, little since 1920 has been distinguished, and most has softened to genteel conventionality.

POETS OF WORLD WAR I

Sensitive intellectuals bred in the secure 19th-century atmosphere and sincerely confident of human progress and brotherhood were unspeakably crushed by the collapse of their ordered world and their sudden experience of savage trench warfare. All the "Pride, pomp, and circumstance of glorious war" is vehemently protested by these disillusioned youths confronted with the impersonality of mass slaughter. Brooke's romanticizing of war is the one exception, and this is mostly because he died early before the struggle had settled down for a time to a gory stalemate. Gibson (considered above) and Robert Graves (treated in the final chapter on the Modern Novel) belong to this group but are chiefly noted for works beyond their wartime experience.

Rupert Chawner Brooke (1887–1915). Rupert Brooke was the son of the assistant master at Rugby. After graduating from King's College, Cambridge, he traveled extensively in Europe, America, and the South Seas. Enlisting soon after the outbreak of World War I, he saw duty in Belgium and then was sent to the Dardanelles campaign, dying en route of blood poisoning.

1914 and Other Poems (1915) contains sonnets which Abercrombie rated "among the few supreme utterances of English patriotism." The *Collected Poems* (1916) swept the English-speaking world, for even to many scoffers of poetry here gleamed the ultimate romantic concept of the fighting man, especially in the famous "The Soldier." Brooke was the only significant wartime poet who sustained this dream, and with the postwar reaction against militarism and combat, his verses gradually fell away before the storm of antiwar verse.

Sometimes mentioned with Rupert Brooke because of the popularity of their contributions to poetry of World War I were two non-English poets who died in the war, John McCrae (1872–1918), a Canadian, who wrote "In Flanders Fields," and Alan Seeger (1888–1916), an American, who wrote "I Have a Rendezvous with Death."

Siegfried Lorraine Sassoon (1886–   ). Siegfried Sassoon on his father's side descends from a wealthy and cosmopolitan Persian-Jewish line; on his mother's side are English country gentlemen and the sculptor Thornycroft, his uncle. After graduation from Clare College, Oxford, he published verse reminiscent of the Pre-Raphaelites and Stephen Phillips. Enlisting early, he saw perhaps more action than any other literary figure, both in France and Palestine. Wounded in 1917, he tossed his Military Cross into the Mersey and refused to return to battle. After hospitalization for shell shock, he returned to service, rising to a captaincy. In 1957 he was awarded the Royal Gold Medal for Poetry.

Counter-Attack and Other Poems (1918) and the collected war poems of 1919 are the most powerful and savage English verse ever written about war. Staccato lines, rugged and clashing, graphically picture the filth and futility of war. A lyric idealist at heart, Sassoon was wrenched to bitter, passionate anger. None of his subsequent verses in *Collected Poems* (1961) can match the intense white-heat of his war verse.

Memoirs of a Fox-Hunting Man (1928) won the two most coveted of English literary prizes—the Hawthornden and the James Tait Black Memorial. This prose quasi-autobiography has a Jorrocks quality (Surtees is a favorite of Sassoon) but the remembrance of war and England's decline intrudes upon this lost world of the squirearchy in the country mansions.

Robert Malise Bowyer Nichols (1893–1944). Robert Nichols experienced war during three weeks of front-line service in France during World War I. His *Ardours and Endurances* (1917) approaches Sassoon but just misses the force of that poet. Nichols wrote a notable preface to Sassoon's *Counter-*

Attack, concluding, "War does not ennoble, it degrades." The preface to his *Anthology of War Poetry 1914–18* (1943) was the first significant attempt to contrast the war psychologies of World Wars I and II.

Isaac Rosenberg (1890–1918). Isaac Rosenberg was born of poor Jewish parents in Bristol, but his remarkable artistic talents won him a scholarship to the Slade School and several high art prizes. Ill-health caused him in 1914 to migrate to South Africa, but he returned to enlist the next year. Though frail, he endured two years of trench warfare until he was killed in action.

Poems (1922), edited by Bottomley, and the *Collected Works* (1937) have recently aroused more interest in his verse than in most of his fellow war poets. In the latter collection Sassoon's foreword correctly diagnoses the fresh, vigorous fusion of English and Hebrew culture, an absorbing tension between calm resolution and prophetic fire. Rosenberg brings to poetry the sharp eye of the pictorial artist for shape and movement. Withal, it is great promise rather than great fulfilment.

Wilfred Owen (1893–1918). Born at Oswestry, Shropshire, Wilfred Owen was educated at Birkenhead Institute and London University. He was a private tutor from 1913 until enlisting in 1915. He was killed in action exactly one week before the Armistice.

Poems (1920), edited by his friend Sassoon, first revealed Owen to the world's readers. Of all the war poets he best expresses the prevailing English sentiment of postwar years: restrained bitterness about the slaughter, compassion, and patriotism without maudlin tears, courage amid chaos. Although Owen intended essentially propaganda pieces ("The Poetry," he asserted, "is in the Pity"), the power of "Futility" and "Greater Love," for example, emits true poetry. Almost half his slender volume consists of impressive experiments with assonance rather than rime, an experiment influencing many subsequent English poets. The premature deaths of Owen and Rosenberg are the greatest known losses to 20th-century poetry, as both might have led the subsequent movement to a new poetic idiom.

CLASSICISTS

Scholarly and somewhat withdrawn, certain important poets of this period produced carefully-wrought verse often with classic themes and allusions.

Robert Seymour Bridges (1844–1930). Born at Walmer, Kent, Robert Bridges studied at Eton and Oxford, then traveled extensively through Europe and the Near East. He practiced medicine at St. Bartholomew's Hospital, London, until 1882, when he withdrew for a literary career. He was a "poet's poet," hardly known to the public until his appointment as poet laureate in 1913. In the same year he was the leading spirit in the founding of the Society for Pure English. He was responsible for the initial publication of Hopkins' poetry in 1918. Until his death at an advanced age, he continued a fervid interest in phonetic spelling, harpsicord music, and high-quality printing of books.

Bridges is probably the master in English of a serene classic style. The everyday reader has frequently ignored him because of his very clarity and simplicity, his fastidious concern for metrics (he is one of the most important experimenters and students of English prosody), and his avoidance of the violent and the dramatic. Perhaps, above all, the English have expected a great poet to espouse the tragic view of life, and Bridges did not. Readers of calm temperament and an ear attuned to subtle harmonies have found him virtually unequaled in our language.

Poetical Works (1912) is remarkable for the amount of consistently good verse it contains. Short poems include *vers de société,* restrained love poetry (notably *The Growth of Love,* a sonnet sequence of 1889), and nature verse. *Nero, Part I* (1885) is probably the best of a number of closet dramas in verse upon ancient subjects such as Achilles, Ulysses, and Prometheus.

The Testament of Beauty (1929), Bridges' swan song, would be an astounding product from any man in his eighties, but this ambitious attempt at a long philosophical poem has aroused more general interest by its intrinsic merit than all other Bridges works put together and may survive as an English classic along with Wordsworth's *Prelude.* The central theme is the evolving of the human soul toward perfection as the growth of spiritual love unites all things in the grandeur of God. Arguing from Christian teleology of design in the universe, Bridges perceives the blind instincts in Nature transformed into spiritual forces, chiefly through aesthetic sensibilities. The poem is written in unrimed "loose alexandrines," following the classic pattern of quantitative scansion instead of modern accentual scansion, and permitting a varied number of syllables in each foot as in Anglo-Saxon verse.

Alfred Edward Housman (1859–1936). A. E. Housman was born at Bournheath, Worcestershire. He left St. John's College, Oxford, in 1882 to work as a clerk in the Patent Office until 1892. Receiving his degree in the latter year, he became professor of Latin at University College, London, and then from 1911 until death professor of Latin at Trinity College, Cambridge. Except for three slender volumes of poetry, most of his efforts were expended upon classical studies. He never resided in Shropshire, indissolubly associated with his name.

A Shropshire Lad (1896) has proved the most popular single volume of English poetry for the last hundred years, except for FitzGerald's *Rubáiyát.* The pervasive note, as in FitzGerald, is pessimism. Housman's is a quiet, mature pessimism ("Luck's a chance, but trouble's sure"); nature is not kind; lovers are false; youth will drink, answer the drums of war or life, and die. Yet though they are potentially dismal, Housman's contentions are incomparably glamorized by a classic music of simple restraint and effortless grace. Though narrow in subject and form Housman, nevertheless, is the unquestioned master of the short lyric, generally in four to eight quatrains. "With Rue My Heart Is Laden" and "Loveliest of Trees" have taken their place in the language along with Gray's "Elegy" as the perfect expression of universal emotions.

Last Poems (1922) and *More Poems* (1936), the latter edited by his brother Laurence, continue the same themes and forms, rather surprisingly displaying perhaps an increasing acerbity instead of the mellowness of advancing years. "Epitaph on an Army of Mercenaries," paying tribute to the old regulars sacrificed to hold the Channel ports, may be the best poem of World War I.

The Name and Nature of Poetry (1933), the Leslie Stephen Lecture at Cambridge, exemplifies the excellent prose of Housman. Clear and understated as his verse, it suggests that his poetry has a twofold origin—self-deliverance from his own sense of life's pains, and sympathy for all "ill-treated fellows," his fellow humans.

Robert Laurence Binyon (1869–1943). Laurence Binyon was the son of a Lancaster clergyman. At Trinity College, Oxford, in 1890 he won the Newdigate prize for poetry and in the same year brought out *Primavera*, a collection of his verses and those of his cousin Stephen Phillips. In 1893 he began a lifetime career in the British Museum, serving from 1913 on as chief of Orientalia. In 1929 he lectured in Japan, and in 1933–34 he succeeded T. S. Eliot as Norton Professor of Poetry at Harvard. Much of his writings consists of studies of oriental art, while *English Poetry in Its Relation to Painting and the Other Arts* (1919) remains one of the significant analyses of the interrelations of the arts.

Collected Poems (1931) displays a progress from earlier academicism to increased flexibility and depth, but all touched with careful craftsmanship and classic restraint. "The Sirens" (1924) may be his best work; a stately, slow-moving ode celebrates the inner voices of hope and beauty that sustain man in a drab world. He was a thoroughly competent and unspectacular master of English verse.

His popular reputation will probably rest upon translations, chiefly the East Indian drama *Sakuntala* (1920) and Dante's *Divine Comedy* (*Inferno*, 1933; *Purgatorio*, 1938; *Paradiso*, 1943). Binyon's version of Dante is perhaps the smoothest and most finished in English, but it has been criticized for its dulling of Dante's precision and forcefulness.

Thomas Sturge Moore (1870–1944). Brother of the noted philosopher George E. Moore, Thomas Sturge Moore was the son of a Hastings physician. His early career was that of wood engraver and book designer, first appearing as a poet in *The Vinedresser* (1899). He was a friend of Yeats, who used one of Moore's images in "The Tower."

Poems (four volumes, 1931–33) reveals Moore as one of the most Hellenized of English poets, most of his subjects treating of ancient Greek life and mythology. The cool, Olympian sunlight that bathes his verses produces perhaps the most convincing re-creation in all English of that storied past. Only diffuseness and a traditional idiom deny Moore rank as a major poet.

T. S. ELIOT AND MODERNIST POETRY

The first significant indications of a new poetic era appeared in the Imagist manifesto of 1915, which emphasized the following three main resolutions:

"(1) To use the language of common speech, but to employ always the exact word, not the nearly exact, nor the merely decorative word.

"(2) To produce poetry that is hard and clear, and not to deal in vague generalities, however magnificent and sonorous.

"(3) To create new rhythms and not to copy old rhythms, which merely echo old moods."

These revolutionaries were chiefly Americans: Ezra Pound, Amy Lowell, Hilda Doolittle, with T. S. Eliot and E. E. Cummings a bit later. The chief leader and theorist of the Imagists, however, was the English poet T. E. Hulme (1886–1917), killed in action during World War I. For contemporary British poetry the major influence of the Imagists was to compel a drastic compression and hard objectivity.

From the Imagist school, T. S. Eliot developed into the dominant exponent of "modernist" verse by his poetic practice and by his critical works (*The Sacred Wood* constitutes a declaration of modernist poetry and sets up a bulwark separating today's poetry from previous poetry). Although some current poets still write somewhat traditionalist verse, the modernist school has so impressed itself upon recent decades that the average reader usually thinks of modernist verse as the poetry of our era. All poets for the rest of this chapter (except the concluding traditionalists) are modernists or followers of the modernists.

Modernist verse is characterized by the following features:

(1) A blanket condemnation of modern life and modern society. The confident bourgeois world before 1914 has been irrevocably shattered, and the modernist poet believes that the collapse of modern civilization into vulgarity and triviality presages the complete dissolution of Western culture.

(2) Autonomy of the individual and the poem. Living in the midst of chaos the modernist poet abandons all hope of social structure and contemplates essentially the role of life for the isolated individual. Each poem

is therefore an island unto itself, not to be related to other works but solely to its own evocation.

(3) The private symbol. The loss of any conscious universal symbols in our fragmented society results in the purely personal symbol, often incomprehensible to the uninitiated and often failing to communicate to many readers.

(4) Purposeful difficulty. As T. S. Eliot states, a confused and complicated age requires comparable expression, not a false simplification.

(5) Tension. Modernist poetry emphasizes tension rather than seeking the time-honored resolution of it through poetry. Such verse tends to disturb rather than soothe, reflecting the contemporary temper instead of placating it.

(6) Irrationality. Regarding as grotesquely naïve the pre-1914 belief in man as a creature capable of solving his problems rationally, modernist poets tend to write by free association (though their revisions are frequently quite cerebral). Ideally, modernist poetry consists solely of symbolic and descriptive images, ignoring the propositional, the denotative, and the explicit.

(7) Myth. Not conscious but unconscious symbols, archetypes from the collective unconscious of man, fascinate modernists. Tapping such deep veins of hidden emotive concepts constitutes the one means of communication with others.

(8) Aggressive unpopularity. Modernist poetry has sought to create a new élite, since the 19th-century bourgeois triumph obliterated the old stratification of society. José Ortega y Gasset explains recent 20th-century art as "the art of a privileged aristocracy of finer senses" united less by aesthetic theory than by scorn for the non-intellectual mass.

(9) Defiantly urban contemporary. The Nature escape of the Georgians is blatantly scorned, as the subject now is the tortured spirit in the industrialized jungle. Modernist poets in their language frequently spout the idiom of today. Instead of the traditional poetic emphasis upon the cosmic, modernists concern themselves with the everyday.

(10) Unceasing experiment in form and technique. Modernists have vastly increased the scope of poetry by subjects, allusions, and phrasings never previously deemed appropriate to poetry. Daring rhythms and irregular metrical patterns have often created an exciting freshness unknown to earlier verse. Some modernist verse has explored perhaps the limits of verbal magic and mood, minimizing rational content.

With all their adventurous newness, the modernists have affinities with earlier English poets. Especially they favor Donne, whose tension-wracked Mannerism accords with today's spirit; Blake, whose subjectivity and probing of the unconscious parallel the modernist impulses; and Hopkins, whose experiments with language and meter have shaken the complacency of poetic expression. It must be remembered that the strikingly individual talents of many modernists have produced some poems of un-modernist quality with wide popularity and impressive clarity.

Oversimplifying, we may categorize British poets who reached their maturity in the 1930s or since as tending toward the cool discipline and aloofness of the New Classicism of T. S. Eliot or the explosive energy of the New Romanticism of Dylan Thomas.

Thomas Stearns Eliot (1888–   ). Of a distinguished New England ancestry, T. S. Eliot was born at St. Louis, Missouri. Entering Harvard University in 1906, he became editor of the *Harvard Advocate,* which printed some of his early verse. His subsequent education was at the Sorbonne, Paris, and Merton College, Oxford. Since 1913 his residence has been in England. During World War I he taught school, worked as a bank clerk, and then became editor of the Imagist periodical, *The Egoist,* from 1917 to 1919. In 1922 he established his own critical journal, *The Criterion,* lasting until 1939. Since World War I he has been associated with the London publishing house of Faber and Faber. In 1927 he became a British subject and a member of the Anglo-Catholic wing of the Church of England. The Nobel Prize for literature and the British Order of Merit in 1948 climaxed national and international honors.

T. S. Eliot has secured for English poetry a majestic prestige unknown since the days of Tennyson. His influence has extended to virtually every poet in the English language since the 1920s. Many suggest that his prose, meticulously clear and precise, may rank as high as his verse; certainly his position as literary and cultural critic surpasses that of any other in 20th-century English. All following entries are poetry, except (D) for poetic drama and (P) for prose criticism.

FIRST PERIOD (TO 1927). A scathing indictment of current culture reverberates through early Eliot verse. This general, as opposed to specific, satire employs ironic juxtaposing of reality and ideal, determinedly contemporary references counterpointed by subtle allusions or quotations from past literature, and a poetic appropriateness instead of conventional logic to link episodes and images. No subsequent Eliot verse has aroused the furor and exerted the compelling influence of this early work.

Prufrock and Other Observations (1917), Eliot's first published volume, is chiefly inspired by the 17th-century metaphysicals (confrontation and fusion of discordant opposites) and by the 19th-century French poet Jules Laforgue (mock-heroic irony to attack the clichés and shams of trivial modern life).

"The Love Song of J. Alfred Prufrock" (*1909–11*) is titled ironically, for its theme is desire that falls off in frustrated inertia. The name *Prufrock* seems a combination of "prudence" or "prudishness" with "frock," the frock coat of respectable upper-class Englishmen. The bearer of the name is symbolic of modern social and sexual failure. He is interpreted as the arena for a threefold Freudian struggle: the "I" is the ego, his weakened impulse to individuality and self-creativity; the "you" is the superego, the overriding, built-in regulator of modern society that demands conformity and decorum; the buried id, only momentarily asserting itself, is the unconscious, intuitive drives to natural, instinctive life. The modern world (London) is stigmatized as tawdry ("one-night cheap hotels") and creatively dead, listlessly "talking of Michelangelo," a giant of the long-past days of energetic art. Cognizant that he is an underling, Prufrock cringes at what "they" will say about him. Water is the symbol of life and of destruction. At the poem's climax Prufrock's selfhood glimpses the mermaids, the symbol of spontaneous life-rhythm, but the challenge of life is too great, and Prufrock is drowned by the superego's insistence upon his inane, subordinate role. As the prefatory quotation from Dante indicates, Prufrock is trapped in his own psychic inferno. Metaphor and symbol replace statement in this, the first significant "modernist" poem. Associations are psychological rather than grammatical, with a rich interweaving of references (e.g. "oyster shells" in the opening contrast with the sea freedom of the concluding lines). Influential was "Crapy Cornelia" (1909) by Henry James, picturing a frustrated bachelor.

"Portrait of a Lady" (*1915*) is not a portrait of a woman but of an adolescent Prufrock. A love affair runs through a year from bleak December to gray October, the youth passing from a feeling of assurance to uncertainty and eventually to ignominious retreat. Baffled and confused by a life challenge too great for him, he takes refuge in polite, futile conventions and pathetic wishful thinking. The verse form develops from speech rather than song, employing functional rime and meter, disregarding set patterns to capture the flow of mood.

"Rhapsody on a Windy Night" (*1915*) recounts a man's night-time walk to his lodgings. Each successive street lamp offers memory-stimulating images, each a twisting of unprofitable, sterile existence. The last lamp twists him to the present, a monotonous round of the meaningless everyday routine. The atmosphere and theme seem derived from Charles-Louis Philippe's *Bubu de Montparnasse*, for which Eliot wrote a preface to the English translation of 1932.

"Mr. Apollinax" (*1916*) brings the modern "son of Apollo" into proper Bostonian society. The exact opposite of Prufrock, Apollinax dominates the gathering by his laughter, at once crude and shy, animalistic and intellectual. Inspiration was Bertrand Russell, lecturing at Harvard in 1914. Russell is more Dionysian than Apollonian, and Eliot sympathizes with his shocking vitality in contrast with New England desiccation.

"La Figlia che Piange" ("The Weeping Maiden") (*1916*) depicts, as do many of these early poems, the frustrated failure in man-woman relationships. Uncertainty and inadequacy cause the man to desert the girl whose arms are filled with flowers.

Ara Vos Prec (1920) in title is a quotation, "Now I pray you," from the 12th-century French poet, Arnaut Daniel, petitioning for relief from mental pain.

"The Hippopotamus" (*1917*) uses the animal as a symbol of the relatively innocent materialism of the secular world compared with the hypocritical materialism of the "True Church." God is more willing to accept the innocent hippo than the stained church. Not religion but religious abuses are the target of this and the next poem.

"Mr. Eliot's Sunday Morning Service" (*1918*) contrasts the pure religion of an Italian "primitive" mural with the modern perversion of religion into subtle sectarian squabbles and sordid money grubbing. The poem parallels "Les Pauvres à l'église" by the 19th-century French poet Arthur Rimbaud.

"Whispers of Immortality" (*1918*) contrasts Webster and Donne with the modern spirit, which Eliot in prose has labeled the "dissociation of sensibility." Possessed by death, these Renaissance poets could see beyond the flesh, while the flesh (symbolized by the "pneumatic bliss" of the Russian siren Grishkin) so overwhelms today's world that the concept of immortality is reduced to a dry metaphysical whisper.

"Sweeney among the Nightingales" (*1918*) is the most famous of the "Sweeney" poems. Sweeney, the coarse, cultureless, sensual ape man of modern society, is a composite, but seems chiefly inspired by Steve O'Donnell, a pugilist who gave Eliot boxing lessons during his Harvard days. The framework is the Agamemnon story of antiquity, but this tawdry display of lechery in a public house rebukes today's sordid materialism, remote from the heroic stature of an earlier culture founded upon ritual and religion.

"Sweeney Erect" (*1919*) is an ironic retort to Emerson's definition, "The lengthened shadow of a man is history" (quoted in the seventh stanza). In the modern Sweeney history becomes the lengthened shadow of an anthropoid ape. Sweeney and the epileptic woman with whom he has been sleeping are scathingly contrasted with Polyphemus and Nausicaä of Greek mythology. As the epileptic sees the naked Sweeney shaving, she has a seizure, feeling vulgar desolation in contrast to the spiritual desolation indicated by the prefatory quotation from *The Maid's Tragedy* by Beaumont and Fletcher.

"Burbank with a Baedeker: Bleistein with a Cigar" (*1919*), like the opening of Byron's fourth canto of *Childe Harold's Pilgrimage,* laments the low estate today of once glorious Venice. The former aristocracy of the city has degenerated into Princess Volupine ("fox") who consorts with the fur merchant Sir Ferdinand Klein ("little"). Two Americans experience the glory and decay of Venice: the grossly materialistic and unheeding Bleistein (the metal "lead" + "stone"), and the receptive Burbank (apparently "hybridizer" from the American plant wizard) who feels enervated and impotent.

"A Cooking Egg" (*1919*) in title means "an old egg," not strictly fresh. The speaker is an "old egg" like the François Villon quoted in the poem's epigraph. The subject of the poem is the frustration of time and career, as the speaker ironically ticks off his disappointments in Honour, Capital, Society, and Pipit (a childhood love now withered into spinsterhood). Youthful hopes have vanished to leave only tawdry meals in A.B.C.'s (restaurants of the Aerated Bread Company).

"Gerontion" ("Little old man") (*1920*) is Eliot's most powerful work before *The Waste Land*. The title seems to derive from Newman's *Dream of Gerontius*, but the diminutive implies a complete falling away from the serene joy and faith of the Victorian poem. The speaker of this dramatic monologue is an aged intellectual whose career recapitulates the futility and desolation of European secular life, contrasted with the disregarded assurance of salvation through Christ. Anticipating the mythic symbolism of *The Waste Land*, Gerontion is "waiting for rain," life-giving moisture in a sterile world. Christ comes as a tiger, creative energy as in Blake's "Tyger," but Humanism has been a "flowering judas," ignoring the redeemer for the hollow gods of disembodied art and materialism worshiped by rootless beings such as Silvero and Hakagawa.

The Sacred Wood: Essays on Poetry and Criticism (1920) (P), the most famous and most influential of Eliot's prose works, derives its title from the consecrated grove through which the Cumaean Sibyl guided Aeneas to the underworld (Dante also begins his journey amid this forest). In an era of intellectual chaos when the romantic tradition has petered out in Georgian bucolics, Eliot made himself the initiator of a new "classical" criticism, seeking in these collected essays to establish the value of poetry in light of an orderly tradition much older than modern romanticism. His main position rests upon these interrelated contentions: the necessity of cultural continuity and tradition instead of romantic egotism and self-expression; intellectual discipline and honesty instead of literature as indulgence or play; and objective, factual criticism instead of platitudes and emotionalism.

"Tradition and the Individual Talent" (1919), his best-known essay, keynotes all his subsequent criticism:

(1) Possessing the historical sense, a poet properly sets himself amid all the body of previous poetry, which represents symmetrical order. Each work of art modifies the meaning of preceding literature and is itself inseparable from the past.

(2) The poet rightfully expresses not an individual "personality" (the self or subjective life, as chiefly projected since the Renaissance) but the ethos of his age and his society (as in the essentially objective art of pre-Renais-

sance times). The justifiable individual response of the poet is his recognition of his sharing of the cultural tradition.

"Ben Jonson" (1919) sees the highly conscious form, the absence of sentiment, and the biting dissection of human foibles by Jonson as making him more attractive to the 20th-century intelligentsia than Shakespeare.

"Hamlet and His Problems" (1919) calls the Shakespearean drama "an artistic failure," because Hamlet "is dominated by an emotion [antipathy to his mother's guilt] which is inexpressible, because it is in *excess* of the facts as they appear." Eliot here coined the phrase "objective correlative," subsequently widely popular, to refer to concrete facts that fully evoke an emotional response.

"William Blake" (1920) extends more praise to Blake than Eliot gives to any other Romantic. Nonetheless, Blake remains an honest genius rather than a classic, like Dante, because he worked independently of the major cultural framework.

The Waste Land (1922) is the most discussed poem of the 20th century, and because of its complexity we shall deal with it in detail.

(1) Theme. *The Waste Land* is a condemnation of the sterile futility of modern life. It follows the immemorial pattern of death-and-resurrection, with the assertion that our age is willing to settle for death instead of accepting the challenge to renewed life, but the way to salvation is open if we will but heed it.

(2) Underlying myth. By Eliot's own admission, the central myth as well as the title of the poem is derived from Jessie L. Weston's *From Ritual to Romance* (1920), with assists from the writings of Frazer. Weston sees the legend of the Holy Grail as ultimately resting upon ancient myths of the vegetation and fertility cycle. The fundamental story concerns the Fisher King who through illness or wound is rendered sexually impotent. The land correspondingly is blighted, an arid waste desperately in need of water. The curse may be removed, and the King and the land restored to fertility, by a valiant quester who endures agonizing hardships to secure a magic cup and spear (sex symbols).

(3) Application of myth to theme. The debility of the Fisher King is the modern weakness of Christianity and of all moderns in their loss of religious faith. Though timeless, the poem corresponds to the painful period between Good Friday and Easter, a time when there appears no hope of resurrection.

(4) Technique. Essentially a ritual drama, the poem employs what the cinema terms *montage*, a dazzling succession of shots ranging through much of Western art and life to illuminate its theme. The rapid sequence proves more impressively effective than a logical transition from one example of the theme to another.

(5) Analysis of *The Waste Land*. The epigraph, from the *Satyricon* of

Petronius Arbiter, is the first enunciation of repeated instances of the degeneration of prophecy in today's world.

Part I. The Burial of the Dead. In April the Vegetation God, Christ, is crucified, and the postwar cafés of central Europe murmur with hopelessness, preferring a wintry hibernation to the stimulus of reawakened life. The angry denunciations of the prophet are followed by taunting pictures of modern sterility and the debasement of the oracle into the fortune-teller. One of the shuffling walkers on the way to work in London is accosted with the question whether the buried corpse of the Vegetation God will arise to renew the blighted land and the darkened spirit.

Part II. A Game of Chess. Futility in the upper classes is demonstrated by a frustrated neurasthenic lady, a desert of the spirit amid sumptuous magnificence. The surrounding grandeur of the ancient and Renaissance past has become meaningless to a vulgarized era. Futility in the lower classes is demonstrated by a cockney girl who in a London pub near closing time relates a sordid tale of sexual desire, abortion, and life denial. The title for this section comes from *Women Beware Women* by Thomas Middleton, where a game of chess is a cover-up for a seduction.

Part III. The Fire Sermon. Futility in the middle classes is demonstrated by a series of tawdry fornications, perverse materialisms of the life principle. From this inferno of unholy loves sound the warnings of St. Augustine, Zechariah, and Buddha (whose Fire Sermon provides the title), who call for transcendence of the spirit over the flesh, and heavenly love instead of bodily lust.

Part IV. Death by Water. As throughout the poem, water is the symbol of life regeneration, but to many the womb of life has proved their tomb.

Part V. What the Thunder Said. The betrayal and crucifixion of Christ keynote the depths of despondency and hallucinatory pangs for life-giving rain in a parched land. His mind almost broken from pain and delirium, the quester (Parsifal) finally reaches the Chapel Perilous, and the rains now come. From the thunder God announces the disciplines for life: Datta (give), Dayadhvam (sympathize), Damyata (control). Although the path to a new and fruitful life is proffered, the concluding lines remind us that modern society is still marooned in the waste land.

Homage to John Dryden (1924) (P) collected the essays published since *The Sacred Wood.*

"John Dryden" (1921) has been instrumental in furthering the 20th-century's admiration for Dryden. Dryden is favorably compared with Milton and especially praised for his range and precision.

"The Metaphysical Poets" (1921) more than any other single work has established this age's regard for Donne and his successors. In a famous phrase, "dissociation of sensibility," Eliot sees all poetry since the metaphysicals as sundering thought and feeling.

"The Function of Criticism" (1923) specifies the critic's task as "the elucidation of works of art and the correction of taste." Eliot supports classicism, "Outside Authority," against the Romantic reliance upon the "Inner Voice."

Poems 1909–1925 (1925) collected the previous verse and printed the following poem:

"The Hollow Men" (1924–25) takes its title from Shakespeare's *Julius Caesar*. Like the Old Guy (straw figure of Guy Fawkes used by English children to solicit pennies for fireworks on November 5), modern men are effigies stuffed with straw. The beginning and the conclusion present a church service, vitiated for our age by the loss of meaning to the communicant. Instead of the heavenly rose of Dante, the prickly cactus is the reality of today's hollow men. The Shadow of paralyzed will thwarts the agonized monologuists, depicting the world as ending "Not with a bang but a whimper."

SECOND PERIOD (1927–   ). In 1928 Eliot proclaimed himself "an Anglo-Catholic in religion, a classicist in literature, and a royalist in politics." Instead of the earlier cynical and nihilistic skeptic, he now emerges as the restrained asserter of penitential hope and faith in what his essay on Dante terms "a coherent traditional system of dogma and morals."

Dante (1929) (P) augments a shorter essay of the same title in *The Sacred Wood*. Eliot has proved the most important influence in establishing today's high reputation of Dante in the English-speaking world. As a pure poet (impersonal, objective), Dante employed the cultural framework of Western society to create an orderly world standing apart from Dante the man.

Ash-Wednesday (1930) completed publication of a work printed as excerpts in periodicals from 1927. Inspired by Dante's *Purgatorio*, the poet prayerfully mounts the ascending spiral of purgatory, hoping in humility and penance to cleanse himself of the world and to focus his life upon God. The first of Eliot's poems to be wholly pervaded by Christian acceptance bears striking resemblance to the Middle English *Cloud of Unknowing*, with its yearning for mystic union with God. The words of Church ritual echo through this penitential plea on the first day of Lent.

Part I. Renouncing all earthly things, the penitent waits passively, seeking salvation but not deeming himself of any worth; all rests upon the decision of God.

Part II. Asking the intercession of Our Lady, the poet proffers himself as dry bones of faith, stripped of all worldly attributes. The bones sing that the loss of fleshly desires and of life itself is no deprivation but offers surpassing joy in the Paradise of divine love.

Part III. The loveliness of the physical world tempts the poet, who in shamed humility cries to God that he is unworthy.

Part IV. The poet pleads with Our Lady to redeem our sinful and oblivious era, and to bring him to God. She offers him encouragement.

Part V. In the last stages of purgatory, in the agony of affirmation and denial, the poet perceives God as the Unmoved Mover at the heart of the universe, even if flesh-shrouded man knows Him not. Again he seeks Our Lady's intercession.

Part VI. Now, at consummation, he calls for Our Lady's help in submitting his will unreservedly in calm passivity to the divine will.

Realizing that in our age it is extremely difficult for an individual fully to accept any belief, Eliot honestly records his sense of tension and wavering. Fulfilling his own criterion of poetry, he expresses not what he would like to feel but what he genuinely does feel.

The Use of Poetry and the Use of Criticism (1933) (P) reinforces Eliot's earlier contentions about the role of criticism and considerably amplifies his scrutiny of the poetic process. Poetry arises from the interplay of the conscious and the unconscious within the poet. Though frequently the pressure of inner incubation (commonly termed "inspiration") compels the writer to relieve internal tension and counter the dullness of his everyday living, the greatest of poetry imposes structure and poetic form upon the expression.

Murder in the Cathedral (1935) (D) was prepared for the Canterbury Festival of 1935 for original performance in the very cathedral where Becket was slain. The six published versions display only minor differences except for the film version (1952), which offers extensive though not monumentally significant additions. The 1951 British motion picture is certainly the most sumptuous and impressive cinema treatment of a 20th-century poetic drama.

The title is misleading, for the actual subjects are the spiritual condition of a churchman facing martyrdom, the spiritual education of the witnesses to martyrdom, and the unwarranted secular usurpation of spiritual powers. Archbishop Becket, as protagonist, is torn between acting and suffering.

Part I portrays the inner sufferings of Becket and his refusal to act. The chorus of women and the cathedral priests see Becket as their defense against arbitrary rule by the monarch. In the fashion of a medieval morality play, the temptations in the mind of the archbishop are represented by four Tempters: worldly pleasure and worldly success, temporal power, statesmanship to protect the visible church, and, most vexatious, pride in martyrdom ("to do the right deed for the wrong reason").

The prose Christmas Day sermon by Becket binds the two parts of the drama as the archbishop reconciles the irreconcilables by wholly submitting his will to the will of God, "the eternal design." Perfect serenity at the heart of the play balances the mental suffering of the first part and the physical suffering of the second part.

Part II bridges to December 29 and the slaying of Becket by four Knights, as he willingly suffers because of the actions of others. The killers attempt to justify their act to the audience: their act was unselfish, Becket had set the church against the state and thereby caused national disunity, Becket's determination to suffer martyrdom made him a madman committing suicide. The chorus recognizes, however, that Becket died for the sins of man. By his redemptive blood, fertility is restored to the waste land, and "the eternal design" is securely ordained.

Form largely follows ancient Greek tragedy. Versification is frequently modeled upon the medieval morality *Everyman.* Deliberately poetic and usually liturgical, the verse ranges adroitly from lyricism to suave argument. The success of this work encouraged Eliot to devote most of his later verse to the drama and to the same theme—the elevation of society by the example of the spiritually élite.

The Idea of a Christian Society (1939) (P) propounds the Eliot theory of the Christian community as constituting the "guardians," whose task is to initiate others into lives of service and illumination. This thesis runs through his subsequent dramas.

The Music of Poetry (1942) (P) chiefly asserts the following concepts:

(1) Poetic music is not "melody" but the harmony of words in ordered significance.

(2) The poet must obtain his music from the potentials of ordinary current speech. Eliot sees the poet as *explorer* in his return to common speech or as *consolidator* in perfecting the new diction. Shakespeare is cited for the relatively rare dual role of both *explorer* and *consolidator.*

(3) Metrical form must underlie even the "freest" verse, for poetic music is tension between meaning and sound.

Four Quartets (1943) brought together four complex poems, published originally in periodicals over a period of six years. It presents the most significant non-dramatic verse of Eliot since *Murder in the Cathedral.* "Burnt Norton" (1936) takes its title from a country house at Ebrington, Gloucester, visited by Eliot in 1934. "East Coker" (1940) refers to the Somersetshire village from which Eliot's ancestors came. "The Dry Salvages" (1941) derives its title from a small outcropping of rocks off the coast of Cape Ann, Massachusetts, familiar to the poet from summer holidays in childhood. "Little Gidding" (1942) refers in title to the religious community established by Nicholas Ferrar in 1625, the first in the Church of England following the dissolution of the monasteries during the Reformation.

The four poems, based on musical structure, can be read on many levels. Among other things—including Eliot's own life and thought, and the nature of art—they deal with the revelation of the nature of God to man in time: in the first poem as God the Father (Air), (the source, the still point, the creator, the prime mover); in the second poem as God the Son (Earth), the Incarnation, the redeemer, the surgeon who is himself wounded; in the third, the feminine element, Saint Mary (Water) (the Middle Ages was the age of Our Lady); and in the fourth, the Holy Spirit (Fire) (whose age we are now in, according to some theologians). These four persons, and poems, form a quaternity, in the Jungian sense.

What Is a Classic? (1945) (P) defines a classic as the maximum success in realizing the potentials of a language within its limitations. Vergil is cited as a true classic, but generally the potentialities of a language are realized only in piecemeal fashion by many authors over an extended period. A culture must provide the facilities for a poet, and he must grasp and expound his culture fully.

Milton (1947) (P) arises from a 1936 essay in which Milton is denied the position of a classic because he created a completely individual idiom instead of elevating contemporary speech, but in the 1947 essay Eliot admits the beneficial influence of Milton while deploring imitation of his unorthodox handling of English.

Notes towards the Definition of Culture (1949) (P), though modest in title, effectively defines an all-important term. While culture may be considered in the individual or in the group, fundamental is the culture of the total society. The component elements of culture are: manners, knowledge (of all types), philosophy, the arts. Instead of an intellectual élite in a classless society, the best sustainer of high culture is a classed society, flexible enough, however, to permit the genuinely worthy to move upward to a higher class. Contending sub-cultures are acceptable as they create a healthful tension and stimulus.

The Three Voices of Poetry (1953) (P) classifies poetry as: (1) "the poet talking to himself or to nobody" (lyric), (2) "the poet addressing an audience" (non-dramatic verse of Dryden and Eliot), (3) "the poet when he attempts to create a dramatic character speaking in verse" (the plays of Shakespeare and Eliot).

PLAYS. *The Family Reunion* (1939) (D), Eliot's first drama for the secular stage, sets the pattern for his subsequent plays. While unalterable in his theological position, he shifts his tactics: the religious symbolism is concealed instead of openly preaching to worldly theatergoers, and the verse is purposely "unpoetic" partly because of the realistic conventions of today's theater but chiefly from Eliot's poetical theory (deriving a verse idiom from contemporary speech). As a "transitional" piece, however, and with strong parallels to ancient Greek tragedy, the verse of this drama shows many of the characteristic images of Eliot's non-dramatic poetry. Many critics see Eliot's poetic idiom as revolutionizing and revitalizing the otherwise sporadic and meager verse drama of this century.

At the ancestral estate of Wishwood, Amy, Lady Monchensey, awaits her three sons to complete the family reunion. Only Harry appears, pursued by the Eumenides of conscience, for he believes himself guilty of pushing his wife overboard on an Atlantic trip. His aunt Agatha reveals that Harry's father had plotted Amy's murder while she was pregnant with Harry. Harry departs on the eve of Lady Monchensey's death.

Harry corresponds to Orestes in the Aeschylus trilogy. Possibly no crime has been perpetrated, but in Christian fashion the intentions of both father and son are as evil as the deed (contrary to ancient Greek ascription of guilt solely to the evildoer). Instead of being the Divine Wrath of antiquity, the Eumenides are the Divine Love of conscience. Harry's departure at their direction is for his mother's redemption. The central concept is Harry's developing apprehension of spiritual election.

The Cocktail Party (1949) (D), deceptively comic in general handling, completely eschews any "poetic" effects in favor of a precise, lucid verse artfully intended to stir poetic awareness without making the audience painfully conscious that it hears poetry. There are considerable echoes from *Alcestis* by Euripides.

At his London flat Edward Chamberlayne lamely conceals from his cocktail guests that his wife Lavinia has left him because of his interest in Celia. Now he actually wants Lavinia back. The gin-drinking psychiatrist, Sir Henry Harcourt-Reilly, aids the Chamberlaynes to a viable marriage and encourages Celia to a life of devoted service. At their cocktail party two years later, the Chamberlaynes learn that Celia, working as a nurse in the tropics, has been killed in a native uprising.

On the surface this is a comedy of manners, but the actual subject is salvation for the entire group of characters. For the Chamberlaynes a patched-up marriage is their capacity and their achievement. Minor characters also achieve fulfilment within their capabilities. For the exceptional being, Celia, martyrdom in the service of mankind is her high calling. The Christian "guardian," Sir Henry, is the Unidentified Guest at the party, persuading each to do the will of God, for in His plan men and society are reborn, each as his measure permits.

The Confidential Clerk (1953) (D), though related to the *Ion* of Euripides, is Eliot's closest approximation to farce, perhaps because the play contains no such extraordinary characters as Harry or Celia. A tangled web of family relationships, confusing the parentage of all the young, reveals the Divine Father of all.

The Elder Statesman (1958) (D), indebted to the *Oedipus at Colonus* by Sophocles, is Eliot's nearest approach to melodrama. Lord Claverton, after a long and distinguished public career, realizes in retirement that he is a "hollow man," a failure in his private life, haunted by guilt for his sins. His acceptance of responsibilites and his free assumption of an unprecedented altruism permit his serene death.

OTHER MODERNIST POETS

Dame **Edith Sitwell** (1887–   ). Born at Scarborough, Edith Sitwell is the daughter of Sir George Sitwell and is the sister of Osbert and Sacheverell Sitwell. The family has held the superb estate Renishaw (in Derbyshire) for over six centuries. Dame Edith was educated privately after informing her startled parents that she intended to be a genius. In opposition to Georgian poetry she edited the annual *Wheels* (1916–18, 1921). Her hostility to the vulgar modern world in part inspired her critical study of *Alexander Pope* (1930), one of her own favorite works. In 1954 she became a Dame of the British Empire, and also became a convert to Roman Catholicism. Although she had previously written novels, few were prepared for the impressive panorama of *The Queens and the Hive* (1962), fictionalized biography brilliantly depicting the personalities surrounding Elizabeth I and centering upon the theme of sacrifice of personal happiness in the national welfare. This was a sequel to her *Fanfare for Elizabeth* (1946).

First period (to 1929) made her perhaps the most talked-about English poet of this century, culminating in a spectacular 1922 poetry reading in London's Aeolian Hall. In reaction to Georgian bucolics and the banal horrors of our century she produced a "non-representational" verse parallel to the work of contemporary pictorial artists such as Picasso and the Cubists. Notably in *Façade* (1922) she reveled in a fantastic dream world of sensuous mood and tonal patterns, perhaps the nearest thing in English to the "pure poetry" envisaged by Continental theorists.

Second period (1929–40) parallels the aggressive mood of Eliot in his *The Waste Land. Gold Coast Customs* (1929) drops the unreal beauty of her early verse for a savage denunciation of modern society. The cannibal world of African natives is the image for a far more darkened "civilized" world of heartless hypocrisy, futility, and cruelty.

Third period (1940 to present) finds her turning, like Eliot, to traditional faith and the bulwark of the Church. *The Shadow of Cain* (1946) sees mankind emerging from the primordial glacial age as the Tiger and the Bird (the exploiters and the exploited). The spiritual cleavage culminates in the atomic bombing of Hiroshima. From terrible suffering and inhumanity the poet hopes to see man's rise to love and unity in faith.

Richard Aldington (1892–   ). A native of Hampshire, Richard Aldington was educated at Dover College and London University. Military service in World War I. Married to the American poet Hilda Doolittle ("H.D.") from 1913 to 1937, he resided in America and in several European countries. His diverse literary talents have featured novels, many excellent trans-

lations from classic and modern languages, and in later years certain widely
discussed debunking biographies.

Images, Old and New (1915) established Aldington as the leading practitioner of the Imagist school in England, largely from the influence of Ezra
Pound. His free verse concentrated upon sharp pictures and incisive language corresponding to the Imagist credo. *A Fool i' the Forest* (1925) in its
despairing mood and poetic dissonances resembles *The Waste Land.*

Dylan Marlais Thomas (dil'en) (1914–1953). Born at Swansea, Wales,
Dylan Thomas was educated at the local grammar school. Hackwork
journalism occupied him until the quick response to his poems in 1934.
His health not permitting military service, he worked for the B.B.C. during
World War II. Most of his life was spent at Laugharne, S.W. Wales. He died
in New York during one of his frequent tours of this country for lecturing
and poetry reading. Since the beginning of mechanical recordings there
has probably been no reader of poetry to equal him.

More than the British, the Americans were fascinated by Thomas. He
was the bourgeois image of a poet—magnificently bibulous, blasphemous,
and bardic. His wild intensity gripped the common reader, and his surrealistic imagery appealed to the literati. In an era when most poetry
seemed austere and coldly cerebral, he could generate powerful excitement
through volcanic energy and eloquence. Much of his freshness springs from
native sources, though he knew very little Welsh. Erudite analysts have
probably overstated Thomas' intellectuality. His preoccupation with birth,
death, and the life force is an immemorial concern of poets, not the invention of Freud. The Authorized Version of the Bible provides much of his
phrasing, and Hopkins is the strongest influence upon his poetic technique.
Poems follow the order in *Collected Poems* (1953):

Eighteen Poems (1934), containing some of his most successful work,
belongs by the poet's own statement to his "womb-tomb period."

"The Force That through the Green Fuse Drives the Flower" (1933)
made Thomas famous. The forces compelling the growth and decay of men
are those same forces operating in outside Nature. We live and die by bewildering contraries and parallels. The first two lines of each stanza employ regular scansion, while the two concluding lines of each stanza are
Hopkins-type counterpointing.

"Especially When the October Wind" discusses the creative and ener-
vating process of poetry writing. October, the month of the poet's birth,
heralds death and symbolizes time. Like an ancient Welsh bard at incanta-
tion, the poet with painful effort constructs words and images as citadels of
life against death.

"When, like a Running Grave" is a young man's dilemma between head
and heart, desire and frustration. Time will conquer through death, but live
and act today in spite of life's aching contradictions.

Twenty-five Poems (1936) contains verse written at much the same time and in the same spirit as those in the previous volume.

"I, in My Intricate Image" (1935) examines the nature of man in which flesh and spirit war. Neither power should be subordinated within man, for their fusion and free play will open up to vigorous, triumphant life.

"The Hand That Signed the Paper" (*1933*, 1935), one of Thomas' clearest poems, is perhaps the most ringing condemnation in all English poetry of any form of tyranny.

"And Death Shall Have No Dominion" (1933), his earliest published poem, is lyric ecstasy celebrating resurrection. All shall be saved in spite of life's pain and even if faith itself is lost.

"Altarwise by Owl-light" consists of ten sonnets (though irregularly rimed and even with sestets preceding octaves). No other Thomas poem has aroused such extensive and contradictory interpretation. A modest appraisal suggests that the sonnets survey the poet's life from begetting to initial publication of verse, and the dominant theme seems to be a reconciliation of the creative and destructive aspects of sexuality. Many readers believe that Thomas is affirming confidence in Christ's mercy amid a chaotic world, though the poet is generally the celebrator of life rather than God.

The Map of Love (1939) marks an emergence into themes more specific and concrete. Marriage to Caitlin and the immanence of war have their effects.

"When All My Five and Country Senses See" (1938) implies that poetic vision arises from the heart and from the senses, not from the mind. Though the senses and love will alter, love will endure.

Deaths and Entrances (1946) contains probably the most powerful poems by Thomas, bred of the horribly real war years and intense personal experience.

"A Refusal to Mourn the Death, by Fire, of a Child in London" (1945) majestically employs religious imagery for a purely humanistic and secular consolation. The child's death during a German fire-bombing fits her into the cosmic plan of destruction and renewal.

"Poem in October" (1945), another birthday piece, is perhaps the poet's most buoyant, smoothly flowing verse. The beauty of the world and the adult's screened view of childhood convince him that human life offers ample joy and certitude.

"Do Not Go Gentle into That Good Night" was occasioned by the fatal illness of the poet's father in 1945. With remarkable skill he employs the villanelle for an impassioned plea for life assertion right to the moment of extinction.

"In My Craft or Sullen Art" (1945) is a poetic manifesto that looks in its very coolness and precision a riposte to Yeats's "Sailing to Byzantium."

"Among Those Killed in the Dawn Raid Was a Man Aged a Hundred" (1941) is an almost regular sonnet singing of death and resurrection. The ironic jest of a bombing raid killing a man doomed to early death produces a metaphysical wit of joyous sorrow.

"Ballad of the Long-legged Bait" (1941), though highly puzzling, is explained by the poet himself as the sexual wantoning of a boy that eventually turns to sober maturity and responsibility.

"Holy Spring" (1945), as the poet wakes in springtime after a night of air raids, greets the morning sun as a symbol of life and poetry, defying the dark world of death.

In Country Sleep (1952) shows Dylan Thomas at his mellowest. The major poems of this collection were intended as parts of a long poem, "In Country Heaven," but the poet's premature death intervened.

"In Country Sleep" (1947) is a father's poem for his daughter. He wishes her to emerge from childish fears to a consciousness that "In Nature there is nothing melancholy" and from childish unawareness to a realization that death is a co-operative element in Nature's scheme.

"In the White Giant's Thigh" (1950) observes the fecundity principle overriding all. Even though sterile themselves, the bearers of the life force will by their unceasing efforts at life carry on the great cycle. Thomas conceived of the White Giant as one of the several chalk figures cut in British turf, but this fertility god seems the poet's imagining.

Under Milk Wood (1954), first performed on the B.B.C. after the author's death, is not so much a radio drama as a poetic mood painting of an imaginary Welsh town, Llaregyb (originally "Llareggub," which in reverse is a British impropriety). The theme suggests the concealed naughtiness behind the façade of Welsh piety and respectability. Thomas indicates his preference for those who follow the life force rather than Mrs. Grundy. Its chief interest lies in the verbal ingenuity and pyrotechnics.

Adventures in the Skin Trade and Other Stories (1955) collects the most important prose fiction of Thomas. Instead of the conventional Aristotelian plotting, he offers wildly poetic mood pictures employing the themes of his verse. The title piece imaginatively portrays in the person of Samuel Bennet young Thomas himself first swept into the human maelstrom of London. According to Vernon Watkins, seven skins, allegorical of the layers of life, were to be stripped away successively, leaving Bennet in naked disillusion. The frenetic gaiety of the three written chapters (*c. 1941*) ill accorded with the poet's somber tone generated by the war, and the work was therefore left incomplete.

George Granville Barker (1913–   ). George Barker was born in Loughton, Essex. He attended the Marlborough Road School and the Regent Street Polytechnic in London, but quit school at fourteen to pass through a wide variety of jobs from automobile mechanic to wallpaper designer. His first volume of poetry in 1933 caused him to be the youngest poet anthologized in Yeats's *Oxford Book of Modern Verse* (1936). In 1939 Barker lectured on English literature at the Imperial Tohoku University in Japan, and in the next year began an American residence that lasted until 1943. Since then he has resided at Haslemere, Surrey.

Collected Poems (1957) includes most of Barker's verses. In sex and religion—his favorite themes—he experiences only blinding ecstasy or terrible agony. His forte is daring, unexpected fireworks in imagery and words. The earlier Barker poems react bitterly to the hardships and instability of his formative years. Less personal, later verse in "Channel Crossing" can rise to prophetic grandeur in contemplating the diminished stature of England. Omitted at the request of his fastidious publishers, *The True Confession of George Barker* (1950) explores sexuality with a scatology and loathing of bodily functions matched in English only by Swift. Like Dylan Thomas, Barker is enraged and entranced by the chaotic paradoxes of life and human nature.

David Emery Gascoyne (1916–   ). A native of Harrow, David Gascoyne was educated at Salisbury Cathedral Choir School and the Regent Street Polytechnic. He resided for some years in France and briefly in America.

Poems (1948) reveals Gascoyne as the most surrealistic poet in English. In 1935 he published *A Short Survey of Surrealism*, arising from his study of the movement while in France. His poems are characterized by vehement hostility to the bourgeois world, a powerful release of unconscious associations, and an exploration of hidden guilts and horrors. More than any other "modernist" he achieves a tragic vision of poetry as a helpless defiant gesture against a hostile universe. Militating against him, however, is his lack of splendid phrase.

Night Thoughts (1956) was commissioned by the B.B.C. for radio première in 1955. This poetic mood piece resembles Thomson's "City of Dreadful Night" in its denunciation of a blighted London.

NEW SIGNATURES POETS

Certain important modern English poets are referred to together as the New Signatures poets or New Country poets because their works were largely introduced in the volumes *New Signatures* (1932) and *New Country* (1933).

In *A Hope for Poetry* (1933) C. Day Lewis specified Hopkins, Owen, and Eliot as the "immediate ancestors" of these poets; D. H. Lawrence and the later Yeats also influenced them. Marx and Freud held sway in their politics and psychology. The New Signatures poets followed the modernists with the important difference of a fervid Marxist propaganda line.

These were not proletarians but bourgeoisie who had suddenly discovered the dustman to be a human being bedeviled with a similar libido. Scorning "luxury poetry," these poets wrote a slangy idiom employing extensive references to everyday life in order to achieve a new virility and a contact with the general reading public. Their militant left-wing politics combined with Eliot symbolism prevented them, however, from gaining much of an appeal beyond the highbrows. They also have tended to become far less radical in verse and politics as they have aged.

Wystan Hugh Auden (1907–   ). Son of a York physician, W. H. Auden was educated at Christ Church, Oxford. After travels in Germany, he settled down as a schoolmaster and poet until the Spanish Civil War induced him to serve on the Loyalist side as an ambulance driver. In 1935 he married Erika Mann, daughter of Thomas Mann, and in 1937 he received King George's Gold Medal for Poetry. In 1939 he established residence in the United States and became an American citizen in 1946. The Pulitzer prize of 1948 was awarded to Auden's *The Age of Anxiety* (1947) and in 1953 he received the Bollingen poetry prize. Since 1950 he has taught at the University of Michigan, Swarthmore, Smith College, and Oxford University.

The most protean figure in 20th-century poetry, Auden seems capable of everything except dullness. The very brilliance and quick-darting mind of Auden have bewildered readers and critics, and have apparently prevented any consistent, long-sustained work; but Auden certainly appears to be the most important poet born in England proper during this century.

BRITISH PERIOD (TO 1940). The earlier verse of Auden seems largely the improvisation of a youthful genius, often inspired by current political events or purely personal encounters. Pervasive is a condemnation of the middle-class failure to create the good society and a plea for the ideal communist state. Here is the archetype of the left-wing intellectual.

Poems (1930) tolls the knell of a doomed civilization, haunted by the death wish and symbolized in ruined factories and ripped-up railway tracks. Most powerful are "XVI," an extended meditation on growth and dissolution in modern culture, and the concluding sonnet, "Petition," with its plea for "a change of heart" to build a new world.

The Orators, an English Study (1932) seeks to create a romantic male solidarity among gifted, discontented young men in a period of social decay. Leaning heavily upon the psychoanalyst Georg Groddeck, Auden sees the modern disease and death wish of society as psychological.

Look, Stranger! (1936, American title *On This Island*) is perhaps the most Marxian of Auden's collections. In the class war he derides a decaying middle-class society but realizes the difficulties of the revolutionary in the conflicting pulls of man between security and a change for the better.

Letters from Iceland (1937), in collaboration with MacNeice, includes the brilliant "Letter to Lord Byron," using a seven-line modification of the *Don Juan* stanza. Auden has often been termed the 20th-century Byron because of his similar diatribes against stuffy English society and his insistence upon freedom, as well as a parallel verve and gentlemanly offhandedness. The contemporary poet rivals the wit and topicality of his predecessor, especially in the wry, autobiographical Part IV.

Journey to a War (1939), in collaboration with Isherwood, contains Auden's sonnet sequence "In Time of War," perhaps his most impressive sustained effort. Though man has spent centuries increasing knowledge of himself and his physical surroundings, he is sick and unhappy because he has learned in theory and not in fact.

Another Time (1940) is perhaps the most dazzlingly varied single volume of verse from any English poet. The amount and facility of his light verse (he also edited the *Oxford Book of Light Verse*, 1938) have caused some, like Robert Graves, to label Auden as primarily a writer of light verse. Villanelles and sestinas jostle with street ballads and syncopated "blues." Experiments in syllabic scansion, in assonance and consonance, clash with heroic couplets. The collection also includes perhaps the only true love poetry (notably "Lay your sleeping head, my love") from Auden and, especially, the majestic "In Memory of W. B. Yeats," proclaiming the efficacy of poetry to solace mankind amid our catastrophic century.

AMERICAN PERIOD (SINCE 1940). Auden's move to America has effected such a change, or at least change of emphases, in his work that his later period properly belongs wholly to American literature. An 18th-century formalism and a growing respect for tradition inform his later pieces. His tone tends toward greater evenness and sobriety, with less puzzling allusions and constructions. The class struggle and the communist ideal have vanished from his verse, and his position has become essentially that of the uncommitted Christian intellectual. Without espousal of any sect, he has apparently accepted a moderate Protestant viewpoint, seeing salvation as an individual rather than a collective problem. Faith and spiritual love for the brethren are the advocacies of *The Age of Anxiety* (1947), a "baroque" dialogue among four speakers that bids fair to bequeath its title as a label for our entire era.

Stephen Harold Spender (1909–). Son of a London journalist, Stephen Spender published his first volume of poetry, *Nine Experiments* (1928), the year after entering University College, Oxford. As an undergraduate he completed the group of noteworthy young Oxford poets that included Louis MacNeice (with whom he edited *Oxford Poetry* in 1929) and C. Day Lewis, with Auden as leading figure. After friendships on the continent with Christopher Isherwood in Germany and André Malraux in Spain, he returned to London as co-editor of *Horizon*. During the war he worked for the Foreign Office and served as a fireman during the blitz. Since World

War II he has become an unofficial ambassador of modern letters, especially to America. Since 1953 he has been co-editor of *Encounter*. His autobiography, *World within World* (1951), may be the classic portrayal of the idealistic intellectual during the 1930s and 1940s, and *The Struggle of the Modern* (1963) pinpoints the intellectual's view after midcentury.

Spender has often been termed the modern Shelley, the idealist as rebel lyricist. In Shelleyan fashion his early devotion to communism arose from a deeply sensitive concern for contemporary suffering and a fervent hope for a utopian future. *Life and the Poet* (1942) renounces communism in favor of the cultivation of art in individual experience. While some critics have deprecated Spender, his lucid, pulsatingly emotional lyricism has probably made him the general reading public's favorite among the New Signatures poets.

Collected Poems, 1928–53 (1954) shows Spender at his weakest in collectivist propaganda and at his strongest in lyric contemplation of the machine age and man's painful lot.

"The Express" (1933) defies the bucolics of Georgian poetry to proclaim that the steam engine can surpass in beauty the familiar nature symbols of poetry. This is probably the best of Spender's impassioned tributes to the products of this mechanical era.

"The Pylons" (1933) sees electric power lines as promising the brave new cities of the future, disdainfully shouldering aside the picturesque past and picturesque landscape.

"Not Palaces, an Era's Crown" (1933) is Spender's most successful revolutionary poem, intensely earnest in its cry for an end to human hunger, inequality, and exploitation.

"I Think Continually" (1933) is possibly the best tribute in English to military aviators.

"Ultima Ratio Regum" ("The last argument of kings," inscribed on the cannons of Louis XIV) (1939) calls war cruel financial rivalry pointlessly destroying the lives of simple, harmless people.

"The Double Shame" (1942) indicates a turn to more personal lyricism. The twofold shame is, first, not loving enough, second, then loving too much. The sharply etched scene is grief for a departed loved one.

"Responsibility: The Pilots Who Destroyed Germany, Spring, 1945" (1949) works upon the psychic tension of mixed joy in Germany's destruction from the air and regret for the horrible slaughter of fellow human beings.

Louis MacNeice (mak-nēs') (1907–1963). Louis MacNeice was born in Belfast, son of the Anglican bishop of Down, Connor, and Dromore. After a brilliant career at Merton College, Oxford, he was appointed lecturer in classics at Birmingham University in 1930. Traveling widely, he was lecturing at Cornell in 1941 when the Battle of Britain caused his return to England. From 1941 to 1949 he wrote and produced radio broadcasts for the B.B.C. Since the war he has continued extensive writing and lecturing, especially in radio drama (*The Dark Tower*, 1946, is a notable collection of radio scripts).

Collected Poems (1949) displays the easiest colloquial tone and most casual manner of the group. Unlike his colleagues, MacNeice has experienced relatively few changes. He never became genuinely attached to communism, and he has managed to retain remarkably similar viewpoints throughout his writing. Always he has been the sensitive intellectual protesting the world's disorder but offering no panacea. As in the powerful "Prayer before Birth," where he demands freedom for the individual, he is skeptical of the Welfare State and of all systems. In *Solstices* (1961) his is still a voice for the self-constituted personality in an ever-narrowing society.

Goethe's Faust (1951) is probably the most effective verse translation of the German work by a British author. Only the C. F. MacIntyre translation can so adequately convince the English reader of the greatness of the original. MacNeice cuts almost one third, since the work was intended for the B.B.C. Goethe celebration.

Cecil Day Lewis (1904–). Son of an English clergyman in Ballintober, Queen's County (now Leix), Ireland, C. Day Lewis is a descendant on his mother's side of Oliver Goldsmith. The family moved to England when the poet was only three, and by six he was already writing poetry. At Wadham College, Oxford, he was particularly interested in Latin poetry; he published *Beechen Vigil and Other Poems* (1925) while still an undergraduate, and in 1927 was co-editor with Auden of *Oxford Poetry*. He taught in English and Scottish schools until World War II, when he worked for the Ministry of Information. Since the war he has lectured widely on poetry and served as director of the publishing house of Chatto and Windus. To supplement the meager financial rewards of poetry he has written expert detective stories under the pseudonym of Nicholas Blake.

Collected Poems (1954) demonstrates the pilgrimage of Day Lewis. His earlier work is Georgian, followed by radical propaganda verse, the most perfervid leftist of the New Signatures poets. His 1930s verse rings the changes on the symbols of "kestrel" (imagination), "airman" (liberating poet), and "magnetic mountain" (the communist co-operative society). Before World War II, however, he had found his true vein in lyricism, reminiscent of Hardy and Meredith. His later verse has proved singularly clear and competent, more consistent than that of other New Signatures poets.

The Eclogues of Virgil (1963) brings to conclusion the long task of the poet in translating the whole of Vergil (*Georgics*, 1941; *Aeneid*, 1952). The six-stress line (with occasional "bob-lines") permits a faithful line-by-line translation, probably the best in English. Dryden's famous translation (better a "re-creation") is baroque splendor, while Day Lewis accurately catches the occasional colloquial ("if you've time to take a breather") and homey touches of Vergil. Dryden created a monument, but Day Lewis has created a moving version by which Vergil speaks to our age in our idiom.

Christopher Isherwood (full name **Christopher William Bradshaw-Isherwood**) (1904–   ). Christopher Isherwood was born at High Lane, Cheshire. After Corpus Christi College, Cambridge, and medical training at King's College, London, he taught English in Berlin, 1930–33. Back in England he collaborated with Auden in three dramas and accompanied Auden to China in 1938. Emigrating to the United States in 1939, he became an American citizen in 1946. His experiences in Germany were the basis for his notable novel *Prater Violet* (1945) and *The Berlin Stories* (1946). Since the 1940s he and Aldous Huxley have been deeply interested in Vedanta and oriental thought generally.

The Ascent of F. 6 (1937), a drama partly in verse and partly in prose, is the most impressive of the Auden-Isherwood collaborations.

Because the natives believe that the first white man to conquer the mountain F. 6 will rule them for a thousand years, Michael Ransom heads a party of climbers. The Abbot of a monastery upon the lower slopes urges Ransom to renounce power and will, but he pushes upward even though three members of his group perish. At the summit just before he expires he finds a Veiled Figure, who proves to be his mother. As a counterpoint Mr. and Mrs. A. in England, envying the adventurous quest of Ransom, bemoan their humdrum lot.

Many subjects engage the authors: imperialism, newspaper distortion of facts, bourgeois society. The major problem, however, is Ransom's dilemma. Power seems inevitably to bring corruption, yet the renunciation of will results in nullity and is itself a form of self-pride. Each of the climbers has a different but equally wrong-headed reason for his effort. With all the complex problems posed, the climax appears weak in its mother-fixation, a Freudian explanation for all Ransom's strivings; Michael has chiefly yearned to displace his brother James in his mother's affections.

OTHER TWENTIETH-CENTURY POETS

THE SCOTTISH RENAISSANCE

The Victorian doldrums of Scottish vernacular verse have been swept away by the vigorous upsurge in the 20th-century of Lallans ("Lowlands") poetry. Scottish poets, like Edwin Muir, writing London English are considered elsewhere. Here we will treat the first significant Lallans verse since Burns. The Scottish Literary Revival forms part of the 20th-century separatist movement in Scotland, politically centered in the Scottish National Party, founded in 1928. Unlike the parallel separatist drive in Wales, the Scottish impulse has arisen not from the universities but from individual authors. Douglas Young (1913–   ) and Alexander Scott (1920–   ) have translated much Gaelic and London English verse into Lallans and have contributed commendable original Lallans verse. William Soutar (1898–1943), an invalid most of his life, has produced perhaps the most sensitive and reflective poetry ever written in Lallans. But the towering figure of 20th-century Lallans verse is:

Hugh MacDiarmid (real name Christopher Murray Grieve) (1892–   ). Born in Langholm, Dumfriesshire, Scotland, Hugh MacDiarmid became a socialist and member of the Independent Labour Party while at Edinburgh University. After graduation he was a labor journalist in Scotland and Wales. During World War I he served in the Royal Army Medical Corps in Greece, Italy, and France. His first published work, *Rural Reform* (1922), was a Fabian Society pamphlet. Always an unreconstructed rebel, he was expelled from the Scottish National Party (which he helped found) for joining the Communist Party, and then was expelled by the communists for advocating Scottish separation. In 1936 he received a national testimonial from virtually every prominent Scot hailing his devotion and accomplishments in Scottish letters and culture. From his Shetland Island home he issues forth periodically to excoriate the English far more scathingly than Dr. Johnson ever denounced the Scots. In *Who's Who* he lists Anglophobia as his sole recreation.

With heroic rage MacDiarmid belabors "all the touts and toadies and lickspittles of the English Ascendancy, and their infernal womenfolk, and all their skunkoil skulduggery." His career has been a one-man crusade to re-create an indigenous Scottish culture that nonetheless is European and world-wide in its viewpoint. As his pen name indicates, he conceives the essential Scottish character as Gaelic, with a "whole" response to life impossible to contemporary capitalism.

Collected Poems (1962) is chiefly written in "synthetic Scots," a modern adaptation of the "makaris," especially Dunbar, MacDiarmid's favorite Scots author (he despises the sentimental Burns cult as "pawky"). Like the New Signatures poets, MacDiarmid in the 1930s was a rabid communist, notably in "First Hymn to Lenin" (1931), foreseeing the inevitable triumph of Marxism. MacDiarmid's most remarkable achievement lies in the sequence of poems, *A Drunk Man Looks at the Thistle* (1926), where in drunkenness (counterpart of the medieval dream vision) a Scot ranges the whole spectrum of Scottish life with the swift changes of mood, wild grotesquerie, homey meditation, and robust realism peculiar to the Scots verse tradition. MacDiarmid's lyric gift produced the remarkable "Water

Music" (1934), which equals Joyce's paean to Anna Livia Plurabelle (though MacDiarmid naturally preferred the streams of Scotland). Untranslatable into London English, this poem utilizes the full melody of Lallans.

POETS OF WORLD WAR II

In contrast to the response of English poets in World War I, the second great upheaval of this century produced little agonized protest against war. Civilization and life were at fault, and there was virtually no diatribe against the Germans or the Japanese. To the combat poets, war was a brutal fact, another of the senseless ironies against the lonely individual of the age. Critics have suggested Alun Lewis (1915–44), killed in the Burma campaign, and Sidney Keyes (1922–43), killed in Tunisia, as the most accomplished of the war poets and the most tragic war loss to English poetry. The *Collected Poems of Keith Douglas* (1920–44) did not appear until 1951, when the interest in war poets had considerably waned, but his sinewy and concentrated power may eventually rate him highest among the poets of World War II.

NEW LINES POETS OR POETS OF "THE MOVEMENT"

A *Spectator* article of 1954 provided the vague label of "The Movement" for the most vocal of postwar poets, and the anthology *New Lines* (1956) offered another. This recent verse parallels "the theater of the absurd." Characteristic is a colloquial ease, allusion to the apparently trivial in everyday life, disillusioned and ironic self-scrutiny, and a calm acceptance of living as a mad, mad thing. Dropping any heroic or tragic view of life, these poets spin poetry out of the very inadequacy and pointlessness of modern existence. Unlike the New Signatures poets, the New Lines writers even in the flush of youth never had a utopian vision. Literary ancestry is extensive, but Eliot and Auden are the chief influences.

Philip Arthur Larkin (1922–   ). Philip Larkin was born in Coventry and educated there at the King Henry VIII School. At St. John's College, Oxford, he was a friend of Kingsley Amis. Since 1943 he has been a college librarian, chiefly at Hull University. Though his productivity is not extensive, he is the best known of the New Lines poets.

The Less Deceived (1955) has established Larkin's reputation. From this work he has been termed Auden's successor as Pope followed Dryden. Lacking the scope and versatility of his predecessor, he has proved within a limited range more precise and disciplined as a craftsman. "Church Going" has been frequently cited as the major example of New Lines verse. A skeptical contemporary in an era of withered faith wanders through an old church. After casual boredom he suggests in a solemn peroration no religious conviction but a quiet regeneration effected by a place where men for centuries have sought peace and solace. The absence of any poetic posturing and the presence of honest perception of today's everyday have made Larkin seem the genuine voice of poetry for this time.

The Whitsun Weddings (1964) maintains the same excellent craftsmanship as the preceding volume and establishes Larkin as the outstanding successor to Hardy. Like Hardy, Larkin dwells upon the poignant pointlessness of life and the ignominious ignorance of man, but far more than his master Larkin can stoically accept the grimness of change and decay.

Roy Broadbent Fuller (1912–   ). A native of Oldham, Lancashire, Roy Broadbent Fuller is an attorney by profession. He is a bridge between the New Signatures poets and "The Movement," his first volume, *Poems* (1939), echoing Auden. Fuller's wartime service (1941–46) with the Royal Navy produced one of the notable volumes of war verse, *The Middle of a War* (1942).

Collected Poems (1962) is strongest when Fuller follows the idiom of New Lines verse. Holding little or no hope for the future of mankind and no belief in personal immortality, he nonetheless counsels endurance and dignity. In "Expostulation and Inadequate Reply" and "To Posterity" Fuller finds somber grandeur in the prospect of man as a dying species upon a doomed planet. Like many of his fellows, Fuller seems a Hardy without the pain.

Donald Davie (1922–   ). Born in Barnsley, Donald Davie was educated at St. Catherine's College, Cambridge. After wartime service (1941–46) in the Royal Navy, he became a professor of English at Trinity College (Dublin), the University of California, and since 1938 at Cambridge.

Davie is a devoted admirer of 18th-century poetry as is demonstrated in *Brides of Reason* (1955). *A Sequence for Francis Parkman* (1961) in scrutinizing America's role in Western culture displays perhaps a larger grasp of history than that held by any other poet of the 1960s and reveals an experimental, independent spirit boding well for future poetic development.

TRADITIONALIST POETS

While few poets from the 1920s on have escaped the influence of the modernists, the following have trended to relatively traditional patterns or at least to an idiosyncratic style of writing which has alienated them from the modernists.

Edmund Charles Blunden (1896–   ). A native of Yalding, Kent, Edmund Blunden was educated at Christ's Hospital and Queen's College, Oxford. During World War I he served with distinction in the Royal Sussex Regiment, 1915–19. Between wars he taught at Oxford and Tokyo University. Since 1948 he has resided in Hong Kong, teaching English at the local university. In 1956 he was awarded the Queen's Gold Medal for Poetry. *Undertones of War* (1928) in prose takes its place with the most prominent of the antiwar autobiographies. Blunden has also written significant biographies of Lamb, Leigh Hunt, Hardy, and Shelley.

With surprisingly little change, Blunden's verse has treated of war and Nature from *Poems* (1914) to *A Hong Kong House* (1962). Early listed with the Georgian poets, he has consistently depicted not mere bucolics but a genuine countryman's Nature, often as gnarled in verse as the bent trees he loves. He seems more the poet of the immemorial landscape than the follower of any 20th-century school.

Edwin Muir (1887–1958). Edwin Muir was born at Deerness in the Orkney Islands of Scotland. Formal schooling ending at fourteen, he became a clerk in Glasgow. From 1921 to 1928 he lived on the continent, especially in Prague from whence issued his translations of Kafka, introducing that author to English readers. Until his later years Muir was regarded chiefly as a critic, especially for *The Structure of the Novel* (1928) and *Essays on Literature and Society* (1949).

Collected Poems 1921–58 (1960) reveals a poet who probably would have achieved major fame in another era, whose temper would run counter to ours. Muir's verse is reflective, not of modern tension and irony, but of "emotion recollected in tranquillity." Archetypal dreams and mythology rather than the pains of this century occupy him. Especially antipathetic to recent 20th-century poetry is his quiet optimism. He sees the powers of good as greater than those of evil, because goodness is more primordial, humble, and close to elemental simplicity. Militating against his revival is a thinness of lyricism, though his lines are commendably clean and smooth.

William Charles Franklyn Plomer (1903–). William Plomer was born at Pietersburg, North Transvaal, Africa. After education in England at Rugby, he roamed through South Africa, Japan, and Greece before settling down in England. Between 1940 and 1945 he served with the Royal Admiralty. For the coronation of Elizabeth II in 1953 he provided the libretto for *Gloriana*, an opera by Benjamin Britten.

Collected Poems (1960) offers Plomer as a leading 20th-century writer of light verse and poetic satire. His laughter at the smug Edwardians and Georgians and their seedy, run-down successors is barbed and witty. Unlike his English predecessors in this lively genre, his is the underlying conviction that the era is hopelessly rotten and man is "the self-destroyer."

John Betjeman (bet′je-men) (1906–). Of Dutch ancestry, John Betjeman was born in London and educated at Marlborough and Magdalen College, Oxford. Although at Oxford at the same time as the New Signatures poets, Betjeman was not of their group. Except for World War II service with the British government, he has been a free-lance writer with wide interests. As a founder of the Victorian Society, he has been perhaps the leading spirit in the resurrected English taste for Victorianism, especially in architecture. As a book reviewer for the *Daily Telegraph* and as a famed television personality, he has surpassed any other 20th-century poet as a public figure. In 1960 he received the Queen's Gold Medal for poetry.

Collected Poems (1958) has sold more copies to the British reading public than any other volume of poetry since Tennyson, and, except perhaps for Kipling, no other poet in England has gained so wide and sympathetic an audience since Tennyson. Reviewing the book, Larkin almost enviously notes that Betjeman writes as though Eliot, Empson, Leavis, and in fact all modern literature since the 1920s never existed. Betjeman, who has little appeal outside of Great Britain, sounds precisely the right notes to fascinate the British middle class. He pokes fun at the Welfare State and summons his readers nostalgically from the present of television commercials and neon movie signs to the (perhaps imaginary) paradise of pre-1914 England. Betjeman's passionate love for "Dear old, bloody old England" has endeared him to thousands who never read poetry before except in school.

Summoned by Bells (1960), the first installment of a projected autobiography in relaxed blank verse ("as near prose as he dare," admits Betjeman), carries the account of wistful memoirs from infancy to the author's first employment after graduation from Oxford. Probably this work will continue Betjeman's great popularity with the English.

NEO-ROMANTICS

The 1940s, perhaps largely from reaction against war's reality, witnessed a new romanticism from some British poets, who might best be described as Dylan Thomas without the "modernism."

Vernon Phillips Watkins (1906–   ). Born of Welsh-speaking parents in Maesteg, Wales, Vernon Watkins studied modern languages at Magdalen College, Cambridge. Except for service with the Royal Air Force during World War II, he has lived near Swansea, Wales, as a bank executive. A record of his friendship with Dylan Thomas appears in *Letters to Vernon Watkins by Dylan Thomas* (1957). Although writing verse since childhood, Watkins first published his poetry in *The Ballad of the Mari Lwyd* (1941).

The Lady with the Unicorn (1948), comprising most Watkins poetry to that date, is his best volume. Strongly influenced by Blake, Watkins seeks to interpret the visible world symbolically, the sensuous experience spiritually, thereby perceiving all things as transformed by the visionary power of imagination. Irony and humor, the modern world and its problems, are absent as he sings of birth, death, the cycles of Nature, and always the invisible world of which this world is an emblem.

John Francis Heath-Stubbs (1918–   ). A London native, John Francis Heath-Stubbs studied English at Queen's College, Oxford, where he was a friend of Sidney Keyes. He has taught English at Leeds University, Alexandria University in Egypt, and the University of Michigan. His wide-ranging interests have included anthologies and critical studies of Victorian and 20th-century literature, translations and adaptations from Sappho and Hafiz to Leopardi and Mallarmé.

The four volumes of Heath-Stubbs verse published between 1942 and 1950 are best described as academic romanticism, treating generally of art and literature of the past in a learned diction alien to the modern idiom and contemporary spirit. One of his most moving poems, "The Divided Ways," is an elegy to Sidney Keyes. His three subsequent volumes, especially *The Blue-Fly in His Head* (1962), display increasing vigor, approaching modern irony and colloquialism. Nonetheless, he remains an incongruous figure among today's intelligentsia poets, a moderate, orthodox Christian and a scholarly romantic.

TRANSLATIONS

In addition to the translations noted elsewhere, the following have been significant verse renderings of other languages into English.

Translation from the classic tongues into English proceeds apace, but much in this century offers English prose for the poetic originals or, as in the case of Maurice Hewlett's blank-verse *Iliad* (1928), receives high accolade upon publication only to fade within a few years. Among the most distinguished verse translations of this century are versions of the ancient Greek tragedies by Gilbert Murray (1866–1957), his earliest being *Hippolytus* by Euripides (1902) and his last *Prometheus Bound* by Aeschylus (1931).

The wealth of Chinese and Japanese literature, both in poetry and prose, has largely been revealed for the first time to English readers in this century by Arthur David Waley (1889–   ), beginning with *170 Chinese Poems* (1919). His translations are gems in their own right and have extensively influenced both English and American poets. Helen Waddell (1889–   ), born in Tokyo, actually preceded Waley with her *Lyrics from the Chinese* (1913) but her subsequent interests have turned to medieval Europe, producing a scholarly and artistic triumph of translation in *Medieval Latin Lyrics* (1929).

Famous as a writer of sophisticated detective novels, Dorothy L. Sayers (1893–1957) turned her interest in the 1940s to Dante and produced translations of the *Inferno* (1949), *Purgatorio* (1955), *Paradiso* (finished by Barbara Reynolds after Miss Sayers' death and published in 1962). Although the translation by the American poet John Ciardi appears the best poetic version for today's reader, Dorothy Sayers' meticulous translation aided by her lucid scholarly apparatus is probably the most revealing and satisfying re-creation of Dante for English readers.

Chapter 10

Prose of the Twentieth Century

LITERARY CRITICISM AND LITERARY SCHOLARSHIP

The most remarkable development in 20th-century prose has been so vast an increase in criticism as to justify the label "The Age of Criticism" for our era. It is no coincidence that T. S. Eliot, the most distinguished poet in 20th-century England, is almost as famed for criticism as for verse; he has indicated that he values the critical impulse about as highly as the creative impulse. As never before in English literature, novelists and poets have written extensively in criticism of other authors and have searchingly analyzed their own art. Philip Larkin, the poet, seems virtually unique among current writers in his unwillingness to scrutinize his artistic principles. Criticism has so proliferated that many observers protest that the public often reads more about an author's writings than it reads in the works themselves.

It is helpful in studying the major figures to group them according to the major schools of criticism, and within each school to follow an essentially chronological order.

IMPRESSIONISM. The approach of Pater, himself an academician, was sustained by a number of college dons at the turn of the century and shortly afterward. These gentlemen in relaxed fashion announced their literary judgments as "the word," based solely upon their own good taste. Although their voluminous tomes upon library shelves may still have influence, significant critics since World War I have almost universally deprecated these purely subjective criticisms.

George Edward Bateman Saintsbury (1845–1933). George Saintsbury read widely and published extensively from *Primer of French Literature* (1880) to *A Consideration of Thackeray* (1931). As a literary historian he still carries weight, especially in his studies of prosody, but his critical opinions, though delivered with unflagging gusto, are not greatly honored at present.

Oliver Elton (1861–1945). Oliver Elton in six volumes reviews the course of English literature from 1730 to 1880, an unmatched one-man job, trustworthy as long as he treads the road of factual presentation. After retirement his energy turned to Slavic studies, resulting in perhaps the best English translations of Pushkin (1935, 1938) and other Slavonic poets.

Sir **Arthur Thomas Quiller-Couch** (1863–1944). Arthur Quiller-Couch in his wide humanism and stimulating manner seemed the oracle of literary criticism in a host of works upon English literature since the Renaissance. But if the romantic "Q" is to be refurbished in reputation, his novels may turn the trick (in 1897 he was selected to finished Stevenson's incomplete *St. Ives*).

ROMANTICISM. It may well be claimed that the main line of English criticism is romantic, emphasizing the power of self-expression in literature and seeking therein the revelation of transcendental truth. Though decried by the newer critical schools, romanticism is the forte of two of the century's most prolific and influential critics.

John Middleton Murry (1889–1957). Son of a London clerk, John Middleton Murry was educated at Christ's Hospital and Brasenose College, Oxford. After journalistic apprenticeship he proved the distinguished editor of the *Athenaeum* (1919–21), the *Adelphi* (1923–48), and *Peace News* (1940–46). His first wife was Katherine Mansfield, whom he married in 1913 and whose works he edited after her death in 1923. They were connected with the D. H. Lawrence group.

Between *Fyodor Dostoevsky* (1916) and *Jonathan Swift* (1954) Murry averaged a book a year, perhaps most notably in the Keats volumes of 1925 and 1930. His approach was to seek a personal identification with an author and to examine the author's success in projecting into his writings his inward spirit. He proclaimed that literature is "what is good for man," and encouraged the fullest achievement of selfhood. In the contemporary world he has proved a somewhat incongruous platonist and humanist.

Sir **Herbert Edward Read** (1893–   ). Son of a farmer of Kirkby Moorside, Yorkshire, Herbert Read attended Leeds University. He served with notable bravery as an infantry officer in World War I. After work on the staff of the Victoria and Albert Museum (1922–31), he has lectured, edited, and written extensively upon art and literature. He is a pioneer in industrial art and has made commendable explorations in sociology, politics, and education.

The True Voice of Feeling (1953) is the fullest statement of Read's critical pronouncements, which extend from medieval stained glass to surrealism (of which he was a leading English supporter), with strong concentration upon the English Romantic poets. Elemental naturalness is his chief criterion of art, and he vigorously opposes the current emphasis upon imposed form, elevating, instead, inherent organic structure. Terming himself a "philosophic anarchist," he envisages the good society as conforming solely to "natural law," granting to each man ample scope for rich spiritual development. In an era derogating romanticism, he has been perhaps the most stalwart champion of Wordsworth, Shelley, and Byron.

Collected Poems (1946) and *Moon's Farm* (1955) show Read as a faithful follower of virtually every 20th-century trend, from Sassoon-like verse of World War I to recent poems resembling those of the "Movement." In poetry he has cultivated "the innocent eye" (also the title of his 1933 autobiography), making him fundamentally an Imagist of romantic leanings.

FACTUAL SCHOLARSHIP. On safer and surer ground, 20th-century academicians have labored devotedly to amass information casting light upon literary works. Although such effort has produced many doctoral dissertations of deadly dullness and dubious value, some scholars, conscious that they are supposed to deepen our comprehension of art itself, have added immensely to our understanding and appreciation.

Andrew Cecil Bradley (1851–1935). A. C. Bradley in *Shakespearian Tragedy* (1904) produced perhaps the most important single volume of Shakespearean criticism by an English scholar of this century. Bringing to consummation the school of character-analysis begun by Maurice Morgan in the 18th century, Bradley shows Shakespearean characters to be as true to life as any character in today's novels.

William Paton Ker (1855–1923). W. P. Ker revolutionized European concepts of the epic with *Epic and Romance* (1897) and subsequent volumes to his death. With an unprecedented knowledge of most of the world's literatures, including those of obscure primitive societies, he established the oral epic tradition as a pervasive tendency among all peoples in early cultural development. More than any other single scholar, he is responsible for establishing the sound historical basis for comparative literature.

Sir **Edmund Kerchever Chambers** (1866–1954). E. K. Chambers has often been rated as the greatest pure scholar of English letters. *The Mediaeval Stage* (1903), *The Elizabethan Stage* (1923), and *William Shakespeare* (1930) still remain the definitive factual studies of the English theater; although minor additions and corrections can be made, their solid substance remains unshaken.

Sir **Herbert John Clifford Grierson** (1866–1960). Herbert John Grierson as scholar and editor was responsible along with the critic T. S. Eliot for the 20th century's impressive revival of Donne and the metaphysical poets. From *The First Half of the Seventeenth Century* (1905) he has consistently written a graceful, fluent prose perhaps superior to that of any of his fellow scholars, except Tillyard. He has been a leader in the study of the history of ideas.

John Dover Wilson (1881–   ). Dover Wilson has utilized the remarkable new development of scientific bibliography (study of the physical creation of a printed book) in the New Cambridge edition of Shakespeare (1921–   ). In seeking to reconstruct the text from the time it left Shakespeare's hand until it emerged in the extant printed form, he exercises an imaginative boldness which sometimes dismays the conservative.

Eustace Mandeville Wetenhall Tillyard (1889–1962). In *Milton* (1930), interpreting Milton's poetry through the development of the poet's thought and emotion, E. M. W. Tillyard has largely determined the 20th-century evaluation of Milton. Equally thoughtful and balanced are his studies of Shakespeare and *The English Epic and Its Background* (1954).

Sir Cecil Maurice Bowra (1898–   ). Expert in ancient and modern languages, C. M. Bowra has proved the outstanding English authority upon the classics since *Tradition and Design in the Iliad* (1930), but his wide-ranging mind has explored contemporary literature with the same penetration.

Geoffrey Tillotson (1905–   ). Geoffrey Tillotson as editor and scholar is the chief authority upon Pope since *On the Poetry of Pope* (1938), helping to refurbish a reputation somewhat dimmed ever since the Romantics.

MARXIAN ANALYSIS. Repudiating aesthetic approaches, Marxian critics explore the social and political implications of literature and their dovetailing into the Marxian dialectic. For example, *Aeschylus and Athens* (1941) by G. D. Thomson examines the first great dramatist of Western society for his illumination of Athens' social evolution and class struggle. Marxism, however, has had meager appeal to the British. Their one significant Marxian critic has been Christopher Caudwell (pseudonym of Christopher St. John Sprigg, 1907–37), whose principal work, *Illusion and Reality* (1937), scrutinizes the whole realm of poetry to discover that it is generated by economics. The present low state of poetry is ascribed to the breakdown of bourgeois society, and communism is prescribed to stimulate and reunite economic and poetic productivity. While Caudwell's approach often yields impressive sociological insights, it also produces such bizarre interpretations as Shakespeare's Ariel termed "the free wage-labourer."

FREUDIAN ANALYSIS. The widespread conviction, especially French, that man is a victim of heredity and environment was fertile ground for the Freudian interpretation of a man as a victim of his own compulsive libido and social repressions. The study of the unconscious as manifested in literature and the search for sex symbols caused Dr. Ernest Jones as early as 1910 to propound a theory that after considerable reworking was published as *Hamlet and Oedipus* (1949), explaining Hamlet's delays as arising from Oedipal tendencies, a suggestion attractive to the 20th century no matter how much it might have startled Shakespeare. Since Freud, no critic can be unaffected by psychoanalytic theories, and much of the world's literature is dealt with in current professional journals of psychology. The most important English practitioner of this school is Geoffrey Gorer.

SEMANTIC ANALYSIS. It is in the area of semantic analysis that we come to the work of I. A. Richards, one of the most brilliant and influential of 20th-century critics.

Ivor Armstrong Richards (1893–   ). A native of Sandbach, Cheshire, I. A. Richards was educated at Magdalen College, Cambridge. After lecturing on English at Cambridge and in China, he established residence in America where he has been a Harvard professor since 1944. He is widely hailed as the "father of modern criticism."

The Foundations of Aesthetics (1922) in collaboration with C. K. Ogden and James Wood explores all theories of aesthetics and concludes by finding beauty an experience or state of being in the perceiver which confers synaesthetic balance. The entire basis for the subsequent criticism of Richards and for most other notable criticism of today is thus shifted from the previous poet-poem relationship to a poem-audience relationship. Precisely what does a work of art communicate to the beholder?

The Meaning of Meaning (1923), in collaboration with Ogden, lays the foundation for the now vast study of semantics. Seeking a science of linguistic communication, the authors developed an elaborate but now familiar terminology to determine how meaning about a "referent" (a non-verbal object, experience, or concept) is transmitted by the symbolism of words. The distinction between "symbolic" meaning of science (or factual prose generally) and the "emotive" or "evocative" meaning of poetry really parallels Mill's 19th-century distinction between "denotative" and "connotative" writing.

Principles of Literary Criticism (1924), by Richards' own statement, "endeavors to provide for the emotive function of language the same critical foundation" as provided for "symbolic" in the previous work. Generally recognized as the most important single critical work of this century, it seeks a scientific (psychological) basis for ascertaining the meaning of poetry. Poetic meaning transcends sense alone and necessitates an understanding of intention, tone, and aura of feeling; Richards brushes aside the time-honored paraphernalia of history, biography, and all other background apparatus for examining a poem, and demands a thorough dissection of the poem solely as it stands. "Anything is valuable that satisfies an appetency," and the greatest success of a poem consists in satisfying the maximum of appetencies while offering the minimum of frustrations to other appetencies. The ideal poem creates in the reader the fullest possible balance or patterning of impulses.

Practical Criticism (1929), applying the theory of the previous volume, is hailed as the basic work in contemporary objective criticism. Its aim is the general improvement of reading comprehension and therefore a general increase in literary appreciation. Asking Cambridge students to read wholly unidentified poems, Richards discovered lamentable blundering in interpretation. He counterpoints their stumblings by precise semantic analysis following the *Principles*. All criticism discussed below ultimately takes its cue from the meticulous examples of this book.

Subsequent writings by Richards, attempting further supplementing and extension of his argument, have sometimes dulled rather than sharpened his fundamental position. Since his works of monumental influence, his most impressive effort has been the urging of Basic English, a simplified version of standard English that might be the best vehicle for a truly universal language.

VERBAL ANALYSIS OR THE "NEW CRITICISM." Arising from Richards, the New Criticism has become largely identified with a brilliant American group, including Cleanth Brooks, Allen Tate, Robert Penn Warren, R. P. Blackmur, and John Crowe Ransom (whose *New Criticism* of 1941 has provided the label). *Explication de texte* is the technique of these critics who emphasize the poetic use of "tension," "irony," and "paradox" to achieve an "equilibrium of opposed forces."

William Empson (1906–   ). Born at Howden, Yorkshire, William Empson was educated at Magdalen College, Cambridge. After extensive teaching in China and Japan, he settled down in 1953 as professor of English literature at Sheffield University.

Seven Types of Ambiguity (1930), perhaps the most remarkable and influential critical work by so young a man, announces ambiguity as the very core of poetic significance. Where earlier analysts would write "either . . . or" for meanings of Shakespeare, Empson writes "both . . . and," thereby making a sort of *Finnegans Wake* (with its purposeful many-layered meanings) out of most literature. Empson finds ambiguity concentrating at the point of highest poetic effectiveness to produce "tension." His example has set "New Critics" scrambling desperately to unearth paradox or oxymoron in even the most apparently lucid verse.

Some Versions of Pastoral (1935, American title *English Pastoral Poetry* in 1938) is the nearest thing to Gestalt literary criticism in English. Seeking to apply his ambiguity concept to the totality (Gestalt) of a poem, he simply reverses the familiar concepts of form and content. To Empson "pastoral" is not the traditional genre of verses about shepherds but the artificial cult of simplicity. The work has been instrumental in suggesting a complete revision of the idea of genre into artistic intent instead of outward form.

Collected Poems (1955) rode the crest of highbrow popularity enjoyed by Empson's self-confessedly "clotted poetry" in the 1950s. John Wain in

1950 started the cult with his recommendation of Empson poetry to counteract the new poetic romanticism. As a poet Empson fully exemplifies the ambiguity he praises as a critic. For a while many poets were imitating his unlyrical, perplexing, highly cerebral verse, but the fashion died before the decade ended.

TRADITION ANALYSIS. Stemming largely from Eliot but with strong indebtedness to Richards are the critics who examine literature to find the maintenance of cultural patterns.

Frank Raymond Leavis (lē'vis) (1895–). F. R. Leavis is strictly a Cambridge product, born there, educated at Emmanuel College (Cambridge), and a Cambridge don since 1935. He edited *Scrutiny* during its entire existence, 1932–53. Much of his critical writing is collected or expanded from his articles in *Scrutiny*. Probably no other 20th-century critic has so profoundly influenced the actual teaching of English literature in British schools and colleges. Acutely aware of the breakdown of modern faith, Leavis sees literature as superseding the church in sustaining cultural awareness and moral values.

New Bearings in English Poetry (1932) employs verbal analysis to establish Hopkins and T. S. Eliot in the great continuity of English religious culture, while the Victorians and Georgians are portrayed as deviationists.

The Great Tradition (1948) interprets the great tradition in English fiction as serious moral concern, which Leavis finds projected best in the novels of George Eliot, Henry James, and Joseph Conrad.

IMAGERY ANALYSIS. Although her technique is certainly as old as Walter Whiter's Shakespearean studies of 1794, Caroline F. E. Spurgeon (1869–1942) truly inaugurated the contemporary vogue of imagery analysis, particularly with *Shakespeare's Imagery and What It Tells Us* (1935). She notes two major clusters of Shakespearean imagery: bodily performance and personification, food-drink-cooking and sickness-disease-medicine. Further, each play revolves about recurrent images, e.g. sickness and corruption in *Hamlet,* anguished contortions of the body in *King Lear.* Her explorations have proved invaluable in questions of disputed authorship (the image clusters of Bacon are quite alien to Shakespeare) and seem quite revelatory of the concerns of an author and his era. Non Freudian, she tends to interpret Shakespeare's riding images, for example, as proving him a devoted horseman, ignoring the possibility of their unconscious symbolism. A sizable segment of academic criticism of literature has since followed Spurgeon's lead.

MYTH ANALYSIS. In his modification of Freudian psychoanalysis Carl Jung emphasized "archetypes," age-old patterns symbolizing central human experience (e.g. the rebel in Prometheus, Blake's Orc, and the Byronic hero). Such archetypes endlessly recur as configurations in the artist's unconscious and in the unconscious of his audience. The collective unconscious of man generated mythic heroes in antiquity, and the mythopoetic urge continues to generate these archetypes today. Maud Bodkin's *Archetypal Patterns in Poetry* (1934) explores archetypes such as the rebirth theme in "The Ancient Mariner," the heaven-hell theme in Milton and Dante, the archetypal devil and hero in *Othello*. Though sometimes deviating far from the Jungian line, George Wilson Knight (1897–   ) in more than a score of volumes since *Myth and Miracle* (1929) has proved the most prolific British critic of this type, particularly in his studies of Shakespeare. Except in application to Blake, literary criticism generally has ignored most of Jung's concepts beyond the archetype.

ESSAYISTS AND PROSE STYLISTS

RELIGIOUS EMPHASIS

Gilbert Keith Chesterton (1874–1936). Son of a London estate agent, G. K. Chesterton attended St. Paul's and the Slade School of Art. In 1900 he began a lifetime journalistic career, strangely enough usually with liberal publications hostile to his viewpoints. From *Orthodoxy* (1909) his conservative bent was obvious, but he did not enter the Roman Catholic Church until 1922. "Ballad of the White Horse" and "Lepanto" (both 1911) are lively rhetoric, but poetry was not his outstanding talent.

Chesterton proved the antithesis of Shaw in attitude (Shaw's revolutionary plan for the future he countered with a reactionary plan from the past), but he utilized Shaw's two most potent weapons—witty dogmatic assertion and striking paradox. With his friend Hilaire Belloc (they were nicknamed Chesterbelloc) he fashioned a dream world of medieval England, a "merrie England" of staunch faith and unselfish brotherhood. Opposed to modern capitalism, he sought to lead men back toward a neo-medievalism of trade guilds. *The Everlasting Man* (1925) is typical of his colorful arguments against the trends of today's world, the liveliest piety and the most delightfully expressed conservatism imaginable. He also wrote a popular series of detective stories featuring the character Father Brown.

Hilaire Belloc (full name, **Joseph Peter René Hilaire Belloc**) (bel'ok) (1870–1953). Son of a French barrister and an Englishwoman, Hilaire Belloc was born at St. Cloud, near Paris. At Oratory School, Birmingham, Cardinal Newman was his preceptor. After Balliol College, Oxford, he served in the French artillery and in 1891 married an American, Elodie Hogan. He became a naturalized British subject in 1902 and sat in parliament from 1906 to 1910 as the Liberal member from Salford.

Admiring the prose of William Ralph Inge, Belloc opposed the Anglican dean at every other point. *History of England* (1925–31) is less a history than an argument that European culture is a unity, fundamentally Latin and Christian, derived from the Roman Empire and perpetuated by Roman Catholicism. Numerous ostensible essays, biographies, travelogues, and novels are essentially restatements of his basic thesis. His most influential volume, *The Servile State* (1912), attacks both industrial capitalism and socialist utopias, exalting the 13th century as the best and happiest period of Western culture. Always his prose displayed Gallic wit and precision.

Clive Staples Lewis (1898–1963). A native of Belfast, Ireland, C. S. Lewis was swept into World War I, where he served as a lieutenant in the Somerset Light Infantry. In 1918 he began a lifelong association with Oxford University as undergraduate and later as its most popular professor. Perhaps time will most respect *The Allegory of Love* (1936), the standard work on the Courtly Love tradition in European literature, *A Preface to Paradise Lost* (1942), and *English Literature in the Sixteenth Century* (1954), the culmination of his studies in medieval and Renaissance literature. In his non-scholarly works Lewis proved the most persuasive advocate of orthodox Anglicanism in this century.

The Screwtape Letters (1942, rev. ed. 1961) created an enormous popular reputation for Lewis, going through twenty English and fourteen American printings within three years. A fiendishly knowledgeable member of Hell's "Lowerarchy," Screwtape, indites admonitory letters to his nephew, Wormwood, an apprentice demon just starting the task of winning human souls to the Infernal Cause. Lewis' phenomenal success lies in startling and ingenious methods of hammering home good, old-fashioned Christian orthodoxy. Thousands of readers, of all Christian sects and beyond, were astounded to find that conventional faith could bounce and fence with unconventional gusto and ironic humor.

The Lewis trilogy (*Out of the Silent Planet*, 1938; *Perelandra*, 1943; *That Hideous Strength*, 1945) is a science fiction *Pilgrim's Progress*. The war of Christian Good and Satanic Evil becomes an interplanetary struggle within the entire solar system. Consistently the villains are scientists, who, to Lewis, embody the sin of pride.

Surprised by Joy (1955), Lewis' spiritual autobiography, claims a purely intellectual conversion. An atheist at twelve, at eighteen he read *Phantastes* by George Macdonald, a Scottish Presbyterian, and came to believe that plain Christianity is the plain truth.

HUMANISTIC EMPHASIS

Arthur Christopher Benson (1862–1925). Arthur Christopher Benson was the son of the Archbishop of Canterbury. Eton and Cambridge were his schools, and he thereafter taught at Eton (1885–1905) and at Cambridge (1905 until death). Queen Victoria and Ruskin were among his friends, but he generally remained the quiet, academic recluse.

Until World War I his essays were remarkably popular on both sides of the Atlantic. Of his many volumes, *From a College Window* (1905) is typical in its charming academic world of good books and congenial, gentlemanly scholars. It is a graceful, placid, good-humored life unbelievably remote from the storms that since have swept our era.

Edward Verall Lucas (1868–1938). From a long line of Quakers, E. V. Lucas was born at Eltham, Kent. Except for service in Italy with the Red Cross during World War I, he pursued a journalistic and editorial career, including the *London Globe, Punch,* and in 1925 chairmanship of Methuen and Co., the publishers.

Between 1905 and 1938 he published over thirty volumes of familiar essays, the most extensive one-man effort in this genre during the 20th century. Although Lamb was his avowed master, a meditative agnosticism precludes the sunniness of Lamb. Urbane wit and shrewd observation of persons and places make his books delightful companions. Perhaps his *Life of Lamb* (1905) will be considered his most important effort.

Sir **Max Beerbohm** (bēr'bōm) (1872–1956). A native Londoner, Max Beerbohm attended Charterhouse and Merton College, Oxford. During the 1890s he wrote for the *Yellow Book* and in 1898 succeeded Shaw as drama critic for the *Saturday Review*. In 1910 he married Florence Kahn, an American, and resided until his death in Rapallo, Italy. In the 1930s he became a noted radio personality, reading his own sketches with mellow good humor.

Shaw gave him a lasting label, "The Incomparable Max," and Rebecca West termed him "the last civilized man on earth." Not the epical but the livable concerns Beerbohm, whose pen could create pictures and words of a light, elegant, debonaire existence now irretrievably lost, if in fact it ever existed outside of his essay collections from *The Happy Hypocrite* (1897) to *Mainly on the Air* (1947).

Beerbohm's chief popular fame arose from a unique combination of pictorial cartoons and vivacious annotations, beginning with *Twenty-five Gentlemen* (1896). The amusing and cleverly distorted caricatures have memorialized some of the greats and immortalized some otherwise forgotten political and literary figures of the 1890s and later. Any picture collection of recent English literature must include the reading of "Ulysses" to Victoria by Tennyson, Browning taking tea with the fawning Browning Society, and the lanky, cranelike specter of Strachey, ready to pounce upon the Victorians.

A Christmas Garland (1912), parodying the mannerisms of seventeen contemporary authors in writing Christmas stories, contains the most delicious prose parodies of this century. The imitation of Henry James is the most famous, while the one of Kipling (whom Beerbohm disliked wholly) is the most crushing.

He is also remembered for a novel, *Zuleika Dobson* (1911).

Percy Wyndham Lewis (1884–1957). Wyndham Lewis was born in Nova Scotia of English parents. He was educated at Rugby and the Slade School of Art. Like Beerbohm he was a remarkable amalgam of author and pictorial artist. Founder of vorticism, the first English abstractionism in painting, he edited *Blast* (1914–15) and *Tyro* (1921–22), organs of the new movement. Later he abandoned these innovations. One of his famous paintings is a portrait of T. S. Eliot. He should not be confused with the biographer, D. B. Wyndham Lewis.

Strongly influenced by T. E. Hulme and Ezra Pound, and conditioned throughout his writing career by the holocaust of World War I, Wyndham Lewis proved one of the most eloquent denouncers of contemporary culture. A series of angry volumes, climaxed by *Time and Western Man* (1927), saw art and righteousness menaced by the democratic mob and the selfish manipulations of capitalists. Lewis' bludgeon descended on the cults of primitivism, childishness, feminism, relativism, anti-intellectualism, and the unconscious. His bitter scorn of both capitalism and communism led him toward fascism, but that way also produced disillusion, resulting in *The Human Age* (1955), a fable of today's society in total collapse.

Sacheverell Sitwell (1897–   ). Brother of Dame Edith and Sir Osbert Sitwell, Sacheverell Sitwell studied at Eton, but left Balliol College, Oxford, for World War I service with the Grenadier Guards. His travels have carried him through much of the world. Though writing extensive poetry, classically deliberate in tone, his excellence seems clearest in prose. He is the founder and secretary of the Magnasco Society, furthering interest in Italian art of the 17th and 18th centuries.

The Gothick North, a Study of Mediaeval Life, Art, and Thought (1929) is his most impressive achievement, a uniquely individual evocation of the past suggested by surviving mementos. Disgusted, like his brother and sister, with this vulgar age, he finds refuge in a dreamlike past of exquisite beauty.

The Homing of the Winds (1942), Sitwell's own anthology from his work, contains some of the best 20th-century writing in personality and grace. The prevailing note is an aristocratic yearning for order and the decencies in a debased, chaotic world.

Cyril Vernon Connolly (1903–   ). Born in Coventry, Cyril Connolly was educated at Eton and Balliol College, Oxford. He was editor of *Horizon* for its entire existence (1939–50). He continues to be a regular contributor to literary journals and writes weekly for the *Sunday Times*.

Since *Enemies of Promise* (1938) Connolly has appraised the literary scene with a provocative mixture of pessimism and vivacity. His pseudonym, Palinurus, is appropriate, for like the helmsman of Aeneas he will hold to his steering though fated to be lost. His valedictory in the last issue of *Horizon* stated: "It is closing-time in the gardens of the West and from now on an artist will be judged only by the resonance of his solitude or the quality of his despair."

Two of the most engaging humorists of the age began quite seriously. Stephen Potter (1900–   ) started as a sober literary critic, but with *Gamemanship* (1947) he launched a series of mock-serious do-it-yourself volumes showing how to browbeat and exasperate all comers on all social occasions. Cyril Northcote Parkinson (1909–   ), after sedate books on political science and business, bedazzled the world with *Parkinson's Law* (1957), burlesquing the theorists in a series of tongue-in-cheek pseudo-laws on social and bureaucratic behavior.

BIOGRAPHY

Giles Lytton Strachey (strā'chē) (1880–1932). London-born son of General Sir Richard Strachey, Lytton Strachey attended the universities of Liverpool and Cambridge. From 1907 to 1909 he was drama critic for the *Spectator*. Closely associated with the "Bloomsbury Group," he was a close friend of Virginia Woolf and E. M. Forster.

Eminent Victorians (1918), short studies of Cardinal Manning, Florence Nightingale, General Gordon, and Thomas Arnold, instituted a new era in biography writing which has sloughed off the dreary "Life and Times of . . ." Victorian biography and made biography rise from an outcast position to be consistently the best seller among non-fiction today. Strachey's new pattern consisted of:

(1) Acid portraits instead of the wearisome adulation of previous biographies. Strachey fingered his subjects with aloof irony, puncturing the idealized image they still retained in English eyes. American "debunking" biographers have followed this Strachey tendency more than have the British.

(2) Reversal of biographical approach. Traditionally, biographers were engrossed in their subject's personality and perused the subject's background as influencing and being influenced by the notable man. Strachey and many succeeding biographers have chosen an era and then have selected within it a man to reflect and reveal the spirit of the age.

(3) Techniques of fiction, Strachey's most significant contribution, largely lifted biography to its present prestige. With a novelist's eye and structural sense, Strachey ignored much of the memorabilia about a figure and instead emphasized a few dramatic highlights which showed the essence of character and mind-set. Strachey's influence has tended to blur the line between novel and biography, resulting in extensive fictionalized biographies; but his technique has elevated biography to an art form as it had not been since Boswell.

Queen Victoria (1921) is Strachey's best work and probably still the finest biography of this century. Readers had anticipated withering sarcasm against the monarch, but Strachey, while cynically ironic about much Victorianism, is strongly sympathetic to Victoria. Recognizing her severe intellectual deficiencies and her parochialism, he nonetheless constructs neat scene after scene to demonstrate how Victoria's goodness and simple sincerity made her an empire's symbol of stability and character. The subsequent biographies by Strachey, though *Elizabeth and Essex* (1928) virtually constitutes an intriguing movie scenario, could not match this work.

The current popularity of biography, stemming from Strachey, has created a new specialist, the professional biographer, producing an unprecedented amount of eminently readable biography. From this numerous group Philip Guedalla (1889–1944) and Hector Bolitho (1898–), both writing extensively on the Victorian era, stand out for colorful style and flourish, while Sir Harold George Nicolson (1886–), Lord David Cecil (1902–), Cecil Woodham-Smith (1896–), and Peter Quennell (1905–) are notable for Strachey-like powers of organization.

AUTOBIOGRAPHY

WAR BETWEEN GENERATIONS

Sir **Edmund Gosse** (gos) (1849–1928). A native Londoner, Edmund Gosse was librarian at the British Museum (1867–75), translator for the Board of Trade (1875–84), lecturer in English literature at Cambridge (1884–90), librarian of the House of Lords (1904–14). His first half century was a struggle, with meager recognition, but during his later life in the 20th century he enjoyed remarkable eminence in journalism and literary criticism, especially through his column in the *Sunday Times,* written up to the day of his death.

Father and Son (1907) is perhaps surpassed only by Joyce's *Portrait* as a 20th-century examination of youth's spiritual crises. His father, Philip Henry Gosse, a distinguished zoologist, in private life headed the Plymouth Brethren, a highly pietistic and evangelical sect. Seeking desperately to reconcile his scientific and religious viewpoints, the father imposed a rigid dogma upon Edmund. The child's fanatical adherence to the father and the youth's agonizing withdrawal from the father to a broader, more tolerant vista look like the classic non-fictional portrait of the revolt against Victorianism and, in ampler scope, the eternal contest of the younger generation against its elders. Withal, the elder Gosse is depicted as wholly sincere and well-intentioned.

Sir **Osbert Sitwell** (full name, **Francis Osbert Sacheverell Sitwell**) (1892–). Brother of Edith and Sacheverell Sitwell, London-born Osbert Sitwell after his education at Eton served in France as an officer in the Grenadier Guards. His war verse is Sassoon-like, and his subsequent poetry "modernist" but often with meaning very clear. He worked assiduously to publicize the verse of his sister. His more recent writings have concentrated upon prose.

Left Hand! Right Hand! (five volumes, 1944–50) is the collective title for one of the most engaging and well-phrased autobiographies in English. Sir Osbert blandly satirizes his father, Sir George Sitwell, and the Edwardian era of his adolescence, all with the debonair touch of a sophisticated aristocrat. Nonetheless, a mellowness surrounds Sir George and ancient Renishaw, the ancestral estate, with the aura of a lost innocence.

POETIC AUTOBIOGRAPHY

Other competent and conventional autobiographies are discussed elsewhere, but here is noted what many, such as V. de Sola Pinto, consider an outstanding creation of mid-20th-century English imagination, the poetic autobiography. Reaction to bald naturalism has produced accounts that in earlier eras would have induced poems like Wordsworth's *Prelude,* but in this prosaic age resemble the novel. Joyce's *Portrait* and Lawrence's *Sons and Lovers* have created not only the poetic autobiographical novel but also poetic autobiography itself.

Memorable lyric evocations of working-class childhood have appeared from Richard Church (1893–   ) in *Over the Bridge* (1955), James Kirkup (1923–   ) in *The Only Child* (1957), Laurie Lee (1914–   ) in *Cider with Rosie* (1959), and Clifford Dyment (1914–   ) in *The Railway Game* (1962). All four are highly gifted poets whose appeal has proved more potent in poetic prose than in verse.

An unsuccessful poet, Paul Potts (c. 1912–   ) in *Dante Called You Beatrice* (1960) has probably produced *the* autobiography for the "angry young men," a headlong Barker-Gascoyne race through life.

A remarkable new talent is that of Dom Moraes (1938–   ), the youngest person ever to receive the Hawthornden prize for poetry (1958). Though East Indian by birth and blood, his native tongue is English. *Gone Away* (1960) ostensibly is a travel account of his revisiting of India, but even more engrossing is the spectacle of a Westernized Oriental, alien to his own origins, searching for his own identity.

Difficult to classify is *A House in Bryanston Square* (1944) by Algernon Cecil. Often likened to *The Education of Henry Adams,* it is the Odyssey of a mind and a soul. The affirmative, constructive elements within the author debate with the negative, critical elements, all in the framework of passage from room to room of his London residence. The Christian humanist wins out after an imaginative and philosophic journey through the world of ideas swirling about Cecil and our age.

HISTORY

George Macaulay Trevelyan (tri-vel′yan) (1876–1962). A grand-nephew of Lord Macaulay, G. M. Trevelyan was born in Shakespeare's town, Stratford-on-Avon. After education at Harrow and Trinity College, Cambridge, he served in an ambulance unit during World War I. From 1927 to 1940 he was regius professor of modern history at Cambridge, and from 1940 to 1951 was master of Trinity College.

Fighting for history as an art (*Clio a Muse*, 1913), Trevelyan is largely responsible for the 20th-century school of English historians, whose imaginative, well-written works have rivaled the new biography for current reader interest. Of Trevelyan's numerous books perhaps most outstanding are *British History in the Nineteenth Century, 1782–1901* (1922), *History of England* (1926), and *English Social History* (1942), all about as readable as the history of his great-uncle but in a less flamboyant style and with recognition of areas omitted by Lord Macaulay.

Sir **Winston Leonard Spencer Churchill** (1874–   ). Winston Churchill was born at Blenheim Palace, Oxfordshire, the mansion given by a grateful nation to his ancestor John Churchill, Duke of Marlborough. His mother, Jennie Jerome, was an American. After Harrow, Sir Winston was trained at the Royal Military College, Sandhurst, and fought thereafter with distinction in Cuba, India, and the Sudan. As war correspondent for the London *Morning Post*, he was captured by the South African Boers but escaped to fight against them. His long and eminent career in parliament began in 1900, and by 1911 he had risen through executive positions to be the first lord of the admiralty. His strengthening of the navy prevented the German surface fleet from offering any real challenge to the British in World War I, and the Royal Air Force originated under his ministry. With the failure of his pet project, the Gallipoli campaign, Churchill resigned in 1915 to see active service on the Western front until recalled for high post, serving as secretary of state for war and air from 1918 to 1921.

Between wars he irked war-weary Britons by his incessant prophecy of renewed conflict, but the onslaught of World War II caused his elevation by popular clamor in 1940 to prime minister. Through the worst days of the blitz and throughout the war Churchill was the world symbol for unswerving resistance to the Axis Powers. Defeated, however, at the polls in 1945, he continued his superb phrase-making by coining "iron curtain" in 1946 to describe the tightly clamped borders of the communist world. He was again prime minister from 1951 until his retirement from office in 1955. Churchill was awarded the Nobel prize for literature in 1953 and in 1962 was designated an honorary citizen of the United States by congressional action.

The Second World War (six volumes, 1948–54) is intended by Churchill as a continuation of his study of World War I, *The World Crisis* (four volumes, 1923–29). While some figures high in war councils have objected that the work ascribes too much prescience and momentous decision to Churchill, the chief factual objection has been to his thesis that professional politicians have surpassed professional soldiers on military policy. Those hostile to the British are annoyed at Churchill's John Bullish certainty that English leadership of the world is wholly right and necessary. Perhaps Lord Keynes's comment on Churchill's World War I account ("brilliant but not history") may be applied to *The Second World War,* but it is an imaginative handling of a vast canvas that dims any avowed fiction and comes from the only man who stood always at the heart of the conflict. Churchill reveals himself as the greatest master of English prose in this century, especially in the speeches that with incomparable sonority and majestic eloquence steeled a people to their supreme effort in history.

A History of the English-Speaking Peoples (four volumes, 1956–58), would do credit to any historian, though critics suggest that it is more revelatory of Churchill than of the history he recounts.

Sir **Arthur Wynne Morgan Bryant** (1899–   ). Born at Dersingham, Norfolk, Arthur Wynne Morgan Bryant has been an Oxford don but is best known as book reviewer for *The Illustrated London News,* taking over the column "Our Note Book" upon the death of Chesterton in 1936.

The Years of Endurance (1942) began a study of the Napoleonic period to reinvigorate the English with memories of how their ancestors withstood the rampages of an earlier continental tyrant. *Years of Victory* (1944) carried the account further, paralleling again the earlier resurgence of England. Even more nostalgic, *The Age of Elegance* (1950) deals with the post-Napoleonic era when England emerged as dominant world power, unpleasantly contrasting with current diminution of England's stature. The entire trilogy sparkles with vivacious writing.

Alfred Leslie Rowse (rŏs) (1903–   ). A native of St. Austell, Cornwall, A. L. Rowse was educated at Christ Church, Oxford, and has since been an Oxford don, though serving as Trevelyan Lecturer at Cambridge in 1958 and as research associate at the Huntington Library, California, 1961–63.

The England of Elizabeth (1950) and *The Expansion of Elizabethan England* (1955) challenge Froude as the epic account of the first Elizabethan age. Unlike his Victorian predecessor, Rowse skeptically dislikes all extremists but bends over backward to present their viewpoints. *William Shakespeare* (1963) is perhaps the best historian's study of the outstanding Elizabethan literary figure, and its treatment of Shakespeare's sonnets has aroused much discussion.

Cicely Veronica Wedgwood (1910–   ). Cicely Veronica Wedgwood of the famous pottery-making family was educated at Lady Margaret Hall, Oxford. Her diverse interests include membership in the Princeton Institute for Advanced Study and a trusteeship in the English National Gallery of Art.

The Great Rebellion, when complete, will attempt a revaluation of the era about which the Earl of Clarendon wrote in the first notable literary history of England. *The King's Peace, 1637–1641* (1955), the first installment, views the tragic struggle not as a contest of good versus evil but as a painful misunderstanding among proud, well-intentioned men, all equally praise-and blameworthy. The calm, fluent, workmanlike prose is among the most competent of our time. *The King's War, 1641–1657* (1958) continues the account with the same lucid phrasing and the same sympathetic balance of both Royalist and Parliamentarian causes.

INTERPRETATIONS OF HISTORY

Richard Henry Tawney (1880–1962). Born in Calcutta, India, R. H. Tawney was educated at Rugby and Balliol College, Oxford. Thereafter he taught at the universities of Glasgow, Oxford, and London. Author of *The Acquisitive Society* (1920), Tawney, probably the leading economic historian of this century, was heavily biased in favor of Fabian socialism.

Religion and the Rise of Capitalism (1926) has effected a significant reconsideration of the Reformation, demonstrating the economic origins of Protestantism in modern capitalism and the rise of the bourgeoisie.

Herbert Butterfield (1900–   ). Herbert Butterfield of Yorkshire has been associated with Cambridge ever since his undergraduate days at Peterhouse (master of his old college since 1955). He has lectured widely and holds honorary degrees from as remote universities as Hong Kong, Harvard, and Columbia. His first published work was *The Historical Novel* (1924).

The Whig Interpretation of History (1931) has powerfully influenced recent study of English history, as it questions the liberal interpretation fostered by Burnet early in the 18th century and consistently followed since. Also, the contemporary resurgence of concern for tradition and continuity, both secular and Anglo-Catholic, has stimulated such a work as Keith Feiling's *History of England* (1950), seeking to supplant Green's *Short History* with a Tory perspective of English history.

Alan John Percivale Taylor (1906–   ). A native of Birkdale, Lancashire, A. J. P. Taylor was educated at Oriel College, Oxford. He has remained at Oxford but has lectured widely, including in 1958 the first college lectures ever presented over B.B.C. television.

The Origins of the Second World War (1961), after Taylor's extensive and rather conventional studies of recent German history, exploded a bombshell. Admitting that Hitler was a wickedly ambitious dictator, Taylor nonetheless insists that Hitler was pursuing the logical and necessary steps of a national leader in trying to readjust the European balance of power in favor of Germany. Allied statesmen, alternately severe (as in the Versailles Treaty) and weak (when yielding to Nazi invasion of the demilitarized Rhineland), are accorded the major blame. No matter how acceptable this thesis, the English willingness to consider Taylor's argument while they still suffer acutely from the wounds of World War II seems a remarkable tribute to their fair-mindedness.

Arnold Joseph Toynbee (1889–   ). Arnold Toynbee was born in London and attended Winchester and Balliol College, Oxford. He worked for the British Foreign Office during both World Wars and was a member of the British delegation to both peace conferences. From 1919 until his retirement in 1955 he was a professor of history at London University, and also from 1925 to 1955 director of studies at the Royal Institute of International Affairs. His first wife was Gilbert Murray's daughter, and his son Philip is a well-known novelist.

A Study of History (twelve volumes, 1934–61) rivals the works of the German Oswald Spengler and the Russian-American Pitirim Sorokin in a stupendous all-embracing theory of history. Arguing that civilizations rather than nations are the true units of history, Toynbee counts twenty-eight known civilizations throughout history; contemporary Western civilization he optimistically notes is the only one not obviously dead or dying. Civilization, he suggests, arises only in response to a challenge (absence of a real challenge forestalled a Polynesian civilization, and too great a challenge prevented an Eskimo civilization). A creative minority senses the challenge and provides the techniques to solve it (e.g. the ancient Egyptian engineers who transformed the Nile from a morass into the world's most fertile river valley). Civilizations fall because the creative minority refuses to alter its responses in the face of a new challenge and thus becomes a dominant minority, driving instead of leading the masses. Collapse occurs from assaults upon a civilization by the internal proletariat (*in* but no longer *of* the civilization) and the external proletariat (formerly *of* but now *against* the civilization which it borders). Consoling, however, is the emergence of a great religion like a phoenix from the ashes of a guttering civilization (Christianity is thus seen as a product of the internal proletariat of the moribund Greco-Roman civilization). In the concluding volumes Toynbee reveals himself as a religious prophet, proclaiming that civilizations are purposeful divine creations existing not for themselves but as means to gestate religions, that history therefore is "a vision of God's creation on the move." Though elevating Christianity above the other great faiths, he suggests that hope for the future lies in a syncretic religion embracing all mankind in one universal civilization.

Critics retort that Toynbee is truly a Christian apologist rather than a historian, that he willfully imposes his predetermined pattern upon historical events (ignoring what fails to substantiate his thesis), and that his novelty consists more in a new terminology than in violently new theory. Cognizant of these objections, the usually reserved *Manchester Guardian* in 1947 said, "The high qualities of Mr. Toynbee's great work lie rather in his poetic vision, in his freedom from the trammels of time and space, and in the Olympian sweep of his glance across the centuries." Sober historians consequently often wish to relegate Toynbee's work to the realm of immensely stimulating imaginative literature. Unlike any kindred study, Toynbee's work in abridgement has been a best seller.

EXPLORATION AND ADVENTURE

Ours is the last century to fill in the blanks of the world map, preparatory to man's exploration of space. Left over from the 19th century was the last great citadel of the unknown, Antarctica. Sir Robert Falcon Scott (1868–1912) and Sir Ernest Henry Shackleton (1874–1922), were representatives of the last era to pit man's naked stamina against the globe's most hostile geography. Scott's *Voyage of Discovery* (1905) and Shackleton's *Heart of the Antarctic* (1909) conjure up the bleak majesty and awesome stillness of the frozen continent. One of the most moving of all human documents is the verbatim diary of Scott in 1912; in the race for the South Pole he was beaten by the Norwegian, Roald Amundsen. Scott reached the pole, dying in a blizzard on the way back. Shackleton in his diary for 1916 matter-of-factly records the most incredible and perilous of all sea voyages in his determination to rescue his men, trapped when their ship *Endurance* was crushed by pack ice.

Robert Bontine Cunningham Graham (1852–1936). Although a Londoner by birth, Cunningham Graham proudly boasted of blood three-quarters Scottish and one-quarter Spanish. Restless at Harrow, he roamed the Americas from the far south to Texas. In 1879 he married a Chilean and in 1884 returned to claim his inheritance at Gartmore, Scotland. From 1886 to 1892 as a Liberal member of parliament he militantly supported labor, suffering imprisonment in 1887 for leading strikers in a charge against the police. He was the first member of the House of Commons ever to be suspended for uttering "Damn" upon the floor. Turning to writing at the century's end, he published frequently until death.

A Renaissance hidalgo strayed into this century, Cunningham Graham strides through far places with chivalric gusto and gazes upon our regimented society with aristocratic contempt. The modern civilized world appears to Graham as vulgar, brutal, and impotent. *Mogreb-el-Acksa* ("Morocco of the West") (1898) sends the author to the remote, forbidden city of Tarudant; Shaw's play *Captain Brassbound's Conversion* in part seeks to correct Graham's elevation of wild justice and "natural" virtues of the

North African Arab over decadent civilization. *The Conquest of New Granada* (1922) is one of the few English works since World War I to glorify war as the dashing, valorous prerogative of manhood.

Henry Major Tomlinson (1873—1958). Born and bred in London's East End, H. M. Tomlinson went to work at twelve. After two decades of spare-time writing, he escaped the drudgery of clerkship to work on the *Morning Leader* in 1904. Outspoken as a war correspondent (1914–17), he returned to London as literary editor of *Nation* and *Athenaeum*. After 1923 he was a free-lance author.

The Sea and the Jungle (1912), faintly heeded at its appearance, has risen in critical opinion to rank as perhaps the one genuine classic of modern travel literature. The voyage of the *Capella* is faithfully chronicled from Swansea to Para, Brazil, thence up the Amazon to Porto Velho, and on to the Barbados and Tampa, Florida. The descriptions of the ocean and the tropical rain forests rank with Conrad's, and in both phenomena Tomlinson senses the brooding, enigmatic giant of Nature silently tolerating human invasion but not yielding its secret heart. Fleeing the drab everyday, Tomlinson perceives the comradeship of men upon far adventures as the bond of brotherhood and work, revealing the basic humanity.

Out of Soundings (1931) contains Tomlinson's maturest essays and most stately poetic prose. Mechanism, he laments, has replaced fundamental human values in today's world. Only by the restoration of natural rhythms and a sense of mankind's responsibility to his fellows and to the globe which is his heritage can we prevent the dissolution of our culture.

Thomas Edward Lawrence (1888–1935). Born at Tremadoc, Wales, T. E. Lawrence attended Jesus College, Oxford, spending his vacations studying archaeology in France and Syria. After graduating in 1910 he participated in archaeological diggings in the Middle East until the outbreak of World War I, when he was attached to British Intelligence in Cairo. His disdain for military discipline made his superiors happy to assign him in 1916 to the task of stirring the Arab tribes to rebellion against Turkish rule. After the war he served at the Peace Conference and in the Colonial Office, but refused a diplomatic career because England and France had reneged on their promises to the Arabs. Bitterly seeking anonymity, he enlisted in the RAF as Aircraftsman Ross in 1922, and, after the discovery of his identity, as Shaw (a name he legally assumed) in the Royal Tank Corps in 1923. In 1925 he transferred back to the RAF. His prose translation of the *Odyssey* (1932) is generally acknowledged to have captured the rugged quality of the original. Shortly after leaving the service in 1935 he died of injuries received in a motorcycle accident.

Lawrence remains one of the most intriguing and baffling personalities of this century. Other Englishmen, such as Glubb Pasha, have equaled or excelled his exploits among the Arabs, but the American journalist Lowell

Thomas made him a commanding legend as "Lawrence of Arabia." Apparently the sting of his illegitimate birth induced Lawrence to foster the legend, which was increased by his very diffidence and attempt to hide.

Seven Pillars of Wisdom (title from Proverbs 9:1) was privately published in 1926 and circulated generally only in 1935. Until Lawrence's death, most readers knew only the abridged version, *Revolt in the Desert* (1927). Aldington with righteous indignation has demonstrated the impossibility or inconsistency of many of Lawrence's statements about the military campaign (1916–18), but no one can challenge Lawrence's graphic analysis of the Arabs and their extraordinary adaptation to the intractable desert.

PHILOSOPHY

Bertrand Arthur William Russell, third **Earl Russell** (1872–   ). Bertrand Russell was born in Trelleck, Wales. At Trinity College, Cambridge, he was led to a scientific realism by the noted philosopher, George Edward Moore, brother of the poet, T. Sturge Moore. Amid his philosophical studies Russell vigorously pursued political and social causes, supporting the Fabian principles of the Webbs. As a conscientious objector during World War I, he served six months in jail. His extensive lecturing throughout the world made him apprehensive of totalitarianism and caused his abandonment of pacifism by 1940. In the same year his appointment at City College of New York was revoked by court order on the allegation of his support of "free love." Honors have mounted during his later years, climaxed by the Nobel prize for literature in 1950.

Russell's greatest kinship lies with Hume, and he may be considered a transposed 18th-century *philosophe,* an empiricist in the major tradition of English philosophy. Although his range is astounding, his fundamental position has never changed. "Logical analysis" is perhaps the best label for his viewpoint that philosophy should avoid all system building in favor of a rigorous, unmoralizing analysis based on the principles of science. Although brushing aside any spiritual or supernatural world, Russell has maintained an almost romantic conviction that men may improve themselves and their world by reason. Among leading intellectuals of this century he stands almost alone in consistent optimism (though qualified) for the future.

Principia Mathematica (three volumes, 1910–13), in collaboration with Alfred North Whitehead, may remain his most significant philosophical pronouncement. In revolt against Idealism, such as Bradley's, he tried to set forth all of logic and mathematics as pure fact devoid of moral, religious, or emotional implications. The keynote for much of modern science and philosophy is sounded in a modification of older materialism: the truth of the universe consists of facts, not things, and events, not "substance."

Our Knowledge of the External World (1914) is often claimed as the best study to date on the theory of knowledge.

A History of Western Philosophy (1945), though clearly demonstrating a worldly philosopher's biases (e.g. Aquinas is summarily dismissed), is probably the best written work on the subject. Complex ideas are expressed wth lucid, witty elegance. Confidently, Russell perceives man's history as essentially an upward surge toward truth.

Unpopular Essays (1950), collecting many previous items, contributes less to philosophy than many other Russell works, but shows a stylistic mastery of the language. Informing the essays is a passionate concern for human welfare and a profound indignation at the irrationality of man. Utilitarian in his approach to morality, Russell denounces humbug and cruelty, and demands justice and freedom.

Alfred North Whitehead (1861–1947). A native of Ramsgate, Kent, Alfred North Whitehead attended Trinity College, Cambridge. A lifelong college professor, he significantly changed from a professor of mathematics at English institutions (1885–1924) to professor of philosophy at Harvard (1924–37).

Some maintain that Whitehead is the outstanding philosopher of this century, and none can deny that his is one of the most important minds of this era, touching wide areas of human knowledge with new illumination. In agreement with Russell until 1914, he then diverged to become the most famous philosophical Idealist of this century. Beginning with the concept of nature as a web of events (instead of the older concept of matter), he propounds a philosophy of "organism." The electron is itself an organism with the capacity for creative development. The final principle is God, the poet of the universe, who is all creative impulse, eternal becoming, who informs and thrusts forward the organisms of his world. *Process and Reality* (1929) best expounds his 20th-century version of Platonism.

Science and the Modern World (1925) is on everyone's list of "most influential books of the 20th century." In a survey beginning with the 16th century, Whitehead analyzes the patterns of cultural development of Western society. In an impressive synthesis he sees the aesthetic and scientific approaches of the last five centuries as shaping toward his philosophy of organism. The changes of the world and thought would be only random chance unless a guiding principle informed the universe.

Robin George Collingwood (1889–1943). R. G. Collingwood was associated with Oxford from his undergraduate days until his retirement in 1941. His *Autobiography* (1939) is, along with Mill's, the most impressive scrutiny by an English philosopher of his intellectual growth. Collingwood traces a suspiciously smooth and logical progress from his initial archaeological concerns to his eventual historicism. More in the vein of continental than British philosophers, he came to see philosophy not as epistemology but as the history of human culture. Claiming in *Speculum Mentis* (1924) that the only proper philosophy is a "critical review of the chief forms of human experience," he sought to explore the experience of the artist and the saint as well as that of the scientist, for all are constructing maps of the same territory, "mind's knowledge of itself."

The result was some of the most stimulating and suavely-phrased books of this century. *Principles of Art* (1937) examines art not as an eternal entity but as the response of sensitive men to specific problems encountered in time and place. *The New Leviathan* (1942) studies human government not as a principle of regulating human behavior but as a shifting adaptation to new problems; democracy is calmly supported not because it is any ideal but because it best fits contemporary needs and experience. Even *The Idea of Nature* (1945) claims history as the fundamental genetic science; the theories of the physicists arise from a man making certain observations at this time and this place.

Cyril Edwin Mitchinson Joad (1891–1953). After Balliol College, Oxford, C. E. M. Joad was a civil servant until 1930, and thereafter head of the department of philosophy, Birkberk College, University of London.

Except for Russell, Joad has been the most prolific writer among the British philosophers of this period. He has proved the most thoroughgoing Platonist of this century, perceiving a static realm beyond the stream of life where values are complete and eternally changeless. *The Recovery of Belief* (1952) is a remarkable spiritual autobiography in which Joad traces his course from atheism to sanctuary in the Church of England. Few other notable secular philosophers of the age have argued so wholly for orthodoxy.

ECONOMICS, POLITICS, AND THE SOCIAL SCIENCES

John Maynard Keynes, first Baron of Tilton, commonly **Lord Keynes** (kānz) (1883–1946). Son of the distinguished economist John Neville Keynes, John Maynard Keynes was born at Cambridge. A boy genius, he easily went through Eton, King's College (Cambridge), and the stiff civil service examinations. Before the age of thirty he was member of the Royal Commission on East Indian finances and editor of *Economic Journal* (1912–46), the leading British journal on economics. From World War I until death he was the world's leading theoretical economist both in theory and as an eminent international consultant. Judicious investments kited a few pounds into a private fortune of almost a million pounds.

The Economic Consequences of the Peace (1919) is one of the most prescient books ever written. Before anyone else, Keynes with uncanny vision foresaw the effects of the Versailles Treaty. The book is enlivened by sharp and unflattering portraits of the statesmen who after one horrendous war unwittingly laid the foundations for the next.

The General Theory of Employment, Interest and Money (1936) is as revolutionary a volume in economics as Smith's *Wealth of Nations* or Marx's *Das Kapital*. In retort to Marx, the "Keynesian Revolution" proposed that capitalism could be fully sustained. Keynes noted that contrary to the traditional optimists a capitalistic depression does not inherently contain the promise of recharging and elevating the economy; private investment is not a dependable drive wheel to restore prosperity. Government "pump priming," deficit financing, and tax withholding are Keynes's constructive proposals for reinvigorating the economy. Especially in America the "Keynesian Revolution" was quickly implemented in an almost unique tribute to an economist in his own age. Ironically, many capitalists, for whom Keynes proposed salvation, have suspiciously distrusted his shoring up of capitalism as "creeping socialism."

George Douglas Howard Cole (1889–1959). After St. Paul's School, G. D. H. Cole was student and professor for a lifetime at Oxford. He long supported guild socialism and was president of the Fabian Society, 1939–46 and 1948–50 (Beatrice Webb expected him to become prime minister). To make money, he and his wife Margaret collaborated upon over thirty detective novels. His heart, however, lay with socialist interpretation of politics and economics, which he eloquently supported in over fifty volumes.

Harold Joseph Laski (1893–1950). A native of Manchester, Harold Laski proved so brilliant at New College, Oxford, that upon graduation in 1914 he started as lecturer in McGill University, Montreal, Canada. His cosmopolitanism and excellent delivery made him a coveted speaker throughout the world, but from 1920 until death his base of operations was the London School of Economics.

Probably no other person has grasped so solidly the political institutions of the entire English-speaking world from *The Problem of Sovereignty* (1917) to *The American Democracy* (1948). Posterity, however, may cherish most *The Holmes-Laski Correspondence* (1954). Although the American jurist, Oliver Wendell Holmes, was fifty years older than Laski, the two carried on a memorable exchange of wise and witty letters, a correspondence between profound minds and rich personalities.

Edward Alexander Westermarck (1862–1939). Of Swedish parentage, Edward Alexander Westermarck was born in Finland, and came to England in 1890. For most of his life he was a professor of sociology at the University of London. *The History of Human Marriage* (1891) began a series of studies that remain the classics on marriage. His versatility classifies him with anthropologists, sociologists, psychologists, philosophers—and competent masters of English prose.

Henry Havelock Ellis (1859–1939). Born at Croyden, Surrey, Havelock Ellis came from a seafaring family. At the age of six he spent a year at sea. After private schooling, he taught in Australia (1875–79) and returned to England to study medicine at St. Thomas' Hospital. After a brief practice of medicine, he turned to criticism and editing of literature, especially of Elizabethan dramatists.

Studies in the Psychology of Sex (seven volumes, 1897–1928) initially produced violent distaste and lawsuits on charges of obscenity, but no other works in the English language have so altered the general attitude toward sex, influencing much recent British conduct and legislation. Ellis' approach is anthropo-sociological, exploring every manifestation of sex, normal and abnormal, without moral stigmatizing. Like the works of Frazer, Ellis' in their brilliant examples and flowing diction have become more the prize of literature than science.

The Dance of Life (1923) is a sort of prose *Marriage of Heaven and Hell* (Blake), for its essence is a mystical view of life's harmonies not by any restricting of the human potentials but by their full realization. "To be the serene spectator of the Absurdity of the world, to be at the same time the strenuous worker in the Rationalization of the world—that is of the function of the complete man."

PHYSICAL AND NATURAL SCIENCES

In the tradition of T. H. Huxley, many British scientists of this era often surpass avowedly belletristic writers in their fluent, effective prose. Many think that the sober articles in *Nature*, the British scientific journal, chronicling such fundamental yet varied successes as the efforts of Lord Rutherford in atomic fission and the team of researchers exploring DNA (deoxyribonucleic acid—"the coil of life") constitute the most enthralling and imagination-stirring writing of this century.

Sir James Hopwood Jeans (1877–1946). Born at Ormskirk, Lancashire, James Jeans attended Merchant Taylors' School and Trinity College, Cambridge. After teaching mathematics at Princeton University (1905–10), he returned to Cambridge. He was president of the Royal Astronomical Society (1925–27) and president of the British Association for the Advancement of Science (1934).

Jeans made important contributions to the dynamic theory of gases, radiation mechanism, and the quantum theory. Though now superseded, his concepts of stellar structure and evolution, and the nature of the universe, were immensely stimulating. Laymen were persuasively introduced to the new physics and new cosmology in *The Universe Around Us* (1929) and *The Mysterious Universe* (1930).

Sir Arthur Stanley Eddington (1882–1944). A native of Kendal, Arthur

Eddington spent most of his life at Cambridge University. In 1916 he began an epoch-making study of the internal structure of stars which revolutionized current theory and established much of our present knowledge about cosmography. One of the first to grasp the importance of Einstein's theory, he led a 1919 expedition whose observation of a solar eclipse provided the first confirmation of Einstein.

The Nature of the Physical World (1928) is an expository masterpiece, whose enormous exploration from the electron to the galaxies handles fantastically difficult concepts with lucidity and grace. Though more recent study can add to this volume, it remains the English science classic for the laity in this century.

Sir **Julian Sorell Huxley** (1887–   ). Grandson of T. H. Huxley and nephew of Matthew Arnold, Julian Huxley is a brother of Aldous Huxley. Born in London, he was educated at Eton and Balliol College, Oxford. After teaching at Rice Institute, Houston, Texas (1912–16), he saw service in Italy during World War I. Then followed a distinguished professorial career in the British educational world. In 1946 he became the first director general of the United Nations Educational, Scientific, and Cultural Organization. Since leaving UNESCO in 1948 he has lectured widely. His extensive writings include poetry and travel accounts.

Like the American James brothers (William and Henry) the Huxley brothers of today are split between science and belles lettres, but the scientific brother is every whit as absorbing and capable a writer as the novelist. Sir Julian, as a world-renowned biologist, has made substantial contributions to embryology, evolution, and the behavior of organisms; but the general public values him highest as a leader in relating science to human social life and religion, ever since *The Individual in the Animal Kingdom* (1912). Essentially in the *Ethics and Evolution* spirit of his grandfather, T. H. Huxley, Sir Julian is today's leading expounder of the evolutionary theory, culminating in *Evolution as a Process* (1954) and *Toward a New Humanism* (1957). He sees three stages of evolution: inorganic, organic, social and mental. Although man has at least momentarily ceased appreciable biological evolution, Sir Julian interprets the present social and intellectual changes of mankind as providing the most rapid and challenging of all evolutions.

Fred Hoyle (1915–   ). A native of Bingley, Yorkshire, Fred Hoyle has been associated with Cambridge University since undergraduate days at St. John's College, though his study of astronomy has taken him over much of the world and includes service with Palomar and other American observatories. Hoyle has succeeded Jeans and Eddington as a distinguished apostle of science to the layman. Significantly, he has also published verse, drama, and science fiction.

The Nature of the Universe (1950) is based upon Hoyle's B.B.C. lectures on astronomy. To the public this work first propounded his and Lyttleton's theory of continuous creation by which the expanding universe constantly replaces its receding galaxies, and the theory of planetary origin from the destruction of a twin star accompanying our sun. Subsequent astronomical theory has cast doubts upon Hoyle's conjectures, but not upon his imaginative powers and excellent prose.

LITERARY PERIODICALS

World War I marked the end of the golden age of English periodicals. Since then the increased tempo of modern life and the uneasy sense of living constantly over a volcano have militated against the leisurely reading of magazines. Especially important, however, is the sudden rise of mass media for communication. Movies, radio, and television now occupy much of the time that 19th-century Englishmen gave to the reading of periodicals. The English are now the most voracious newspaper readers in the world, purchasing more newspapers per capita than any other nation.

GENERAL LITERARY PERIODICALS. Though significant periodicals founded in this century are few, there are two notable weeklies. *The New Statesman* (1913–   ), absorbing *The Nation* in 1930 and the *Weekend Review* in 1934, was created by the Webbs as a vehicle for Fabian socialism, but its interest is as much literary as propagandist. *The New Statesman* has been consistently the outstanding literary weekly of this century. *Times Literary Supplement* (1902–   ) has actually been a separate publication since 1914. Although maintaining discreet anonymity, its reviewers have included many excellent English writers and critics from Virginia Woolf and E. M. Forster to the present. Its scope includes scholarly and foreign publications far beyond its American counterparts. "T.L.S." for most of this century has proved the most prestigious review in the English language.

THE "LITTLE MAGAZINES." Taking its generic term and much of its attitude from *The Little Review* (1914–29) edited in Chicago and New York by Margaret Anderson, the "little magazine" has been an outstanding literary phenomenon from World War I through World War II. Its dominant characteristic has been a bold desire to print contemporary intellectual literature that seldom sees print in the general literary periodicals. The "little magazines" are symptoms of a conscious revolt against mass-communication media and of the intellectuals' sense of isolation from the general populace. A distinct coterie appeal and a defiant artiness characterized most of these publications, but collectively they served as a necessary outlet for progressive new writing of their era. Only a few can be mentioned from a multitudinous array.

The Egoist (1914–19), with T. S. Eliot as an assistant editor, was the first notable British "little magazine." It was a vehicle for Imagist verse, but also offered the initial printing of Joyce's *Portrait* and selections from *Ulysses*.

Horizon (1939–50) under Cyril Connolly was the outstanding all-round "little magazine." In the opening editorial Connolly declared: "At the moment civilization is on the operating table and we sit in the waiting room." Connolly's editorship displayed a competence in balancing viewpoints and in extracting the unexpected from the best writers of the time.

Scrutiny (1932–53) under Leavis enjoyed the longest life of the genre, and by general admission is the most important critical review of this century. Its fundamental basis was the tradition analysis of its editor, who with warrant judged this periodical to be the greatest influence "affecting radically the prevailing sense of the past."

The fate of the "little magazines" can be traced in *New Writing,* started by John Lehmann in 1936. In 1940 Lehmann contracted with Penguin Books to bring out small paperbound anthologies titled *Penguin New Writing.* By the end of World War II the "little magazines" were virtually played out, and they have in the main been succeeded since by a host of inexpensive paperbacks, now the chief outlet for progressive new British authors.

Chapter 11

Fiction of the Twentieth Century

The outstanding literary achievement of 20th-century English literature is the novel. Almost every English literary figure of this era has attempted the genre; and many writers who are primarily poets or essayists have found the novel their one sure way of securing an income and commanding an audience.

NOVELISTS EMPHASIZING SOCIAL PROBLEMS

This phase of the novel continues the pattern inaugurated under late Victorian fiction. Most of the following writers have suffered considerable reduction in reputation. Critics today often label them "middlebrows," because their appeal is largely to the more sensitive members of the middle class. They are deviants from the bourgeois novel rather than breakers of new paths.

John Galsworthy (1867–1933). Descendant of a long line of Devonshire yeomen, John Galsworthy was the son of a Kingston, Surrey, attorney. He was a capable athlete at Harrow and New College, Oxford. Although called to the bar in 1890, he preferred to travel, establishing in 1893 a life-long friendship with Conrad, then first mate of the ship in which Galsworthy was sailing. Early novels appeared under the pseudonym of John Sinjohn. By the close of the 1920s he was often considered the greatest living English novelist, and in 1932 he was awarded the Nobel prize for literature. His reputation has diminished considerably, but he is still highly regarded for the following novels. His plays and their importance have been discussed in Chapter 8.

The Forsyte Saga consists of *The Man of Property* (1906), *In Chancery* (1920), and *To Let* (1921) with two short connecting pieces.

To please his unhappy wife Irene, Soames Forsyte hires Philip Bosinney to build a country mansion; the young architect is engaged to June, daughter of young Jolyon Forsyte. Irene and Philip fall in love, and Soames sues Philip for breach of contract. Soames wins the suit, Philip is killed in a traffic accident, and Irene leaves Soames. Seeking divorce from Irene, Soames forces her and young Jolyon together. After a divorce scandal, Irene and young Jolyon marry to have a son Jon, and Soames secures an heir, Fleur, through a second wife. Later Fleur and Jon wish to marry, but the old family quarrels keep the younger generation apart. With the death of Timothy, last Forsyte of the oldest generation, Soames senses the passing of the Forsyte era.

The Irene-Jolyon romance is based upon that of the novelist's wife Ada and the novelist. She had been unhappily married to his cousin Arthur Galsworthy, but in deference to the father of the novelist they waited for a divorce until the aged man's death. Galsworthy himself states his theme as the disturbance of beauty in the lives of men, but this is strictly true only of the first volume. Pervasive is the condemnation of the upper middle class (Galsworthy's own social stratum) for its narrow mind and especially for its consuming desire for wealth (Forsyte-foresight). However, Galsworthy's substitute, the Art-*cum*-Beauty vision of the artists, Bosinney and young Jolyon, seems unconvincing. Most memorable is the superb writing, which possesses a gentlemanly grace that can rise to sheer poetry in the interpiece, "Indian Summer of a Forsyte" (1917), relating the death of old Jolyon. Technically, the banal plot of the sensitive wife seeking refuge from an insensitive husband in the grand passion is lifted above the commonplace by narrative from the viewpoint of the injured husband and by masterful dramatic handling.

A Modern Comedy is a sequel composed of *The White Monkey* (1924), *The Silver Spoon* (1926), and *Swan Song* (1928) with two interpieces. Fleur is central to a skeptical exhibition of every fad and foible of the 1920s, a "lost generation," drifting aimlessly. The novelist's sympathies turn increasingly to Soames, who is far more attractive in later years than in his prime. The death of Soames in the last volume induced front-page headlines, for this Victorian holdover had by this time won not only the novelist but also much of the English reading public. Though the writing continues its excellence, the novelist is too close to the era depicted and, rebel as he had been once, feels rather repelled by the younger generation.

Herbert George Wells (1866–1946). H. G. Wells was the son of a Bromley, Kent, professional cricket player whose attempt at the crockery business failed miserably. After many odd jobs Wells in 1884 won a scholarship to the Normal School of Science in London where T. H. Huxley inspired him to be a biology instructor. After textbook writing he turned in 1893 to journalism. He proved one of the most prolific writers in this century, a fluent storyteller.

Tono-Bungay (1909), generally acclaimed as Wells's masterwork, is largely socialist propaganda. The earlier portion of the novel is quite autobiographical.

George Ponderevo, after a miserable early life at Bladesover House, where his mother is housekeeper, secures a B.S. from the University of London. His uncle Edward gives him a high-paying job involving Tono-Bungay, a cheap patent medicine only slightly injurious to its consumers. Edward parlays Tono-Bungay into a huge corporation, Domestic Utilities (Do-Ut), which crashes to disaster. George, an amateur aviator, flies his uncle to France in evasion of the law, but Edward dies and George turns to building war munitions.

The fake medicine and the rise and fall of its opportunistic promoter symbolize a disintegrating society. The old England of Bladesover is a class-ridden sham, and Edward is not so much a villain as the inevitable product of an iniquitous social system. Trapped by the system, George, like Shaw's Undershaft, turns science and constructive talents into the weapons of destruction.

Although Jules Verne may properly be termed the father of modern science fiction, Wells was its English progenitor, beginning with *The Time Machine* (1895). *The Invisible Man* (1897) remains a favorite, and even in 1938 the American public was panicked when Wells's *The War of the Worlds* (1898) was dramatized over the radio. Social criticism is omnipresent in these works. Graham of *When the Sleeper Awakes* (1899) is aroused two centuries hence to a mechanical horror of fascist despotism, only to realize "how necessarily this state of things had developed from the Victorian city."

The Outline of History (1920) now suggests history instead of socialism as the means of salvation. The best-selling history of our century, it proclaims that progress is the law of history, with momentary pauses (such as the Dark Ages) only accelerating man's inevitable movement upward. Aldous Huxley mercilessly derides this contention in *Point Counter Point*.

The New World Order (1941) would now offer education as man's hope, but hope has largely departed from Wells. In his last years Wells shocked the sedate British by opposing the monarchy and advocating a republic, but his influence had considerably waned before his death.

Enoch Arnold Bennett (1867–1931). Arnold Bennett early dropped his first name, reminiscent of his evangelical origin at Hanley, Staffordshire, in the "Potteries." In 1888 he came to London, largely to escape his lawyer father and the atmosphere of his native community. In 1893 he began a journalistic career that was to make him one of the most financially successful of recent British authors. His range and quantity were enormous. Seeking to be a cosmopolite, Bennett resided frequently in France, marrying a Frenchwoman in 1907 and separating from her in 1921.

The Old Wives' Tale (1908), his best-known work, is the classic example of the English naturalistic novel under the influence of Balzac and Flaubert. Like most of Bennett's serious novels, it derives its impact chiefly from the solid re-creation of the stuffy, grimy "Five Towns" of his Staffordshire youth.

Constance and Sophia Baines are youthfully restive in their parents' draper's shop (dry goods store) in 1864. Constance, however, marries the uninspiring clerk, Samuel Povey, and settles down to a quiet tradesman's existence. Sophia elopes with a traveling salesman, Gerald Scales, who abandons her in Paris. Sophia fends for herself, eventually becoming a comfortable Parisian landlady, even weathering the horrible siege of Paris in 1870. A chance boarder from the "Five Towns" causes the reunion of the sisters, who die in 1907 amid the bustle of the new century and the indifference of their only heir, Cyril, son of Constance.

Like his French masters, Bennett resolutely depicts smug, self-satisfied bourgeoisie, complicated only in their emotional life. The central motif of this work is the relentless march of time that imperceptibly transforms vivacious girls into dowdy old women. Plot is subordinated to a masterful building upon small details. The invalidism of Mr. Baines symbolizes the impotence of the 19th century, and Sophia's rebellion against castor oil symbolizes the revolt against Victorianism. Each scene begins with a concrete picture and is realized with such photographic accuracy as to make the reader live amid the stairways, overfurnished rooms, and cellars of the Baines establishment. Admirally driven home is Bennett's contention that possessiveness and tangible objects wholly govern these narrow lives. The title is ironically transferred from the romantic Elizabethan comedy by Peele.

The Clayhanger Trilogy, probably Bennett's greatest achievement, consists of *Clayhanger* (1910), *Hilda Lessways* (1911), and *These Twain* (1915). The love affair of Edwin Clayhanger and Hilda Lessways is first told from the man's viewpoint, next from the woman's, and in the final volume from both as they are united in marriage. This may be the definitive English fictional study of non-romantic love and marriage with all the normal little frictions and happinesses. The canvas of the "Five Towns" is rich in atmosphere and sociological interest. Virginia Woolf particularly derided this work because her concerns quite transcended Bennett's thesis that these people are solely what their environment, chiefly physical, makes of them.

The Journals of Arnold Bennett (three volumes, 1932–33) provides one of the most fascinating literary source books ever printed. Daily entries from 1896 until death show the ceaseless process by which the novelist recorded everything he saw and felt as grist for his fiction.

George Augustus Moore (1857–1933). Son of an Irish member of parliament, George Moore was born at Moore Hall, County Mayo, Ireland. Restive under formal education, he went to Paris in 1870 to study art and to associate with most of the noted French artists and writers during a stimulating period of French creativity. After a decade and a half in France he returned to England where he resided until 1901, when his detestation of the Boer War caused him to move back to his native Ireland. After 1905 he lived in England except for occasional travel abroad, publishing as late as 1931. His relation with the Irish writers of the Celtic Renaissance was important, but he is most often considered among English novelists.

Gissing's dedicated art, though often drably unpleasant to contemporary readers, was solidly, understandably in the English realistic tradition. Moore's dedication to art was aesthetic and more Gallic than English. Though one of the consummate prose stylists in English and though considered by capable judges to be one of the greatest writers of his period, Moore has therefore suffered something of the neglect accorded an alien voice. Moore's extraordinary sensitivity to art trends caused him to alter with intellectual movements, thereby displaying a protean quality rare among English writers and often disturbing to English readers.

FRENCH NATURALISM. *A Mummer's Wife* (1885) is the first novel in English to exemplify fully the Zola pattern, in tracing the slow degeneration of an actor's wife.

Esther Waters (1894), Moore's most famous novel, shows strong Balzac influence.

Forced from home by a drunken stepfather, Esther works as a kitchenmaid at the Barfield residence, Woodview. She is seduced by William Latch, the cook's son, and, when pregnant, is forced to leave Woodview and return to her squalid home. Her brutal stepfather causes her again to leave home for the birth of Jackie, her son. After years of struggle to support herself and child, Esther is courted by honest Fred Parsons, but Latch reappears and plays on her religious beliefs to marry her. Latch loses heavily as a racetrack bookie, eventually dying poverty-stricken from tuberculosis. Esther returns to Woodview, proudly showing to Mrs. Barfield her Jackie, now a British soldier.

In its unsentimentally honest picture of lower-class life, and its minute depiction of sordid experiences, *Esther Waters* has been declared the first truly naturalistic novel in English ("Naturalism" goes further than realism in delineating the coarse proletariat, brutalized surroundings, and situations of violence and lust). Although many circulating libraries followed the lead of W. H. Smith & Son in barring *Esther Waters,* Gladstone recognized its fidelity to life and approved of its humble, pious heroine.

FRENCH AESTHETICISM AND DECADENCE. The influence of Huysmans is paramount in *Evelyn Innes* (1898). Evelyn is moved by music to sensual and erotic ecstasies, yet is equally urged to her religion. The conflict between music and faith becomes a major theme. And it is continued by Moore in a sequel, *Sister Teresa* (1901).

FRENCH SYMBOLISM. Though owing something to the Celtic Renaissance and though set in Ireland, *The Lake* (1905) owes most to Mallarmé. Father Gogarty realizes that jealousy rather than Christian morality caused him to hound Nora Glynn from the community. Recognizing "There is a lake in every man's heart," he swims the lake and starts a new life in America.

FRENCH BIBLICAL REVISIONISM. *The Brook Kerith* (1916), often termed Moore's most flawless and beautiful narrative, shows the influence of Renan and Anatole France. Christ is portrayed as a mystical Essene revived from unconsciousness after crucifixion to be shocked later by Paul's perversion of his creed and by the proliferation of dogma and ecclesiastical bickering. Although not entering into the mystic perceptions of Jesus, the work is a marvel of pellucid clarity and simple, reverent beauty.

LATER YEARS. Moore continued to write works of great stylistic importance, notably *Heloïse and Abelard* (1921). And his fine talents later turned to themes from the lore of his native Ireland.

AUTOBIOGRAPHICAL WRITINGS. Moore, in *Hail and Farewell* (1911–1914) discussed not only the events of his life but the meaning for him of the Celtic Renaissance and his relation with the key figures who remained in Ireland when he sought to find himself abroad.

May Sinclair (1865–1946). May Sinclair was greatly interested in psychological studies, and this is very evident in her novels. She had won an audience with *The Divine Fire* (1904); but it was her early recognition of the overwhelming significance of Freud and psychoanalysis and her use of Freudian approaches in such novels as *Mary Olivier* (1919) and *Arnold Waterlow* (1924) which give her a prominent place among the novelists of the period.

William Somerset Maugham (môm) (1874–   ). W. Somerset Maugham was born in Paris, where his father was attached to the British Embassy. England seemed a dull foreign country when he first settled there in 1884. After desultory education, he began medical training at St. Thomas' Hospital in London in 1892. His first novel, *Liza of Lambeth* (1897), derived from his visits to slum patients. He has traveled widely and during both World Wars performed secret missions for the British government. The land of his birth, however, proves more congenial, and most of his later life has been spent in France.

Maugham, certainly in America, has proved the most popular English novelist of this century and the outstanding naturalistic writer in Britain. He is a born storyteller, unmatched since Kipling. Unlike Kipling, however, his mood has paralleled that of readers during recent decades—a cynical contemplation of human unpredictability and the painful or ludicrous entrapment of man by his passions; as a materialist he finds no significance in life. His important contribution to the theater is discussed in Chapter 8.

Of Human Bondage (1915) takes its title from Spinoza's *Ethics*—"Of human bondage, or the strength of the emotions." Maugham, tubercular in his youth, admits the strong autobiographical element.

Philip Carey finds his fellows cruel and himself forced to self-introspection by his congenital deformity, a clubfoot. He is consumed by love for Mildred Rogers, a waitress of only moderate attractiveness and no virtue. Philip cannot free himself from his bondage, although he clearly recognizes Mildred for what she is. He provides for the illegitimate child she has by another man, and Mildred descends to public prostitution. Later he marries Sally Athelny, a wholesome, natural girl who offers him a normal home and security.

Maugham seeks to develop his hero toward the next chapter in Spinoza's *Ethics*—"Of human freedom, or the control of the understanding." Philip rises quite above the young men of previous English novels, who are the slaves of passion, for he is able to change as soon as the film is removed from his eyes. From the beginning he knows the truth and is inwardly torn asunder by his own diagnosis. Relieving himself from the early restraints of Victorianism by discarding all belief in God, Philip finds his tortures multiplying as amid a painful existence he then conceives of pleasure as the meaning of life. Finding later (in the famous perusal of Cronshaw's Persian rug) that life is meaningless, "the world was robbed of its cruelty." Happiness and pain are simply parts of the individual design, and he is now free to live in the present (not the past or the future). Philip is undoubtedly one of the major creations of 20th-century fiction. With this novel Maugham was hailed by the critics as potentially the greatest English novelist of this century, but his subsequent efforts never again reached as high.

The Summing-Up (1938) is perhaps the most honest self-evaluation by any author, as it certainly is the most disarming. No erudite critic so unfailingly dissects Maugham, demonstrating capabilities and limitations, as does Maugham himself. "I have a clear and logical brain, but not a very subtle nor a very powerful one."

NOVELISTS EMPHASIZING NEW FORMS AND NEW THEMES

The modern experimental novel has added previously unknown dimensions to both the longer and the shorter works of fiction, and has established the novel as the most versatile and, at least potentially, the most all-embracing of literary forms. Sterne's *Tristram Shandy* in the 18th century shows more affinities with the experimental novel than any previous English work, but this novel stands in isolation.

In many respects the inspirer of the modern experimental novel was Henry James (1843–1916). Although he is generally treated in the study of American literature because many of his characters are Americans and because he remained an American citizen until a short time before his death, he lived in England through much of his mature life and he is the acknowledged master of Conrad and many subsequent English novelists.

Beginning in the familiar tradition of the novel, James increasingly turned his attention to aspects of the novel heretofore almost unnoted, aspects which characterize the experimental novel.

(1) Technique. Dickens was distinctly English, a born storyteller who wrote as it came to him in the immemorial fashion of an omniscient narrator. When he consciously considered how a story might be told, he stumbled, as in the clumsy use of Esther Summerson as narrator in *Bleak House*. A more conscious craftsman such as Thackeray refined traditional storytelling methods but essentially was no innovator. James displayed a previously unknown concern for how a story should be presented. Although experiments with "viewpoint" (or angle of narration) chiefly occupied James, he triggered the extensive 20th-century search for new novelistic techniques.

(2) Purpose of the novel. The novelists considered in English literature up to this point sought above all to create memorable characters. The experimental novel asks instead: "What is the actual experience of living?" James purposely made his characters financially independent so that he could ignore the economic pressures omnipresent with other novelists. The immense scope now opened to the novel has forced a critical reappraisal. The erudite could earlier dismiss the novel as essentially recreation and amusement, though possessing some sociological interest. Now the explorations of the experimental novel must be treated quite seriously by the professional psychologist and philosopher.

(3) Withering away of external plot. Readers of James protested that very little "happened" in his novels, and ordinary readers of many 20th-century novels in bewilderment aver that nothing at all "happens." The arena of the novelist's concern has shifted from outside events to the inner life, and the conflict has not infrequently been transferred entirely to warring elements within a character.

(4) Absence of the hero. In the bourgeois novel and in the antibourgeois novel the hero and the villain (even if society) were obvious. Heroism has largely departed from the experimental novel, and today's novel reader seldom finds a truly likable character.

(5) Complexity. Seeking to portray not so much what people do or say as what they actually are, the experimental novelist finds none of the old ethical simplicity but discovers a vast and chaotic world within even the outwardly mundane character. Change and alteration produce within a

personality a ceaseless fluidity which destroys the old rigidity of character and reveals disturbing contradictions and complexities.

(6) Irrationality. Increasingly the experimental novel, in exploring the inner life, has found that man does not act from reason, as earlier novels assumed, but rather is motivated by deep unconscious sources of primordial origin.

We turn now to novelists whose work was experimental either in the ways just mentioned or in other important respects.

Joseph Conrad (real name **Jósef Teodor Konrad Korzeniowski**) (1857–1924). Joseph Conrad was born at Berdyczew, Poland, then under Russian rule. Orphaned in 1869, he was educated at Kraków, but partly because of Russian distrust of his family's association with Polish nationalism, he proceeded to France in 1874 for greater opportunity. Until his majority he knew no English at all. At Marseille (1874–78) he was caught up in the Carlist conspiracy to gain the Spanish throne, smuggling arms for the cause. He first followed the sea in French vessels (1875) but joined an English ship in 1878. In the British merchant marine he worked his way up to master by 1886, the year in which he was naturalized. A journey up the Congo in 1890 sapped his health and forced him to abandon the sea in 1894. His first novel, *Almayer's Folly,* was published in the next year. Revisiting Poland in 1914, he was aided by the American ambassador to Austria in returning to England from war-torn Europe. He lost a son in World War I and served the British Admiralty. Late in achieving fame, he made a triumphant tour of the United States in 1923 shortly before his death.

To the English novel Conrad brought a greater and truer cosmopolitanism than any previous author. Instead of falling into the conventions of the English novel, he boldly experimented in form and language. With no concern for the familiar problems of the contemporary novel, his themes were honor, guilt, moral alienation, and expiation. He was not interested in his characters "getting on" in life; he was preoccupied with man's responsibility to himself, which he believed ultimately hinged on fidelity, i.e. brotherhood. Many readers regarded him as an excellent but unduly difficult writer of adventure stories; however, Conrad was only employing his real life experience and, more especially, using locales and conflicts alien to everyday bourgeois society so that he could more easily lead men to ultimate appraisals of their nature and moral duties.

SEARCH FOR TECHNIQUE (TO 1904). *The Nigger of the Narcissus* (1897) brought literary fame but not fortune to Conrad. Flaubert and de Maupassant were the chief influences.

A huge Negro, James Wait, boards the British freighter *Narcissus* (actual name of a vessel on which Conrad was second mate) at Bombay but claims to be too sick from the outset to do any work. On the long sail around the Cape of Good Hope he grows increasingly worse, disrupting the entire crew with his demands for care. When he dies within sight of the Flores islands and is buried at sea, the ship seems lighter, as though Death itself had departed.

The name Wait suggests a malingerer, and the dying man, truly sick in mind as well as body, breaks up the human solidarity necessary for ship operation. The ship is a microcosm of the world of men, where only the unified efforts and fellow feelings of mankind can save our species from the destruction of impersonal Nature. The work is a classic of poetic realism, a profound analysis of the mingled moral responses of men confronted with the mysterious and unfathomable in human spirit and relationship. In a preface to this book written a few months later, Conrad produced his best non-fictional work; the preface states an artistic credo of impressionism, perhaps indebted to Pater.

Lord Jim (1900), most notable of Conrad's early works, is the first important British experimental novel of our era. Story elements come from a variety of sources.

Seeking to exemplify the romantic British naval hero, Jim on the spur of the moment abandons the pilgrim-laden *Patna* along with his cowardly fellow white officers. The ship, however, does not sink, and disgraced and ashamed to return to England, Jim wanders through the East, pursued by the name of coward. Marlow, the partial narrator of the story, secures him a trading-post job under the wise Stein in distant Patusan. There the young Britisher becomes Tuan Jim ("Lord Jim") to the natives. When Gentleman Brown, a modern pirate, besieges Patusan, Jim lets the cutthroat depart, but Brown viciously murders the son of the local chieftain. Jim has himself killed by the chieftain in return.

The theme is guilt and atonement. Unlike Wait, Jim is "one of us," Conrad asserts, the full-fledged product of the British code. As Conrad sees it, Jim's failure was due not so much to cowardice as it was to a paralysis of the will, a strange devil in every man that is inexplicable, which overrides training and conscious purpose. Jim finds expiation for his mistakes in sacrifice of himself.

To analyze the mystery of Jim, Conrad presents the story not in orthodox chronological pattern but as a curious questioner might unearth the facts. The time sequence is therefore completely askew, and events are not related in the order of occurrence but as they are ascertained by the questioner. Imagistic detail and highly conscious symbol (such as Stein's ring) bring characteristics of contemporary poetry to the novel.

Youth (1902) marks the first appearance of Marlow, the novelist's alter ego, who was to figure in many subsequent works as narrator (this work was written before *Lord Jim*).

The *Judea* (obviously named for the *Palestine*, one of Conrad's ships) is a jinxed vessel on which Marlow serves as second mate. Every sort of nautical accident plagues the ship, which is finally destroyed in the Indian Ocean by spontaneous combustion from wet coal. Though derelict, her crew has at last reached the fabled East.

As the title indicates, this novel is a paean to youth and to the unquenchable endurance of men, even in a hopeless cause. The retrospective glance of Marlow sees the poignancy of youth's vivacity and freshness, hinting of the shadows to come.

"Heart of Darkness," included in this volume, is recognized as one of the most noteworthy pieces of fiction of this century; it provides the epigraph, "Mistah Kurtz, he dead," for Eliot's "Hollow Men." It is based upon Conrad's 1890 trip up the Congo.

Marlow journeys up the Congo River for a Belgian concern to find the hideously degenerated Kurtz, a god-devil of the wretched natives whom he exploits. Kurtz dies in conscience-stricken horror, but Marlow feels himself obliged to relate a glib fiction to Kurtz's fiancée back home.

Probably no other writing brings so glaringly to life the teeming, sinister Congo. Kurtz had first come here as a brilliant young idealist, but greed for power and wealth transformed him into a monster. This is not so much an indictment of imperialism as it is a horrified comment on the complete loss of moral responsibility by a civilization devoted to selfish materialism.

"The End of the Tether" portrays as transgressor Captain Whalley, who must continue his seamanship to provide for his daughter. His vision failing, he loses his ship because of the scoundrel Massy's interference with the compass. Whalley's deception and compromise with his conscience send him to death for violation of his duty to his men. Conrad saw this piece as concluding within this volume his study of the three ages of man: youth, maturity, age.

Typhoon (1903), the most memorable tale in English upon the simple conflict of man versus Nature, contains the best description of a sea storm in literature. In the Pacific, Captain MacWhirr saves his rusty tub, the *Nan-Shan,* in spite of a merciless pounding from the sea and a panicked crew. An imaginative man would have failed, but the invincible determination of MacWhirr is a tribute to men of limited intellectual range but great heart and faithfulness to duty. Conrad served on the *Highland Forest* under a Captain McWhirr, but the story was hearsay.

POLITICAL AND SOCIAL PERIOD (1904–14). *Nostromo* (1904), Conrad's masterpiece, belongs to that tiny number of the world's novels that may seriously be compared to Tolstoy's *War and Peace.*

Nostromo ("our man") is an Italian sailor, Gian' Battista, foreman of the stevedores at Sulaco, seaport of revolution-torn Costaguana in Central America. Dominating the entire western part of the nation is the San Tomé silver mine, a concession originally forced upon the family of Charles Gould, an Englishman. To prevent silver ingots from falling into the hands of insurrectionists, Nostromo and Decoud (the local journalist) carry away the silver in a lighter that is sunk by collision with the revolutionists' ships. Decoud is lost, but Nostromo then acts as messenger to bring other troops who eventually break off this segment of Costaguana to form the Occidental Republic (parallel to Panama's secession from Colombia). Everyone presuming the lighter of silver lost, Nostromo is able to salvage silver for his own gain. In a night jaunt for more of his hidden treasure, Nostromo is accidentally slain.

No other work in English so vividly brings to life an entire nation, with every class of society represented and with majestic land- and seascapes completely portrayed. But Conrad's main purpose is a scrutiny of all Western history in miniature. The course of the eventual Occidental Republic is traced from the first conquistadors until the communists are agitating at the novel's close. Conrad analyzes the spectrum of motives producing modern capitalism, and although selfish greed and exploitation represent only part of capitalistic drive, the end product seems to Conrad to be the economic crushing of freedom and brotherhood, as evidenced in Gould, the owner of the San Tomé mine. Outwardly prosperous and bustling, the Occidental Republic (or, rather, the impersonal silver that rules all its inhabitants) has imposed a tyranny more devastating though less overtly brutal than that of the conquistadors.

The infection of the silver destroys Nostromo. Nostromo was based on a real figure, an audacious scamp who, according to Central American anecdotes, had actually stolen a boatload of silver. Conrad transforms him into a typical Conradian figure, a noble though naïve man of action who gradually realizes that he is simply being used by those struggling for power and wealth. In succumbing to this selfish code, he alienates himself from his brothers and, a hollow man, insures his own destruction.

The impressionistic technique of novel writing reaches its height in this work. Expecting conventional narrative, the reader is intrigued but bewildered by brilliantly swirling events and descriptions for almost the first two hundred pages. This, Conrad contends, is how any observer learns from experience. We enter the harbor, catch glimpses of Sulaco, hear varying and irreconcilable accounts about the community, and only gradually begin to form fixed judgments about the Occidental Republic and its people. The thematic rhythms of Conrad exceed those of any previous English novel. For example, the superlative description of the harbor at the outset establishes symbols of greed, darkness, and disorder that will be played upon throughout, much as T. S. Eliot does in *The Waste Land*. Unlike later experimenters, Conrad creates his microcosm by having each individual represent an essentially simple human trait (e.g. Nostromo=action,

Decoud=thought) instead of concentrating in depth on one character to reveal the human mystery.

The Secret Agent (1907), Conrad's first story set in London, was suggested by the 1894 attempt of anarchists to blow up the Greenwich Observatory. The pathetic efforts at conspiracy by Adolf Verloc (a tool of the Russians) are set in a grimy, inhuman city. Ironically, Conrad castigates the bourgeois world of science and materialism, which produces a drab prison atmosphere hostile to the human spirit.

A Set of Six (1908) consists of a half dozen short stories, the most significant of which is "Il Conde," a portrait of a retiring European count, enjoying the quiet, art-loving life possible to the privileged before World War I. The theme asserts that true humanity and ethical responsibility must surpass self-seeking acquisitiveness.

Under Western Eyes (1911), seeking to explain the baffling Russian nature to the West, is strongly reminiscent of Dostoevsky, though Conrad denied any Russian influence. Razumov, the revolutionary, is the most fully realized and analyzed of all Conrad's characters. Denouncing the cruel autocracy of Czarist Russia, Conrad sees as equally perverse the wild revolutionaries reacting in tyranny. The theme again is guilt and atonement.

'Twixt Land and Sea (1912) contained three stories, most notably "The Secret Sharer." A youthful Captain helps a fugitive, Leggatt (who physically is almost his double), to escape by concealing him on board his ship. The themes are initiation into maturity, brotherhood, and ethical responsibility. For all its surface simplicity, psychologists have found it a classic study of the *doppelgänger*.

Chance (1914), first serialized by the New York *Herald* (1912), is the most complex of all Conrad novels in technique, but his first popular success. It seems the least dependent of any Conrad works upon his experience or reading. The theme is emotional isolation represented in Flora de Barral, Conrad's most fully examined woman. Despite his Roman Catholic upbringing, Conrad here as elsewhere posits a strictly man-centered universe. Flora must turn inward altogether for her resources, and Conrad's position parallels the self-responsibility of existentialism.

MORE CONVENTIONAL TECHNIQUE (1915 TO DEATH). *Victory* (1915), widely hailed and thus belatedly granting fame to Conrad, was the author's own favorite along with *Nostromo*.

Axel Heyst, a Swede influenced by his pessimistic father, detaches himself from life, living alone on a tropic island in the Pacific. To save Lena, an English girl, from the lecherous advances of Schomberg, an inn-keeper, he bears her off to his hideaway, still cognizant of his father's warning that "he who forms a tie is lost." In revenge, Schomberg enlists the aid of the villainous Mr. Jones and his accomplice, Ricardo, against Heyst. Lena gives her life in futile but loving defense of Heyst.

Too late Heyst realizes the active role he should have performed among his fellow humans. The novel has been interpreted as an indictment of all Western art and society before World War I. In shirking their responsibility as their brothers' keepers, well-intentioned Western men brought upon mankind the holocausts of this century. Heyst's dying cry is "to put trust in life." In defeat Heyst and Lena are victorious.

The Shadow-Line (1917), relating the vicissitudes of the young Captain of the *Melita* with a sick crew and a stagnant sea, is virtually an allegory of human victory in the face of bitter adversity.

Subsequent novels by Conrad are competent romances, like *The Arrow of Gold* (1919), harking back to his gun-running days, or *The Rover* (1923), a historical tale of Napoleonic days on the Escampobar Peninsula. In his more individual style is *The Rescue* (1920).

William Henry Hudson (1841–1922). W. H. Hudson achieved recognition when he was well along in years. His grandfather had emigrated from England to Massachusetts, and his father emigrated from New England to the pampas of the Argentine, west of Buenos Aires, where Hudson was born. After roaming about South America, Hudson went to England in 1870, becoming a British subject in 1900. It was in the circle of Edward Garnett and his family that Hudson came to know Joseph Conrad. Many of Hudson's works are essays on Nature in England or South America, but his fame rests on his works of fiction—romances and short stories—and upon his autobiographical reminiscences.

The Purple Land That England Lost (1885) is picaresque fiction, partly disguised autobiography, carrying young Richard Lamb through colorful episodes in Uruguay. Hudson, a naturalist at heart, proves himself a master of sensuous prose, calling forth the convincing atmosphere of the pampas. Although the ostensible theme is regret that England's law and order do not extend to this troubled land, the underlying assertion is the superiority of the natural rhythms of the Banda Oriental to the age of the machine. The work was highly praised by Theodore Roosevelt.

Green Mansions (1904) first attracted widespread attention to Hudson, and this poetic romance of the forests remains a classic legend of our century. Galsworthy wrote the laudatory introduction.

Though the Indians believe the forest to be haunted, Abel explores it and finds Rima, an exquisite, strange, birdlike girl, with whom he falls in love. Much of the story deals with his search for Rima's home. When the savages trap Rima and set fire to the tree in which she is seeking to hide, Abel sorrowfully bears away Rima's charred remains and avenges her murder.

Although never having visited the jungles of Guiana in northern South America, Hudson imagined them so completely as to impress the knowledgeable American scientist William Beebe. But the fascinating focus of the novel is the amazing Rima, emblem of the Eternal Feminine and of Nature herself. The lonely, mysterious beauty of Nature can never be fully grasped by man. Instead, like the savages in *Green Mansions,* he resents his ignorance and alien isolation, and viciously destroys true loveliness.

Other characteristically poetic works of Hudson during this period are *A Little Boy Lost* (1905), a fantasy, and *A Shepherd's Life* (1910), narrative prose. His short stories are collected as *Tales of the Pampas* (1902).

Far Away and Long Ago (1918), written by Hudson in his old age, relives his early Argentinian days. Many consider it the best re-creation of childhood in our language. Sensuous prose poetry caresses the violent, amoral society and the spacious, untamed landscapes of his distant youth. Most notable is "A Boy's Animism," a chapter recounting young Hudson's progress from a physical to a mystical response to Nature. Unlike Wordsworth, the older Hudson never lost the "vision splendid," but retained until death an exultation at the numinous presence in Nature.

Ford Madox Ford (1873–1939). Ford Madox Ford was born with the surname Hueffer which he changed to Ford in 1919. He was the grandson of the artist Ford Madox Brown. Born in Merton, Surrey, he was educated at University College School, London. He was received into the Roman Catholic Church in 1891. He collaborated with Conrad in writing *The Inheritors* (1901) and *Romance* (1903), and in 1908–09 edited the *English Review*. During World War I he served in France with a Welsh regiment. After the war he resided in Paris, associating with Ezra Pound and James Joyce, and editing *transatlantic review* (1923–24). His novels securing better acceptance in America than in England, he spent most of his later life in the United States or France, where he died. Although he was essentially a follower of the novelistic experiments of others, interest in his writing has been mounting steadily.

Parade's End is the 1950 title given to Ford's Tietjens tetralogy, consisting of *Some Do Not* (1924), *No More Parades* (1925), *A Man Could Stand Up* (1926), and *The Last Post* (1928). Ford's theme here is lost causes. Christopher Tietjens is the last 18th-century Englishman: Protestant in his beliefs, humane in his relationships, feudal in outlook, a classicist by training, and a Tory in politics. God, man, and the world seem a harmony to him, and England is the treasured abode of reason and balance. The whole scheme of things, however, is against him, especially World War I, which is a monstrous refutation of all Tietjens knew and stood for. From his vindictive Roman Catholic wife, Sylvia, to the errant German mortar shell that wrongfully causes him to be relieved of his front-line command, everything and everybody seem to conspire to obliterate the sane existence Tietjens tried to create for himself. In the agonies of Tietjens, Ford symbolizes the foundering of all modern society. The passing of the Tietjens clan is the vanishing of an anachronism, of those true to principles in a world that has abandoned any fixed principles. Just or unjust, it is the law of history.

Time-shift and stream of consciousness are Ford's major techniques. Particularly impressive is the interior monologue of *A Man Could Stand Up,* where Tietjens struggles amidst the insanity of the trenches to retain his own sanity. The last volume consists of nine interconnected interior monologues climaxing in the moment-of-truth perception of Mark, Christopher's brother, dying of a paralytic stroke.

THE NOVELS AND SHORT STORIES OF JAMES JOYCE

James Augustine Aloysius Joyce (1882–1941). James Joyce was the son of lower middle-class parents in Rathgar, a suburb of Dublin. Destined from infancy for the Roman Catholic priesthood, he was sent at six to Clongowes Wood College and in 1893 to Belvedere College, both Jesuit institutions. During studies at University College, Dublin, from 1898 to 1902 he became an avowed atheist, vehemently hostile to a Roman Catholicism which he could never entirely shake off. In 1902 he went to Paris only to be summoned home the next year by his mother's death. When he left Dublin with his new bride in 1904, he was never to return to Ireland again except for brief visits, the last in 1912. In Trieste, Rome, and Zürich he supported his family chiefly by teaching foreign languages, in which he was immensely fluent. His later years in Paris were devoted entirely to writing.

The most discussed novelist in our language during this century, Joyce is the archetype of the rebellious artist of our era, though T. S. Eliot has always recognized Joyce as thoroughly in the Catholic tradition, and Thomas Merton has declared that the reading of Joyce sent him into the Church. Indeed, many Catholics believe that Joyce would have returned to the fold, had he lived longer. Over his own Dublin (never absent from his blood during all his exile) and over all modern society Joyce sensed an atmosphere of frustration and disintegration. His refuge was in art, the most absolute and brilliant experimentation ever performed upon the novel. A remarkable combination of realist and symbolist, he stated without too much exaggeration that if all other writings of our period were lost, the age could be reconstructed *in toto* from his writings.

Dubliners (*1905* started, 1914), long delayed from publication as a volume because of censorship, consists of fifteen short stories in which Joyce intended "to betray the soul of that hemiplegia or paralysis which many consider a city"; the paralysis is intellectual, moral, and spiritual. This study in environment, notably in "Araby," "The Dead," and "Counterparts," is militantly opposed to the contemporary Celtic Renaissance. To the dreamy or patriotic effusions of his fellow Irishmen, Joyce countered with uncompromising depictions of Irish decay, banality, and tawdriness. Although quite Chekhovian, the series began some time before Joyce read Chekhov.

A Portrait of the Artist as a Young Man (1916) is a complete revision of an early ms. of 1906 which was first published in 1944 in its surviving fragment (about one third of the original) as *Stephen Hero*. The central character is Stephen Dedalus (Stephen was the first Christian martyr; Daedalus was the mythical artisan who constructed waxen wings with which to fly out of the Labyrinth). Joyce actually used this pseudonym for early periodical publication of *Dubliners* stories.

This autobiographical novel traces Stephen from infancy until, like his creator, he departs for Paris and the life of the self-exiled artist. Family, country, and Church are oppressive instruments to trap and deform Stephen's spirit. His father Simon is a shiftless good fellow incapable of providing for the large family. At Clongowes Wood College the frail child (suffering like Joyce from poor eyesight) is mistreated by the arbitrary priests who teach him. A horribly vulgar quarrel about Parnell and Irish patriotism disgusts little Stephen. His brilliance causes the Jesuits to seek him for their order, and for a while the youth is fanatically pious. The inculcation of a sense of sin results in Stephen's terrible inward turmoil over a sexual adventure. In college he gradually undergoes a conversion from faith and the Church to life and art. Finally he flees to Paris.

The *Portrait* has set a fashion for the poetized autobiographical novel, but none since (except perhaps Lawrence's *Sons and Lovers*) has matched its power. It is the definitive presentation of the 20th-century artist in rebellion, breaking from his matrix and becoming himself. Art is a spiritual exaltation, requiring such unstinted devotion that lesser claims must be wholly brushed aside. The artist is presented as the supreme hero, and he is the outsider.

The impact of the novel arises in large part from the interior monologue, the direct presentation of Stephen's thoughts. Conditioned by traditional novel techniques, readers protest that they cannot learn the exact age of the central character until half way through and cannot describe Mrs. Dedalus at all. Unlike any previous novel, the work follows the strengthening mind of the artist from the infantile language of the opening through increased complexity and depth of monologue until in conclusion the reader is confronted with the inner verbalizings of an artistic genius. Like a musical composition (and Joyce was a gifted vocalist and music lover) the novel establishes in embryo at the outset the leitmotifs that will run through the entire work. The dominant motif, like Eliot's, is mythological; the artist Stephen is the daedal fabricator of wings by which to fly over walls and escape. Like a Celtic bard or a Christian saint, Joyce finds epiphanies (i.e. revelations) in even the most commonplace of experiences. Though not as obvious as the Daedalus motif, the theme of the Christ-like artist therefore emerges in the everyday ministrations of the artist, his assumption of the priesthood of art, and his crucifixion by his fellows.

Exiles (1918), Joyce's only drama, was rejected by Shaw as "obscure." Like Joyce, the central figure returns to Dublin from exile in 1912, but his name is Richard Rowan ("rowan" is an ash tree, a tree of life, like the ashplant carried by Stephen). Richard is the lonely rebel, a victim of jealousy and possessiveness, who nonetheless maintains the moral principle of artistic freedom.

Ulysses (1922) is possibly the most talked-about and most controversial piece of literature in this century. Initial publication was in Paris, and censorship in the English-speaking world delayed the first legal printings in the United States until 1933 and in England until 1936; the work is still banned in Ireland.

The title shows the mythological framework of the novel; Joyce declared that in its portrayal of the life quest the *Odyssey* was the fundamental book of Western literature. Paralleling Odysseus is Leopold Bloom, a little man of Jewish origins but successively a Protestant and Roman Catholic (in his urge to belong he embodies the three major strains of European culture and represents Everyman). Paralleling Telemachus is Stephen Dedalus, representing the intellect, in search of a father, as Bloom (whose only son died in infancy) seeks a son. Paralleling Penelope is Molly Bloom, the flesh, who represents the fecund earth mother in her sensuality. The apparently trivial experiences of these characters on June 16, 1904, constitute the entire universe of human impulses in the modern bourgeois world (the more gracious aspects of Dublin are sacrificed for a vision of the cheap and the run-down).

The pervasive technique is the interior monologue, apparently introduced to recent literature by Edouard Dujardin in 1887 in "Les lauriers sont coupés" ("The laurels are cut"). The method was further substantiated for Joyce by Remy de Gourmont who in *Promenades Philosophiques* (2° *Série*, 1908) claimed language as a sixth sense, the machinery through which the human organism reveals its innermost processes. The result is presentation of a character's interior world through "the stream of consciousness," every sense impression from the outer world triggering a string of associated thoughts and memories, highly imaginative and creative in Stephen's case, quite physical and sensual from Molly.

In the following brief summary and comment the numbers refer to pages in the Random House edition (New York); the John Lane edition (London) runs to about thirty pages less. The subtitles were Joyce's original intention, omitted from the printed text to prevent overemphasis on the Homeric allusions.

The Telemachiad (4–51) depicts the isolation of Stephen the artist from his fellows. Incomplete, he needs the shared life with others but finds no contact.

I Telemachus (4–24), 8 AM. Interior monologue of Stephen. The artist shares an old Martello tower near Dublin with the blasphemous medical student Buck Mulligan (Oliver Gogarty) and Haines (S. C. Trench), a rabid English convert to Irish nationalism. With parallels to Hamlet as well as the Odyssey, Stephen is shown in need of atonement, of becoming one with the father, and removing the feeling of guilt for his mother's death.

II Nestor (25–37), 10 AM. Interior monologue of Stephen. Stephen's history class in a boys' school at Dalkey is mercifully cut short by a half-holiday. The freedom-loving poet wishes to escape from history and his own past, though such a renegade Catholic and Jesuit will not find it possible. Nestor is the garrulous headmaster, Mr. Deasy.

III Proteus (38–51), 11 AM. Interior monologue of Stephen. In free association, Stephen on the beach at Sandymount near Dublin contemplates the protean nature of the world and of human experience, illusion and reality, seeking the fixation of flux by form, i.e. by the imposition and composition of philosophy and art.

The Voyage of Odysseus (54–593) follows Bloom in his life journey through Dublin, increasingly crossing the path of Stephen until the two are united.

IV Calypso (54–69), 8 AM. Interior monologue of Bloom. Like Odysseus, trapped for seven years on the isle of the enchantress Calypso, Bloom of 7 Eccles Street has had no marital relations since the death of his son Rudy ten years ago and therefore takes refuge in amatory fantasies. He and Molly chat briefly and after her breakfast Bloom sets off for a public bath, preparatory to attending a funeral.

V Lotus Eaters (70–85), 10 AM. Interior monologue of Bloom. The public bath is a sensual sex substitute for Bloom, a narcotic like the ancient lotus.

VI Hades (86–114), 11 AM. Interior monologue of Bloom. Proceeding to Paddy Dignam's funeral at Glasnevin Cemetery, Bloom is conducted through the modern hell of Dublin. Burial, commerce, and the empty death of the present community pervade this chapter. En route Bloom spots Stephen for the first time that day, at a distance.

VII Aeolus (115–148), noon. In a truly windy chapter, set in a newspaper office, the headlines, interrupting a naturalistic narrative, mark the tempo by a formal opening but gradually jazz up to the blatant vulgarity of current journalism. Stephen comes with a letter that Mr. Deasy wishes printed, and Bloom, as a canvasser for advertisements, again almost meets him. This age needs an oracle, a true prophet, but it ignores Stephen and offers only newspaper sensationalism.

VIII Lestrygonians (149–181), 1 PM. Interior monologue of Bloom.

The Homeric originals were cannibals. Mr. Bloom stops for lunch but discards the idea when observing the filthy eating habits of the diners. He hungers for the message, the way of life, but is repelled by the purely sensual solutions of the modern world.

IX Scylla and Charybdis (182–215), 2 PM. Interior monologue of Stephen. Like the ancient monsters of the Sicilian narrows, Aristotelianism and Platonism, the real and the ideal, await Stephen, George Russell (A.E.), John Eglinton (pen name for W. K. Magee of the Celtic Renaissance), and others in the National Library as they discuss Hamlet. The marvelously ingenious theory of Stephen reveals little about Shakespeare but intensifies his search for a father. Looking up a newspaper file, Bloom again passes by.

X Wandering Rocks (216–251), 3 PM. Terming his method here "labyrinthine," Joyce at the novel's center presents eighteen vignettes of the disordered city, this age of simultaneity but not of genuine integration. The strange intrusions of apparently unrelated items are cross links to other vignettes occurring at precisely the same time. Church, state, and family all teem in the crowded Dublin streets, a maze without a plan.

XI Sirens (252–286), 4 PM. Bloom steps into the Ormond Hotel for food at the time Blazes Boylan, Molly's manager, has a drink in the Ormond bar preparatory to an assignation with Bloom's wife. The lyric yearning and pain of Bloom are appropriately handled in a four-part fugue. The phrases beginning this chapter are leitmotifs for the musical variations to follow. Syntax itself is completely distorted to achieve polyphonic effects. Lyrically, the themes of lost love and the betrayed youth are united into "Siopold," fusing Stephen's two fathers. The barmaids are ineffectual sirens.

XII Cyclops (287–339), 5 PM. Stopping in Barney Kiernan's pub, Bloom is confronted by the most offensive version of Irishism in "the citizen." "Gigantism" is Joyce's term for this technique that presents the same accounts in two constantly contrasted and diametrically opposite fashions—the inflated heroic and the debased vulgar. Perhaps the true vision lies between. The Irish in the pub display disgusting bigotry and brutality, while Bloom approaches a Christ figure in his doctrine of love and brotherhood.

XIII Nausicaa (340–376), 8 PM. At Sandymount beach, where Stephen had been this morning, Bloom is a voyeur, partly of a Dublin fireworks display (symbol of his orgasm) but chiefly of the vulgarly flirtatious Gerty MacDowell. His sensuality like that of his era results in impotence and onanism. The interior monologue of Bloom is counterpointed by that of Gerty, which wickedly parodies the romantic fiction of cheap women's magazines.

XIV Oxen of the Sun (377–421), 10 PM. At the National Maternity

Hospital, Bloom meets Stephen and uproarious medical students while Mrs. Purefoy suffers upstairs in her third day of labor. The disrespect of Odysseus' crew for the fertility symbol of the sacred cattle is matched by the maudlin revelers. Bloom counters their mockery with humane compassion and reverence for life. The technique here is the idea of creation and development presented through coruscating parodies of Western literature beginning with the Latin fathers and Anglo-Saxon, and bowling through Swift, Sterne, Carlyle, and so on to modern journalism and Billy Sunday.

XV Circe (422–593), midnight. Bloom protectively follows Stephen and the drunken crew to Bella Cohen's brothel where Stephen wrecks a chandelier but is rescued and carried off by Bloom as Odysseus saved his men from Circe's sty. This nightmare scene, which Joyce called a *Walpurgisnacht,* is presented as a sort of hallucinatory Strindberg drama; exhaustion and inebriation cause the wildest of memories and bizarre associations to leap to life in the minds of Bloom and Stephen. Jung saw every psychological fear of this century dramatized in this section. In its purgation it cleanses the spirits of the two men. In smashing the chandelier Stephen destroys the gnawing sense of sin he has felt because of supposed unkindness that killed his mother ("Cancer did it, not I"). Bloom throws off his sensuality for parental love toward Stephen. Epiphanies have caused the rebirth of both.

Ithaca (596–end) brings momentary togetherness of Stephen and Bloom, and ends the voyage at the great principle of sustaining life.

XVI Eumaeus (596–649), 1 AM. Paralleling the revelation of Odysseus' identity to his son in the hut of Eumaeus, the swineherd, Bloom becomes a father surrogate to the befuddled Stephen, sobered in a cabman's shelter. The straight narrative is purposely tired and flabby.

XVII Ithaca (650–722), 2 AM. Bloom brings Stephen home for cocoa, invites him to stay, and regretfully bids him farewell. The chapter is told in a lengthy parody of the Longer Catechism. Much previously puzzling is made clear, though the weary hours purposely compel an almost deadly boredom. Stephen's quest has been for maturity, humanity, and self. Bloom's love and Stephen's apprehension briefly unite and elevate them. Bloom has done his job and found his purpose; the vagrant artist, recharged by the humanity of Bloom, must now depart from the bourgeois society that created him in order to be a veritable creator in his own right.

XVIII Penelope (723–end), 2:45 PM. The concluding monologue from the somnolent Molly Bloom is a fantastic *tour de force,* almost fifty pages of reverie without punctuation, to reproduce the continuous thinking of the dreamer. Bloom's goal has been home, Stephen's (prepared for by Bloom) is reality. Here indeed is that reality in the paean to life by the eternal feminine principle of fructifying earth. In spite of her long estrangement from her husband, she recognizes him as all aspects of maleness. Home and reality and all the sought-for human goals of security and meaning rise in this soliloquy to the ecstatic concluding affirmation: "and yes I said yes I will YES." With all the debasement of Dublin and the modern world, Molly's deep instinct and intuition promise abiding hope.

Finnegans Wake (1939) was the final title for Joyce's last effort, which previously had been termed "Work in Progress" since its first fragment had been printed in 1924 by the *transatlantic review*. The work is so fantastically all-embracing and so bewilderingly difficult that outside of several major points few interpreters are in agreement; Joyce suggested that the reader could profitably devote a lifetime to this work.

Most obvious difficulty is the language, a unique Joycean creation. It seems an entire volume written with portmanteau words such as Carroll used only sparingly in *Alice*. Seeking multiple layers in the meaning of each word, Joyce jams together several English words and even foreign words into one. "Oystrygods gaggin fishygods" contains at least these multiple meanings:

Oystrygods=Ostrogoths; shellfish-eaters believed to have preceded fish-eaters on the Irish coast; Oyster Haven, a bay at Cork, Ireland; shell-fish versus other fish in chaotic contest during the Deluge.

gaggin=ramming something down the throats of the conquered; attempting to silence; against (German *gegen*).

fishgods=Visigoths; fish-eaters following shell-eaters on Irish coast. There seems no end to the *multum-in-parvo* idea-hunt, and scholarly articles often consume multitudes of pages dissecting only a few phrases from *Finnegans Wake*.

While much of Joyce's language seems a dismaying conundrum, his new tongue can produce some of the most mellifluous phrasing in English. The "Anna Livia Plurabelle" passage, frequently anthologized as poetry, starts from the Liffey river of Dublin to soar ecstatically in the life force represented by all the rivers of the world.

As the title indicates, the starting point is the old vaudeville patter song about an Irish hodcarrier who falls off a ladder in a drunken fit and is believed dead. At his wake, bibulous grievers spill whiskey upon him, and Finnegan comes to life to join the general celebration. "Finn-again" is thus interpreted as another of the death-and-resurrection myths of mankind, and Finn becomes all such resurrected ones—Dionysus, Adonis, Osiris, Christ. Likewise the fall of Finnegan is symbolic of every fall, from the Fall of Man to the crash of Wall Street.

The entire course of history and human destiny is the actual subject. From *La Scienza Nuova* of the 18th-century Italian philosopher Giambattista Vico, Joyce adopts, as the four divisions of the work indicate, a classification of every cycle of history into four phases: theocratic, aristocratic, democratic, chaotic. The last phase, in which modern society now stands, is characterized by individualism and sterility. The collapse of a civilization, however, liberates energy that will recharge mankind and precipitate a new cycle. Pessimistic about modern culture, as are most of today's intellectuals, Joyce nonetheless sounds a note of triumphant optimism in the assurance that a new and vigorous era shall rise even from our ashes. To exemplify the circular movement of the entire scheme, *Finnegans Wake* begins in mid-sentence and concludes with the first half of the initial sentence; by Joyce's own declaration the reader may begin anywhere in the work and read circularly.

To embody his thesis Joyce presents as central character Humphrey Chimpden Earwicker (HCE), a Dublin tavernkeeper who as the universal progenitor constantly pops up as Here Comes Everybody, Haveth Childers Everywhere, Howth Castle and Environs, etc. His wife Anna is the eternal principle of love and fertility, but especially the river of life. The couple have two sons, Jerry (Shem in symbolic sense) and Kerry (Shaun in symbolic sense); in the ceaseless war of brothers Shem the Penman is the poet and seer, while Shaun is the man of action and exploitation. Within this family and its ramifications struggle all the polarities of life: male and female, thinking and doing, age and youth, love and hate, life and death. Amid the apparent diversity of humanity these polarities forever abide and forever provide the energy that sustains the individual and sweeps all our species into the eternal *corso-recorso* of Vico.

NOVELISTS EXPERIMENTING WITH FORM AND CONTENT

Virginia Woolf (1882–1941). Daughter of Sir Leslie Stephen, Virginia Woolf was born in London. She had family connections with Thackeray, Symonds, and Darwin. In a household of remarkable culture and intellect she was reading Gibbon and Hume in childhood. From 1904 she resided in Bloomsbury to become the focal figure in the "Bloomsbury Group," a brilliant circle of intellectuals including Lord Keynes, Lytton Strachey, and E. M. Forster. She married one of the group, Leonard Woolf, in 1912. She and her husband founded the Hogarth Press, which proved the leading British avant-garde publisher, giving T. S. Eliot and Katherine Mansfield a hearing before conservative publishers picked them up. Her first novel, *The Voyage Out* (1915), was rather conventional. Although a shy, retiring creature, she vigorously supported feminism and controversial new literature against all opponents. Living for literature and art, she could not endure the horrors of World War II and drowned herself.

From a fastidious feminine viewpoint (free of violence in action or language) Mrs. Woolf attempted experiments paralleling Joyce's, yet she was also strongly influenced by Dorothy Richardson and the Frenchmen Henri Bergson and Marcel Proust. Discarding the conventional "character" and altogether ignoring "plot," Mrs. Woolf sought to re-create the inner complexities of experience. She searched the eternal fluctuation of life to find illuminations, chiefly of what meaning there is in personal relationships and what life actually is to the psyche. Never a popular writer, she has had an enormous impact upon modern intellectuals.

Jacob's Room (1922) is her first stream-of-consciousness novel. The title character is a commonplace, easy-going chap familiar in the prewar years. Jacob Flanders is not a Joycean rebel but a quiet seeker for reality, whose room or rather sequence of rooms represents his attempt to construct meaning for himself from the eddying of experience. Killed in World War I, Jacob never finds his plan or purpose. Plotless, unsensational, it remains one of the world's most sensitive perceptions of what youth actually is.

Mrs. Dalloway (1925) in the stream-of-consciousness technique is an experiment with time, mingling present experience with memory, chiefly in the mind of the fashionable, middle-aged Mrs. Dalloway. All action occurs upon one day in June.

Clarissa Dalloway, whose husband Richard is a member of parliament, is giving a splendid party that night. Visiting her is Peter Walsh, her lover of thirty years ago. In the Park, Peter sees the shell-shocked veteran Septimus Warren Smith with his Italian wife, Lucrezia. The awkward, unattractive tutor Miss Kilman tries to draw to herself Clarissa's lovely daughter Elizabeth. The party is a resounding success largely because the prime minister attends, but the noted specialist Sir William Bradshaw is late because of the suicide of Septimus.

The London of stone and brick and macadam is an inhuman world, deluding the lovers of life into believing that it is life. The reality is love itself. Mrs. Dalloway is a catalyst to make others "connect," but this envied hostess realizes the ultimate mystery of human isolation. Instead of the security of Richard she should have taken the love of Peter. Even her daughter is being drawn away from her by the painfully spinsterish Miss Kilman. Septimus is her double, another victim of the shallow emptiness of the modern world. In her identification with him and her piercing through Bradshaw she justifies her existence and momentarily penetrates beneath the surface of life.

The entire novel is structured in the two dimensions of time and space. It either stands still in time and moves about in space (as the consciousness of a number of Londoners is explored) or it stands still in space and moves about in time (as Mrs. Dalloway lives much of a lifetime in a few moments). Clock time, symbolized by the recurring chimes of Big Ben, is not the reality; the truth is subjective felt time by which at any given moment we may be living in the past, present, or future—or any combination or sum of them.

To the Lighthouse (1927), her masterpiece, might better be entitled "Going to the Lighthouse," for the lighthouse is the symbolic focus of every character's desires, the object of their attainment or fulfillment. Technique is stream of consciousness.

"The Window" (Integration) is present time lived through. Mr. and Mrs. Ramsay (Woolf's parents) are summering with their numerous offspring at their cottage in the Hebrides. Son James is intent upon a trip the next day to the lighthouse, but Mr. Ramsay with meteorological exactitude squashes the plan. Minta Doyle and Paul Rayley are enraptured by their engagement, but all the other adults are unhappy: Tansley, a crabbed scholar; Carmichael, a not-too-successful poet; Lily Briscoe, an unsuccessful painter; William Banks, a scientist. Especially troubled is Mr. Ramsay, who wrote a brilliant philosophical study at the age of twenty-five and nothing quite so good thereafter. By her act of will and love Mrs. Ramsay makes time stand still. She has created the home, filling it with children, warmth, and security; she strengthens the fragile male ego of her husband and brings the scattered guests together in at least momentary communion. In her and the unity she creates, life has achieved meaning, a window to reality.

"Time Passes" (Disintegration) is external clock time, the war period when the summer cottage slowly decays, showing the breakup of the Ramsays, as a son is killed in the war, a daughter dies in childbirth, and Mrs. Ramsay herself dies. The impersonality of Nature to the destruction of human hopes is celebrated in one of the notable prose poems of English.

"The Lighthouse" (Reintegration) handles time in a twofold fashion. For James and his father making the long-delayed trip to the lighthouse it is actually time extended into the future as the family sundered by Mrs. Ramsay's death fuses into a new working combination. For Lily Briscoe, remaining at the cottage, time moves backward as she re-creates the meaning of Mrs. Ramsay and comprehends Mrs. Ramsay's creation of the family and of life.

Much of Woolf's writing purposely seeks the symbolic setting of the sea. On this remote isle in the ocean of life these people are a microcosm of mankind, not concerned with the economic and other values omnipresent to most humans but exploring the essence of live experience. Mrs. Ramsay is herself the lighthouse, bringing shelter and coherence to those weltering upon the chaotic sea of life. The concerns of this slender volume are momentous: marriage, family, feminine and masculine worlds, the mystery of personality, life and death. But the overriding contention is that womanly love is the great creator of meaning in an otherwise senseless universe.

Orlando (1928) in rather conventional narrative relates a bizarre fantasy. Orlando is an English boy during the Renaissance. During the reign of Charles II, Orlando, on embassy to Constantinople, is transformed into a woman. We last see her in 1928 when, according to an accompanying picture, she looks exactly like Victoria Sackville-West, a literary friend of Virginia Woolf's. As a *jeu d'espirit* on the Tiresias theme it is joyously imaginative, tellingly jocular in depicting what Victorianism expected a lady to be, and scintillating in such descriptions as the Great Frost which froze the Thames solid. Interpretations suggest that it is allegorical for the history of the Sackville-West family and/or English literature. Certainly it looks like a devoted feminist's assertion that the complexion of England has changed from the masculine dominance of Elizabethan days to the feminization of recent generations. It is easily Woolf's most brilliant work but in many respects her lightest.

The Waves (1931) is a search for identity in today's world where the impersonal machine of outside things virtually obliterates the self. The gradual unfolding of consciousness from youth to age is depicted in six persons (Bernard, Neville, Louis, Susan, Rhoda, and Jinny) whose rich cultural background, sensitivity, and intelligence parallel Woolf's but not the general reader's.

In form the novel resembles a classic ballet, rigidly formalized, with each dancer stepping forth to deliver a lyric solo. There are nine sections, carrying the six persons from childhood to approaching death. Interludes beginning each section are a counterpointing from Nature, the rhythms of the physical world passing from dawn to sunset, paralleling the human minds. Bernard, an artist surrogate for Virginia Woolf, feels most poignantly the loneliness of mankind and enunciates the fruit of Mrs. Woolf's vision: do not fight against the difficulties of life but love one another, thus fabricating the only possible meaning for life. Paradoxically, the more we strive for independent selfhood, the less identity and less happiness we form.

Flush (1932), a study of Elizabeth Barrett Browning, is the most extraordinary biography ever written. All is told from the viewpoint of the poetess' pet dog. Consequently smell and taste predominate over sight, the most employed of human senses, and instincts far exceed thoughts. Although a fantastic feat of imagination and not without its recognition of the seamy side of Victorian existence, it cannot penetrate the surface of life as do her other works, and it remains essentially a fascinating fable.

From *Mr. Bennett and Mrs. Brown* (1924) to *The Captain's Death-Bed* (1950) Virginia Woolf issued over a dozen volumes of criticism. Best known are the two series of *The Common Reader* (1925, 1932), revealing her as a most uncommon reader. She deemed criticism quite inferior to the creative impulse, but these essays in a far more conventional guise than her fiction have perhaps intrigued more readers. Dominating them is her revolt from the realistic-naturalistic school in the inner exploration of the truth of experience.

Dorothy Miller Richardson (1873–1957). Dorothy M. Richardson has been reticent about her biography, but she is a native of Berkshire whose formal education ended at seventeen. She has been a teacher and clerk, critic and translator. Though an English pioneer in the stream-of-consciousness technique, she has been unduly neglected except for a faithful band of admirers.

Pilgrimage (1938) is the collective title for twelve essentially autobiographical novels from *Pointed Roofs* (1915) to *Dimple Hill* (1938). The entire series is the exploration of the mind of Miriam Henderson; nothing is given except as it impinges upon her consciousness. No conventional plot exists. Miriam teaches school in Germany and London, and successively works as governess, secretary, and dental assistant. She falls in love with a Russian Jew but quits him to become the mistress later of a writer. In Switzerland she briefly experiences spiritual freedom. Ordered to rest, she finds peace with a Quaker family at Dimple Hill, where we leave her. Enthusiasts such as J. C. Powys see *Pilgrimage* as the fullest probing of a woman's consciousness in all literature. Many are distressed that no goal is apparent in the pilgrimage except possibly a quasimystical quietude.

David Herbert Lawrence (1885–1930). D. H. Lawrence was the son of an illiterate coal miner and a genteel schoolteacher in Eastwood, Nottinghamshire. From early years he was plagued with tuberculosis, which, growing acute in his forties, eventually killed him. Starting work with clerical jobs he went on to Nottingham University College, qualifying as a teacher in 1908. After four years of teaching he eloped to Italy in 1912 with Frieda, wife of his professor, Ernest Weekley; by birth she was a von Richthoven of a proud German Junker family. After her divorce, Lawrence married Frieda in 1914 and returned to England. During World War I they were suspect because of her German origin and his conscientious objection to war. Permitted to leave England after the war, Lawrence roamed over much of the world—Europe, Australia, Mexico, and New Mexico—revisiting England intermittently. He died in France at Vence, near Nice.

Lawrence belies all the usual generalizations about Englishmen. No other of the world's writers lived and wrote with such passionate intensity. To Lawrence the novel was a religious art in which he could speak of and to the whole man. In his significant fiction his central figure is always proceeding from a partial or mechanical existence into organic wholeness. Such a struggle ignores the traditional "character" in its search for the subconscious powers of mankind.

AUTOBIOGRAPHICAL FICTION (1909–12). *The White Peacock* (1911) inaugurates the modern novel of poetic autobiography. Its diffuseness and its yielding to traditional novelistic patterns by transposing Lawrence's background to the middle class weakens it as a novel, but it displays the exciting lyricism of Nature that is a hallmark of the novelist.

The narrator, Cyril Beardsall, is Lawrence (Beardsall was his mother's maiden name), and his frustrated love affair with Emily is that of Lawrence and Jessie Chambers. The major conflict involves Lettie (Lawrence's own sister) and two suitors, George Saxton and Leslie Tempest. Lettie marries Leslie and becomes preoccupied with the empty surface life of the bourgeoisie. George in drunkenness suffers mental and physical degeneration.

Almost heedless of their significance, Lawrence first presents themes that will dominate his later works: the male-female war, the contest for a woman between a supercivilized man and an inarticulate man of earth, antagonism toward the father and all imposed authority, degradation of the man who thwarts his own potentialities. Beneath all is the dark subterranean world of the subconscious that battles with the modern world, its fellows, and itself.

Sons and Lovers (1913) vies with Joyce's *Portrait,* which it preceded, as the most notable autobiographical novel of this century.

Gertrude Morel, of a bourgeois family fallen in fortune, is married to the coarse miner Walter Morel. The children turn to her, especially the sensitive Paul (Lawrence) who has a talent for painting. Encouraged to education and social climbing by his mother, Paul becomes a factory clerk. Miriam Leivers, a charming and affectionate girl, encourages Paul's art work but cannot woo him from his mother fixation. He has a passionate relationship with Clara Dawes, a factory worker estranged from her husband; the puritanical Mrs. Morel condones the affair because Paul will not be taken from her. His mother's death is heartbreaking to Paul, but he resolves to remake his life.

Many consider this the greatest Lawrence novel, for its realistic quality is never approached in the later works, and its *Bildungsroman* structure surpasses that of all other Lawrence novels. The war between the parents is the conflict between conscious, mental puritanism and unconscious, primitive sensuality, a contest that Lawrence would subsequently define as between Spirit (intellect) and Soul (body). Paul is caught in an obvious Oedipal situation (though that inverted puritan Lawrence excoriated Freud as indecent). As the son-lover he cannot bring fulfilment to himself or to his mother. In striving for normal relationships Paul is a split being, seeking spiritual attachment in Miriam and physical attachment in Clara. This inability to function as an integrated man is seen by Lawrence as the sterility of today's industrialized society. While the outward form of the novel is not unusual, except for its fervid lyricism, the experimental quality lies in an unprecedented search not for the outward manifestations but for the inner reality. Unlike Joyce and Woolf, Lawrence probes inwardly not for thoughts or verbalized experience but for feelings that are seldom phrased but which in Lawrence's world are the wellsprings of our nature. Frustration is the keynote of the autobiographical works, while the next period of Lawrence will seek a solution for the individual.

EMOTIONAL ADJUSTMENT IN THE MODERN ERA (1913–20). *The Rainbow*

(1915), banned upon publication, is the first half of a novel that Lawrence variously titled "The Sisters," "The Wedding Ring," and "Noah's Ark." The sequel should be considered in conjunction with this work. A summary suggests that this is a family chronicle like *The Forsyte Saga*, but, breaking new trails, its history traces essentially the changing patterns of psychic relationships.

Tom Brangwen and his forebears had long held Marsh Farm in Nottinghamshire. His marriage to the Polish widow Lydia Lensky in the 1840s introduced an exotic element into the earthy English farm family. Tom's stepdaughter, Anna, marries Tom's nephew Will Brangwen and proceeds to have numerous children. Will's favorite child, Ursula, was fortunate as a late 19th-century girl to receive a college education. She has a stormy love affair with Anton Skrebensky, a Polish officer in the British army. After his departure Ursula finds herself pregnant, but Anton has married his commander's daughter. Ursula loses the child but during convalescence sees the rainbow promise in the sky.

Lawrence ignores the stock-in-trade of the English novel—manners and worldly careers. He offers the first novel in English to examine basic sexual relationships, normal and otherwise (hence the prompt banning). Also, his is the first novel to trace what the social revolution of the past hundred years has meant in the passionate life of individuals. The first Brangwen generation is the product of earth's eternal rhythms. Tom's marital problems with Lydia are conveyed with a previously unknown symbolizing of the inarticulate waves of human emotion; Lydia's foreignness points up the eternal enigma of male-female union, but for all their disturbances, Tom's outgoing responses are the last primordial vitality in a community sloping toward dissolution. The next generation is swamped in the bourgeois world of the 19th century; Anna and Will share the first contemporary marriage. In the manner of Victorian standards, sex is equated with sensuality, and their lives fritter away in unrealized disorganization: Anna as a wholly child-centered housewife, Will as a successful, "public-spirited" teacher. Ursula is the first truly modern woman, totally dispossessed of the spirit and totally exploratory in the vagaries of the flesh. Ursula's search momentarily becomes homosexual in her adoration of Winifred Inger, that mannish new woman, and she experiments with Skrebensky, the weak, false-valuing male of today. However, the entire conditioning of the present world renders impossible a viable relationship between them. Ursula is like a monstrous female spider destroying the diminutive male. After a bizarre hallucinatory episode of being threatened by wild Freudian horses, Ursula glimpses the rainbow which even in this blighted era is earth's promise of a possible readjustment of human values to wholeness.

The telling of the story is an extension of the thematic and symbolic technique of Conrad. Loosely organized by conventional standards, the novel achieves coherence by rhythms, nuances, subsurface tones that counterpoint each other instead of following one unbroken line. The opening paragraph announces motifs such as "inward," "outward," "unresolved," which are repeated, expanded, and varied throughout.

Women in Love (1920) is a continuation of the previous novel, seeking here the terms with life only promised at the conclusion of *The Rainbow*. Admittedly the concept of Ursula is altered by Lawrence's perception of Frieda. We pick up about three years after the conclusion of *The Rainbow*.

The Brangwen sisters, Ursula the teacher and Gudrun the artist (she was only a minor child in the previous book), are emancipated modern women. Gudrun (Katherine Mansfield) becomes involved with Gerald Crich (J. M. Murry), wealthy young colliery owner, and Ursula with Rupert Birkin, young inspector of schools (Lawrence). Ursula and Birkin find fulfilment in marriage, but Gudrun and Gerald break further and further apart until in the Alps he skis off to die of exposure at the heights.

Many of Lawrence's acquaintances appear in this book; Bertrand Russell appears as Sir Joshua Malleson only to be refuted, supposedly, by the hero Birkin. Lawrence's major assault is against Crich, symbol of the modern male. Crich is the industrial tycoon who makes the machine his god, a god that fails. The strength of Crich is mechanical, the strength of modern "will power," "personality," and "ideals" (terms used derogatively by Lawrence). He therefore lacks the emotional depth necessary for genuine human relationships, and his death symbolizes the suicidal course of today's mechanical man.

Birkin-Lawrence feels deep revulsion against the entire mechanical wilderness of modern society. Love to Birkin is a relationship between "fulfilled" persons who retain their selfhood ("balanced conjunction") but through the "door" of love gain access to the supreme life force which is inaccessible to the Christian ethos or modern bourgeois culture. The Gerald-Gudrun failure is symptomatic of the sterility of the modern love ethic. The Rupert-Ursula success is achieved only after her modern woman's titanic opposition is overcome, but she must yield for her own nature to come to terms with the great male god in Birkin.

Almost equally important, and running at crosscurrents, is the "blood brothership" theme. Not merely the man-woman relationship has been poisoned in modern society, but also the man-man relationship. In the famous wrestling passage Gerald and Rupert sense a mystic bond and communion in contact with each other. Lawrence detested homosexuality, at least consciously, proclaiming a meeting of males that like male-female love should through the flesh transcend the flesh to the great life force.

Like Joyce, but with far less thoroughness, Lawrence sets his work within a mythological framework: Gudrun (wife of Siegfried in the Eddas), Gerald ("spear-bearer" in German), Loerke (Loki, the evil one). Ursula, of course, is "she-bear." Apparently he saw in the Northern myth, as Shaw discerned in the Wagnerian version, a symbolism of modern industrial society.

Most important, however, is the realization that Lawrence is frankly out to poetize man's inner nature. Episodes such as Birkin's stoning of the moon-lit pool are poetic symbols, not realistic events. Trying to express what novelists had never before expressed, Lawrence tries to present not "characters" but emotional depths in mankind.

THE MYSTIC PROPHET (1920 TO DEATH). Searchers for anything resembling a conventional novel in the later works of Lawrence frequently complain that the seer has overpowered the artist. Several thousand years ago in establishing the pattern we now follow, men, claimed Lawrence, had created a false civilization, dividing the individual human by emphasizing selfish acquisitiveness and the use of the mind to compel Nature to their purposes. Lawrence's travels were a feverish attempt to find in more primitive men the wholeness and balance lost by civilization.

The Plumed Serpent (1926) discovers among the Mexican Indians an esoteric life source missing among Europeans. To European conquerors the Indians were devil-worshipers, but that Devil is now re-examined as containing all the psychic riches repressed and scorned by European culture.

An Irish widow, Kate Leslie, disgusted at the savage slaughter of the Mexico City bullring, is escorted away by General Cipriano Viedma, a full-blooded Indian. The general and his landowner friend, Don Ramón Carrasco, draw her into their revival of the worship of ancient Mexican deities. Don Ramón is the reincarnation of Quetzalcoatl, and Cipriano is the reincarnation of Huitzilopochtli. In pagan rites Kate as Malintzi is united to Cipriano. The Roman Catholic Church opposes the old faith, but it spreads like wildfire until it becomes the official religion of the republic. Kate tries to break away and return to Britain, but the dark maleness of Cipriano and the primitive religion of Mexico enthrall and contain her.

The central concept is the re-education of Kate from egotistical, unhappy modern womanhood into a profound and inarticulate communion. She is properly skeptical about the incredible happenings about her and only gradually finds fulfilment in the deep, dark (both words are chanted throughout by Lawrence) sensual mysticism of primitive religion. Lawrence creates a whole ritual and virtually a whole theology for the Quetzalcoatl faith, with only slender hints from Indian sources. He seeks in hymns, hypnotic chants solely of his creation, to embody the worship of man's buried instincts. The whole man, without any of civilization's corruption, is henceforth to be supercharged with energy and creativity.

Lady Chatterley's Lover could not legally be circulated in Britain in unexpurgated form until 1960. Lawrence wrote three versions, and the censored text of the initial printing at Florence, Italy, (1928) makes a fourth.

Crippled and impotent by a war wound, Sir Clifford Chatterley becomes a noted writer. Oppressed by emptiness, his wife Constance turns to Mellors, her husband's gamekeeper, for satisfaction. Meanwhile her husband finds pleasure in building up his colliery business. She elopes with the gamekeeper to start a fresh life upon a quiet English farm.

The banality of the plot is relieved by a poetical revelation of the direct sexual experience, an innovation in literature. Erotica had minutely and factually detailed such events, but most novels heretofore had concentrated exclusively on preliminaries or subsequent reactions. Considering sensuality a high moment of life and believing sexual maladjustment to be the symptom and curse of our age, Lawrence eschews all reticence. He employs socially forbidden Anglo-Saxon words; clearly his intent is to treat natural acts with natural language, but the lewd and facetious currency of such terms is hard to counteract, as the pornographer's interest in the novel all too obviously demonstrates. Clifford's impotence is symbolic of modern mechanical man, and his growing concern with business is a lust for power, while his wife is expanding her nature by the warmth and tenderness of sensual love. In a familiar Lawrence symbolism, Mellors is the dark, sensual, full man set against the blond, sterile, incomplete Clifford. Lawrence's experiment has apparently led to a far more specific and frank scrutiny of personal relationships by the English novel and has apparently shifted the amatory interest of novelists largely from courtship to concrete marital problems.

SHORT STORIES. From *The Prussian Officer* (1914) to *A Prelude* (1949) Lawrence issued over a dozen collections of short stories, which rank him among the best practitioners of this genre in English. The themes and subjects of the short works generally parallel those of the novels, where his major points and changes of position are first hammered out. Actually Lawrence achieved his highest artistry in short pieces such as "The Rocking Horse Winner," "The Captain's Doll," "The Woman Who Rode Away," and "The Man Who Died." His impassioned, suggestive prose casts its spell most effectively in the confines of the short story.

VERSE. Published verse from 1913 to 1940 is chiefly represented by *Collected Poems* (1932). It is hard to say where to draw the line between Lawrence prose and verse. The avowed poetry could usually be printed as a paragraph or so from the novels with few readers aware of it, for his favorite was intensely rhythmic free-verse. Most of Lawrence's verse seems a running commentary upon his prose fiction. Unlike most poems, his are miniature essays charged by pulsating emotion. They start with meticulous observation, select a single and generally surprising aspect, then complete with an imaginative unification and celebration. Remarkable is the tortoise series in which poems covering the entire life of the beast represent the most impressive attempt in English to identify with an alien form of life.

TRAVEL ACCOUNTS. For sheer magnificence of writing and the poetic summoning up of places *Mornings in Mexico* (1927) and *Etruscan Places* (1932) are almost unmatched in English. Some think that these lyric pieces are Lawrence's most memorable accomplishment. Pervasive is the osmotic perception of greater psychic power in the less civilized world than in the more civilized.

CORRESPONDENCE. *The Letters of D. H. Lawrence* (1932), edited by Aldous Huxley, reveal some of the most individualistic letters written in English. Lawrence assailing censorship, conventions, and the whole premise of modern society is a master of invective. His letters confirm the judgment of all who knew him: a most exciting and stimulating personality, and one hard to get along with.

Joyce Cary (full name, **Arthur Joyce Lunel Cary**) (1888–1957). Joyce Cary was born in Londonderry, Ireland. From early years he was interested in painting, and after Trinity College, Oxford, he studied art in Edinburgh and Paris. In 1913 he joined the Nigerian political service. During 1915–16 he was an officer in a Nigerian regiment fighting the Germans. Invalided out of the political service in 1920, he settled in Oxford. He did not begin novel writing until *Aissa Saved* (1932). Thereafter his production was prodigious and his fame rapid in its rise until his death. His reputation has slacked off since his death.

Mister Johnson (1939), recalling Cary's experiences in Nigeria, was his first great success and perhaps his best novel.

Johnson is a Nigerian native employed by the British government. He makes down payment on Bamu, the ferryman's beautiful daughter, and hopes to make her a lady and himself a gentleman, as *Mister* Johnson indicates. Getting into debt and losing his wife because of failure to meet installments, he becomes a paid spy for the Waziri. Crime mounts until he kills Sergeant Gollop and in turn is executed by his white superior, Harry Rudbeck.

In some respects Cary is a traditionalist in novel writing; by his own statement, characters first interest him, and he creates characters with an intense vitality virtually unknown since Dickens. His chief interest lies in the abundantly creative man who seeks to construct his own life as a work of art. Such a man is perforce a transgressor in modern society; defeat is inevitable, but in every creation he finds fulfilment and meaning. The summary of *Mister Johnson* sounds like the tragedy of a half-savage man pathetically seeking membership in an alien civilization, but Johnson is a bubbling extrovert, and a poet (Cary fashions his appropriate ditties). Cary favors neither white man's civilization nor black man's primitivism; the conflict breeds its own destruction, yet it brings, too, vivacious living and creativity.

Herself Surprised (1941), *To Be a Pilgrim* (1942), and *The Horse's Mouth* (1944) constitute a trilogy, dominated respectively by Sara Monday, Thomas Wilcher, and Gulley Jimson. For all three the theme is entrapment, the lonely bondage of freedom in an idiotic world. Cary's three major character types here appear in their classic stature: Jimson as the artist rejected by the world but driven to creativity, Wilcher as the conservative bound by tradition seeking to hold out against the world's mad swing, and Sara as the eternal feminine trapped between her woman's moral sense and the world's moral code. The last and greatest of the trilogy suggests that the artist gets his truth right from the horse's mouth, for he is the interpreter to men of the vision of life. Jimson is a rogue and a wastrel, but he is the artist. Outcast from society, he must continue to create, even upon the walls of a condemned building which is falling before a demolition crew.

A Fearful Joy (1949) in title refers to the hold that con-man Dick Bonser exerts upon Tabitha Baskett. Knowing what a scoundrel he is, she cannot escape from him and from life. In the picaresque tradition this seems to be a modern version of Defoe's *Moll Flanders,* but unlike the earlier work this is a panorama of English culture and history for a fifty-year period beginning with the *fin de siècle* 1890s and going through every *ism* and trend almost to midcentury.

Prisoner of Grace (1952), *Except the Lord* (1953), and *Not Honour More* (1955) constitute Cary's political trilogy. Chester Nimmo (Lord Nimmo at the end) is a famous and controversial Labour politician, assailed by his public enemies and in private by the love affair of his wife and Jim Latter. The volumes are told successively by Nina, Chester, and Jim. The question arises, is Nimmo a hypocritical fraud in private life and a temporizing politico in public affairs, or a conscientious husband and realistic public servant? Each account is shockingly different and irreconcilable. Cary seems to sympathize with Nimmo as a man stained by the world and his own deficiencies but trying to effect viable relations between nations and individuals in an impossible world.

Lawrence George Durrell (dûr'el) (1912–   ). Lawrence Durrell was born in India of Irish Protestant parents. Private school there and in England constitute his formal education; he never attended a university. His residence in England has been quite brief, largely as a nightclub pianist and automobile racer. The fascinating escapades of the Durrell family on the Greek island of Corfu are related by his biologist brother Gerald in *My Family and Other Animals* (1956), probably the most delightful of all the recent spate of whimsical accounts of families. Lawrence has resided extensively in France, Greece, Argentina, the Mediterranean, and the Orient.

Few other English authors are so obviously the rootless cosmopolite, the 20th-century wanderer without a home.

The Alexandria Quartet is the collective title for a tetralogy consisting of *Justine* (1957), *Balthazar* (1958), *Mountolive* (1959), and *Clea* (1960). Critics and intellectuals throughout the English-speaking world have displayed more interest in this work than in any other since Joyce, while enthusiastic French reviewers have claimed for Durrell a rank with Joyce and Proust.

The author himself states that the time concept of relativity has guided his technique. The first three novels cover the same events; "Time is stayed." Only in the last novel, the one true sequel, do the survivors of the initial three novels move ahead in time. World War II intrudes peripherally.

The first novel, supposedly written by Darley (the author's alter ego), centers about a Jewess, Justine, whose life has been warped by two blows: her own rape in childhood and the kidnaping of her baby daughter, child of her first marriage to Arnauti (she spends much time fruitlessly searching the child-brothels of Alexandria). She is now married to Nessim Hosnani, a rich Coptic Christian who plots an uprising against the Moslems. Swirling about her are the European drifters: Darley, Melissa (his mistress, a Greek dancer), Pursewarden (another novelist much admired by Darley), Balthazar (a pederastic physician), Clea (a beautiful girl with a frustrated talent for painting), and Scobie (one of fiction's great comic characters, a former British merchant seaman now an Egyptian police officer and transvestite). Central is the suicide of Pursewarden.

The second volume is Balthazar's "great interlinear" to *Justine*. With this revision, the account shifts upon its axis, forcing a revision of the entire story. Darley is surprised along with other revelations to learn that Pursewarden, not himself, was the object of Justine's affections.

The third volume from the cool heights of Mountolive, the British ambassador to Egypt, again twists the entire account with more remarkable revelations, especially the anti-British, pro-Zionist combine symbolized by Justine and Nessim.

The concluding volume is Darley's escape from Alexandria and into true love with Clea, a breakthrough from time and space.

"The central topic . . . ," states Durrell, "is an investigation of modern love." The lush city of Alexandria is one of the superlative feats of novelistic imagination (E. M. Forster in *Alexandria,* 1922, 1938, and others who know the city find it quite otherwise), an embodiment of all sensualism of all time but especially of our time. In the last volume Darley and Clea break the space-time continuum in a symbolic underwater crucifixion and rebirth. The thwarted artist Clea is nailed to an undersea wreck by a discharged harpoon. Darley frees her, but she loses her hand. Forced to paint with an artificial hand, she actually finds release, as both she and

Darley escape Alexandrianism and the romantic love bonds of time and space to achieve what Pursewarden termed the "heraldic universe."

Hostile critics point out that Durrell's almost lifelong overseas residence has made him an anachronism, a belated practitioner of the experimental novel in an era when that exciting attempt has otherwise petered out. The style, they suggest, seems a holdover from Wilde's *Salome,* but the baroque style is appropriate to the unreal glitter of Alexandria and the intertwined tale of the *Quartet.*

VERSE. *Collected Poems* (1960) reveals that the poetic novelist is in fact a sizable poet in verse. Probably no other writing in English so hauntingly re-creates the atmosphere of the Eastern Mediterranean, especially the Greece of today. Strangely enough, the quality is hushed and meditative instead of the coruscating phrases and images of the *Quartet.* "As a poet of the historic consciousness" (Durrell speaking of himself) Durrell seems to preside over the subsiding of our culture, finding beauty in death, proclaiming dignity in the face of purposeless history.

TRAVEL ACCOUNTS. *Bitter Lemons* (1958) is no conventional collection of impressions but the essentially tragic depiction of the alteration of Cyprus during 1953–56, Durrell's years of residence there, from the quasi-understanding of Briton and Cypriot to the intense hostility that since has taken Cyprus away from British administration. The English could not grasp the Byzantine nature of Cypriot culture. Durrell respects and admires both peoples, both sincere and noble, sundered by alien views of life. His departure is a lyric farewell to an idyllic existence and a world forever shattered.

CRITICISM. *A Key to Modern British Poetry* (1952) illuminates much of 20th-century English poetry but even more of Durrell himself as it considers the impact chiefly of the theory of relativity and psychoanalysis upon modern art.

SHORT STORY WRITERS

Katherine Mansfield (real name **Kathleen Mansfield Beauchamp**) (1888–1923). Katherine Mansfield was born at Wellington, New Zealand, daughter of a banker. She planned a musical career after training at Queen's College School, London, but instead married George Bowden in 1909. She met J. M. Murry in 1911 and married him in 1913 after divorce from her first husband. With Murry and D. H. Lawrence she edited *Signature* (1915). Tuberculosis forced her to live and travel on the continent after 1918. After her death in France, Murry edited most of her writings.

Mansfield's short stories are the closest approximations in English of Chekhov short stories, though Murry denies direct influence. Discarding the well-made short stories of Kipling and Maugham, her pieces rarely display either plot or climax. From *In a German Pension* (1911) to *Something*

Childish (1924) and collected stories in 1937, she is interested not in what happens in the outside world but in moments of illumination when a human being learns something about himself or life.

Katherine Mansfield may well be termed the Imagist of the short story as she re-creates the mood and atmosphere of a New Zealand day in "At the Bay." Nuances, casual remarks, and apparently trivial mannerisms reveal the true nature of a person as a man's peeling of an orange in "The Dill Pickle" demonstrates why the young woman cannot return to him. Her insistence that the short story present "slices of experience" rather than a moral or a narrative has strongly influenced all serious practitioners of the form since.

Alfred Edgar Coppard (1878–1957). A. E. Coppard was born to working-class parents in Folkestone, Kent. Poor health terminated his education at the age of nine. Until the end of World War I he made a living variously as tailor's apprentice, office boy, messenger, professional athlete, and clerk. First touching intellectual circles at Oxford in 1907, he began writing in 1911, gaining initial attention with *Adam and Eve and Pinch Me* (1921). His more than one hundred short stories in seventeen volumes form one of the most impressive collections of 20th-century English short fiction.

Although Coppard's range is remarkable, most of his characters are simple people, countrymen or laborers. Character is revealed in action, but plot is subordinated to a poetic perception of the comic and tragic. Pervasive is a wry pity for humans defeated by the thoughtless actions of others or by their own incomplete comprehension.

Saki (wine-bearer in the *Rubáiyát*) (real name Hector Hugh Munro) (1870–1916). H. H. Munro was born in Akyab, Burma, where his father was inspector general of police. At the age of two he was brought to England for public and private education until in 1893 he returned to Burma to join the Burma Military Police. Broken in health, he came back to England and began a writing career in 1896. From 1902 until 1908 he was foreign correspondent for the London *Morning Post*, roaming the continent. He enlisted in the Royal Fusiliers and was killed in action in France.

Saki's fame rests upon impish short stories in volumes from *Reginald* (1904) to *The Square Egg and Other Sketches* (1924). The omnibus edition of 1930 ran through ten American printings in thirteen years. Saki's place is among the witty social satirists like Oscar Wilde and Evelyn Waugh. His heroes, Reginald and Clovis, are the ancestors of P. G. Wodehouse's Bertie Wooster, but in contrast they are highly intelligent, suave, and subtle in their devastating assaults upon upper class conventionality and stupidity. Saki's bizarre humor, sometimes tinged with the macabre, is conveyed by a deft touch that can create a swift effect in a sentence or two and then delicately astonish the reader at the climax.

Arthur Machen (mak'un) (1863–1947). Born in Wales and deeply imbued with the mystic sensitivity which is such an important element in the Welsh tradition, Arthur Machen is the author of some of the most beautifully written and fascinatingly strange short stories in English. One of the earliest of these was "The Great God Pan" (1894), later included with others in the volume *The House of Souls*. Machen also wrote novels filled with his individual fantasy, *The Hill of Dreams* (1907) and *The Secret Glory* (1922).

Victor Sawdon Pritchett (1900–   ). A native of Ipswich, Suffolk, V. S. Pritchett was educated at Alleyn's School, London. In the 1920s he became a newspaper correspondent, and by the end of the decade a novelist. His critical writings have established an international reputation. He has lectured extensively in the United States, notably at Princeton and California.

The title of Pritchett's second short-story collection, *You Make Your Own Life* (1938), suggests his viewpoint and method. He sees "disclosure" as the purpose of the short story and finds disclosure in the everyday doings of commonplace people. In a pub conversation, in moving furniture, in the dentist's chair, men and women reveal themselves. Less sensitive than Mansfield to inner nuances, Pritchett gives the general reader even more of the shock of recognition about himself and the persons around him. Without any moralizing he displays remarkable perceptivity in observing and understanding slices of actual living. Pritchett's wry mixture of realism and caricature brings to life the eccentrics of *The Key to My Heart* (1963).

Herbert Ernest Bates (1905–   ). Born in Rushden, Northamptonshire, H. E. Bates was educated at the Kettering Grammar School. After newspaper writing and clerking, he published his first novel at twenty. During World War II he rose to the post of squadron leader in the R.A.F. and published war accounts under the pseudonym of "Flying Officer X." His best-known novel, *The Purple Plain* (1947), arose from his wartime experiences. His fiction has been translated into at least sixteen languages, and he appears more often than any other author in the O'Brien annuals, *Best British Short Stories*.

Although a competent novelist, Bates is best known for short-story collections beginning with *Day's End* (1928). More than any other significant British short-story writer, he is strongly indebted to the Americans such as Faulkner and Hemingway, and frequently shows their preoccupation with violence, lust, and decadence. Cinematic and colloquial effects exemplify the incisive, impressionistic style which Bates praises in his perceptive study *The Modern Short Story* (1941).

OTHER TWENTIETH-CENTURY NOVELISTS

Although the experimental novel was the most spectacular form of 20th-century novel writing, it represents only a small fraction of the total output of English fiction. Many 20th-century novelists have used an essentially conventional technique and style that seemed readily accessible to the general reader; profoundly disturbing to many was the serious novelist's abandonment of the older viewpoints. The antibourgeois novelist as well as the bourgeois novelist assumed that society must and could function to provide the matrix of a good world. The intellectual novelist has now largely discarded the idea of individual adjustment to society; instead he searches for an individual way of life in a culture seemingly doomed.

CRITICS AND SATIRISTS OF TODAY'S WORLD

Norman Douglas (full name **George Norman Douglas**) (1868–1952). Norman Douglas was born to an old Scottish family at Tilquhillie Castle, Deeside, Scotland. Restive at Uppingham School, he was sent in 1883 to the Gymnasium at Karlsruhe, Germany, where he became proficient in several modern languages. He served with the British Foreign Office from 1893 until 1896, mainly in Russia. Thereafter he lived mainly in Italy and France, staging a melodramatic escape from the latter country during the Nazi *blitzkrieg* of 1940. Many believe that his memorable travel account ot southern Italy, *Old Calabria* (1915), is his best work.

South Wind (1917), coming during the darkest year of World War I, is one of the gayest, blithest novels in English. In the manner of Thomas Love Peacock, Douglas brings to Nepenthe (Capri) a fantastic assortment of Britons and Americans, all relaxed by the salubrious climate and uninhibited atmosphere of this Mediterranean isle.

Unlike most English novelists, Douglas displays no moral concerns, only a gentlemanly hedonism and a cultured epicureanism. Like Anatole France, who influenced him, he derides all modern society with satiric, ironic detachment. Sanity has been lost, he contends, in the triumph of democracy, puritanism, and religion. Subsequent novelists such as Aldous Huxley and Evelyn Waugh take from Douglas their position that witty satire is the only sensible attitude of truly civilized man toward the insanity of the present world.

Ronald Firbank (1886–1926). Ronald Firbank enjoyed a spurt of fame in the 1920s for *Caprice* (1917) and *Santal* (1921), sophisticated novels of brilliant and often indelicate delicacy. Renewed interest in the era has recently revived Firbank's reputation. Wittily he sweeps over a brittle, pointless society. (*The Green Hat* [1924] by Michael Arlen [1895–1956] should also be mentioned as epitomizing the frenetic 1920s.)

David Garnett (1892–   ). Satire and fantasy combine in David Garnett's best-known work, *Lady into Fox* (1923). This is a short novel telling gently of the surprising gradual change by which a married woman becomes a pet fox in her husband's home. David Garnett's style gives great piquancy to the story. He used a comparable approach in other short novels, as in *The Man in the Zoo* (1924). His recent *Two by Two* (1963) is a fabulous, realistic retelling of the Noah's Ark account, guaranteed to convince the most sceptical.

David Garnett's family has long been well known in English letters. His father Edward Garnett (1868–1937) was a noted critic and a friend and adviser of Joseph Conrad, W. H. Hudson, and John Galsworthy. Constance Garnett (Mrs. Edward Garnett) (1862–1946) was the noted translator of major Russian novelists, especially Tolstoy and Dostoevsky. David Garnett's grandfather Richard Garnett (1835–1906), a distinguished writer, was for many years librarian of the British Museum.

Kenneth Grahame (1859–1931). Though he was writing somewhat earlier than the novelists just discussed, this seems an appropriate place to mention Kenneth Grahame because there is a kindly satiric and fable-like quality in his most famous work, *The Wind in the Willows* (1908), a masterpiece among books for children, ranking close to Lewis Carroll's *Alice in Wonderland* and *Through the Looking-Glass*. The principal characters in *The Wind in the Willows* are small animals, notably Mr. Toad. Like the Alice books, Grahame's story has a great fascination for adults.

Ivy Compton-Burnett (1892–   ). Ivy Compton-Burnett has published almost a score of novels since *Dolores* (1911).

Two Worlds and Their Ways (1949) is representative of her consistent practice of attacking the distinctly contemporary world by placing its setting in the microcosm of a late Victorian family.

Maria Shelley is eager that her two children, Clemence and Sefton, by Sir Roderick, shall excel their half brother Oliver, child of Sir Roderick's first wife, Mary. At school both youngsters are expelled for cheating. Their parents react with surprising insouciance. The world of childhood and the world of adulthood are both cheats.

Part of the humor of Compton-Burnett is the disillusioning opposite of the legendary idyllic Victorian family. Her families are battlegrounds, ruthless power struggles as much as the outer world, and in this novel the parents determine action and crush all spirit. With feminine astuteness Compton-Burnett confines herself to the household, but within this limited area she marshals a searing indictment of a whole society erected upon such a false basis. The light treatment masks it as comedy.

Aldous Leonard Huxley (1894–1963). Like Virginia Woolf, Aldous Huxley stemmed from some of the most noted intellectuals of the 19th century. Grandson of T. H. Huxley and nephew of Matthew Arnold, he was the brother of Julian Huxley, the noted scientist. Born in Godalming, Surrey, he majored in biology at Eton. After graduation from Balliol College, Oxford, he was on the staff of the *Athenaeum* and the *Westminster Gazette* from 1919 to 1924. Poor eyesight barred him from military service and plagued him constantly. In 1923 he began world travels that would encompass almost two decades. In Italy he established a friendship with D. H. Lawrence that, unlike most friendships with Lawrence, lasted throughout life. From 1947 he was a resident of Southern California.

By general admission, Aldous Huxley was primarily an essayist resorting to the novel for a hearing in this age. Actually a moralist and preacher, he expounded ideas rather than character or life as it is individually lived. His enormous versatility permitted him to range over more of the modern situation than perhaps any other belletristic writer of this century. Though probably not a major novelist, he was a major voice of this era.

DETERMINATION BY THE BODY (TO 1936). *Crome Yellow* (1921), his first novel, takes its title from the country estate of Henry Wimbush where it is set.

A shy young poet, Denis Stone, is in love with Wimbush's niece, Anne, but she ignores him. Other guests include the implacable rationalist Scrogan, the artist Gombauld, deaf but shrewdly observant Jenny Mullion, and Mary Bracegirdle, worried about her Freudian dreams. Finding himself the butt of Jenny's caricatures and Scrogan's unpoetic realism, Denis arranges for a fake telegram to drag him back to London. Too late he realizes that Anne has changed her mind and deeply regrets his departure.

The major themes of Huxley's earlier period all appear in *Crome Yellow*. All these people are frauds—futile, spiritually bankrupt "hollow men"—who try to evade life and reality. What *The Waste Land* was to contemporary poetry, these early Huxley works were to the novel.

Dominating this and subsequent Huxley novels is a thoroughgoing Behavioristic psychology otherwise rare in the English novel. The body is represented as the complete determiner of the spirit, all too logically in a materialistic era. Huxley can never forgive the body for its implacable attachment to the spirit, and he likewise mocks the pretensions of the spirit to independence of bodily functions.

Antic Hay (1923), even more witty and more devastating, brings together a similar band of futilitarians: Shearwater, engrossed in meaningless scientific experiments; Mercaptan, the sybaritic dilettante; Lypiatt, the pseudo-artist with a messianic complex; Myra Viveash, a sensualist. The play within the novel symbolizes Huxley's theme: the pitiful Monster who wrecks his life and ends on the dissecting table is modern humanity—only half alive, perverted in values, and diseased in mind and body. With irresponsibility and nullity the leitmotifs of modern life, Huxley chants: "Nil . . . Nil . . . Nothing at all." Unlike the urbane Douglas, Huxley as fundamentally a humanist and moralist feels deep distress and profound anger at the modern predicament.

Point Counter Point (1928), Huxley's important contribution to the experimental novel, derives its technique, as the title suggests, from music. Instead of musical language, the effects are to be secured by the stating of a theme and of a countertheme, then the separate development of each, and the restatement of each, repeating motifs and offering abrupt transitions. Joyce's *Ulysses* and Gide's *Counterfeiters* are the chief influences. Many contemporaries are portrayed under pseudonyms; the one favorable portrait is that of D. H. Lawrence as Rampion, whose "blood consciousness" is the only praiseworthy spirit Huxley finds.

Philip Quarles (surrogate for Huxley) is a novelist planning a work based upon his acquaintances. As Rampion, the peasant-born "whole man," sees it, the novel should depict the contemporary world as "an asylum of perverts." The themes to be counterpointed are basic: birth, love, and death. Almost every conceivable form of these themes is played within the circle of people known to Quarles, but the patterns endlessly repeat themselves as perversions: sadism in Lucy Tantamount, adolescent thrill-seeking in the cynical Spandrell, pseudo-artiness in Burlap, fascism in Webley, lechery in Quarles senior, selfish egotism in John Bidlake, and so on. Human dignity and meaning have gone out of these people in their perversions of all the basic themes. We conclude with Burlap and his mistress, Beatrice Gilray, merrily splashing water together in the bath like children; sensual irresponsibility is the lasting tone of modern times.

Critics complain that Huxley is deficient in character creation and that his plotting creaks (since Rampion does not belong to this social and artistic class, he must be anchored in a Soho restaurant talking vigorously). The powerful impact of the work, however, cannot be denied by anyone.

Brave New World (1932), its ironic title taken from Shakespeare's *Tempest*, is a humanist's horrified prediction of how today's world will develop. Although Wells had in part set the course, recent inverted Utopias largely spring from Huxley's contemplation. Disturbing today is the picture even in pulp magazine science fiction of a nightmarish future, hideous and inhuman.

As the Director of the Central London Hatchery and Conditioning Centre tells his students in this year 632 A.F. (After Ford), Community, Identity, and Stability are society's glorious achievements. To this end art and religion have been exterminated. Human beings are created by artificial fertilization of eggs on an assembly line and are scientifically treated in embryo to produce the necessary range from Alpha Plus Intellectuals to Epsilon Minus Morons. Lenina Crowne and Bernard Marx, hatchery workers, holiday in the Savage Reservation of New Mexico where old-fashioned-type human beings are preserved as a curiosity. There they find John, son of

Linda and the Hatchery director, and bring him to London. Disclosed as a *father* (!), the shamed director is forced to resign. Linda dies from an overdose of *soma*, the lethe drug lulling poor humans to accept their plight. John, believing in god and poetry, is a curiosity for sightseers. Driven berserk, he slays Lenina whom he desired and hangs himself. Human emotions are obviously impossible and disastrous in this brave new world.

In perhaps the nearest thing to Swiftian satire since the master, Huxley introduces the natural man, John the Savage, who chooses the way of freedom and life against the consciously determined environment and predetermined human organism toward which our culture trends. The mass-produced humanity six hundred years hence will believe their world perfect, but it is the living death that cares for the flesh by destroying the spirit. To the Marxist and pseudoscientific cries for a changed and improved society and world, Huxley retorts with an implied plea for the changed and reinvigorated individual.

THE MYSTICAL PATH (FROM 1936). *Eyeless in Gaza* (1936) takes its title from Milton's *Samson Agonistes,* suggesting the chaining of our blinded era. Huxley experiments in form by shifting the time in each chapter (e.g. 1933 in Chap 1, 1934 in Chap 2, 1933 in Chap 3, 1902 in Chap 4, 1926 in Chap 5, and so on), but the reader actually finds this essentially the familiar flashback method.

Here message overrides fiction altogether. Essentially the account is the conversion of Anthony Beavis from a cynical hedonist to the way of the mystic. Not the selfish sensualism of men, not even the "blood consciousness" of Lawrence, will suffice. Beavis learns that selflessness is the proper course, complete detachment from the self, the world, all mankind—not commitment. In mystic contemplation of cones resembling those of Yeats, Beavis feels "the source and substance of all truth."

Ends and Means (1937), frankly composed of essays, clearly proclaims the new Huxley. Here he advocates a spiritual revival for the individual, who should become the nonattached man, uncommitted to power, fame, love, even to art and intelligence. The disinterested spirit, operating in perfect freedom, should espouse the perennial philosophy (title of Huxley's 1946 volume on mysticism) beyond the world and the flesh, a union of all contraries.

Huxley's subsequent course continued to elevate mysticism as the one right path for the individual. Body and mind intervene, as he sees it, between our true selves and the infinite spiritual consciousness ("the divine ground"). When we let the body or mind rule us, we are indeed purely physical beings, chained to the natural order, but our truest self is spirit, which makes us inhabitants of another order, the mystical spirit world of truth and freedom.

Evelyn Arthur St. John Waugh (wô) (1903–   ). Evelyn Waugh is the younger brother of the novelist Alec Waugh. Evelyn was born in Hampstead, London, son of a publisher. After art study and teaching he turned to writing, publishing his first novel, *Decline and Fall* in 1928. After divorce from his first wife in 1930 he entered the Roman Catholic Church. During World War II he served with the Royal Marines and Commandos.

Vile Bodies (1930) is probably the best of his six earlier satires.

Adam Fenwick-Symes, a young writer, wishes to marry Nina Blount, but every bizarre mishap imaginable occurs. Finally he borrows money from a Captain Littlejohn and lets him marry Nina. Characters flit about at the most incredible tasks and die as haphazardly and trivially, but the monstrous death of Superwar crashes at the finale with liquid-fire guns and leprosy bombs, while the drunken general (or was he only a major?) seduces a stray girl in a stranded automobile.

Absolute inbecility and frenetic confusion reign here. Without the writhing anger of Huxley, Waugh plunges along with a gaiety that is unspeakably appalling. The whole thing is as artificial as an ebony Christmas tree and even more emblematic of a perverted, unnatural society. The witty ingenuity rivals Wilde, as Waugh tops one wild nonsense with a greater nonsense.

Brideshead Revisited (1945) is the first and still the best Waugh novel of his later manner. The hilarious satirist has become a Catholic moralist, but Graham Greene cannot be matched on these grounds.

Captain Charles Ryder, an agnostic, while stationed near the old estate of Brideshead relives his memories of the 1920s with the ancient Catholic family of the Flytes, Lord and Lady Marchmain. Although Lady Marchmain is saintly, all the other members of the family have been pulled away from the Church by the world. Though sinners, each member of the family is pulled back toward grace, as far as his or her weak nature will permit.

It is sin and the world that eventually bring man to God. Through even the most sordid of lives develops the theme of divine purpose making itself apparent, and man's flight (Flyte) must be to his Creator. Waugh's predilection for the aristocratic tradition is clear, but when he now treats seriously the social class he had earlier satirized so uproariously, his hand is less effective and impressive.

George Orwell (real name **Eric Hugh Blair)** (1903–1950). George Orwell was the son of a civil servant in Bengal, India. After Eton he served with the Imperial Police in Burma (1922—27). From 1927 to 1934 in England and France he lived from hand to mouth, for some of this period as a tramp. In 1936 he went to Spain theoretically as a free-lance reporter, but on arrival enlisted in the Socialist militia. He was wounded in front-line service and street fighting in Barcelona. During World War II he worked for the B.B.C., but ill health clouded most of his last decade and a half.

Animal Farm (1945) represents Orwell's disillusionment with Russian communism. Before his Spanish experiences he had been strongly sympathetic to Marxians, but was almost killed in Barcelona as a "Trotskyite." Earlier he had regarded the common man as his hero, but now he fears that the common man will all too frequently let himself be manipulated by demagogues.

Inspired by a dream of Old Major, a prize boar, the animals of the Manor Farm drive out farmer Jones and establish an Animals' Republic. The attempts of the animals to create a free and equal community after expelling their exploiter ingeniously parallels Russian history from 1917 to the Teheran Conference. The pigs with their superior intelligence dominate, and in the final card game between pig Napoleon and human Pilkington the animal spectators find it impossible to distinguish between pig and human.

The supposed saviors have proved every bit as much the tyrannical exploiters as the original despots, but so blithe and good-humored is the telling of this depressing moral that children, totally ignorant of its implications, can read it with joy for its farmyard whimsy. Orwell himself termed it a "fairy tale." Few English works of this century have been translated into so many languages, as remote as Persian and Japanese.

Nineteen Eighty-Four (1949), one of the most widely disseminated books of this century, was written by the ill Orwell on the eve of his death.

Winston Smith, with a flair for newspeak, the official language, is a minor functionary at the Ministry of Truth on Airstrip One (British Isles). In 1984 there are only three world empires, Oceania (America and the British Commonwealth), Eurasia, and Eastasia. These three maintain desultory war with each other solely to keep their populaces under wartime conditions. Heading the Party, and probably fictitious, is the unseen Big Brother. The Inner Party actually rules. Winston belongs to the Outer Party, chiefly secretarial and technical specialists. The remaining 85 per cent of the population consists of the "proles" (proletariat) who are ignored or treated like animals by the Party; if any prole shows intelligence or thinking for himself, he is promptly liquidated by the Thought Police. By *doublethink* the Party states whatever it wishes, no matter how contradictory, and history is regularly rewritten to show the omniscience and perfection of the Party. Party members are ceaselessly scrutinized by microphone and telescreen (two-way television) to keep them in line. Winston falls in love with Julia, a fellow worker, and both hope to overthrow the Party tyranny. A valid history supposedly from O'Brien causes them to plot with him, but O'Brien betrays them, for the actual history is only a lure to trap unwary Party members. Under torture Winston breaks until he even betrays Julia. Released, he at last feels cleansed. Now beatifically he loves Big Brother.

Even more monstrous than *Brave New World* is Orwell's picture of a regimented world of the future, ruthlessly controlled by the Inner Party in its

lust for power, as the last glimmers of human freedom and dignity have
been totally obliterated. The gentler manner of *Animal Farm* gives way to
a grim denunciation of the whole trend of modern society. "Big Brother"
and "doublethink" have been nightmarish catch-phrases to scare our world.

James Hilton (1900–1954). With *Lost Horizon* (1933), a novel about a
highly civilized valley hidden away in the mountains of Tibet, James Hilton
gave the world and the language a new name for a remote place where
life moves along untouched by the wars and tensions of modern civilization. Hilton called his imaginary valley Shangri-La, and Franklin D. Roosevelt used it as the name for his presidential mountain retreat.

William Golding (1911–   ). William Golding in *Lord of the Flies*
(1954) is concerned with moral aimlessness. A group of small boys stranded
on a desert island completely shake off their civilized behavior. Dividing
into the keepers of the fire (the contemplatives, the poets) and the hunters
(the doers, the predatory creatures), they begin a complete reconstitution of
society. Primitive passion and bloodlust, the inherent evil within, start them
savagely battling with each other. A rescue party from an atomic fighting
group chides the boys for not carrying on better, but obviously the mur-
derous adults are no better.

"The Angry Young Men" take their label from Leslie Allen Paul's autobiography, *Angry Young Man* (1951), though several of the group angrily
disclaim the label. Iconoclasm is the dominant note, "honesty" the incessant cry. The central figures are anti-heroes, disgusted young men who
find the whole world reprehensible. Language and actions are determinedly
coarse and slangy. Underlying their anger is a profound desire for lost innocence, for a world that would throw off its pretensions and hypocrisies in
favor of genuinely "natural" conduct in a "natural" society. Representative
is *Lucky Jim* (1954) by Kingsley Amis (1922–   ). In *Room at the Top*
(1957) John Braine (1922–   ) pictures a cynical hustler in Joe Lampton,
who is a modern Crusoe in making his way financially; en route he sacrifices
love and all else to the vacuous god of success. *The Contenders* (1958),
probably the best novel by John Wain (1925–   ) is related by Joe Shaw,
a journalist, who sees no point to the violent competitive spirit of his artist
friend Robert Lamb and his businessman friend Ned Roper. To an unprecedented degree, Alan Sillitoe (1928–   ) has explored the working-class
world of England to find it a jungle; in the novel *Saturday Night and Sunday Morning* (1958) and the short-story collection *The Loneliness of the
Long-Distance Runner* (1960). The depressed classes with a cocky "I'm all
right, Jack" cynically fight for survival in a brutal, materialistic society. Joyce
and the American J. D. Salinger seem the important influences upon Sillitoe,
whose vigorous style and acute perception may rate him as the outstanding
talent of the group.

HUMANISTIC SEARCH FOR THE INDIVIDUAL WAY

The typical English novel, as opposed to the experimental novel or the satiric novel, has usually meant a well-written, dignified story about good-intentioned Britishers trying to live relatively decent, pleasant lives. At the same time, serious novelists have recognized the complexity and chaos of the modern world and have sought conscientiously to find meaning and happiness for the individual. The extraordinary diversity of approaches to the plight of the individual demonstrate the fragmentation of our era and pay tribute to the vitality and versatility of today's English novel.

Edward Morgan Forster (1879–   ). A London native, E. M. Forster attended King's College, Cambridge. For some time he lived in Italy; he also visited India and was in Alexandria, Egypt, during World War I. He proved one of the central personages of the "Bloomsbury Group" in the 1920s. His Clark lectures at Cambridge constitute the impressive *Aspects of the Novel* (1927), and *Abinger Harvest* (1936) and *Two Cheers for Democracy* (1951) are notable essay collections.

Howards End (1910), by its author's statement, is a "hunt for a home." The Schlegel family, dissatisfied with German militarism and reactionism, now live in England. Helen Schlegel is interested in Paul Wilcox, son of the successful businessman Henry Wilcox, but the families part them. Margaret Schlegel, however, becomes friendly with Mrs. Henry Wilcox, who at her death wills the country house Howards End to Margaret. The Wilcox family destroys the document, but the widowed Henry later marries Margaret. Helen has a child by a Leonard Bast, and Henry's son Charles strikes Bast, who dies of a weak heart. Henry Wilcox wills his money to his children by the first marriage but leaves Howards End to Margaret and Helen's illegitimate child.

"English to the backbone," the Wilcox family is awesome in its practical handling of the material world, but it is pitifully ignorant of private values. Its holding of the country estate Howards End is symptomatic of the late 19th-century assumption of the landowners' position by the industrial moguls. Margaret's creed is Forster's: "to be humble and kind, to go straight ahead, to love people rather than pity them, to remember the submerged." Howards End is therefore the focus of a symbolic battle over England's destiny. A balance of body and mind, female and male, humanism and materialism, must be achieved to civilize those who would otherwise reduce the whole world to cost accountancy.

A Passage to India (1924) is Forster's acknowledged masterpiece.

Accompanied by her son's fiancée, Adela Quested, Mrs. Moore comes to India to visit Ronald Heaslop. Adela accuses a young Moslem surgeon, Dr. Aziz, of attempting to attack her in the Marabar Caves. The trial becomes a bitter contest between the English and the natives, but at the crucial point in the trial Adela changes her mind and withdraws the charges. Heaslop packs off Adela and marries another Englishwoman. Although Indian and Briton try to make some rapprochement, too great a gap stretches between them.

It is Ronald's belief that Indians and Britons are apart not because of Indian venality but because of fundamental cultural differences in temperament, social concepts, and religious viewpoints. The one hope would seem to be personal contacts, yet even the good intentions of Mrs. Moore and Cyril Fielding, the intelligent principal of the Chandrapore Government College, cannot bridge to the good intentions of the abused Dr. Aziz. No passage can be effected, for there is a hopeless breach between man's powers and man's needs. The rational individualism of the West collides vainly with the depersonalized mystery of India.

The Cave scenes are the symbolic heart of the novel where India confronts the Westerner with illusion and disillusion. Always willing to seek rapport and always willing to alter his mind, the story seems to say, man must nonetheless acquiesce to the restrictions of that part of the world which he knows and which formed him.

Henry Handel Richardson (real name **Mrs. Henrietta Richardson Robertson**) (1870–1946). Henry Handel Richardson was Australian by birth but wrote her novels in England.

The Fortunes of Richard Mahoney was the 1930 title for a trilogy composed of *Australia Felix* (1917), *The Way Home* (1925), and *Ultima Thule* (1929). Irish-born Mahoney varies between England and Australia in speculation and in the practice of medicine, related in novels as toughly realistic as those by male novelists. Always the alien and always in pursuit of material wealth, Mahoney ends in an Australian madhouse. The moderate ideals with which he started cannot withstand the assaults of purely worldly values in a self-centered society.

John Cowper Powys (1872–1963). John Cowper Powys was the eldest of three remarkable brothers, the other two, Theodore Francis Powys and Llewelyn Powys. All three are novelists of remarkable poetic style.

The Glastonbury Romance (1929) has an hypnotic quality of mysticism and the aura of storied places as it recreates the Grail myth in a modern context. The melodramatic narrative is less impressive than the powerful descriptions of places.

Theodore Francis Powys (1875–1953). Theodore Francis Powys recreates the English rural tradition, seeking within it a pre-Christian sense of the universal rhythms of life.

Mr. Weston's Good Wine (1927) is a rare combination of poetry and comedy, its title meaning the awareness and acceptance of life. God is the creation of human art; the reality is the rich maturity that drinks to the full the draughts of life and death.

Leopold Hamilton Myers (1881–1944). Leopold Hamilton Myers was born at Cambridge and educated there at Trinity College. Financially affluent, he never had to earn a living, though during World War I he worked for the Board of Trade. After the war he was prominent amid the "Bloomsbury Group." He traveled extensively, especially in the Orient. Death was at his own hand.

The Near and the Far is a tetralogy consisting of *The Near and the Far* (1929), *Prince Jali* (1931), *Rajah Amar* (1935), and *The Pool of Vishnu* (1940). Set in 16th-century India at the height of the great Akbar, the series seems to bring an Oriental world to life more vividly than any other work in English, but by the author's own admission, the exotic locale is primarily to "give prominence to certain chosen aspects of human life." The resultant exploration of most avenues of life produces one of the most impressive philosophical novels of 20th-century English. Myers divides men into the Fastidious and the Trivial, and for all his grandeur Akbar is a materialist and trivial. Spokesman for the Fastidious and for Myers is the Guru, the wise man, who calls for the spiritualization of the community of men. The Rajah Amar, who gives up his kingdom to be a beggar monk (and incredibly Myers makes the Westerner accept this decision as right), finds in the life of denial and spiritual wholeness a serenity he never knew in temporal power.

Charles Langbridge Morgan (1894–1958). Charles Morgan has been perhaps more appreciated on the continent than in the English-speaking world, for he is distinctly the art novelist.

Portrait in a Mirror (1929), *The Fountain* (1932), and *Sparkenbroke* (1936) actually form a trilogy concerned with love, contemplation (the mystic contemplation that eventuates in art), and death. Sparkenbroke is a poet-novelist who seeks in art a defense against love and death. Just short of the consummation of his love for Mary Leward he dies, but not before he has had the beatific vision that lifts him from the temporal and the self to the mystic union and harmony of all three themes.

Leslie Poles Hartley (1895–   ). While enjoying small international repute, L. P. Hartley ranks quite high in England.

Eustace and Hilda is the collective title for four pieces, *The Shrimp and the Anemone* (1944), *Hilda's Letter* (1945), *The Sixth Heaven* (1946), and *Eustace and Hilda* (1947). Hartley seems a misplaced late Victorian in his slow-paced, genteel progress, unaffected by the experimental novel. His subject, however, would be extremely distasteful to the last century. Brother and sister are drawn together too closely, and Eustace commits suicide to release her from their bond. Their opposites attract: her asceticism, puritanism, straining, and inflexibility versus his hedonism, wilfulness, apathy, and flexibility. Betjeman, Lord Cecil, and other Englishmen united in praising Hartley's evocation of place and mood as a classic of youth's vicissitudes in a world where it is thrown back upon personal attachments solely.

Elizabeth Dorothea Cole Bowen (1899–   ). Though born in Dublin and still owner of the ancestral estate Bowen's Court, in County Cork, Elizabeth Bowen was educated at Downe House, Kent, and has resided in England since the age of nineteen. In 1923 she married A. C. Cameron and published her first work, *Encounters,* a collection of short stories. Everything she has written has been distinguished by fastidious restraint and feminine sensitivity.

The Death of the Heart (1938), probably her most brilliant novel, is representative in characters and themes of her entire output.

Portia Quayne, sixteen-year-old half-sister of advertising man Tom Quayne is a disturbing newcomer to the Quayne household. Aging Major Brutt, a retired army officer, is the only person she likes until she meets Eddie, twenty-three-year-old employee of the Quayne advertising company. Portia falls in love with Eddie (or perhaps more in love with love), but the young man is just romancing. While the Quaynes are holidaying on the continent, Portia stays at Seale with friends of the Quaynes and manages an invitation for Eddie. The young man's conduct with the pretty girls at Seale disillusions Portia, and things are worse when she learns that Mrs. Quayne has been examining her diary. Bursting in upon Major Brutt, she pleads with him to marry her and take her away, but that mellow gentleman patches things up and packs her off to the Quaynes.

Portia is the typically sensitive girl of a Bowen novel, what Virginia Woolf probably was at the same age. The failure of any of her associates to provide the love Portia wants causes the death of her heart. Innocent, seeking rapport, Portia is doomed to the loneliness of a society grown mechanical and selfish. Like D. H. Lawrence (but wholly ladylike), Elizabeth Bowen believes that today's world has stripped away the genuine feelings that would save mankind, but her delicate womanly perception finds no likelihood of regeneration.

Richard Arthur Warren Hughes (1900–   ). Richard Hughes was educated at Charterhouse and Oriel College, Oxford, where he was a friend of Coppard and Aldous Huxley. Between wars he lived adventurously in Europe and Canada, and even worked as a deckhand on sailing ships.

A High Wind in Jamaica (1929, American title *The Innocent Voyage*) is an extraordinary melodrama of the seven Bas-Thornton children captured by pirates on their way to England. Seduction, murder, and other terrible experiences surround the youngsters, but they are insulated from the adult world of fear, frustration, and compulsion by their amorality. A remarkable penetration of the child's psyche suggests that behavior and morality are artificial constructions of a culture, and plastic humanity has fantastic powers of adaptability and resilience.

The Human Predicament is the collective title for a projected series of novels starting with *The Fox in the Attic* (1961). Exploring the Nazi mentality, Hughes seeks to interpret the problems of today's world as arising from the polarities in human nature; man cannot conceive of a good without likewise positing an evil, and therefore his search for the right way will inevitably compel attendant hate and cruelty.

Henry Graham Greene (1904–   ). Son of a Berkhamstead schoolmaster, Graham Greene was trained at Balliol College, Oxford. From 1926 to 1930 he was subeditor on *The Times,* and from 1935 to 1941 a staff editor for *The Spectator.* He was converted to Roman Catholicism late in the 1920s. During World War II he served in the Foreign Office. His wide travels have assured a cosmopolitan viewpoint.

Greene is unquestionably a major novelist of this century, in style and content, "among the few, the very few, of our great living novelists," says Bowen. The contest of good and evil rages throughout his novels. He applies the label "entertainments" to works such as *The Third Man* (1950) and *Our Man in Havana* (1958), which are adventure thrillers. But in all his fiction is the ceaseless struggle for grace that frees men of the bondage of sin. In the strange ambiguity of the world, it is sin that draws men most powerfully back to God. He rivals the Frenchman François Mauriac as a great Catholic novelist of this era.

The Power and the Glory (1940, also published as *The Labyrinthine Ways*) arose from Greene's extensive travels in Mexico in 1938.

The Roman Catholic Church has been outlawed in a state of Mexico. Priests have vanished, some like Father José renouncing the Church and marrying. Father Montez in secret continues his ministry, although, as a whiskey priest with an illegitimate child, he realizes that he is a weak vessel of the Lord. The government seeks an American bandit and the fugitive Father Montez, but the revolutionary lieutenant pursues the priest more zealously than he does the bandit. The priest is jailed ironically for illegal possession of liquor and is released without his identity being discovered. However, he goes to give the last rites to the dying American bandit and is trapped by the police. Cowardly Father José refusing him the last rites, Father Montez is executed. That very day another priest secretly arrives to continue the work of the Church.

The lieutenant in consecration to the world often seems a more exemplary figure than the disreputable priest, but incomprehensible are the workings of God, who chooses the least likely as the instruments of His goodness. In broader application the lieutenant and the priest are staging the modern warfare for the souls of men: materialism versus spirituality. The devotion and idealism of the materialists cannot be gainsaid, but they are staking all upon worldly chance. In Father Montez, Greene for the first time in this century has re-created the hero. Of course, he appears to be the familiar antihero of 20th-century fiction, but his downfall is that of a hero in the tragic Greek drama, and his succession is proof that the throwing of oneself upon the mercies of God will mean not death but eternal life. In revising the Christian novel, Greene substitutes for the quest of the good man for virtue (as in *Pilgrim's Progress*) the quest of the sinner for God.

The Heart of the Matter (1948) says that faith is the heart of the matter. Greene draws symbolism also from the resemblance of the continent of Africa to a giant heart.

Major Scobie is disappointed in being passed over for the district commissionership of this African colony in favor of a younger man. His wife, already distressed by the loss of their only child, thereupon wants a holiday in South Africa. Scobie borrows money from a dubious Syrian merchant, Yusef. Helen Rolt, victim of German torpedoing, and Scobie fall in love. Using their adultery as blackmail, Yusef forces Scobie to aid in diamond smuggling. Unable to make his peace with man or god, Scobie commits suicide.

Scobie desperately needs Helen, but his very human needs seem to damn his soul. Miracles do not happen in a Greene novel; so a soul must undergo extreme suffering and inner conflict à la Dostoevsky, whom Greene resembles more than does any other English novelist. Though his wife at the end denounces Scobie to the priest, the cleric assures her that no man can call Scobie wicked or damned, for no man fully comprehends God's mercy.

Henry Green (real name **Henry Vincent Yorke**) (1905–   ). Henry Green is the son of a wealthy Midland manufacturer and nephew of a peer. After education at Eton and Oxford, he rose to become managing director of a Birmingham industrial firm. For years the novelist's identity was concealed, as Yorke has strictly maintained his separate natures as artist and businessman.

His first novel *Blindness* (1926) was stream of consciousness, but all his noted novels from *Party Going* (1939) to *Doting* (1952) have offered a laconic style stripping away the author's role as far as possible to let the characters reveal themselves through dialogue. Superficially, Green appears a superb comic novelist of a frustrated age where people have no plans or get nowhere with the plans they concoct. Actually he is close in spirit to Cary and Bowen. His position seems to be that thinking will be of little avail in this disorganized age. Right feeling, genuine emotional response, is the only hope for individual sanity and perhaps a fragmentary togetherness amid our chaos.

Sir Charles Percy Snow (1905–   ). C. P. Snow is the Leicester-born son of a shoe-factory clerk. His brilliant intellect won him scholarships first to University College, Leicester, and then to Christ Church, Cambridge. At the famous Cavendish Laboratory during the epochal work of Lord Rutherford, Snow was a researcher and instructor in physics. Writing fascinated him, and he produced *Death under Sail* (1932), a detective story, as his first printed novel. Scientific writing continued as he edited the Cambridge Library of Modern Science and *Discovery*. During World War II he was chief of scientific personnel for the Ministry of Labour. While still a civil servant after the war, he became an international figure with the controversial *Two Cultures and the Scientific Revolution* (1959), in which he diagnosed the split of the intellectuals between science and humanism and championed the scientific view against the defeatist spirit of many contemporary artists. In 1950 he was knighted, and in 1962 he was installed as lord rector of the University of St. Andrews.

The Search (1934) has often been compared with Sinclair Lewis' *Arrowsmith*. Probably no other novel has so effectively presented the life of the scientist and his motivations. In many respects the central character Arthur Miles is Snow.

Strangers and Brothers is the collective label for about a dozen novels beginning with a 1940 volume bearing this title and numbering nine by *The Corridors of Power* (1964). When complete, it will cover English life from 1914 to the present day. With his almost unprecedented range of experience from the working classes to high government post, in science and in letters, Snow is perhaps better qualified than any other Englishman to interpret our century. In the preface to *The Conscience of the Rich* (1958) Snow states two purposes of his series: to offer "some insights into society" and to trace the moral growth of his central character, Lewis Eliot. Like his creator, Eliot rises from provincial clerk to upper civil servant and at the same time from vigorous leftist to genteel conservative. "Society" has become "contacts" and the goal is less social distinction than effective power. The traditional British touchstones to success are no longer manners and culture but shrewd ability and, above all, a gift for picking the winning side. This modern power struggle shows itself as much in the academic world of *The Masters* (1951) as in the atomic contests of scientists and bureaucrats of *The New Men* (1954). The 20th-century British movement from industrial power to government power and the entire social atmosphere of 20th-century England are painstakingly documented. Like Snow, Eliot is a man of good will, a pure secularist, with no illusions about men but a profound desire to help man. Eliot obtains power only to renounce it, for as the series title indicates he sees brotherhood as the one purpose of life. The strangers seek power for self; the brothers find meaning in human relations, the creation of a decent and sympathetic atmosphere for the lonely ones of our time.

Anthony Dymoke Powell (1905–   ). Anthony Powell in *The Music of Time* has presented a series of novels beginning with *A Question of Upbringing* (1951) that roughly parallel Snow's series; *The Acceptance World* (1955) appears the most significant in the series. His narrator is

Nicholas Jenkins, who knows all the upper middle class who are somehow sustaining a mad world. Powell's material somewhat resembles Firbank's and Waugh's, but his central figure makes do, finding that acceptance of the state of things while far from adequate permits a modicum of happiness.

Angus Frank Johnstone Wilson (1913–). Angus Wilson in *Anglo-Saxon Attitudes* (1956) has written one of the most mature novels of this period. Belated maturity is the achievement of Gerald Middleton, a historian, finding confusion and fraud in his private life and in the "great Melpham find" of archaeology. Not asking too much of people or life, but seeing them clearly and unsentimentally, he steadies himself for the onward push.

RELIVING THE LIFE OF THE DISTANT PAST

Robert Ranke Graves (1895–). Robert Graves was the Wimbledon-born son of the poet Alfred Percival Graves. He left Charterhouse to serve as an officer in the Royal Welch Fusiliers during World War I. After the war he settled in Oxford. After World War II he established permanent residence in Majorca. In 1961 he was elected Professor of Poetry at Oxford.

Graves is so boldly original a talent that perhaps another generation will be necessary to assay adequately his contribution. His autobiography, *Goodbye to All That* (1929), is the harrowing, definitive testament of the generation crucified by World War I. His first and eternal love is poetry, from his first printed volume, *Over the Brazier* (1916), to the *Collected Poems* of 1961. An intimate friend of Sassoon, he was a fellow "trench" poet. In the 1920s to escape he sought refuge in Georgian bucolics. Poems about 1930 anticipate the manner of Auden. The later verse, as Graves hopes, may establish his future literary reputation. Without a propaganda message to our age, either social or religious, he presents verse of classic clarity and workmanship suggesting stoic virtues in this dark age. Yet to our day he is most noted for historical fiction, which he freely admits is written for money to sustain him as a poet.

I, Claudius (1934) won both the James Tait Black and the Hawthornden prizes. In the court intrigue of imperial Rome, Claudius escapes destruction because he is a retiring scholar, a hesitant stammerer that no one considers worth poisoning or stabbing. Thus he survives the reigns of Tiberius and Caligula to become emperor himself.

The historical romance still lives with us, but with this novel Graves opened a new fictional world that has proved to be a most distinctive literary accomplishment of our time. The new historical novel is distinguished by the following characteristics:

(1) Choice of period of cultural change. Modern historical novels of significance are less interested in past glamour than in eras which like our

own are ones of momentous alteration. Historical fiction now offers readers actually a scrutiny of their own time from the vantage point of similar transitional eras of the past.

(2) The vanished hero. The Walter Scott form of historical fiction was largely motivated by a search for the heroic in the past. From Graves on, historical fiction has generally eschewed the hero concept of history, and considered men of the past realistically as our companions in the toils of fortune and fate.

(3) Today's diction. Graves dropped any attempts at a pseudo-language such as "the Wardour Street" phrasing for medieval tales. Characters here speak colloquial (not slangy) modern English instead of a noble Latin imitated in English.

(4) Competent scholarship. Unpedantic and lively as it is, Graves's historical fiction is the product of considerable erudition instead of a little library hunting to get dates right and make a romance seen "based upon actual history." The new historical novel tries not to form history to its purposes but to take acknowledged events of history and supply character and dialogue to render them credible.

(5) Mind-set true for the times. Genuine historical fiction since Graves has tried to see the ancient mind as ancient, and the medieval as medieval. The very modernity of the language and realism of character portrayal have set off more intensely the aspects of Claudius that are strange to the mind of today; we recognize Claudius as completely a man like ourselves but with cultural views we do not share.

Claudius the God (1934) continues the previous novel through the emperor's reign. *Count Belisarius* (1938) concludes this "Roman trilogy" with the great general of Justinian, last of the old Romans.

The Golden Fleece (1944, American title *Hercules, My Shipmate*) is an even more daring attempt at historical re-creation. This account of Jason and the Argonauts places the mythological story in the primitive cultural era when the Mother Goddess of the indigenous Mediterranean peoples was being supplanted by the patriarchal deity of the Indo-Europeans. Instead of classic Greek glamorizing, the story reeks with sudden violence and primordial rites and superstitions of a culture almost as remote from Periclean Athens as from us. Although as in his learned exposition of *The Greek Myths* (1955) Graves may unduly ride some of his anthropological theories such as the tanist, he renders believable much that countless generations have dismissed as impossible fancy.

Bryher (real name **Annie Winifred Ellerman MacPherson**) (1894–   ). One of the outstanding historical novelists today, Bryher likewise concentrates upon periods of cultural change, ranging from the contest of barbarism vs. Hellenism in the 4th century B.C. in *Gate to the Sea* (1948) to the fallaway of Elizabethanism into Jacobeanism in *The Player's Boy* (1954).

Alfred Leo Duggan (1903–   ). Alfred Duggan prefers Pre-Norman Britain, seeking the great dividing points in national history. His style is determinedly realistic and underplayed, with history often sticking out more obviously than character creation. *The Cunning of the Dove* (1960) brings the Norman and a new age.

Mary Renault (real name **Mary Challans)** (1905–   ). Mary Renault has charged picturesque Greek mythology with extraordinary vitality, especially in *The King Must Die* (1958) and *The Bull from the Sea* (1962), interpretations of the Theseus legend. She may have produced the outstanding historical novels of this century in these works, which breathe the very air of ancient Greece.

Henry Treece (1912–   ). Henry Treece was the leading poet in the 1940s movement ambitiously termed "The Apocalypse," but his literary reputation has been established by a tetralogy on early Britain beginning with *The Dark Island* (1952). Often melodramatic, his works are concerned with divided loyalties in eras of cultural conflict.

Terence Hanbury White (1906–1964). T. H. White, in *The Once and Future King* (1958) (consisting of three short novels published earlier) used the story of King Arthur imaginatively, aiming to gain perspective on the lonely individual who seeks to understand his world and is constantly forced into painful compromises.

John Ronald Reuel Tolkien (1892–   ). J. R. R. Tolkien's work *The Lord of the Rings* (1954–55), as befits a distinguished linguist and medievalist, incredibly fashions an entire primitive world, replete with its own language and mythology, that still confronts its characters with the painful problems our era thinks peculiar to itself.

MISCELLANEOUS NOVELS

THE BEST SELLER. England has been rich in this century with numerous authors whose craftsmanship has regularly earned high rank among best sellers throughout the English-speaking world. The appeal to a mass audience has caused the familiar pattern of repetition today of formulae from the pioneer novelists of previous generations.

The historical romance flourishes like the green bay tree in the manner of Scott, adding, usually, the properly indecorous to interest today's un-Victorian taste. The romantic treatment of the past is well represented by the "Herries Chronicles" (1930–33) of Sir Hugh Walpole (1884–1941); in *The Cathedral* (1922) this highly talented novelist did once achieve a notable novel. Recently prominent has been C. S. Forester (1899–   ) whose English naval hero of the Napoleonic period, Horatio Hornblower, sailed through many novels from 1927 to 1952. In *The Sky and the Forest* (1948) he created probably his best work in an impressive scrutiny of the primitive African mind.

The best seller in handling contemporary themes falls into two opposite camps. The realistic-naturalistic style is exemplified by *The Cruel Sea* (1951) by Nicholas Montsarrat (1910–   ). This may be the best novel in English upon World War II; unlike the psychoanalytic concerns of American war novels, these British seamen are wholly occupied by struggle for survival against relentless Nature and even more vindictive human enemies. The sentimental treatment of an ex-army officer in *Sorrel and Son* (1925) by Warwick Deeping (1877–1950) has proved equally popular.

THE DETECTIVE STORY. Because its essence is deception of the reader and because narrative must by nature dominate it, the detective story has seldom achieved literary stature, although it has claimed endless practitioners. With over 150 novels to his credit Edgar Wallace (1875–1932) is probably the most prolific of 20th-century writers, but by a newer generation he and his exciting crime tales have been almost forgotten. Chesterton's Father Brown rates with Doyle's Sherlock Holmes as a notable detective character, but otherwise the one work in this genre to approach genuine literary level is *Trent's Last Case* (1913) by Edmund Clerihew Bentley (1875–1956) whose lasting fame may arise from the nonsense verses called *Clerihews.*

CHILDREN'S BOOKS. Both the verse and the stories of Alan Alexander Milne (1882–1956) appeal immediately to children, and at the same time have fascinated the maturest of adult readers by their sensitive explorations of the world through the eyes of childhood. A. A. Milne's verse includes *When We Were Very Young* (1924) and his best stories are the *Winnie the Pooh* series (1926–28). Milne also wrote some very popular plays in a skillful high-comedy vein.

EPILOGUE

No other language in world history has grown so rapidly or come so close to being a truly universal tongue as English. Just four centuries ago, French, German, Spanish, and Italian each counted more speakers than English. Today English claims almost as many speakers as these four together. A very large percentage of newspapers, magazines (including scientific journals), and radio and television broadcasts throughout the world employ English.

In viewing the history of English literature we have limited ourselves to the writings of the British Isles. The student who wishes to see the literature of the language as a whole must include in his range the remarkable works appearing in Canada, New Zealand, and Australia, and also the writings of the Danish baroness Isak Dinesen. It goes without saying that such a student will also turn enthusiastically to the past and present great writers who have given us our own American literature.

INDEX

Index

Page numbers in **bold face** signify major references to the subject.